Adam Nathan

with Daniel Lehenbauer,
Lead Developer Responsible for WPF 3D

Windows®
Presentation
Foundation

UNLEASHED

SAMS | 800 East 96th Street, Indianapolis, Indiana 46240 USA

Windows Presentation Foundation Unleashed

International Standard Book Number: 0-672-32891-7

Library of Congress Cataloging-in-Publication Data

Nathan, Adam.

Windows presentation foundation unleashed / Adam Nathan.

p. cm.

ISBN 0-672-32891-7

1. Windows presentation foundation. 2. Application software. 3. Microsoft .NET Framework. I. Title.

QA76.76.A65N38 2007

005.2'768—dc22

2006038586

Printed in the United States of America

First Printing: December, 2006

10   09   08   07   8   7   6   5   4

Trademarks

Warning and Disclaimer

Bulk Sales

Pearson Education offers excellent discounts on this book when ordered in quantity for bulk purchases or special sales. For more information, please contact

U.S. Corporate and Government Sales
1-800-382-3419
corpsales@pearsontechgroup.com

For sales outside of the U.S., please contact

International Sales
international@pearsoned.com

Safari BOOKS ONLINE ENABLED

The Safari® Enabled icon on the cover of your favorite technology book means the book is available through Safari Bookshelf. When you buy this book, you get free access to the online edition for 45 days. Safari Bookshelf is an electronic reference library that lets you easily search thousands of technical books, find code samples, download chapters, and access technical information whenever and wherever you need it.

To gain 45-day Safari Enabled access to this book:

▶ Go to http://www.samspublishing.com/safarienabled
▶ Complete the brief registration form
▶ Enter the coupon code **VTGS-KQSI-NJGK-KYID-KMGR**

If you have difficulty registering on Safari Bookshelf or accessing the online edition, please e-mail customer-service@safaribooksonline.com.

Editor-in-Chief
Karen Gettman

Acquisitions Editor
Neil Rowe

Development Editor
Mark Renfrow

Managing Editor
Gina Kanouse

Project Editor
Betsy Harris

Copy Editor
Karen Annett

Indexers
Lisa Stumpf
Ken Johnson

Proofreader
Kathy Bidwell

Publishing Coordinator
Cindy Teeters

Book Designer
Gary Adair

Technical Editor
Robert Hogue

Composition
Jake McFarland

Contents at a Glance

Table of Contents

About the Authors

Adam Nathan is a senior software development engineer in Microsoft's Developer Division. He is the author of the acclaimed *.NET and COM: The Complete Interoperability Guide* (SAMS, 2002), a coauthor of *ASP.NET: Tips, Tutorials, and Code* (SAMS, 2001), and a contributor to books such as *.NET Framework Standard Library Annotated Reference, Vol. 2* (Addison-Wesley, 2005) and *Windows Developer Power Tools* (O'Reilly, 2006).

Adam regularly speaks at development conferences and to groups within Microsoft about a variety of .NET Framework topics. Having started his career on Microsoft's Common Language Runtime team in 1999, Adam has been at the core of .NET technologies since the very beginning. Adam is also the creator of popular tools and websites for .NET developers, such as PINVOKE.NET, CLR SPY (and its Visual Studio add-in), and XAMLshare.com. You can find him online at www.adamnathan.net.

Daniel Lehenbauer is the lead software design engineer responsible for the 3D features in Windows Presentation Foundation. Prior to WPF, he worked on multiple graphics and UI technologies, including mobile controls for ASP.NET and Windows Forms. Daniel is active in the WPF community and blogs about 3D graphics using WPF at www.viewport3D.com.

Dedication

To Lindsay and Tyler.

Acknowledgments

First and foremost, I'd like to not only thank my wife, Lindsay, but somehow attempt to apologize to her. Unfortunately, I know that nothing I write can come close to making up for what I've put her through over the last year. In the midst of writing this book, I realized two things that I'm sure my wife has known all along: I can't write a book shorter than 500 pages, and I can't write a book without neglecting my family.

As if it weren't bad enough that I wrote my first book during our first year of marriage, I wrote this book during our first year of parenthood. Although I was able to do most of the writing after our son went to bed, I robbed the two of us of any significant quality time for far too long. Yet Lindsay showed incredible patience and understanding throughout the entire process—much more than I deserved. As my schedule got extra hectic toward the end, she kept me on track, helped me get out of bed at 5 AM, and helped me stay healthy. She even weighed in (over my shoulder) with her own thoughts as I revised chapters! In short, she took care of me, our son, our house, and all aspects of our life while I was preoccupied in front of my silly little computer. And she did all this with grace and humility. Lindsay, I love you, and I'm sorry.

Although most of the process of writing a book is very solitary, this book came together because of the work of many talented and hard-working people. I'd like to take a moment to thank some of them by name.

Daniel Lehenbauer, the lead developer responsible for the 3D features in WPF, deserves an enormous amount of thanks for agreeing to contribute a chapter on 3D that is far better than anything I could have written myself. Having Daniel's perspective and advice captured on paper is a huge benefit for any readers thinking about dabbling in 3D. Daniel also thoroughly reviewed other chapters in this book and provided invaluable feedback.

Many other Microsoft co-workers graciously agreed to review chapters and provided wonderful feedback. I'd like to thank (in alphabetical order) Beatriz de Oliveira Costa, Robert Hogue, Neil Kronlage, Mike Mueller, Oleg Ovetchkine, S. Ramini, Rob Relyea, Adam Smith, and Tim Sneath. I also thank Lori Pearce and David Treadwell for giving me permission to write this book in the first place.

I'd like to sincerely thank the folks at Sams—especially Neil Rowe—because I couldn't have asked for a better publishing team. Never once was I told that my content was too long or too short or too different from a typical "Unleashed" title. I was never even told that I was taking too much time (although I did get some gentle hints along the way)! They gave me the complete freedom to write the kind of book I wanted to write. And when I asked Neil if there was any way that we could print the book in full color, he not only made it happen but came up with the innovative idea to print the code samples with complete syntax coloring!

Introduction

Thank you for picking up *Windows Presentation Foundation Unleashed*! To avoid unsatisfied customers, I want to clarify that this is *not* a book about Microsoft PowerPoint (which many people consider to be the *foundation* of *Windows presentations*)! Windows Presentation Foundation (WPF) is Microsoft's latest technology for creating graphical user interfaces, whether they consist of plain forms, document-centric windows, animated cartoons, videos, immersive 3D environments, or all of the above! This is a technology that makes it easier than ever to create a broad range of applications. For example, WPF makes it relatively straightforward to implement applications similar to Windows Media Player, Microsoft Word (or at least WordPad), and, yes, even Microsoft PowerPoint!

Ever since WPF was publicly announced in 2003 (with the code name of "Avalon"), it has gotten considerable (and deserved) attention for the ways in which it revolutionizes the process of creating software—especially for Windows programmers used to Windows Forms and GDI. It's relatively easy to create fun, useful, and shareable WPF samples that demonstrate all kinds of techniques that are difficult to accomplish in other technologies. But WPF is quite a departure from previous technologies in terms of its programming model, underlying concepts, and basic terminology. Even viewing the source code for WPF (by cracking open its components with a tool like .NET Reflector) is a confusing experience because the code you're looking for often doesn't reside where you'd expect. When you combine all of this with the fact that there are often several ways to accomplish any task, you arrive at a conclusion shared by many: *WPF has a very steep learning curve.*

That's where this book comes in. Five years ago, I wrote *.NET and COM: The Complete Interoperability Guide* because I felt there was a need for an entire book to guide people through such a deep and complex topic. As WPF was developed, it was obvious that there would be no shortage of WPF books in the marketplace. But it wasn't clear to me that the books would have the right balance to guide people through the technology and its unique concepts while showing practical ways to exploit it. Therefore, I wrote *Windows Presentation Foundation Unleashed* with the following goals in mind:

▶ To provide a solid grounding in the underlying concepts in a practical and approachable fashion

▶ To answer the questions most people have when learning the technology, and to show how commonly desired tasks are accomplished

▶ To be an authoritative source, thanks to input from members of the WPF team who designed, implemented, and tested the technology

▶ To be clear about where the technology falls short, rather than selling the technology as the answer to all problems

▶ To be an easily navigated reference that you can constantly come back to

I hope you find this book to exhibit all of these attributes.

Who Should Read This Book?

This book is for software developers who are interested in user interfaces. Regardless of whether you're creating line-of-business applications, consumer-facing applications, or reusable controls, this book contains a lot of content that helps you get the most out of the platform. It's designed to be understandable even for folks who are new to .NET. And if you are already well versed in WPF, I'm confident that this book still has things to teach you. At the very least, it should be an invaluable reference for your bookshelf.

Because WPF enables you to create not only standalone Windows applications but also content hosted in a web browser, anyone interested in alternatives to Adobe Flash might find this book interesting. And although the more lightweight and cross-platform Silverlight technology does not have significant coverage in this book, many of the same concepts in this book will apply to WPF/E once it is released.

Although this book's content is not optimized for graphic designers, reading this book can be a great way to understand more of the "guts" behind a product like Microsoft Expression Blend.

To summarize, this book

- ▶ Covers everything you need to know about Extensible Application Markup Language (XAML), the new XML-based language for creating declarative user interfaces that can be easily restyled

- ▶ Examines the WPF feature areas in incredible depth: controls, layout, resources, data binding, styling, graphics, animation, and more

- ▶ Delves into topics that aren't covered by most books: 3D, speech, audio/video, documents, bitmap effects, and more

- ▶ Shows how to create popular UI elements, such as features introduced in the 2007 Microsoft Office System: Galleries, ScreenTips, custom control layouts, and more

- ▶ Demonstrates how to create sophisticated UI mechanisms, such as Visual Studio-like collapsible/dockable panes

- ▶ Explains how to develop and deploy all types of applications, including navigation-based applications, applications hosted in a web browser, and applications with great-looking nonrectangular windows

- ▶ Explains how to create first-class custom controls for WPF

- ▶ Demonstrates how to create hybrid WPF software that leverages Windows Forms, ActiveX, or other non-WPF technologies

- ▶ Explains how to exploit new Windows Vista features in WPF applications, and how to go beyond certain limitations of WPF

This book doesn't cover every last bit of WPF. (In particular, XML Paper Specification [XPS] documents are only given a small bit of attention.) WPF's surface area is so large that I don't believe any single book can. But I think you'll be pleased with the breadth and depth achieved by this book.

Examples in this book appear in XAML and C#, plus C++/CLI for interoperability discussions. XAML is used heavily for a number of reasons: It's often the most concise way to express source code, it can often be pasted into tools like XamlPad (in the Windows SDK) to see instant results without any compilation, WPF-based tools generate XAML rather than procedural code, and XAML is applicable no matter what .NET language you use, such as Visual Basic instead of C#. Whenever the mapping between XAML and a language like C# is not obvious, examples are shown in both representations.

Software Requirements

This book targets the final release of version 3.0 of Windows Presentation Foundation, the corresponding Windows SDK, and the October 2006 release of .NET Framework 3.0 extensions to Visual Studio 2005.

The following software is required:

▶ A version of Windows that supports the .NET Framework 3.0. This can be Windows XP with Service Pack 2 (including Media Center, Tablet PC, and x64 editions), Windows Server 2003 with Service Pack 1 (including the R2 edition), Windows Vista, or later versions.

▶ The .NET Framework 3.0, which is installed by default starting with Windows Vista. For earlier versions of Windows, you can download it for free from http://msdn.com.

In addition, the following software is recommended:

▶ The Windows Software Development Kit (SDK), specifically the .NET tools it includes. This is also a free download from http://msdn.com.

▶ Visual Studio 2005 or later, which can be a free Express edition downloaded from http://msdn.com. If you're using a 2005 edition of Visual Studio (Express or otherwise), you should download the extensions for .NET Framework 3.0 development available from MSDN. This is not necessary for later versions of Visual Studio.

If you want additional tool support for WPF-based graphic design, Microsoft Expression can be extremely helpful. See the appendix, "Helpful Tools," for other pieces of software that can be helpful for WPF design and development.

A few examples in Chapter 7, "Structuring and Deploying an Application," are specific to Windows Vista, but the rest of the book applies equally to all relevant versions of Windows.

...ue Examples

The source code for examples in this book can be downloaded via www.samspublishing.com or www.adamnathan.net/wpf.

How This Book Is Organized

This book is arranged into five main parts, representing the progression of feature areas that you typically need to understand to use WPF effectively. But if you're dying to jump ahead and learn about a topic such as 3D or animation, the book is set up to allow for nonlinear journeys as well. The following sections provide a summary of each part.

Part I: Background

The book introduces WPF by comparing it to alternative technologies and helping you make decisions about when WPF is appropriate for your needs. Chapter 2 explores XAML in great depth, giving you the foundation to understand the XAML you'll encounter in the rest of the book and in real life. Chapter 3 highlights the most unique pieces of WPF's programming model above and beyond what .NET programmers already understand.

- ▶ Chapter 1: Why Windows Presentation Foundation?

- ▶ Chapter 2: XAML Demystified

- ▶ Chapter 3: Important New Concepts in WPF

Part II: Building a WPF Application

Part II equips you with the knowledge to assemble and deploy a traditional-looking application (although some fancier effects like transforms, non-rectangular windows, and Aero glass are also covered). It begins by introducing WPF's implementation of controls you'd expect to have available, plus a few that you might not expect. It then devotes two chapters to arranging such controls (and other elements) in a user interface. Chapter 7 ends this part by examining several different ways to take WPF-based user interfaces and package and deploy complete applications. This not only includes traditional standalone Windows applications, but also applications that are more like web pages.

- ▶ Chapter 4: Introducing WPF's Controls

- ▶ Chapter 5: Sizing, Positioning, and Transforming Elements

- ▶ Chapter 6: Layout with Panels

- ▶ Chapter 7: Structuring and Deploying an Application

Part III: Features for Professional Developers

The features covered in Part III are not always necessary to use in WPF applications, but they can greatly enhance the development process. Therefore, they tend to be indispensable for professional developers who are serious about creating maintainable and robust applications or components.

- ▶ Chapter 8: Resources

- ▶ Chapter 9: Data Binding

- ▶ Chapter 10: Styles, Templates, Skins, and Themes

Part IV: Going Beyond Today's Applications with Rich Media

This part of the book covers the features in WPF that typically get the most attention. The support for 2D and 3D graphics, animation, video, and more enable you to create a stunning experience. These features—and the way they are exposed—set WPF apart from previous systems. WPF lowers the barrier to incorporating such content in your software, so you might try some of these features that you never would have dared to in the past!

- ▶ Chapter 11: 2D Graphics

- ▶ Chapter 12: 3D Graphics

- ▶ Chapter 13: Animation

- ▶ Chapter 14: Audio, Video, Speech, and Documents

Part V: Advanced Topics

The topics covered in Part V are relevant for advanced application developers, or developers of WPF-based controls. Because existing WPF controls can be radically restyled, the need for creating custom controls is greatly reduced.

- ▶ Chapter 15: Interoperability with Win32, Windows Forms, and ActiveX

- ▶ Chapter 16: User Controls and Custom Controls

- ▶ Chapter 17: Layout with Custom Panels

Conventions Used in This Book

Various typefaces in this book identify terms and other special items. These typefaces include the following:

Typeface	Meaning
Italic	Italic is used for new terms or phrases when they are initially defined, and occasionally for emphasis.
`Monospace`	Monospace is used for screen messages, code listings, and command samples, as well as filenames. In code listings, `italic monospace type` is used for placeholder text.
	Code listings are colorized similar to the way they are colorized in Visual Studio. `Blue monospace type` is used for XML elements and C#/C++ keywords, `brown monospace type` is used for XML element names and C#/C++ strings, `green monospace type` is used for comments, `red monospace type` is used for XML attributes, and `teal monospace type` is used for type names in C# and C++.

Throughout this book, you'll find the following sidebar elements:

▶ FAQ (Frequently Asked Question) sidebars present a question readers might have regarding the subject matter in a particular spot in the book—then it provides a concise answer.

▶ Digging Deeper sidebars present advanced or more detailed information on a subject than is provided in the text surrounding them. Think of Digging Deeper material as stuff you can look into if you're curious, but can ignore if you're not.

▶ Tips are bits of information that can help you in real-world situations. They often offer shortcuts or alternative approaches to make a task easier, quicker, or produce better results.

▶ Warnings alert you to an action or condition that can lead to an unexpected or unpredictable result, and then tell you how to avoid it.

PART I

Background

IN THIS PART

Why Windows Presentation Foundation?

In movies and on TV, the main characters are typically an exaggeration of the people you encounter in real life. They're more attractive, they react quicker, and they somehow always know exactly what to do. The same could be said about the software they use.

This first struck me back in 1994 when watching the movie *Disclosure*, starring Michael Douglas, Demi Moore, and an email program that looks nothing like Microsoft Outlook! Throughout the movie, we're treated to various visual features of the program: a spinning three-dimensional "e," messages that unfold when you open them and crumple when you delete them, hints of inking support, and slick animations when you print messages. (The email program isn't even the most unrealistic software in the movie. I'll just say "virtual reality database" and leave it at that.)

Usability issues aside, Hollywood has been telling us for a long time that software in the real world isn't as compelling as it should be. You can probably think of several examples on your own of TV shows and movies with comically unrealistic software. But real-world software is starting to catch up to Hollywood's standards! You can already see it in traditional operating systems (such as Mac OS and more recently Windows Vista), in software for devices such as TiVo or Xbox, and on the Web thanks to Adobe Flash. Users have increasing expectations for the experience of using software, and companies are spending a great deal of time and money on user interfaces that differentiate themselves from the competition.

Microsoft now has a solution for helping people create 21ˢᵗ-century software that meets these high demands, using less time and less money. This solution is Windows Presentation Foundation (WPF).

A Look at the Past

The primary technologies behind most of today's Windows-based user interfaces—the GDI and USER subsystems—were introduced with Windows 1.0 in 1985. That's almost prehistoric in the world of technology! In the early 1990s, OpenGL (created by Silicon Graphics) became a popular graphics library for doing advanced 2D and 3D graphics on both Windows and non-Windows systems. This was leveraged by people creating computer-aided design (CAD) programs, scientific visualization programs, and games. DirectX, a Microsoft technology introduced in 1995, provided a new high-performance alternative for 2D graphics, input, communication, sound, and eventually 3D (introduced with DirectX 2 in 1996).

Over the years, many enhancements have been made to both GDI and DirectX. GDI+, introduced in the Windows XP time frame, builds on top of GDI and adds support for features such as alpha blending and gradient brushes. DirectX (which, by the way, is the technology behind Xbox) continually comes out with new versions that push the limits of what can be done with computer graphics. With the introduction of .NET and managed code in 2002, developers were treated to a highly productive model for creating Windows (and web) applications. In this world, Windows Forms (built on top of GDI+) became the primary way a C#, Visual Basic, and (to a lesser degree) C++ developer started to create new user interfaces on Windows. But it still has all the fundamental limitations of GDI+ and USER.

Starting with DirectX 9, Microsoft shipped a DirectX framework for managed code (much like it shipped libraries specifically for Visual Basic in the past), which eventually morphed into the XNA framework. Although this enables C# developers to use DirectX without most of the complications of .NET/COM interoperability, these managed frameworks aren't significantly easier to use than their unmanaged counterparts unless you're writing a game. (Writing a game is easier because the XNA Framework includes new libraries specifically for game development and works with compelling tools such as the XNA Framework Content Pipeline and XNA Game Studio Express.)

So although you could have developed a Windows-based email program with the 3D effects seen in *Disclosure* ever since the mid-1990s with non-GDI technologies (actually, probably mixing DirectX or OpenGL with GDI), such technologies are rarely used in mainstream Windows applications even a decade later. There are several reasons for this: The hardware required to get a decent experience hasn't been ubiquitous until recently, it has been at least an order of magnitude harder to use alternative technologies, and GDI-based experiences have been considered "good enough."

Graphics hardware continues to get better (and cheaper) and consumer expectations continue to rise, but until now, the development experience has not improved significantly. In recent years, developers started to take matters into their own hands to get custom-branded applications and controls on Windows. A simple example of this is using bitmaps for buttons instead of the standard button control. These types of customizations can not only be expensive to develop, but they also often produce a flakier experience. Such applications often aren't as accessible as they should be, can't run in partial-trust environments, don't render well over Remote Desktop, don't handle high dots-per-inch (DPI) settings very well, and have other visual glitches.

Enter WPF

Microsoft recognized that something brand new was needed that escaped the limitations of GDI+ and USER yet provided the kind of productivity that people enjoy with frameworks like Windows Forms. Windows Presentation Foundation (WPF) is the answer for software developers and graphic designers who want to create modern user experiences without having to master several difficult technologies. Although "Presentation" sounds like a lofty term for what I would simply call a user interface, it's probably more appropriate for describing the higher level of visual polish that's expected of today's applications and the wide range of functionality included in WPF.

The highlights of WPF include the following:

▶ **Broad integration**—Prior to WPF, a Windows developer who wanted to use 3D, video, speech, and rich document viewing in addition to normal 2D graphics and controls would have to learn several independent technologies with a number of inconsistencies and attempt to blend them together without much built-in support. But WPF covers all these areas with a consistent programming model as well as tight integration when each type of media gets composited and rendered. You can apply the same kind of effects consistently across different media types, and many of the techniques you learn in one area apply to all the other areas.

▶ **Resolution independence**—Imagine a world in which moving to a higher resolution or DPI setting doesn't mean that everything gets smaller; instead, graphics and text simply get crisper! Envision user interfaces that look reasonable on a tiny Ultra-Mobile PC screen as well as on a 50-inch TV! WPF makes this easy, and gives you the power to shrink or enlarge elements on the screen independently from the screen's resolution. A lot of this is possible because of WPF's emphasis on vector graphics. This impact can be easily seen with the Windows Vista Magnifier application, which has intrinsic support for WPF vector graphics. Figure 1.1 shows Magnifier being used on a dialog in Microsoft Expression, in which half of the content is implemented with WPF and the other half is not. Notice the smooth scaling of the two WPF buttons compared to the jagged enlargement of the non-WPF combobox and tab control border (and even the mouse pointer)!

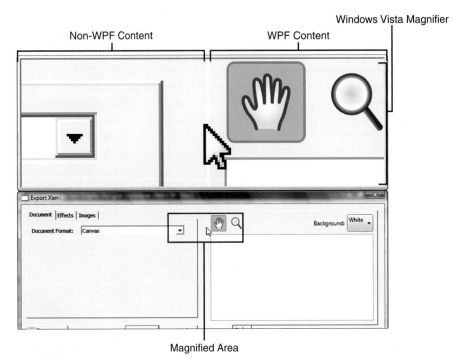

FIGURE 1.1   Vector-based WPF content scales beautifully even under the Windows Vista Magnifier program.

▶ **Hardware acceleration**—Although WPF is a new technology, it is built on top of Direct3D. Specifically, content in a WPF application—whether 2D or 3D, graphics, or text—is converted to 3D triangles, textures, and other Direct3D objects and then rendered by hardware. This means that, unlike GDI-based systems, WPF applications get the benefits of hardware acceleration for smoother graphics and all-around better performance (due to work being off-loaded to graphics processing units [GPUs] instead of central processor units [CPUs]). It also ensures that all WPF applications—not just high-end games—receive the maximum benefit from new hardware and drivers, whose advances typically focus on 3D capabilities. But WPF doesn't *require* high-end graphics hardware; it has a software rendering pipeline as well. This enables features not yet supported by hardware, enables high-fidelity printing of any content on the screen, and is used as a fallback mechanism when encountering inadequate hardware resources (such as an outdated graphics card or even a high-end one that has simply run out of GPU resources such as video memory).

More than that, though, WPF and the other new pieces of the .NET Framework 3.0 are the first major set of libraries from Microsoft *implemented* largely in managed code. In contrast, Managed DirectX, Windows Forms, and a lot of the .NET Framework base class libraries consist of relatively thin wrappers on top of unmanaged code. (That said, WPF does have core pieces implemented in unmanaged code and even exposes some low-level unmanaged APIs for writing your own imaging CODECs or bitmap effects.)

Emphasis on Declarative Descriptions

Throughout the new additions to the .NET Framework, XAML and XML are often used to expose functionality in a transparent and declarative fashion. In WPF, XAML is typically used to express a user interface. In Windows Workflow Foundation (WF), programs can also use XAML to express workflow-related activities. In Windows Communication Foundation (WCF), programs can use XML configuration files to separate their infrastructure protocol from their application protocol, and can use XML messages and contracts (Simple Object Access Protocol [SOAP] and Web Services Description Language [WSDL]) to communicate with other programs.

The point of all this is to make it easy for programmers to work together with experts in other fields. XAML and XML become the common language spoken by all parties (most likely via development tools and field-specific design tools). With WPF, the "field experts" are graphic designers, who can use a design tool to create a slick user interface while developers independently write code. But what enables the developer/designer cooperation in WPF is not just the common language of XAML, but the fact that great care went into making functionality exposed by WPF APIs accessible declaratively. This gives design tools a wide range of expressiveness without having to worry about generating procedural code.

FAQ

? Are there any differences with WPF on Windows Vista versus earlier versions of Windows?

WPF doesn't expose any Windows Vista–specific APIs. But two interesting implicit features were unable to be supported on earlier versions of Windows:

- ▶ 3D objects only get anti-aliasing on Windows Vista or later
- ▶ Non-rectangular or translucent windows only get hardware acceleration on Windows Vista or later

And of course, WPF controls have different default themes to match their host operating system (Aero on Windows Vista versus Luna or Classic on earlier systems).

One significant improvement in Windows Vista that helps WPF applications is a new driver model that helps with resource contention. It virtualizes and schedules GPU resources, making your system perform better when multiple GPU-intensive programs are running. Running multiple WPF or DirectX applications might bog down a Windows XP system, but shouldn't cause performance issues on a Windows Vista system.

Conclusion

As time passes, more software is delivering high-quality—sometimes *cinematic*—experiences, and those that don't risk looking old-fashioned. However, the effort involved in creating such user interfaces—especially on Windows—has been far too difficult in the past. WPF makes it easier than ever before to create all kinds of user interfaces, whether you want to create a "traditional-looking" Windows application or an immersive 3D experience worthy of a role in a summer blockbuster! But don't just take my word on it; read on to see for yourself how it's done!

CHAPTER 2

XAML Demystified

The preceding chapter touched on the new Extensible Application Markup Language known as XAML and its importance in integrating graphic designers into the development process. Even if you have no plans to work with graphic designers, you should still become familiar with XAML for the following reasons:

▶ XAML is usually the most concise way to represent user interfaces or other hierarchies of objects.

▶ The use of XAML encourages a separation of front-end appearance and back-end logic, which is helpful for maintenance even if you're only a team of one.

▶ XAML can often be pasted into tools like XamlPad (in the Windows SDK) to see results without any compilation.

▶ XAML is the language that almost all WPF-related tools emit.

Therefore, this chapter jumps right into the mechanics of XAML, examining its syntax in depth and showing how it relates to procedural code. Unlike the preceding chapter, this is a fairly deep dive! However, having this background knowledge before proceeding with the rest of the book will help you not only understand the code examples but also have better insights into why the APIs in each feature area were designed the way they were.

> **TIP**
>
> There are several ways to run the XAML examples in this chapter, which you can download in electronic form with the rest of this book's source code. For example, you can
>
> ▶ Save the content in a .xaml file and open it inside Internet Explorer (as long as you have the .NET Framework 3.0 or later installed)
>
> ▶ Open the XamlPad tool from the Windows SDK (described in the appendix, "Helpful Tools") and enter the content into its bottom pane
>
> ▶ Create a WPF-based Visual Studio project and replace the content of the main Window or Page with the desired content, which might require some code changes
>
> The first two options are great ways to get started and do a lot of experimentation. Mixing XAML with other content in a Visual Studio project is covered at the end of the chapter.

XAML Defined

XAML is a relatively simple and general-purpose declarative programming language suitable for constructing and initializing .NET objects. The .NET Framework 3.0 includes a compiler and run-time parser for XAML, as well as a plug-in that enables you to view standalone WPF-based XAML files (sometimes called loose XAML pages) inside Internet Explorer.

Because XAML is just a way to use .NET APIs, attempts to compare it to HTML, Scalable Vector Graphics (SVG), or other domain-specific formats/languages are misguided. XAML consists of rules for how parsers/compilers must treat XML and has some keywords, but it doesn't define any interesting elements by itself. So, talking about XAML without a framework like WPF is like talking about C# without the .NET Framework.

The role XAML plays in relation to WPF is often confused, so the first thing to realize is that WPF and XAML can be used independently from each other. Although XAML was originally designed for WPF, it applies to other technologies as well (such as Windows Workflow Foundation [WF]). Because of its general-purpose nature, XAML can be applied to just about any .NET technology if you really want it to be. Furthermore, using XAML with WPF is optional. Everything done with XAML can be done entirely in your favorite .NET language instead (but note that the reverse is not true). However, because of the benefits listed at the beginning of the chapter, it's rare to see WPF used in the real world without XAML.

Elements and Attributes

The XAML specification defines rules that map .NET namespaces, types, properties, and events into XML namespaces, elements, and attributes. This can be seen by examining the following simple (but complete) XAML file that declares a WPF Button and comparing it to the equivalent C# code:

XAML:

```
<Button xmlns="http://schemas.microsoft.com/winfx/2006/xaml/presentation"
  Content="OK"/>
```

C#:

```
System.Windows.Controls.Button b = new System.Windows.Controls.Button();
b.Content = "OK";
```

Although these two snippets are equivalent, you can instantly view the XAML in Internet Explorer and see a live button fill the browser window, as pictured in Figure 2.1, whereas the C# code must be compiled with additional code to be usable.

Declaring an XML element in XAML (known as an *object element*) is equivalent to instantiating the corresponding .NET object (always via a default constructor). Setting an attribute on the object element is equivalent to setting a property of the same name (called a *property attribute*) or hooking up a handler for an event of the same name (called an *event attribute*). For example, here's an update to the Button that not only sets its Content property, but also attaches an event handler to its Click event:

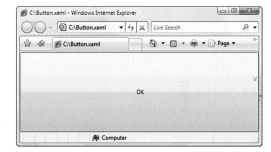

FIGURE 2.1   A simple WPF Button declared in a .xaml file.

XAML:

```
<Button xmlns="http://schemas.microsoft.com/winfx/2006/xaml/presentation"
  Content="OK" Click="button_Click"/>
```

C#:

```
System.Windows.Controls.Button b = new System.Windows.Controls.Button();
b.Click += new System.Windows.RoutedEventHandler(button_Click);
b.Content = "OK";
```

This requires a method called button_Click to be defined with the appropriate signature, which means that the XAML file can no longer be rendered standalone, as in Figure 2.1. The "Compilation: Mixing XAML with Procedural Code" section at the end of this chapter explains how to work with XAML that requires additional code. Note that XAML, like C#, is a case-sensitive language.

DIGGING DEEPER

Order of Property and Event Processing

At run-time, event handlers are always attached *before* any properties are set for an object declared in XAML (excluding the Name property, described toward the end of the chapter, which is set immediately after object construction). This enables appropriate events to be raised in response to properties being set, without worrying about the order of attributes used in XAML.

As for the ordering of multiple property sets or multiple event handler attachments, these are always performed in the relative order that property attributes and event attributes are specified on the object element. Fortunately, this ordering shouldn't matter in practice because .NET design guidelines dictate that classes should allow properties to be set in any order, and the same holds true for attaching event handlers.

Namespaces

The most mysterious part about comparing the previous XAML examples with the equivalent C# examples is how the XML namespace http://schemas.microsoft.com/winfx/2006/xaml/presentation maps to the .NET namespace System.Windows.Controls. It turns out that the mapping to this and other WPF namespaces is hard-coded inside the WPF assemblies with several instances of an XmlnsDefinitionAttribute custom attribute. (In case you're wondering, no web page exists at that schemas.microsoft.com URL—it's just an arbitrary string like any namespace.)

The root object element in a XAML file must specify at least one XML namespace that is used to qualify itself and any child elements. You can declare additional XML namespaces (on the root or on children), but each one must be given a distinct prefix to be used on any identifiers from that namespace. For example, WPF XAML files typically use a second namespace with the prefix x (denoted by using xmlns:x instead of just xmlns):

```
xmlns:x="http://schemas.microsoft.com/winfx/2006/xaml"
```

This is the XAML language namespace, which maps to types in the System.Windows.Markup namespace but also defines some special directives for the XAML compiler or parser. These directives often appear as attributes to XML elements, so they look like properties of the host element but actually are not. For a list of XAML keywords, see the "XAML Keywords" section later in this chapter.

Using http://schemas.microsoft.com/winfx/2006/xaml/presentation as a default namespace and http://schemas.microsoft.com/winfx/2006/xaml as a secondary namespace with the prefix x is just a convention, just like it's a convention to begin a C# file with a using System; directive. You could have written the original XAML file as follows and it would mean the same thing:

```
<WpfNamespace:Button
  xmlns:WpfNamespace="http://schemas.microsoft.com/winfx/2006/xaml/presentation"
  Content="OK"/>
```

Of course, for readability it makes sense to have your most commonly used namespace be prefix-free (also known as the *primary* XML namespace) and use short prefixes for any additional namespaces.

DIGGING DEEPER

The Implicit .NET Namespaces

WPF maps all of the following .NET namespaces to the `http://schemas.microsoft.com/winfx/2006/xaml/presentation` XML namespace used throughout this book:

- ▶ `System.Windows`
- ▶ `System.Windows.Automation`
- ▶ `System.Windows.Controls`
- ▶ `System.Windows.Controls.Primitives`
- ▶ `System.Windows.Data`
- ▶ `System.Windows.Documents`
- ▶ `System.Windows.Forms.Integration`
- ▶ `System.Windows.Ink`
- ▶ `System.Windows.Input`
- ▶ `System.Windows.Media`
- ▶ `System.Windows.Media.Animation`
- ▶ `System.Windows.Media.Effects`
- ▶ `System.Windows.Media.Imaging`
- ▶ `System.Windows.Media.Media3D`
- ▶ `System.Windows.Media.TextFormatting`
- ▶ `System.Windows.Navigation`
- ▶ `System.Windows.Shapes`

Because this is a many-to-one mapping, the designers of WPF needed to take care not to introduce two classes with the same name, despite being in separate .NET namespaces.

TIP

The standalone XAML examples in this chapter explicitly specify their namespaces, but in the remainder of the book, most examples assume that `http://schemas.microsoft.com/winfx/2006/xaml/presentation` is declared as the primary namespace and `http://schemas.microsoft.com/winfx/2006/xaml` is declared as a secondary namespace with the prefix x. If you want to view such content in Internet Explorer or copy them into a program like XamlPad, be sure to add these explicitly.

Property Elements

Chapter 1, "Why Windows Presentation Foundation," mentioned that rich composition is one of the highlights of WPF. This can be demonstrated with the simple `Button` from Figure 2.1, because you can put arbitrary content inside it; you're not limited to just text! To demonstrate this, the following code embeds a simple square to make a VCR-style Stop button:

```
System.Windows.Controls.Button b = new System.Windows.Controls.Button();
System.Windows.Shapes.Rectangle r = new System.Windows.Shapes.Rectangle();
r.Width = 40;
r.Height = 40;
r.Fill = System.Windows.Media.Brushes.Black;
b.Content = r; // Make the square the content of the Button
```

Button's `Content` property is of type `System.Object`, so it can easily be set to the 40x40 `Rectangle` object. The result is pictured in Figure 2.2.

That's pretty neat, but how can you do the same thing in XAML with property attribute syntax? What kind of string could you possibly set `Content` to that is equivalent to the preceding `Rectangle` declared in C#? There is no such string, but XAML fortunately provides an alternative (and more verbose) syntax for setting complex property values: *property elements*. This looks like the following:

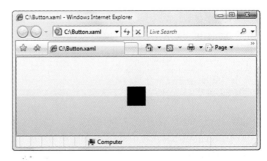

FIGURE 2.2   Updating the WPF `Button` with complex content.

```
<Button xmlns="http://schemas.microsoft.com/winfx/2006/xaml/presentation">
<Button.Content>
  <Rectangle Height="40" Width="40" Fill="Black"/>
</Button.Content>
</Button>
```

The `Content` property is now set with an XML element instead of an XML attribute, making it equivalent to the previous C# code. The period in `Button.Content` is what distinguishes property elements from object elements. They always take the form *TypeName.PropertyName*, they are always contained inside a *TypeName* object element, and they can never have attributes of their own.

Property element syntax can be used for simple property values as well. The following `Button` that sets two properties with attributes (`Content` and `Background`):

```
<Button xmlns="http://schemas.microsoft.com/winfx/2006/xaml/presentation"
  Content="OK" Background="White"/>
```

is equivalent to this `Button` that sets the same two properties with elements:

```
<Button xmlns="http://schemas.microsoft.com/winfx/2006/xaml/presentation">
<Button.Content>
  OK
</Button.Content>
<Button.Background>
  White
</Button.Background>
</Button>
```

Of course, using attributes when you can is a nice shortcut when hand-typing XAML.

Type Converters

Let's look at the C# code equivalent to the preceding `Button` declaration that sets both `Content` and `Background` properties:

```
System.Windows.Controls.Button b = new System.Windows.Controls.Button();
b.Content = "OK";
b.Background = System.Windows.Media.Brushes.White;
```

Wait a minute—how can `"White"` in the previous XAML file be equivalent to the static `System.Windows.Media.Brushes.White` field (of type `System.Windows.Media.SolidColorBrush`) in the C# code? Indeed, this example exposes a subtlety with using strings to set properties in XAML that are a different data type than `System.String` or `System.Object`. In such cases, the XAML parser or compiler must look for a *type converter* that knows how to convert the string representation to the desired data type. WPF provides type converters for many common data types: `Brush`, `Color`, `FontWeight`, `Point`, and so on. They are all classes deriving from `TypeConverter` (`BrushConverter`, `ColorConverter`, and so on). You can also write your own type converters for custom data types. Unlike the XAML language, type converters generally support case-insensitive strings.

Without a type converter for `Brush`, you would have to use property element syntax to set the `Background` in XAML, as follows:

```
<Button xmlns="http://schemas.microsoft.com/winfx/2006/xaml/presentation"
  Content="OK">
<Button.Background>
  <SolidColorBrush Color="White"/>
</Button.Background>
</Button>
```

And even that is only possible because of a type converter for Color that can make sense of the "White" string. If there were no Color type converter, you could still write:

```
<Button xmlns="http://schemas.microsoft.com/winfx/2006/xaml/presentation"
Content="OK">
<Button.Background>
  <SolidColorBrush>
  <SolidColorBrush.Color>
    <Color A="255" R="255" G="255" B="255"/>
  </SolidColorBrush.Color>
  </SolidColorBrush>
</Button.Background>
</Button>
```

But *that's* only possible because of a type converter that can convert each "255" string into a Byte value expected by the A, R, G, and B properties of the Color type. Without this type converter, you would be stuck. Therefore, type converters don't just enhance the readability of XAML, but they also enable concepts to be expressed that wouldn't otherwise be expressible.

DIGGING DEEPER

Using Type Converters in Procedural Code

Although the C# code that sets Background to System.Windows.Media.Brushes.White produces the same result as the XAML declaration that assigns it to the "White" string, it doesn't actually use the same type conversion mechanism employed by the XAML parser or compiler. The following code more accurately represents the run-time retrieval and execution of the appropriate type converter for Brush:

```
System.Windows.Controls.Button b = new System.Windows.Controls.Button();
b.Content = "OK";
b.Background = (Brush)System.ComponentModel.TypeDescriptor.GetConverter(
  typeof(Brush)).ConvertFromInvariantString("White");
```

Unlike the previous C# code, misspelling White would not cause a compilation error but would cause an exception at run-time, as with XAML. (Although Visual Studio does provide compile-time warnings for mistakes in XAML such as this.)

Markup Extensions

Markup extensions, like type converters, enable you to extend the expressibility of XAML. Both can evaluate a string attribute value at run-time (except for a few built-in markup extensions that are evaluated at compile time for performance reasons) and produce an appropriate object based on the string. Just like with type converters, WPF ships with several markup extensions built in. You can find them as classes deriving from MarkupExtension on the book's front inside cover.

Unlike type converters, however, markup extensions are invoked from XAML with explicit and consistent syntax. For this reason, markup extensions are a preferred approach for extending XAML. In addition, markup extensions enable you to overcome potential limitations in existing type converters that you don't have the power to change. For example, if you want to set a control's background to a fancy gradient brush with a simple string value, you can write a custom markup extension that supports it even though the built-in `BrushConverter` does not.

Whenever an attribute value is enclosed in curly braces ({}), the XAML compiler/parser treats it as a markup extension value rather than a literal string (or something that needs to be type-converted). The following `Button` uses three different markup extension values with three different properties:

Markup extension class

```
<Button xmlns="http://schemas.microsoft.com/winfx/2006/xaml/presentation"
        xmlns:x="http://schemas.microsoft.com/winfx/2006/xaml"
        Background="{x:Null}"
        Height="{x:Static SystemParameters.IconHeight}"
        Content="{Binding Path=Height, RelativeSource={RelativeSource Self}}"/>
```

Positional parameter

Named parameters

The first identifier in each set of curly braces is the name of the markup extension class. By convention, such classes end with an `Extension` suffix, but you can leave it off when using it in XAML. In this example, `NullExtension` (seen as `x:Null`) and `StaticExtension` (seen as `x:Static`) are classes in the `System.Windows.Markup` namespace, so the x prefix must be used to locate them. `Binding` (which doesn't have the `Extension` suffix) is in the `System.Windows.Data` namespace, so it can be found in the default XML namespace.

If a markup extension supports it, comma-delimited parameters can be specified. Positional parameters (such as `SystemParameters.IconHeight` in the example) are treated as string arguments for the extension class's appropriate constructor. Named parameters (`Path` and `RelativeSource` in the example) enable you to set properties with matching names on the constructed extension object. The values for these properties can be markup extension values themselves (using nested curly braces, as done with the value for `RelativeSource`) or literal values that can undergo the normal type conversion process. If you're familiar with .NET custom attributes (the .NET Framework's popular extensibility mechanism), you've probably noticed that the design and usage of markup extensions closely mirrors the design and usage of custom attributes. That is intentional.

In the preceding `Button` declaration, `NullExtension` enables the `Background` brush to be set to `null`, which isn't natively supported by `BrushConverter` (or many other type converters for that matter). This is just done for demonstration purposes, for a `null` `Background` is not very useful. `StaticExtension` enables the use of static properties, fields, constants, and enumeration values rather than hard-coding literals in XAML. In this case, the `Button`'s `Height` is set to the operating system's current height setting for icons, exposed by the static `IconHeight` field on a `System.Windows.SystemParameters` class. `Binding`, covered in depth in Chapter 9, "Data Binding," enables `Content` to be set to the same value as its `Height` property.

DIGGING DEEPER

Escaping the Curly Braces

If you ever want a property attribute value to be set to a literal string beginning with an open curly brace ({), you must escape it so it doesn't get treated as a markup extension. This can be done by preceding it with an empty pair of curly braces. For example:

```
<Button xmlns="http://schemas.microsoft.com/winfx/2006/xaml/presentation"
        Content="{}{This is not a markup extension!}"/>
```

Alternatively, you could use property element syntax without any escaping because the curly braces do not have special meaning in this context. The preceding `Button` could be rewritten as follows (with implicit property element syntax because `Content` is the content property):

```
<Button xmlns="http://schemas.microsoft.com/winfx/2006/xaml/presentation">
  {This is not a markup extension!}
</Button>
```

Because markup extensions are just classes with default constructors, they can be used with property element syntax. The following `Button` is identical to the preceding one:

```
<Button xmlns="http://schemas.microsoft.com/winfx/2006/xaml/presentation"
        xmlns:x="http://schemas.microsoft.com/winfx/2006/xaml">
<Button.Background>
  <x:Null/>
</Button.Background>
<Button.Height>
  <x:Static Member="SystemParameters.IconHeight"/>
</Button.Height>
<Button.Content>
  <Binding Path="Height">
  <Binding.RelativeSource>
    <RelativeSource Mode="Self"/>
  </Binding.RelativeSource>
  </Binding>
</Button.Content>
</Button>
```

This transformation works because these markup extensions all have properties corresponding to their parameterized constructor arguments (the positional parameters used with property attribute syntax). For example, `StaticExtension` has a `Member` property that has the same meaning as the argument that was previously passed to its parameterized constructor, and `RelativeSource` has a `Mode` property corresponding to its constructor argument.

> **DIGGING DEEPER**
>
> **Markup Extensions and Procedural Code**
>
> The actual work done by a markup extension is specific to each extension. For example, the following C# code is equivalent to the XAML-based `Button` that uses `NullExtension`, `StaticExtension`, and `Binding`:
>
> ```
> System.Windows.Controls.Button b = new System.Windows.Controls.Button();
> // Set Background:
> b.Background = null;
> // Set Height:
> b.Height = System.Windows.SystemParameters.IconHeight;
> // Set Content:
> System.Windows.Data.Binding binding = new System.Windows.Data.Binding();
> binding.Path = new System.Windows.PropertyPath("Height");
> binding.RelativeSource = System.Windows.Data.RelativeSource.Self;
> b.SetBinding(System.Windows.Controls.Button.ContentProperty, binding);
> ```
>
> However, this code doesn't use the same mechanism as the XAML parser or compiler, which rely on each markup extension to set the appropriate values at run-time (essentially by invoking each one's `ProvideValue` method). The procedural code equivalent of this mechanism is often complex, sometimes requiring context that only a parser would have (like how to resolve an XML namespace prefix that could be used in `StaticExtension`'s `Member`). Fortunately, there is no reason to use markup extensions this way in procedural code!

Children of Object Elements

A XAML file, like all XML files, must have a single root object element. Therefore, it should come as no surprise that object elements can support child object elements (not just property elements, which aren't children as far as XAML is concerned). An object element can have three types of children: a value for a content property, collection items, or a value that can be type-converted to its parent.

The Content Property

Most WPF classes designate a property (via a custom attribute) that should be set to whatever content is inside the XML element. This property is called the *content property*, and is really just a convenient shortcut to make the XAML representation more compact. In some ways, these content properties are like (often-maligned) default properties in Visual Basic.

`Button`'s `Content` property is (appropriately) given this special designation, so the following `Button`:

```
<Button xmlns="http://schemas.microsoft.com/winfx/2006/xaml/presentation"
  Content="OK"/>
```

could be rewritten as:

```
<Button xmlns="http://schemas.microsoft.com/winfx/2006/xaml/presentation">
  OK
</Button>
```

Or more usefully, the Button with more complex content:

```
<Button xmlns="http://schemas.microsoft.com/winfx/2006/xaml/presentation">
<Button.Content>
  <Rectangle Height="40" Width="40" Fill="Black"/>
</Button.Content>
</Button>
```

could be rewritten as:

```
<Button xmlns="http://schemas.microsoft.com/winfx/2006/xaml/presentation">
  <Rectangle Height="40" Width="40" Fill="Black"/>
</Button>
```

There is no requirement that the content property must actually be called Content; classes such as ComboBox, ListBox, and TabControl (also in the System.Windows.Controls namespace) use their Items property as the content property.

Collection Items

XAML enables you to add items to the two main types of collections that support indexing: lists and dictionaries.

Lists

A *list* is any collection implementing System.Collections.IList, such as System.Collections.ArrayList or numerous collection classes defined by WPF. For example, the following XAML adds two items to a ListBox, whose Items property is an ItemCollection that implements IList:

```
<ListBox xmlns="http://schemas.microsoft.com/winfx/2006/xaml/presentation">
<ListBox.Items>
  <ListBoxItem Content="Item 1"/>
  <ListBoxItem Content="Item 2"/>
</ListBox.Items>
</ListBox>
```

This is equivalent to the following C# code:

```
System.Windows.Controls.ListBox listbox = new System.Windows.Controls.ListBox();
System.Windows.Controls.ListBoxItem item1 =
  new System.Windows.Controls.ListBoxItem();
System.Windows.Controls.ListBoxItem item2 =
```

```
      new System.Windows.Controls.ListBoxItem();
item1.Content = "Item 1";
item2.Content = "Item 2";
listbox.Items.Add(item1);
listbox.Items.Add(item2);
```

Furthermore, because `Items` is the content property for `ListBox`, you can shorten the XAML even further as follows:

```
<ListBox xmlns="http://schemas.microsoft.com/winfx/2006/xaml/presentation">
  <ListBoxItem Content="Item 1"/>
  <ListBoxItem Content="Item 2"/>
</ListBox>
```

In all of these cases, the code works because `ListBox`'s `Items` property is automatically initialized to any empty collection object. If a collection property is initially `null` instead (and is read/write, unlike `ListBox`'s read-only `Items` property), you would need to wrap the items in an explicit element that instantiates the collection.

Dictionaries

`System.Windows.ResourceDictionary` is a commonly used collection type in WPF that you'll see more of in Chapter 8, "Resources." It implements `System.Collections.IDictionary` so it supports adding, removing, and enumerating key/value pairs in procedural code, as you would do with a typical hash table. In XAML, you can add key/value pairs to any collection implementing `IDictionary`. For example, the following XAML adds two `Colors` to a `ResourceDictionary`:

```
<ResourceDictionary
    xmlns="http://schemas.microsoft.com/winfx/2006/xaml/presentation"
    xmlns:x="http://schemas.microsoft.com/winfx/2006/xaml">
    <Color x:Key="1" A="255" R="255" G="255" B="255"/>
    <Color x:Key="2" A="0" R="0" G="0" B="0"/>
</ResourceDictionary>
```

This leverages the XAML `Key` keyword (defined in the secondary XML namespace) that is processed specially and enables us to attach a key to each `Color` value. (The `Color` type does not define a `Key` property.) Therefore, the XAML is equivalent to the following C# code:

```
System.Windows.ResourceDictionary d = new System.Windows.ResourceDictionary();
System.Windows.Media.Color color1 = new System.Windows.Media.Color();
System.Windows.Media.Color color2 = new System.Windows.Media.Color();
color1.A = 255; color1.R = 255; color1.G = 255; color1.B = 255;
color2.A = 0;   color2.R = 0;   color2.G = 0;   color2.B = 0;
d.Add("1", color1);
d.Add("2", color2);
```

Note that the value specified in XAML with x:Key is always treated as a string unless a markup extension is used; no type conversion is attempted.

More Type Conversion

Plain text can often be used as the child of an object element, such as in the following XAML declaration of a SolidColorBrush:

```
<SolidColorBrush>White</SolidColorBrush>
```

This is equivalent to:

```
<SolidColorBrush Color="White"/>
```

even though Color has not been designated as a content property. In this case, the first XAML snippet works because a type converter exists that can convert strings such as "White" (or "white" or "#FFFFFF") into a SolidColorBrush object.

Although type converters play a huge role in making XAML readable, the downside is that they can make XAML appear a bit "magical" and harder to understand how it maps to instances of .NET objects. Using what you know so far, it would be reasonable to assume that you can't declare an abstract class element in XAML because there's no way to instantiate it. However, even though System.Windows.Media.Brush is an abstract base class for SolidColorBrush, GradientBrush, and other concrete brushes, you can express the preceding XAML snippets as simply:

```
<Brush>White</Brush>
```

because the type converter for Brushes understands that this is still a SolidColorBrush. This may seem like an unusual feature, but it's important for supporting the ability to express primitive types in XAML, as demonstrated in the "The Extensible Part of XAML" sidebar.

DIGGING DEEPER

The Extensible Part of XAML

Because XAML was designed to work with the .NET type system, you can use it with just about any .NET object (or even *COM objects*, thanks to COM interoperability), including ones you define yourself. It doesn't matter whether these objects have anything to do with a user interface. However, the objects need to be designed in a "declarative-friendly" way. For example, if a class doesn't have a default constructor and doesn't expose useful instance properties, it's not going to be directly usable from XAML. A lot of care went into the design of the WPF APIs (above and beyond the usual .NET design guidelines) to fit XAML's declarative model.

The WPF assemblies are marked with XmlnsDefinitionAttribute to map their .NET namespaces to XML namespaces in a XAML file, but what about assemblies that weren't designed with XAML in mind and, therefore, don't use this attribute? Their types can still be used; you just need to use a special directive as the XML namespace. For example, here's some plain old C# code using .NET Framework APIs contained in mscorlib.dll:

Continued

```
System.Collections.Hashtable h = new System.Collections.Hashtable();
h.Add("key1", 7);
h.Add("key2", 23);
```

and here's how it can be represented in XAML:

```
<collections:Hashtable
   xmlns:collections="clr-namespace:System.Collections;assembly=mscorlib"
   xmlns:sys="clr-namespace:System;assembly=mscorlib"
   xmlns:x="http://schemas.microsoft.com/winfx/2006/xaml">
   <sys:Int32 x:Key="key1">7</sys:Int32>
   <sys:Int32 x:Key="key2">23</sys:Int32>
</collections:Hashtable>
```

The `clr-namespace` directive enables you to place a .NET namespace directly inside XAML. The assembly specification at the end is only necessary if the desired types don't reside in the same assembly that the XAML is compiled into. Typically the assembly's simple name is used (as with `mscorlib`), but you can use the canonical representation supported by `System.Reflection.Assembly.Load` (although with no spaces allowed) that includes additional information such as a version and/or public key token.

Two key points about this example highlight the integration with not only the .NET type system but also with specific types in the .NET Framework base class libraries:

▶ Child elements can be added to the parent `Hashtable` with the standard XAML `x:Key` syntax because `Hashtable` and other collection classes in the .NET Framework have implemented the `IDictionary` interface since version 1.0.

▶ `System.Int32` can be used in this simple fashion because a type converter already exists that supports converting strings to integers. This is because the type converters supported by XAML are simply classes that derive from `System.ComponentModel.TypeConverter`, a class that has also been around since version 1.0 of the .NET Framework. This is the same type conversion mechanism used by Windows Forms (enabling you to type strings into the Visual Studio property grid, for example, and have them converted to the appropriate type).

XAML Processing Rules for Object Element Children

You've now seen the three types of object element children. To avoid ambiguity, the following rules are followed by any valid XAML parser or compiler when encountering and interpreting child elements:

1. If the type implements `IList`, call `IList.Add` for each child.

2. Otherwise, if the type implements `IDictionary`, call `IDictionary.Add` for each child, using the `x:Key` attribute value for the key and the element for the value.

3. Otherwise, if the parent supports a content property (indicated by `System.Windows.Markup.ContentPropertyAttribute`) and the type of the child is compatible with that property, treat the child as its value.

Continues

DIGGING DEEPER

Continued

4. Otherwise, if the child is plain text and a type converter exists to transform the child into the parent type (*and* no properties are set on the parent element), treat the child as the input to the type converter and use the output as the parent object instance.

5. Otherwise, raise an error.

Rules 1 and 2 enable the behavior described in the previous "Collection Items" section, Rule 3 enables the behavior described in the "The Content Property" section, and Rule 4 explains the often-confusing behavior described in the "More Type Conversion" section.

Compilation: Mixing XAML with Procedural Code

WPF applications can be written entirely in procedural code in any .NET language. In addition, certain types of simple applications can be written entirely in XAML, thanks to the data-binding features described in Chapter 9, the triggers introduced in the next chapter, and the fact that loose XAML pages can be rendered in Internet Explorer. However, most WPF applications are a mix of XAML with procedural code. This section covers the two ways that XAML and code can be mixed together, then looks at all the keywords in the XAML language namespace that help to control the interaction between XAML and code.

Loading and Parsing XAML at Run-Time

WPF's run-time XAML parser is exposed as two classes in the `System.Windows.Markup` namespace: `XamlReader` and `XamlWriter`. And their APIs couldn't be much simpler. `XamlReader` contains a few overloads of a static `Load` method, and `XamlWriter` contains a few overloads of a static `Save` method. Therefore, programs written in any .NET language can leverage XAML at run-time without much effort.

XamlReader

The set of `XamlReader.Load` methods parse XAML, create the appropriate .NET objects, and return an instance of the root element. So, if a XAML file named `MyWindow.xaml` in the current directory contains a `Window` object (explained in depth in Chapter 7, "Structuring and Deploying an Application") as its root node, the following code could be used to load and retrieve the `Window`:

```
Window window = null;
using (FileStream fs =
  new FileStream("MyWindow.xaml", FileMode.Open, FileAccess.Read))
{
  // Get the root element, which we know is a Window
  window = (Window)XamlReader.Load(fs);
}
```

In this case, Load is called with a FileStream (from the System.IO namespace). After Load returns, the entire hierarchy of objects in the XAML file is instantiated in memory, so the XAML file is no longer needed. In the preceding code, the FileStream is instantly closed by exiting the using block. Because XamlReader can be passed an arbitrary Stream (or System.Xml. XmlReader via a different overload), you have a lot of flexibility in retrieving XAML content.

> **TIP**
>
> XamlReader also defines LoadAsync instance methods that load and parse XAML content asynchronously. You'll want to use LoadAsync to keep a responsive user interface during the loading of large files or files over the network, for example. Accompanying these methods are a CancelAsync method for halting the processing and a LoadCompleted event for knowing when the processing is complete.

Now that an instance of the root element exists, you can retrieve child elements by making use of the appropriate content properties or collection properties. The following code assumes that the Window has a child of type StackPanel whose fifth child is an OK Button:

```
Window window = null;
using (FileStream fs =
  new FileStream("MyWindow.xaml", FileMode.Open, FileAccess.Read))
{
  // Get the root element, which we know is a Window
  window = (Window)XamlReader.Load(fs);
}
// Grab the OK button by walking the children (with hard-coded knowledge!)
StackPanel panel = (StackPanel)window.Content;
Button okButton = (Button)panel.Children[4];
```

With a reference to the Button, you can do whatever you want: set additional properties (perhaps using logic that is hard or impossible to express in XAML), attach event handlers, or perform additional actions that you can't do from XAML, such as calling its methods.

Of course, the code that uses a hard-coded index and other assumptions about the user interface structure isn't very satisfying, as simple changes to the XAML can break it. Instead, you could have written code to process the elements more generically and look for a Button element whose content is an "OK" string, but that would be a lot of work for such a simple task. In addition, if you want the Button to contain graphical content, how can you easily identify it in the presence of multiple Buttons?

Fortunately, XAML supports naming of elements so they can be found and used reliably from procedural code.

Naming XAML Elements

The XAML language namespace has a `Name` keyword that enables you to give any element a name. For the simple OK `Button` that we're imagining is embedded somewhere inside a `Window`, the `Name` keyword can be used as follows:

```
<Button x:Name="okButton">OK</Button>
```

With this in place, you can update the preceding C# code to use `Window`'s `FindName` method that searches its children (recursively) and returns the desired instance:

```
Window window = null;
using (FileStream fs =
  new FileStream("MyWindow.xaml", FileMode.Open, FileAccess.Read))
{
  // Get the root element, which we know is a Window
  window = (Window)XamlReader.Load(fs);
}
// Grab the OK button, knowing only its name
Button okButton = (Button)window.FindName("okButton");
```

`FindName` is not unique to `Window`; it is defined on `FrameworkElement` and `FrameworkContentElement`, base classes for many important classes in WPF, as you can see on the inside back cover of this book.

DIGGING DEEPER

Naming Elements Without `x:Name`

The `x:Name` syntax can be used to name elements, but some classes define their own property that can be treated as the element's name (by marking themselves with `System.Windows.Markup.RuntimeNamePropertyAttribute`). For example, `FrameworkElement` and `FrameworkContentElement` have a `Name` property, so they mark themselves with `RuntimeNameProperty("Name")`. This means that on such elements you can simply set its `Name` property to a string rather than using the `x:Name` syntax. You can use either mechanism, but you can't use both simultaneously. Having two ways to set a name is a bit confusing, but it's handy for these classes to have a `Name` property for use by procedural code, and without this special treatment you'd be able to set both `x:Name` and `Name` simultaneously in XAML, which would be even more confusing!

Compiling XAML

Loading and parsing XAML at run-time is interesting for dynamic skinning scenarios (demonstrated in Chapter 10, "Styles, Templates, Skins, and Themes"), or for .NET languages that don't have the necessary support for XAML compilation. Most WPF projects, however, will leverage the XAML compilation supported by MSBuild and Visual Studio. XAML compilation involves three things: converting a XAML file into a special binary format, embedding the converted content as a binary resource in the assembly being built, and performing the plumbing that connects XAML with procedural code automatically. At the time of writing, C# and Visual Basic are the two languages with the best support for XAML compilation.

If you don't care about mixing procedural code with your XAML file, then all you need to do to compile it is add it to WPF project in Visual Studio with a Build Action of Page. (Chapter 7 explains ways to make use of the content in the context of an application.) But for the typical case of compiling a XAML file *and* mixing it with procedural code, the first step is specifying a subclass for the root element in a XAML file. This can be done with the Class keyword defined in the XAML language namespace, for example:

> **DIGGING DEEPER**
>
> **Supporting Compiled XAML with any .NET Language**
>
> If you want to leverage XAML compilation with an arbitrary .NET language, there are two basic requirements for enabling this: having a corresponding CodeDom provider and having an MSBuild target file. In addition, language support for partial classes is helpful but not strictly required.

```
<Window xmlns="http://schemas.microsoft.com/winfx/2006/xaml/presentation"
        xmlns:x="http://schemas.microsoft.com/winfx/2006/xaml"
        x:Class="MyNamespace.MyWindow">
  ...
</Window>
```

In a separate source file (but in the same project), you can define that subclass and add whatever members you want:

```
namespace MyNamespace
{
  partial class MyWindow : Window
  {
    public MyWindow
    {
      // Necessary to call in order to load XAML-defined content!
      InitializeComponent();
      ...
    }
    Any other members can go here...
  }
}
```

This is often referred to as the *code-behind file*. If you reference any event handlers in XAML (via event attributes such as Click on Button), this is where they should be defined.

The `partial` keyword in the class definition is important, as the class's implementation is spread across more than one file. If the .NET language doesn't support partial classes (as with C++/CLI and J#), the XAML file must also use a `Subclass` keyword in the root element as follows:

```
<Window xmlns="http://schemas.microsoft.com/winfx/2006/xaml/presentation"
        xmlns:x="http://schemas.microsoft.com/winfx/2006/xaml"
        x:Class="MyNamespace.MyWindow" x:Subclass="MyNamespace.MyWindow2">
  …
</Window>
```

With this change, the XAML file completely defines the `Subclass` (`MyWindow2` in this case) but uses the `Class` in the code-behind file (`MyWindow`) as its base class. Therefore, this simulates the ability to split the implementationacross two files by relying on inheritance.

When creating a WPF-based C# or Visual Basic project in Visual Studio, or when you use Add New Item… to add certain WPF items to a project, Visual Studio automatically creates a XAML file with x:Class on its root, creates the code-behind source file with the partial class definition, and links the two together so they are built properly.

If you're an MSBuild user and want to understand the contents of the project file that enables code-behind, you can open any of the C# project files included with this book's source code in a simple text editor such as Notepad. But the relevant part of a typical project is as follows:

```
<ItemGroup>
  <Page Include="MyWindow.xaml"/>
</ItemGroup>
<ItemGroup>
  <Compile Include="MyWindow.xaml.cs">
    <DependentUpon>MyWindow.xaml</DependentUpon>
    <SubType>Code</SubType>
  </Compile>
</ItemGroup>
```

For such a project, the build system generates several items when processing `MyWindow.xaml`, including

- A BAML file (`MyWindow.baml`), which gets embedded in the assembly as a binary resource by default.

- A C# source file (`MyWindow.g.cs`), which gets compiled into the assembly like all other source code.

BAML

BAML, which stands for Binary Application Markup Language, is simply XAML that has been parsed, tokenized, and converted into binary form. Although any chunk of XAML can be represented by procedural code, the XAML-to-BAML compilation process *does not* generate procedural source code. So, BAML is not like Microsoft intermediate language (MSIL); it is a compressed declarative format that is faster to load and parse (and smaller in size) than plain XAML. BAML is just an implementation detail of the XAML compilation process without any direct public exposure, so it could be replaced with something different in the future. Nevertheless, it's interesting to be aware of its existence.

Generated Source Code

Some procedural code does get generated in the XAML compilation process (if you use x:Class), but it's just some "glue code" similar to what had to be written to load and parse a loose XAML file at run-time. Such files are given a suffix like .g.cs (or .g.vb), where the g stands for generated.

Each generated source file contains a partial class definition for the class specified with x:Class on the root object element. This partial class contains a field (private by default) for every named element in the XAML file, using the element name as the field name. It also contains an InitializeComponent method that does the grunt work of loading the embedded BAML resource, assigning the fields to the appropriate instances originally declared in XAML, and hooking up any event handlers (if any event handlers were specified in the XAML file).

> **TIP**
>
> x:Class can only be used in a XAML file that gets compiled. But you can sometimes compile a XAML file with no x:Class without problems. This simply means that there is no corresponding code-behind file, so you can't use any features that rely on the presence of procedural code. Therefore, adding a XAML file to a Visual Studio project without an x:Class directive can be a handy way to get the deployment and performance benefits of compiled XAML without having to create an unnecessary code-behind file.

> **DIGGING DEEPER**
>
> **There Once Was a CAML...**
>
> Early prerelease versions of WPF had the ability to compile XAML into BAML or MSIL. This MSIL output was called CAML, which stood for *Compiled* Application Markup Language. The idea was to enable the choice of optimizing for size (BAML) or speed (CAML). But the team decided not to burden the WPF code base with these two independent implementations that did essentially the same thing. BAML won out over CAML because it has several advantages: It's less of a security threat than MSIL execution, it's more compact (resulting in smaller download sizes for web scenarios), and it can be localized postcompilation. Furthermore, using CAML was not appreciably faster than using BAML, as people had theorized.

Because the glue code tucked away in the generated source file is part of the same class you've defined in the code-behind file (and because BAML gets embedded as a resource), you often don't need to be aware of the existence of BAML or the process of loading and parsing it. You simply write code that references named elements just like any other class member, and let the build system worry about hooking things together. The only thing you need to remember is to call InitializeComponent in your code-behind class's constructor.

WARNING

Don't forget to call InitializeComponent in the constructor of your code-behind class!

If you fail to do so, your root element won't contain any of the content you defined in XAML (because the corresponding BAML doesn't get loaded) and all the fields representing named object elements will be null.

DIGGING DEEPER

Procedural Code Inside XAML!

XAML actually supports "code inside" in addition to code behind (somewhat like in ASP.NET). This can be done with the Code keyword in the XAML language namespace, as follows:

```
<Window xmlns="http://schemas.microsoft.com/winfx/2006/xaml/presentation"
        xmlns:x="http://schemas.microsoft.com/winfx/2006/xaml">
  <Button Click="button_Click">OK</Button>
  <x:Code><![CDATA[
    void button_Click(object sender, RoutedEventArgs e)
    {
        this.Close();
    }
  ]]></x:Code>
</Window>
```

When such a XAML file is compiled, the contents inside the x:Code element get plopped inside the partial class in the .g.cs file. Note that the procedural language is not specified in the XAML file; it is determined by the project containing this file.

Wrapping the code in <![CDATA[...]]> isn't required, but it avoids the need to escape less-than signs as <, and ampersands as &. That's because CDATA sections are ignored by XML parsers, whereas anything else is processed as XML. (The tradeoff is that you must avoid using]]> anywhere in the code, because that terminates the CDATA section!)

Of course, there's no good reason to pollute your XAML files with this "code inside" feature. Besides making the division between UI and logic messier, loose XAML pages don't support it and Visual Studio doesn't show syntax coloring.

FAQ

 Can BAML be decompiled back into XAML?

Sure, because an instance of any public .NET class can be serialized as XAML, regardless of how it was originally declared. The first step is to retrieve an instance that you want to be the root. If you don't already have this object, you can call the static `System.Windows.Application.LoadComponent` method as follows:

```
System.Uri uri = new System.Uri("MyWindow.xaml", System.UriKind.Relative);
Window window = (Window)Application.LoadComponent(uri);
```

This differs from previous code that uses `FileStream` to load a `.xaml` file because with `LoadComponent`, the name specified as the Uniform Resource Identifier (URI) does not have to physically exist as a standalone `.xaml` file. `LoadComponent` can automatically retrieve BAML embedded as a resource when given the appropriate URI (which, by MSBuild convention, is the name of the original XAML source file). In fact, Visual Studio's autogenerated `InitializeComponent` method calls `Application.LoadComponent` to load embedded BAML, although it uses a different overload. Chapter 8 has more details about this mechanism of retrieving embedded resources with URIs.

After you've gotten a hold of the root element instance, you can use the `System.Windows.Markup.XamlWriter` class to get a XAML representation of the root element (and, therefore, any of its children). `XamlWriter` contains five overloads of a static `Save` method, the simplest of which accepts an object instance and returns appropriate XAML as a string. For example:

```
string xaml = XamlWriter.Save(window);
```

It might sound a little troubling that BAML can be so easily "cracked open," but it's really no different from any other software running locally or displaying UI locally. (For example, you can easily dig into a website's HTML, JavaScript, and Cascading Style Sheets [CSS] files.)

XAML Keywords

The XAML language namespace (`http://schemas.microsoft.com/winfx/2006/xaml`) defines a handful of keywords that must be treated specially by any XAML compiler or parser. They mostly control aspects of how elements get exposed to procedural code, but a few are useful even without any procedural code. You've already seen some of them (Key, Name, Class, Subclass, and Code), but Table 2.1 lists them all. They are listed with the conventional x prefix because that is how they usually appear in XAML and in documentation.

DIGGING DEEPER

Special Attributes Defined by the W3C

In addition to keywords in the XAML language namespace, XAML also supports two special attributes defined for XML by the World Wide Web Consortium (W3C): `xml:space` for controlling whitespace parsing, and `xml:lang` for declaring the document's language and culture. The `xml` prefix is implicitly mapped to the standard XML namespace: `http://www.w3.org/XML/1998/namespace`.

TABLE 2.1   Keywords in the XAML Language Namespace, Assuming the Conventional x Namespace Prefix

Keyword	Valid As	Meaning
x:Class	Attribute on root element	Defines a class for the root element that derives from the element type, optionally prefixed with a .NET namespace
x:ClassModifier	Attribute on root element, and must be used with x:Class	Defines the visibility of the class specified by x:Class (which is public by default). The attribute value must be specified in terms of the procedural language being used (e.g. public or internal for C#)
x:Code	Element anywhere in XAML, but must be used with x:Class	Embeds procedural code to be inserted into the class specified by x:Class
x:FieldModifier	Attribute on any nonroot element, but must be used with x:Name (or equivalent)	Defines the visibility of the field to be generated for the element (which is internal by default). As with x:ClassModifier, the value must be specified in terms of the procedural language (e.g. public, private, ... for C#)
x:Key	Attribute on an element whose parent implements IDictionary	Specifies the key for the item when added to the parent dictionary
x:Name	Attribute on any nonroot element, but must be used with x:Class	Chooses a name for the field to be generated for the element, so it can be referenced from procedural code
x:Shared	Attribute on any element in a ResourceDictionary, but only works if XAML is compiled	Can be set to false to avoid sharing the same resource instance in multiple places, as explained in Chapter 8
x:Subclass	Attribute on root element, and must be used with x:Class	Specifies a subclass of the x:Class class that holds the content defined in XAML, optionally prefixed with a .NET namespace (used with languages without support for partial classes)
x:TypeArguments	Attribute on root element, and must be used with x:Class	Makes the root class generic (e.g. List<T>) with the specified generic argument instantiations (e.g. List<Int32> or List<String>). Can be set to a comma-delimited list of generic arguments, with XML namespace prefixes for any types not in the default namespace

Keyword	Valid As	Meaning
x:Uid	Attribute on any element	Marks an element with an identifier used for localization, as described in Chapter 8
x:XData	Element used as the value for any property of type IXmlSerializable	An arbitrary XML data island that remains opaque to the XAML parser, as explained in Chapter 9

Table 2.2 contains additional items in the XAML language namespace that can be confused as keywords but are actually just markup extensions (e.g. real .NET classes in the System.Windows.Markup namespace). Each class's Extension suffix is omitted from the table because they are typically used without the suffix.

TABLE 2.2   Markup Extensions in the XAML Language Namespace, Assuming the Conventional x Namespace Prefix

Extension	Meaning
x:Array	Represents a .NET array. An x:Array element's children are the elements of the array. It must be used with x:Type to define the type of the array.
x:Null	Represents a null reference.
x:Static	References any static property, field, constant, or enumeration value defined in procedural code. This can even be a nonpublic member in the same assembly, when XAML is compiled. Its Member string must be qualified with an XML namespace prefix if the type is not in the default namespace.
x:Type	Represents an instance of System.Type, just like the typeof operator in C#. Its TypeName string must be qualified with an XML namespace prefix if the type is not in the default namespace.

Conclusion

You have now seen how XAML fits in with WPF, and most important, you now have the information needed to translate most XAML examples into a language such as C# and vice versa. However, because type converters and markup extensions are "black boxes," a straightforward translation is not always going to be obvious. That said, invoking a type converter directly from procedural code is always an option if you can't figure out the conversion it's doing internally! (Many classes with corresponding type converters even expose a static Parse method that does the same work, for the sake of simpler procedural code.)

I love the fact that simple concepts that could have been treated specially by XAML (such as null) are expressed using the same markup extension mechanism to be used by third parties. It keeps the XAML language as simple as possible, and it ensures that the extensibility mechanism works really well.

As you proceed further with WPF, you might find that some WPF APIs can be a little clunky from procedural code because their design is often optimized for XAML use. For example, WPF exposes many small building blocks (enabling the rich composition described in the previous chapter), so a WPF application generally must create far more objects manually than, say, a Windows Forms application. Besides the fact the XAML excels at expressing deep hierarchies of objects concisely, the WPF team spent more time implementing features to effectively hide intermediate objects in XAML (such as type converters) rather than features to hide them from procedural code (such as constructors that create inner objects on your behalf).

Most people understand the benefit of WPF having the separate declarative model provided by XAML, but some lament XML as the choice of format. The following sections are two common complaints and my attempt to debunk them.

Complaint #1: XML Is Too Verbose to Type

That's true—almost nobody enjoys typing lots of XML, but that's where tools come in. The appendix outlines some tools that can cut down on the amount of typing. This can come in the form of autocompletion based on the appropriate XML Schema Definition (XSD), or visual designers that can spare you from typing a single angle bracket! The transparent and well-specified nature of XML makes it easy to integrate new tools into the development process (creating a XAML exporter for your favorite tool, for example), and also enables easy hand-tweaking or troubleshooting.

In some areas of WPF, typing XAML by hand isn't even practical: complicated paths and shapes, 3D models, and so on. In fact, the trend from when XAML was first introduced in beta form has been to remove some of the handy human-typeable shortcuts in favor of a more predictable and extensible format that can be supported well by tools. But I still believe that being familiar with XAML and seeing the WPF APIs through both a procedural and declarative perspective is the best way to learn the technology. It's like understanding how HTML works without relying on a tool like Microsoft FrontPage.

Complaint #2: XML-Based Systems Have Poor Performance

XML is about interoperability, not about an efficient representation of data. So, why should most WPF applications be saddled with a bunch of data that is relatively large and slow to parse?

The good news is that in a normal WPF scenario, XAML is compiled into BAML, so you don't pay the full penalties of size and parsing performance at run-time. BAML is both smaller in size than the original XAML and optimized for efficient use at run-time. Performance pitfalls from XML are therefore limited to development time, which is when the benefits of XML are needed the most.

Imp
Concep

3

implement
(im′plə-mĕnt′, ĭm′plə-mənt)
She has the experience to **implement** our plans,
putting ideas to work. These regulations will be
implements for quality control.

To finish Part I of this book, and befo
really fun topics, it's helpful to examine
concepts that WPF introduces above an
.NET programmers are already familiar w
this chapter are some of the main culprit
WPF's notoriously steep learning curve. By ....ng
yourself with these concepts now, you'll be able to
approach the rest of this book (or any other WPF documentation) with confidence.

Some of this chapter's concepts are brand new (such as
logical and visual trees), but others are just extensions of
concepts that should be quite familiar (such as properties
and events). As you learn about each one, you'll also see
how to apply it to a very simple piece of user interface that
most programs need—an *About dialog*.

Logical and Visual Trees

XAML is natural for representing a user interface because of
its hierarchical nature. In WPF, user interfaces are
constructed from a tree of objects known as a *logical tree*.

Listing 3.1 defines the beginnings of a hypothetical About
dialog, using a Window as the root of the logical tree. The
Window has a StackPanel child element (described in
Chapter 6, "Layout with Panels") containing a few simple
controls plus another StackPanel which contains Buttons.

LISTING 3.1   A Simple About Dialog in XAML

```xml
<Window xmlns="http://schemas.microsoft.com/winfx/2006/xaml/presentation"
  Title="About WPF Unleashed" SizeToContent="WidthAndHeight"
  Background="OrangeRed">
  <StackPanel>
    <Label FontWeight="Bold" FontSize="20" Foreground="White">
      WPF Unleashed (Version 3.0)
    </Label>
    <Label>© 2006 SAMS Publishing</Label>
    <Label>Installed Chapters:</Label>
    <ListBox>
      <ListBoxItem>Chapter 1</ListBoxItem>
      <ListBoxItem>Chapter 2</ListBoxItem>
    </ListBox>
    <StackPanel Orientation="Horizontal" HorizontalAlignment="Center">
      <Button MinWidth="75" Margin="10">Help</Button>
      <Button MinWidth="75" Margin="10">OK</Button>
    </StackPanel>
    <StatusBar>You have successfully registered this product.</StatusBar>
  </StackPanel>
</Window>
```

Figure 3.1 shows the rendered dialog (which you can easily produce by pasting the content of Listing 3.1 into a tool such as XamlPad), and Figure 3.2 illustrates the logical tree for this dialog.

Note that a logical tree exists even for WPF user interfaces that aren't created in XAML. Listing 3.1 could be implemented entirely in procedural code and the logical tree would be identical.

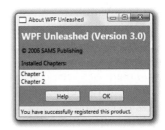

FIGURE 3.1   The rendered dialog from Listing 3.1.

The logical tree concept is straightforward, but why should you care about it? Because just about every aspect of WPF (properties, events, resources, and so on) has behavior tied to the logical tree. For example, property values are sometimes propagated down the tree to child elements automatically, and raised events can travel up or down the tree. Both of these behaviors are discussed later in this chapter.

A similar concept to the logical tree is the *visual tree*. A visual tree is basically an expansion of a logical tree, in which nodes are broken down into their core visual components. Rather than leaving each element as a "black box," a visual tree exposes the visual implementation details. For example, although a ListBox is logically a single control, its default visual representation is composed of more primitive WPF elements: a Border, two ScrollBars, and more.

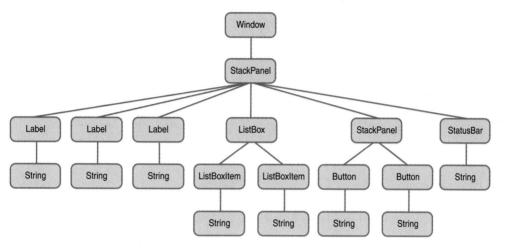

FIGURE 3.2   The logical tree for Listing 3.1.

Not all logical tree nodes appear in the visual tree; only the elements that derive from `System.Windows.Media.Visual` or `System.Windows.Media.Visual3D` are included. Other elements (and simple string content, as in Listing 3.1) are not included because they don't have inherent rendering behavior of their own.

Figure 3.3 illustrates the default visual tree for Listing 3.1 when running on Windows Vista with the Aero theme. This diagram exposes some inner components of the UI that are currently invisible, such as the `ListBox`'s two `ScrollBars` and each `Label`'s `Border`. It also reveals that `Button`, `Label`, and `ListBoxItem` are all comprised of the same elements, except `Button` uses an obscure `ButtonChrome` element rather than a `Border`. (These controls have other visual differences as the result of different default property values. For example, `Button` has a default `Margin` of 10 on all sides whereas `Label` has a default `Margin` of 0.)

> **TIP**
>
> XamlPad contains a button in its toolbar that reveals the visual tree (and property values) for any XAML that it renders. It doesn't work when hosting a `Window` (as in Figure 3.1), but you can change the `Window` element to a `Page` (and remove the `SizeToContent` property) to take advantage of this functionality.

Because they enable you to peer inside the deep composition of WPF elements, visual trees can be surprisingly complex. Fortunately, although visual trees are an essential part of the WPF infrastructure, you often don't need to worry about them unless you're radically restyling controls (covered in Chapter 10, "Styles, Templates, Skins, and Themes") or doing low-level drawing (covered in Chapter 11, "2D Graphics"). Writing code that depends on a specific visual tree for a `Button`, for example, breaks one of WPF's core tenets—the separation of look and logic. When someone restyles a control like `Button` using the techniques described in Chapter 10, its entire visual tree is replaced with something that could be completely different.

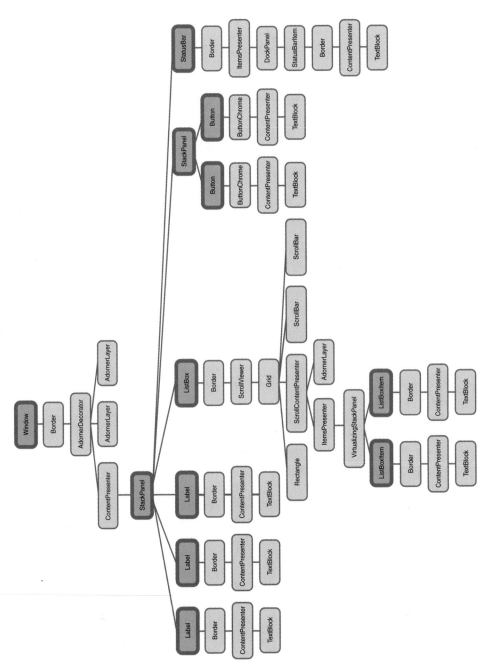

FIGURE 3.3   The visual tree for Listing 3.1, with logical tree nodes emphasized.

That said, you can easily traverse both the logical and visual trees using the somewhat symmetrical `System.Windows.LogicalTreeHelper` and `System.Windows.Media.VisualTreeHelper` classes. Listing 3.2 contains a code-behind file for Listing 3.1 that, when run under a debugger, outputs a simple depth-first representation of both the logical and visual trees for the About dialog. (This requires adding `x:Class="AboutDialog"` and the corresponding `xmlns:x` directive to Listing 3.1 in order to hook it up to this procedural code.)

> **WARNING**
>
> **Avoid writing code that depends on a specific visual tree!**
>
> Whereas a logical tree is static without programmer intervention (such as dynamically adding/removing elements), a visual tree can change simply by a user switching to a different Windows theme!

LISTING 3.2   Walking and Printing the Logical and Visual Trees

```
using System;
using System.Diagnostics;
using System.Windows;
using System.Windows.Media;

public partial class AboutDialog : Window
{
  public AboutDialog()
  {
    InitializeComponent();
    PrintLogicalTree(0, this);
  }

  protected override void OnContentRendered(EventArgs e)
  {
    base.OnContentRendered(e);
    PrintVisualTree(0, this);
  }

  void PrintLogicalTree(int depth, object obj)
  {
    // Print the object with preceding spaces that represent its depth
    Debug.WriteLine(new string(' ', depth) + obj);

    // Sometimes leaf nodes aren't DependencyObjects (e.g. strings)
    if (!(obj is DependencyObject)) return;

    // Recursive call for each logical child
    foreach (object child in LogicalTreeHelper.GetChildren(
      obj as DependencyObject))
```

LISTING 3.2   Continued

```
      PrintLogicalTree(depth + 1, child);
  }

  void PrintVisualTree(int depth, DependencyObject obj)
  {
    // Print the object with preceding spaces that represent its depth
    Debug.WriteLine(new string(' ', depth) + obj);

    // Recursive call for each visual child
    for (int i = 0; i < VisualTreeHelper.GetChildrenCount(obj); i++)
      PrintVisualTree(depth + 1, VisualTreeHelper.GetChild(obj, i));
  }
}
```

When calling these methods with a depth of 0 and the current Window instance, the result is a text-based tree with the exact same nodes shown in Figures 3.2 and 3.3. Although the logical tree can be traversed within the Window's constructor, the visual tree is empty until the Window undergoes layout at least once. That is why PrintVisualTree is called within OnContentRendered, which doesn't get called until after layout occurs.

Navigating either tree can sometimes be done with instance methods on the elements themselves. For example, the Visual class contains three protected members (VisualParent, VisualChildrenCount, and GetVisualChild) for examining its visual parent and children. FrameworkElement, a common base class for controls such as Button and Label, defines a public Parent property representing the logical parent. Specific subclasses of FrameworkElement expose their logical children in different ways. For example, some classes expose a Children collection, and other classes (such as Button and Label) expose a Content property, enforcing that the element can only have one logical child.

TIP

Visual trees like the one in represented in Figure 3.3 are often referred to simply as *element trees*, because they encompass both elements in the logical tree and elements specific to the visual tree. The term *visual tree* is then used to describe any subtree that contains visual-only (illogical?) elements. For example, most people would say that Window's default visual tree consists of a Border, AdornerDecorator, two AdornerLayers, a ContentPresenter, and nothing more. In Figure 3.3, the top-most StackPanel is generally *not* considered to be the visual child of the ContentPresenter, despite the fact that VisualTreeHelper presents it as one.

Dependency Properties

WPF introduces a new type of property called a *dependency property*, used throughout the platform to enable styling, automatic data binding, animation, and more. You might first meet this concept with skepticism, as it complicates the picture of .NET types having simple fields, properties, methods, and events. But after you understand the problems that dependency properties solve, you will likely accept them as a welcome addition.

A dependency property *depends* on multiple providers for determining its value at any point in time. These providers could be an animation continuously changing its value, a parent element whose property value trickles down to its children, and so on. Arguably the biggest feature of a dependency property is its built-in ability to provide change notification.

The motivation for adding such intelligence to properties is to enable rich functionality directly from declarative markup. The key to WPF's declarative-friendly design is its heavy use of properties. Button, for example, has 96 public properties! Properties can be easily set in XAML (directly or by a design tool) without any procedural code. But without the extra plumbing in dependency properties, it would be hard for the simple action of setting properties to get the desired results without writing additional code.

In this section, we'll briefly look at the implementation of a dependency property to make this discussion more concrete, and then we'll dig deeper into some of the ways that dependency properties add value on top of plain .NET properties:

▶ Change notification

▶ Property value inheritance

▶ Support for multiple providers

Understanding most of the nuances of dependency properties is usually only important for custom control authors. However, even casual users of WPF end up needing to be aware of what they are and how they work. For example, you can only style and animate dependency properties. After working with WPF for a while you might find yourself wishing that all properties would be dependency properties!

A Dependency Property Implementation

In practice, dependency properties are just normal .NET properties hooked into some extra WPF infrastructure. This is all accomplished via WPF APIs; no .NET languages (other than XAML) have an intrinsic understanding of a dependency property.

Listing 3.3 demonstrates how Button effectively implements one of its dependency properties called IsDefault.

LISTING 3.3   A Standard Dependency Property Implementation

```
public class Button : ButtonBase
{
  // The dependency property
  public static readonly DependencyProperty IsDefaultProperty;

  static Button()
  {
    // Register the property
    Button.IsDefaultProperty = DependencyProperty.Register("IsDefault",
      typeof(bool), typeof(Button),
      new FrameworkPropertyMetadata(false,
      new PropertyChangedCallback(OnIsDefaultChanged)));
    …
  }

  // A .NET property wrapper (optional)
  public bool IsDefault
  {
    get { return (bool)GetValue(Button.IsDefaultProperty); }
    set { SetValue(Button.IsDefaultProperty, value); }
  }

  // A property changed callback (optional)
  private static void OnIsDefaultChanged(
    DependencyObject o, DependencyPropertyChangedEventArgs e) { … }
  …
}
```

The static IsDefaultProperty field is the actual dependency property, represented by the System.Windows.DependencyProperty class. By convention all DependencyProperty fields are public, static, and have a Property suffix. Dependency properties are usually created by calling the static DependencyProperty.Register method, which requires a name (IsDefault), a property type (bool), and the type of the class claiming to own the property (Button). Optionally (via different overloads of Register), you can pass metadata that customizes how the property is treated by WPF, as well as callbacks for handling property value changes, coercing values, and validating values. Button calls an overload of Register in its static constructor to give the dependency property a default value of false and to attach a delegate for change notifications.

Finally, the traditional .NET property called IsDefault implements its accessors by calling GetValue and SetValue methods inherited from System.Windows.DependencyObject, a low-level base class from which all classes with dependency properties must derive. GetValue returns the last value passed to SetValue or, if SetValue has never been called, the default value registered with the property. The IsDefault .NET property (sometimes called a *property wrapper* in this context) is not strictly necessary; consumers of Button could always directly call the GetValue/SetValue methods because they are exposed publicly. But the .NET property makes programmatic reading and writing of the property much more natural for consumers, and it enables the property to be set via XAML.

WARNING

.NET property wrappers are bypassed at run-time when setting dependency properties in XAML!

Although the XAML compiler depends on the property wrapper at compile-time, at run-time WPF calls the underlying GetValue and SetValue methods directly! Therefore, to maintain parity between setting a property in XAML and procedural code, it's crucial that property wrappers do not contain any logic in addition to the GetValue/SetValue calls. If you want to add custom logic, that's what the registered callbacks are for. All of WPF's built-in property wrappers abide by this rule, so this warning is for anyone writing a custom class with its own dependency properties.

On the surface, Listing 3.3 looks like an overly verbose way of representing a simple Boolean property. However, because GetValue and SetValue internally use an efficient sparse storage system and because IsDefaultProperty is a static field (rather than an instance field), the dependency property implementation saves per-instance memory compared to a typical .NET property. If all the properties on WPF controls were wrappers around instance fields (as most .NET properties are), they would consume a significant amount of memory because of all the local data attached to each instance. Having 96 fields for each Button, 89 fields for each Label, and so forth would add up quickly! Instead, 78 out of Button's 96 properties are dependency properties, and 71 out of Label's 89 properties are dependency properties.

The benefits of the dependency property implementation extend to more than just memory usage, however. It centralizes and standardizes a fair amount of code that property implementers would have to write to check thread access, prompt the containing element to be re-rendered, and so on. For example, if a property requires its element to be re-rendered when its value changes (such as Button's Background property), it can simply pass the FrameworkPropertyMetadataOptions.AffectsRender flag to an overload of DependencyProperty.Register. In addition, this implementation enables the three features listed earlier that we'll now examine one-by-one, starting with change notification.

Change Notification

Whenever the value of a dependency property changes, WPF can automatically trigger a number of actions depending on the property's metadata. These actions can be re-rendering the appropriate elements, updating the current layout, refreshing data bindings, and much more. One of the most interesting features enabled by this built-in change notification is *property triggers*, which enable you to perform your own custom actions when a property value changes without writing any procedural code.

For example, imagine that you want the text in each Button from the About dialog in Listing 3.1 to turn blue when the mouse pointer hovers over it. Without property triggers, you can attach two event handlers to each Button, one for its MouseEnter event and one for its MouseLeave event:

```
<Button MouseEnter="Button_MouseEnter" MouseLeave="Button_MouseLeave"
        MinWidth="75" Margin="10">Help</Button>
<Button MouseEnter="Button_MouseEnter" MouseLeave="Button_MouseLeave"
        MinWidth="75" Margin="10">OK</Button>
```

These two handlers could be implemented in a C# code-behind file as follows:

```
// Change the foreground to blue when the mouse enters the button
void Button_MouseEnter(object sender, MouseEventArgs e)
{
  Button b = sender as Button;
  if (b != null) b.Foreground = Brushes.Blue;
}

// Restore the foreground to black when the mouse exits the button
void Button_MouseLeave(object sender, MouseEventArgs e)
{
  Button b = sender as Button;
  if (b != null) b.Foreground = Brushes.Black;
}
```

With a property trigger, however, you can accomplish this same behavior purely in XAML. The following concise Trigger object is (just about) all you need:

```
<Trigger Property="IsMouseOver" Value="True">
  <Setter Property="Foreground" Value="Blue"/>
</Trigger>
```

This trigger can act upon Button's IsMouseOver property, which becomes true at the same time the MouseEnter event is raised and false at the same time the MouseLeave event is raised. Note that you don't have to worry about reverting Foreground to black when IsMouseOver changes to false. This is automatically done by WPF!

The only trick is assigning this Trigger to each Button. Unfortunately, because of an artificial limitation in WPF version 3.0, you can't apply property triggers directly to elements such as Button. They can only be applied inside a Style object, so an in-depth examination of property triggers is saved for Chapter 10. In the meantime, if you want to experiment with property triggers, you could apply the preceding Trigger to a Button by wrapping it in a few intermediate XML elements as follows:

```
<Button MinWidth="75" Margin="10">
<Button.Style>
  <Style TargetType="{x:Type Button}">
```

```
<Style.Triggers>
  <Trigger Property="IsMouseOver" Value="True">
    <Setter Property="Foreground" Value="Blue"/>
  </Trigger>
</Style.Triggers>
</Style>
</Button.Style>
  OK
</Button>
```

Property triggers are just one of three types of triggers supported by WPF. A *data trigger* is a form of property trigger that works for all .NET properties (not just dependency properties), also covered in Chapter 10. An *event trigger* enables you to declaratively specify actions to take when a routed event (covered later in the chapter) is raised. Event triggers always involve working with animations or sounds, so they aren't covered until Chapter 13, "Animation."

WARNING

Don't be fooled by an element's `Triggers` collection!

`FrameworkElement`'s `Triggers` property is a read/write collection of `TriggerBase` items (the common base class for all three types of triggers), so it looks like an easy way to attach property triggers to controls such as `Button`. Unfortunately, this collection can only contain event triggers in version 3.0 of WPF simply because the WPF team didn't have time to implement this support. Attempting to add a property trigger (or data trigger) to the collection causes an exception to be thrown at run-time.

Property Value Inheritance

The term *property value inheritance* (or *property inheritance* for short) doesn't refer to traditional object oriented class-based inheritance, but rather the flowing of property values down the element tree. A simple example of this can be seen in Listing 3.4, which updates the `Window` from Listing 3.1 by explicitly setting its `FontSize` and `FontStyle` dependency properties. Figure 3.4 shows the result of this change. (Notice that the `Window` automatically resizes to fit all the content thanks to its slick `SizeToContent` setting!)

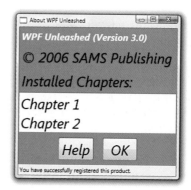

FIGURE 3.4   The About dialog with `FontSize` and `FontStyle` set on the root `Window`.

LISTING 3.4   The About Dialog with Font Properties Set on the Root Window

```xaml
<Window xmlns="http://schemas.microsoft.com/winfx/2006/xaml/presentation"
  Title="About WPF Unleashed" SizeToContent="WidthAndHeight"
  FontSize="30" FontStyle="Italic"
  Background="OrangeRed">
  <StackPanel>
    <Label FontWeight="Bold" FontSize="20" Foreground="White">
      WPF Unleashed (Version 3.0)
    </Label>
    <Label>© 2006 SAMS Publishing</Label>
    <Label>Installed Chapters:</Label>
    <ListBox>
      <ListBoxItem>Chapter 1</ListBoxItem>
      <ListBoxItem>Chapter 2</ListBoxItem>
    </ListBox>
    <StackPanel Orientation="Horizontal" HorizontalAlignment="Center">
      <Button MinWidth="75" Margin="10">Help</Button>
      <Button MinWidth="75" Margin="10">OK</Button>
    </StackPanel>
    <StatusBar>You have successfully registered this product.</StatusBar>
  </StackPanel>
</Window>
```

For the most part, these two settings flow all the way down the tree and are inherited by children. This affects even the Buttons and ListBoxItems, which are three levels down the logical tree. The first Label's FontSize does not change because it is explicitly marked with a FontSize of 20, overriding the inherited value of 30. The inherited FontStyle setting of Italic affects all Labels, ListBoxItems, and Buttons, however, because none of them have this set explicitly.

Notice that the text in the StatusBar is unaffected by either of these values, despite the fact that it supports these two properties just like the other controls. The behavior of property value inheritance can be subtle in cases like this for two reasons:

▶ Not every dependency property participates in property value inheritance. (Internally, dependency properties can opt in to inheritance by passing FrameworkPropertyMetadataOptions.Inherits to DependencyProperty.Register.)

▶ There may be other higher-priority sources setting the property value, as explained in the next section.

In this case, the latter reason is to blame. A few controls such as StatusBar, Menu, and ToolTip internally set their font properties to match current system settings. This way, users get the familiar experience of controlling their font via Control Panel. The result can be confusing, however, because such controls end up "swallowing" any inheritance from proceeding further down the element tree. For example, if you add a Button as a logical child of the StatusBar in Listing 3.4, its FontSize and FontStyle would be the default values of 12 and Normal, respectively, unlike the other Buttons outside of the StatusBar.

DIGGING DEEPER

Property Value Inheritance in Additional Places

Property value inheritance was originally designed to operate on the element tree, but it has been extended to work in a few other contexts as well. For example, values can be passed down to certain elements that *look like* children in the XML sense (because of XAML's property element syntax) but *are not* children in terms of the logical or visual trees. These pseudochildren can be an element's triggers or the value of *any* property (not just Content or Children) as long as it is an object deriving from Freezable. This may sound arbitrary and isn't well documented, but the intention is that several XAML-based scenarios "just work" as you would expect without having to think about it.

Support for Multiple Providers

WPF contains many powerful mechanisms that independently attempt to set the value of dependency properties. Without a well-defined mechanism for handling these disparate property value providers, the system would be a bit chaotic and property values could be unstable. Of course, as their name indicates, dependency properties were designed to depend on these providers in a consistent and orderly manner.

Figure 3.5 illustrates the five-step process that WPF runs each dependency property through in order to calculate its final value. This process happens automatically thanks to the built-in change notification in dependency properties.

FIGURE 3.5   The pipeline for calculating the value of a dependency property.

Step 1: Determine Base Value

Most of the property value providers factor into the base value calculation. The following list reveals the eight providers that can set the value of most dependency properties, in order from highest to lowest precedence:

1. Local value
2. Style triggers
3. Template triggers
4. Style setters
5. Theme style triggers
6. Theme style setters
7. Property value inheritance
8. Default value

You've already seen some of the property value providers, such as property value inheritance. *Local value* technically means any call to DependencyObject.SetValue, but this is typically seen with a simple property assignment in XAML or procedural code (because of the way dependency properties are implemented, as shown previously with Button.IsDefault). *Default value* refers to the initial value registered with the dependency property, which naturally has the lowest precedence. The other providers, which all involve styles and templates, are explained further in Chapter 10.

This order of precedence explains why StatusBar's FontSize and FontStyle were not impacted by property value inheritance in Listing 3.4. The setting of StatusBar's font properties to match system settings is done via theme style setters (#6 in the list). Although this has precedence over property value inheritance (#7 in the list), you can still override these font settings using any mechanism with a higher precedence, such as simply setting local values on the StatusBar.

Step 2: Evaluate
If the value from step one is an *expression* (an object deriving from System.Windows.Expression), then WPF performs a special evaluation step to convert the expression into a concrete result. In version 3.0 of WPF, expressions only come into play when using dynamic resources (covered in Chapter 8, "Resources") or data binding (the topic of Chapter 9, "Data Binding"). Future versions of WPF may enable additional kinds of expressions.

Step 3: Apply Animations
If one or more animations are running, they have the power to alter the current property value (using the value after step 2 as input) or completely replace it. Therefore, animations (the topic of Chapter 13) can trump all other property value providers—even local values! This is often a stumbling block for people who are new to WPF.

Step 4: Coerce
After all the property value providers have had their say, WPF takes the almost-final property value and passes it to a CoerceValueCallback delegate, if one was registered with the dependency property. The callback is responsible for returning a new value, based on custom logic. For example, built-in WPF controls such as ProgressBar use this callback to constrain its Value dependency property to a value between its Minimum and Maximum values, returning Minimum if the input value is less than Minimum or Maximum if the input value is greater than Maximum.

Step 5: Validate
Finally, the potentially-coerced value is passed to a ValidateValueCallback delegate, if one was registered with the dependency property. This callback must return true if the input value is valid or false otherwise. Returning false causes an exception to be thrown, cancelling the entire process.

TIP

If you can't figure out where a given dependency property is getting its current value from, you can use the static `DependencyPropertyHelper.GetValueSource` method as a debugging aid. This returns a `ValueSource` structure that contains a few pieces of data: a `BaseValueSource` enumeration that reveals where the base value came from (step 1 in the process) and Boolean `IsExpression`, `IsAnimated`, and `IsCoerced` properties that reveal information about steps 2-4.

When calling this method on the `StatusBar` instance from Listing 3.1 or 3.4 with the `FontSize` or `FontStyle` property, the returned `BaseValueSource` is `DefaultStyle`, revealing that the value comes from a theme style setter. (Theme styles are sometimes referred to as *default styles*. The enumeration value for a theme style trigger is `DefaultStyleTrigger`.)

Do *not* use this method in production code! Future versions of WPF could break assumptions you've made about the value calculation, plus treating a property value differently depending on its source goes against the way things are supposed to work in WPF applications.

DIGGING DEEPER

Clearing a Local Value

The earlier "Change Notification" section demonstrated the use of procedural code to change a `Button`'s `Foreground` to blue in response to the `MouseEnter` event, and then changing it back to black in response to the `MouseLeave` event. The problem with this approach is that black is set as a local value inside `MouseLeave`, which is much different from the `Button`'s initial state in which its black `Foreground` comes from a setter in its theme style. If the theme is changed and the new theme tries to change the default `Foreground` color (or if other providers with higher precedence try to do the same), it gets trumped by the local setting of black.

What you likely want to do instead is *clear* the local value and let WPF set the value from the relevant provider with the next-highest precedence. Fortunately, `DependencyObject` provides exactly this kind of mechanism with its `ClearValue` method. This can be called on a `Button` b as follows in C#:

```
b.ClearValue(Button.ForegroundProperty);
```

(`Button.ForegroundProperty` is the static `DependencyProperty` field.) After calling `ClearValue`, the local value is simply removed from the equation when WPF recalculates the base value.

Note that the trigger on the `IsMouseOver` property from the "Change Notification" section does not have the same problem as the implementation with event handlers. A trigger is either active or inactive, and when inactive it is simply ignored in the property value calculation.

Attached Properties

An attached property is a special form of dependency property that can effectively be *attached* to arbitrary objects. This may sound strange at first, but this mechanism has several applications in WPF.

For the About dialog example, imagine that rather than setting `FontSize` and `FontStyle` for the entire `Window` (as done in Listing 3.4), you would rather set them on the inner `StackPanel` so they are inherited only by the two `Buttons`. Moving the property attributes to the inner `StackPanel` element doesn't work, however, because `StackPanel` doesn't have any font-related properties of its own! Instead, you must use the `FontSize` and `FontStyle` attached properties that happen to be defined on a class called `TextElement`. Listing 3.5 demonstrates this, introducing new XAML syntax designed especially for attached properties. This enables the desired property value inheritance, as shown in Figure 3.6.

FIGURE 3.6   The About dialog with `FontSize` and `FontStyle` set on both `Buttons` via inheritance from the inner `StackPanel`.

LISTING 3.5   The About Dialog with Font Properties Moved to the Inner StackPanel

```
<Window xmlns="http://schemas.microsoft.com/winfx/2006/xaml/presentation"
  Title="About WPF Unleashed" SizeToContent="WidthAndHeight"
  Background="OrangeRed">
  <StackPanel>
    <Label FontWeight="Bold" FontSize="20" Foreground="White">
      WPF Unleashed (Version 3.0)
    </Label>
    <Label>© 2006 SAMS Publishing</Label>
    <Label>Installed Chapters:</Label>
    <ListBox>
      <ListBoxItem>Chapter 1</ListBoxItem>
      <ListBoxItem>Chapter 2</ListBoxItem>
    </ListBox>
    <StackPanel TextElement.FontSize="30" TextElement.FontStyle="Italic"
      Orientation="Horizontal" HorizontalAlignment="Center">
      <Button MinWidth="75" Margin="10">Help</Button>
      <Button MinWidth="75" Margin="10">OK</Button>
    </StackPanel>
    <StatusBar>You have successfully registered this product.</StatusBar>
  </StackPanel>
</Window>
```

`TextElement.FontSize` and `TextElement.FontStyle` (rather than simply `FontSize` and `FontStyle`) must be used in the `StackPanel` element because `StackPanel` does not have these properties. When a XAML parser or compiler encounters this syntax, it requires that `TextElement` (sometimes called the *attached property provider*) has static methods called `SetFontSize` and `SetFontStyle` that can set the value accordingly. Therefore, the `StackPanel` declaration in Listing 3.5 is equivalent to the following C# code:

```
StackPanel panel = new StackPanel();
TextElement.SetFontSize(panel, 30);
TextElement.SetFontStyle(panel, FontStyles.Italic);
panel.Orientation = Orientation.Horizontal;
panel.HorizontalAlignment = HorizontalAlignment.Center;
Button helpButton = new Button();
helpButton.MinWidth = 75;
helpButton.Margin = new Thickness(10);
helpButton.Content = "Help";
Button okButton = new Button();
okButton.MinWidth = 75;
okButton.Margin = new Thickness(10);
okButton.Content = "OK";
panel.Children.Add(helpButton);
panel.Children.Add(okButton);
```

Notice that the enumeration values such as `FontStyles.Italic`, `Orientation.Horizontal`, and `HorizontalAlignment.Center` were previously specified in XAML simply as `Italic`, `Horizontal`, and `Center`, respectively. This is possible thanks to the `EnumConverter` type converter in the .NET Framework, which can convert any case-insensitive string.

Although the XAML in Listing 3.5 nicely represents the logical attachment of `FontSize` and `FontStyle` to `StackPanel`, the C# code reveals that there's no real magic here; just a method call that associates an element with an otherwise-unrelated property. One of the interesting things about the attached property abstraction is that no .NET property is a part of it!

Internally, methods like `SetFontSize` simply call the same `DependencyObject.SetValue` method that a normal dependency property accessor calls, but on the passed-in `DependencyObject` rather than the current instance:

```
public static void SetFontSize(DependencyObject element, double value)
{
   element.SetValue(TextElement.FontSizeProperty, value);
}
```

Similarly, attached properties also define a static Get*XXX* method (where *XXX* is the name of the property) that calls the familiar `DependencyObject.GetValue` method:

```
public static double GetFontSize(DependencyObject element)
{
  return (double)element.GetValue(TextElement.FontSizeProperty);
}
```

As with property wrappers for normal dependency properties, these Get*XXX* and Set*XXX* methods must not do anything other than making a call to GetValue and SetValue.

DIGGING DEEPER

Understanding the Attached Property Provider

The most confusing part about the FontSize and FontStyle attached properties used in Listing 3.5 is that they aren't defined by Button or even Control, the base class that defines the normal FontSize and FontStyle dependency properties! Instead, they are defined by the seemingly unrelated TextElement class (and also by the TextBlock class, which could also be used in the preceding examples).

How can this possibly work when TextElement.FontSizeProperty is a separate DependencyProperty field from Control.FontSizeProperty (and TextElement. FontStyleProperty is separate from Control.FontStyleProperty)? The key is the way these dependency properties are internally registered. If you were to look at the source code for TextElement, you would see something like the following:

```
TextElement.FontSizeProperty = DependencyProperty.RegisterAttached(
  "FontSize", typeof(double), typeof(TextElement), new FrameworkPropertyMetadata(
  SystemFonts.MessageFontSize, FrameworkPropertyMetadataOptions.Inherits |
  FrameworkPropertyMetadataOptions.AffectsRender |
  FrameworkPropertyMetadataOptions.AffectsMeasure),
  new ValidateValueCallback(TextElement.IsValidFontSize));
```

This is similar to the earlier example of registering Button's IsDefault dependency property, except that the RegisterAttached method optimizes the handling of property metadata for attached property scenarios.

Control, on the other hand, doesn't register its FontSize dependency property! Instead, it calls AddOwner on TextElement's already-registered property, getting a reference to the exact same instance:

```
Control.FontSizeProperty = TextElement.FontSizeProperty.AddOwner(
  typeof(Control), new FrameworkPropertyMetadata(SystemFonts.MessageFontSize,
  FrameworkPropertyMetadataOptions.Inherits));
```

Therefore, the FontSize, FontStyle, and other font-related dependency properties inherited by all controls *are* the same properties exposed by TextElement!

Fortunately, in most cases, the class that exposes an attached property (e.g. Get*XXX* and Set*XXX* methods) is the same class that defines the normal dependency property, avoiding this confusion.

Although the About dialog example uses attached properties for advanced property value inheritance, attached properties are most commonly used for layout of user interface elements. (In fact, attached properties were originally designed for WPF's layout system.) Various Panel-derived classes define attached properties designed to be attached to their children for controlling how they are arranged. This way, each Panel can apply its own custom behavior to arbitrary children without requiring all possible child elements to be burdened with their own set of relevant properties. It also enables systems like layout to be easily extensible, because anyone can write a new Panel with custom attached properties. Chapter 6, "Layout with Panels," and Chapter 17, "Layout with Custom Panels," have all the details.

DIGGING DEEPER

Attached Properties as an Extensibility Mechanism

Just like previous technologies such as Windows Forms, many classes in WPF define a Tag property (of type System.Object) intended for storing arbitrary custom data with each instance. But attached properties are a more powerful and flexible mechanism for attaching custom data to any object deriving from DependencyObject. It's often overlooked that attached properties enable you to effectively add custom data to instances of sealed classes (something that WPF has plenty of)!

A further twist to the story of attached properties is that although setting them in XAML relies on the presence of the static Set*XXX* method, you can bypass this method in procedural code and call DependencyObject.SetValue directly. This means that you can use *any* dependency property as an attached property in procedural code. For example, the following line of code attaches ListBox's IsTextSearchEnabled property to a Button and assigns it a value:

```
// Attach an unrelated property to a Button and set its value to true:
okButton.SetValue(ListBox.IsTextSearchEnabledProperty, true);
```

Although this seems nonsensical, and it certainly doesn't magically enable new functionality on this Button, you have the freedom to consume this property value in a way that makes sense to your application or component.

There are more interesting ways to extend elements in this manner. For example, FrameworkElement's Tag property is a dependency property, so you can attach it to an instance of a GeometryModel3D (a class you'll see again in Chapter 12, "3D Graphics," that is sealed and does *not* have a Tag property) as follows:

```
GeometryModel3D model = new GeometryModel3D();
model.SetValue(FrameworkElement.TagProperty, "my custom data");
```

This is just one of the ways in which WPF provides extensibility without the need for traditional inheritance.

Routed Events

Just as WPF adds more infrastructure on top of the simple notion of .NET properties, it also adds more infrastructure on top of the simple notion of .NET events. *Routed events* are events that are designed to work well with a tree of elements. When a routed event is raised, it can travel up or down the visual and logical tree, getting raised on each element in a simple and consistent fashion, without the need for any custom code.

Event routing helps most applications remain oblivious to details of the visual tree (which is good for restyling) and is crucial to the success of WPF's element composition. For example, Button exposes a Click event based on handling lower-level MouseLeftButtonDown and KeyDown events. When a user presses the left mouse button with the mouse pointer over a standard Button, however, they are really interacting with its ButtonChrome or TextBlock visual child. Because the event travels up the *visual* tree, the Button eventually sees the event and can handle it. Similarly, for the VCR-style Stop Button in the preceding chapter, a user might press the left mouse button directly over the Rectangle logical child. Because the event travels up the *logical* tree, the Button still sees the event and can handle it as well. (Yet if you really wish to distinguish between an event on the Rectangle versus the outer Button, you have the freedom to do so.)

Therefore, you can embed arbitrarily complex content inside an element like Button or give it an arbitrarily complex visual tree (using the techniques in Chapter 10), and a mouse left-click on any of the internal elements still results in a Click event raised by the parent Button. Without routed events, producers of the inner content or consumers of the Button would have to write code to patch everything together.

The implementation and behavior of routed events have many parallels to dependency properties. As with the dependency property discussion, we'll first look at how a simple routed event is implemented to make things more concrete. Then we'll examine some of the features of routed events and apply them to the About dialog.

A Routed Event Implementation

In most cases, routed events don't look very different from normal .NET events. As with dependency properties, no .NET languages (other than XAML) have an intrinsic understanding of the *routed* designation. The extra support is based on a handful of WPF APIs.

Listing 3.6 demonstrates how Button effectively implements its Click routed event. (Click is actually implemented by Button's base class, but that's not important for this discussion.)

Just as dependency properties are represented as public static DependencyProperty fields with a conventional Property suffix, routed events are represented as public static RoutedEvent fields with a conventional Event suffix. The routed event is registered much like a dependency property in the static constructor, and a normal .NET event—or *event wrapper*—is defined to enable more familiar use from procedural code and adding a handler in XAML with event attribute syntax. As with a property wrapper, an event wrapper must not do anything in its accessors other than call AddHandler and RemoveHandler.

LISTING 3.6   A Standard Routed Event Implementation

```csharp
public class Button : ButtonBase
{
  // The routed event
  public static readonly RoutedEvent ClickEvent;

  static Button()
  {
    // Register the event
    Button.ClickEvent = EventManager.RegisterRoutedEvent("Click",
      RoutingStrategy.Bubble, typeof(RoutedEventHandler), typeof(Button));
    ...
  }

  // A .NET event wrapper (optional)
  public event RoutedEventHandler Click
  {
    add { AddHandler(Button.ClickEvent, value); }
    remove { RemoveHandler(Button.ClickEvent, value); }
  }

  protected override void OnMouseLeftButtonDown(MouseButtonEventArgs e)
  {
    ...
    // Raise the event
    RaiseEvent(new RoutedEventArgs(Button.ClickEvent, this));
    ...
  }
  ...
}
```

These AddHandler and RemoveHandler methods are not inherited from DependencyObject, but rather System.Windows.UIElement, a higher-level base class of elements such as Button. (This class hierarchy is examined in more depth at the end of this chapter.) These methods attach and remove a delegate to the appropriate routed event. Inside OnMouseLeftButtonDown, RaiseEvent (also defined on the base UIElement class) is called with the appropriate RoutedEvent field to raise the Click event. The current Button instance (this) is passed as the source element of the event. It's not shown in this listing, but Button's Click event is also raised in response to a KeyDown event to support clicking with the spacebar or sometimes the Enter key.

Routing Strategies and Event Handlers

When registered, every routed event chooses one of three *routing strategies*—the way in which the event raising travels through the element tree. These strategies are exposed as values of a RoutingStrategy enumeration:

- ▶ **Tunneling**—The event is first raised on the root, then on each element down the tree until the source element is reached (or until a handler halts the tunneling by marking the event as handled).

- ▶ **Bubbling**—The event is first raised on the source element, then on each element up the tree until the root is reached (or until a handler halts the bubbling by marking the event as handled).

- ▶ **Direct**—The event is only raised on the source element. This is the same behavior as a plain .NET event, except that such events can still participate in mechanisms specific to routed events such as event triggers.

Handlers for routed events have a signature matching the pattern for general .NET event handlers: The first parameter is a System.Object typically named sender, and the second parameter (typically named e) is a class that derives from System.EventArgs. The sender parameter passed to a handler is always the element to which the handler was attached. The e parameter is (or derives from) an instance of RoutedEventArgs, a subclass of EventArgs that exposes four useful properties:

- ▶ **Source**—The element in the logical tree that originally raised the event.

- ▶ **OriginalSource**—The element in the visual tree that originally raised the event (for example, the TextBlock or ButtonChrome child of a standard Button).

- ▶ **Handled**—A Boolean that can be set to true to mark the event as handled. This is precisely what halts any tunneling or bubbling.

- ▶ **RoutedEvent**—The actual routed event object (such as Button.ClickEvent), which can be helpful for identifying the raised event when the same handler is used for multiple routed events.

The presence of both Source and OriginalSource enable you to work with the higher-level logical tree or the lower-level visual tree. This distinction only applies to physical events like mouse events, however. For more abstract events that don't necessarily have a direct relationship with an element in the visual tree (like Click due to its keyboard support), the same object is passed for both Source and OriginalSource.

Routed Events in Action

The UIElement class defines many routed events for keyboard, mouse, and stylus input. Most of these are bubbling events, but many of them are paired with a tunneling event. Tunneling events can be easily identified because, by convention, they are named with a Preview prefix. These events, also by convention, are raised immediately before their bubbling counterpart. For example, `PreviewMouseMove` is a tunneling event raised before the `MouseMove` bubbling event.

The idea behind having a pair of events for various activities is to give elements a chance to effectively cancel or otherwise modify an event that's about to occur. By convention, WPF's built-in elements only take action in response to a bubbling event (when a bubbling and tunneling pair is defined), ensuring that the tunneling event lives up to its "preview" name. For example, imagine you want to implement a `TextBox` that restricts its input to a certain pattern or regular expression (such as a phone number or zip code). If you handle `TextBox`'s `KeyDown` event, the best you can do is remove text that has already been displayed inside the `TextBox`. But if you handle `TextBox`'s `PreviewKeyDown` event instead, you can mark it as "handled" to not only stop the tunneling but also stop the bubbling `KeyDown` event from being raised. In this case, the `TextBox` will never receive the `KeyDown` notification and the current character will not get displayed.

> **DIGGING DEEPER**
>
> **Using Stylus Events**
>
> A *stylus*—the pen-like device used by Tablet PCs—acts like a mouse by default. In other words, its use raises events such as `MouseMove`, `MouseDown`, and `MouseUp`. This behavior is essential for a stylus to be usable with programs that aren't designed specifically for a Tablet PC. However, if you want to provide an experience that is *optimized* for a stylus, you can handle stylus-specific events such as `StylusMove`, `StylusDown`, and `StylusUp`. A stylus can do more "tricks" than a mouse, as evidenced by some of its events that have no mouse counterpart, such as `StylusInAirMove`, `StylusSystemGesture`, `StylusInRange`, and `StylusOutOfRange`. There are other ways to exploit a stylus without handling these events directly, however. The next chapter, "Introducing WPF's Controls," shows how this can be done with a powerful `InkCanvas` element.

To demonstrate the use of a simple bubbling event, Listing 3.7 updates the original About dialog from Listing 3.1 by attaching an event handler to `Window`'s `MouseRightButtonDown` event. Listing 3.8 contains the C# code-behind file with the event handler implementation.

LISTING 3.7   The About Dialog with an Event Handler on the Root `Window`

```xml
<Window xmlns="http://schemas.microsoft.com/winfx/2006/xaml/presentation"
  xmlns:x="http://schemas.microsoft.com/winfx/2006/xaml"
  x:Class="AboutDialog" MouseRightButtonDown="AboutDialog_MouseRightButtonDown"
  Title="About WPF Unleashed" SizeToContent="WidthAndHeight"
  Background="OrangeRed">
<StackPanel>
  <Label FontWeight="Bold" FontSize="20" Foreground="White">
    WPF Unleashed (Version 3.0)
  </Label>
  <Label>© 2006 SAMS Publishing</Label>
  <Label>Installed Chapters:</Label>
  <ListBox>
```

LISTING 3.7   Continued

```
      <ListBoxItem>Chapter 1</ListBoxItem>
      <ListBoxItem>Chapter 2</ListBoxItem>
    </ListBox>
    <StackPanel Orientation="Horizontal" HorizontalAlignment="Center">
      <Button MinWidth="75" Margin="10">Help</Button>
      <Button MinWidth="75" Margin="10">OK</Button>
    </StackPanel>
    <StatusBar>You have successfully registered this product.</StatusBar>
  </StackPanel>
</Window>
```

LISTING 3.8   The Code-Behind File for Listing 3.7

```
using System.Windows;
using System.Windows.Input;
using System.Windows.Media;
using System.Windows.Controls;

public partial class AboutDialog : Window
{
  public AboutDialog()
  {
    InitializeComponent();
  }

  void AboutDialog_MouseRightButtonDown(object sender, MouseButtonEventArgs e)
  {
    // Display information about this event
    this.Title = "Source = " + e.Source.GetType().Name + ", OriginalSource = " +
      e.OriginalSource.GetType().Name + " @ " + e.Timestamp;

    // In this example, all possible sources derive from Control
    Control source = e.Source as Control;

    // Toggle the border on the source control
    if (source.BorderThickness != new Thickness(5))
    {
      source.BorderThickness = new Thickness(5);
      source.BorderBrush = Brushes.Black;
    }
    else
      source.BorderThickness = new Thickness(0);
  }
}
```

The AboutDialog_MouseRightButtonDown
handler performs two actions whenever
a right-click bubbles up to the Window: It
prints information about the event to
the Window's title bar, and it adds (then
subsequently removes) a thick black
border around the specific element in
the logical tree that was right-clicked.
Figure 3.7 shows the result. Notice that
right-clicking on the Label reveals
Source set to the Label but
OriginalSource set to its TextBlock
visual child.

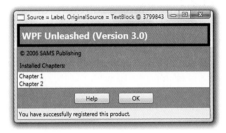

FIGURE 3.7   The modified About dialog, after
the first Label is right-clicked.

If you run this example and right-click on everything, you'll notice two interesting
behaviors:

▶ Window never receives the MouseRightButtonDown event when you right-click on
  either ListBoxItem. That's because ListBoxItem internally handles this event as
  well as the MouseLeftButtonDown event (halting the bubbling) to implement item
  selection.

▶ Window receives the MouseRightButtonDown event when you right-click on a Button,
  but setting Button's Border property has no visual effect. This is due to Button's
  default visual tree, which was shown back in Figure 3.3. Unlike Window, Label,
  ListBox, ListBoxItem, and StatusBar, the visual tree for Button has no Border
  element.

FAQ

 Where is the event for handling the pressing of a mouse's *middle* button?

If you browse through the various mouse events exposed by UIElement or ContentElement,
you'll find events for MouseLeftButtonDown, MouseLeftButtonUp, MouseRightButtonDown,
and MouseRightButtonUp (as well as the tunneling Preview version of each event). But
what about the additional buttons present on some mice?

This information can be retrieved via the more generic MouseDown and MouseUp events (which
also have Preview counterparts). The arguments passed to such event handlers include a
MouseButton enumeration that indicates which button's state just changed: Left, Right,
Middle, XButton1, or XButton2. A corresponding MouseButtonState enumeration indicates
whether that button is Pressed or Released.

DIGGING DEEPER

Halting a Routed Event Is an Illusion

Although setting the `RoutedEventArgs` parameter's `Handled` property to `true` in a routed event handler appears to stop the tunneling or bubbling, individual handlers further up or down the tree can opt to receive the events anyway! This can only be done from procedural code, using an overload of AddHandler that adds a Boolean `handledEventsToo` parameter.

For example, the event attribute could be removed from Listing 3.7 and replaced with the following AddHandler call in AboutDialog's constructor:

```
public AboutDialog()
{
  InitializeComponent();
  this.AddHandler(Window.MouseRightButtonDownEvent,
    new MouseButtonEventHandler(AboutDialog_MouseRightButtonDown), true);
}
```

With `true` passed as a third parameter, AboutDialog_MouseRightButtonDown now receives events when you right-click on a `ListBoxItem`, and can add the black border!

You should avoid processing handled events whenever possible, because there is likely a reason the event is handled in the first place. Attaching a handler to the `Preview` version of an event is the preferred alternative.

The bottom line, however, is that the halting of tunneling or bubbling is really just an illusion. It's more correct to say that tunneling and bubbling still continue when a routed event is marked as handled, but that event handlers only see unhandled events by default.

Attached Events

The tunneling and bubbling of a routed event is natural when every element in the tree exposes that event. But WPF supports tunneling and bubbling of routed events through elements that don't even define that event! This is possible thanks to the notion of *attached events*.

Attached events operate much like attached properties (and their use with tunneling or bubbling is very similar to using attached properties with property value inheritance). Listing 3.9 changes the About dialog again by handing the bubbling `SelectionChanged` event raised by its `ListBox` and the bubbling `Click` event raised by both of its `Buttons` directly on the root `Window`. Because `Window` doesn't define its own `SelectionChanged` or `Click` events, the event attribute names must be prefixed with the class name defining these events. Listing 3.10 contains the corresponding code-behind file that implements the two event handlers. Both event handlers simply show a `MessageBox` with information about what just happened.

LISTING 3.9   The About Dialog with Two Attached Event Handlers on the Root Window

```xml
<Window xmlns="http://schemas.microsoft.com/winfx/2006/xaml/presentation"
  xmlns:x="http://schemas.microsoft.com/winfx/2006/xaml"
  x:Class="AboutDialog" ListBox.SelectionChanged="ListBox_SelectionChanged"
  Button.Click="Button_Click"
  Title="About WPF Unleashed" SizeToContent="WidthAndHeight"
  Background="OrangeRed">
  <StackPanel>
    <Label FontWeight="Bold" FontSize="20" Foreground="White">
      WPF Unleashed (Version 3.0)
    </Label>
    <Label>© 2006 SAMS Publishing</Label>
    <Label>Installed Chapters:</Label>
    <ListBox>
      <ListBoxItem>Chapter 1</ListBoxItem>
      <ListBoxItem>Chapter 2</ListBoxItem>
    </ListBox>
    <StackPanel Orientation="Horizontal" HorizontalAlignment="Center">
      <Button MinWidth="75" Margin="10">Help</Button>
      <Button MinWidth="75" Margin="10">OK</Button>
    </StackPanel>
    <StatusBar>You have successfully registered this product.</StatusBar>
  </StackPanel>
</Window>
```

LISTING 3.10   The Code-Behind File for Listing 3.9

```csharp
using System.Windows;
using System.Windows.Controls;

public partial class AboutDialog : Window
{
  public AboutDialog()
  {
    InitializeComponent();
  }

  void ListBox_SelectionChanged(object sender, SelectionChangedEventArgs e)
  {
    if (e.AddedItems.Count > 0)
      MessageBox.Show("You just selected " + e.AddedItems[0]);
  }
```

LISTING 3.10   Continued

```
  void Button_Click(object sender, RoutedEventArgs e)
  {
      MessageBox.Show("You just clicked " + e.Source);
  }
}
```

Every routed event can be used as an attached event. The attached event syntax used in Listing 3.9 is valid because the XAML compiler sees the SelectionChanged .NET event defined on ListBox and the Click .NET event defined on Button. At run-time, however, AddHandler is directly called to attach these two events to the Window. Therefore, the two event attributes are equivalent to placing the following code inside the Window's constructor:

```
public AboutDialog()
{
  InitializeComponent();
  this.AddHandler(ListBox.SelectionChangedEvent,
    new SelectionChangedEventHandler(ListBox_SelectionChanged));
  this.AddHandler(Button.ClickEvent, new RoutedEventHandler(Button_Click));
}
```

DIGGING DEEPER

Consolidating Routed Event Handlers

Because of the rich information passed to routed events, you could handle every event that tunnels or bubbles with one top-level "megahandler" if you really wanted to! This handler could examine the RoutedEvent object to determine which event got raised, cast the RoutedEventArgs parameter to an appropriate subclass (such as KeyEventArgs, MouseButtonEventArgs, and so on) and go from there.

For example, Listing 3.9 could be changed to assign both ListBox.SelectionChanged and Button.Click to the same GenericHandler method, defined as follows:

```
void GenericHandler(object sender, RoutedEventArgs e)
{
  if (e.RoutedEvent == Button.ClickEvent)
  {
    MessageBox.Show("You just clicked " + e.Source);
  }
  else if (e.RoutedEvent == ListBox.SelectionChangedEvent)
  {
```

Continued

```
    SelectionChangedEventArgs sce = (SelectionChangedEventArgs)e;
    if (sce.AddedItems.Count > 0)
      MessageBox.Show("You just selected " + sce.AddedItems[0]);
  }
}
```

This is also made possible by the *delegate contravariance* feature added in version 2.0 of the .NET Framework, enabling a delegate to be used with a method whose signature uses a base class of an expected parameter (e.g. RoutedEventArgs instead of SelectionChangedEventArgs). GenericHandler simply casts the RoutedEventArgs parameter when necessary to get the extra information specific to the SelectionChanged event.

Commands

WPF provides built-in support for *commands*, a more abstract and loosely-coupled version of events. Whereas events are tied to details about specific user actions (such as a Button being clicked or a ListBoxItem being selected), commands represent actions independent from their user interface exposure. Canonical examples of commands are Cut, Copy, and Paste. Applications often expose these actions through many mechanisms simultaneously: MenuItems in a Menu, MenuItems on a ContextMenu, Buttons on a ToolBar, keyboard shortcuts, and so on.

You could handle the multiple exposures of commands such as Cut, Copy, and Paste with events fairly well. For example, you could define a generic event handler for each of the three actions and then attach each handler to the appropriate events on the relevant elements (the Click event on a Button, the KeyDown event on the main Window, and so on). In addition, you'd probably want to enable and disable the appropriate controls whenever the corresponding actions are invalid (for example, disabling any user interface for Paste when there is nothing on the clipboard). This two-way communication gets a bit more cumbersome, especially if you don't want to hard-code a list of controls that need updating.

Fortunately, WPF's support for commands is designed to make such scenarios very easy. The support reduces the amount of code you need to write (and in some cases eliminating all procedural code), and it gives you more flexibility to change your user interface without breaking the back-end logic. Commands are not a new invention of WPF; older technologies such as Microsoft Foundation Classes (MFC) have a similar mechanism. Of course, even if you're familiar with MFC, commands in WPF have their own unique traits to learn about.

Much of the power of commands comes from the following three features:

▸ WPF defines a number of built-in commands.

▸ Commands have automatic support for input gestures (such as keyboard shortcuts).

▸ Some of WPF's controls have built-in behavior tied to various commands.

Built-In Commands

A command is any object implementing the ICommand interface (from System.Windows.Input), which defines three simple members:

▸ **Execute**—The method that executes the command-specific logic

▸ **CanExecute**—A method returning true if the command is enabled or false if it is disabled

▸ **CanExecuteChanged**—An event that is raised whenever the value of CanExecute changes

If you want to create Cut, Copy, and Paste commands, you could define and implement three classes implementing ICommand, find a place to store them (perhaps as static fields of your main Window), call Execute from relevant event handlers (when CanExecute returns true), and handle the CanExecuteChanged event to toggle the IsEnabled property on the relevant pieces of user interface. This doesn't sound much better than simply using events, however.

Fortunately, controls such as Button, CheckBox, and MenuItem have logic to interact with any command on your behalf. They expose a simple Command property (of type ICommand). When set, these controls automatically call the command's Execute method (when CanExecute returns true) whenever their Click event is raised. In addition, they automatically keep their value for IsEnabled synchronized with the value of CanExecute by leveraging the CanExecuteChanged event. By supporting all this via a simple property assignment, all of this logic is available from XAML.

Even more fortunately, WPF defines a bunch of commands already, so you don't have to implement ICommand objects for Cut, Copy, and Paste and worry about where to store them. WPF's built-in commands are exposed as static properties of five different classes:

▸ **ApplicationCommands**—Close, Copy, Cut, Delete, Find, Help, New, Open, Paste, Print, PrintPreview, Properties, Redo, Replace, Save, SaveAs, SelectAll, Stop, Undo, and more

▸ **ComponentCommands**—MoveDown, MoveLeft, MoveRight, MoveUp, ScrollByLine, ScrollPageDown, ScrollPageLeft, ScrollPageRight, ScrollPageUp, SelectToEnd, SelectToHome, SelectToPageDown, SelectToPageUp, and more

▸ **MediaCommands**—ChannelDown, ChannelUp, DecreaseVolume, FastForward, IncreaseVolume, MuteVolume, NextTrack, Pause, Play, PreviousTrack, Record, Rewind, Select, Stop, and more

- ▶ **NavigationCommands**—BrowseBack, BrowseForward, BrowseHome, BrowseStop, Favorites, FirstPage, GoToPage, LastPage, NextPage, PreviousPage, Refresh, Search, Zoom, and more

- ▶ **EditingCommands**—AlignCenter, AlignJustify, AlignLeft, AlignRight, CorrectSpellingError, DecreaseFontSize, DecreaseIndentation, EnterLineBreak, EnterParagraphBreak, IgnoreSpellingError, IncreaseFontSize, IncreaseIndentation, MoveDownByLine, MoveDownByPage, MoveDownByParagraph, MoveLeftByCharacter, MoveLeftByWord, MoveRightByCharacter, MoveRightByWord, and more

Each of these properties does not return a unique type implementing ICommand. Instead, they are all instances of RoutedUICommand, a class that not only implements ICommand, but supports bubbling just like a routed event.

The About dialog has a "Help" Button that currently does nothing, so let's demonstrate how these built-in commands work by attaching some logic with the Help command defined in ApplicationCommands. Assuming the Button is named helpButton, you can associate it with the Help command in C# as follows:

```
helpButton.Command = ApplicationCommands.Help;
```

All RoutedUICommand objects define a Text property containing a name for the command that's appropriate to show in a user interface. (This property is the only difference between RoutedUICommand and its base RoutedCommand class.) For example, the Help command's Text property is (unsurprisingly) set to the string Help. The hard-coded Content on this Button could therefore be replaced as follows:

```
helpButton.Content = ApplicationCom-
mands.Help.Text;
```

If you were to run the About dialog with this change, you would see that the Button is now permanently disabled. That's because the built-in commands can't possibly know when they should be enabled or disabled, or even what action to take when they are executed. They delegate this logic to consumers of the commands.

To plug in custom logic, you need to add a CommandBinding to the element that will execute the command *or any parent element* (thanks to the bubbling behavior of routed commands). All classes deriving from UIElement (and

> **TIP**
>
> The Text string defined by all RoutedUICommands is automatically localized into every language supported by WPF! This means that a Button whose Content is assigned to ApplicationCommands. Help.Text automatically displays "Ayuda" rather than "Help" when the thread's current UI culture represents Spanish rather than English. Even in a context where you want to expose images rather than text (perhaps on a ToolBar), you can still leverage this localized string elsewhere, such as in a ToolTip.
>
> Of course, you're still responsible for localizing any of your own strings that get displayed in your user interface. Leveraging Text on commands can simply cut down on the number of terms you need to translate.

ContentElement) contain a CommandBindings collection that can hold one or more CommandBinding objects. Therefore, you can add a CommandBinding for Help to the About dialog's root Window as follows in its code-behind file:

```
this.CommandBindings.Add(new CommandBinding(ApplicationCommands.Help,
  HelpExecuted, HelpCanExecute));
```

This assumes that methods called HelpExecuted and HelpCanExecute have been defined. These methods will be called back at appropriate times in order to plug in an implementation for the Help command's CanExecute and Execute methods.

Listings 3.11 and 3.12 change the About dialog one last time, binding the Help Button to the Help command entirely in XAML (although the two handlers must be defined in the code-behind file).

LISTING 3.11   The About Dialog Supporting the Help Command

```xml
<Window xmlns="http://schemas.microsoft.com/winfx/2006/xaml/presentation"
  xmlns:x="http://schemas.microsoft.com/winfx/2006/xaml"
  x:Class="AboutDialog"
  Title="About WPF Unleashed" SizeToContent="WidthAndHeight"
  Background="OrangeRed">
<Window.CommandBindings>
  <CommandBinding Command="Help"
    CanExecute="HelpCanExecute" Executed="HelpExecuted"/>
</Window.CommandBindings>
  <StackPanel>
    <Label FontWeight="Bold" FontSize="20" Foreground="White">
      WPF Unleashed (Version 3.0)
    </Label>
    <Label>© 2006 SAMS Publishing</Label>
    <Label>Installed Chapters:</Label>
    <ListBox>
      <ListBoxItem>Chapter 1</ListBoxItem>
      <ListBoxItem>Chapter 2</ListBoxItem>
    </ListBox>
    <StackPanel Orientation="Horizontal" HorizontalAlignment="Center">
      <Button MinWidth="75" Margin="10" Command="Help" Content=
        "{Binding RelativeSource={RelativeSource Self}, Path=Command.Text}"/>
      <Button MinWidth="75" Margin="10">OK</Button>
    </StackPanel>
    <StatusBar>You have successfully registered this product.</StatusBar>
  </StackPanel>
</Window>
```

LISTING 3.12   The Code-Behind File for Listing 3.11

```
using System.Windows;
using System.Windows.Input;

public partial class AboutDialog : Window
{
  public AboutDialog()
  {
    InitializeComponent();
  }

  void HelpCanExecute(object sender, CanExecuteRoutedEventArgs e)
  {
    e.CanExecute = true;
  }

  void HelpExecuted(object sender, ExecutedRoutedEventArgs e)
  {
    System.Diagnostics.Process.Start("http://www.adamnathan.net/wpf");
  }
}
```

Window's CommandBinding can be set in XAML because it defines a default constructor and enables its data to be set with properties. Button's Content can even be set to the chosen command's Text property in XAML thanks to a popular data binding technique discussed in Chapter 9. In addition, notice that a type converter simplifies specifying the Help command in XAML. A CommandConverter class knows about all the built-in commands, so the Command property can be set to Help in both places rather than the more verbose {x:Static ApplicationCommands.Help}. (Custom commands don't get the same special treatment.) In the code-behind file, HelpCanExecute keeps the command enabled at all times, and HelpExecuted launches a web browser with an appropriate help URL.

Executing Commands with Input Gestures

Using the Help command in such a simple dialog may seem like overkill when a simple event handler for Click would do, but the command has provided an extra benefit (other than localized text): automatic binding to a keyboard shortcut.

Applications typically invoke their version of help when the user presses the F1 key. Sure enough, if you press F1 while displaying the dialog defined in Listing 3.10, the Help command is automatically launched, as if you clicked the Help Button! That's because commands such as Help define a default *input gesture* that executes the command. You can bind your own input gestures to a command by adding KeyBinding and/or MouseBinding objects to the relevant element's InputBindings collection. For example, to assign F2 as a keyboard shortcut that executes Help, you could add the following state-ment to AboutDialog's constructor:

```
this.InputBindings.Add(
  new KeyBinding(ApplicationCommands.Help, new KeyGesture(Key.F2)));
```

This would make *both* F1 and F2 execute Help, however. You could additionally suppress the default F1 behavior by binding F1 to a special NotACommand command as follows:

```
this.InputBindings.Add(
  new KeyBinding(ApplicationCommands.NotACommand, new KeyGesture(Key.F1)));
```

Both of these statements could alternatively be represented in XAML as follows:

```
<Window.InputBindings>
  <KeyBinding Command="Help" Key="F2"/>
  <KeyBinding Command="NotACommand" Key="F1"/>
</Window.InputBindings>
```

Controls with Built-In Command Bindings

It can seem almost magical when you encounter it, but some controls in WPF contain their own command bindings. The simplest example of this is the TextBox control, which has its own built-in bindings for the Cut, Copy, and Paste commands that interact with the clipboard, as well as Undo and Redo commands. This not only means that TextBox responds to the standard Ctrl+X, Ctrl+C, Ctrl+V, Ctrl+Z, and Ctrl+Y keyboard shortcuts, but that it's easy for additional elements to participate in these actions.

The following standalone XAML demonstrates the power of these built-in command bindings:

```
<StackPanel xmlns="http://schemas.microsoft.com/winfx/2006/xaml/presentation"
  xmlns:x="http://schemas.microsoft.com/winfx/2006/xaml"
  Orientation="Horizontal" Height="25">
  <Button Command="Cut" CommandTarget="{Binding ElementName=textBox}"
    Content="{Binding RelativeSource={RelativeSource Self}, Path=Command.Text}"/>
  <Button Command="Copy" CommandTarget="{Binding ElementName=textBox}"
    Content="{Binding RelativeSource={RelativeSource Self}, Path=Command.Text}"/>
  <Button Command="Paste" CommandTarget="{Binding ElementName=textBox}"
    Content="{Binding RelativeSource={RelativeSource Self}, Path=Command.Text}"/>
  <Button Command="Undo" CommandTarget="{Binding ElementName=textBox}"
    Content="{Binding RelativeSource={RelativeSource Self}, Path=Command.Text}"/>
  <Button Command="Redo" CommandTarget="{Binding ElementName=textBox}"
    Content="{Binding RelativeSource={RelativeSource Self}, Path=Command.Text}"/>
  <TextBox x:Name="textBox" Width="200"/>
</StackPanel>
```

You can paste this content into XamlPad or save it as a .xaml file to view in Internet Explorer, because no procedural code is necessary. Each of the five Buttons is associated with one of the commands and sets its `Content` to the string returned by each command's `Text` property. The only new thing here is the setting of each `Button`'s `CommandTarget` property to the instance of the `TextBox` (again using data binding functionality discussed in Chapter 9). This causes the command to be executed from the `TextBox` rather than the `Button`, which is necessary in order for it to react to the commands.

This XAML produces the result in Figure 3.8. The first two `Button`s are automatically disabled when no text in the `TextBox` is selected, and automatically enabled when there is a selection. Similarly, the Paste `Button` is automatically enabled whenever there is text content on the clipboard, or disabled otherwise.

FIGURE 3.8   The five `Button`s work as expected without any procedural code, thanks to `TextBox`'s built-in bindings.

`Button` and `TextBox` have no direct knowledge of each other, yet though commands they can achieve rich interaction. This is why WPF's long list of built-in commands is so important. The more that third-party controls standardize on WPF's built-in commands, the more seamless (and declarative) interaction can be achieved among controls that have no direct knowledge of each other.

A Tour of the Class Hierarchy

WPF's classes have a very deep inheritance hierarchy, so it can be hard to get your head wrapped around the significance of various classes and their relationships. The inside cover of this book contains a map of these classes to help you put them in perspective as you encounter new ones. It is incomplete due to space constraints, but the major classes are covered.

A handful of classes are fundamental to the inner-workings of WPF, and deserve a quick explanation before we get any further in the book. Some of these have been mentioned in passing already. Figure 3.9 shows these important classes and their relationships without all the extra clutter from the inside cover.

These ten classes have the following significance:

▶ **Object**—The base class for all .NET classes.

▶ **DispatcherObject**—The base class for any object that wishes to be accessed only on the thread that created it. Most WPF classes derive from `DispatcherObject`, and are therefore inherently thread-unsafe. The `Dispatcher` part of the name refers to WPF's version of a Win32-like message loop, discussed further in Chapter 7, "Structuring and Deploying an Application."

▶ **DependencyObject**—The base class for any object that can support dependency properties. `DependencyObject` defines the `GetValue` and `SetValue` methods that are central to the operation of dependency properties.

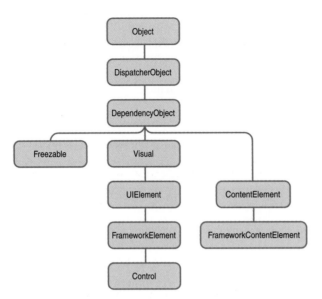

FIGURE 3.9   The core classes in the WPF Presentation Framework.

▶ **Freezable**—The base class for objects that can be "frozen" into a read-only state for performance reasons. Freezables, once frozen, can even be safely shared among multiple threads, unlike all other DispatcherObjects. Frozen objects can never be unfrozen, but you can clone them to create unfrozen copies.

▶ **Visual**—The base class for all objects that have their own visual representation. Visuals are discussed in depth in Chapter 11.

▶ **UIElement**—The base class for all visual objects with support for routed events, command binding, layout, and focus.

▶ **ContentElement**—A base class similar to UIElement, but for pieces of content that don't have rendering behavior on their own. Instead, ContentElements are hosted in a Visual-derived class to be rendered on the screen.

▶ **FrameworkElement**—The base class that adds support for styles, data binding, resources, and a few common mechanisms for Windows-based controls such as tooltips and context menus.

▶ **FrameworkContentElement**—The analog to FrameworkElement for content. Chapter 14 examines the FrameworkContentElements in WPF.

▶ **Control**—The base class for familiar controls such as Button, ListBox, and StatusBar. Control adds many properties to its FrameworkElement base class, such as Foreground, Background, and FontSize. Controls also support templates that enable you to completely replace their visual tree, discussed in Chapter 10. The next chapter examines WPF's Controls in depth.

Throughout the book, the simple term *element* is used to refer to an object that derives from UIElement or FrameworkElement, and sometimes ContentElement or FrameworkContentElement. The distinction between UIElement versus FrameworkElement or ContentElement versus FrameworkContentElement is not important because WPF doesn't ship any other public subclasses of UIElement and ContentElement.

Conclusion

In this chapter and the preceding two chapters, you've learned about all the major ways that WPF builds on top of the foundation of the .NET Framework. The WPF team could have exposed its features via typical .NET APIs similar to Windows Forms and still have an interesting technology. Instead, the team added several fundamental concepts that enable a wide range of features to be exposed in a way that can provide great productivity for developers and designers.

Indeed, when you focus on these core concepts (as this chapter has done), you can see that the landscape isn't quite as simple as it used to be: There are multiple types of properties, multiple types of events, multiple trees, and multiple ways of achieving the same results (such as writing declarative versus procedural code)! Hopefully you can now appreciate some of the value of these new mechanisms. Throughout the rest of the book, these concepts generally fade into the background as we focus on accomplishing specific development tasks.

Because of the (primitive) examples used in this chapter, you should now have a feel for some of WPF's controls and how WPF user interfaces are arranged. The next three chapters build on this by formally introducing you to WPF's controls and layout mechanisms.

PART II

Building a WPF Application

Introducing WPF's Controls

No modern presentation framework would be complete without a standard set of controls that enables you to quickly assemble traditional user interfaces. And Windows Presentation Foundation has plenty of such controls included "in the box." You've seen a few of them in previous chapters, but this chapter takes you on a tour of the major built-in controls, highlighting some of what makes each control unique.

The figures in this book show WPF controls under Windows Vista's default Aero theme. Most WPF controls contain several distinct default appearances, however. That's because WPF ships with theme DLLs containing control templates for the following Windows themes:

▶ Aero (the default Windows Vista theme)

▶ Luna (the default Windows XP theme)

▶ Royale (the theme from Windows XP Media Center Edition 2005 and Windows XP Tablet PC Edition 2005)

▶ Classic (the theme available in Windows 2000 and later)

For example, Figure 4.1 displays the default appearance of a WPF Button control under each of the supported Windows themes. If WPF encounters an unknown theme, such as the Zune theme released by Microsoft in 2006, it defaults to Classic.

FIGURE 4.1   The WPF Button's theme-specific default appearances.

In most cases, the difference in appearance is very subtle. Of course, you can give the controls a radically different look (based on the current theme or theme-independent) using custom control templates, as discussed in Chapter 10, "Styles, Templates, Skins, and Themes."

The controls covered in this chapter can be grouped into four main categories, which mostly coincide with their inheritance hierarchy (seen on the inside back cover of this book):

▶ Content Controls

▶ Items Controls

▶ Range Controls

▶ Text and Ink Controls

Content Controls

Content controls are simply controls that are constrained to contain a single item. Content controls all derive from System.Windows.Controls.ContentControl, which has a Content property of type Object that contains the single item (first shown with Button in Chapter 2, "XAML Demystified").

Because a content control's single item can be any arbitrary object, the control can contain a potentially large tree of objects. There just can only be one *direct* child. Besides Content, the other interesting member of the ContentControl class is the Boolean HasContent property. This simply returns false if Content is null, or true otherwise.

FAQ

 Why does ContentControl define a HasContent property? Checking for Content==null is just as easy as checking for HasContent==false!

Welcome to the world of WPF APIs, which don't always look like your typical .NET APIs! From a C# perspective, the HasContent property is redundant. But from a XAML perspective, the property is useful. For example, it makes it easy to use a property trigger to set various property values when HasContent becomes true.

DIGGING DEEPER

Content and Arbitrary Objects

Given that a content control's Content can be set to any managed object, it's natural to wonder what happens if you set the content to a non-UI object, such as an instance of a Hashtable or RegistryKey. The way it works is fairly simple. If the content derives from WPF's UIElement class, it gets rendered via UIElement's OnRender method. Otherwise, if a data template is applied to the item (described in Chapter 9, "Data Binding"), this template can provide the rendering behavior on behalf of the object. Otherwise, the content's ToString method is called and the returned text gets rendered inside a TextBlock.

The built-in content controls come in three major varieties:

▶ Buttons

▶ Simple containers

▶ Containers with a header

The Window class is also a content control, but an examination of Window is reserved for Chapter 7, "Structuring and Deploying an Application."

Buttons

Buttons are probably the most familiar and essential user interface element. WPF's Button, pictured in Figure 4.1, has already made several appearances in this book.

Although everyone intuitively knows what a button is, its precise definition (at least in WPF) might not be obvious. A basic button is a content control that can be clicked, but not double-clicked. This behavior is actually captured by an abstract class called ButtonBase, from which a few different controls are derived.

The ButtonBase class contains the Click event and contains the logic that defines what it means to be clicked. As with typical Windows buttons, a click can occur from a mouse's left button being pressed down then up, or from the keyboard (with Enter or spacebar if the button has focus).

ButtonBase also defines a Boolean IsPressed property, in case you want to act upon the pressed state (when the left mouse button or spacebar is held down but not yet released).

The most interesting feature of ButtonBase, however, is its ClickMode property. This can be set to a value of a ClickMode enumeration to control exactly when the Click event gets raised. Its values are Release (the default), Press, and Hover. Although changing the ClickMode on standard buttons would likely confuse users, this capability is very handy for buttons that have been restyled to look like something completely different. In these cases, it's a common expectation that *pressing* an object should be the same as *clicking* it.

Several controls ultimately derive from `ButtonBase`, and the following sections examine each of them in turn:

- ▶ `Button`
- ▶ `RepeatButton`
- ▶ `ToggleButton`
- ▶ `CheckBox`
- ▶ `RadioButton`

Button

The WPF `Button` class only adds two simple concepts on top of what `ButtonBase` already provides: being a *cancel button* or a *default button*. These two mechanisms are handy shortcuts for dialogs. If `Button.IsCancel` is set to `true` on a `Button` inside a dialog (that is, a `Window` shown via its `ShowDialog` method), the `Window` is automatically closed with a `DialogResult` of `false`. If `Button.IsDefault` is set to `true`, pressing Enter causes the `Button` to be clicked unless focus is explicitly taken away from it.

FAQ

 What's the difference between `Button`'s `IsDefault` and `IsDefaulted` properties?

`IsDefault` is a read/write property that enables you to decide whether a `Button` should be the default one. The poorly named `IsDefaulted` property, on the other hand, is read-only. It indicates when a default button is in a state such that pressing Enter causes it to be clicked. In other words, `IsDefaulted` can only be `true` when `IsDefault` is `true` *and* either the default button or a `TextBox` (with `AcceptsReturn` set to `false`) has focus. The latter condition enables the Enter key to click the default button without tabbing out of a `TextBox`.

FAQ

 How can I programmatically click a `Button`?

`Button`, like many other WPF controls, has a peer class in the `System.Windows.Automation.Peers` namespace to support UI Automation: `ButtonAutomationPeer`. It can be used as follows with a `Button` called `myButton`:

```
ButtonAutomationPeer bap = new ButtonAutomationPeer(myButton);
IInvokeProvider iip = bap.GetPattern(PatternInterface.Invoke) as IInvokeProvider;
iip.Invoke(); // This clicks the Button
```

These UI Automation classes have several members that are extremely useful for automated testing and accessibility.

RepeatButton

RepeatButton acts just like Button except that it continually raises the Click event as long as the button is being pressed. (It also doesn't have Button's cancel and default behaviors because it derives directly from ButtonBase.) The frequency of the raised Click events depends on the values of RepeatButton's Delay and Interval properties, whose default values are SystemParameters.KeyboardDelay and SystemParameters.Keyboard-Speed, respectively. The default look of a RepeatButton is exactly the same as Button (shown in Figure 4.1).

The behavior of RepeatButton might sound strange at first, but it is useful (and standard) for buttons that increment or decrement a value each time they are pressed. For example, the buttons at the ends of a scrollbar exhibit the repeat-press behavior when clicking them and holding the mouse button down. Or, if you were to build a numeric "up-down" control (which WPF currently does not have built in), you would likely want to use two RepeatButtons to control the numeric value. RepeatButton is in the System.Windows.Controls.**Primitives** namespace because it is likely that you would only use this control as part of a more sophisticated control rather than using it directly.

ToggleButton

ToggleButton is a "sticky" button that holds its state when it is clicked (again without Button's cancel and default behaviors). Clicking it the first time sets its IsChecked property to true, and clicking it again sets IsChecked to false. The default appearance of ToggleButton is exactly the same as Button and RepeatButton.

ToggleButton also has an IsThreeState property that, if set to true, gives IsChecked three possible values: true, false, or null. In fact, IsChecked is of type Nullable<Boolean> (bool? in C#). In the three-state case, the first click sets IsChecked to true, the second click sets it to null, the third click sets it to false, and so on.

In addition to the IsChecked property, ToggleButton defines a separate event for each value of IsChecked: Checked for true, Unchecked for false, and Indeterminate for null. It might seem odd that ToggleButton doesn't have a single IsCheckedChanged event, but the three separate events are handy for declarative scenarios.

As with RepeatButton, ToggleButton is in the System.Windows.Controls.Primitives namespace, which essentially means that the WPF designers don't expect people to use ToggleButtons directly or without additional customizations. It is quite natural, however, to use ToggleButtons directly inside a ToolBar, which is done later in this chapter.

CheckBox

CheckBox is a familiar control, shown in Figure 4.2. But wait a minute…isn't this section supposed to be about buttons? Yes, but consider the characteristics of a WPF CheckBox:

▶ It has a single piece of *externally supplied* content (so this doesn't count the standard check box).

▶ It has a notion of being clicked by mouse or keyboard.

▶ It retains a state of being checked or unchecked when clicked.

▶ It supports a three-state mode, where the state toggles from checked to indeterminate to unchecked.

Does this sound familiar? It should, because a `CheckBox` is nothing more than a `ToggleButton` with a different appearance! `CheckBox` is a simple class deriving from `ToggleButton` that does little more than overriding its default style to the visuals shown in Figure 4.2.

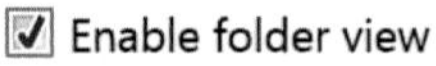

RadioButton

RadioButton is another control that derives from `ToggleButton`, but is unique because it has built-in support for mutual exclusion. When multiple `RadioButton`s are grouped together, only one can be checked at a time. Checking one `RadioButton` automatically unchecks all others in the same group. In fact, users can't even directly uncheck a `RadioButton` by clicking it; unchecking can only be done programmatically. Therefore, `RadioButton` is designed for a multiple choice question. The default appearance of a `RadioButton` is shown in Figure 4.3.

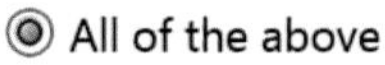

☑ Enable folder view

FIGURE 4.2   The WPF `CheckBox`.

DIGGING DEEPER

CheckBox Keyboard Support

CheckBox supports one additional behavior that `ToggleButton` does not, for parity with a little-known feature of Win32 check boxes. When a `CheckBox` has focus, pressing the plus (+) key checks the control and pressing the minus (–) key unchecks the control!

◉ All of the above

FIGURE 4.3   The WPF `RadioButton`.

Placing several WPF `RadioButton`s in the same group is very straightforward. By default, any `RadioButton`s that share the same direct logical parent are automatically grouped together. For example, only one of the following `RadioButton`s can be checked at any point in time:

```
<StackPanel>
  <RadioButton>Option 1</RadioButton>
  <RadioButton>Option 2</RadioButton>
  <RadioButton>Option 3</RadioButton>
</StackPanel>
```

If you need to group `RadioButton`s in a custom manner, however, you can use its `GroupName` property, which is a simple string. Any `RadioButton`s with the same `GroupName` value get grouped together (as long as they have the same logical root). Therefore, you can group them across different parents:

```
<StackPanel>
  <StackPanel>
    <RadioButton GroupName="A">Option 1</RadioButton>
```

```
      <RadioButton GroupName="A">Option 2</RadioButton>
    </StackPanel>
    <StackPanel>
      <RadioButton GroupName="A">Option 3</RadioButton>
    </StackPanel>
</StackPanel>
```

Or even create subgroups inside the same parent:

```
<StackPanel>
    <RadioButton GroupName="A">Option 1</RadioButton>
    <RadioButton GroupName="A">Option 2</RadioButton>
    <RadioButton GroupName="B">A Different Option 1</RadioButton>
    <RadioButton GroupName="B">A Different Option 2</RadioButton>
</StackPanel>
```

Different groups

Although that last example would be a confusing piece of UI without an extra visual element separating the two subgroups!

Simple Containers

WPF includes several built-in content controls that *don't* have a notion of being clicked like a button, but each has its own unique features to justify its existence.

Label

Label is a classic control that, as in previous technologies, can be used to hold some text. Being a WPF content control, it can hold arbitrary content in its Content property—a Button, a Menu, and so on—but Label is really only useful for text.

You can place text on the screen with WPF in several different ways, such as using a TextBlock element, but what makes Label unique is its support for access keys. With an access key, you can designate a letter in a Label's text that gets special treatment when the user presses the Alt key and that letter. Label enables you to specify an arbitrary element that should receive focus when the user does this. Designating the letter (which can appear underlined, depending on Windows settings) is done by simply preceding it with an underscore, and choosing the target element is done with Label's Target property (of type UIElement).

The classic case of using a Label's access key support with another control is pairing it with a TextBox. For example, the following XAML snippet gives focus to the TextBox when Alt+U is pressed:

```
<Label Target="{Binding ElementName=userNameBox}">_User Name:</Label>
<TextBox x:Name="userNameBox" />
```

The value of `Target` is set using data binding, which is covered in Chapter 9. In C#, you can simply set the property to the instance of the `TextBox` control as follows (assuming the `Label` is named `userNameLabel`):

```
userNameLabel.Target = userNameBox;
```

> **TIP**
>
> Controls like `Label` and `Button` support access keys by treating an underscore before the appropriate letter specially, as in `_Open` or `Save _As`. (Win32 and Windows Forms use an ampersand [&] instead, but the underscore is much more XML-friendly.) If you really want an underscore to appear in your text, use two consecutive underscores.

ToolTip

The `ToolTip` control holds its content in a floating box that appears when you hover over an associated control and disappears when you move the mouse away. Figure 4.4 shows a typical `ToolTip` in action, created from the following XAML:

```
<Button>
  OK
<Button.ToolTip>
  <ToolTip>
    Clicking this will submit your request.
  </ToolTip>
</Button.ToolTip>
</Button>
```

The `ToolTip` class can never be placed directly in a tree of UI elements. Instead, it must be assigned as the value of a separate element's `ToolTip` property (defined on both `FrameworkElement` and `FrameworkContentElement`).

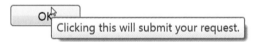

FIGURE 4.4   The WPF `ToolTip`.

> **TIP**
>
> You don't even need to use the `ToolTip` class when setting an element's `ToolTip` property! The property is of type `Object`, and if you set it to any non-`ToolTip` object, the property's implementation automatically creates a `ToolTip` and uses the property value as the `ToolTip`'s content. Therefore, the XAML for Figure 4.4 could be simplified to the following and give the same result:
>
> ```
> <Button>
>   OK
> <Button.ToolTip>
>   Clicking this will submit your request.
> </Button.ToolTip>
> </Button>
> ```
>
> or more simply:
>
> ```
> <Button Content="OK" ToolTip="Clicking this will submit your request."/>
> ```

Of course, because of the flexibility of WPF's content controls, a WPF ToolTip can hold anything you want! Listing 4.1 shows how you might construct a Microsoft Office-style ScreenTip. The result is shown in Figure 4.5.

LISTING 4.1   A Complex ToolTip, Similar to a Microsoft Office ScreenTip

```
<CheckBox>
  CheckBox
<CheckBox.ToolTip>
  <StackPanel>
    <Label FontWeight="Bold" Background="Blue" Foreground="White">
      The CheckBox
    </Label>
    <TextBlock Padding="10" TextWrapping="WrapWithOverflow" Width="200">
      CheckBox is a familiar control. But in WPF, it's not much
      more than a ToggleButton styled differently!
    </TextBlock>
    <Line Stroke="Black" StrokeThickness="1" X2="200"/>
    <StackPanel Orientation="Horizontal">
      <Image Margin="2" Source="help.gif"/>
      <Label FontWeight="Bold">Press F1 for more help.</Label>
    </StackPanel>
  </StackPanel>
</CheckBox.ToolTip>
</CheckBox>
```

Although the content of a ToolTip can contain interactive controls such as Buttons, they never get focus, and you can't click or otherwise interact with them.

ToolTip defines Open and Closed events in case you want to act upon its appearance and disappearance. It also defines several properties for tweaking its behavior, such as its placement, whether it should stay open until explicitly closed, or even whether a drop shadow should be rendered. Sometimes you might want

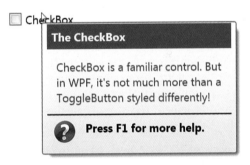

FIGURE 4.5   A ScreenTip, like the kind introduced in the 2007 Office System, couldn't be any easier to create in WPF.

to apply the same ToolTip on multiple controls, yet you might want the ToolTip to behave differently depending on the control to which it is attached. For such cases, a separate ToolTipService static class can meet your needs.

ToolTipService defines a handful of attached properties that can be set on any element using the ToolTip (rather than on the ToolTip itself). It has several of the same properties as ToolTip (which have a higher precedence in case the ToolTip in question has conflicting values), but adds several more. For example, ShowDuration controls how long the ToolTip should be displayed while the mouse pointer is paused over an element, and InitialShowDelay controls the length of time between the pause occurring and the ToolTip first being shown. You can add ShowDuration to the first ToolTip example as follows:

```
<Button ToolTipService.ShowDuration="3000">
  …
</Button>
```

FAQ

 How do I get a ToolTip to appear when hovering over a disabled element?|

Simply use the ShowOnDisabled attached property of the ToolTipService class! From XAML, this would look like the following on a Button:

```
<Button ToolTipService.ShowOnDisabled="True">
  …
</Button>
```

Or from C# code, you can call the static method corresponding to the attached property:

```
ToolTipService.SetShowOnDisabled(myButton, true);
```

Frame

The Frame control holds arbitrary content, just like all other content controls, but it isolates the content from the rest of the UI. For example, properties that would normally be inherited down the element tree stop when they reach the Frame. In many respects, WPF Frames act like frames in HTML.

FAQ

 How can I forcibly close a ToolTip that is currently showing?

Set its IsOpen property to false.

Speaking of HTML, Frame's claim to fame is that it can render HTML content in addition to WPF content! Frame has a Source property of type System.Uri that can be set to any HTML (or XAML) page. For example:

```
<Frame Source="http://www.pinvoke.net"/>
```

Frame has built-in support for WPF's navigation tracking that applies to both HTML and XAML content. This is examined in Chapter 7.

So, you can think of the Frame control as a more powerful version of the "Microsoft Web Browser" ActiveX control or the Windows Forms WebBrowser control. Unfortunately, when Frame hosts HTML it has several limitations that don't apply to other WPF controls (due to relying on Win32 for its implementation of HTML rendering). For example, the HTML content is always rendered on top of WPF content, it can't have bitmap effects applied to it, its Opacity can't be changed, and so on. Frame also does not support rendering an arbitrary string or stream of HTML; the content must be a path or URL pointing to a loose file. (If you require the ability to display HTML embedded as a resource, the best option is to use the Windows Forms WebBrowser control via the techniques discussed in Chapter 15, "Interoperability with Win32, Windows Forms, and ActiveX.")

TIP

The Image element is another WPF class with a Source property that can be used to hold images stored at a URL, on the local disk, or even embedded in an assembly. Image is used a few times in this chapter and is revisited in Chapter 8, "Resources."

DIGGING DEEPER

Frame's Content Property

Although Frame is a content control and has a property called Content, it does not treat Content as a content property in the XAML sense. In other words, the Frame element in XAML doesn't support a child element. You must explicitly use the Content property as follows:

```
<Frame>
<Frame.Content>

  …
</Frame.Content>
</Frame>
```

Frame accomplishes this by marking itself with an empty ContentPropertyAttribute, overriding the [ContentProperty("Content")] marking on the base ContentControl class. But why does it bother?

According to the designers of WPF, this was done to deemphasize the use of Frame's Content property, as setting its Source property to an external file is the typical expected usage of Frame. And the only reason Frame is a ContentControl is for consistency with NavigationWindow, discussed in Chapter 7. Note that if you set both the Source and Content properties, Content takes precedence!

Containers with a Header

All the previous content controls either add very simple default visuals around the content (button chrome, a check box, and so on) or don't add any visuals at all. The following two controls are a little different because they add a customizable *header* to the main content. These controls derive from a subclass of ContentControl named HeaderedContentControl, which adds a Header property of type Object.

GroupBox

GroupBox is a familiar control for organizing chunks of controls. Figure 4.6 shows a GroupBox surrounding CheckBoxes, created from the following XAML:

```
<GroupBox Header="Grammar">
  <StackPanel>
    <CheckBox>Check grammar as you type</CheckBox>
    <CheckBox>Hide grammatical errors in this document</CheckBox>
    <CheckBox>Check grammar with spelling</CheckBox>
  </StackPanel>
</GroupBox>
```

GroupBox is typically used to contain multiple items, but because it is a content control, it can only directly contain a single item. Therefore, you typically need to set GroupBox's content to an intermediate control that can contain multiple children. In the preceding XAML snippet, a StackPanel is used, which is discussed in depth in Chapter 6, "Layout with Panels."

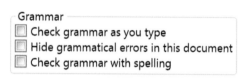

FIGURE 4.6   The WPF GroupBox.

Just like the Content property, the Header property can be set to an arbitrary object, and if it derives from UIElement it gets rendered as expected. For example, changing Header to be a Button as follows produces the result in Figure 4.7:

```
<GroupBox>
<GroupBox.Header>
  <Button>Grammar</Button>
</GroupBox.Header>
  <StackPanel>
    <CheckBox>Check grammar as you type</CheckBox>
    <CheckBox>Hide grammatical errors in this document</CheckBox>
    <CheckBox>Check grammar with spelling</CheckBox>
  </StackPanel>
</GroupBox>
```

In Figure 4.7, the Button used in the header is fully functional. It can get focus, it can be clicked, and so on.

Expander

Expander is exciting because it's the first control examined in this chapter that doesn't already exist in Win32-based UI technologies such as Windows Forms!

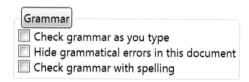

FIGURE 4.7   This GroupBox has a Button as a header, just to reinforce WPF's flexible content model.

Expander is very much like GroupBox, but contains a button that enables you to expand and collapse the inner content. (By default, the Expander starts out collapsed.)

Figure 4.8 displays the Expander control in its two states. This Expander was created with the same XAML used in Figure 4.6, but with the opening and closing GroupBox tags replaced with Expander tags:

```
<Expander Header="Grammar">
  <StackPanel>
    <CheckBox>Check grammar as you type</CheckBox>
    <CheckBox>Hide grammatical errors in this document</CheckBox>
    <CheckBox>Check grammar with spelling</CheckBox>
  </StackPanel>
</Expander>
```

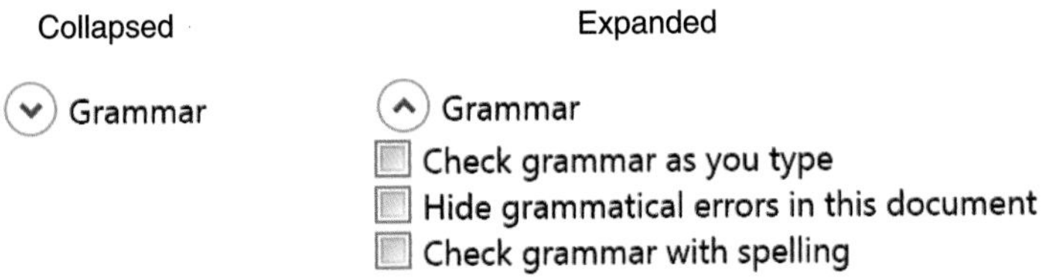

Collapsed   Expanded

⌄ Grammar   ⌃ Grammar
                                  ☐ Check grammar as you type
                                  ☐ Hide grammatical errors in this document
                                  ☐ Check grammar with spelling

FIGURE 4.8   The WPF Expander.

Expander defines an IsExpanded property and Expanded/Collapsed events. It also enables you to control which direction the expansion happens (Up, Down, Left, or Right) with an ExpandDirection property.

The button inside the Expander is actually a restyled ToggleButton! The more primitive controls such as ToggleButton and RepeatButton are used internally by several of the more complicated controls.

Items Controls

Another major category of WPF controls are *items controls*, which can contain an unbounded collection of items rather than just a single piece of content. All items controls derive from the abstract ItemsControl class, a direct subclass of Control (just like the ContentControl class).

ItemsControl stores its content in an Items property (of type ItemCollection). Each item can be an arbitrary object, which by default gets rendered just like it would inside a content control. In other words, any UIElement gets rendered as expected, and (ignoring data templates) any other type is rendered as a TextBlock containing the string returned by its ToString method.

The ListBox control used by the two preceding chapters is an items control. These chapters always added ListBoxItems to the Items collection, but here's an example that adds arbitrary objects to Items:

```
<ListBox xmlns="http://schemas.microsoft.com/winfx/2006/xaml/presentation"
  xmlns:sys="clr-namespace:System;assembly=mscorlib">
  <Button>Button</Button>
  <Expander Header="Expander" />
  <sys:DateTime>1/1/2007</sys:DateTime>
  <sys:DateTime>1/2/2007</sys:DateTime>
  <sys:DateTime>1/3/2007</sys:DateTime>
</ListBox>
```

The child elements are implicitly added to the Items collection because Items is a content property. This ListBox is shown in Figure 4.9. The two UIElements (Button and Expander) are rendered normally and are fully interactive, and the three DateTime objects are rendered according to their ToString method.

As mentioned in Chapter 2, the Items property is read-only. This means that you can add objects to the initially empty collection or remove objects, but you can't point Items to an entirely different collection. ItemsControl has a separate property that supports filling its items with an existing arbitrary collection, called ItemsSource. The use of ItemsSource is examined further in Chapter 9.

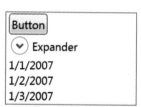

FIGURE 4.9   A ListBox containing arbitrary objects.

Besides Items and ItemsSource, ItemsControl has a few additional interesting properties, such as

▶ **HasItems**—A read-only Boolean property that makes it easy to act upon the control's empty state from declarative XAML. From C#, you can either use this property or simply check the value of Items.Count.

▶ **IsGrouping**—Another read-only Boolean property that tells you if the control's items are divided into top-level groups. This grouping is done directly within the ItemsCollection class, which contains several properties for managing and naming groups of items. You'll see more about grouping in Chapter 9.

▶ **DisplayMemberPath**—A string property that can be set to the name of a property on each item (or a more complicated expression) that changes how each object gets rendered.

To illustrate DisplayMemberPath, Figure 4.10 demonstrates what happens when it is applied to the preceding ListBox as follows:

```
<ListBox xmlns="http://schemas.microsoft.com/winfx/2006/xaml/presentation"
  xmlns:sys="clr-namespace:System;assembly=mscorlib" DisplayMemberPath="DayOfWeek">
  <Button>Button</Button>
```

```
  <Expander Header="Expander"/>
  <sys:DateTime>1/1/2007</sys:DateTime>
  <sys:DateTime>1/2/2007</sys:DateTime>
  <sys:DateTime>1/3/2007</sys:DateTime>
</ListBox>
```

Setting DisplayMemberPath to DayOfWeek tells WPF to render the value of each item's DayOfWeek property rather than each item itself. That is why the three DateTime objects render as Monday, Tuesday, and Wednesday in Figure 4.10. (This is the ToString-based rendering of each DayOfWeek enumeration value returned by the DayOfWeek property.) Because Button and Expander don't have a DayOfWeek property, they are rendered as empty TextBlocks.

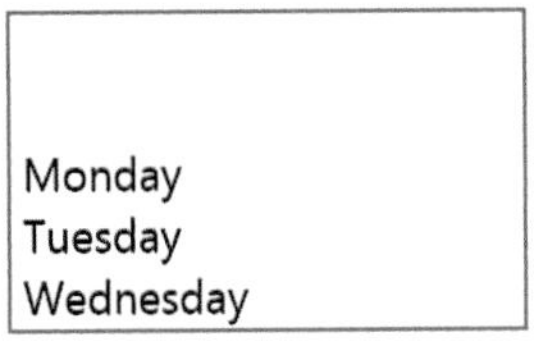

Monday
Tuesday
Wednesday

FIGURE 4.10   The ListBox from Figure 4.9 with DisplayMemberPath set to DayOfWeek.

DIGGING DEEPER

Property Paths in WPF

DisplayMemberPath supports syntax known as a *property path* that is used in several areas of WPF, such as data binding and animation. The basic idea of a property path is to represent a sequence of one or more properties that you could also use in procedural code to get a desired value. The simplest example of a property path is a single property name, but if the value of that property is a complex object, you can invoke one of its own properties (and so on) by delimiting the property names with periods, just like in C#. This syntax even supports indexers and arrays.

For example, imagine an object that defines a FirstButton property of type Button, whose Content property is currently set to an "OK" string. The following property path represents the value of the string ("OK"):

```
FirstButton.Content
```

The following property path represents the length of the string (2):

```
FirstButton.Content.Length
```

And the following property path represents the first character of the string ('O'):

```
FirstButton.Content[0]
```

These expressions match what you would use in C#, except that no casting is required.

ListBox is not the only items control, of course. Items controls can be divided into three main groups: selectors, menus, and everything else.

Selectors

Selectors are items controls whose items can be indexed and, most important, selected. The abstract Selector class, which derives from ItemsControl, adds a few properties to handle selection. For example, three similar properties for getting or setting the current selection are

- ▶ **SelectedIndex**—A zero-based integer that indicates what item is selected or -1 if nothing is selected. Items are numbered in the order they are added to the collection.

- ▶ **SelectedItem**—The actual item instance that is currently selected.

- ▶ **SelectedValue**—The *value* of the currently selected item. By default this value is the item itself, making SelectedValue identical to SelectedItem. You can set SelectedValuePath, however, to choose an arbitrary property or expression that should represent each item's value. (SelectedValuePath works just like DisplayMemberPath.)

All three properties are read/write, so you use them to change the current selection as well as retrieve it.

Selector also supports two attached properties that can be applied to individual items:

- ▶ **IsSelected**—A Boolean that can be used to select or unselect an item (or to retrieve its current selection state)

- ▶ **IsSelectionActive**—A read-only Boolean that tells you if the selection has focus

Selector also defines an event—SelectionChanged—that makes it possible to listen for changes to the current selection. The preceding chapter used this with a ListBox when demonstrating attached events.

WPF ships four Selector-derived controls:

- ▶ ComboBox

- ▶ ListBox

- ▶ ListView

- ▶ TabControl

ComboBox

The ComboBox control, shown in Figure 4.11, enables users to select one item from a list. ComboBox is a popular control because it doesn't occupy much space. It displays only the current selection in a *selection box,* with the rest of the list shown on demand in a *drop-down.* The drop-down can be opened and closed by clicking the button or by pressing Alt+Up, Alt+Down, or F4.

ComboBox defines two events—
DropDownOpened and DropDownClosed—
and a property—IsDropDownOpen—that
enable you to act on the drop-down
being opened or closed. For example,
you can delay the filling of ComboBox
items until the drop-down is opened by
handling the DropDownOpened event.
Note that IsDropDownOpen is a read/write
property, so you can set it directly to
change the state of the drop-down.

FIGURE 4.11   The WPF ComboBox, with its
drop-down showing.

Customizing the Selection Box

ComboBox supports a mode in which the user can type arbitrary text into the selection
box. If the text matches one of the existing items, that item automatically becomes
selected. Otherwise, no item gets selected but the custom text gets stored in ComboBox's
Text property so you can act on it appropriately. This mode can be controlled with two
poorly named properties: IsEditable and IsReadOnly, which are both false by default.
In addition, a StaysOpenOnEdit property can be set to true to keep the drop-down open if
the user clicks on the selection box (matching the behavior of drop-downs in Microsoft
Office as opposed to normal Win32 drop-downs).

FAQ

What's the difference between ComboBox's IsEditable and IsReadOnly properties?

Setting IsEditable to true turns ComboBox's selection box into a text box. IsReadOnly
controls whether that text box can be edited, just like TextBox's IsReadOnly property. This
means that IsReadOnly is meaningless unless IsEditable is true, and IsEditable being
true doesn't necessarily mean that the selection text can be edited. Table 4.1 sums up the
behavior of ComboBox based on the values of these two properties.

TABLE 4.1   The Behavior for All Combinations of IsEditable and IsReadOnly

IsEditable	IsReadOnly	Meaning
false	false	The selection box displays a visual copy of the selected item and it doesn't allow the typing of arbitrary text. (The default behavior.)
false	true	Same as above.
true	false	The selection box displays a textual representation of the selected item and it allows the typing of arbitrary text.
true	true	The selection box displays a textual representation of the selected item but it doesn't allow the typing of arbitrary text.

When the selection box is a text box, the selected item can only be displayed as a simple string. This isn't a problem when items in the ComboBox are strings (or content controls containing strings), but when they are more complicated items, you must tell ComboBox what to use as the string representation for its items.

Listing 4.2 contains XAML for a ComboBox with complex items. Each item displays an old PowerPoint design in a way that makes the ComboBox look like a Microsoft Office-style "gallery," showing a preview and description for each item. A typical gallery in Office restricts the selection box to simple text, however, rather than keeping the full richness of the selected item. Figure 4.12 shows the rendered result of Listing 4.2, as well as what happens by default when this ComboBox is marked with IsEditable set to true.

LISTING 4.2   A ComboBox with Complex Items, such as a Microsoft Office Gallery

```
<ComboBox>
  <!-- Item #1 -->
  <StackPanel Orientation="Horizontal" Margin="5">
    <Image Source="CurtainCall.bmp"/>
    <StackPanel Width="200">
      <TextBlock Margin="5,0" FontSize="14" FontWeight="Bold"
        VerticalAlignment="center">Curtain Call</TextBlock>
      <TextBlock Margin="5" VerticalAlignment="center" TextWrapping="Wrap">
        Whimsical, with a red curtain background that represents a stage.
      </TextBlock>
    </StackPanel>
  </StackPanel>
  <!-- Item #2 -->
  <StackPanel Orientation="Horizontal" Margin="5">
    <Image Source="Fireworks.bmp"/>
    <StackPanel Width="200">
      <TextBlock Margin="5,0" FontSize="14" FontWeight="Bold"
        VerticalAlignment="center">Fireworks</TextBlock>
      <TextBlock Margin="5" VerticalAlignment="center" TextWrapping="Wrap">
        Sleek, with a black sky containing fireworks. When you need to
        celebrate PowerPoint-style, this design is for you!
      </TextBlock>
    </StackPanel>
  </StackPanel>
  …more items…
</ComboBox>
```

IsEditable="False" (default)   IsEditable="True"

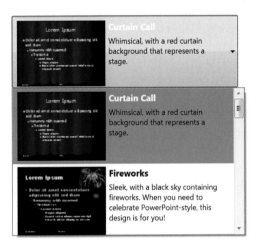

FIGURE 4.12   By default, setting `IsEditable` to true causes `ToString`-based rendering in the selection box.

Obviously, displaying the type name of `"System.Windows.Controls.StackPanel"` in the selection box is not acceptable, so that's where the `TextSearch` class comes in. `TextSearch` defines two attached properties that provide control over the text that gets displayed in an editable selection box.

A `TextSearch.TextPath` property can be attached to the `ComboBox` to designate the property (or subproperty) of each item to use as the selection box text. This works just like the `DisplayMemberPath` and `SelectedValuePath` properties; the only difference between these three properties is how the final value gets used.

For each item in Listing 4.2, the obvious text to use in the selection box is the content of the first `TextBlock` because it contains the title (such as "Curtain Call" or "Fireworks"). Because the `TextBlock` is nested within two `StackPanel`s, the desired property path involves referencing the inner `StackPanel` (the second child of each item) before referencing the `TextBlock` (the first child of each inner `StackPanel`). Therefore, the `TextPath` attached property can be applied to Listing 4.2 as follows:

```
<ComboBox IsEditable="True" TextSearch.TextPath="Children[1].Children[0].Text">
  …
</ComboBox>
```

This is a bit fragile, however, because the property path will stop working if the structure of the items is changed. It also doesn't handle heterogeneous items; any item that doesn't match the structure of `TextPath` is displayed as an empty string in the selection box.

`TextSearch`'s other attached property—`Text`—is more flexible, but must be applied to individual items in the `ComboBox`. You can set `Text` to the literal text you want to be displayed in the selection box for each item. It could be applied to Listing 4.2 as follows:

```
<ComboBox IsEditable="True">
  <!-- Item #1 -->
  <StackPanel TextSearch.Text="Curtain Call" Orientation="Horizontal" Margin="5">
    …
  </StackPanel>
  <!-- Item #2 -->
  <StackPanel TextSearch.Text="Fireworks" Orientation="Horizontal" Margin="5">
    …
  </StackPanel>
  …more items…
</ComboBox>
```

You can use `TextSearch.TextPath` on the `ComboBox` and `TextSearch.Text` on individual items simultaneously. In this case, `TextPath` provides the default selection box representation and `Text` overrides this representation for any marked items.

The result of using either `TextSearch.TextPath` on `TextSearch.Text` as done in the preceding snippets is shown in Figure 4.13.

FIGURE 4.13   A proper looking Office-style gallery, thanks to the use of `TextSearch` attached properties.

FAQ

 When the `SelectionChanged` event gets raised, how do I get the new selection?

The `SelectionChanged` event is designed to handle controls that allow multiple selections, so it can be a little confusing for a single-selection selector such as `ComboBox`. The `SelectionChangedEventArgs` type passed to event handlers has two properties of type `IList`: `AddedItems` and `RemovedItems`. `AddedItems` contains the new selection and `RemovedItems` contains the previous selection. For example:

Continues

> **Continued**
>
> ```
> void ComboBox_SelectionChanged(object sender, SelectionChangedEventArgs e)
> {
>   if (e.AddedItems.Count > 0)
>     object newSelection = e.AddedItems[0];
> }
> ```
>
> Like this code, never assume that there's a selected item! Besides the fact that ComboBox's selection can be cleared programmatically, it can get cleared by the user when IsEditable is true and IsReadOnly is false. In this case, if the user changes the selection box text to something that doesn't match any item, the SelectionChanged event is raised with an empty AddedItems collection.

ComboBoxItem

ComboBox implicitly wraps each of its items in a ComboBoxItem object. (You can see this from code if you traverse up the visual tree from any of the items.) But you can explicitly wrap any item in a ComboBoxItem, which happens to be a content control. This can be applied to each item in Listing 4.2 as follows:

```
<!-- Item #1 -->
<ComboBoxItem TextSearch.Text="Curtain Call">
  <StackPanel Orientation="Horizontal" Margin="5">
    ...
  </StackPanel>
</ComboBoxItem>
<!-- Item #2 -->
<ComboBoxItem TextSearch.Text="Fireworks">
  <StackPanel Orientation="Horizontal" Margin="5">
    ...
  </StackPanel>
</ComboBoxItem>
...more items...
```

Notice that if you're using the TextSearch.Text attached property, you need to move it to the ComboBoxItem element now that StackPanel is not the outermost element for each item. Similarly, the TextSearch.TextPath value used earlier would need to be changed to **Content**.Children[1].Children[0].Text.

ListBox

The familiar ListBox control is similar to ComboBox, except that all items are displayed directly within the control's bounds (or you can scroll to view additional items if they don't all fit). Figure 4.14 shows a ListBox containing the same items used in Listing 4.2.

> **TIP**
>
> The preferred approach for items controls such as ComboBox and ListBox is to actually give it nonvisual items (for example, custom business objects) and then use a data template to define how each item gets rendered. Chapter 9 discusses data templates in depth.

FAQ

Why should I bother wrapping items in a ComboBoxItem?

ComboBoxItem exposes some useful properties—IsSelected and IsHighlighted—and useful events—Selected and Unselected. Using ComboBoxItem also avoids a quirky behavior with showing content controls in the selection box (when IsEditable is false): If an item in a ComboBox is a content control, the entire control doesn't get displayed in the selection box. Instead, the inner content is extracted and shown. By using ComboBoxItem as the outermost content control, the inner content is now the entire control that you probably wanted to be displayed in the first place.

Because ComboBoxItem is a content control, it is also handy for adding simple strings to a ComboBox (rather than using something like TextBlock or Label). For example:

```
<ComboBox>
  <ComboBoxItem>Item 1</ComboBoxItem>
  <ComboBoxItem>Item 2</ComboBoxItem>
</ComboBox>
```

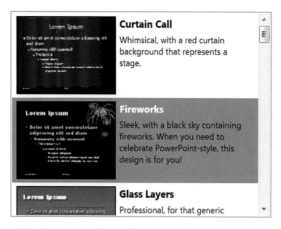

FIGURE 4.14   The WPF ListBox.

Probably the most important feature of ListBox is that it can support multiple simultaneous selections. This is controllable via the SelectionMode property, which accepts three values (from a SelectionMode enumeration):

▶ **Single** (default)—Only one item can be selected at a time, just like with ComboBox.

▶ **Multiple**—Any number of items can be selected simultaneously. Clicking an unselected item adds it to ListBox's SelectedItems collection, and clicking a selected item removes it from the collection.

▶ **Extended**—Any number of items can be selected simultaneously, but the behavior is optimized for the single selection case. To select multiple items in this mode, you must hold down Shift (for contiguous items) or Ctrl (for noncontiguous items) while clicking. This matches the behavior of the Win32 ListBox control.

DIGGING DEEPER

ListBox **Properties and Multiple Selection**

Although ListBox has a SelectedItems property that can be used no matter which SelectionMode is used, it still inherits the SelectedIndex, SelectedItem, and SelectedValue properties from Selector that don't fit in with the multiselect model.

When multiple items are selected, SelectedItem simply points to the first item in the SelectedItems collection (which is the item selected the earliest by the user), and SelectedIndex/SelectedValue simply give the index and value for that item. But it's best not to use these properties on a control supporting multiple selections. Note that ListBox does *not* define a SelectedIndices or SelectedValues property, however.

Just like ComboBox has its companion ComboBoxItem class, ListBox has a ListBoxItem class as seen in the preceding two chapters. In fact, ComboBoxItem derives from ListBoxItem, which defines the IsSelected property and Selected/Unselected events.

TIP

The TextSearch technique shown with ComboBox in the preceding section is important for ListBox, too. For example, if the items in Figure 4.14 are marked with the appropriate TextSearch.Text values, then typing "F" while the ListBox has focus makes the selection jump to the "Fireworks" item. Without the use of TextSearch, the items would get focus by pressing "S," because that's the first letter in System.Windows.Controls.StackPanel. (And that would be a weird user experience!)

FAQ

 How can I make ListBox arrange its items horizontally instead of vertically?

One way is to define a new control template (as discussed in Chapter 10), but all ItemsControls provide a shortcut with its ItemsPanel property. ItemsPanel enables you to swap out the panel used to arrange items while leaving everything else about the control intact. ListBox uses a panel called VirtualizingStackPanel to arrange its items vertically, but the following code replaces it with a new VirtualizingStackPanel that explicitly sets its Orientation to Horizontal:

```
<ListBox>
<ListBox.ItemsPanel>
  <ItemsPanelTemplate>
    <VirtualizingStackPanel Orientation="Horizontal"/>
```

Continues

FAQ

Continued

```
  </ItemsPanelTemplate>
</ListBox.ItemsPanel>
   …
</ListBox>
```

The translation of this XAML to procedural code is not straightforward, but here's how you can accomplish the same task in C#:

```csharp
FrameworkElementFactory panelFactory =
  new FrameworkElementFactory(typeof(VirtualizingStackPanel));
panelFactory.SetValue(VirtualizingStackPanel.OrientationProperty,
  Orientation.Horizontal);
myListBox.ItemsPanel = new ItemsPanelTemplate(panelFactory);
```

The result is shown in Figure 4.15. Because ItemsPanel is defined on ItemsControl, you can do the same thing with a ComboBox as well.

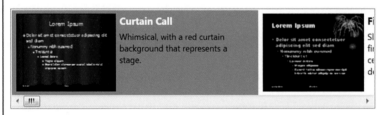

FIGURE 4.15   ListBox with a Horizontal panel used as its ItemsPanel.

Chapter 6 examines all the built-in panels, some of which can be very useful as an ItemsPanel.

FAQ

How can I get ListBox to scroll smoothly?

By default, ListBox scrolls on an item-by-item basis. Because the scrolling is based on each item's height, it can look quite choppy if you have large items. If you want smooth scrolling, such that each scrolling action shifts the items by a small number of pixels regardless of their heights, the easiest solution is to set the ScrollViewer.CanContentScroll attached property to false on the ListBox.

Be aware, however, that by making this change you lose ListBox's *virtualization* functionality. Virtualization refers to the optimization of creating child elements only when they become visible on the screen. Virtualization is only possible when using data binding to fill the control's items, so setting CanContentScroll to false can negatively impact the performance of data-bound scenarios only.

FAQ

 How can I sort items in a `ListBox` (or any other `ItemsControl`)?

Sorting can be done via a mechanism on the `ItemsCollection` object, so it applies equally to all `ItemsControls`. `ItemsCollection` has a `SortDescriptions` property that can hold any number of `System.ComponentModel.SortDescription` instances. Each `SortDescription` describes which property of the items should be used for sorting and whether the sort is ascending or descending. For example, the following code sorts a bunch of `ContentControl` items based on their `Content` property:

```
// Clear any existing sorting first
myItemsControl.Items.SortDescriptions.Clear();
// Sort by the Content property
myItemsControl.Items.SortDescriptions.Add(
  new SortDescription("Content", ListSortDirection.Ascending));
```

FAQ

 How do I get the items in my `ItemsControl` to have Automation IDs, as seen in tools like UISpy?

The easiest way to give any `FrameworkElement` an Automation ID is to set its `Name` property, as that gets used by default for automation purposes. However, if you want to give an element an ID that is different from its name, simply set the `AutomationProperties.AutomationID` attached property (from the `System.Windows.Automation` namespace) to the desired string.

ListView

The `ListView` control, which derives from `ListBox`, looks and acts just like a `ListBox`, except that it uses the `Extended SelectionMode` by default. But `ListView` also adds a property called `View` that enables you to customize the view in a richer way than choosing a custom `ItemsPanel`.

The `View` property is of type `ViewBase`, an abstract class. WPF ships with one concrete subclass, and that class is called `GridView`. Its default experience is much like Windows Explorer's Details view. (In fact, in beta versions of WPF, `GridView` was even called `DetailsView`.)

Figure 4.16 displays a simple `ListView` created from the following XAML, which assumes that the sys prefix corresponds to the `System` .NET namespace in `mscorlib.dll`:

```
<ListView>
<ListView.View>
  <GridView>
    <GridViewColumn Header="Date"/>
    <GridViewColumn Header="Day of Week"
      DisplayMemberBinding="{Binding DayOfWeek}"/>
```

```
    <GridViewColumn Header="Year" DisplayMemberBinding="{Binding Year}"/>
  </GridView>
</ListView.View>
  <sys:DateTime>1/1/2007</sys:DateTime>
  <sys:DateTime>1/2/2007</sys:DateTime>
  <sys:DateTime>1/3/2007</sys:DateTime>
</ListView>
```

GridView has a Columns content property that holds a collection of
GridViewColumn objects, as well as other
properties to control the behavior of the
column headers. WPF defines a
ListViewItem element that derives from
ListBoxItem. In this case, the DateTime
objects are implicitly wrapped in
ListViewItems because they are not
used explicitly.

Date	Day of Week	Year
1/1/2007	Monday	2007
1/2/2007	Tuesday	2007
1/3/2007	Wednesday	2007

FIGURE 4.16   The WPF ListView, using
GridView.

ListView's items are specified as a simple list as with ListBox, so the key to displaying
different data in each column is the DisplayMemberBinding property of GridViewColumn.
The idea is that ListView contains a complex object for each row, and the value for every
column is a property or subproperty of each object. Unlike ItemsControl's
DisplayMemberPath property, however, DisplayMemberBinding requires the use of data
binding techniques described in Chapter 9.

What's nice about GridView is that it automatically supports some of the more advanced
features of Windows Explorer's Details view:

▶ Columns can be reordered by dragging and dropping them.

▶ Columns can be resized by dragging the column separators.

▶ Columns can automatically resize to "just fit" their content by double-clicking their
separators.

It doesn't, however, support automatic sorting by clicking on a column header, which is
an unfortunate gap in functionality. The code to sort items when a header is clicked is
not complicated (because you can use the SortDescriptions property mentioned in the
previous section), but you would also have to manually create the little arrow in the
header that typically indicates which column is being used for sorting and whether it's
ascending or descending.

TabControl
The final selector—TabControl—is useful for switching between multiple pages of
content. Figure 4.17 shows what a basic TabControl looks like. Tabs in a TabControl are
typically placed on the top, but with TabControl's TabStripPlacement property (of type
Dock), you can also set their placement to Left, Right, or Bottom.

TabControl is pretty easy to use. Simply add items, and each item is placed on a separate tab. For example:

```
<TabControl>
  <TextBlock>Content for Tab 1.</TextBlock>
  <TextBlock>Content for Tab 2.</TextBlock>
  <TextBlock>Content for Tab 3.</TextBlock>
</TabControl>
```

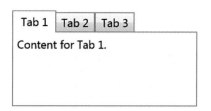

FIGURE 4.17   The WPF TabControl.

Much like ComboBox with ComboBoxItem, ListBox with ListBoxItem, and so on, TabControl implicitly wraps each item in its companion TabItem type. It's unlikely you'd add non-TabItem children directly to TabControl, however, because without an explicit TabItem there's no way to label the corresponding tab. For example, the following XAML is the source for Figure 4.17:

```
<TabControl>
  <TabItem Header="Tab 1">Content for Tab 1.</TabItem>
  <TabItem Header="Tab 2">Content for Tab 2.</TabItem>
  <TabItem Header="Tab 3">Content for Tab 3.</TabItem>
</TabControl>
```

TabItem is a headered content control, so Header can be any arbitrary object, just like with GroupBox or Expander.

Unlike the other selectors, the first item is selected by default. However, you can programmatically unselect all tabs by setting SelectedItem to null (or SelectedIndex to -1).

Menus

WPF has both of the familiar menu controls built-in—Menu and ContextMenu. Unlike in Win32-based technologies, WPF menus are not special-cased over other controls to have distinct prominence or limitations. They are just another set of items controls, designed for the hierarchical display of items in a series of cascading pop-ups.

Menu

Menu simply stacks its items horizontally with the characteristic gray bar (by default) as its background. The only public API that Menu adds to its ItemsControl base class is the IsMainMenu property. When true (which it is by default) the Menu gets focus when the user presses the Alt or F10 key, matching user expectations for Win32 menus.

As with any other items control, Menu's items can be anything, but it's expected that you'll use MenuItem and Separator objects. Figure 4.18 displays a typical menu created from the XAML in Listing 4.3.

LISTING 4.3   A Typical Menu, with MenuItem and Separator Children

```
<Menu>
  <MenuItem Header="_File">
    <MenuItem Header="_New..."/>
    <MenuItem Header="_Open..."/>
    <Separator/>
    <MenuItem Header="Sen_d To">
      <MenuItem Header="Mail Recipient"/>
      <MenuItem Header="My Documents"/>
    </MenuItem>
  </MenuItem>
  <MenuItem Header="_Edit">
    ...
  </MenuItem>
  <MenuItem Header="_View">
    ...
  </MenuItem>
</Menu>
```

FIGURE 4.18   The WPF Menu.

MenuItem is a *headered items control* (deriving from HeaderedItemsControl), which is much like a headered content control. For MenuItem, the Header is actually the main object (typically text, as in Figure 4.18). The Items, if any, are the child elements that get displayed as a submenu. Like Button and Label, MenuItem supports access keys by using the underscore prefix.

Separator is a simple control that, when placed in a MenuItem, gets rendered as the horizontal line shown in Figure 4.18. Separator is also designed for two other items controls discussed later in this chapter: ToolBar and StatusBar.

Although Menu is a simple control, MenuItem contains many properties for customizing its behavior. Some of the interesting ones are as follows:

▶ **Icon**—Enables you to add an arbitrary object to be placed alongside the Header. The Icon object gets rendered just like Header, although typically a small image or drawing is used.

▶ **IsCheckable**—Enables you to make a MenuItem act like a CheckBox control.

▶ **InputGestureText**—Enables you to label an item with an associated gesture (most commonly, a keyboard shortcut such as Ctrl+O).

MenuItem also defines five events: Checked, Unchecked, SubmenuOpened, SubmenuClosed, and Click. Although handling a Click event is a common way to attach behavior to a MenuItem, you can alternatively assign a command to MenuItem's Command property.

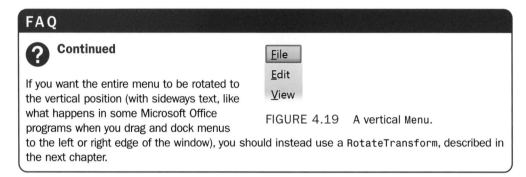

FAQ

? Continued

If you want the entire menu to be rotated to
the vertical position (with sideways text, like
what happens in some Microsoft Office
programs when you drag and dock menus
to the left or right edge of the window), you should instead use a `RotateTransform`, described in
the next chapter.

File
Edit
View

FIGURE 4.19   A vertical Menu.

ContextMenu

`ContextMenu` works just like `Menu`; it's a simple container designed to hold `MenuItems` and
`Separators`. You can't embed `ContextMenu` directly in an element tree, however. You must
attach it to a control via an appropriate property, such as the `ContextMenu` property
defined on `FrameworkElement` and `FrameworkContentElement`. When a user right-clicks on
the control (or presses Shift+F10), the context menu is displayed.

Figure 4.20 displays a context menu applied to a `ListBox` as follows, using the exact same
`MenuItems` from Listing 4.3:

```
<ListBox>
<ListBox.ContextMenu>
  <ContextMenu>
    …The three MenuItems from Listing 4.3…
  </ContextMenu>
</ListBox.ContextMenu>

  …
</ListBox>
```

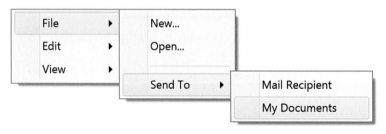

FIGURE 4.20   The WPF `ContextMenu`.

Besides the expected `IsOpen` property land `Opened/Closed` events, `ContextMenu` defines
many properties for customizing the placement of the menu. By default, the menu
appears with its upper-left corner directly under the mouse pointer. But you can change
its `Placement` to something other than `MousePoint` (such as `Absolute`), and/or set its
`HorizontalOffset` and `VerticalOffset`, for example, to adjust this behavior.

Just as `ToolTip` has a companion `ToolTipService` static class for controlling properties
from the `ToolTip`'s target, `ContextMenu` has a `ContextMenuService` static class for the same

purpose. It contains several attached properties corresponding to many of the properties defined directly on ContextMenu.

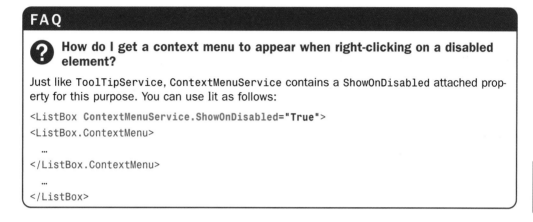

FAQ

? **How do I get a context menu to appear when right-clicking on a disabled element?**

Just like ToolTipService, ContextMenuService contains a ShowOnDisabled attached property for this purpose. You can use lit as follows:

```
<ListBox ContextMenuService.ShowOnDisabled="True">
<ListBox.ContextMenu>
  …
</ListBox.ContextMenu>
  …
</ListBox>
```

Other Items Controls

The remaining items controls—TreeView, ToolBar, and StatusBar—are neither selectors nor menus, but can still contain an unbounded number of arbitrary objects.

TreeView

TreeView is a popular control for displaying hierarchical data with nodes that can be expanded and collapsed, as shown in Figure 4.21. Under the Aero theme, nodes have triangles indicating their expanded/collapsed state, but on the other themes (such as Luna) nodes have the familiar plus and minus indicators.

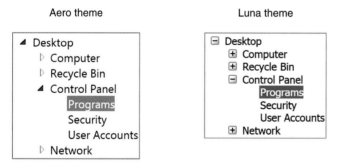

FIGURE 4.21   The WPF TreeView.

TreeView, like Menu, is a very simple control. It can contain any items, and stacks them vertically. But TreeView is pretty pointless unless you fill it with TreeViewItems.

TreeViewItem, just like MenuItem, is a headered items control. TreeViewItem's Header property contains the current item, and its Items collection contains subitems (which, again, are expected to be TreeViewItems).

The TreeView in Figure 4.21 can be created with the following XAML:

```
<TreeView>
  <TreeViewItem Header="Desktop">
    <TreeViewItem Header="Computer">

      ...

    </TreeViewItem>
    <TreeViewItem Header="Recycle Bin">

      ...

    </TreeViewItem>
    <TreeViewItem Header="Control Panel">
      <TreeViewItem Header="Programs"/>
      <TreeViewItem Header="Security"/>
      <TreeViewItem Header="User Accounts"/>
    </TreeViewItem>
    <TreeViewItem Header="Network">

      ...

    </TreeViewItem>
  </TreeViewItem>
</TreeView>
```

TreeViewItem contains handy IsExpanded and IsSelected properties, as well as four events covering all four states from these properties: Expanded, Collapsed, Selected, and Unselected. TreeViewItem also supports rich keyboard navigation, with the plus (+) and minus (-) keys expanding and collapsing an item, and the arrow keys, Page Up, Page Down, Home, and End keys enabling several ways to move focus from one item to another.

WARNING

Always use `TreeViewItem` to explicitly wrap items in a `TreeView`!

It might be tempting to use simple TextBlocks as leaf nodes, but you can run into a subtle property value inheritance trap that can make the text in such TextBlocks seem to disappear. For example, highlighting a parent node can change its Foreground to white, and if TextBlocks are direct logical children, their text turns white as well. (Although the implicit TreeViewItem is the visual parent for each TextBlock, the logical parent takes precedence for inheritance.) Against the default white background, such text cannot be seen. If you make TreeViewItem the explicit (logical) parent of each TextBlock, however, the undesirable inheritance no longer occurs.

DIGGING DEEPER

TreeView Versus Selector

TreeView's APIs make it look a lot like a `Selector`, but it does not derive from `Selector` only because its hierarchical items can't be naturally indexed with a simple integer. Therefore, the `TreeView` class defines its own `SelectedItem` and `SelectedValue` properties (but not `SelectedIndex`). It also defines a `SelectedItemChanged` event that passes simple `OldValue` and `NewValue` items to event handlers, as `TreeView` only handles single selections.

ToolBar

The `ToolBar` control is typically used to group together many small buttons (or other controls) as an enhancement to a traditional menu system. Figure 4.22 displays a `ToolBar` created from the following XAML:

```
<ToolBar>
  <Button><Image Source="copy.gif"/></Button>
  <Separator/>
  <ToggleButton><Image Source="bold.gif"/></ToggleButton>
  <ToggleButton><Image Source="italic.gif"/></ToggleButton>
  <ToggleButton><Image Source="underline.gif"/></ToggleButton>
  <Separator/>
  <ToggleButton><Image Source="left.gif"/></ToggleButton>
  <ToggleButton><Image Source="right.gif"/></ToggleButton>
  <ToggleButton><Image Source="justify.gif"/></ToggleButton>
  <Separator/>
  <Label>Zoom</Label>
  <ComboBox>
    ...
  </ComboBox>
  <Separator/>
  <Button><Image Source="superscript.gif"/></Button>
  <Button><Image Source="subscript.gif"/></Button>
  ...
</ToolBar>
```

FIGURE 4.22   The WPF `ToolBar`.

Notice that the `Button`s and `ComboBox` used in the `ToolBar` look different than they normally do. In addition, `Separator` now gets rendered as a vertical line instead of the horizontal line seen when placing one inside a `Menu`. `ToolBar` overrides the default styles of its items, so they automatically get the look that most people expect from a `ToolBar` when placed inside one.

ToolBars can be placed anywhere in an element tree, but they are typically placed inside a FrameworkElement called ToolBarTray. ToolBarTray holds a collection of ToolBars (in its content property called ToolBars) and, unless its IsLocked property is set to true, enables users to drag and reposition the ToolBars. (ToolBarTray also defines an IsLocked attached property that can be placed on individual ToolBars.) ToolBarTray has an Orientation property that can be set to Vertical to make all of its ToolBars arrange its items vertically.

If a ToolBar contains more items than it can fit within its bounds, the extra items move to an overflow area. This overflow area is a pop-up that can be accessed by clicking the little arrow at the end of the control, as shown in Figure 4.23. By default, the last item is the first to move to the overflow area, but you can control the overflow behavior of individual items with ToolBar's OverflowMode attached property. With this, you can mark an item to overflow AsNeeded (the default), Always, or Never.

TIP

You can create a Visual Studio-style customizable ToolBar by setting ToolBar.OverflowMode to Never on each item, then adding a Menu with the header "_Add or Remove Buttons" and ToolBar.OverflowMode set to Always (so it always remains in the overflow area). You can then add MenuItems to this Menu that users can check/uncheck to add/remove the corresponding item to/from the ToolBar.

FIGURE 4.23   ToolBar has an overflow area for items that don't fit.

DIGGING DEEPER

Customizing Keyboard Navigation

The following ToolBar exhibits potentially problematic keyboard behavior:

```
<ToolBar>
  <Button>A</Button>
  <Menu>
    <MenuItem Header="B"/>
    <MenuItem Header="C"/>
  </Menu>
  <Button>D</Button>
</ToolBar>
```

Continued

If you give focus to the ToolBar and repeatedly press Tab, the focus gets "stuck" in a cycle from A to B to C to D to A to B, and so on. And if you use the left or right arrow key to focus on either MenuItem, the focus gets stuck oscillating between B and C as you keep pressing the arrow key.

The KeyboardNavigation class in the System.Windows.Input namespace defines a handful of attached properties for customizing this (and other) keyboard behavior. For example, to avoid the cycle when tabbing through a ToolBar, you can set KeyboardNavigation.TabNavigation to Continue (rather than Cycle) on the ToolBar. To avoid the cycle when navigating through a Menu with arrow keys, you can set KeyboardNavigation.DirectionalNavigation to Continue on the Menu.

DIGGING DEEPER

ToolBar's Unused Header Property

ToolBar is actually a headered items control (like MenuItem and TreeViewItem). Its Header property is never displayed, but it can be useful for implementing extra features for ToolBarTray. For example, you could add a context menu that lists all the ToolBars (using their Header), enabling users to add or remove them. Or, you could implement "tear off" ToolBars (like in Visual Studio) and show the Header on the floating ToolBar.

StatusBar

StatusBar behaves just like Menu; it just stacks its items horizontally, as shown in Figure 4.24. But it's typically used along the bottom of a Window to display status information.

The StatusBar in Figure 4.24 can be created with the following XAML:

FIGURE 4.24   The WPF StatusBar.

```
<StatusBar>
  <Label>27 Items</Label>
  <Separator/>
  <Label>Zoom</Label>
  <ComboBox>

    ...

  </ComboBox>
  <Separator/>
  <Button><Image Source="justify.gif"/></Button>
</StatusBar>
```

By default, StatusBar gives Separator a control template that renders it as a vertical line, just like when it is within a ToolBar. Items in a StatusBar (other than Separator) are implicitly wrapped in a StatusBarItem, but you can also do this wrapping explicitly. This enables you to customize their position with layout-related attached properties discussed in Chapter 6.

FAQ

How can I get items in a StatusBar to grow proportionally?

It's common to want StatusBar panes that remain proportionately sized. For example, perhaps you want a left pane that occupies 25% of the StatusBar's width and a right pane that occupies 75% of the width. This can be done by overriding StatusBar's ItemsPanel with a Grid and configuring the Grid's columns appropriately. Chapter 6 shows how to do this.

Range Controls

Range controls do not render arbitrary content like content controls or items controls. They simply store and display a numeric value that falls within a specified range.

The core functionality of range controls come from an abstract class called RangeBase. This class defines properties of type double that store the current value and the endpoints of the range: Value, Minimum, and Maximum. It also defines a simple ValueChanged event.

This section examines the two major built-in range controls—ProgressBar and Slider. WPF also has a primitive ScrollBar control that derives from RangeBase, but you're unlikely to want to use it directly. Instead, you would use a ScrollViewer object, which is described in Chapter 6.

ProgressBar

In an ideal world, we would never need to use a ProgressBar in our software. But when faced with long-running operations, showing users a ProgressBar helps them realize that progress is indeed being made. Therefore, using a ProgressBar in the right places can dramatically improve usability. (Of course, not as much as making the slow operation fast enough in the first place!) Figure 4.25 displays the default look for WPF's ProgressBar control.

ProgressBar has a default Minimum of 0 and a default Maximum of 100. It only adds two public properties to what RangeBase already provides:

FIGURE 4.25   The WPF ProgressBar.

▶ **IsIndeterminate**—When set to true, ProgressBar shows a generic animation (so the values of Minimum, Maximum, and Value don't matter). This is a great feature for when you have no clue how long something will take, or are too lazy to do the work required for showing true progress!

▶ **Orientation**—Horizontal by default, but can be set to Vertical to make progress go from bottom-to-top rather than left-to-right. I haven't seen applications use "thermometer-style" vertical progress bars other than the old-fashioned full-screen installation applications, but this nevertheless makes it easy to achieve such an effect!

FAQ

? How can I give `ProgressBar` paused or stopped/error states, as seen in Windows Vista?

Starting with Windows Vista, the Win32 progress bar can show a paused (yellow) state and a stopped/error (red) state. Unfortunately, the WPF `ProgressBar` does not have built-in support for this. If you want to achieve a similar effect, you need to create new templates for these states and apply them to the control programmatically using techniques described in Chapter 10.

Slider

`Slider` is a bit more complicated than `ProgressBar` because it enables users to change the current value by moving its *thumb* through any number of optional *ticks*. `Slider` is shown in Figure 4.26.

`Slider` also has a default `Minimum` of `0`, but a default `Maximum` of `10`. It also defines an `Orientation` property (and is `Horizontal` by default), but it contains

FIGURE 4.26   The WPF `Slider`.

several properties for adjusting the placement and frequency of ticks, the placement and precision of `ToolTips` that can show the current value as the thumb is moved, and whether the thumb snaps to tick values or moves smoothly to any arbitrary value. For keyboard navigation purposes, `Slider` also contains `Delay` and `Interval` properties that work just like `RepeatButton`'s properties of the same name.

Ticks are enabled by setting `TickPlacement` to `TopLeft`, `BottomRight`, or `Both`. The values for `TickPlacement` have odd names, but they cover both orientations of the `Slider`. When `TickPlacement` is set to `BottomRight`, the ticks are on the bottom when the `Slider` is horizontal and on the right when the `Slider` is vertical. Similarly, when `TickPlacement` is set to `TopLeft`, the ticks are on the top when the `Slider` is horizontal and on the left when the `Slider` is vertical. When `TickPlacement` is set to `None` (the default value), the thumb is given a simpler look, shown in Figure 4.27.

One interesting feature of `Slider` is its support for displaying a smaller range within the current range, as shown in Figure 4.28. If `IsSelectionRangeEnabled` is set to `true`, `SelectionStart` and `SelectionEnd` can be set to the desired values of this "subrange." There's nothing built into the control that enables a user to set the subrange via keyboard, mouse, or stylus, nor does it

FIGURE 4.27   A `Slider` without any ticks.

FIGURE 4.28   `Slider` supports a selection range, which can be a subset of the main range.

enforce that the thumb stays within the subrange. But with this feature, you could make `Slider` act like the one in Windows Media Player, where a "background bar" indicates how much of the current media has been downloaded.

Text and Ink Controls

WPF contains a handful of controls for displaying and editing text, whether typed with a keyboard or hand-written with a stylus:

► TextBox

► RichTextBox

► PasswordBox

► InkCanvas

TextBox

The TextBox control, pictured in Figure 4.29, enables users to type one or more lines of text into it. Unlike most other controls in WPF, the content is not stored as a generic System.Object. Instead, TextBox stores it in a string property called Text.

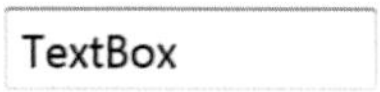

Although it appears like a simple control on the surface, TextBox has built-in support for a variety of features: bindings for Cut, Copy, Paste, Undo, and Redo commands (as seen in the preceding chapter), and even spell checking!

TextBox

FIGURE 4.29   The WPF TextBox.

TextBox contains several methods and properties for grabbing chunks of text (by selection, by line number, and so on) as well as methods for converting between a character index, line index, and physical point within the control. It also defines TextChanged and SelectionChanged events.

Unless the size of the TextBox is constrained by its surroundings (or given an explicit size), it grows as the text inside of it grows. But when the TextBox's width is constrained, you can make the text wrap to form additional lines by setting its TextWrapping property to Wrap or WrapWithOverflow. Wrap never allows a line to go beyond the control's bounds, forcing wrapping even if it's in the middle of a word. WrapWithOverflow only breaks a line if there's an opportunity, so long words could get cut off.

FAQ

 How can I make TextBox support multiple lines of text?

Setting AcceptsReturn to true allows users to press the Enter key to create a new line of text. Note that TextBox *always* supports multiple lines of text programmatically. If its Text is set to a string containing NewLine characters, it displays the multiple lines regardless of the value of AcceptsReturn. Also, the multiline support is completely independent from text wrapping. Text wrapping only applies to individual lines of text that are wider than the TextBox.

> **DIGGING DEEPER**
>
> **Spell Checking**
>
> To enable spell checking in a TextBox (or RichTextBox), set the attached SpellCheck.IsEnabled property to true. The result is an experience similar to Microsoft Word, in which misspelled words get underlined in red and you can right-click to view and apply suggestions. The dictionary used by WPF matches the one used by Microsoft Office, and is available for multiple languages (along with the corresponding language pack). WPF does not support custom dictionaries, however, in version 3.0.

RichTextBox

RichTextBox is a more advanced TextBox that can contain formatted text (and arbitrary objects embedded among the text). Figure 4.30 displays a RichTextBox with simple formatted text.

RichTextBox and TextBox share the same base class (TextBoxBase), so many of the features described with TextBox apply to RichTextBox as well.

FIGURE 4.30   The WPF RichTextBox.

RichTextBox has more sophisticated versions of various TextBox properties. Whereas TextBox exposes simple integer properties like CaretIndex, SelectionStart, and SelectionEnd, RichTextBox exposes a CaretPosition property of type TextPointer and a Selection property of type TextSelection. In addition, RichTextBox's content is stored in a Document property of type FlowDocument rather than the simple string Text property. FlowDocuments are discussed in Chapter 14, "Audio, Video, Speech, and Documents."

PasswordBox

PasswordBox is a simpler TextBox designed for the entry of a password. Rather than displaying the text typed in, it displays little circles, as shown in Figure 4.31.

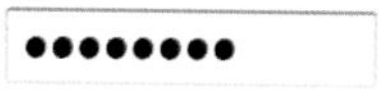

PasswordBox does not derive from TextBoxBase like the two previous controls, so it doesn't support Cut, Copy, Undo, and Redo commands (although it

FIGURE 4.31   The WPF PasswordBox.

does support Paste) and it doesn't support spell checking. This is, of course, quite sensible for a control meant to store passwords! If you don't like the circle character used to represent each letter of the password, you can choose a new one via the PasswordChar property. (The default character is an asterisk, special-cased to look like a circle.)

PasswordBox's text is stored in a string property called Password. Internally, the password is stored in a System.Security.SecureString object for a little bit of extra protection. The contents of a SecureString are encrypted and aggressively cleared, unlike a plain System.String whose unencrypted contents can remain in the garbage-collected heap for an indefinite amount of time.

Rather than having TextChanged and SelectionChanged events, PasswordBox only defines
a PasswordChanged event. In addition, this event uses the plain RoutedEventHandler delegate, so no information about the old and new password is sent with the event. If you
must know the current password, you can simply check the Password property within
such an event handler.

InkCanvas

The amazing InkCanvas is a versatile element whose primary purpose is to capture handwriting (via a mouse or stylus), as pictured in Figure 4.32. InkCanvas is technically not a
control, as it derives directly from FrameworkElement, but it acts very much like a control
(except for the fact that you can't restyle it with a new template).

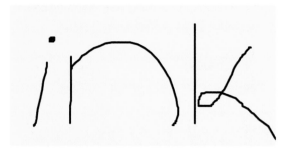

FIGURE 4.32   The WPF InkCanvas.

In its default mode, InkCanvas enables simple writing or drawing on its surface. When
using a stylus, its tip automatically writes and its back end automatically erases. Each
stroke is captured as a System.Windows.Ink.Stroke object and stored in InkCanvas's
Strokes collection. But InkCanvas also supports holding any number of arbitrary
UIElements in its Children collection (a content property). This makes it easy to annotate
just about anything with ink, as shown in Figure 4.33.

This figure was created by drawing on top of the following Window:

```
<Window xmlns="http://schemas.microsoft.com/winfx/2006/xaml/presentation"
  SizeToContent="WidthAndHeight">
  <Grid>
    <InkCanvas>
      <Image Source="http://pinvoke.net/blog/images/anathan.png"/>
    </InkCanvas>
  </Grid>
</Window>
```

(The SizeToContent setting is pretty interesting in this example, because if you draw out
of bounds, the Window automatically resizes to fit your ink strokes if you haven't resized it
manually!)

With InkCanvas's DefaultDrawingAttributes property, you can change the appearance of future strokes (width, color, and so on). Stroke has its own DrawingAttributes property, so appearance can be modified on a stroke-by-stroke basis.

FIGURE 4.33   A creative ink annotation on top of an image.

InkCanvas supports several modes, and they can be applied independently to the stylus tip (or mouse) via an EditingMode property and the stylus's back end via an EditingModeInverted property. A read-only ActiveEditingMode property tells you which of the two modes is currently being used. All three of these properties are of type InkCanvasEditingMode, which has the following values:

▶ **Ink** (default for EditingMode)—Draws strokes with the mouse or stylus.

▶ **InkAndGesture**—Like Ink, but also recognizes gestures made by the user. A list of gestures (such as Up, Down, Circle, ScratchOut, or Tap) can be found in the System.Windows.Ink.ApplicationGesture enumeration.

▶ **GestureOnly**—Only recognizes gestures; does not draw any strokes from user input.

▶ **EraseByStroke** (default for EditingModeInverted)—Erases an entire stroke when it is touched.

▶ **EraseByPoint**—Erases only the part of a stroke that is directly touched (like a traditional pencil eraser).

▶ **Select**—Selects strokes *or any UIElements* when touched, such that they can be deleted, moved, or resized within the bounds of the InkCanvas.

▶ **None**—Does nothing in response to mouse or stylus input.

Using the Select mode with normal elements that have nothing to do with ink is pretty interesting, as it automatically gives you a poor-man's run-time design surface for arranging controls. InkCanvas also defines 15 events, covering everything from changing the editing mode, changing/moving/resizing selections, collecting or erasing strokes, or performing gestures.

Of course, enabling ink in an application is about more than drawing mustaches on people's faces! Often, you want to apply handwriting recognition to a collection of strokes so you can interpret it as if it were typed text. WPF has a built-in gesture recognition, but no handwriting recognition engine.

Conclusion

You've now seen the major built-in controls that can be used for creating traditional (and perhaps some not-so-traditional) user interfaces. Two sidebars have also highlighted WPF's built-in support for UI automation, making it easy to programmatically control a user interface without resorting to lower-level techniques of controlling the mouse, keyboard, or other input devices. Although you can radically change the *look* of these controls using techniques that are discussed in Chapter 10, the core *behavior* described in this chapter remains the same.

This chapter focused on over 25 controls, but there are still many more covered in later chapters! For example, several special-purpose controls are covered in Chapter 14. In addition, a variety of panels are covered in Chapter 6.

CHAPTER 5

Sizing, Positioning, and Transforming Elements

When building a WPF application, one of the first things you must do is arrange a bunch of controls on the application's surface. This sizing and positioning of controls (and other elements) is called *layout*, and WPF contains a lot of infrastructure to provide a feature-rich layout system.

Layout in WPF boils down to interactions between parent elements and their child elements. Parents and their children work together to determine their final sizes and positions. Although parents ultimately tell their children where to render and how much space they get, they are more like collaborators than dictators; parents also *ask* their children how much space they would like before making their final decision.

These parent elements that support the arrangement of multiple children are known as *panels*, and derive from the abstract `System.Windows.Controls.Panel` class. All the elements involved in the layout process (both parents and children) derive from `System.Windows.UIElement`.

Because layout in WPF is such a big and important topic, this book dedicates three chapters to it:

▶ Chapter 5, "Sizing, Positioning, and Transforming Elements"

▶ Chapter 6, "Layout with Panels"

▶ Chapter 17, "Layout with Custom Panels"

This chapter focuses on the children, examining the common ways that you can control layout on a child-by-child basis. Several properties control these aspects, most of which are summarized in Figure 5.1 for an arbitrary element inside an arbitrary panel. Size-related properties are shown in blue, and position-related properties are shown in red. In addition, elements can have transforms applied to them (shown in green) that can affect both size and position.

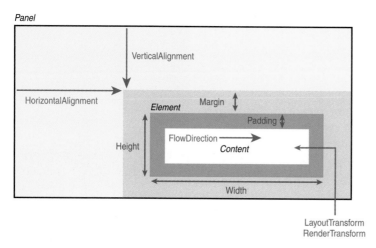

FIGURE 5.1   The main child layout properties examined in this chapter.

The next chapter continues the layout story by examining the variety of parent panels built in to WPF, each of which arranges their children in unique ways. Creating custom panels is an advanced topic reserved for the final part of the book.

Controlling Size

Every time layout occurs (such as when a window is resized), child elements tell their parent panel their desired size. WPF elements tend to *size to their content*, meaning that they try to be large enough to fit their content and no larger. (Even `Window` does this, but only when you explicitly set its `SizeToContent` property as done in Chapters 3 and 4.) This size can be influenced on individual instances of children via several straightforward properties.

Height and Width

All `FrameworkElements` have simple `Height` and `Width` properties (of type `double`), but they also have `MinHeight`, `MaxHeight`, `MinWidth`, and `MaxWidth` properties that can be used to specify a range of acceptable values. Any or all of these can be easily set on elements in procedural code or in XAML.

An element naturally stays as small as possible, so if you use `MinHeight` or `MinWidth`, it is rendered at that height/width unless its content forces it to grow. In addition, that growth can be limited by using `MaxHeight` and `MaxWidth` (as long as these values are larger than their Min counterparts). When using an explicit Height and Width at the same time as their Min and Max counterparts, Height and Width take precedence as long as they are in the range from Min to Max. The default value of MinHeight and MinWidth is 0, and the default value of MaxHeight and MaxWidth is Double.PositiveInfinity (which can be set in XAML as simply "Infinity").

WARNING

Avoid setting explicit sizes!

Giving controls explicit sizes, especially ContentControls such as Button and Label, opens up the risk of cutting off text when users change system font settings or if the text gets translated into other languages. Therefore, you should avoid setting explicit sizes unless absolutely necessary. Thankfully, setting explicit sizes is rarely necessary thanks to the panels described in the next chapter.

DIGGING DEEPER

The Special "Auto" Length

FrameworkElement's Height and Width have a default value of Double.NaN (*Not a Number*), meaning that the element will only be as large as its content needs it to be. This setting can also be explicitly specified in XAML using "NaN" (which is case sensitive) or the preferred "Auto" (which is not case sensitive), thanks to the LengthConverter type converter associated with these properties. To check if one of these properties is autosized, you can use the static Double.IsNaN method.

To complicate matters, FrameworkElement also contains a few more size-related properties:

▶ DesiredSize (inherited from UIElement)

▶ RenderSize (inherited from UIElement)

▶ ActualHeight and ActualWidth

Unlike the other six properties that are *input* to the layout process, however, these are read-only properties representing *output* from the layout process. An element's DesiredSize is calculated during layout based on other property values (such as the aforementioned Width, Height, MinXXX, and MaxXXX properties) and the amount of space its parent is currently giving it. It is used internally by panels.

RenderSize represents the final size of an element after layout is complete, and ActualHeight and ActualWidth are exactly the same as RenderSize.Height and RenderSize.Width, respectively. That's right—whether an element specified an explicit size, a range of acceptable sizes, or didn't specify anything at all, the behavior of the parent can alter an element's final size on the screen. These three properties are, therefore, useful for advanced scenarios in which you need to programmatically act upon an element's size. The values of all the other size-related properties, on the other hand, aren't very interesting to base logic upon. For example, when not set explicitly, the value of Height and Width are Double.NaN regardless of the element's true size.

All these properties are put into context in Chapter 17.

WARNING

Be careful when writing code that uses ActualHeight and ActualWidth (or RenderSize)!

Every time the layout process occurs, it updates the values of each element's RenderSize (and, therefore, ActualHeight and ActualWidth as well). However, layout occurs asynchronously, so you can't rely on the values of these properties at all times. It's only safe to access them within an event handler for the LayoutUpdated event defined on UIElement.

Alternatively, UIElement defines an UpdateLayout method to force any pending layout updates to finish synchronously, but you should avoid using this method. Besides the fact that frequent calls to UpdateLayout can harm performance because of the excess layout processing, there's no guarantee that the elements you're using properly handle the potential reentrancy in their layout-related methods.

Margin and Padding

Margin and Padding are two very similar properties that also are related to an element's size. All FrameworkElements have a Margin property, and all Controls (plus Border) have a Padding property. Their only difference is that Margin controls how much extra space gets placed around the *outside* edges of the element, whereas Padding controls how much extra space gets placed around the *inside* edges of the element.

Both Margin and Padding are of type System.Windows.Thickness, an interesting class that can represent 1, 2, or 4 double values. The meaning of these values is demonstrated in Listing 5.1, which applies various Paddings and Margins to Label controls. The second set of Labels is wrapped in Borders because the margin settings would not be noticeable otherwise. Figure 5.2 shows the rendered result for each Label if each one is individually placed in a Canvas (a panel covered in the next chapter).

LISTING 5.1   Applying Padding and Margin Values with 1, 2, or 4 Digits

```
<!-- PADDING: -->

<!-- 1 value: The same padding on all four sides: -->
<Label Padding="0" Background="Orange">0</Label>
<Label Padding="10" Background="Orange">10</Label>

<!-- 2 values: Left & Right get the 1st value,
              Top & Bottom get the 2nd value: -->
<Label Padding="20,5" Background="Orange">20,5</Label>
```

```xml
<!-- 4 values: Left,Top,Right,Bottom: -->
<Label Padding="0,10,20,30" Background="Orange">0,10,20,30</Label>


<!-- MARGIN: -->

<Border BorderBrush="Black" BorderThickness="1">
  <!-- No margin: -->
  <Label Background="Aqua">0</Label>
</Border>

<Border BorderBrush="Black" BorderThickness="1">
  <!-- 1 value: The same margin on all four sides: -->
  <Label Margin="10" Background="Aqua">10</Label>
</Border>

<Border BorderBrush="Black" BorderThickness="1">
  <!-- 2 values: Left & Right get the 1st value,
                Top & Bottom get the 2nd value: -->
  <Label Margin="20,5" Background="Aqua">20,5</Label>
</Border>

<Border BorderBrush="Black" BorderThickness="1">
  <!-- 4 values: Left,Top,Right,Bottom: -->
  <Label Margin="0,10,20,30" Background="Aqua">0,10,20,30</Label>
</Border>
```

Label has a default Padding of 5, but it can be overridden to any valid value. That is why Listing 5.1 explicitly sets the first Label's Padding to 0. Without the explicit setting, it would look like the fifth Label (the one demonstrating the implicit Margin of 0) and the visual comparison to the other Padding values would be confusing.

Four different Paddings:

Four different Margins:

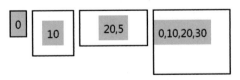

FIGURE 5.2   The effects of Padding and Margin.

DIGGING DEEPER

The Syntax for Thickness

The comma-delimited syntax supported by Margin and Padding are enabled by (what else?) a type converter. System.Windows.ThicknessConverter constructs a Thickness object based on the input string. Thickness has two constructors, one that accepts a single double, and one that expects four. Therefore, it can be used in C# as follows:

```
myLabel.Margin = new Thickness(10);          // Same as Margin="10" in XAML
myLabel.Margin = new Thickness(20,5,20,5);   // Same as Margin="20,5" in XAML
myLabel.Margin = new Thickness(0,10,20,30);  // Same as Margin="0,10,20,30" in XAML
```

Note that the handy two-number syntax is a shortcut only available through the type converter!

FAQ

 What unit of measurement is used by WPF?

All absolute measurements, such as the numbers used in this section's size-related properties, are specified in *device-independent pixels*. These "logical pixels" are meant to represent 1/96th of an inch, regardless of the screen's DPI setting. Note that device-independent pixels are always specified as double values, so they can be fractional.

The exact measurement of 1/96th of an inch isn't important, although it was chosen because on a typical 96 DPI display, one device-independent pixel is identical to one physical pixel. Of course, the notion of a true "inch" depends on the physical display device. If an application draws a one-inch line on my laptop screen, that line will certainly be longer than one inch if I hook up my laptop to a projector!

What *is* important is that all such measurements are DPI independent. But this functionality alone doesn't prevent items from shrinking when you increase the screen resolution. To get this resolution independence, you need the automatic scaling functionality discussed in the next chapter.

Visibility

Visibility (defined on UIElement) might sound like a strange property to talk about in the context of layout, but it is indeed relevant. An element's Visibility property actually isn't Boolean, but rather a three-state System.Windows.Visibility enumeration. Its values and meanings are as follows:

▶ **Visible**—The element gets rendered and participates in layout.

▶ **Collapsed**—The element is invisible and does not participate in layout.

▶ **Hidden**—The element is invisible *yet still participates in layout.*

A `Collapsed` element effectively has a size of zero, whereas a `Hidden` element retains its original size. (Its `ActualHeight` and `ActualWidth` values don't change, for example.) The difference between `Collapsed` and `Hidden` is demonstrated in Figure 5.3, which compares the following `StackPanel` with a `Collapsed Button`:

```
<StackPanel Height="100" Background="Aqua">
  <Button Visibility="Collapsed">Collapsed Button</Button>
  <Button>Below a Collapsed Button</Button>
</StackPanel>
```

to the following `StackPanel` with a `Hidden Button`:

```
<StackPanel Height="100" Background="Aqua">
  <Button Visibility="Hidden">Hidden Button</Button>
  <Button>Below a Hidden Button</Button>
</StackPanel>
```

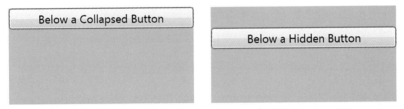

FIGURE 5.3   A `Hidden Button` still occupies space, unlike a `Collapsed Button`.

Controlling Position

This section doesn't discuss positioning elements with (X,Y) coordinates, as you might expect. Parent panels define their own unique mechanisms for enabling children to position themselves (via attached properties or simply the order in which children are added to the parent). A few mechanisms are common to all `FrameworkElement` children, however, and that's what this section examines. These mechanisms are related to alignment and a concept called *flow direction*.

Alignment

The `HorizontalAlignment` and `VerticalAlignment` properties enable an element to control what it does with any extra space given to it by its parent panel. Each property has a corresponding enumeration with the same name in the `System.Windows` namespace, giving the following options:

   `HorizontalAlignment`: `Left`, `Center`, `Right`, and `Stretch`

   `VerticalAlignment`:   `Top`, `Center`, `Bottom`, and `Stretch`

`Stretch` is the default value for both properties, although various controls override the setting in their theme styles. The effects of `HorizontalAlignment` can easily be seen by placing a few Buttons in a StackPanel and marking them with each value from the enumeration:

```
<StackPanel>
  <Button HorizontalAlignment="Left" Background="Red">Left</Button>
  <Button HorizontalAlignment="Center" Background="Orange">Center</Button>
  <Button HorizontalAlignment="Right" Background="Yellow">Right</Button>
  <Button HorizontalAlignment="Stretch" Background="Lime">Stretch</Button>
</StackPanel>
```

The rendered result appears in Figure 5.4.

These two properties are only useful when a parent panel gives the child element more space than it needs. For example, adding VerticalAlignment values to elements in the StackPanel used in Figure 5.4 would make no difference, as each element is already given the exact amount of height it needs (no more, no less).

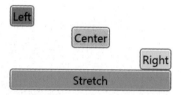

FIGURE 5.4   The effects of Horizontal-Alignment on Buttons in a StackPanel.

DIGGING DEEPER

Interaction Between Stretch Alignment and Explicit Element Size

When an element uses Stretch alignment (horizontally or vertically), an explicit Height or Width setting still takes precedence. MaxHeight and MaxWidth also take precedence, but only when their values are smaller than the natural stretched size. Similarly, MinHeight and MinWidth take precedence only when their values are *larger* than the natural stretched size. When Stretch is used in a context that constrains the element's size, it acts like an alignment of Center.

Content Alignment

In addition to HorizontalAlignment and VerticalAlignment properties, the Control class also has HorizontalContentAlignment and VerticalContentAlignment properties. These properties determine how a control's content fills the space *within* the control. (Therefore, the relationship between alignment and content alignment is somewhat like the relationship between Margin and Padding.)

The content alignment properties are of the same enumeration types as the corresponding alignment properties, so they provide the same options. However, the default value for HorizontalContentAlignment is Left and the default value for VerticalContentAlignment is Top. This wasn't the case for the previous Buttons, however, because their theme style overrides these settings. (Recall the order of precedence for dependency property value providers in Chapter 3, "Important New Concepts in WPF." Default values have the lowest priority, and are trumped by styles.)

Figure 5.5 demonstrates the effects of HorizontalContentAlignment, simply by taking the previous XAML snippet and changing the property name as follows:

```
<StackPanel>
  <Button HorizontalContentAlignment="Left" Background="Red">Left</Button>
  <Button HorizontalContentAlignment="Center" Background="Orange">Center</Button>
  <Button HorizontalContentAlignment="Right" Background="Yellow">Right</Button>
  <Button HorizontalContentAlignment="Stretch" Background="Lime">Stretch</Button>
</StackPanel>
```

In Figure 5.5, the Button with HorizontalContentAlignment= "Stretch" might not appear as you expected. Its inner TextBlock is indeed stretched, but TextBlock is not a true Control (rather than just a FrameworkElement) and, therefore, doesn't have the same notion for stretching its inner text.

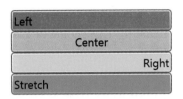

FIGURE 5.5   The effects of Horizontal-ContentAlignment on Buttons in a StackPanel.

FlowDirection

FlowDirection is a property on FrameworkElement (and several other classes) that can reverse the way an element's inner content flows. It applies to some panels and their arrangement of children, but it also applies to the way content is aligned inside child controls. The property is of type System.Windows.FlowDirection, with two values: LeftToRight (FrameworkElement's default) and RightToLeft.

The idea of FlowDirection is that it should be set to RightToLeft when the current culture corresponds to a language that is read from right-to-left. This reverses the meaning of left and right for settings such as content alignment. The following XAML demonstrates this, with Buttons that force their content alignment to Top and Left, but then apply each of the two FlowDirection values:

```
<StackPanel>
  <Button FlowDirection="LeftToRight"
          HorizontalContentAlignment="Left" VerticalContentAlignment="Top"
          Height="40" Background="Red">LeftToRight</Button>
  <Button FlowDirection="RightToLeft"
          HorizontalContentAlignment="Left" VerticalContentAlignment="Top"
          Height="40" Background="Orange">RightToLeft</Button>
</StackPanel>
```

The result is shown in Figure 5.6.

Notice that FlowDirection does not affect the flow of letters within these Buttons. English letters always flow left to right and Arabic letters always flow right to left, for example. But FlowDirection reverses the notion of left and right for other pieces of UI, which typically need to match the flow direction of letters.

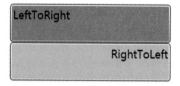

FIGURE 5.6   The effects of FlowDirection on Buttons with Top and Left content alignment.

FlowDirection must be explicitly set to match the current culture (and can be done on a single, top-level element). This should be part of the localization process described in Chapter 8, "Resources."

Applying Transforms

WPF contains a handful of built-in 2D transform classes (deriving from System.Windows.Media.Transform) that enable you to change the size and position of elements independently from the previously discussed properties. Some also enable you to alter elements in more exotic ways, such as rotating or skewing them.

All FrameworkElements have two properties of type Transform that can be used to apply such transforms:

▶ LayoutTransform, which is applied *before* the element is laid out

▶ RenderTransform (inherited from UIElement), which is applied *after* the layout process has finished (immediately before the element is rendered)

Figure 5.7 demonstrates the difference between applying a transform called Rotate-Transform as a LayoutTransform versus a RenderTransform. In both cases, the transform is applied to the second of three consecutive Buttons in a StackPanel. When applied as a LayoutTransform, the third Button is pushed out of the way. But when applied as a RenderTransform, the third Button is placed as if the second Button weren't rotated.

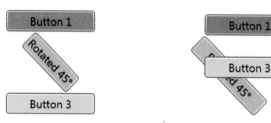

Rotation as a LayoutTransform   Rotation as a RenderTransform

FIGURE 5.7   The difference between LayoutTransform and RenderTransform on the middle of three Buttons in a StackPanel.

UIElements also have a handy `RenderTransformOrigin` property that represents the starting point of the transform (the point that remains stationary). For the `RotateTransform` used in Figure 5.7, the origin is the `Button`'s top-left corner, which the rest of the `Button` pivots around. `LayoutTransforms`, on the other hand, don't have the notion of an origin because the positioning of the transformed element is completely dictated by the parent panel's layout rules.

`RenderTransformOrigin` can be set to a `System.Windows.Point`, with (0,0) being the default value. This represents the top-left corner, as in Figure 5.7. An origin of (0,1) represents the bottom-left corner, (1,0) is the top-right corner, and (1,1) is the bottom-right corner. You can use numbers greater than 1 to set the origin to a point outside the bounds of an element, and you can use fractional values. Therefore, (0.5,0.5) represents the middle of the object. Figure 5.8 demonstrates the five most common origins used with the `RenderTransform` from Figure 5.7.

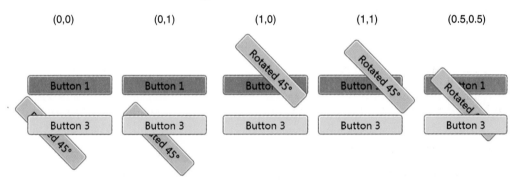

FIGURE 5.8   Five common `RenderTransformOrigins` used on the rotated `Button` from Figure 5.7.

Thanks to `System.Windows.PointConverter`, the value for `RenderTransformOrigin` can be specified in XAML with two comma-delimited numbers (and no parentheses). For example, the `Button` rotated around its center at the far right of Figure 5.8 can be created as follows:

```
<Button RenderTransformOrigin="0.5,0.5" Background="Orange">
<Button.RenderTransform>
  <RotateTransform Angle="45"/>
</Button.RenderTransform>
  Rotated 45°
</Button>
```

At this point, you might be wondering why you would ever want to have a rotated `Button` in your application! Indeed, such transforms look silly on standard controls with their default style. They often make more sense in a heavily themed application, but even with default-styled controls, transforms can add a nice touch when used within animations.

This section looks at the five built-in 2D transforms, all in the `System.Windows.Media` namespace:

- ▶ RotateTransform

- ▶ ScaleTransform

- ▶ SkewTransform

- ▶ TranslateTransform

- ▶ MatrixTransform

RotateTransform

RotateTransform, demonstrated in the preceding section, rotates an element according to the values of three double properties:

- ▶ **Angle**—Angle of rotation, specified in degrees (default value = 0)

- ▶ **CenterX**—Horizontal center of rotation (default value = 0)

- ▶ **CenterY**—Vertical center of rotation (default value = 0)

The default (CenterX,CenterY) point of (0,0) represents the top-left corner. CenterX and CenterY are only useful when RotateTransform is applied as a RenderTransform because when LayoutTransforms are applied the position is still dictated by the parent panel.

FAQ

 Why do transforms such as RotateTransform have CenterX and CenterY properties when all UIElements already have a RenderTransformOrigin property?

The CenterX and CenterY properties do appear to be redundant with RenderTransformOrigin at first. Both mechanisms control the origin of the transform, and both mechanisms only work when the transform is applied as a RenderTransform.

However, CenterX and CenterY enable absolute positioning of the origin rather than the relative positioning of RenderTransformOrigin. Their values are specified as device-independent pixels, so the top-right corner of an element with a Width of 20 would be specified with CenterX set to 20 and CenterY set to 0 rather than the point (1,0). Also, when multiple RenderTransforms are applied to the same element (described later in the chapter), RenderTransformOrigin applies to all of them, whereas CenterX and CenterY on individual transforms enables more fine-grained control. Finally, the individual double values of CenterX and CenterY are easier to use with data binding than the Point value of RenderTransformOrigin.

That said, RenderTransformOrigin is generally more useful than CenterX and CenterY. For the common case of transforming an element around its middle, the relative (0.5,0.5) RenderTransformOrigin is easy to specify in XAML, whereas accomplishing the same thing with CenterX and CenterY would require writing some procedural code to calculate the absolute offsets.

Note that you can use RenderTransformOrigin on an element simultaneously with using CenterX and CenterY on its transform. In this case, the two X values and two Y values are combined to calculate the final origin point.

Although the preceding two figures (Figures 5.7 and 5.8) showed rotated Buttons, Figure 5.9 demonstrates what happens when RotateTransform is applied as a RenderTransform *to the inner content* of Buttons, with two different values of RenderTransformOrigin. To achieve this, the simple string inside each Button is replaced with an explicit TextBlock. For example:

```
<Button Background="Orange">
  <TextBlock RenderTransformOrigin="0.5,0.5">
  <TextBlock.RenderTransform>
    <RotateTransform Angle="45"/>
  </TextBlock.RenderTransform>
    45°
  </TextBlock>
</Button>
```

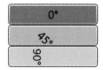

Text rotation around the top-left corner

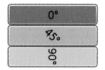

Text rotation around the middle

FIGURE 5.9   Using RotateTransform on the content of Buttons in a StackPanel.

The TextBlocks in the Buttons on the left side of Figure 5.9 might not seem to be rotated around their top-left corners, but that's because the TextBlocks are slightly larger than the text. By giving the TextBlocks an explicit aqua Background, the rotation makes more sense. Figure 5.10 demonstrates this.

RotateTransform has parameterized constructors that accept an angle or both angle and center values, for the convenience of creating it from procedural code.

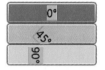

FIGURE 5.10   Inner TextBlocks rotated around their top-left corner, with an explicit background.

ScaleTransform

ScaleTransform enlarges or shrinks an element horizontally, vertically, or in both directions. This transform has four straightforward double properties:

- ▶ **ScaleX**—Multiplier for the element's width (default value = 1)

- ▶ **ScaleY**—Multiplier for the element's height (default value = 1)

- ▶ **CenterX**—Origin for horizontal scaling (default value = 0)

- ▶ **CenterY**—Origin for vertical scaling (default value = 0)

A ScaleX value of 0.5 shrinks an element's rendered width in half, whereas a ScaleX value of 2 doubles the width. CenterX and CenterY work the same way as with RotateTransform.

Listing 5.2 applies ScaleTransform to three Buttons in a StackPanel, demonstrating the ability to stretch them independently in height or in width. The result is shown in Figure 5.11.

LISTING 5.2   Applying ScaleTransform to Buttons in a StackPanel

```
<StackPanel Width="100">
  <Button Background="Red">No Scaling</Button>
  <Button Background="Orange">
  <Button.RenderTransform>
    <ScaleTransform ScaleX="2"/>
  </Button.RenderTransform>
    X</Button>
  <Button Background="Yellow">
  <Button.RenderTransform>
    <ScaleTransform ScaleX="2" ScaleY="2"/>
  </Button.RenderTransform>
    X + Y</Button>
  <Button Background="Lime">
  <Button.RenderTransform>
    <ScaleTransform ScaleY="2"/>
  </Button.RenderTransform>
    Y</Button>
</StackPanel>
```

Figure 5.12 displays the same Buttons from Listing 5.2 (and Figure 5.11), but with explicit CenterX and CenterY values set. The point represented by each pair of these values is displayed in each Button's text. Notice that the lime Button isn't moved to the left like the orange Button is, despite being marked with the same CenterX of 70. That's because CenterX is only relevant when ScaleX is a value other than 1, and CenterY is only relevant when ScaleY is a value other than 1.

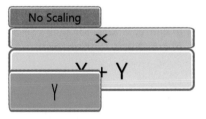

FIGURE 5.11   The scaled Buttons from Listing 5.2.

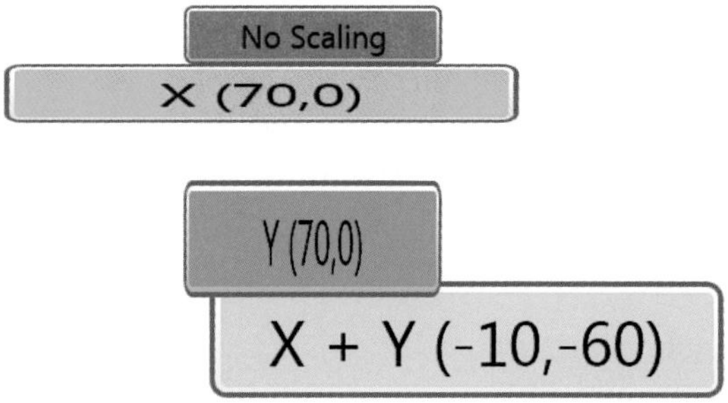

No Scaling

X (70,0)

Y (70,0)

X + Y (-10,-60)

FIGURE 5.12   The Buttons from Listing 5.2, but with explicit scaling centers.

As with other transforms, ScaleTransform has a few parameterized constructors for the convenience of creating it from procedural code.

DIGGING DEEPER

Interaction Between ScaleTransform and Stretch Alignment

When applying ScaleTransform as a LayoutTransform on an element that is already stretching in the dimension of scaling, it only has an effect if the amount of scaling is greater than the amount the natural-sized control is already being stretched.

FAQ

 How do transforms such as ScaleTransform affect FrameworkElement's ActualHeight and ActualWidth properties or UIElement's RenderSize property?

Applying a transform to a FrameworkElement never changes the values of these properties. This is true whether it is applied as a RenderTransform or LayoutTransform. Therefore, because of transforms, these properties can "lie" about the size of an element on the screen. For example, all the Buttons in Figures 5.11 and 5.12 have the same ActualHeight, ActualWidth, and RenderSize.

Such "lies" might surprise you, but it's for the best. First, it's debatable how such values should even be expressed for some transforms. More important, the point of transforms is to alter an element's appearance without the element's knowledge. Giving elements the illusion that they are being rendered normally enables arbitrary controls to be plugged in and transformed without special handling.

FAQ

 How does ScaleTransform affect Margin and Padding?

Padding is scaled along with the rest of the content (because Padding is internal to the element), but Margin does not get scaled. As with ActualHeight and ActualWidth, the numeric Padding property value does not change despite the visual scaling.

SkewTransform

SkewTransform slants an element according to the values of four `double` properties:

- ▶ **AngleX**—Amount of horizontal skew (default value = 0)
- ▶ **AngleY**—Amount of vertical skew (default value = 0)
- ▶ **CenterX**—Origin for horizontal skew (default value = 0)
- ▶ **CenterY**—Origin for vertical skew (default value = 0)

These properties behave much like the properties of the previous transforms. Figure 5.13 demonstrates SkewTransform applied as a RenderTransform on several Buttons, using the default center of the top-left corner.

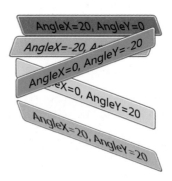

FIGURE 5.13   SkewTransform applied to Buttons in a StackPanel.

TranslateTransform

TranslateTransform simply moves an element according to two `double` properties:

- ▶ **X**—Amount to move horizontally (default value = 0)
- ▶ **Y**—Amount to move vertically (default value = 0)

TranslateTransform has no effect when you apply it as a LayoutTransform, but applying it as a RenderTransform is an easy way to "nudge" elements one way or another. Most likely, you'd do this dynamically based on user actions (and perhaps in an animation). With all the panels described in the next chapter, it's unlikely you'd need to use TranslateTransform to arrange a static user interface.

MatrixTransform

MatrixTransform is a low-level mechanism that can be used to create custom 2D transforms. MatrixTransform has a single Matrix property (of type System.Windows.Media.Matrix) representing a 3x3 affine transformation matrix. In case you're not a linear algebra buff, this basically means that all of the previous transforms (or any combination of them) can also be expressed using MatrixTransform.

The 3x3 matrix has the following values:

$$\begin{bmatrix} M11 & M12 & 0 \\ M21 & M22 & 0 \\ OffsetX & OffsetY & 1 \end{bmatrix}$$

The final column's values are fixed, but the other six values can be set as properties of the `Matrix` type (with the same names as shown) or via a constructor that accepts the six values in row-major order.

DIGGING DEEPER

`MatrixTransform`'s Type Converter

`MatrixTransform` is the only transform that has a type converter to enable its use as a simple string in XAML. (The type converter is called `TransformConverter` and is actually associated with the abstract `Transform` class, but it only supports `MatrixTransform`.) For example, you can translate a `Button` 10 units to the right and 20 units down with the following syntax:

```
<Button RenderTransform="1,0,0,1,10,20" />
```

The comma-delimited list represents the `M11`, `M12`, `M21`, `M22`, `OffsetX`, and `OffsetY` values, respectively. Values of `1,0,0,1,0,0` give you the identity matrix (meaning no transform is done), so making `MatrixTransform` act like `TranslateTransform` is as simple as starting with the identity matrix and then using `OffsetX` and `OffsetY` as `TranslateTransform`'s X and Y values. Scaling can be done by treating the first and fourth values (the 1s in the identity matrix) as `ScaleX` and `ScaleY`, respectively. Rotation and skewing are more complicated as they involve `sin`, `cos`, and angles specified in radians.

But if you're comfortable with the matrix notation, representing transforms with this concise (and less-readable) syntax can be a time-saver when writing XAML by hand.

Combining Transforms

A few different options exist for combining multiple transforms, such as rotating an element while simultaneously scaling it. You can apply both a `LayoutTransform` and a `RenderTransform` simultaneously. Or, you could figure out the correct `MatrixTransform` representation to get the combined effect. Most likely, however, you would take advantage of the `TransformGroup` class.

`TransformGroup` is just another `Transform`-derived class (so it can be used wherever the previous classes are used) whose purpose is to combine child `Transform` objects. From procedural code, you can add transforms to its `Children` collection, or from XAML, you could use it as follows:

```
<Button>
<Button.RenderTransform>
  <TransformGroup>
    <RotateTransform Angle="45"/>
    <ScaleTransform ScaleX="5" ScaleY="1"/>
    <SkewTransform AngleX="30"/>
  </TransformGroup>
</Button.RenderTransform>
  OK
</Button>
```

The result of all three transforms being applied to the Button is shown in Figure 5.14.

FIGURE 5.14   A Button that has been thoroughly tortured by being rotated, scaled, and skewed.

For maximum performance, WPF calculates a combined transform out of a TransformGroup's children and applies it as a single transform (much like if you had used MatrixTransform). Note that you can apply multiple instances of the same transform to a TransformGroup. For example, applying two separate 45° RotateTransforms would result in a 90° rotation.

WARNING

Not all FrameworkElements support transforms!

Elements hosting content that isn't native to WPF do not support transforms, despite inheriting the LayoutTransform and RenderTransform properties. For example, HwndHost, used to host GDI-based content and discussed in Chapter 15, "Interoperability with Win32, Windows Forms, and ActiveX," does not support them. Frame supports them unless it is used to host HTML. In both cases, ScaleTransform can still be applied to scale the size of such elements, but the inner content won't scale.

Figure 5.15 demonstrates this with a StackPanel containing some Buttons and a Frame containing a webpage (constrained to be 100x100). When the entire StackPanel is rotated and scaled, the Frame does its best to scale but doesn't rotate at all. It ends up hiding most of the rotated Buttons.

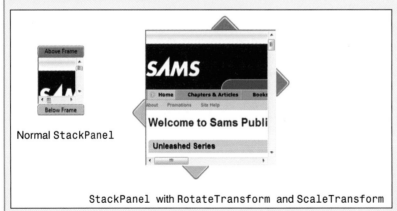

FIGURE 5.15   A Frame with HTML content responds somewhat to ScaleTransform, but no other transforms.

Conclusion

That concludes our tour of the layout properties that child elements can use to influence the way they appear on the screen. In this chapter, you also got some first glimpses into user-visible features unlike anything you'd see in Win32 or Windows Forms: rotated and skewed controls!

But the most important part of layout is the parent panels. This chapter repeatedly used a simple `StackPanel` for simplicity, but the next chapter formally introduces this panel and all the other panels as well.

5

CHAPTER 6

Layout with Panels

Layout is a critical component of an application's usability on a wide range of devices, but without good platform support it can be extremely hard to get right. Arranging the pieces of your user interface simply with static pixel-based coordinates and static pixel-based sizes can work in limited environments, but these types of interfaces start to crumble under the influence of many varying factors: different screen resolutions and dimensions, user settings such as font sizes, or content that changes in unpredictable ways (such as text being translated into different languages). Plus, applications that don't allow users to resize them (and take advantage of the extra space intelligently) frustrate most users.

Figure 6.1 shows two simple examples where bad layout rears its ugly head on my widescreen laptop with 1680x1050 resolution. Applications (or dialogs) that don't allow resizing are invariably too small. Some applications stretch out to fill the space, but their content doesn't scale as you might like it to. And even web pages frequently fail to take advantage of the screen real estate on widescreen displays. Although HTML does have features for flexible layout, it's often hard to use them and still get the exact look that designers insist upon.

WPF contains built-in panels that can make it easy to avoid layout pitfalls like the ones shown in Figure 6.1. This chapter begins by examining the five main built-in panels, all in the `System.Windows.Controls` namespace, in increasing order of complexity (and general usefulness):

- ▶ Canvas
- ▶ StackPanel

- ▶ WrapPanel

- ▶ DockPanel

- ▶ Grid

The Windows Calculator is
small and doesn't resize.

The old Microsoft home page doesn't
take advantage of the extra width.

FIGURE 6.1   Bad layout can be found just about anywhere.

For completeness, this chapter also looks at a few rarely used "primitive panels." Then, after a section on content overflow (which happens when parents and children can't agree on the use of available space), this chapter ends with a large example. This example applies a variety of layout techniques to make a relatively sophisticated user interface found in applications such as Visual Studio that would be hard to construct without the help of WPF's layout features.

Canvas

Canvas is the most basic panel. So basic, in fact, that you probably should never bother using it for arranging typical user interfaces. Canvas only supports the "classic" notion of positioning elements with explicit coordinates, although at least those coordinates are device-independent pixels, unlike older UI systems. Canvas also enables you to specify coordinates relative to *any* corner of it; not just the top-left corner.

You can position elements in a Canvas using its attached properties: Left, Top, Right, and Bottom. By setting a value for Left or Right, you're stating that the closest edge of the element should remain a fixed distance from the left or right edge of the Canvas. And the same goes for setting a value for Top or Bottom. In essence, you choose the corner in which to "dock" each element, and the attached property values serve as margins (to which the element's own Margin values are added). If an element doesn't use any of these attached properties (leaving them with their default value of Double.NaN), it is placed in the top-left corner of the Canvas (the equivalent of setting Left and Top to 0). This is demonstrated in Listing 6.1, with the result shown in Figure 6.2.

LISTING 6.1   Buttons Arranged in a Canvas

```
<Window xmlns="http://schemas.microsoft.com/winfx/2006/xaml/presentation"
        Title="Buttons in a Canvas">
  <Canvas>
    <Button Background="Red">Left=0, Top=0</Button>
    <Button Canvas.Left="18" Canvas.Top="18"
            Background="Orange">Left=18, Top=18</Button>
    <Button Canvas.Right="18" Canvas.Bottom="18"
            Background="Yellow">Right=18, Bottom=18</Button>
    <Button Canvas.Right="0" Canvas.Bottom="0"
            Background="Lime">Right=0, Bottom=0</Button>
    <Button Canvas.Right="0" Canvas.Top="0"
            Background="Aqua">Right=0, Top=0</Button>
    <Button Canvas.Left="0" Canvas.Bottom="0"
            Background="Magenta">Left=0, Bottom=0</Button>
  </Canvas>
</Window>
```

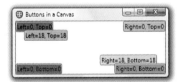

FIGURE 6.2   The Buttons in a Canvas from Listing 6.1.

> **WARNING**
>
> **Elements can't use more than two of the Canvas attached properties!**
>
> If you attempt to set Canvas.Left and Canvas.Right simultaneously, Canvas.Right gets ignored. And if you attempt to set Canvas.Top and Canvas.Bottom simultaneously, Canvas.Bottom gets ignored. Therefore, you can't dock an element to more than one corner of the Canvas at a time.

> ## TIP
>
> The default Z order (defining which elements are "on top of" other elements) is determined by the order in which the children are added to the parent. In XAML, this translates to the order children are listed in the file. Elements added later are placed on top of elements added earlier. So in Figure 6.2, the orange `Button` is on top of the red `Button`, and the green `Button` is on top of the yellow `Button`. This is relevant not just for the built-in panels that enable elements to overlap (like `Canvas`), but whenever a `RenderTransform` causes an element to overlap another (as shown in Figures 5.7, 5.8, 5.11, 5.12, and 5.13 in the preceding chapter).
>
> However, you can customize the Z order of any child element by marking it with the `ZIndex` attached property that is defined on `Panel` (so it is inherited by all panels). `ZIndex` is an integer with a default value of `0` that you can set to any number (positive or negative). Elements with larger `ZIndex` values are rendered on top of smaller `ZIndex` values, so the element with the smallest value is in the back, and the element with the largest value is in the front. In the following example, `ZIndex` causes the red button to be on top of the orange button, despite being an earlier child of the `Canvas`:
>
> ```
> <Canvas>
>   <Button Canvas.ZIndex="1" Background="Red">On Top!</Button>
>   <Button Background="Orange">On Bottom with a Default ZIndex=0</Button>
> </Canvas>
> ```
>
> If multiple children have the same `ZIndex` value, the order is determined by their order in the panel's `Children` collection, as in the default case.
>
> Therefore, programmatically manipulating Z order is as simple as adjusting the `ZIndex` value. To make the preceding red button get rendered behind the orange button, you can set the attached property value to any number less than or equal to zero. The following line of C# does just that (assuming the red button's name is `redButton`):
>
> ```
> Canvas.SetZIndex(redButton, 0);
> ```

Table 6.1 evaluates the way that some of the child layout properties discussed in the preceding chapter apply to elements inside a `Canvas`.

TABLE 6.1   Canvas's Interaction with Child Layout Properties

Properties	Usable Inside a `Canvas`?
`Margin`	Partially. On the two sides used to position the element (`Top` and `Left` by default), the relevant two out of four margin values are added to the attached property values.
`HorizontalAlignment` and `VerticalAlignment`	No. Elements are only given the exact space they need.
`LayoutTransform`	Yes. Differs from `RenderTransform` because when `LayoutTransform` is used, elements always remain the specified distance from the selected corner of the `Canvas`.

Although Canvas is too primitive a panel for creating flexible user interfaces, it is the most lightweight panel. So, you should keep it in mind for maximum performance when you really do need precise control over the placement of elements. For example, Canvas is very handy for precise positioning of primitive shapes in vector-based drawings, discussed in Chapter 11, "2D Graphics."

StackPanel

StackPanel is a popular panel because of its simplicity and usefulness. As its name suggests, it simply stacks its children sequentially. Examples in previous chapters used StackPanel because it doesn't require the use of any attached properties to get a reasonable-looking UI. In fact, StackPanel is one of the few panels that doesn't even define any of its own attached properties!

With no attached properties for arranging children, you just have one way to customize the behavior of StackPanel—setting its Orientation property (of type System.Windows.Controls.Orientation) to Horizontal or Vertical. Vertical is the default Orientation. Figure 6.3 shows simple Buttons, with no properties set other than Background and Content, in two StackPanels with only their Orientation set.

Vertical stacks elements from top to bottom.

Horizontal stacks elements from left to right.

FIGURE 6.3   Buttons in a StackPanel, using both Orientations.

DIGGING DEEPER

StackPanel **and Right-To-Left Environments**

When FlowDirection is set to RightToLeft, stacking occurs right to left for a StackPanel with Horizontal Orientation, rather than the default left-to-right behavior.

Table 6.2 evaluates the way that some of the child layout properties apply to elements inside a StackPanel.

TABLE 6.2   StackPanel's Interaction with Child Layout Properties

Properties	Usable Inside a StackPanel?
Margin	Yes. Margin controls the space between an element and the StackPanel's edges as well as space between elements.
HorizontalAlignment and VerticalAlignment	Partially, because alignment is effectively ignored in the direction of stacking (because children get the exact amount of space they need). For Orientation="Vertical", VerticalAlignment is meaningless. For Orientation="Horizontal", HorizontalAlignment is meaningless.
LayoutTransform	Yes. Differs from RenderTransform because when LayoutTransform is used, the remaining elements in the stack are pushed out further to make room. When combining Stretch layout with RotateTransform or SkewTransform as a LayoutTransform, the stretching only occurs for angles that are multiples of 90°.

The final sentence discussing LayoutTransform in Table 6.2 needs a little more explanation. Figure 6.4 reveals that when an element that normally would be stretched is rotated, the stretching only occurs when edges of the element are parallel or perpendicular to the direction of stretching. This behavior isn't specific to StackPanel, but can be seen whenever an element is stretched in only one direction. This odd-looking behavior only applies to LayoutTransform; it doesn't happen with RenderTransform.

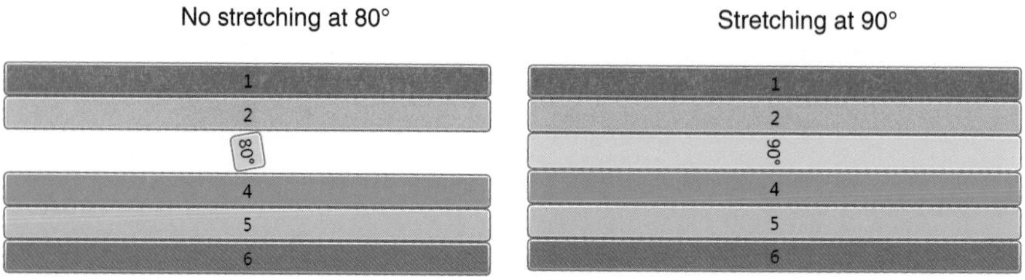

FIGURE 6.4   The yellow Button is rotated 80° then 90° using a LayoutTransform.

WrapPanel

WrapPanel is similar to StackPanel. But in addition to stacking its child elements, it wraps them to additional rows or columns when there's not enough space for a single stack. This is useful for displaying an indeterminate number of items with a more interesting layout than a simple list, much like Windows Explorer does.

Like StackPanel, WrapPanel has no attached properties for controlling element positions. It defines three properties for controlling its behavior:

- **Orientation**—This is just like StackPanel's property, except Horizontal is the default. Horizontal Orientation is like Windows Explorer's Thumbnails view: Elements are stacked left to right, then wrap top to bottom. Vertical Orientation is like Windows Explorer's List view: Elements are stacked top to bottom, then wrap left to right.

- **ItemHeight**—A uniform height for all child elements. The way each child fills that height depends on its own VerticalAlignment, Height, and so forth. Any elements taller than ItemHeight get clipped.

- **ItemWidth**—A uniform width for all child elements. The way each child fills that width depends on its own HorizontalAlignment, Width, and so forth. Any elements wider than ItemWidth get clipped.

By default, ItemHeight and ItemWidth are not set (or rather, set to Double.NaN). In this case, a WrapPanel with Vertical Orientation gives each column the width of its widest element, whereas a WrapPanel with Horizontal Orientation gives each row the height of its tallest element. So no intra-WrapPanel clipping occurs by default.

Figure 6.5 shows four snapshots of a WrapPanel with Horizontal Orientation in action, because it is inside a Window being resized. Figure 6.6 shows the same thing for a WrapPanel with Vertical Orientation. When a WrapPanel has plenty of space and ItemHeight/ItemWidth aren't set, WrapPanel looks just like a StackPanel.

> **TIP**
>
> You can force WrapPanel to arrange elements in a single row or column by setting its Width (for Horizontal Orientation) or Height (for Vertical Orientation) to Double.MaxValue or Double.PositiveInfinity. In XAML, this must be done with the x:Static markup extension because neither of these values is supported by the type converter for System.Double.

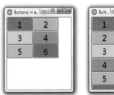

FIGURE 6.5   Buttons arranged in a WrapPanel with its default Horizontal Orientation, as the Window width shrinks.

FIGURE 6.6   Buttons arranged in a WrapPanel with Vertical Orientation, as the Window height shrinks.

DIGGING DEEPER

WrapPanel and Right-to-Left Environments

When FlowDirection is set to RightToLeft, wrapping occurs right to left for a WrapPanel with Vertical Orientation, and stacking occurs right to left for a WrapPanel with Horizontal Orientation.

Table 6.3 evaluates the way that some of the child layout properties apply to elements inside a WrapPanel.

TABLE 6.3   WrapPanel's Interaction with Child Layout Properties

Properties	Usable Inside a WrapPanel?
Margin	Yes. Margins are included when WrapPanel calculates the size of each item for determining default stack widths or heights.
HorizontalAlignment and VerticalAlignment	Partially. Alignment can be used in the opposite direction of stacking, just like with StackPanel. But alignment can also be useful in the direction of stacking when WrapPanel's ItemHeight or ItemWidth gives an element extra space to align within.
LayoutTransform	Yes. Differs from RenderTransform because when LayoutTransform is used, the remaining elements are pushed out further to make room, but only if WrapPanel's ItemHeight or ItemWidth (depending on the Orientation) is not set. When combining Stretch layout with RotateTransform or SkewTransform as a LayoutTransform, the stretching only occurs for angles that are multiples of 90°, as with StackPanel.

WrapPanel is most commonly used as an items panel for an items control. For example, if you want to support user selection of wrapping items (as in Windows Explorer), it makes sense to use a ListBox but replace its default panel with a WrapPanel as follows:

```
<ListBox>
<ListBox.ItemsPanel>
```

```
  <ItemsPanelTemplate>
    <WrapPanel/>
  </ItemsPanelTemplate>
</ListBox.ItemsPanel>

  ...

</ListBox>
```

DockPanel

DockPanel enables easy docking of elements to an entire side of the panel, stretching it to fill the entire width or height. (This is unlike Canvas, which enables you to dock elements to a corner only.) It also enables a single element to fill all the remaining space unused by the docked elements.

DockPanel has a Dock attached property (of type System.Windows.Controls.Dock), so children can control their docking with one of four possible values: Left (the default when Dock isn't applied), Top, Right, and Bottom. Note that there is no Fill value for Dock. Instead, the last child added to a DockPanel fills the remaining space unless DockPanel's LastChildFill property is set to false. With LastChildFill set to true (the default), the last child's Dock setting is ignored. With it set to false, it can be docked in any direction (Left by default).

Figure 6.7 displays the following five Buttons in a DockPanel (with LastChildFill left as true), each marked with their Dock setting:

```
<DockPanel>
  <Button DockPanel.Dock="Top" Background="Red">1 (Top)</Button>
  <Button DockPanel.Dock="Left" Background="Orange">2 (Left)</Button>
  <Button DockPanel.Dock="Right" Background="Yellow">3 (Right)</Button>
  <Button DockPanel.Dock="Bottom" Background="Lime">4 (Bottom)</Button>
  <Button Background="Aqua">5</Button>
</DockPanel>
```

The order in which they are added to the DockPanel is indicated by their number (and color). As with StackPanel, any stretching of elements is due to their default HorizontalAlignment or VerticalAlignment values of Stretch. Individual elements can choose different alignments if they don't want to fill the entire space that DockPanel gives them.

DockPanel is useful for arranging your top-level UI in a Window or Page, where most docked elements are actually other panels containing the real meat. For example, applications typically dock a Menu on top, perhaps a panel on the side, a StatusBar on the bottom, and then fill the remaining space with the main content.

The order children are added to DockPanel matters because each child is given all the space remaining on the docking edge. (This is somewhat like people selfishly claiming both armrests when they're the first to sit down in an airplane or auditorium!)

6

Figure 6.8 displays five Buttons in a DockPanel as in Figure 6.7, but added in a different order (indicated by their number and color). Notice how the layout differs from the preceding figure.

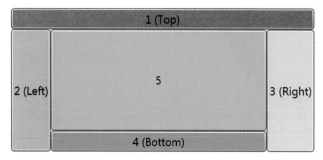

FIGURE 6.7   Buttons arranged in a DockPanel.

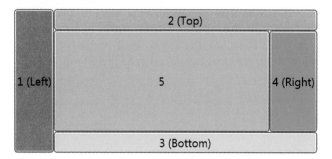

FIGURE 6.8   Buttons arranged in a DockPanel in a different order than Figure 6.7.

But DockPanel supports an indefinite number of children—not just five. When multiple elements are docked in the same direction, they are simply stacked in the appropriate direction. Figure 6.9 shows a DockPanel with eight elements—three docked on the left, two docked on the top, and two docked on the bottom.

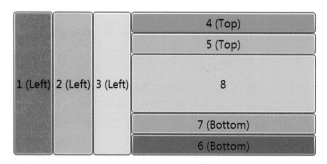

FIGURE 6.9   Multiple elements can be docked in all directions.

Therefore, DockPanel's functionality is actually a superset of StackPanel's functionality. With LastChildFill set to false, DockPanel behaves like a horizontal StackPanel when all children are docked to the left, and it behaves like a vertical StackPanel when all children are docked to the top.

Table 6.4 evaluates the way that some of the child layout properties apply to elements inside a DockPanel.

TABLE 6.4   DockPanel's Interaction with Child Layout Properties

Properties	Usable Inside a DockPanel?
Margin	Yes. Margin controls the space between an element and the DockPanel's edges as well as space between elements.
HorizontalAlignment and VerticalAlignment	Partially. Like StackPanel, alignment is effectively ignored in the direction of docking. For Left or Right, HorizontalAlignment is meaningless. For Top or Bottom, VerticalAlignment is meaningless. For the element filling the remaining space, however, both HorizontalAlignment and VerticalAlignment can be useful.
LayoutTransform	Yes. Differs from RenderTransform because when LayoutTransform is used, the remaining elements are pushed out further to make room. When combining Stretch layout with RotateTransform or SkewTransform as a LayoutTransform, the stretching only occurs for angles that are multiples of 90°, except for the element filling the remaining space (because it can stretch in both directions).

Grid

Grid is the most versatile panel, and probably the one you'll use most often. (Visual Studio and Expression Blend use Grid by default for their projects.) It enables you to arrange its children in a multirow and multicolumn fashion without relying on wrapping (like WrapPanel), and provides a number of features to control the rows and columns in interesting ways. Working with Grid is a lot like working with a Table in HTML.

> **TIP**
>
> WPF also contains a class called Table in the System.Windows.Documents namespace that exposes similar features to Grid. However, Table is optimized for the display of documents, whereas Grid is optimized for the display of elements in a more typical user interface. Table is covered in Chapter 14, "Audio, Video, Speech, and Documents."

Rather than continuing to use simple colored buttons to demonstrate layout, Listing 6.2 uses Grid to build a UI similar to Visual Studio's start page. It defines a 4x2 Grid and arranges a Label and four GroupBoxes in some of its cells.

LISTING 6.2   First Attempt at a Visual Studio-Like Start Page with a Grid

```xml
<Grid Background="LightBlue">

  <!-- Define four rows: -->
  <Grid.RowDefinitions>
    <RowDefinition/>
    <RowDefinition/>
    <RowDefinition/>
    <RowDefinition/>
  </Grid.RowDefinitions>

  <!-- Define two columns: -->
  <Grid.ColumnDefinitions>
    <ColumnDefinition/>
    <ColumnDefinition/>
  </Grid.ColumnDefinitions>

  <!-- Arrange the children: -->
  <Label    Grid.Row="0" Grid.Column="0" Background="Blue" Foreground="White"
            HorizontalContentAlignment="Center">Start Page</Label>
  <GroupBox Grid.Row="1" Grid.Column="0" Background="White"
            Header="Recent Projects">…</GroupBox>
  <GroupBox Grid.Row="2" Grid.Column="0" Background="White"
            Header="Getting Started">…</GroupBox>
  <GroupBox Grid.Row="3" Grid.Column="0" Background="White"
    Header="Headlines">…</GroupBox>
  <GroupBox Grid.Row="1" Grid.Column="1" Background="White"
    Header="Online Articles">
    <ListBox>
      <ListBoxItem>Article #1</ListBoxItem>
      <ListBoxItem>Article #2</ListBoxItem>
      <ListBoxItem>Article #3</ListBoxItem>
      <ListBoxItem>Article #4</ListBoxItem>
    </ListBox>
  </GroupBox>
</Grid>
```

For the basic usage of Grid, you define the number of rows and columns by adding that number of RowDefinition and ColumnDefinition elements to its RowDefinitions and ColumnDefinitions properties. (It's a little verbose, but handy for giving individual rows and columns distinct sizes.) You can then position child elements in the Grid using its Row and Column attached properties, which are zero-based integers. When you don't explicitly specify any rows or columns, a Grid is implicitly given a single cell. And when you don't explicitly set Grid.Row or Grid.Column on child elements, the value 0 is used for each.

Grid cells can be left empty, and multiple elements can appear in the same Grid cell. In the latter case, elements are simply rendered on top of one another according to their Z order. As with Canvas, child elements in the same cell don't interact with each other in terms of layout—they simply overlap.

Figure 6.10 shows the rendered result of Listing 6.2.

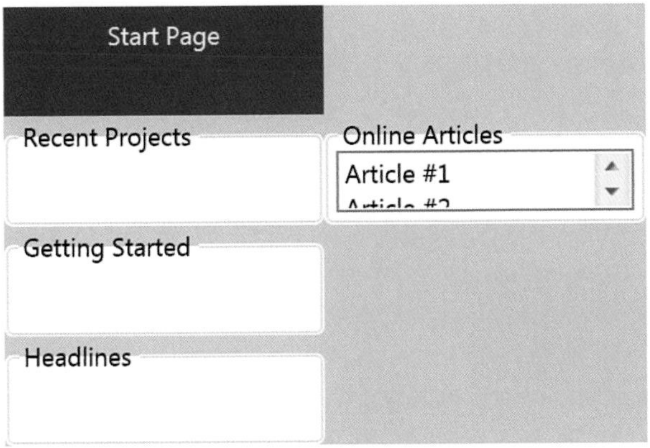

FIGURE 6.10   The first attempt at a Visual Studio-like start page is not very satisfactory.

The most noticeable problem with Figure 6.10 is that the list of online articles is too small. Also, it would probably look better if the "Start Page" label spanned across the entire width of the Grid. Fortunately, we can solve both of these problems with two more attached properties defined by Grid: RowSpan and ColumnSpan.

RowSpan and ColumnSpan are set to 1 by default, and can be set to any number greater than 1 to make an element span that many rows or columns. (If a value greater than the number of rows or columns is given, the element simply spans the maximum number that it can.) Therefore, by simply adding:

```
Grid.RowSpan="3"
```

to the last GroupBox in Listing 6.2, and adding:

```
Grid.ColumnSpan="2"
```

to the Label in Listing 6.2, you get a much better result, shown in Figure 6.11.

The Grid in Figure 6.11 still looks a little strange, however, because by default the heights of all rows and the widths of all columns are equal. Ideally, we'd make more room for the list of online articles and we wouldn't let the Label on top take up so much space. We can easily fix this by making the first row and first column size to their content. This *autosizing* can be done by setting the appropriate RowDefinition's Height and ColumnDefinition's Width to the case-insensitive string Auto. Therefore, updating the definitions in Listing 6.2 as follows gives the result shown in Figure 6.12:

```
<!-- Define four rows: -->
<Grid.RowDefinitions>
  <RowDefinition Height="Auto"/>
  <RowDefinition/>
  <RowDefinition/>
  <RowDefinition/>
</Grid.RowDefinitions>

<!-- Define two columns: -->
<Grid.ColumnDefinitions>
  <ColumnDefinition Width="Auto"/>
  <ColumnDefinition/>
</Grid.ColumnDefinitions>
```

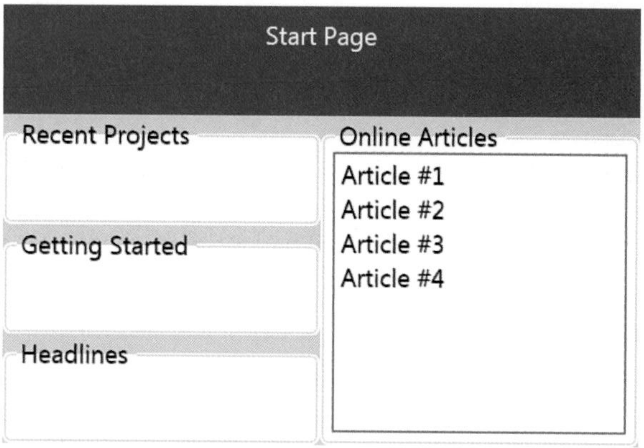

FIGURE 6.11   Using `RowSpan` and `ColumnSpan` improves the Visual Studio-like start page.

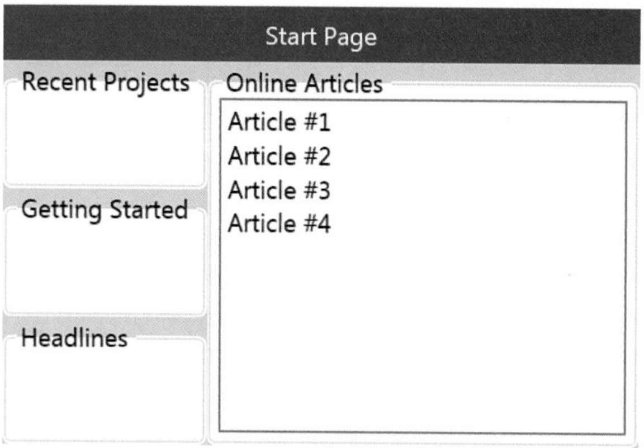

FIGURE 6.12   The final Visual Studio-like start page uses autosizing in the first row and first column.

FAQ

How can I give `Grid` cells background colors, padding, and borders like I can with cells of an HTML `Table`?

There is no intrinsic mechanism to give `Grid` cells such properties, but you can simulate them pretty easily thanks to the fact that multiple elements can appear in any `Grid` cell. To give a cell a background color, you can simply plop in a `Rectangle` with the appropriate `Fill`, which stretches to fill the cell by default. To give a cell padding, you can use autosizing and set the `Margin` on the appropriate child element. For borders, you can again use a `Rectangle` but give it an explicit `Stroke` of the appropriate color, or you can simply use a `Border` element instead.

Just be sure to add such `Rectangles` or `Borders` to the `Grid` *before* any of the other children (or explicitly mark them with the `ZIndex` attached property), so their Z order puts them behind the main content.

TIP

`Grid` has a simple `ShowGridLines` property that can be set to `true` to highlight the edges of cells with blue and yellow dashed lines. Applications in production have no use for this, but it can be a helpful aid to "debug" the layout of your `Grid`. Figure 6.13 shows the result of setting `ShowGridLines="True"` on the `Grid` used in Figure 6.12.

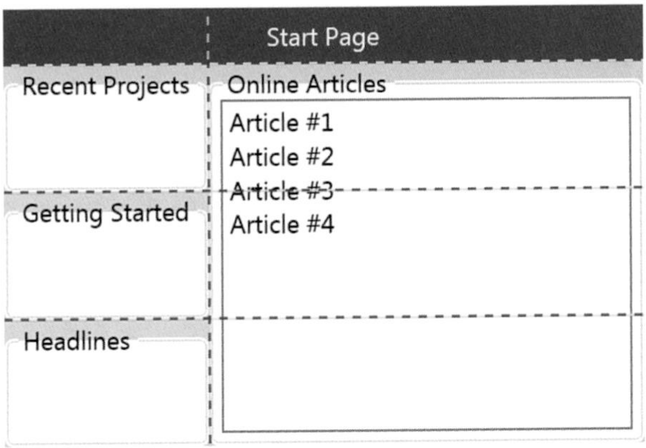

	Start Page
Recent Projects	Online Articles
	Article #1
	Article #2
Getting Started	Article #3
	Article #4
Headlines	

FIGURE 6.13   Using `ShowGridLines` on a Grid.

Sizing the Rows and Columns

Unlike `FrameworkElement`'s `Height` and `Width` properties, `RowDefinition`'s and `ColumnDefinition`'s corresponding properties do not default to `Auto` (or `Double.NaN`). And unlike almost all other `Height` and `Width` properties in WPF, theirs are of type

System.Windows.GridLength rather than double. This way, Grid can uniquely support three different types of RowDefinition and ColumnDefinition sizing:

▶ **Absolute sizing**—Setting Height or Width to a numeric value representing device-independent pixels (like all other Heights and Widths in WPF). Unlike the other types of sizing, an absolute-sized row or column does not grow or shrink as the size of the Grid or size of the elements changes.

▶ **Autosizing**—Setting Height or Width to Auto (seen previously), which gives child elements the space that they need and no more (like the default setting for other Heights and Widths in WPF). For a row, this is the height of the tallest element, and for a column, this is the width of the widest element. This is a better choice than absolute sizing whenever text is involved to be sure it doesn't get cut off because of different font settings or localization.

▶ **Proportional sizing (sometimes called star sizing)**—Setting Height or Width to special syntax to divide available space into equal-sized regions or regions based on fixed ratios. A proportional-sized row or column grows and shrinks as the Grid is resized.

Absolute and autosizing are straightforward, but proportional sizing needs more explanation. It is done with *star syntax*, and works as follows:

▶ When a row's height or column's width is set to *, it occupies all the remaining space.

▶ When multiple rows or columns use *, the remaining space is divided equally between them.

▶ Rows and columns can place a coefficient in front of the asterisk (like 2* or 5.5*) to take proportionately more space than other columns using the asterisk notation. A column with width 2* is always twice the width of a column with width * (which is shorthand for 1*) *in the same Grid*. A column with width 5.5* is always twice the width of a column with width 2.75* *in the same Grid*.

The "remaining space" is the height or width of the Grid minus any rows or columns that use absolute or autosizing. Figure 6.14 demonstrates these different scenarios with simple columns in a Grid.

The default height and width for Grid rows and columns is *. That's why the rows and columns are evenly distributed in Figures 6.10 and 6.11.

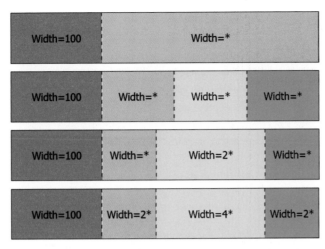

FIGURE 6.14   Proportional-sized Grid columns in action.

FAQ

 Why doesn't WPF provide built-in support for percentage sizing, like HTML?

The most common use of percentage sizing in HTML—setting the width or height of an item to 100%—is handled by setting an element's HorizontalAlignment or VerticalAlignment property to Stretch inside most panels. For more complicated scenarios, Grid's proportional sizing effectively provides percentage sizing, just with a syntax that takes a little getting used to. For example, to have a column always occupy 25% of a Grid's width, you can mark it with * and ensure that the remaining columns have a total width of 3*.

The WPF team chose this syntax so developers wouldn't have to worry about keeping the sum of percentages equal to 100 as rows or columns are dynamically added or removed. In addition, the fact that proportional sizing is specified relative to the remaining space (as opposed to the entire Grid) makes its behavior more understandable than an HTML table when mixing proportional rows or columns with fixed-size rows or columns.

DIGGING DEEPER

Using GridLength from Procedural Code

System.Windows.GridLengthConverter is the type converter that converts strings like "100", "auto", and "2*" to GridLength structures. From C#, you can use one of two constructors to construct the appropriate GridLength. The key is a GridUnitType enumeration that identifies which of the three types of values you're creating.

For absolute sizing, you can use the constructor that takes a simple double value (such as 100):

```
GridLength length = new GridLength(100);
```

Continues

DIGGING DEEPER

Continued

or you can use another constructor that accepts a `GridUnitType`:

```
GridLength length = new GridLength(100, GridUnitType.Pixel);
```

In both examples, the length is 100 device-independent pixels.

`Double.NaN` isn't a supported value for the `GridLength` constructors, so for autosizing you must use `GridUnitType.Auto`:

```
GridLength length = new GridLength(0, GridUnitType.Auto);
```

The number passed as the first parameter is ignored. However, the preferred approach is to simply use the static `GridLength.Auto` property, which returns an instance of `GridLength` just like the one created by the preceding line of code. For proportional sizing, you can pass a number along with `GridUnitType.Star`:

```
GridLength length = new GridLength(2, GridUnitType.Star);
```

This example is equivalent to specifying 2* in XAML. You can pass 1 with `GridUnitType.Star` to get the equivalent of *.

Interactive Sizing with `GridSplitter`

Another attractive feature of `Grid` is its support for interactive resizing of rows and columns using a mouse, keyboard, or stylus. This is accomplished with a `GridSplitter` class from the same namespace. You can add any number of `GridSplitter` children to a `Grid` and give them `Grid.Row`, `Grid.Column`, `Grid.RowSpan`, and/or `Grid.ColumnSpan` attached property values like any other children. Dragging the `GridSplitter` resizes at least one cell. Whether the other cells resize or simply move depend on whether they use proportional or nonproportional sizing.

By default, which cells get directly affected by the resizing depends on `GridSplitter's` alignment values. Table 6.5 summarizes the behavior, and also indicates in blue what the `GridSplitter` looks like with the various settings, treating the cells of the table as cells of a `Grid`.

GridSplitter has a default HorizontalAlignment of Right and a default VerticalAlignment of Stretch, so it docks to the right side of the specified cell by default. Any reasonable use of GridSplitter should set Stretch alignment in at least one direction, otherwise it ends up looking like a small dot, as seen in Table 6.5.

TIP

Although GridSplitter fits in one cell by default, its resizing behavior always affects the entire column (when dragging horizontally) or the entire row (when dragging vertically). Therefore, it's best to give it a ColumnSpan or RowSpan value to ensure it stretches across the entire height or width of the Grid.

TABLE 6.5   The Cells Directly Affected When Dragging a GridSplitter with Various Alignment Settings

| | | HorizontalAlignment | | | |
		Left	Right	Center	Stretch
VerticalAlignment	Top	Current cell and cell to the left	Current cell and cell to the right	Cells to the left and right	Current cell and cell above
	Bottom	Current cell and cell to the left	Current cell and cell to the right	Cells to the left and right	Current cell and cell above
	Center	Current cell and cell to the left	Current cell and cell to the right	Cells to the left and right	Cells above and below
	Stretch	Current cell and cell to the left	Current cell and cell to the right	Cells to the left and right	Cells to the left and right if GridSplitter is taller than it is wide, or cells to the top and bottom if GridSplitter is wider than it is tall

When all rows or columns are proportional-sized, dragging the GridSplitter changes the coefficients for the two affected rows or columns accordingly. When all rows or columns are absolute-sized, dragging the GridSplitter only changes the size of the topmost or leftmost of the two affected cells (depending on the resize direction). The remaining cells get pushed down or to the right to make room. This same behavior applies for autosized rows and columns, although the row or column that gets resized is switched to absolute sizing on the fly.

Although you can control all aspects of the resizing behavior and direction with GridSplitter's alignment properties, it also has two properties for explicitly and independently controlling these aspects: ResizeDirection (of type GridResizeDirection) and ResizeBehavior (of type GridResizeBehavior). ResizeDirection defaults to Auto, and can be changed to Rows or Columns, *but this only has an effect when* GridSplitter *is stretching in both directions* (the bottom-right cell in Table 6.5). ResizeBehavior defaults to BasedOnAlignment to get the behavior in Table 6.5, but can be set to PreviousAndCurrent, CurrentAndNext, or PreviousAndNext to control which two rows or columns should be directly affected by the resizing.

> **TIP**
>
> The best way to use GridSplitter is to place it in its own autosized row or column. That way, it doesn't overlap the existing content in the adjacent cells. If you do place it in a cell with other elements, however, be sure to add it last (or choose an appropriate ZIndex value) so it has the topmost Z order!

Sharing Row and Column Sizes

RowDefinitions and ColumnDefinitions have a property called SharedSizeGroup that enables multiple rows and/or columns to remain the same length as each other, even as any of them change length at runtime (via GridSplitter, for example). SharedSizeGroup can be set to a simple case-sensitive string value representing an arbitrary group name, and any rows or columns with that same group name are kept in sync.

For a simple example, consider the following three-column Grid shown in Figure 6.15 that doesn't use SharedSizeGroup:

```
<Grid>
<Grid.ColumnDefinitions>
  <ColumnDefinition Width="Auto" />
  <ColumnDefinition/>
  <ColumnDefinition/>
</Grid.ColumnDefinitions>

  <Label Grid.Column="0" Background="Red"
    HorizontalContentAlignment="Center" VerticalContentAlignment="Center">1
  </Label>
  <GridSplitter Grid.Column="0" Width="5" />
  <Label Grid.Column="1" Background="Orange"
    HorizontalContentAlignment="Center" VerticalContentAlignment="Center">2
  </Label>
  <Label Grid.Column="2" Background="Yellow"
    HorizontalContentAlignment="Center" VerticalContentAlignment="Center">3
  </Label>
</Grid>
```

The first column is autosized and has both a Label and a GridSplitter. The two remaining columns are both *-sized and only contain a Label. As the first column is enlarged, the remaining two *-sized columns split the shrunken space evenly.

> **TIP**
>
> GridSplitter must be given an explicit Width (or Height, depending on orientation) in order to be seen and be useable!

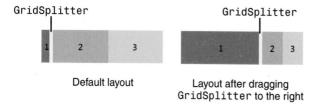

FIGURE 6.15   A simple Grid that doesn't use SharedSizeGroup.

In contrast, Figure 6.16 shows what happens with the same Grid when the first and last columns are marked with the same SharedSizeGroup. First, all members in the SharedSizeGroup are initialized to the largest auto or absolute size. Then, as the first column is enlarged, the last column is enlarged to match. The middle column is now effectively the only *-sized column, and fills whatever space remains.

The XAML for the Grid shown in Figure 6.16 is as follows:

```
<Grid IsSharedSizeScope="True">
<Grid.ColumnDefinitions>
  <ColumnDefinition Width="Auto" SharedSizeGroup="myGroup"/>
  <ColumnDefinition/>
  <ColumnDefinition SharedSizeGroup="myGroup"/>
</Grid.ColumnDefinitions>
  <Label Grid.Column="0" Background="Red"
    HorizontalContentAlignment="Center" VerticalContentAlignment="Center">1
  </Label>
  <GridSplitter Grid.Column="0" Width="5"/>
  <Label Grid.Column="1" Background="Orange"
    HorizontalContentAlignment="Center" VerticalContentAlignment="Center">2
  </Label>
  <Label Grid.Column="2" Background="Yellow"
    HorizontalContentAlignment="Center" VerticalContentAlignment="Center">3
  </Label>
</Grid>
```

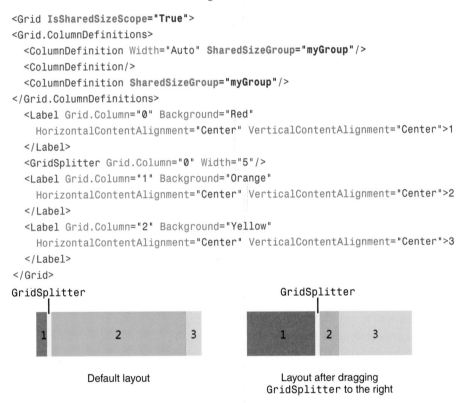

FIGURE 6.16   The Grid from Figure 6.15, but with the first and last columns in the same SharedSizeGroup.

The reason that the IsSharedSizeScope property needs to be set is that size groups can be shared *across multiple grids*! To avoid potential name collisions (and to cut down on the amount of logical tree walking that needs to be done), all uses of the same SharedSizeGroup must be under a common parent with IsSharedSizeScope set to true. Besides being a dependency property of Grid, it's also an attached property that can be used on non-Grid parents. For example:

```
<StackPanel Grid.IsSharedSizeScope="True">
  <Grid>…can use SharedSizeGroup…</Grid>
  <Grid>…can use SharedSizeGroup…</Grid>
  <WrapPanel>
```

```
    <Grid>…can use SharedSizeGroup…</Grid>
  </WrapPanel>
</StackPanel>
```

The "Putting It All Together: Creating a Visual Studio-Like Collapsible, Dockable, Resizable Pane" section at the end this chapter leverages SharedSizeGroup across multiple Grids to create a useful user interface.

Comparing Grid to Other Panels

Grid is usually the best choice for most layout scenarios because it can do everything done by the previous panels and more, except for the wrapping feature of WrapPanel. Grid can also accomplish layout for which you would otherwise need multiple panels. For example, the start page displayed in Figure 6.12 could have been created with a DockPanel and a StackPanel. The DockPanel would be the outermost element, with the Label docked on top, the StackPanel docked to the left (which would contain the first three GroupBoxes), and the last GroupBox would be left to fill the DockPanel's remaining space.

To prove that Grid is usually the best choice, it's interesting to see how to mimic the behavior of the other panels with Grid, knowing that you can take advantage of Grid's extra features at any time.

Mimicking a Canvas with Grid

If you leave Grid with a single row and column and set the HorizontalAlignment and VerticalAlignment of all children to values other than Stretch, the children get added to the single cell just like a Canvas. Setting HorizontalAlignment to Left and VerticalAlignment to Top is like setting Canvas.Left and Canvas.Top to 0. Setting HorizontalAlignment to Right and VerticalAlignment to Bottom is like setting Canvas.Right and Canvas.Bottom to 0. Furthermore, applying Margin values to each element can give you the same effect as setting Canvas's attached properties to the same values.

Mimicking a StackPanel with Grid

A single-column Grid with autosized rows looks just like a vertical StackPanel when each element is manually placed in consecutive rows. Similarly, a single-row Grid with auto-sized columns looks just like a horizontal StackPanel when each element is manually placed in consecutive columns.

Mimicking a DockPanel with Grid

With RowSpan and ColumnSpan, you can easily arrange the outermost elements to be docked and stretched against a Grid's edges just like what you would see with DockPanel. In Figure 6.12, the start page's Label is effectively docked along the top.

As with the previous panels, Table 6.6 evaluates the way that some of the child layout properties apply to elements inside a Grid.

TABLE 6.6   Grid's Interaction with Child Layout Properties

Properties	Usable Inside a Grid?
Margin	Yes. Margin controls the space between an element and the edges of its cell.
HorizontalAlignment and VerticalAlignment	Yes. Unlike the previous panels, both directions are completely usable unless an autosized cell causes an element to have no extra room. Therefore, by default, most elements completely stretch to fill their cell.
LayoutTransform	Yes. Differs from RenderTransform because when LayoutTransform is used, elements remain inside their cells (when they can) and respect their Margin. Unlike with RenderTransform, an element scaled outside the bounds of a cell gets clipped.

> **TIP**
>
> Although Grid looks like it can practically do it all, StackPanel and WrapPanel are better choices when dealing with an indeterminate number of child elements (typically as an items panel for an items control). Also, a DockPanel with complicated subpanels is sometimes a better choice than a single Grid because the isolation provided by subpanels is more manageable when your UI changes. With a single Grid, you might need to adjust RowSpan and ColumnSpan values to keep the docking illusion while rows and columns are added to the Grid.

Primitive Panels

The previous panels are generally useful for both application layout and control layout. But WPF also ships a few lightweight panels that are only likely to be useful inside controls, whether you're simply restyling a built-in control (covered in Chapter 10, "Styles, Templates, Skins, and Themes") or creating a custom control (covered in Chapter 16, "User Controls and Custom Controls"). They aren't nearly as general purpose as the previous panels, but are worth a quick look. All of these panels are in the System.Windows.Controls.Primitives namespace, except for ToolBarTray, which is in System.Windows.Controls.

TabPanel

TabPanel is a lot like a WrapPanel, but with limitations in some areas and extra features in other areas. As its name indicates, it is used in the default style for TabControl to arrange its tabs. Unlike WrapPanel, it only supports left-to-right stacking (when FlowDirection is LeftToRight, that is) and top-to-bottom wrapping. When wrapping occurs, it evenly stretches elements so that all rows consume the entire width of the panel.

ToolBarOverflowPanel

ToolBarOverflowPanel is also a simplified WrapPanel that only supports left-to-right stacking and top-to-bottom wrapping, used by the default style of ToolBar to display the extra elements that don't fit in its main area. Above and beyond WrapPanel's functionality, it adds a WrapWidth property that acts like a Padding property. But there's no compelling reason to use this panel over WrapPanel.

ToolBarTray

ToolBarTray only supports ToolBar children (and throws an InvalidOperationException if you try to add children of any other type). It arranges the ToolBars sequentially horizontally, but also enables you to drag them around to form additional rows or compress/expand neighboring ToolBars.

UniformGrid

UniformGrid is an interesting primitive panel (although its usefulness is questionable). It's a simplified form of Grid, where all rows and columns are of size * and can't be changed. Because of this, UniformGrid has two simple double properties to set the number of rows and columns rather than the more verbose RowDefinitions and ColumnDefinitions collections. It also has no attached properties; children are added in row-major order, and there can only be one child per cell.

Furthermore, if you don't explicitly set the number of rows and columns, UniformGrid automatically chooses suitable values. For example, it automatically places 2–4 elements in a 2x2 arrangement, 5–9 elements in a 3x3 arrangement, 10–16 elements in a 4x4 arrangement, and so on. Figure 6.17 demonstrates UniformGrid's default layout when eight Buttons are added to it.

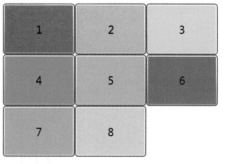

FIGURE 6.17   Eight Buttons added to a UniformGrid.

Handling Content Overflow

The built-in panels make their best effort to accommodate the size needs of their children. But sometimes they are forced to give children smaller space than they would like, and sometimes children refuse to render completely within that smaller space. For example, perhaps an element is marked with an explicit width that's wider than the containing panel! Or perhaps a control like ListBox contains so many items that they all can't fit within the containing Window. In such cases, a content overflow problem exists.

You can deal with content overflow using several different strategies:

- ▶ Clipping
- ▶ Scrolling
- ▶ Scaling
- ▶ Wrapping
- ▶ Trimming

The first three strategies are examined in this section. You've already seen examples of wrapping with WrapPanel (plus TabPanel and ToolBarOverflowPanel). This is the only built-in way to get wrapping behavior for content other than text (the layout of which is covered in Chapter 14).

As for trimming, that refers to a more intelligent form of clipping. This is only supported for text by the TextBlock and AccessText controls. They have a TextTrimming property (of type System.Windows.TextTrimming) that can be set to None (the default), CharacterEllipsis, or WordEllipsis. With the latter two values, text gets trimmed with ellipses (...) rather than simply being truncated at an arbitrary place.

Clipping

Clipping (that is, truncating or cropping) children is the default way that panels handle them when they are too large. Clipping can happen at the edges of a panel or within a panel (such as at the edges of a Grid cell or the fill area of a DockPanel). This behavior can be controlled to some degree, however.

All UIElements have a Boolean ClipToBounds property that controls whether child elements can be rendered outside of its bounds. If an outer element's edge coincides with the outer Window's or Page's edge, however, clipping still occurs. This mechanism is *not* a means to draw outside the bounds of a Window! (However, nonrectangular windows are discussed in the next chapter.)

Despite the fact that all panels inherit a ClipToBounds property, Canvas is the only one that respects it. The other panels clip content at their edges regardless of the setting. Furthermore, unlike most controls, Canvas sets its ClipToBounds property to false by default.

Figure 6.18 shows the difference that ClipToBounds makes with a Button that isn't entirely contained within its parent Canvas (which has a tan background).

This behavior means that unless you set ClipToBounds to true, the size of a Canvas is irrelevant—it can be given a Height and Width of 0 yet all its contents will be rendered as if the Canvas occupied the whole screen!

ClipToBounds="False"   ClipToBounds="True"

FIGURE 6.18   ClipToBounds determines whether children can be rendered outside their panel.

Controls can also control the clipping of their own content with ClipToBounds. For example, Button has ClipToBounds set to false by default. Figure 6.19 demonstrates the effect of setting it to true when its text is scaled with a ScaleTransform (applied as a RenderTransform).

ClipToBounds="False"   ClipToBounds="True"

FIGURE 6.19   ClipToBounds can also be used on a control like Button to affect the rendering of its inner content.

TIP

Canvas can be used as an intermediate element to prevent clipping in other panels! For example, if a large Button gets clipped at the edge of a Grid, you can make it render past the edge of the Grid if you instead place a Canvas in that cell (which gets sized to fit the cell) and then place the Button inside that Canvas. Of course, you need to write some code if you want the Button to get the same stretching behavior it would have gotten by being a direct child of the Grid.

You can use the same approach to work around clipping within *inner* cells of a Grid, but increasing an element's RowSpan and/or ColumnSpan is usually the best way to enable it to "bleed" into adjacent cells.

WARNING

Clipping occurs before RenderTransforms are applied!

When enlarging an element with ScaleTransform as a RenderTransform, the element can easily surpass the bounds of the parent panel yet doesn't get clipped (unless it reaches the edge of the Window or Page). *Shrinking* an element with ScaleTransform as a RenderTransform is more subtle. If the unscaled element would have been clipped because it exceeds its parent's bounds, the scaled element is still clipped the exact same way even if the entire element can fit! That's because clipping is part of the layout process and already determined by the time RenderTransform is applied. If you need to shrink a large element using ScaleTransform, applying it as a LayoutTransform might suit your needs better.

Scrolling

For many applications, the ability to scroll through content that is too large to view all at once is critical. WPF makes this easy because all you need to do is wrap an element in a `System.Windows.Controls.ScrollViewer` control, and it instantly becomes scrollable. `ScrollViewer` makes use of `ScrollBar` controls, and hooks them up to your content automatically.

`ScrollViewer` has a `Content` property that can be set to a single item, typically an entire panel. Because `Content` is `ScrollViewer`'s content property in the XAML sense, you can place the item requiring scrolling as its child element. For example:

```
<Window Title="Using ScrollViewer"
  xmlns="http://schemas.microsoft.com/winfx/2006/xaml/presentation">
  <ScrollViewer>
    <StackPanel>
      …
    </StackPanel>
  </ScrollViewer>
</Window>
```

Figure 6.20 shows the `Window` containing the simple `StackPanel`, with and without a `ScrollViewer`.

Not using `ScrollViewer`   Using `ScrollViewer`

FIGURE 6.20   `ScrollViewer` enables scrolling of an element that is larger than the space given to it.

The `ScrollBars` respond to a variety of input, such as arrow keys for fine-grained scrolling, Page Up and Page Down for coarser scrolling, and Ctrl+Home or Ctrl+End to jump to the beginning or end, respectively.

`ScrollViewer` exposes several properties and methods for more advanced or programmatic manipulation of scrolling, but its two most important properties are `VerticalScrollBarVisibility` and `HorizontalScrollBarVisibility`. Both of these properties are of type `ScrollBarVisibility`, an enumeration that defines four distinct states specific to its two `ScrollBars`:

▶ **Visible**—The ScrollBar is always visible, regardless of whether it's needed. When it's not needed, it has a disabled look and doesn't respond to input. (But this is different from the ScrollBarVisibility value called Disabled.)

▶ **Auto**—The ScrollBar is visible if the content is big enough to require scrolling in that dimension. Otherwise, the ScrollBar disappears.

▶ **Hidden**—The ScrollBar is always invisible but still logically exists, in that scrolling can still be done with arrow keys. Therefore, the content is still given all the length it wants in that dimension.

▶ **Disabled**—The ScrollBar is not only invisible but doesn't exist, so scrolling is not possible via mouse or keyboard. In this case, the content is only given the length of its parent rather than all the length it wants.

The default value for VerticalScrollBarVisibility is Visible, and the default value for HorizontalScrollBarVisibility is Auto, to match the scrolling behavior used by most applications.

Depending on the content inside ScrollViewer, the subtle difference between Hidden and Disabled can make a big difference. For example, Figure 6.21 shows two different Windows containing a ScrollViewer with the exact same WrapPanel. The only difference is that in one Window the ScrollViewer has HorizontalScrollBarVisibility set to Hidden, and in the other Window the ScrollViewer has it set to Disabled.

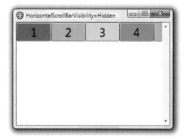

HorizontalScrollBarVisibility="Hidden"

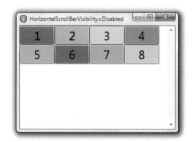

HorizontalScrollBarVisibility="Disabled"

FIGURE 6.21   Although the horizontal ScrollBar is invisible in both cases, the different values for HorizontalScrollBarVisibility drastically alter the layout of the WrapPanel.

In the Hidden case, the WrapPanel is given as much width as it desires (the same as if HorizontalScrollBarVisibility were set to Visible or Auto), so it makes use of it and arranges all children on the same row. In the Disabled case, the WrapPanel is only given the width of the parent Window, so wrapping occurs as if no ScrollViewer existed.

> **TIP**
>
> Chapter 3, "Important New Concepts in WPF," revealed that the default visual tree for `ListBox` contains a `ScrollViewer`. You can set its `VerticalScrollBarVisibility` and `HorizontalScrollBarVisibility` properties as attached properties on the `ListBox` so the values get inherited by the implicit `ScrollViewer`. For example:
>
> ```
> <ListBox ScrollViewer.HorizontalScrollBarVisibility="Disabled">
>   ...
> </ListBox>
> ```

> **TIP**
>
> There's another panel that isn't discussed in this chapter: `System.Windows.Controls.VirtualizingStackPanel`. It acts just like a `StackPanel`, but it temporarily discards any items off-screen to optimize performance (only when data binding). Therefore, `VirtualizingStackPanel` is the best panel for a *really* large number of child elements, and is used internally by `ListBox` by default. `VirtualizingStackPanel` derives from an abstract `VirtualizingPanel` class, but in the first version of WPF, `VirtualizingStackPanel` is the only subclass. Unfortunately, there's no `VirtualizingWrapPanel` (at least yet).

Scaling

Although scrolling is a popular and long-standing way to deal with large content, dynamically shrinking or enlarging content to "just fit" in a given space is more appropriate for several scenarios. As a simple example, imagine that you want to create a card game. You'll need some playing cards, and you'll probably want them to scale proportionally with the game's `Window`.

Figure 6.22 displays some shapes that form a vector representation of a playing card (shown with its source XAML in Chapter 16). These shapes are placed inside a `Canvas`, which is inside a `Window`. Because of their explicit sizes, they do not change size as the `Window` gets resized (even if they were placed in a `Grid` rather than a `Canvas`), and, obviously, the shapes are currently far too big.

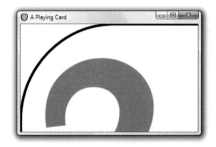

FIGURE 6.22   The shapes representing the playing card do not scale with the `Window`.

`ScaleTransform` can scale elements *relative to their own size* (and easily help the largeness of the playing card), but it doesn't provide a mechanism to scale elements *relative to their available space* without writing some custom code. Fortunately, `System.Windows.Controls.Viewbox` provides an easy mechanism to scale arbitrary content within a given space.

Viewbox is a type of class known as a *decorator*, a panel-like class that can only have one child element. It derives from System.Windows.Controls.Decorator, along with classes such as Border. By default, Viewbox stretches in both dimensions to fill the space given to it (like most controls). But it also has a Stretch property to control how its single child gets scaled within its bounds. The property is a System.Windows.Media.Stretch enumeration, which has the following values (demonstrated in Figure 6.23 by wrapping the Canvas inside a Viewbox):

▶ **None**—No scaling is done. This is the same as not using a Viewbox at all.

▶ **Fill**—The child's dimensions are set to equal the Viewbox's dimensions. Therefore, the child's aspect ratio is not necessarily preserved.

▶ **Uniform** (the default value)—The child is scaled as large as it can be while still fitting entirely within the Viewbox and preserving its aspect ratio. Therefore, there will be extra space in one dimension if its aspect ratio doesn't match.

▶ **UniformToFill**—The child is scaled to entirely fill the Viewbox while preserving its aspect ratio. Therefore, the content will be cropped in one dimension if its aspect ratio doesn't match.

Stretch="None"

Stretch="Fill"

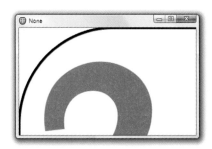
Stretch="Uniform"

Stretch="UniformToFill"

FIGURE 6.23   Each of the four values for Viewbox's Stretch property changes the playing card's layout.

Although it's unrealistic for a card game to want its cards to be the size of the Window, the same techniques apply for making the cards occupy a certain fraction of the Window's size. In Figure 6.23, the Viewbox is the child element of the Window, but in a real application you would likely place the Viewbox inside an appropriately sized Grid cell.

A second property of Viewbox controls whether you only want to use it to shrink content or enlarge content (as opposed to doing either). This property is called StretchDirection, and is a System.Windows.Controls.StretchDirection enumeration with the following values:

▶ **UpOnly**—Enlarges the content, if appropriate. If the content is already too big, the Viewbox leaves the current content size as is.

▶ **DownOnly**—Shrinks the content, if appropriate. If the content is already small enough, the Viewbox leaves the current content size as is.

▶ **Both** (the default value)—Enlarges or shrinks the content, whichever is needed to get the stretching described earlier.

What's pretty amazing is how easy it is to choose between a scrolling versus scaling strategy for dealing with large content. Consider the following Window that was shown in Figure 6.20:

```
<Window Title="Using ScrollViewer"
  xmlns="http://schemas.microsoft.com/winfx/2006/xaml/presentation">
  <ScrollViewer>
    <StackPanel>
      ...
    </StackPanel>
  </ScrollViewer>
</Window>
```

Simply changing the ScrollViewer element to a Viewbox (and updating the Window's Title):

```
<Window Title="Using Viewbox"
  xmlns="http://schemas.microsoft.com/winfx/2006/xaml/presentation">
  <Viewbox>
    <StackPanel>
      ...
    </StackPanel>
  </Viewbox>
</Window>
```

produces the result in Figure 6.24. Just like that, you can now see all eight buttons regardless of the Window size!

FIGURE 6.24   The StackPanel used in Figure 6.20, but now wrapped in a Viewbox instead of a ScrollViewer.

WARNING

Viewbox **removes all wrapping!**

Viewbox is very handy for many situations, but it's not a good choice for content you'd normally like to wrap, such as a paragraph of text or any content in a WrapPanel. That's because the content is given as much space as it needs in both directions before it is potentially scaled. Figure 6.25 demonstrates this by using the WrapPanel with eight Buttons from Figure 6.21, but replacing the ScrollViewer with a Viewbox.

The result is a single line of content that could potentially be much smaller than you would have liked. Giving the Viewbox a StretchDirection of UpOnly rather than the default of Both doesn't help either. The layout of the Viewbox's content happens before any potential scaling. Therefore, UpOnly prevents the Buttons from shrinking, but they are still arranged in a single line. This is shown in Figure 6.26.

The result of this is similar to the use of HorizontalScrollBarVisibility= "Hidden" in Figure 6.21, except that there's no way to scroll to the remaining content, even with the keyboard!

FIGURE 6.25   The WrapPanel used in Figure 6.21 has no need to wrap when placed in a Viewbox instead of a ScrollViewer.

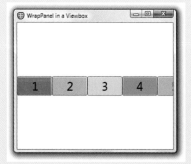

FIGURE 6.26   Giving the Viewbox from Figure 6.25 a StretchDirection="UpOnly" prevents the Buttons from shrinking, but doesn't affect the inner WrapPanel's layout.

Putting It All Together: Creating a Visual Studio-Like Collapsible, Dockable, Resizable Pane

Let's put WPF's layout features to the test and create a more complex piece of UI. In this section, we'll create some Visual Studio-like panes that can be docked next to the window's main content or collapsed to a button along the edge of the window. In this collapsed form, hovering over the button shows the pane but rather than being docked, it overlaps on top of the main content. Whether docked or undocked, each pane is resizable using a splitter. Figures 6.27 through 6.33 walk through several sequential states of the user interface as it is being used.

FIGURE 6.27   Both panes start out hidden, so you only see their buttons docked on the right.

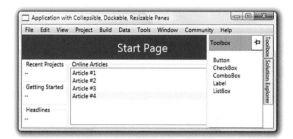

FIGURE 6.28   Hovering over the Toolbox button presents the undocked Toolbox pane, which stays open unless the mouse wanders onto the main content or a different pane's button.

FIGURE 6.29   An undocked pane can be resized, still overlapping the main content.

FIGURE 6.30   The Toolbox pane is docked by clicking the pushpin, making the main content shrink to fit beside it and making the Toolbox button on the right disappear.

FIGURE 6.31   The docked pane can still be resized with the `GridSplitter`, but this time the main content stretches and shrinks in unison.

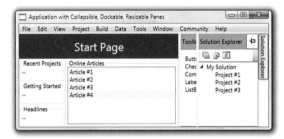

FIGURE 6.32   Hovering over the Solution Explorer button presents the undocked Solution Explorer pane, which overlaps all other content (including the docked Toolbox pane). The undocked pane can be resized independently to overlap more or less of the other content.

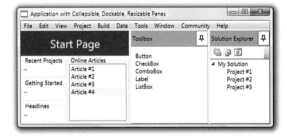

FIGURE 6.33   The Solution Explorer pane is docked by clicking the pushpin, pushing the Toolbox pane over and making the entire rightmost bar disappear because there are no more undocked pane buttons to show.

With both panes undocked, they resize independently from the main content and each other. With both panes docked (as in Figure 6.33), the UI behaves like a single Grid with three cells that can be resized but never overlap.

So, how do you go about implementing such a UI? Because splitters are needed for interactive resizing, using Grid with GridSplitters is a natural choice. No other built-in panels provide an interactive splitter. But because undocked panes need to overlap and resize independently from one another, a single Grid won't do. Instead, this example uses three independent Grids—one for the main content and one for each pane—layered on top of each other. SharedSizeGroups are then used to keep these three independent Grids in sync when they need to be (that is, the docked case). Figure 6.34 illustrates the structure of these three Grids and how they are tied together.

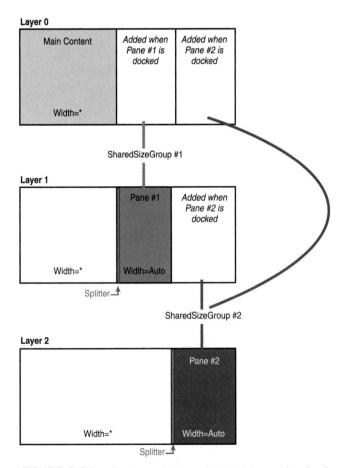

FIGURE 6.34   The three independent Grids used to implement two collapsible, dockable, resizable panes.

The bottom layer (Layer 0) contains the main content that stretches to fill the Grid when both panes are collapsed. Hovering over either pane's button switches the appropriate pane's visibility in Layers 1 or 2 from `Collapsed` to `Visible`. Each pane's splitter can be used to adjust the space between itself and the column to the left (which is empty, revealing the content from Layer 0 behind it).

The main trickery occurs when it's time to dock a panel. When docking Pane #1, the main content needs to be squeezed to match the width of the empty 0th column in Layer 1. Therefore, an empty column is dynamically added to Layer 0 and given the same width as Pane #1. Because a `SharedSizeGroup` is used rather than a hard-coded width, the bottom layer stays up to date as the splitter in Layer 1 is used.

The same technique is used when docking Pane #2, except that the dummy column needs to be added to all layers underneath (both Layers 0 and 1). This enables both docked panes to be seen simultaneously with no overlap, and enables the main content on Layer 0 to be sized appropriately in the presence of zero, one, or two docked panes. Note that the ordering of the panes when both are docked is predetermined.

These three `Grid`s are placed in (what else?) a `Grid` with a single row and column, so they can completely overlap each other while stretching to completely fill the space given to them. Although Layer 0 always has the bottommost Z order, the Z order between the other layers can get swapped so the current undocked pane is always on top.

Listing 6.3 contains the XAML for the application shown in Figures 6.27 to 6.33, with some of the irrelevant parts removed for brevity. The entire project appears with this book's source code.

LISTING 6.3   `VisualStudioLikePanes.xaml`—The XAML Implementation of the Application in Figures 6.27 to 6.33

```
<Window x:Class="MainWindow"
        xmlns="http://schemas.microsoft.com/winfx/2006/xaml/presentation"
        xmlns:x="http://schemas.microsoft.com/winfx/2006/xaml"
        Title="Application with Collapsible, Dockable, Resizable Panes"
>
  <DockPanel>
    <Menu DockPanel.Dock="Top">
      ...
    </Menu>

    <!-- The bar of buttons docked along the right edge: -->
    <StackPanel Name="buttonBar" Orientation="Horizontal" DockPanel.Dock="Right">
      <StackPanel.LayoutTransform>
        <RotateTransform Angle="90"/>
      </StackPanel.LayoutTransform>
        <Button Name="pane1Button" MouseEnter="pane1Button_MouseEnter">
          Toolbox
        </Button>
        <Button Name="pane2Button" MouseEnter="pane2Button_MouseEnter">
          Solution Explorer
```

LISTING 6.3   Continued

```
    </Button>
  </StackPanel>

  <!-- The Grid containing the three child Grids fills the DockPanel: -->
  <Grid Name="parentGrid" Grid.IsSharedSizeScope="True">

    <!-- Layer 0: -->
    <Grid Name="layer0" MouseEnter="layer0_MouseEnter">
      … (content of this Grid is similar to Listing 6.2)
    </Grid>

    <!-- Layer 1: -->
    <Grid Name="layer1" Visibility="Collapsed">
    <Grid.ColumnDefinitions>
      <ColumnDefinition/>
      <ColumnDefinition SharedSizeGroup="column1" Width="auto"/>
    </Grid.ColumnDefinitions>
      <!-- Column 0 is empty,
           but column 1 contains a Grid and a GridSplitter: -->
      <Grid Grid.Column="1" MouseEnter="pane1_MouseEnter"
            Background="{DynamicResource
                          {x:Static SystemColors.ActiveCaptionBrushKey}}">
      <Grid.RowDefinitions>
        <RowDefinition Height="auto"/>
        <RowDefinition/>
      </Grid.RowDefinitions>
        <!-- Row 0 contains a header,
             and row 1 contains pane-specific content: -->
        <DockPanel Grid.Row="0">
          <Button Name="pane1Pin" Width="26" DockPanel.Dock="Right"
                  Click="pane1Pin_Click" Background="White">
            <Image Name="pane1PinImage" Source="pinHorizontal.gif"/>
          </Button>
          <TextBlock Padding="8" TextTrimming="CharacterEllipsis"
            Foreground="{DynamicResource
                          {x:Static SystemColors.ActiveCaptionTextBrushKey}}"
            DockPanel.Dock="Left">Toolbox</TextBlock>
        </DockPanel>
        … (pane-specific content fills row 1)
      </Grid>
      <GridSplitter Width="5" Grid.Column="1" HorizontalAlignment="Left"/>
    </Grid>

    <!-- Layer 2: -->
```

LISTING 6.3   Continued

```xml
        <Grid Name="layer2" Visibility="Collapsed">
        <Grid.ColumnDefinitions>
          <ColumnDefinition/>
          <ColumnDefinition SharedSizeGroup="column2" Width="auto"/>
        </Grid.ColumnDefinitions>
          <!-- Column 0 is empty,
               but column 1 contains a Grid and a GridSplitter: -->
          <Grid Grid.Column="1" MouseEnter="pane2_MouseEnter"
                Background="{DynamicResource
                           {x:Static SystemColors.ActiveCaptionBrushKey}}">
          <Grid.RowDefinitions>
            <RowDefinition Height="auto"/>
            <RowDefinition Height="auto"/>
            <RowDefinition/>
          </Grid.RowDefinitions>
            <!-- Row 0 contains a header,
                 and rows 1 & 2 contain pane-specific content: -->
            <DockPanel Grid.Row="0">
              <Button Name="pane2Pin" Width="26" DockPanel.Dock="Right"
                      Click="pane2Pin_Click" Background="White">
                <Image Name="pane2PinImage" Source="pinHorizontal.gif"/>
              </Button>
              <TextBlock Padding="8" TextTrimming="CharacterEllipsis"
                 Foreground="{DynamicResource
                           {x:Static SystemColors.ActiveCaptionTextBrushKey}}"
                 DockPanel.Dock="Left">Solution Explorer</TextBlock>
            </DockPanel>
            … (pane-specific content fills rows 1 & 2)
          </Grid>
          <GridSplitter Width="5" Grid.Column="1" HorizontalAlignment="Left"/>
        </Grid>
      </Grid>
    </DockPanel>
</Window>
```

The Window's top-level panel is a DockPanel, which arranges a Menu, the "button bar"
StackPanel (rotated 90° with a RotateTransform), and a single-cell grid containing the
three "layer" Grids. Notice that the Menu is added to the DockPanel before the StackPanel
so it stretches all the way across the top.

Each layer Grid only has one column containing any content, and that content happens
to be encased in a Grid in all three cases. Each GridSplitter is docked on the left inside
the column with the content so it doesn't overlap any content from the other layers. One
subtlety is that TextBlocks are used for each pane's header instead of Labels, so that

TextTrimming="CharacterEllipsis" can be set to get a more polished effect than simply clipping the text when the pane is resized.

Listing 6.4 contains the C# code behind file for Listing 6.3.

LISTING 6.4   VisualStudioLikePanes.xaml.cs—The C# Implementation of the Application in Figures 6.27 to 6.33

```csharp
using System;
using System.Windows;
using System.Windows.Controls;
using System.Windows.Media.Imaging;

public partial class MainWindow : Window
{
  // Dummy columns for layers 0 and 1:
  ColumnDefinition column1CloneForLayer0;
  ColumnDefinition column2CloneForLayer0;
  ColumnDefinition column2CloneForLayer1;

  public MainWindow()
  {
    InitializeComponent();

    // Initialize the dummy columns used when docking:
    column1CloneForLayer0 = new ColumnDefinition();
    column1CloneForLayer0.SharedSizeGroup = "column1";
    column2CloneForLayer0 = new ColumnDefinition();
    column2CloneForLayer0.SharedSizeGroup = "column2";
    column2CloneForLayer1 = new ColumnDefinition();
    column2CloneForLayer1.SharedSizeGroup = "column2";
  }

  // Toggle between docked and undocked states (Pane 1)
  public void pane1Pin_Click(object sender, RoutedEventArgs e)
  {
    if (pane1Button.Visibility == Visibility.Collapsed)
      UndockPane(1);
    else
      DockPane(1);
  }

  // Toggle between docked and undocked states (Pane 2)
  public void pane2Pin_Click(object sender, RoutedEventArgs e)
  {
    if (pane2Button.Visibility == Visibility.Collapsed)
      UndockPane(2);
```

9

LISTING 6.4   Continued

```
  else
    DockPane(2);
}

// Show Pane 1 when hovering over its button
public void pane1Button_MouseEnter(object sender, RoutedEventArgs e)
{
  layer1.Visibility = Visibility.Visible;

  // Adjust Z order to ensure the pane is on top:
  Grid.SetZIndex(layer1, 1);
  Grid.SetZIndex(layer2, 0);

  // Ensure the other pane is hidden if it is undocked
  if (pane2Button.Visibility == Visibility.Visible)
    layer2.Visibility = Visibility.Collapsed;
}

// Show Pane 2 when hovering over its button
public void pane2Button_MouseEnter(object sender, RoutedEventArgs e)
{
  layer2.Visibility = Visibility.Visible;

  // Adjust Z order to ensure the pane is on top:
  Grid.SetZIndex(layer2, 1);
  Grid.SetZIndex(layer1, 0);

  // Ensure the other pane is hidden if it is undocked
  if (pane1Button.Visibility == Visibility.Visible)
    layer1.Visibility = Visibility.Collapsed;
}

// Hide any undocked panes when the mouse enters Layer 0
public void layer0_MouseEnter(object sender, RoutedEventArgs e)
{
  if (pane1Button.Visibility == Visibility.Visible)
    layer1.Visibility = Visibility.Collapsed;
  if (pane2Button.Visibility == Visibility.Visible)
    layer2.Visibility = Visibility.Collapsed;
}

// Hide the other pane if undocked when the mouse enters Pane 1
public void pane1_MouseEnter(object sender, RoutedEventArgs e)
{
```

LISTING 6.4   Continued

```csharp
    // Ensure the other pane is hidden if it is undocked
    if (pane2Button.Visibility == Visibility.Visible)
      layer2.Visibility = Visibility.Collapsed;
  }

  // Hide the other pane if undocked when the mouse enters Pane 2
  public void pane2_MouseEnter(object sender, RoutedEventArgs e)
  {
    // Ensure the other pane is hidden if it is undocked
    if (pane1Button.Visibility == Visibility.Visible)
      layer1.Visibility = Visibility.Collapsed;
  }

  // Docks a pane, which hides the corresponding pane button
  public void DockPane(int paneNumber)
  {
    if (paneNumber == 1)
    {
      pane1Button.Visibility = Visibility.Collapsed;
      pane1PinImage.Source = new BitmapImage(new Uri("pin.gif", UriKind.Relative));

      // Add the cloned column to layer 0:
      layer0.ColumnDefinitions.Add(column1CloneForLayer0);
      // Add the cloned column to layer 1, but only if pane 2 is docked:
      if (pane2Button.Visibility == Visibility.Collapsed)
        layer1.ColumnDefinitions.Add(column2CloneForLayer1);
    }
    else if (paneNumber == 2)
    {
      pane2Button.Visibility = Visibility.Collapsed;
      pane2PinImage.Source = new BitmapImage(new Uri("pin.gif", UriKind.Relative));

      // Add the cloned column to layer 0:
      layer0.ColumnDefinitions.Add(column2CloneForLayer0);
      // Add the cloned column to layer 1, but only if pane 1 is docked:
      if (pane1Button.Visibility == Visibility.Collapsed)
        layer1.ColumnDefinitions.Add(column2CloneForLayer1);
    }
  }

  // Undocks a pane, which reveals the corresponding pane button
  public void UndockPane(int paneNumber)
  {
```

6

LISTING 6.4   Continued

```
    if (paneNumber == 1)
    {
      layer1.Visibility = Visibility.Visible;
      pane1Button.Visibility = Visibility.Visible;
      pane1PinImage.Source = new BitmapImage
        (new Uri("pinHorizontal.gif", UriKind.Relative));

      // Remove the cloned columns from layers 0 and 1:
      layer0.ColumnDefinitions.Remove(column1CloneForLayer0);
      // This won't always be present, but Remove silently ignores bad columns:
      layer1.ColumnDefinitions.Remove(column2CloneForLayer1);
    }
    else if (paneNumber == 2)
    {
      layer2.Visibility = Visibility.Visible;
      pane2Button.Visibility = Visibility.Visible;
      pane2PinImage.Source = new BitmapImage
        (new Uri("pinHorizontal.gif", UriKind.Relative));

      // Remove the cloned columns from layers 0 and 1:
      layer0.ColumnDefinitions.Remove(column2CloneForLayer0);
      // This won't always be present, but Remove silently ignores bad columns:
      layer1.ColumnDefinitions.Remove(column2CloneForLayer1);
    }
  }
}
```

The C# code is hard-coded to work with exactly two panes. More likely, you'd generalize the code and abstract it into a custom control, but as far as layout goes the concepts are the same.

Notice that there is no code to hide the "button bar" when all panes have been docked or to reveal it when at least one pane is undocked. This happens automatically because the StackPanel sizes to its content by default, so collapsing both Buttons ends up collapsing the StackPanel.

Listing 6.4 doesn't contain very much code (or any complex code) yet achieves a relatively sophisticated user interface. Compared with Visual Studio's panes, one noticeable lacking feature is the animated effect for panes gliding in and out. But don't worry—such an animation can easily be added using the techniques described in Chapter 13, "Animation."

Conclusion

With all the features described in this chapter and the preceding chapter, you can control layout in many interesting ways! This isn't like the old days, where your only options were pretty much just choosing a size and choosing an (X,Y) point on the screen!

The built-in panels—notably `Grid`—are a key part of WPF's capability to enable rapid application development. But one of the most powerful aspects of WPF's layout is that parent panels can themselves be children of other panels. Although each panel was examined in isolation, the versatility enabled by arbitrary nesting of panels is quite impressive.

CHAPTER 7

Structuring and Deploying an Application

We've covered all the basics for assembling a WPF-based user interface and hooking it up to logic. Now it's time to see how to package it up as an application. There's no single canonical way to structure a WPF application. WPF supports standard Windows applications that take full advantage of the local computer, web-based applications that can still provide a compelling experience despite being restricted by Internet zone security, and a lot of other variations on these themes.

To help you explore the differences between each type of application (rather than just reading about them), this book's source code contains a collection of sample "Photo Gallery" applications that are inspired by the Windows Photo Gallery introduced in Windows Vista. Each variation of Photo Gallery corresponds to each application type covered here.

Standard Windows Applications

A standard Windows application runs locally on your computer and displays its user interface in one or more windows. The "standard" version of the Photo Gallery application is shown in Figure 7.1.

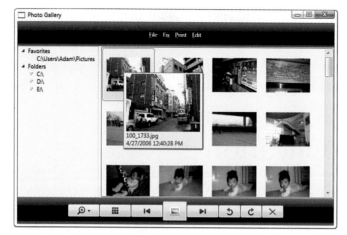

FIGURE 7.1   Using the Photo Gallery application to browse local photos.

When creating a new WPF Windows Application project in Visual Studio, several files are generated for you. Most of them are familiar to .NET developers, such as `AssemblyInfo.*`, `Resources.*`, and `Settings.*`. But the WPF-specific meat of the project can be found in `App.xaml` and `Window1.xaml` (along with their corresponding code-behind files). These contain the `Application` and `Window` objects that are central to this type of application.

The Window Class

`Window` is the main element that traditional applications use to contain their content. A WPF `Window` is really just a Win32 window under the covers. The operating system doesn't distinguish between windows with WPF content and windows with Win32 content; it renders the chrome the same way for both, both appear in the Windows taskbar in the same manner, and so on. (*Chrome* is another name for the nonclient area, which contains the Minimize, Maximize, and Close buttons among other things.)

Therefore, `Window` provides a straightforward abstraction for a Win32 window (like the `Form` class in Windows Forms), with a handful of simple methods and properties. After instantiating a `Window`, you can call `Show` to make it appear, `Hide` to make it disappear (which is the same as setting `Visibility` to `Hidden` or `Collapsed`), and `Close` to make it disappear for good. Despite being a `Control`, `Window`'s Win32 dependency means that you cannot do certain advanced things like apply a transform to it.

`Window`'s appearance can be controlled by properties such as `Icon`, `Title` (which is used as its caption), and `WindowStyle`. Its position can be controlled via `Left` and `Top` properties, or you can set its `WindowStartupLocation` to `CenterScreen` or `CenterOwner` to get more sophisticated behavior. In short, you can do just about everything you'd expect with `Window` by setting properties: Set `Topmost` to `true` to give it "always on top" behavior, set `ShowInTaskbar` to `false` if you don't want the typical item to appear in the taskbar, and so on.

A Window can spawn any number of additional Windows by instantiating a Window-derived class and calling Show. But it can also designate any of these additional Windows as child Windows. A child Window is just like any other top-level Window, but it automatically gets closed when the parent is closed and minimized when the parent is minimized. Such a Window is sometimes called a *modeless dialog*.

For a Window to make another Window its child, it must set the child Window's Owner property (of type Window) to a reference to itself, but only after the parent has been shown. It can enumerate its children via a read-only OwnedWindows property.

Every time a Window becomes active or inactive (for example, from the user flipping between her windows), a corresponding Activated and Deactivated event is raised. You can also attempt to force a Window to become active by calling Window's Activate method (which behaves like the Win32 SetForegroundWindow API).

Listing 7.1 contains portions of the MainWindow class defined by the Photo Gallery application.

LISTING 7.1   Portions of MainWindow.xaml.cs Related to Window Management

```
public partial class MainWindow : Window
{
  public MainWindow()
  {
    InitializeComponent();
  }

  protected override void OnClosing(CancelEventArgs e)
  {
    base.OnClosing(e);

    if (MessageBox.Show("Are you sure you want to close Photo Gallery?",
      "Annoying Prompt", MessageBoxButton.YesNo, MessageBoxImage.Question)
      == MessageBoxResult.No)
        e.Cancel = true;
  }

  protected override void OnClosed(EventArgs e)
  {
    base.OnClosed(e);

    // Persist the list of favorites
    ...
  }

  protected override void OnInitialized(EventArgs e)
  {
```

LISTING 7.1   Continued

```
    base.OnInitialized(e);

    // Retrieve the persisted list of favorites
    ...
  }
...
  void exitMenu_Click(object sender, RoutedEventArgs e)
  {
    this.Close();
  }
...
}
```

MainWindow calls InitializeComponent in its constructor to initialize the part of the Window defined in XAML. It then takes action on the Closing, Closed, and Initialized events. But it does this by overriding Window's OnEventName methods rather than attaching event handlers to each event. It's conventional for managed classes to expose protected OnEventName methods corresponding to each event, and WPF classes follow this convention. The end result is the same whether you override the method or attach an event handler, but the overriding mechanism tends to be a bit faster. The .NET Framework designers also felt that the override approach is a more natural way for a subclass to handle base class events.

The Closing event is raised when someone attempts to close the Window, whether it's done programmatically or via the user clicking the Close button, pressing Alt+F4, and so on. Any event handler can veto the closure, however, by setting the Cancel property in the passed-in CancelEventArgs object (the same one used by Windows Forms for the same purpose) to true. Inside this listing's OnClosing method, the user is presented with a confirmation dialog, and the closing is canceled if the user clicks the No button. In this example, the dialog is just an annoyance because there's no data for the user to poten-

tially save. But a typical usage of this event is to prompt the user to save some data that they haven't already saved. If the closing process is not vetoed, the Window is closed and the Closed event (which can't be canceled) gets raised.

In Listing 7.1, MainWindow handles Closed to persist the list of favorite folders that the user might have designated while running the application. It also handles the Initialized event to retrieve that persisted list and update the user interface appropriately. (The

> **WARNING**
>
> **Don't forget to call InitializeComponent!**
>
> This was mentioned in Chapter 2, "XAML Demystified," but it's worth repeating. If you don't call InitializeComponent in the constructor of any class that has corresponding compiled XAML, the object will not get constructed correctly. That's because all the runtime processing of the compiled XAML happens inside this method. Fortunately, Visual Studio automatically generates calls to InitializeComponent, so it should be hard to accidentally omit.

upcoming "Persisting and Restoring Application State" section shows the code that does this.) The listing ends with an event handler for the File, Exit menu, which closes the `Window` when selected.

The Application Class

Now that we know how to create and show `Windows`, our application simply needs an entry point to do this work. You might expect to write a `Main` method as follows, given a `MainWindow` class as defined in Listing 7.1:

```
public static void Main()
{
  MainWindow window = new MainWindow();
  window.Show();
}
```

This is incorrect for two reasons. First, threads in a WPF application must run in a single-threaded apartment (STA). Therefore, `Main` must be marked with an `STAThread` attribute. But more important, `Show` is a nonblocking call; it shows the `Window` (by calling the Win32 `ShowWindow` API) and then immediately returns. But the call to `Show` is the last line of `Main`, so the application then exits. The result is `MainWindow` flashing on the screen for a fraction of a second!

FAQ

  Please tell me that I did not just read the words *single-threaded apartment*! Isn't that a legacy COM thing?

Yes, apartments are a COM mechanism. And like previous Win32-based UI frameworks (including Windows Forms), WPF requires the main thread to live in a single-threaded apartment. This is mainly the case to enable seamless interoperability with non-WPF technologies (the topic of Chapter 15, "Interoperability with Win32, Windows Forms, and ActiveX"). But even without the interoperability requirement, the STA model—in which developers don't need to worry about correctly handling calls from arbitrary threads—is valuable for making programming with WPF easier. When an object is created on an STA thread, it can only be called on that same thread.

WPF enforces that many of its APIs (on `DispatcherObject`-derived classes) are called from the correct thread by throwing an exception if the call comes from any other thread. That way, there's no chance of accidentally calling such members from the wrong thread and only seeing it fail intermittently (which can be incredibly hard to debug). At the same time, WPF provides an easy mechanism for multiple threads to communicate with the UI thread, as discussed in a later sidebar.

If you don't know anything about COM and don't want to deal with threading, don't worry. Simply mark your `Main` method with `STAThread` and forget about these rules!

To prevent `Main` from instantly existing after showing `MainWindow`, you need to tell the application to dispatch messages from the operating system to `MainWindow` indefinitely until it has been closed. These messages are the same Windows messages that Win32 applications are built upon: `WM_PAINT`, `WM_MOUSEMOVE`, and so on. Internally, WPF must handle these messages to run on Windows. In Win32, you would write a loop (called a *message loop* or *message pump*) that processes incoming messages and sends them to the appropriate window procedure. In WPF, the easiest way to accomplish the same task is by using the `System.Windows.Application` class.

Using `Application.Run`

`Application` defines a `Run` method that keeps the application alive and dispatches messages appropriately. So the previous `Main` implementation can be corrected as follows:

```
[STAThread]
public static void Main()
{
  Application app = new Application();
  MainWindow window = new MainWindow();
  window.Show();
  app.Run(window);
}
```

`Application` also defines a `StartupUri` property that provides an alternate means of showing the application's first `Window`. It can be used as follows:

```
[STAThread]
public static void Main()
{
  Application app = new Application();
  app.StartupUri = new Uri("MainWindow.xaml", UriKind.Relative);
  app.Run();
}
```

This implementation of `Main` is equivalent to the previous one because the instantiation of `MainWindow` and the call to `Show` is done implicitly by `Application`. Notice that `MainWindow` is identified only by the name of the XAML source file as a uniform resource identifier (URI), and that an overload of `Run` is called that doesn't need an instance of a `Window`. WPF's use of URIs is explained in the next chapter, "Resources."

The reason for having the `StartupUri` property is to enable this common initialization to be done in XAML. Indeed, the Visual Studio template for WPF Windows Application projects defines an `Application`-derived class called `App` in XAML and sets the `StartupUri` property to the project's main `Window`. For the Photo Gallery application, the content of `App.xaml` is as follows:

```
<Application x:Class="PhotoGallery.App"
  xmlns="http://schemas.microsoft.com/winfx/2006/xaml/presentation"
```

```
    xmlns:x="http://schemas.microsoft.com/winfx/2006/xaml"
    StartupUri="MainWindow.xaml"/>
```

StartupUri can be set with a simple string thanks to a type converter for Uri.

The corresponding code-behind file—App.xaml.cs—simply has the InitializeComponent call:

```
using System.Windows;

namespace PhotoGallery
{
  public partial class App : Application
  {
    public App()
    {
      InitializeComponent();
    }
  }
}
```

This is the most common approach for structuring a standard WPF application and showing its main Window. Note, however, that if you have nothing custom to add to the Application code-behind file, you can omit it altogether.

FAQ

 Where's the Main method in my WPF application?

When you create a WPF Windows Application in Visual Studio, the generated project has no Main method, yet it still runs as expected! In fact, even attempting to add a Main method gives a compilation error telling you that it is already defined.

Application is special-cased when it is compiled from XAML, because Visual Studio assigns the XAML file a Build Action of ApplicationDefinition. This causes a Main method to be autogenerated. For the Photo Gallery application, this entry point can be found inside App.g.cs:

```
[System.STAThreadAttribute()]
public static void Main() {
  PhotoGallery.App app = new PhotoGallery.App();
  app.InitializeComponent();
  app.Run();
}
```

The App.g.cs file is hidden by Visual Studio unless you select Show All Files in the Solution Explorer.

FAQ

 How do I retrieve command-line arguments in my WPF application?

Command-line arguments are typically retrieved via a string array parameter passed to `Main`, but the common way to define WPF applications doesn't allow you to implement the `Main` method. You can get around this in two different ways. One way is to forego defining an `Application`-derived class in XAML, so you can manually define the `Main` method with a string array parameter. The easier way, however, is to simply call `System.Environment.GetCommandLineArgs` at any point in your application, which returns the same string array you'd get inside `Main`.

Other Uses for `Application`

The `Application` class is more than a simple entry point and message dispatcher. It contains a handful of events, properties, and methods for managing common application-level tasks. The events, which are typically handled by overriding the `OnEventName` methods in an `Application`-derived class (such as the Visual Studio–generated `App` class), include `Startup` and `Exit`, `Activated` and `Deactivated` (which behave like `Window`'s events of the same name but apply to any of `Application`'s `Window`s), and even `SessionEnding`, a cancellable event that occurs when the user logs off or shuts down their computer. The data passed with this event tells you whether it was raised due to logging off or shutting down, via a `ReasonSessionEnding` enumeration.

Because applications often have multiple windows, `Application` defines a read-only `Windows` collection to give you access to all open `Window`s. The initial `Window` is given a special designation, and can be accessed via the `MainWindow` property. This property is read/write, however, so you can give any window the special designation at any time.

By default, `Application` exits (that is, the `Run` method finally returns) when all `Window`s have been closed. But this behavior can be modified by setting the `ShutdownMode` property to various values

WARNING

Don't rely on fixed indices in the `Windows` collection!

Windows are added to `Application`. Windows in the order they are initially shown, and they are removed from the collection when they are closed. Therefore, the index of a given `Window` inside the collection can change over the lifetime of an application. You should not assume that `Windows[2]`, for example, is always going to reference the same `Window`!

of the `ShutdownMode` enumeration. For example, you can make `Application` exit when the main `Window` (designated by the `MainWindow` property) exits, regardless of the state of other `Window`s. Or, you could make `Application` continue to run until its `Shutdown` method is explicitly called, even if all `Window`s have been closed. This behavior is handy for applications that want to "minimize" to the Windows notification area (done by programs such as Skype and Windows Live Messenger).

One very handy property on the `Application` class is the `Properties` collection. `Properties`, much like application state or session state in ASP.NET, is a dictionary for conveniently storing data (as key/value pairs) that can easily be shared among `Windows` or other objects. Rather than defining public fields or properties on your `Application`-derived class, you might want to simply store such data in the `Properties` collection. For example, Photo Gallery stores the filename of the currently selected photo in `Properties` as follows:

```
myApplication.Properties["CurrentPhotoFilename"] = filename;
```

and retrieves it as follows:

```
string filename = myApplication.Properties["CurrentPhotoFilename"] as string;
```

Note that both the key and value are of type `Object`, so they are not constrained to be strings.

TIP

Application-level tasks are usually performed from code within `Windows`, requiring various `Windows` in your application to obtain a reference to the current `Application` instance. Fortunately, you can easily get access to this instance with the static `Application.Current` property. So the `myApplication` variable in the preceding code snippets can be replaced with `Application.Current`. For example:

```
Application.Current.Properties["CurrentPhotoFilename"] = filename;
```

FAQ

 How can I create an MDI (Multiple Document Interface) application using WPF?

The WPF classes don't have built-in support for creating MDI user interfaces, but Windows Forms classes do. Therefore, you can use the interoperability techniques discussed in Chapter 15 to get MDI in a WPF application. That said, you might want to consider an alternative arrangement for your user interface. For example, WPF has built-in support for creating a tabbed interface, which is really just this decade's version of MDI. But MDI and tabbed interfaces tend to feel limiting on multimonitor systems or when using features such as Windows Flip 3D.

FAQ

 How can I create a single-instance application using WPF?

The classic approach to implementing single-instance behavior still applies to WPF applications: Use a named (and, therefore, OS-wide) mutex. The following code shows how you can do this in C#:

```
bool mutexIsNew;
using (System.Threading.Mutex m =
  new System.Threading.Mutex(true, uniqueName, out mutexIsNew))
{
  if (mutexIsNew)
    // This is the first instance. Run the application.
  else
    // There is already an instance running. Exit!
}
```

Just be sure that *uniqueName* won't be chosen by other applications! It's common to generate a globally unique identifier (GUID) at development time and use that as your identifier. Of course, nothing prevents a malicious application from creating a semaphore with the same name to prevent such an application from running!

DIGGING DEEPER

Creating an Application Without `Application`

Although using an `Application` object is the recommended way to structure a WPF application, it's not an absolute requirement. Showing `Windows` without `Application` is easy, but you need to at least handle message dispatching to avoid the "instant exit" problem described in the beginning of this section.

This can be done using Win32 techniques, but WPF also defines a low-level `Dispatcher` class in the `System.Windows.Threading` namespace that enables you to perform dispatching without resorting to calling Win32 APIs.

For example, your `Main` method could call `Dispatcher.Run` rather than `Application.Run` after showing your main `Window`. (In fact, `Application.Run` internally calls `Dispatcher.Run` to get the message dispatching functionality!) But such an application still lacks other important application-management functionality. For example, `Dispatcher.Run` never returns unless you explicitly call `Dispatcher.ExitAllFrames` somewhere (such as in a handler for the main `Window`'s `Closed` event).

DIGGING DEEPER

Multithreaded Applications

A typical WPF application has a single UI thread and a render thread. (The render thread is an implementation detail that is never directly exposed to developers. It runs in the background and handles low-level tasks such as composition.) You can spawn additional threads to perform background work, but you must not directly communicate with any DispatcherObject-derived objects created on the UI thread from such threads. (There are some exceptions to this, such as a Freezable object that has been frozen.)

Fortunately, WPF makes it easy for an arbitrary thread to schedule code to be run on the UI thread. DispatcherObject defines a Dispatcher property (of type Dispatcher) containing several overloads of Invoke (a synchronous call) and BeginInvoke (an asynchronous call). These methods enable you to pass a delegate to be invoked on the dispatcher's corresponding UI thread. All overloads of Invoke and BeginInvoke require a DispatcherPriority enumeration value. DispatcherPriority defines ten active priorities, ranging from the highest-priority Send (meaning execute immediately) to the lowest-priority SystemIdle (meaning execute only when the dispatcher's queue is otherwise empty).

You can even give your application multiple UI threads by calling Dispatcher.Run in any new thread that you spawn. Therefore, you could make each Window run on a separate thread if your application has more than one top-level Window. Doing this is certainly not necessary for most applications, but such a scheme could improve your application's responsiveness if it's likely that one Window could start activities that would dominate the thread. The Application abstraction starts to break down in this case, however, because it is tied to a single Dispatcher. For example, the Application.Windows collection only contains Window instances created on the same thread as the Application.

Creating and Showing Dialogs

Windows provides a set of common *dialogs* (modal subwindows) that you can leverage to handle common tasks such as opening/saving files, browsing folders, choosing fonts or colors, and printing. You can also create your own custom dialogs with the same modal behavior. (In other words, the dialog doesn't let you return to the current Window until you've dismissed it.)

Common Dialogs

WPF provides built-in exposure to a few of the common dialogs with classes that expose their functionality in a handful of straightforward methods and properties. Note that WPF does not natively render these dialogs; it internally calls Win32 APIs to show them and communicate with them. This is good, however, because it means that the dialogs remain consistent with the version of the operating system on which your application is running.

> **TIP**
>
> Both Windows Forms and WPF define managed classes that wrap Windows common dialogs. But in the current version of WPF, not all of the dialogs have corresponding classes in the WPF assemblies. (Windows Forms has `ColorDialog`, `FontDialog`, and `FolderBrowser`, whereas WPF does not.) Therefore, the easiest way to use these omitted dialogs is to reference `System.Windows.Forms.dll` and use the managed classes defined by Windows Forms.

Using a built-in common dialog is often just a matter of instantiating it, calling its `ShowDialog` method, and then processing the result. For example, Photo Gallery uses `PrintDialog` to print photos as follows:

```
void printMenu_Click(object sender, RoutedEventArgs e)
{
  string filename = (pictureBox.SelectedItem as ListBoxItem).Tag as string;
  Image image = new Image();
  image.Source = new BitmapImage(new Uri(filename, UriKind.RelativeOrAbsolute));

  PrintDialog pd = new PrintDialog();
  if (pd.ShowDialog() == true) // Result could be true, false, or null
    pd.PrintVisual(image, Path.GetFileName(filename) + " from Photo Gallery");
}
```

> **TIP**
>
> Using `PrintDialog` is the easiest way to print from a WPF application. But for advanced printing functionality, check out the `XpsDocumentWriter` class in the `System.Windows.Xps` namespace.

Custom Dialogs

Applications often show their own custom dialogs, such as the Rename Photo dialog used by Photo Gallery, pictured in Figure 7.2.

FIGURE 7.2   A custom dialog enables the user to rename a photo.

In WPF, creating and using such a dialog is almost the same as creating and using a `Window`. In fact, such dialogs *are* just `Windows`, typically with a little extra handling for returning what's known as a *dialog result*.

To show a `Window` as a modal dialog rather than a modeless window, simply call its `ShowDialog` method instead of `Show`. Unlike `Show`, `ShowDialog` is a blocking call (so it doesn't exit until the `Window` is closed) and it returns a nullable Boolean (`bool?` in C#). Here is how Photo Gallery consumes its custom `RenameDialog`:

```
void renameMenu_Click(object sender, RoutedEventArgs e)
{
  string filename = (pictureBox.SelectedItem as ListBoxItem).Tag as string;
  RenameDialog dialog = new RenameDialog(
    Path.GetFileNameWithoutExtension(filename));
  if (dialog.ShowDialog() == true) // Result could be true, false, or null
  {
    // Attempt to rename the file
    try
    {
      File.Move(filename, Path.Combine(Path.GetDirectoryName(filename),
        dialog.NewFilename) + Path.GetExtension(filename));
    }
    catch (Exception ex)
    {
      MessageBox.Show(ex.Message, "Cannot Rename File", MessageBoxButton.OK,
        MessageBoxImage.Error);
    }
  }
}
```

When you develop a `Window` that you know will be used as a dialog (such as `RenameDialog`), you typically want the `ShowDialog` method to return `true` if the action enabled by a dialog is successful, or `false` if it is unsuccessful or canceled. To control what gets returned by this method, simply set `Window`'s `DialogResult` property (of type `bool?`) to the desired value. Setting `DialogResult` implicitly closes the `Window`. Therefore, `RenameDialog`'s OK button could have an event handler like the following:

```
void okButton_Click(object sender, RoutedEventArgs e)
{
  this.DialogResult = true;
}
```

Or it could simply have its `IsDefault` property set to `true`, which accomplishes the same behavior without any procedural code.

> **DIGGING DEEPER**
>
> **Another Use for ShowDialog**
>
> To get its blocking behavior while still allowing message dispatching, Window's ShowDialog method effectively calls Dispatcher.Run just like Application.Run does. So, the following trick could be used to properly launch a WPF Window without using the Application class:
>
> ```
> [STAThread]
> public static void Main()
> {
>   MainWindow window = new MainWindow();
>   window.ShowDialog();
> }
> ```

Persisting and Restoring Application State

A standard Windows application can have full access to the computer (depending on user security settings), so there are many options for storing data, such as using the Windows Registry or the local file system. But an attractive alternative to these classic approaches is to use the .NET Framework's *isolated storage* technology. Besides being easy to use, it works in all environments in which managed code can run.

Photo Gallery uses the following code to persist and retrieve the user's favorites data to/from isolated storage:

LISTING 7.2   Portions of MainWindow.xaml.cs Related to Isolated Storage

```
protected override void OnClosed(EventArgs e)
{
  base.OnClosed(e);


  // Write each favorites item when the application is about to close
  IsolatedStorageFile f = IsolatedStorageFile.GetUserStoreForAssembly();
  using (IsolatedStorageFileStream stream =
    new IsolatedStorageFileStream("myFile", FileMode.Create, f))
  using (StreamWriter writer = new StreamWriter(stream))
  {
    foreach (TreeViewItem item in favoritesItem.Items)
      writer.WriteLine(item.Tag as string);
  }
}


protected override void OnInitialized(EventArgs e)
{
  base.OnInitialized(e);
```

LISTING 7.2   Continued

```csharp
// Read each favorites item when the application is initialized
IsolatedStorageFile f = IsolatedStorageFile.GetUserStoreForAssembly();
using (IsolatedStorageFileStream stream =
  new IsolatedStorageFileStream("myFile", FileMode.OpenOrCreate, f))
using (StreamReader reader = new StreamReader(stream))
{
  string line = reader.ReadLine();
  while (line != null)
  {
    AddFavorite(line);
    line = reader.ReadLine();
  }
}
…
}
```

The `IsolatedStorageFile` and `IsolatedStorageFileStream` classes are in the `System.IO.IsolatedStorage` namespace. All data stored in isolated storage is physically located in a hidden folder under the current user's Documents folder.

TIP

For an even simpler way to persist and retrieve application settings, check out the Visual Studio–generated `Settings` class (under `Properties\Settings.settings`). This mechanism stores data in an application configuration file and provides strongly typed access on top of it.

Deployment: ClickOnce Versus Windows Installer

When you think of deploying standard Windows applications, you probably think of a setup program that places the relevant files in the Program Files directory (or a user-chosen directory), registers the necessary components, adds itself to the installed programs list under Control Panel, and perhaps adds Start menu or desktop shortcuts. You can do all of these things with a WPF application by using Windows Installer technology. Visual Studio contains several "Setup and Deployment" project types for doing just that.

ClickOnce, however, is a more recent and simpler installation technology (introduced with the .NET Framework 2.0). It's an attractive option for installations that don't need the full power of Windows Installer. Visual Studio exposes ClickOnce functionality via a wizard accessed from the Build, Publish menu. If you don't have Visual Studio, the Windows SDK has two tools for using ClickOnce: `mage.exe` is a command-line version and `mageUI.exe` is a graphical version.

In short, Windows Installer has the following benefits over ClickOnce:

▶ Supports customized setup user interface, such as showing an end user license agreement (EULA)

▶ Can give control over where the files are installed

▶ Supports arbitrary code at setup time via custom actions

▶ Supports installing shared assemblies in the Global Assembly Cache

▶ Supports registration of COM components and file associations

▶ Supports machine-wide installation (that is, the program is available for all users)

▶ Supports offline installation from a CD/DVD

ClickOnce has the following benefits over Windows Installer:

▶ Contains built-in support for automatic updates and rolling back to previous versions.

▶ Provides two installation models: a weblike experience where the application is addressed via a URL in a web browser and appears to "go away" when it is closed (although it is still cached for future use), or a more traditional experience where the application can have a Start menu shortcut and show up in Control Panel's list of installed programs.

▶ Guarantees that installation doesn't affect other applications because all files are placed in an isolated area and no custom registration can be done.

▶ Practically guarantees a clean uninstallation because no custom code could be run during installation. (Full-trust applications still have the power to leave artifacts on the computer while they run.)

▶ Integrates with .NET code access security, enabling users to run applications without having to trust them completely.

> **TIP**
>
> Many people don't realize that ClickOnce can still be used even if your application contains unmanaged code, as long as the main executable isn't entirely unmanaged. You might need to alter some aspects of the unmanaged code, however. For example, if COM objects are registered, you would need to set up registration-free COM instead.

Navigation-Based Windows Applications

Although the concept of navigation is usually associated with web browsers, many Windows applications implement some sort of navigation scheme: Windows Explorer, Windows Media Player, Microsoft Money, and, of course, the Windows Photo Gallery application that this chapter's Photo Gallery application is based on.

The first version of Photo Gallery, represented in Figure 7.1, has hand-crafted and primitive navigation functionality for traversing photos and returning to the main gallery screen. It turns out, however, that WPF has a lot of built-in infrastructure for adding rich navigation to an application with minimal effort. With these features, it becomes trivial to implement an application that can browse and navigate content like a web browser.

Although the title of this section makes it sound like the choice of using navigation impacts the design of your entire application, the truth is that navigation support can be integrated into an otherwise-traditional application as little or as much as you want. And even if you don't want to expose a browser-style user interface, you can still use the navigation support to structure your application more like you would structure a website. For example, you can organize various pieces of UI in separate pages identifiable via URIs, and use hyperlinks to navigate from one to another. Or you can just use navigation simply for a small chunk of an application or component, such as a wizard.

This section examines these features and highlights some of the changes made to the "standard" version of Photo Gallery to leverage them. Adding navigation to a WPF application doesn't change the discussions in the previous section about deployment, persisting data, and so on. Instead, it involves becoming familiar with a few additional elements, such as `NavigationWindow` and `Page`.

Pages and Their Navigation Containers

When using navigation in WPF, content is typically organized in `Page` elements. (`Page` is basically a simpler version of the `Window` class.) `Page`s can then be hosted in one of two built-in navigation containers: `NavigationWindow` or `Frame`. These containers provide a way to navigate from one page to another, a "journal" that keeps track of navigation history, and a series of navigation-related events.

FAQ

? **What's the difference between `NavigationWindow` and `Frame`?**

They have almost identical functionality, except that `NavigationWindow` functions more like a top-level browser whereas `Frame` functions more like an HTML FRAME or IFRAME. Whereas `NavigationWindow` is a top-level window, `Frame` can fill an arbitrary (but rectangular) region of its parent element. `Frame`s can be nested inside a `NavigationWindow` or inside other `Frame`s. By default, `NavigationWindow` has a bar along the top with Back/Forward buttons and `Frame` does not, but you can add or remove this bar on either element by setting the `ShowsNavigationUI` property on the `Page` it contains. In addition, `NavigationWindow` has a `ShowsNavigationUI` property and `Frame` has a `NavigationUIVisibility` property for enabling or disabling this bar regardless of `Page` settings.

The navigation-enabled version of Photo Gallery changes the `Application`'s `StartupUri` to point to the following `NavigationWindow`:

```
<NavigationWindow x:Class="PhotoGallery.Container"
  xmlns="http://schemas.microsoft.com/winfx/2006/xaml/presentation"
  xmlns:x="http://schemas.microsoft.com/winfx/2006/xaml"
  Title="Photo Gallery" Source="MainPage.xaml">
</NavigationWindow>
```

The `MainPage.xaml` referenced by the `NavigationWindow` has a `Page` root that contains all the content that the original `MainWindow.xaml` previously had:

```
<Page x:Class="PhotoGallery.MainPage"
  xmlns="http://schemas.microsoft.com/winfx/2006/xaml/presentation"
  xmlns:x="http://schemas.microsoft.com/winfx/2006/xaml"
  Title="Photo Gallery" Loaded="Page_Loaded">
  …Application-specific content…
</Page>
```

Similarly, the code-behind in `MainPage.xaml.cs` corresponds to the code-behind that was previously in `MainWindow.xaml.cs`. The main code difference in `MainPage.xaml.cs` is that the `OnClosing` and `OnClosed` logic has been moved back to the `Window` level because `Pages` don't have these methods (nor would it be appropriate to invoke them every time the `Page` goes away).

As seen in Figure 7.3, this introduction of `NavigationWindow` and `Page` into Photo Gallery doesn't appear to give us much—just a new bar at the top of the window with (disabled) Back and Forward buttons. But it also sets up the application to navigate to other content within the same container, which is covered next.

FIGURE 7.3   When Photo Gallery is hosted in a `NavigationWindow`, an extra bar appears at the top.

A Page can interact with its navigation container by using the NavigationService class, which exposes relevant functionality regardless of whether the container is a NavigationWindow or a Frame. You can get an instance of NavigationService by calling the static NavigationService. GetNavigationService method and passing the instance of the Page. But

> **TIP**
>
> WPF's navigation containers can hold more than Pages; they can also hold HTML files (from the file system or from the Internet)! You can even navigate back and forth between WPF content and HTML content using techniques described in the next section.

even easier than that, you can simply use Page's NavigationService property. For example, you can set a title that is used in the drop-down menu associated with the Back and Forward buttons as follows:

```
this.NavigationService.Title = "Main Photo Gallery Page";
```

Or you could refresh the current Page as follows:

```
this.NavigationService.Refresh();
```

But Page also contains a few of its own properties that control the behavior of the parent container, such as WindowHeight, WindowWidth, and WindowTitle. These are handy because you can easily set them within the XAML for the Page.

Navigating from Page to Page

The purpose of using navigation is to progress from one page to another, whether in a predetermined linear sequence (like a simple wizard), a user-driven path through a hierarchy (like most websites), or a dynamically generated path.

You can perform navigation in three main ways:

- ▶ Calling the Navigate method
- ▶ Using Hyperlinks
- ▶ Using the journal

Calling the Navigate Method

Navigation containers support a Navigate method that enables the current page to be changed. You can call Navigate with an instance of the target page or a URI that points to it:

```
// Navigate to a page instance
PhotoPage nextPage = new PhotoPage();
this.NavigationService.Navigate(nextPage);
// Or navigate to a page via a URI
this.NavigationService.Navigate(new Uri("PhotoPage.xaml", UriKind.Relative));
```

The Page specified by a URI could be a loose XAML file or a compiled resource. (The next chapter explains how such URIs work in WPF.) The root element of this XAML file must be a Page.

If you want to navigate to an HTML page, you must use the overload of Navigate that accepts a URI. For example:

```
this.NavigationService.Navigate(new Uri("http://www.adamnathan.net/wpf"));
```

DIGGING DEEPER

Navigate Exposed as Two Properties

Navigation containers also have two properties that behave identically to these two overloads of the Navigate method. You can navigate to a Page instance by setting the Content property:

```
this.NavigationService.Content = nextPage;
```

or navigate via a URI by setting the Source property:

```
this.NavigationService.Source = new Uri("PhotoPage.xaml", UriKind.Relative);
```

Other than their ability to be set declaratively, there's no reason to use these properties instead of the Navigate method.

Using Hyperlinks

For simple navigation schemes, WPF provides a Hyperlink element that acts much like hyperlinks in HTML. You can embed Hyperlinks inside a TextBlock element and, like the HTML AREA (or A) tag, the content is automatically rendered as a clickable hyperlink that navigates the current page to the desired target page. This target page is specified via Hyperlink's NavigateUri property (the analog to the href attribute in HTML). For example, this XAML:

```
<TextBlock>
Click <Hyperlink NavigateUri="PhotoPage.xaml">here</Hyperlink> to view the photo.
</TextBlock>
```

gets rendered as shown in Figure 7.4.

Click here to view the photo.

Hyperlink, therefore, is really just a more-wordy version of the HTML A tag. Although it can be used programmatically like any other WPF element, its

FIGURE 7.4   A rendered Hyperlink looks like an HTML hyperlink.

purpose is for simple HTML-like links where the target page is known in advance.

FAQ

 How can I have a link in an HTML page that navigates to a WPF `Page`?

Hyperlinks in HTML work automatically, but there's no way to give an HREF value that points to a compiled WPF `Page`. Instead, you can use the technique similar to the previous tip to achieve HTML-to-WPF navigation: Use a sentinel value as the HREF value, listen to the `Navigating` event, and then dynamically change the target by calling `Navigate` yourself. `Navigating` and other events are examined in the next section. Depending on the nature of the desired HTML and WPF interaction, you might also want to consider creating a XAML Browser Application or a loose XAML page. These are discussed at the end of this chapter.

TIP

Hyperlinks support more complex functionality, similar to HTML hyperlinks. For example, to navigate a single `Frame` in the presence of multiple `Frame`s, set `Hyperlink`'s `TargetName` property to the name of the desired `Frame`. To navigate to a section of a `Page` (like using # anchors in HTML), simply append a # and a name to the URI. The name can be the name of any element on the target page.

TIP

If you want to combine the flexibility of programmatic navigation with the convenience of `Hyperlink`'s automatic text formatting, you can use a `Hyperlink` with a dummy `NavigateUri` value, then handle `Hyperlink`'s `Click` event and call `Navigate` however you desire inside this handler.

Using the Journal

Both navigation containers have a *journal* that records navigation history, just like a web browser. This journal provides the logic behind the Back and Forward buttons shown in Figure 7.3. Internally, it maintains two stacks—a back stack and a forward stack—and uses them as shown in Table 7.1.

TABLE 7.1   Navigation Effects on the Journal

Action	Result
Back	Pushes the current page onto the forward stack, pops a page off the back stack, and navigates to it
Forward	Pushes the current page onto the back stack, pops a page off the forward stack, and navigates to it
Any other navigation	Pushes the current page onto the back stack and empties the forward stack

The Back and Forward actions can be initiated by the user, or invoked programmatically by calling the navigation container's GoBack and GoForward methods (after calling CanGoBack or CanGoForward to avoid an exception by trying to pop an empty stack).

NavigationWindow always has a journal, but Frame might not have its own journal, depending on the value of its JournalOwnership property. It has the following settings:

▶ **OwnsJournal**—The Frame has its own journal.

▶ **UsesParentJournal**—The history is stored in the parent container's journal, or not at all if the parent doesn't have a journal.

▶ **Automatic** (the default value)—Equivalent to UsesParentJournal if the Frame is hosted in either of the two navigation containers (NavigationWindow or Frame), or OwnsJournal otherwise.

When Frame gets its own journal, it also gets the built-in navigation buttons. But if you don't want them, you can set NavigationUIVisibility to Hidden.

TIP

When navigating to a Page via a URI (whether done by calling the Navigate method or by using a Hyperlink), a new instance of the Page is created, even if you've already visited it. Therefore, you need to maintain your own state (via static variables or Application.Properties, for example) if you want a page to "remember" its data. (When calling an overload of Navigate that accepts a Page instance, of course, you're in control of whether a new or old instance is used.)

In the case of journal navigation, however, you can force a Page to reuse the same instance by setting its JournalEntry.KeepAlive attached property to true.

FAQ

 Web browser-like Back and Forward actions are handled by the journal, but how do I implement Stop and Refresh?

There's no built-in UI for Stop and Refresh buttons, but navigation containers do have ways to easily accomplish these actions.

To stop a pending navigation at any time, you can call the navigation container's StopLoading method.

To refresh a page, simply call the navigation container's parameterless Refresh method. This acts identically to calling Navigate with the URI or instance for the current page, except that the data passed to the Navigating event contains the NavigationMode.Refresh value, in case any event handlers want to customize their behavior in this situation.

TIP

Pages can opt out of the journal by setting their `RemoveFromJournal` property to `true`. This can be appropriate for pages representing a sequence of steps that shouldn't be randomly visited after the transaction is complete.

DIGGING DEEPER

Using the Journal for Purposes Other Than Navigation

You can add custom entries to the journal that have nothing to do with built-in navigation. For example, you could build an application-specific undo/redo scheme on top of the journal and get most of the functionality for free.

To do this, call the navigation container's `AddBackEntry` method with an instance of a `CustomContentState` object. `CustomContentState` is an abstract class, so you must create a derived class that implements a method called `Replay`. `Replay` is called whenever going back or forward makes the action the current state. You can optionally override the `JournalEntryName` property to give the entry a label in the drop-down list.

Photo Gallery uses this to implement a simple undoable image rotation as follows:

```csharp
[Serializable]
class RotateState : CustomContentState
{
  FrameworkElement element;
  double rotation;

  public RotateState(FrameworkElement element, double rotation)
  {
    this.element = element;
    this.rotation = rotation;
  }
  public override string JournalEntryName
  {
    get { return "Rotate " + rotation + "°"; }
  }

  public override void Replay(NavigationService navigationService, NavigationMode
mode)
  {
    // Rotate the element by the specified amount
    element.LayoutTransform = new RotateTransform(rotation);
  }
}
```

Navigation Events

Regardless of whether navigation occurs via Navigate, Hyperlinks, or the journal, it is performed asynchronously. A number of events are raised during the navigation process that enable you to display rich UI or even cancel the navigation.

Figures 7.5 and 7.6 show the progression of navigation-related events when the first page is loaded, and when navigation occurs from one page to another.

NavigationProgress is raised periodically until Navigated is raised. One event that isn't shown is NavigationStopped. This gets raised instead of LoadCompleted if the navigation is canceled or if an error occurs.

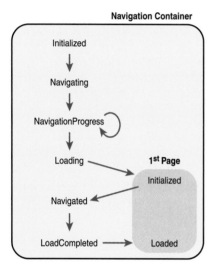

FIGURE 7.5   Navigation events that are raised when the first page is loaded.

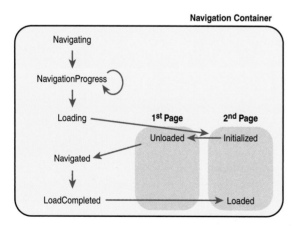

FIGURE 7.6   Navigation events that are raised when navigation occurs between two pages.

> **TIP**
>
> A navigation container raises the events shown in Figures 7.5 and 7.6 when navigation occurs within itself (including child containers). But `Application` also defines these events, enabling you to handle them in one place for all navigation containers within the `Application`.

> **WARNING**
>
> **Navigation events aren't raised when navigating from one HTML page to another!**
>
> The WPF navigation events are raised when navigating from one WPF `Page` to another, from a WPF `Page` to an HTML page, and from an HTML page to a WPF `Page`. In the current version of WPF, however, these events are not raised when navigating from one HTML page to another HTML page. Such HTML-to-HTML navigation also doesn't appear in the journal.

Passing Data Between Pages

When an application employs navigation for more than just document browsing, it likely needs to pass data from one page to another. HTML-based web applications might encode such data as URL parameters, or use server-side variables. In WPF, you can use a variety of techniques for sending or returning data.

Sending Data to Pages

WPF supports a scheme similar to URL parameters via overloads of the `Navigate` method that accept an extra object parameter. There's an overload for the version that accepts a `Page` instance and an overload for the version that accepts a `Uri`. You can pass anything you want via this object parameter (a simple data type, an array, a custom data structure, and so on), and it is sent to the target page. For example:

```
int photoId = 10;
// Navigate to a page instance
PhotoPage nextPage = new PhotoPage();
this.NavigationService.Navigate(nextPage, photoId);
// Or navigate to a page via a URI
this.NavigationService.Navigate(
  new Uri("PhotoPage.xaml", UriKind.Relative), photoId);
```

For the target page to receive this data, it must handle the navigation container's `LoadCompleted` event and check the `ExtraData` parameter of the event argument:

```
this.NavigationService.LoadCompleted += new
LoadCompletedEventHandler(container_LoadCompleted);
...
```

```
void container_LoadCompleted(object sender, NavigationEventArgs e)
{
  if (e.ExtraData != null)
    LoadPhoto((int) e.ExtraData);
}
```

A simpler scheme of passing data, however, is to use the simpler version of Navigate that accepts a Page instance, and define a constructor on the target page that accepts the custom data (using as many parameters as you want). This looks like the following for the Photo Gallery example:

```
int photoId = 10;
// Navigate to a page instance
PhotoPage nextPage = new PhotoPage(photoId);
this.NavigationService.Navigate(nextPage);
```

For this to work, PhotoPage has a constructor defined as follows:

```
public PhotoPage(int id)
{
  LoadPhoto(id);
}
```

An advantage of this approach is that the parameters can be strongly typed, so PhotoPage doesn't need to check that the passed-in data is nonnull or an integer. The type system guarantees it!

A third approach is to globally share the data in the Application object's Properties collection discussed earlier in the chapter. For example:

```
// Navigate to a page by instance or URI
Application.Properties["PhotoId"] = 10;
this.NavigationService.Navigate(…);
```

The target page can then check the value from anywhere in code that gets executed after Navigate is called:

```
  if (Application.Properties["PhotoId"] != null)
    LoadPhoto((int)Application.Properties["PhotoId"]);
```

This might be the desired approach if you want to share the data between multiple pages (rather than explicitly passing it from page to page). However, just like the first scheme, it lacks the convenience of type safety.

Returning Data from Pages with a PageFunction

Perhaps you want the user to navigate to a page, take some action, and then automatically return to a previous page that can act on the action (and, therefore, must receive data from the latter page). A classic example for this is a "settings" or "options" page.

You could simulate this behavior by navigating forward to the old page and passing the data using the first two of the three schemes just discussed. This process is illustrated in Figure 7.7.

FIGURE 7.7   Simulating the return of data by navigating forward to the page on the back stack.

This can be awkward, however. If you're navigating via URI, you'd need to manually reconstruct the state of the new instance of MainPage to match the old instance. Furthermore, navigating forward to simulate the action of navigating back causes undesirable effects in the journal without manually manipulating it.

Instead, you could share the data globally (via Application.Properties) and have the target page call the navigation container's GoBack method to return to the previous page. This works, but is a bit sloppy because of the global (and typeless) sharing of data that might only be relevant to two pages rather than the entire application.

Therefore, WPF provides yet another mechanism to "return" data to the previous page in a type-safe manner and automatically navigate back to it, as illustrated in Figure 7.8.

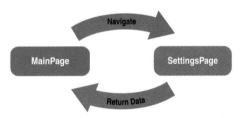

FIGURE 7.8   The commonsense navigation flow can be achieved with a PageFunction.

This can be accomplished with a funny-named class called PageFunction. A PageFunction is really just a Page (because it derives from Page) but it acts like a function because of its mechanism for returning data.

Visual Studio has a template for creating a new PageFunction just like it does for Page. Here's what you get when you add a PageFunction via Visual Studio's Add New Item dialog:

```
<PageFunction
    xmlns="http://schemas.microsoft.com/winfx/2006/xaml/presentation"
    xmlns:x="http://schemas.microsoft.com/winfx/2006/xaml"
    xmlns:sys="clr-namespace:System;assembly=mscorlib"
    x:Class="MyProject.PageFunction1"
    x:TypeArguments="sys:String"
    Title="PageFunction1">
  <Grid>
  </Grid>
</PageFunction>
```

Notice the use of the `TypeArguments` keyword. `PageFunction` is actually a generic class (as in `PageFunction<T>`), where the type argument represents the type of the return value. For the `PageFunction` shown, the returned value must be a string. Although the use of generics makes defining a `PageFunction` a little trickier, the benefit is the type safety that is lacking from some of the earlier schemes.

Because `PageFunction` derives from `Page`, you can navigate to it just like you would with any other page:

```
PageFunction1 nextPage = new PageFunction1<string>();
this.NavigationService.Navigate(nextPage);
```

To receive the return value, the source page must handle the `PageFunction`'s `Return` event:

```
nextPage.Return += new ReturnEventHandler<string>(nextPage_Return);
…
void nextPage_Return(object sender, ReturnEventArgs<string> e)
{
  string returnValue = e.Result;
}
```

Notice that the same generic argument also applies to the `ReturnEventHandler` and `ReturnEventArgs` types. This enables the event argument's `Result` property to be the same type as the data returned by the `PageFunction` (a string in this case).

The `PageFunction` can return data by wrapping it in the `ReturnEventArgs` type and calling `OnReturn`, which it inherits from the base `PageFunction` class:

```
OnReturn(new ReturnEventArgs<string>("the data"));
```

Applications with a Windows Vista Look and Feel

Windows Vista introduces many new features that aren't supported on prior operating systems. These features cover a number of areas—security, reliability, networking, data, and (most relevant for this book) user interface. What surprises many folks is that these new features are exposed via unmanaged APIs. This means that consuming such features in a WPF application can be tricky.

Some of the new UI features, such as the ability to create a "command link" button, are interesting for Win32-based UI frameworks, but not so interesting to WPF, as it's trivial to mimic such a button by nesting a panel with a few elements inside the normal `Button` element. Other features, such as using Aero Glass, are not as easy to mimic. And even if you did, it would be difficult to remain consistent with user preferences (for example, when a user tints their glass or adjusts the opacity) or with different visual styles that will undoubtedly accompany future versions of Windows.

This section looks at how to leverage two common features to make a WPF application feel more at home on Windows Vista:

▶ Task Dialogs

▶ Aero Glass

> **TIP**
>
> When using features that are new to Windows Vista, be sure to have a fallback plan so your application can still run on Windows XP or Windows Server 2003. .NET code can easily check the operating system version using `System.Environment.OSVersion`. For example:
>
> ```
> if (System.Environment.OSVersion.Version.Major >= 6)
>   // Windows Vista or later, so use TaskDialog
> else
>   // Earlier than Windows Vista, so just use MessageBox
> ```

Going Beyond `MessageBox` with `TaskDialog`

It's all too tempting for a developer to use `MessageBox` where it might be more appropriate to craft a custom dialog. But laziness is a fact of life, so Windows Vista introduces a new and improved `MessageBox`—called `TaskDialog`—that gives such developers better results and more flexibility. It matches Windows' new look and feel (which is the focus of this section) and even enables deep customization of the dialog with additional controls.

You can take advantage of this new functionality by calling a Win32 API called `TaskDialog`. If you're using Visual C++, you can call the API directly. But in a language like C# or Visual Basic, PInvoke (that is, using the `DllImport` attribute) enables you to call it. A PInvoke signature for `TaskDialog` and its associated types are shown in Listing 7.3.

LISTING 7.3   TaskDialog Signature and Types in C#
```csharp
[DllImport("comctl32.dll", PreserveSig=false, CharSet=CharSet.Unicode)]
static extern TaskDialogResult TaskDialog(IntPtr hwndParent, IntPtr hInstance,
  string title, string mainInstruction, string content,
  TaskDialogButtons buttons, TaskDialogIcon icon);

enum TaskDialogResult
{
  Ok=1,
  Cancel=2,
  Retry=4,
  Yes=6,
  No=7,
  Close=8
}
```

LISTING 7.3   Continued

```
[Flags]
enum TaskDialogButtons
{
  Ok = 0x0001,
  Yes = 0x0002,
  No = 0x0004,
  Cancel = 0x0008,
  Retry = 0x0010,
  Close = 0x0020
}
enum TaskDialogIcon
{
  Warning = 65535,
  Error = 65534,
  Information = 65533,
  Shield = 65532
}
```

Unlike MessageBox, the TaskDialog API enables you to specify a main instruction that is visually separated from the rest of the content. It also enables you to choose an arbitrary mix of buttons. Figures 7.9 and 7.10 illustrate the difference between MessageBox and TaskDialog, based on the following code:

```
// Using MessageBox
result = MessageBox.Show("Are you sure you want to delete '" + filename + "'?",
  "Delete Picture", MessageBoxButton.YesNo, MessageBoxImage.Warning);

// Using TaskDialog
result = TaskDialog(new System.Windows.Interop.WindowInteropHelper(this).Handle,
  IntPtr.Zero, "Delete Picture",
  "Are you sure you want to delete '" + filename + "'?",
  "This will delete the picture permanently, rather than sending it
    ➥to the Recycle Bin.",
  TaskDialogButtons.Yes | TaskDialogButtons.No, TaskDialogIcon.Warning);
```

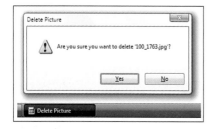

FIGURE 7.9   A MessageBox looks a little old-fashioned on Windows Vista.

FIGURE 7.10   A similar TaskDialog looks much more user-friendly, even in the taskbar!

WARNING

The use of `TaskDialog` requires version 6 of the Windows Common Controls DLL (`ComCtl32.dll`)!

Applications don't bind to this version by default for compatibility reasons. One way to bind to version 6 is to place a manifest file alongside your executable (named `YourAppName.exe.manifest`) with the following content:

```xml
<?xml version="1.0" encoding="UTF-8" standalone="yes"?>
<assembly xmlns="urn:schemas-microsoft-com:asm.v1" manifestVersion="1.0">
  <assemblyIdentity version="1.0.0.0"
      processorArchitecture="X86" name="YourAppName" type="win32" />
  <description>Your description</description>
  <dependency>
    <dependentAssembly>
      <assemblyIdentity
          type="win32" name="Microsoft.Windows.Common-Controls"
          version="6.0.0.0" processorArchitecture="X86"
          publicKeyToken="6595b64144ccf1df" language="*" />
    </dependentAssembly>
  </dependency>
</assembly>
```

This manifest can also be embedded as a Win32 resource inside your executable (with the name RT_MANIFEST and an ID of 1), if you don't want to have the extra standalone file.

If you fail to bind to this version, calling TaskDialog results in an EntryPointNotFoundException with the message, "Unable to find an entry point named 'TaskDialog' in DLL 'comctl32.dll'."

TIP

To customize the `TaskDialog` even further, you can use a more complicated `TaskDialogIndirect` API. The Windows SDK contains samples for using this and other Win32 features in .NET applications. You can also check http://www.pinvoke.net for PInvoke signatures and types for just about any popular Win32 API.

Using Aero Glass

Aero Glass is the blurry, transparent window chrome that can be extended into the client area. The easiest way to use it in a WPF application is to call the `DwmExtendFrameIntoClientArea` API. (The `Dwm` stands for Desktop Window Manager.) With this method, you can make the entire `Window` a sheet of glass (shown in Figure 7.11) or choose to extend the glass a specified amount from any of the `Window`'s four edges (shown in Figure 7.12). Either way, you can add WPF content on top of the glass just like you would if the `Window` background were a simple solid color.

FIGURE 7.11   A glass background for the entire Window.

FIGURE 7.12   Extending glass on the bottom of the Window only.

As with TaskDialog, PInvoke is the key to calling the Desktop Window Manager APIs from C#. Listing 7.4 contains PInvoke signatures and a simple reusable utility method that wraps the PInvoke calls.

LISTING 7.4   Using Glass in C#

```csharp
[StructLayout(LayoutKind.Sequential)]
public struct MARGINS
{
  public MARGINS(Thickness t)
  {
    Left = (int)t.Left;
    Right = (int)t.Right;
    Top = (int)t.Top;
    Bottom = (int)t.Bottom;
  }
  public int Left;
  public int Right;
  public int Top;
  public int Bottom;
}

public class GlassHelper
{
  [DllImport("dwmapi.dll", PreserveSig=false)]
  static extern void DwmExtendFrameIntoClientArea(
    IntPtr hWnd, ref MARGINS pMarInset);

  [DllImport("dwmapi.dll", PreserveSig=false)]
  static extern bool DwmIsCompositionEnabled();

  public static bool ExtendGlassFrame(Window window, Thickness margin)
  {
    if (!DwmIsCompositionEnabled())
      return false;

    IntPtr hwnd = new WindowInteropHelper(window).Handle;
    if (hwnd == IntPtr.Zero)
      throw new InvalidOperationException(
        "The Window must be shown before extending glass.");

    // Set the background to transparent from both the WPF and Win32 perspectives
    window.Background = Brushes.Transparent;
    HwndSource.FromHwnd(hwnd).CompositionTarget.BackgroundColor =
      Colors.Transparent;

    MARGINS margins = new MARGINS(margin);
    DwmExtendFrameIntoClientArea(hwnd, ref margins);
    return true;
  }
}
```

7

The `GlassHelper.ExtendGlassFrame` method accepts a `Window` and a familiar `Thickness` object for representing how much glass should be extended on all four edges. (To get the "sheet of glass" effect, you can pass `-1` for all four sides.) After checking that desktop composition is enabled (a prerequisite for glass), the code maps the `Thickness` object to the `MARGINS` type expected by `DwmExtendFrameIntoClientArea`, and calls this API with the appropriate `HWND`. The `Window`'s `Background` is also set to `Transparent` so the glass is able to show through. For more information about the techniques used here, consult Chapter 15.

Any WPF `Window` can use `GlassHelper.ExtendGlassFrame` as follows:

```
protected override void OnSourceInitialized(EventArgs e)
{
  base.OnSourceInitialized(e);
  // This can't be done any earlier than the SourceInitialized event:
  GlassHelper.ExtendGlassFrame(this, new Thickness(-1));

  // Attach a window procedure in order to detect later enabling of desktop
  // composition
  IntPtr hwnd = new WindowInteropHelper(this).Handle;
  HwndSource.FromHwnd(hwnd).AddHook(new HwndSourceHook(WndProc));
}

private IntPtr WndProc(IntPtr hwnd, int msg, IntPtr wParam, IntPtr lParam, ref bool
  handled)
{
  if (msg == WM_DWMCOMPOSITIONCHANGED)
  {
    // Reenable glass:
    GlassHelper.ExtendGlassFrame(this, new Thickness(-1));
    handled = true;
  }
  return IntPtr.Zero;
}

private const int WM_DWMCOMPOSITIONCHANGED = 0x031E;
```

The method must not only be called during initialization, but whenever desktop composition is disabled and then reenabled. This could happen because of explicit user action, or triggered from something like Remote Desktop. To be notified of changes to desktop composition, you need to intercept a Win32 message (`WM_DWMCOMPOSITIONCHANGED`). See Chapter 15 to get a better understanding of how the preceding code works.

Figure 7.13 shows Photo Gallery using the preceding code to enable a glass bar at the bottom of the `Window`.

FIGURE 7.13   A glass-enabled Photo Gallery.

Gadget-Style Applications

WPF makes it easier than ever to create nonrectangular top-level windows. With this support, you can give an otherwise-standard application custom chrome with a more fun shape. Or, you could create a smaller gadget-style application that looks like a custom object "floating" on the desktop.

To take advantage of this support, just do the following:

1. On your Window, set AllowsTransparency to true. (If you're doing this programmatically, it must be set before the Window has been shown. Otherwise, you'll get an InvalidOperationException.)

2. Set your Window's WindowStyle to None, which removes all the chrome. (Any other setting combined with AllowsTransparency="True" results in an InvalidOperationException.)

3. Set your Window's Background to Transparent. This prevents your content from being surrounded by an opaque rectangle.

4. Decide how you want the user to move your Window around and call Window's DragMove method at the appropriate place to enable it. Technically, this is not a requirement, but an application that can't be moved is not going to result in happy users!

5. Consider adding a custom Close Button so the user doesn't have to right-click the Windows taskbar in order to close your application. This is especially important if you set ShowInTaskbar to false!

Here is a XAML file for such a `Window`, which contains a translucent red circle and a Close Button:

```xml
<Window x:Class="GadgetWindow"
  xmlns="http://schemas.microsoft.com/winfx/2006/xaml/presentation"
  xmlns:x="http://schemas.microsoft.com/winfx/2006/xaml"
  Height="300" Width="300"
  AllowsTransparency="True" WindowStyle="None" Background="Transparent"
  MouseLeftButtonDown="Window_MouseLeftButtonDown">
  <Grid>
    <Ellipse Fill="Red" Opacity="0.5" Margin="20">
    <Ellipse.BitmapEffect>
      <DropShadowBitmapEffect/>
    </Ellipse.BitmapEffect>
    </Ellipse>
    <Button Margin="100" Click="Button_Click">Close</Button>
  </Grid>
</Window>
```

`DropShadowBitmapEffect`, covered in Chapter 11, "2D Graphics," is added to give the circle a bit more visual polish. This `Window` uses the following code-behind file:

```csharp
using System.Windows;
using System.Windows.Input;

public partial class GadgetWindow : Window
{
  public GadgetWindow()
  {
    InitializeComponent();
  }
  void Window_MouseLeftButtonDown(object sender, MouseButtonEventArgs e)
  {
    this.DragMove();
  }
  void Button_Click(object sender, RoutedEventArgs e)
  {
    this.Close();
  }
}
```

To enable the `Window` to be moved, the handler for `MouseLeftButtonDown` simply calls `Window.DragMove`. DragMove handles the rest of the logic automatically. Figure 7.14 shows this little application in action.

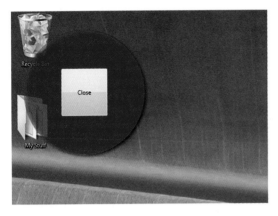

FIGURE 7.14   An invisible `Window` containing nonrectangular (and half-transparent) content.

XAML Browser Applications

This chapter started with a standard Windows application, and basically continued to add features to it to take fuller advantage of WPF or of the underlying operating system. These last two sections are actually about ways to repackage and *restrict* functionality for the sake of achieving broader and easier deployment.

WPF supports the creation of applications that run directly in a web browser. (So does Silverlight, but with less power and broader reach.) They are called XAML Browser Applications (XBAPs), and have a `.xbap` file extension.

The power of this WPF support is that the exact same programming model is used for a XAML Browser Application as for a standard Windows application. Therefore, creating an XBAP isn't much different than creating a standard Windows application. The main differences are as follows:

▶ Not all features in WPF or the .NET Framework are accessible (by default).

▶ Navigation is integrated into the browser (for Internet Explorer 7 or later).

▶ Deployment is handled differently.

FAQ

❓ Do XAML Browser Applications work on any operating system or in any web browser?

No. Just like full WPF applications, they require Windows and they require the .NET Framework 3.0 or later to be installed. And at the time of writing, they are only supported within Internet Explorer or any other browser that hosts the Microsoft `WebBrowser` ActiveX control. If you don't need all the power of WPF and want broader platform exposure, Silverlight is the best choice. (Especially considering that all the power of WPF isn't typically available in the browser anyway due to security restrictions!)

This section drills into these three aspects of XAML Browser Applications.

So how do you create a XAML Browser Application? If you have Visual Studio, you simply follow these steps:

1. Create a new XAML Browser Application project in Visual Studio.

2. Create your user interface inside of a Page and add the appropriate code-behind logic.

3. Compile and run your project, and watch it run inside Internet Explorer!

If you don't have Visual Studio, you can still use MSBuild on project files with the appropriate settings, described in the Digging Deeper sidebar.

DIGGING DEEPER

How XAML Browser Applications Work

There's nothing XBAP-specific about the source files generated by Visual Studio. The key is in a handful of settings in the project file, such as

```
<HostInBrowser>True</HostInBrowser>
<Install>False</Install>
<TargetZone>Internet</TargetZone>
```

plus a few settings to make the debugger launch PresentationHost.exe rather than the output of the compilation.

A standard executable is generated, but it does nothing if run directly because the infrastructure quits if it detects that it's not hosted in a web browser. In addition to the EXE, two XML files are generated:

▶ A .manifest file, which is a ClickOnce application manifest

▶ An .xbap file, which is simply a ClickOnce deployment manifest (typically seen with the .application extension for non-XBAPs)

And that's it. XBAPs are really just online-only ClickOnce applications, but with some special handling by WPF for the browser-integrated experience.

WARNING

Beware of ClickOnce caching!

XBAPs are based on ClickOnce technology, which has caching behavior that can be confusing during development. For maximum performance, ClickOnce applications are stored in a cache when first run. Subsequent requests to run the application go to the cache unless the application's version number changes. (As with isolated storage, the ClickOnce cache is implemented as a hidden folder under the current user's Documents folder.)

Continued

Therefore, if you make a change to your application, recompile it, and then run it, you won't see the result of your changes if you don't also change the version number! The default Visual Studio settings increment your version number each time you recompile (because of the `AssemblyVersion("1.0.*")` marking in the `AssemblyInfo` source file) so you won't encounter this issue unless you give your application a fixed version number.

If you find incrementing the version number on recompilation to be unacceptable, you can clear the cache at any time using the `mage.exe` tool in the Windows SDK. Just run `mage -cc` at a command prompt. Or, you can execute the following command without requiring the SDK to be installed:

```
rundll32 %windir%\system32\dfshim.dll CleanOnlineAppCache
```

Limited Feature Set

For simple enough WPF Windows applications, you can change a few project settings, recompile, and run it just fine as a XAML Browser Application. But that's usually not the case. The only thing that complicates developing a XAML Browser Application is that XBAPs run as partially trusted in the Internet zone, so not all APIs work in this context. For example, if you try to convert the standard Photo Gallery application to an XBAP, you'll quickly find that calls such as the following would throw a (very verbose) security exception:

```
// Whoops! Partially trusted code is not allowed to get this data!
AddFavorite(Environment.GetFolderPath(Environment.SpecialFolder.MyPictures));
```

The .NET Framework's code access security blocks the call because it requires `FileIOPermission`, which is not granted to the Internet zone by default. (Note that individual users could expand the set of allowed permissions in their Internet zone, but they would be crazy to do so because of the security risks.)

For most people, figuring out what works and what doesn't in the Internet zone is a process of trial and error. Some features don't work because of their inherently insecure nature: arbitrary access to the local file system or Registry, interoperability with unmanaged code, or launching new `Windows`. (You can use `Popup` elements, but they won't extend past the `Page`'s bounds.) But some other features that aren't allowed in the Internet zone aren't obvious because the restriction is a result of implementation details.

TIP

If you want to share the same code between a full-trust standard application and a partial-trust XBAP, it's helpful to be able to determine which state you're in at runtime so you can adapt to your environment. This can be done with the static `BrowserInteropHelper.IsBrowserHosted` Boolean property in the `System.Windows.Interop` namespace. In addition, Karen Corby from Microsoft has created a "Flexible Application Template" that enables you to easily switch a single Visual Studio project between producing a standard Windows application and an XBAP. She shares it at http://scorbs.com/2006/06/04/vs-template-flexible-application.

For example, you can't use bitmap effects (covered in Chapter 11) or use WCF to communicate with web services.

Despite the limitations, there is still a lot of functionality to take advantage of in the Internet zone. You still can display rich text and media, read/write to isolated storage (up to 512 KB), and open arbitrary files on the host web server. You can even launch the browser's standard File, Open dialog to interact with local files (with the user's explicit permission). This is done with `Microsoft.Win32.OpenFileDialog` as follows:

```
string fileContents = null;
OpenFileDialog ofd = new OpenFileDialog();
if (ofd.ShowDialog() == true) // Result could be true, false, or null
{
  using (Stream s = ofd.OpenFile())
  using (StreamReader sr = new StreamReader(s))
  {
    fileContents = sr.ReadToEnd();
  }
}
```

TIP

Another difference between a XAML Browser Application and a standard Windows application is the way in which parameters (or really, any external data) are passed in. One simple approach is to send URL parameters to the HTML page hosting an XBAP, and then have the XBAP call `BrowserInteropHelper.Source` to retrieve the complete URL (including parameters). Another approach is to store the information in a browser cookie and then retrieve the cookie using the `Application.GetCookie` method.

FAQ

 How do I enable my own components to run in the Internet zone?

You use the same mechanism that applies to all .NET components. If you mark an assembly with the `AllowPartiallyTrustedCallers` attribute and install it into the Global Assembly Cache (which can only be done if the user trusts your code and decides to run it), any of the assembly's public APIs can be called by any XBAP.

Note that marking an assembly with `AllowPartiallyTrustedCallers` should never be taken lightly. Any security bug or design flaw that makes it inappropriate for the Internet zone could open up your users to a severe security hole. And if that happens, they might never trust code from you again!

FAQ

 How do I create a full-trust XAML Browser Application?

If you want to take advantage of functionality that requires a higher level of trust yet still want to be integrated into a browser, you can indeed configure an XBAP to require full trust. The two actions to enable this are a bit convoluted, however:

1. In the ClickOnce application manifest (`app.manifest`), add `Unrestricted="true"` to the `PermissionSet` XML element. For example:

   ```
   <PermissionSet class="System.Security.PermissionSet" version="1"
    ID="Custom" SameSite="site" Unrestricted="true"/>
   ```

2. In the project file (with the `.csproj` or `.vbproj` extension), change

   ```
   <TargetZone>Internet</TargetZone>
   ```

   to

   ```
   <TargetZone>Custom</TargetZone>
   ```

You can also make this change inside Visual Studio's project properties UI on the Security tab.

After you do this, deploying and running your XBAP in the Local Computer zone should work just fine. It's also possible to run such a full-trust application in the Internet zone, but only if users list you (or more specifically, the certificate used to sign the manifest) as a trusted publisher.

Integrated Navigation

All `Pages` in XBAPs are implicitly hosted in a `NavigationWindow`. In Internet Explorer 6, you see the typical bar with Back and Forward buttons. This is usually not desirable because many XBAPs don't take advantage of navigation. And if they do, having separate Back/Forward buttons right below the browser's Back/Forward buttons is clumsy. To disable this unwanted navigation bar, set `ShowsNavigationUI` to `false` on your `Page`.

Fortunately, versions 7 and later of Internet Explorer merge the `NavigationWindow`'s journal with the browser's own journal, providing a much slicker experience. The separate navigation bar is not shown, and WPF journal entries automatically appear in the browser's Back/Forward list right along with web pages.

TIP

The journal integration in Internet Explorer 7 and later only applies to the top-level `Page`. If you host an XBAP in an HTML IFRAME, you'll still get the navigation bar unless you set `ShowsNavigationUI` to `false` on the WPF `Page`.

Deployment

Deploying an XBAP is as easy as deploying any other ClickOnce application. It's a matter of using Visual Studio's publishing wizard (or the Mage tool in the Windows SDK) and copying the files to a web server or file share. (The web server must also be configured to serve the content correctly.)

What's incredibly compelling about XBAPs is the fact that users install and run them simply by navigating to a URL. In addition, unlike other ClickOnce applications, no security prompts get in the way, assuming you didn't create an XBAP that needs nonstandard permissions. (So you don't even have to *click once* to view such an application!)

FAQ

 There are no security prompts when running an XBAP? Isn't that a huge security issue?

As with any software features, there is some risk of enabling a security breach just by being enabled. But with the multiple layers of security from Windows, Internet Explorer, and the .NET Framework, the WPF team is confident that users are safe from hackers that would try to use the XBAP mechanism to circumvent security. For example, the .NET Framework enforces a sandbox on top of the sandbox already enforced by Internet Explorer. And although this amount of security should be enough in theory, WPF goes one step further and removes additional OS-level privileges from the host process token (such as the ability to load device drivers), just in case all the other layers of security are somehow breached.

FAQ

 Why would you want to create a XAML Browser Application?

XBAPs are suited for relatively full-featured applications that happen to be hosted directly in a web browser. This direct hosting can be desirable for seamless navigation between HTML and WPF content, or simply for the lightweight feel conveyed by such an arrangement. Silverlight is likely to be the preferred approach over creating an XBAP (as it will have broader platform support) for simpler applications that don't require as much functionality.

If you want weblike deployment but don't care about having your application hosted directly in a web browser, you can simply create a standard Windows application rather than an XBAP, decide if you want to constrain it to run under partial trust, and deploy it using ClickOnce.

On the other hand, if your goal is to use WPF to create richer web pages (which tend not to require custom application logic), you should consider creating and deploying a loose XAML page, described in the "Loose XAML Pages" section.

> **TIP**
>
> XBAPs (and Silverlight applications) are the key to using WPF to create applications for diverse environments. For example, Windows Media Center, Windows Sidebar, and live.com enable developers to plug in HTML-based applications. By hosting an XBAP in an HTML page, you can create a WPF Media Center application or a WPF Microsoft Gadget simply by creating an appropriate XBAP!

Downloading Files on Demand

ClickOnce contains support for on-demand downloading of files in your application, so you can design a small application that loads quickly and then downloads additional content as-needed based on arbitrary logic. This support is a great remedy for large XBAPs that would otherwise be slow to load, although it can apply to other types of applications as well.

To take advantage of this support, you can assign a set of loose files in your project to a *download group* in Visual Studio. This functionality can be found under Publish, Application Files in the project's Properties page. You can then programmatically prompt the download and be notified when it completes by using a few APIs in the `System.Deployment.Application` namespace (in `System.Deployment.dll`).

Listing 7.5 demonstrates how this might be done for the simple idea of displaying a custom progress user interface while the application's main content loads. The application is assumed to start by loading `Page1`, whose code-behind file is the content of Listing 7.4. (The specific user interface presumed to be defined in XAML is irrelevant.) `Page1` initiates the download of any files assigned to a download group called "MyGroup," and then navigates to `Page2` (which presumably uses some of these downloaded files) once the download is complete.

LISTING 7.5   Using ClickOnce Support for On-Demand Download

```
using System;
using System.Windows.Controls;
using System.Windows.Threading;
using System.Deployment.Application;

public partial class Page1 : Page
{
  public Page1()
  {
    InitializeComponent();
  }

  protected override void OnInitialized(EventArgs e)
  {
    base.OnInitialized(e);
```

LISTING 7.5   Continued

```
   if (ApplicationDeployment.IsNetworkDeployed)
   {
     // Handle the event that is raised when the download of files
     // in MyGroup is complete.
     ApplicationDeployment.CurrentDeployment.DownloadFileGroupCompleted +=
     delegate {
       // We're on a different thread, so invoke GotoPage2 on the UI thread
       Dispatcher.BeginInvoke(DispatcherPriority.Send,
         new DispatcherOperationCallback(GotoPage2), null);
     };
     ApplicationDeployment.CurrentDeployment.DownloadFileGroupAsync("MyGroup");
   }
   else
   {
     // We're not running in the context of ClickOnce (perhaps because
     // we're being debugged), so just go directly to Page2.
     GotoPage2(null);
   }
 }

 // Navigates to Page2 when ready. Accepts and returns an object simply
 // to match the signature of DispatcherOperationCallback
 private object GotoPage2(object o)
 {
   return NavigationService.Navigate(new Uri("Page2.xaml", UriKind.Relative));
 }
}
```

The download support only applies when the application is run over the network (not locally under a debugger), so the listing first calls ApplicationDeployment.IsNetworkDeployed to determine whether to rely on it. If the application is not network deployed, all files are present locally, so the code immediately navigates to Page2. Otherwise, the download is prompted by calling DownloadFileGroupAsync. Before that call, however, an anonymous delegate is attached to the DownloadFileGroupCompleted event so the navigation can be initiated as soon as the download finishes. ApplicationDeployment defines additional events, in case you want to expose more fine-grained progress during the download process.

Loose XAML Pages

Internet Explorer can navigate to a loose `.xaml` file just like a `.html` file if you've got the .NET Framework 3.0 or later installed. Therefore, in certain environments XAML can be used as a richer form of HTML with better support for layout, text, graphics, and so on.

You can't use any procedural code in this environment, but with data binding (covered in Chapter 9, "Data Binding"), you can still create pretty powerful dynamic user interfaces. Figure 7.15 shows the loose XAML version of Photo Gallery, which displays a static set of pictures from the web server, but uses data binding to keep the snazzy zoom feature.

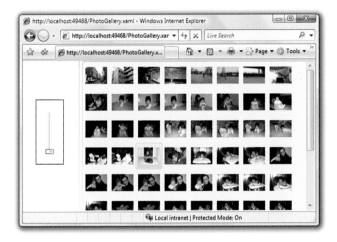

FIGURE 7.15   Photo Gallery can still be very functional as a loose XAML page.

> **TIP**
>
> If you want your website to take advantage of the richness of loose XAML but still want to show HTML to users who won't be able to view XAML, you could maintain two versions of your content and adaptively pick the appropriate one. This is easy to do by checking the user agent string for content such as ".NET CLR 3.0."

> **TIP**
>
> To mix HTML and loose XAML content, simply host one or more `.xaml` files in IFRAMEs on an HTML page.

Conclusion

WPF's rich support for building applications has something for just about everyone. Probably the best part of all is that the same programming model is used for all application types. As demonstrated by the Photo Gallery source code that accompanies this book, you can often take the same user interface implementation and apply it from everything to a traditional Windows application to a code-less "rich web page."

In all cases, the deployment of an application can be fast and easy. The only wrinkle is the prerequisite of having the .NET Framework 3.0 installed. (For example, I would love to use loose XAML or XBAPs for all my websites, if only the majority of the target audience could view it without hassles!) Fortunately, with the .NET Framework 3.0 installed and on by default in Windows Vista, as well as being available via Windows Update for other versions of Windows, this prerequisite becomes less of an issue as time goes on.

PART III

Features for Professional Developers

Resources

The .NET Framework has generic infrastructure for packaging and accessing *resources*—the noncode pieces of an application or component, such as bitmaps, fonts, audio/video files, and string tables. As with many other parts of WPF, WPF not only leverages the core .NET resources system but adds a little more support. WPF supports two distinct types of resources: binary resources and logical resources.

Binary Resources

The first type—*binary resources*—are exactly what the rest of the .NET Framework considers to be resources. In WPF applications, these are typically traditional items like bitmaps. However, even compiled XAML gets stored as such a resource behind the scenes. Binary resources can be packaged in three different ways:

▶ Embedded inside an assembly

▶ Loose files that are known to the application at compile time

▶ Loose files that might not be known to the application at compile time

An application's binary resources are often put into two categories: localizable resources that must change depending on the current culture and language-neutral (or nonlocalizable) resources that don't change based on culture. This section looks at the ways in which binary resources are defined, accessed, and localized.

Defining Binary Resources

The typical procedure for defining a binary resource consists of adding the file to a Visual Studio project and selecting the appropriate build action in the property grid, as shown in Figure 8.1 for an image called `logo.jpg`.

Visual Studio supports several build actions for WPF applications, two of which are relevant for binary resources:

FIGURE 8.1   Marking a file as a binary resource in Visual Studio.

▶ **Resource**—Embeds the resource into the assembly (or a culture-specific satellite assembly).

▶ **Content**—Leaves the resource as a loose file, but adds a custom attribute to the assembly (`AssemblyAssociatedContentFile`) that records the existence and relative location of the file.

If you're an MSBuild user editing a project file by hand, you can add such a file with the following syntax:

```
<BuildAction Include="logo.jpg"/>
```

where *BuildAction* is the name of the build action. Build actions sometimes include child elements that refine its behavior. For example:

```
<Content Include="logo.jpg">
  <CopyToOutputDirectory>Always</CopyToOutputDirectory>
</Content>
```

> **WARNING**
>
> **Avoid the `Embedded Resource` build action!**
>
> The `Resource` build action is confusingly similar to the `EmbeddedResource` build action (`Embedded Resource` in Visual Studio's property grid). Both embed a binary resource inside an assembly, but the latter should be avoided in WPF projects. Whereas `Resource` was added specifically for WPF, `EmbeddedResource` predates WPF (and is the way binary resources are embedded in a Windows Forms project).
>
> WPF's APIs that reference resources via uniform resource identifiers (described in the next section) are designed for resources that use a build action of `Content` or `Resource` only. This also means that resources embedded with the `Content` or `Resource` build action can be referenced easily from XAML, but resources embedded with the `EmbeddedResource` build action cannot be (unless you write some custom code).

If you want to keep your resources as loose files, adding them to your project with a `Content` build action is not required; you could simply put them at the appropriate location when the application runs and not worry about adding them to your project at all. This is not recommended, however, because it makes accessing them a bit less natural (as described in the next section). Still, sometimes using resources that aren't known at compile time is inevitable, such as files that are dynamically generated at run-time.

Resources should be embedded (with the `Resource` build action) if they are localizable, or if you feel the benefits of having a single binary file outweigh the benefits of having a loose file that can be easily replaced independently from the code. If neither of these is true, or if the content needs to be accessible directly from HTML, using the `Content` build action is a good choice.

Accessing Binary Resources

Whether binary resources are embedded with the `Resource` build action, linked as loose files with the `Content` build action, or left as loose files with no special treatment at compile time, WPF provides a mechanism for accessing them from code or XAML with a uniform resource identifier (URI). A type converter enables such URIs to be specified in XAML as simple strings with a few built-in shortcuts for common scenarios.

You can see this by examining the source code for the Photo Gallery application introduced in the preceding chapter. The following XAML snippet from Photo Gallery references several images that are included in the project with a build action of `Resource`:

```
<StackPanel Grid.Column="1" Orientation="Horizontal" HorizontalAlignment="Center">
  <Button x:Name="previousButton" ToolTip="Previous (Left Arrow)" …>
    <Image Height="21" Source="previous.gif"/>
  </Button>
  <Button x:Name="slideshowButton" ToolTip="Play Slide Show (F11)" …>
    <Image Height="21" Source="slideshow.gif"/>
  </Button>
  <Button x:Name="nextButton" ToolTip="Next (Right Arrow)" …>
    <Image Height="21" Source="next.gif"/>
  </Button>
</StackPanel>
```

`System.Windows.Controls.Image` is the control that enables easy access to each binary image. `Image` has a `Source` property of type `System.Windows.Media.ImageSource`, but thanks to a type converter (`System.Windows.Media.ImageSourceConverter`), you can set the property to a simple string in XAML.

Note that this same XAML works even if the `.gif` files are given a build action of `Content` instead of `Resource` (as long as the loose files are copied to the same directory as the executable when it runs). It does not work, however, if the loose `.gif` files are not added to the project.

WARNING

Compiled XAML can't reference a binary resource in the current directory via its simple filename unless it has been added to the project!

It often surprises people that compiled XAML, unlike loose XAML, can't reference an arbitrary file in the current directory as follows:

```
<Image Height="21" Source="slideshow.gif"/>
```

If you require the resource to be loose and do not want to add it to your project, you have a few easy alternatives. One (unsatisfactory) alternative is to qualify the filename with its full path:

```
<Image Height="21" Source="C:\Users\Adam\Documents\slideshow.gif"/>
```

A better alternative is to use the following odd-looking syntax described later in the "Accessing Resources at the Site of Origin" section:

```
<Image Height="21" Source="pack://siteOfOrigin:,,,/slideshow.gif"/>
```

The key to accessing binary resources, whether done with the Image element or other elements, is understanding what URIs you can use to address a resource that could be embedded or loose. Table 8.1 summarizes the main options for URI strings in XAML. Note that not all of these options are available for partial-trust applications.

TABLE 8.1   URIs for Accessing Binary Resources from XAML

Using logo.jpg as the Resource Name

If the URI Is...	The Resource Is...
logo.jpg	▶ Embedded in the current assembly, or ▶ Loose and alongside the current XAML page or assembly (the latter case only if marked as Content in the project)
A/B/logo.jpg	▶ Embedded in the current assembly using an internal subfolder (A\B) structure defined at compile time, or ▶ Loose and in an A\B subfolder relative to the current XAML page or assembly (the latter case only if marked as Content in the project)
c:\temp\logo.jpg	Loose in the local c:\temp folder
file://c:/temp/logo.jpg	Loose in the local c:\temp folder
\\pc1\images\logo.jpg	Loose on the \\pc1\images UNC share
http://pinvoke.net/logo.jpg	Loose and hosted at the pinvoke.net website
MyDll;Component/logo.jpg	Embedded in a different assembly called MyDll.dll or MyDll.exe
MyDll;Component/A/B/logo.jpg	Embedded in a different assembly called MyDll.dll or MyDll.exe using an internal subfolder structure (A\B) defined at compile time

TABLE 8.1   Continued

Using `logo.jpg` as the Resource Name	
If the URI Is...	**The Resource Is...**
`pack://siteOfOrigin:,,,/logo.jpg`	Loose at the site of origin
`pack://siteOfOrigin:,,,/A/B/logo.jpg`	Loose at the site of origin in an A\B subfolder

FAQ

What happens when attempting to access resources on a slow or unavailable network?

Table 8.1 shows that binary resources can be directly referenced from potentially unreliable sources such as a website or a Universal Naming Convention (UNC) share. This access is done synchronously, so you'll unfortunately see an application "hang" while waiting for all the bits to be retrieved. In addition, failure to retrieve the resource results in an unhandled exception.

Note that the first two entries in Table 8.1 can work with both embedded and loose binary resources. This means that you can replace loose resources with embedded ones (or vice versa) without having to change your XAML.

The notion of using subfolders with embedded resources might sound a little odd, but it can be a nice way to organize embedded resources just as you would with loose ones. For example, if you put `logo.jpg` in an `images` folder in your Visual Studio project (using `<Resource Include="images\logo.jpg"/>` or `<Content Include="images\logo.jpg"/>` in the project file), you could access it as follows:

```
<Image Source="images\logo.jpg"/>
```

regardless of whether `logo.jpg` physically resides as a loose file in an `images` subfolder at run-time, or if it's simply embedded in the assembly.

The final four rows of Table 8.1 need a bit more explanation. The first two enable you to access binary resources embedded in another assembly, and the second two enable you to access binary resources at a special place known as a site of origin.

Accessing Resources Embedded in Another Assembly

The ability to easily access binary resources embedded in another assembly is very handy (and gives you more options for updating resources without needing to replace the main executable), but the syntax is a little bizarre. As Table 8.1 implies, the syntax is

```
AssemblyReference;Component/ResourceName
```

where *AssemblyReference* identifies the specific assembly, but `Component` is a keyword and must be used literally. *ResourceName* is the filename (which can include subfolders).

The *AssemblyReference* can be the simple assembly display name, or it can optionally include other pieces of a .NET assembly's identity: version number and public key token (if it's a strong-named assembly). So, you have four options for the *AssemblyReference*:

▶ *AssemblyName*

▶ *AssemblyName*;v*VersionNumber* (the v prefix is required)

▶ *AssemblyName*;*PublicKeyToken*

▶ *AssemblyName*;v*VersionNumber*;*PublicKeyToken*

Accessing Resources at the Site of Origin

Although full-trust applications can hard-code a uniform resource locator (URL) or path for loose binary resources, taking advantage of the site of origin notion is a more maintainable approach. (In addition, it is required for partial-trust applications.) The site of origin gets resolved to different places at run-time, depending how the application is deployed:

▶ For a full-trust application installed with Windows Installer, the site of origin is the application's root folder.

▶ For a full-trust ClickOnce application, the site of origin is the URL or Universal Naming Convention (UNC) path from which the application was deployed.

▶ For a partial-trust XAML Browser Application (XBAP) or ClickOnce application, the site of origin is the URL or UNC path that hosts the application.

▶ For loose XAML pages viewed in Internet Explorer, there is no site of origin. Attempting to use it throws an exception.

The syntax for taking advantage of your site of origin is even stranger than the syntax to reference resources embedded in another assembly! You must use the `pack://siteOfOrigin:,,,/` prefix, followed by the resource name (which can contain subfolders). Note that `siteOfOrigin` is a keyword to be used literally, not a placeholder for other text.

Accessing Resources from Procedural Code

When creating URIs in C# for referencing resources, you aren't able to use the XAML-specific shortcuts from Table 8.1. Instead, such URIs must be constructed with a fully-qualified Pack URI or a fully-qualified path/URL.

For example, the following code assigns an `Image`'s `Source` property to the contents of `logo.jpg`:

```
Image image = new Image();
image.Source = new BitmapImage(new Uri("pack://application:,,,/logo.jpg"));
```

FAQ

 Where does that awful triple-comma syntax come from?

The Pack URI format is part of the XML Paper Specification (XPS), which can be found at http://www.microsoft.com/whdc/xps/xpsspec.mspx. The specified format is:

`pack://packageURI/partPath`

The *packageURI* is actually a URI within a URI, so it is encoded by converting its forward slashes into commas. This *packageURI* could point to an XPS document, such as `file:///C:/Document.xps` encoded as `file:,,,C:,Document.xps`. Or, in WPF programs, it can be one of two URIs treated specially by the platform:

- ► `siteOfOrigin:///` (encoded as `siteOfOrigin:,,,`)
- ► `application:///` (encoded as `application:,,,`)

Therefore, the triple commas are actually encoded forward slashes, not placeholders for optional parameters! (Note that these can also be specified with two slashes/commas rather than three.)

The `application:///` package is implicitly used by all the resource references shown in Table 8.1 that don't use `siteOfOrigin`. In other words, the following URI used in XAML:

`logo.jpg`

is really just shorthand notation for:

`pack://application:,,,/logo.jpg`

and this URI:

`MyDll;Component/logo.jpg`

is shorthand notation for:

`pack://application:,,,/MyDll;Component/logo.jpg`

You can use these longer and more explicit URIs in XAML, but there's no good reason to.

This instantiates a `System.Windows.Media.Imaging.BitmapImage` object (which works with popular image formats such as JPEG, PNG, GIF, and BMP), which ultimately derives from the abstract `ImageSource` type (the type of the `Source` property). The URI is represented by a `System.Uri` object.

The use of `pack://application:,,,/` only works with resources belonging to the current project marked as `Resource` or `Content`. To reference relative loose files with no relation to the project, the easiest approach is to use a `siteOfOrigin`-based URI.

Localization

If your application contains some binary resources that are specific to certain cultures, you can partition them into satellite assemblies (one per culture) that get loaded automatically when appropriate. If you're doing this, then you likely have strings in your user interface that you need to localize as well. LocBaml, a sample tool in the Windows SDK, makes it easy to manage the localization of strings (and some other properties in your user interface) without having to rip them out of your XAML and manually apply a level of indirection. This section walks through the basics steps to get started with LocBaml and satellite assemblies.

Preparing Your Project for Multiple Cultures

To specify a default culture for your resources and automatically build an appropriate satellite assembly, you must add a UICulture element to your project file. Visual Studio 2005 doesn't have a means to set this within its environment, so you can open the project file in your favorite text editor instead.

> **TIP**
>
> You can open a raw project file without leaving Visual Studio if you right-click and unload it from the current solution first. After it's unloaded, right-click the project again and select Edit from the context menu.

The UICulture element should be added under any or all PropertyGroup elements corresponding to the build configurations you want to impact (Debug, Release, and so on). This setting should look as follows for a default culture of American English:

```
<Project …>
  <PropertyGroup>
    <UICulture>en-US</UICulture>
…
```

If you rebuild your project with this setting in place, you'll find an en-US folder alongside your assembly containing the satellite assembly named AssemblyName.resources.dll.

You should also mark your assembly with the assembly-level NeutralResourcesLanguage custom attribute with a value matching your default UICulture as follows:

```
[assembly: NeutralResourcesLanguage("en-US",
  UltimateResourceFallbackLocation.Satellite)]
```

Marking Your User Interface with Localization IDs

The next step is to apply a Uid directive from the XAML language namespace (x:Uid) to every object element that needs to be localized. The value of each directive should be a unique identifier

This would be extremely tedious to do by hand, but it fortunately can be done automatically by invoking MSBuild from a command prompt as follows:

```
msbuild /t:updateuid ProjectName.csproj
```

Running this gives *every* object element in *every* XAML file in the project an x:Uid directive with a unique value.

Creating a New Satellite Assembly with LocBaml

After compiling your project that has been enhanced with Uids, you can run the LocBaml tool from the Windows SDK on a .resources file generated by the build process (found in the obj\debug directory) as follows:

```
LocBaml /parse ProjectName.g.en-US.resources /out:en-US.csv
```

This generates a simple .csv text file containing all the property values you should need to localize. You can edit the contents of this file so it correctly corresponds to a new culture. (There's no magic in this part of localization!) If you save the file, you can then use LocBaml in the reverse direction to generate a new satellite assembly from the .csv file! For example, if you changed the contents of the .csv file to match the French Canadian culture, you could save the file as fr-CA.csv, and then run LocBaml as follows:

```
LocBaml /generate ProjectName.resources.dll /trans:fr-CA.csv /cul:fr-CA
```

This new satellite assembly needs to be copied to a folder alongside the main assembly with a name that matches the culture (fr-CA in this case).

To test a different culture, you can set System.Threading.Thread.CurrentThread.CurrentUICulture (and System.Threading.Thread.CurrentThread.CurrentCulture) to an instance of the desired CultureInfo.

Logical Resources

The second type of resources supported by WPF is a brand-new (and WPF-specific) mechanism. In this chapter, they are called *logical resources* for lack of a better term, but mostly the book refers to them as *resources* in contrast to the *binary resources* just covered. (You might be tempted to call them *XAML resources* but like everything else in XAML, you can create and use them entirely in procedural code.)

These logical resources are arbitrary .NET objects stored (and named) in an element's Resources property, typically meant to be shared by multiple child elements. The FrameworkElement and FrameworkContentElement base classes both have a Resources property (of type System.Windows.ResourceDictionary), so most WPF classes you'll encounter have such a property. These logical resources are often styles (covered in Chapter 10, "Styles, Templates, Skins, and Themes") or data providers (covered in Chapter 9, "Data Binding"). But this chapter demonstrates logical resources by storing some simple Brushes.

Listing 8.1 contains a simple Window with a row of Buttons along the bottom similar to ones from the Photo Gallery user interface. It demonstrates a brute force way to apply a custom Brush to each Button's (and the Window's) Background, as well as each Button's BorderBrush. The result is shown in Figure 8.2.

LISTING 8.1   Applying Custom Color Brushes Without Using Logical Resources

```
<Window xmlns="http://schemas.microsoft.com/winfx/2006/xaml/presentation"
  Title="Simple Window" Background="Yellow">
  <DockPanel>
    <StackPanel DockPanel.Dock="Bottom" Orientation="Horizontal"
      HorizontalAlignment="Center">
      <Button Background="Yellow" BorderBrush="Red" Margin="5">
        <Image Height="21" Source="zoom.gif"/>
      </Button>
      <Button Background="Yellow" BorderBrush="Red" Margin="5">
        <Image Height="21" Source="defaultThumbnailSize.gif"/>
      </Button>
      <Button Background="Yellow" BorderBrush="Red" Margin="5">
        <Image Height="21" Source="previous.gif"/>
      </Button>
      <Button Background="Yellow" BorderBrush="Red" Margin="5">
        <Image Height="21" Source="slideshow.gif"/>
      </Button>
      <Button Background="Yellow" BorderBrush="Red" Margin="5">
        <Image Height="21" Source="next.gif"/>
      </Button>
      <Button Background="Yellow" BorderBrush="Red" Margin="5">
        <Image Height="21" Source="counterclockwise.gif"/>
      </Button>
      <Button Background="Yellow" BorderBrush="Red" Margin="5">
        <Image Height="21" Source="clockwise.gif"/>
      </Button>
      <Button Background="Yellow" BorderBrush="Red" Margin="5">
        <Image Height="21" Source="delete.gif"/>
      </Button>
    </StackPanel>
    <ListBox/>
  </DockPanel>
</Window>
```

Alternatively, you could organize the yellow and red Brushes as logical resources for the Window, and apply them to individual elements as resource references. This is a nice way to separate and consolidate the style information, much like using Cascading Style Sheets (CSS) to control colors and styles in a web page rather than hard-coding them on individual elements. The sharing of

FIGURE 8.2   The rendered Window from Listing 8.1.

objects enabled by the logical resources scheme can also help you consume significantly less memory, depending on the complexity of the objects. Listing 8.2 is an update to Listing 8.1, using logical resources for the two Brushes.

LISTING 8.2   Consolidating Color Brushes with Logical Resources

```xml
<Window xmlns="http://schemas.microsoft.com/winfx/2006/xaml/presentation"
  xmlns:x="http://schemas.microsoft.com/winfx/2006/xaml"
  Title="Simple Window">
<Window.Resources>
  <SolidColorBrush x:Key="backgroundBrush">Yellow</SolidColorBrush>
  <SolidColorBrush x:Key="borderBrush">Red</SolidColorBrush>
</Window.Resources>
<Window.Background>
  <StaticResource ResourceKey="backgroundBrush"/>
</Window.Background>
  <DockPanel>
    <StackPanel DockPanel.Dock="Bottom" Orientation="Horizontal"
      HorizontalAlignment="Center">
      <Button Background="{StaticResource backgroundBrush}"
        BorderBrush="{StaticResource borderBrush}" Margin="5">
        <Image Height="21" Source="zoom.gif"/>
      </Button>
      <Button Background="{StaticResource backgroundBrush}"
        BorderBrush="{StaticResource borderBrush}" Margin="5">
        <Image Height="21" Source="defaultThumbnailSize.gif"/>
      </Button>
      <Button Background="{StaticResource backgroundBrush}"
        BorderBrush="{StaticResource borderBrush}" Margin="5">
        <Image Height="21" Source="previous.gif"/>
      </Button>
      <Button Background="{StaticResource backgroundBrush}"
        BorderBrush="{StaticResource borderBrush}" Margin="5">
        <Image Height="21" Source="slideshow.gif"/>
      </Button>
      <Button Background="{StaticResource backgroundBrush}"
        BorderBrush="{StaticResource borderBrush}" Margin="5">
        <Image Height="21" Source="next.gif"/>
      </Button>
      <Button Background="{StaticResource backgroundBrush}"
        BorderBrush="{StaticResource borderBrush}" Margin="5">
        <Image Height="21" Source="counterclockwise.gif"/>
      </Button>
      <Button Background="{StaticResource backgroundBrush}"
        BorderBrush="{StaticResource borderBrush}" Margin="5">
        <Image Height="21" Source="clockwise.gif"/>
```

8

LISTING 8.2   Continued

```
      </Button>
      <Button Background="{StaticResource backgroundBrush}"
        BorderBrush="{StaticResource borderBrush}" Margin="5">
        <Image Height="21" Source="delete.gif"/>
      </Button>
    </StackPanel>
    <ListBox/>
  </DockPanel>
</Window>
```

The definition of resources and the x:Key syntax should look familiar, from when ResourceDictionary was introduced in Chapter 2, "XAML Demystified." Applying the resource to elements uses the StaticResource markup extension (short for System.Windows.StaticResourceExtension). This is applied to Window.Background with property element syntax, and to Button.Background and Button.BorderBrush with property attribute syntax. Because both resources in this example are Brushes, they can be applied anywhere a Brush is expected.

Because simple yellow and red Brushes are still used in Listing 8.2, the result looks identical to Figure 8.2. But now, you can replace the Brushes in one spot and leave the rest of the XAML alone (as long as you use the same keys in the resource dictionary). For example, replacing the backgroundBrush resource with the following linear gradient produces the result in Figure 8.3:

FIGURE 8.3   The same Window from Listing 8.2, but with a new definition for backgroundBrush.

```
<LinearGradientBrush x:Key="backgroundBrush" StartPoint="0,0" EndPoint="1,1">
  <GradientStop Color="Blue" Offset="0"/>
  <GradientStop Color="White" Offset="0.5"/>
  <GradientStop Color="Red" Offset="1"/>
</LinearGradientBrush>
```

Resource Lookup

The StaticResource markup extension accepts a single parameter representing the key to the item in a resource dictionary. But that item doesn't have to be inside the current element's resource dictionary. It could be in any logical parent's collection, or even in application-level or system-level resource dictionaries.

The markup extension class implements the ability to walk the logical tree to find the item. It first checks the current element's Resources collection (its resource dictionary). If the item is not found, it checks the parent element, its parent, and so on until it reaches the root element. At that point, it checks the Resources collection on the Application object. If it is not found there, it finally checks a system collection (which contains system-defined fonts, colors, and other settings). If the item is in none of these collections, it throws an InvalidOperationException.

Because of this behavior, resources are typically stored in the root element's resource dictionary or in the application-level dictionary for maximum sharing potential. Note that although each individual ResourceDictionary requires unique keys, the same key can be used in multiple collections. The one "closest" to the element accessing the resource will win because of the way the tree gets walked.

Static Versus Dynamic Resources

WPF provides two ways to access a logical resource:

▶ Statically with StaticResource, meaning the resource is applied only once (the first time it's needed)

▶ Dynamically with DynamicResource, meaning the resource is reapplied every time it changes

The DynamicResource markup extension (System.Windows.DynamicResourceExtension) implements the ability to walk the logical tree just like StaticResource does, so DynamicResource can often be used wherever StaticResource is used to get the same effect. Nothing about the resource declarations themselves make them suited for one versus the other; choosing StaticResource or DynamicResource is mostly about deciding if you want consumers of the resource to see updates. In fact, you could even mix and match StaticResource and DynamicResource with the same resource key, although that would be a strange thing to do.

Examining the Differences

The main difference between StaticResource and DynamicResource is that any subsequent updates to the resource are reflected only to those elements that use DynamicResource. Such updates can be done in your own code (changing a yellow Brush to blue, for example) or they can be done by a user changing system settings.

StaticResource and DynamicResource have different performance characteristics. On the one hand, using DynamicResource requires more overhead than StaticResource because of the extra tracking. On the other hand, the use of DynamicResource can potentially improve load time. StaticResource references are always loaded when the Window or Page loads, whereas a DynamicResource reference is not loaded until it is actually used.

In addition, DynamicResource can only be used to set dependency property values, whereas StaticResource can be used just about anywhere. For example, you could use StaticResource as an element to abstract away entire controls! This Window:

```
<Window xmlns="http://schemas.microsoft.com/winfx/2006/xaml/presentation"
  xmlns:x="http://schemas.microsoft.com/winfx/2006/xaml">
  ...
```

```
  <Image Height="21" Source="zoom.gif"/>
  …
</Window>
```

is equivalent to this window:

```
<Window xmlns="http://schemas.microsoft.com/winfx/2006/xaml/presentation"
  xmlns:x="http://schemas.microsoft.com/winfx/2006/xaml">
<Window.Resources>
  <Image x:Key="zoom" Height="21" Source="zoom.gif"/>
</Window.Resources>
  …
  <StaticResource ResourceKey="zoom"/>
  …
</Window>
```

Using elements such as Image as a resource might be an interesting way to factor your XAML, but it doesn't allow you to share the object. Image can only have one parent because it derives from Visual (therefore participating in the logical and visual trees), so any attempt to use the same object as a resource more than once fails. For example, pasting a second but identical StaticResource element in the preceding XAML snippet produces an exception with the message: "Specified Visual is already a child of another Visual or the root of a CompositionTarget."

There's one more (and subtle) difference between static and dynamic resource access. When using StaticResource in XAML, forward references aren't supported. In other words, any uses of the resource must appear *after* it is declared in the XAML file. That means that you can't use StaticResource with property attribute syntax if the resource is defined on the same element (because they appear afterward)! DynamicResource does not have this limitation.

This forward reference rule is the reason that the Window in Listing 8.2 used property element syntax to set its Background. By doing so, it ensures that the resource is defined before it is used.

Although DynamicResource could be used the same way, you can also use it via property attribute syntax in this case because it doesn't matter that the resource is referenced before it is defined. For example:

```
<Window xmlns="http://schemas.microsoft.com/winfx/2006/xaml/presentation"
  xmlns:x="http://schemas.microsoft.com/winfx/2006/xaml"
  Title="Simple Window" Background="{DynamicResource backgroundBrush}">
<Window.Resources>
  <SolidColorBrush x:Key="backgroundBrush">Yellow</SolidColorBrush>
  <SolidColorBrush x:Key="borderBrush">Red</SolidColorBrush>
</Window.Resources>
  …
</Window>
```

DIGGING DEEPER

Factoring XAML

Resources provide a nice way to factor your XAML within a page. And if you store them as application-level resources, they can live in a separate XAML file. But if you want to partition a set of resources into arbitrary XAML files no matter where they are stored in the logical tree (perhaps for maintainability or flexibility), you can leverage the `MergedDictionaries` property of the `ResourceDictionary` class to achieve this.

For example, a `Window` could set its `Resources` collection as follows to merge together multiple resource dictionaries from separate files:

```
<Window.Resources>
  <ResourceDictionary>
    <ResourceDictionary.MergedDictionaries>
      <ResourceDictionary Source="file1.xaml"/>
      <ResourceDictionary Source="file2.xaml"/>
    </ResourceDictionary.MergedDictionaries>
  </ResourceDictionary>
</Window.Resources>
```

The separate files must use `ResourceDictionary` as the root element. For example, `file1.xaml` could contain:

```
<ResourceDictionary
  xmlns="http://schemas.microsoft.com/winfx/2006/xaml/presentation"
  xmlns:x=" http://schemas.microsoft.com/winfx/2006/xaml">
  <Image x:Key="logo" Source="logo.jpg"/>
</ResourceDictionary>
```

If the dictionaries being merged have a duplicate key, the last one wins (unlike the case of having duplicate keys in a single dictionary).

Besides this approach of using resources, creating custom controls (covered in Chapter 16, "User Controls and Custom Controls") is the other way to factor XAML into multiple files. There is no general purpose C++-like `#include` mechanism for XAML.

Resources Without Sharing

By default, when a resource is applied in multiple places, the same object instance is used everywhere. This is usually the desired behavior. However, you can mark items in a `ResourceDictionary` with `x:Shared="False"` to make each application of that resource a distinct instance of the object that can be modified independently of the others.

One case where this behavior can be interesting is the previous example of using an entire `Image` (or any other `Visual`-derived object) as a resource. Such a resource can only be applied once in an element tree because each application is the same instance. But setting `x:Shared="False"` changes this behavior, enabling the resource to be applied multiple times as independent objects! This could be done as follows:

```
<Window xmlns="http://schemas.microsoft.com/winfx/2006/xaml/presentation"
  xmlns:x="http://schemas.microsoft.com/winfx/2006/xaml">
<Window.Resources>
  <Image x:Shared="False" x:Key="zoom" Height="21" Source="zoom.gif"/>
</Window.Resources>
  ...
  <!-- Applying the resource multiple times works! -->
  <StaticResource ResourceKey="zoom"/>
  <StaticResource ResourceKey="zoom"/>
  <StaticResource ResourceKey="zoom"/>
  ...
</Window>
```

Note that x:Shared can only be used in a compiled XAML file.

Defining and Applying Resources in Procedural Code

So far, this chapter has examined how to define and apply logical resources in XAML, but hasn't yet looked at what it means to do the same things in procedural code. Fortunately, *defining* resources in code is straightforward. The two SolidColorBrush resources used in Listing 8.2 can be defined as follows in C#, assuming a Window called window:

```
window.Resources.Add("backgroundBrush", new SolidColorBrush("Yellow"));
window.Resources.Add("borderBrush", new SolidColorBrush("Red"));
```

Applying resources in code is a different story, however. Because StaticResource and DynamicResource are markup extensions, the equivalent C# code to find and apply resources is not obvious.

For StaticResource, you can get the equivalent behavior by setting an element's property to the result from its FindResource method (inherited from FrameworkElement or FrameworkContentElement).

So, the following Button (similar to one declared in Listing 8.2):

```
<Button Background="{StaticResource backgroundBrush}"
        BorderBrush="{StaticResource borderBrush}"/>
```

is equivalent to the following C# code:

```
Button button = new Button();
button.Background = (Brush)button.FindResource("backgroundBrush");
button.BorderBrush = (Brush)button.FindResource("borderBrush");
```

FindResource throws an exception when the resource cannot be found, but you can alternatively call TryFindResource, which returns null when the lookup fails.

For DynamicResource, a call to an element's SetResourceReference (also inherited from FrameworkElement or FrameworkContentElement) does the trick of setting up the updatable binding with the dependency property.

Therefore, replacing both `StaticResource` references with `DynamicResource`:

```
<Button Background="{DynamicResource backgroundBrush}"
        BorderBrush="{DynamicResource borderBrush}"/>
```

is equivalent to the following C# code:

```
Button button = new Button();
button.SetResourceReference(Button.BackgroundProperty, "backgroundBrush");
button.SetResourceReference(Button.BorderBrushProperty, "borderBrush");
```

The forward reference rule with `StaticResource` also applies to procedural code. A call to `FindResource` or `TryFindResource` fails if you call it before adding the resource to an appropriate resource dictionary with the appropriate key. `SetResourceReference`, on the other hand, can be called before the resource has been added.

DIGGING DEEPER

Accessing Resources Directly

Because resource dictionaries are simple collections exposed as public properties, nothing prevents you from accessing its items directly in source code. For example, you could set a Button's Background and BorderBrush properties as follows in C# (assuming a Window object called window):

```
Button button = new Button();
button.Background = (Brush)window.Resources["backgroundBrush"];
button.BorderBrush = (Brush)window.Resources["borderBrush"];
```

This is similar to the use of `StaticResource` in XAML (`FindResource` in code) in that it's a one-time property set. However, it doesn't search the logical tree, application, or system for the named resources. Therefore, this gives you less flexibility and makes the binding between XAML and code more brittle, but also gives you a minor performance boost by avoiding the lookups. Note that there is no way to use this technique in XAML.

Accessing Resources Embedded in Another Assembly

Earlier in the chapter, you saw that you can access binary resources embedded in another assembly with a specially-formed URI. WPF also has special support for retrieving *logical* resources from another assembly via a markup extension called `ComponentResourceKey`. You could retrieve such logical resources without this support, but it would involve getting an instance of the appropriate `ResourceDictionary` first.

To make use of `ComponentResourceKey`, a resource should be assigned a key that is an instance of `ComponentResourceKey` rather than a simple string. For example:

```
<SolidColorBrush
  x:Key="{ComponentResourceKey TypeInTargetAssembly={x:Type local:MyClass},
  ResourceId=MyClassBrush}">Yellow</SolidColorBrush>
```

Consumers can construct an instance of ComponentResourceKey with the same data and use it to reference the resource:

```
<Button Background="{DynamicResource {ComponentResourceKey TypeInTargetAssembly=
   otherAssembly:MyClass, ResourceId=MyClassBrush}}" …/>
```

Often, the assembly defining the resource exposes a property on the relevant class that returns an instance of the ComponentResourceKey to any consumers. This is a nice way to advertise resources that you expect others to use. For example, if MyClass exposes the following property:

```
public object MyClassBrushKey
{
  get { return new ComponentResourceKey(this.GetType(), "MyClassBrush"); }
}
```

Then it can be consumed from another assembly as follows:

```
<Button Background=
  "{DynamicResource {x:Static otherAssembly:MyClass.MyClassBrushKey}}" …/>
```

Interaction with System Resources

One obvious place where it's appropriate to use DynamicResource is in the use of system settings encapsulated by static fields on three classes in the System.Windows namespace: SystemColors, SystemFonts, and SystemParameters. That's because a user can change the settings via Control Panel while your application is running.

Table 8.2 demonstrates the various ways you might try to set a Button's background to the system's currently defined "window color," but only the last approach is completely correct.

Conclusion

Of all the WPF features covered in this part of the book, the support for resources is the one that is practically impossible to live without. It's hard to build a professional-looking application without at least an icon and a few images!

But using resources is about much more than just making your application or control look (or sound, if you're using audio resources) a little better. It's a fundamental piece of enabling your software to be localized into different languages. It also enables higher productivity for developing software because the logical resources support enables you to consolidate information that might otherwise be duplicated, and even factor XAML files into more manageable chunks. The most fun—and perhaps most important—application of logical resources is its use with objects such as styles and templates, covered in Chapter 10.

TABLE 8.2   Potential Options for Setting a System-Defined Background

The Approach	The Result

XAML:
 	
`<Button Background="SystemColors.WindowBrush"/>`
 	
C#:
 	
`Button b = new Button();`
`b.Background = "SystemColors.WindowBrush";`
	This doesn't work. BrushConverter doesn't support such strings.

XAML:
 	
`<Button Background="{x:Static SystemColors.WindowBrush}"/>`
 	
C#:
 	
`Button b = new Button();`
`b.Background = SystemColors.WindowBrush;`
	This sets the color once, but doesn't respond to the user changing the color while the application runs.

XAML:
 	
`<Button Background=`
`  "{StaticResource SystemColors.WindowBrush}"/>`
 	
C#:
 	
`Button b = new Button();`
`b.Background = FindResource("SystemColors.WindowBrush");`
	This doesn't work, unless you defined a Brush resource with a "SystemColors. WindowBrush" key, which would have no relation to the static field you probably want to use.

XAML:
 	
`<Button Background=`
`  "{StaticResource {x:Static SystemColors.WindowBrush}}"/>`
 	
C#:
 	
`Button b = new Button();`
`b.Background = FindResource(SystemColors.WindowBrush);`
	This is like approach #2, but also allows the application to override the color (during initialization) for simple skinning purposes.

XAML:
 	
`<Button Background=`
`  "{DynamicResource {x:Static SystemColors.WindowBrush}}"/>`
 	
C#:
 	
`Button b = new Button();`
`b.Background = SetResourceReference(`
`  Button.BackgroundProperty, SystemColors.WindowBrush);`
	This is the preferred approach. It responds to any user-initiated changes and allows the application to override the values to reskin it at any time.

8

Data Binding

In WPF, the term *data* is generally used to describe an arbitrary .NET object. You can see this naming pattern in terms like *data binding*, *data templates*, and *data triggers*, covered in this chapter and the next chapter. A piece of data could be a collection object, an XML file, a web service, a database table, a custom object, or even a WPF element such as a Button.

Therefore, data binding is about tying together arbitrary .NET objects. The classic scenario is providing a visual representation (for example, in a ListBox or ListView) of items in an XML file, database, or an in-memory collection. For example, instead of iterating through a data source and manually adding a ListBoxItem to a ListBox for each one, it would be nice to just say, "Hey, ListBox! Get your items from over here. And keep them up to date, please. Oh yeah, and format them to look like this." Data binding enables this and much more.

Introducing the Binding Object

The key to data binding is a System.Windows.Data.Binding object that "glues" two properties together and keeps a channel of communication open between them. You can set up a Binding once, and then have it do all the synchronization work for the remainder of the application's lifetime.

Using Binding in Procedural Code

Imagine that you want to add a TextBlock to the Photo Gallery application used in the preceding two chapters that displays the current folder above the ListBox:

```
<TextBlock x:Name="currentFolder" DockPanel.Dock="Top"
  Background="AliceBlue" FontSize="16" />
```

You could update this `TextBlock`'s text manually whenever the `TreeView`'s `SelectedItem` changes:

```
void treeView_SelectedItemChanged(object sender,
  RoutedPropertyChangedEventArgs<object> e)
{
  currentFolder.Text = (treeView.SelectedItem as TreeViewItem).Header.ToString();
  Refresh();
}
```

By using a `Binding` object, you can remove this line of code and replace it with the following one-time initialization inside `MainWindow`'s constructor:

```
public MainWindow()
{
  InitializeComponent();

  Binding binding = new Binding();
  // Set source object
  binding.Source = treeView;
  // Set source property
  binding.Path = new PropertyPath("SelectedItem.Header");
  // Attach to target property
  currentFolder.SetBinding(TextBlock.TextProperty, binding);
}
```

With this change, `currentFolder.Text` updates automatically as `treeView.SelectedItem.Header` changes. If an item in the `TreeView` is ever selected that doesn't have a `Header` property (which doesn't happen in Photo Gallery), the data binding silently fails. (There are ways to get diagnostics, however, discussed later in this chapter.)

This code change doesn't appear to be an improvement, because we've exchanged one line of code for four! Keep in mind, however, that this is a very simple use of data binding! In later examples, the use of data binding greatly reduces the amount of code you would have to write to achieve the same results.

`Binding` has the notion of a *source* property and a *target* property. The source property (`treeView.SelectedItem.Header`, in this case) is set in two steps—assigning the source object to `Source` and the name of its relevant property (or chain of property and subproperties) to `Path` via an instance of `PropertyPath`. To associate the `Binding` with the target property (`currentFolder.Text`, in this case), you can call `SetBinding` (which is inherited by all `FrameworkElements` and `FrameworkContentElements`) with the relevant dependency property and the `Binding` instance.

TIP

There are actually two ways to set a `Binding` in procedural code. One is to call the `SetBinding` instance method on the relevant `FrameworkElement` or `FrameworkContentElement`, as done previously. The other is to call the `SetBinding` static method on a class called `BindingOperations`. You pass this method the same objects you would pass to the instance method, but it has an additional first parameter representing the target object. For example:

```
BindingOperations.SetBinding(currentFolder, TextBlock.TextProperty, binding);
```

The benefit of the static method is that the first parameter is defined as a `DependencyObject`, so it enables data binding on objects that don't derive from `FrameworkElement` or `FrameworkContentElement` (such as `Freezables`).

DIGGING DEEPER

Removing a `Binding`

If you don't want a `Binding` to exist for the remainder of the application's lifespan, you can "disconnect" it at any time with the static `BindingOperations.ClearBinding` method. You pass it the target object and its dependency property. For example:

```
BindingOperations.ClearBinding(currentFolder, TextBlock.TextProperty);
```

If a target object has more than one `Binding` attached to it, you can clear them all in one fell swoop by calling `BindingOperations.ClearAllBindings` like so:

```
BindingOperations.ClearAllBindings(currentFolder);
```

Another way to clear a `Binding` is simply to directly set the target property to a new value, such as:

```
currentFolder.Text = "I am no longer receiving updates.";
```

This only clears one-way `Bindings`, however. (The different types of `Bindings` are discussed in the "Customizing the Data Flow" section toward the end of this chapter.) The `ClearBinding` approach is more flexible anyway, as it still enables the dependency property to receive values from sources with a lower precedence (style triggers, property value inheritance, and so on). Recall the order of precedence for determining a base property value in Chapter 3, "Important New Concepts in WPF." A `Binding` has the same precedence as a local value, and `ClearBinding` removes the value from the property value equation, just like `ClearValue` does for *any* local value. (In fact, all `ClearBinding` does internally is call `ClearValue` on the target object!)

6

Using Binding in XAML

Because you can't call an element's `SetBinding` method from XAML, WPF contains a markup extension to make declarative use of `Binding` possible. In fact, `Binding` itself is a markup extension class (despite the nonstandard name without the `Extension` suffix).

To use `Binding` in XAML, you directly set the target property to a `Binding` instance and then use the standard markup extension syntax to set its properties. Therefore, the preceding `Binding` code could be replaced with the following addition to `currentFolder`'s declaration:

```
<TextBlock x:Name="currentFolder" DockPanel.Dock="Top"
  Text="{Binding ElementName=treeView, Path=SelectedItem.Header}"
  Background="AliceBlue" FontSize="16" />
```

Data binding is now starting to look more attractive than the manual approach! The connection between the source and target properties is not only expressed succinctly, but it's also abstracted away from all procedural code.

TIP

Besides its default constructor, `Binding` has a constructor that accepts `Path` as its single argument. Therefore, you can use alternative markup extension syntax to pass `Path` to the constructor rather than explicitly setting the property. In other words, the preceding XAML snippet could also be expressed as:

```
<TextBlock x:Name="currentFolder" DockPanel.Dock="Top"
  Text="{Binding SelectedItem.Header, ElementName=treeView}"
  Background="AliceBlue" FontSize="16" />
```

There's no difference in functionality, so the choice comes down to personal preference.

Notice that the XAML snippet uses `Binding`'s `ElementName` property to set the source object rather than `Source`, which was used in the preceding section. Both are valid in either context, but `ElementName` is easier to use from XAML because you only need to give it the source element's name. To set `Source` from XAML, the target object would need to be defined as a resource in an appropriate `ResourceDictionary`. In that case, you could write the following, where `treeView` is the resource's key:

```
<TextBlock x:Name="currentFolder" DockPanel.Dock="Top"
  Text="{Binding Source={StaticResource treeView}, Path=SelectedItem.Header}"
  Background="AliceBlue" FontSize="16" />
```

DIGGING DEEPER

Binding's `RelativeSource`

Another way to specify a data source is with `Binding`'s `RelativeSource` property, which refers to an element by its relationship to the target element. The property is of type `RelativeSource`, which also happens to be a markup extension. Here are some of the ways `RelativeSource` can be used:

To make the source element equal the target element:

```
{Binding RelativeSource={RelativeSource Self}}
```

To make the source element equal the target element's `TemplatedParent` (a property discussed in the next chapter):

```
{Binding RelativeSource={RelativeSource TemplatedParent}}
```

To make the source element equal the closest parent of a given type:

```
{Binding RelativeSource={RelativeSource FindAncestor, AncestorType={x:Type
    desiredType}}}
```

To make the source element equal the *n*th closest parent of a given type:

```
{Binding RelativeSource={RelativeSource FindAncestor,
    AncestorLevel=n, AncestorType={x:Type desiredType}}}
```

To make the source element equal the previous data item in a data-bound collection:

```
{Binding RelativeSource={RelativeSource PreviousData}}
```

`RelativeSource` is especially useful for control templates, discussed in the next chapter. But using `RelativeSource` with a mode of `Self` is handy for binding one property of an element to another without having to give the element a name. An interesting example is the following `Slider` whose `ToolTip` is bound to its own value:

```
<Slider ToolTip="{Binding RelativeSource={RelativeSource Self}, Path=Value}"/>
```

Binding to Plain .NET Properties

The example with the `TreeView` and the `Label` works because both the target and source properties are dependency properties. As discussed in Chapter 3, dependency properties have plumbing for change notification built in. This facility is the key to WPF's ability to keep the target property and source property in sync.

However, WPF supports any .NET property on any .NET object as a data-binding source. For example, imagine that you want to add a `Label` to the Photo Gallery application that displays the number of photos in the current folder. Rather than manually updating with the `Count` property from the `photos` collection (of type `Photos`), you can use data binding to connect the `Label`'s Content with the collection's Count property:

```
<Label x:Name="numItemsLabel"
  Content="{Binding Source={StaticResource photos}, Path=Count}"
  DockPanel.Dock="Bottom" />
```

(Here, the collection is assumed to be defined as a resource so it can be set in XAML via Source. ElementName is not an option because the collection is not a FrameworkElement or FrameworkContentElement!) The result of this addition is shown in Figure 9.1. Notice that the label says "54" when we really want it to say "54 item(s)." This can be fixed with an adjacent label with a static " item(s)" string as its content.

FIGURE 9.1   Displaying the value of photos.Count via data binding in the bottom-left corner of Photo Gallery's main Window.

There's a big caveat to using a plain .NET property as a data-binding source, however. Because such properties have no automatic plumbing for change notification, the target is not kept up to date as the source property value changes without doing a little extra work. Therefore, the value displayed in Figure 9.1 does not change as the current folder changes, which is clearly incorrect.

To keep the target and source properties synchronized, the source object must do one of the following:

▶ Implement the System.ComponentModel.INotifyPropertyChanged interface, which has a single PropertyChanged event.

▶ Implement an *XXX*Changed event, where *XXX* is the name of the property whose value changed.

The first technique is recommended, as WPF is optimized for this approach. (WPF only supports *XXX*Changed events for backward compatibility with older classes.) You could fix Photo Gallery by having the photos collection implement INotifyPropertyChanged. This would involve intercepting the relevant operations (such as Add, Remove, Clear, and Insert) and raising the PropertyChanged event. Fortunately, WPF already has a built-in class that does this work for you! It's called ObservableCollection. Therefore, making the binding to photos.Count synchronized is a one-line change from this:

```
public class Photos : Collection<Photo>
```

to this:

```
public class Photos : ObservableCollection<Photo>
```

DIGGING DEEPER

How Binding to a Plain .NET Property Works

When retrieving the value of a source property that's a plain .NET property, WPF uses reflection. However, if the source object implements `ICustomTypeDescriptor`, WPF uses this interface instead. Implementing this interface is an advanced technique, but it can be useful for boosting performance or supporting additional scenarios (such as changing the set of properties exposed on the fly).

WARNING

Data sources and data targets aren't treated equally!

Although the source property can be any .NET property on any .NET object, the same is not true for the data-binding target. The target property *must* be a dependency property. Also note that the source member must be a real property and not just a simple field.

Binding to an Entire Object

Although every example so far has used source objects and source properties, it turns out that the source property (that is, the `Path` in `Binding`) is optional! You can bind a target property to the entire source object.

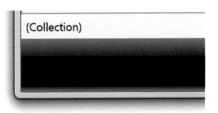

But what does it mean to bind to an entire object? Figure 9.2 shows what the `Label` from Figure 9.1 would look like if the `Path` were omitted:

FIGURE 9.2   Displaying the entire photos object via data binding in the bottom-left corner of Photo Gallery's main `Window`.

```
<Label x:Name="numItemsLabel"
  Content="{Binding Source={StaticResource photos}}"
  DockPanel.Dock="Bottom"/>
```

Because the `photos` object is not a `UIElement`, it gets rendered as the string returned from its `ToString` method. Binding to the whole object is not very useful in this case, but it's essential for elements that can take better advantage of the object, such as the `ListBox` that we'll examine next.

TIP

Binding to an entire object is a handy technique for setting a property from XAML that requires an instance of an object that can't be obtained via a type converter or markup extension.

For example, Photo Gallery contains a Popup that, when shown, is centered over a Button called zoomButton. Popup enables this with its Placement and PlacementTarget properties, the latter of which must be set to a UIElement. This could easily be done in C# as follows:

```
Button zoomButton = new Button();
…
Popup zoomPopup = new Popup();
zoomPopup.Placement = PlacementMode.Center;
zoomPopup.PlacementTarget = zoomButton;
```

But instead, Photo Gallery uses the following XAML to accomplish this:

```
<Button x:Name="zoomButton" … >
  …
</Button>
<Popup PlacementTarget="{Binding ElementName=zoomButton}" Placement="Center" …>
  …
</Popup>
```

In such cases, the use of Binding really isn't *data* binding in the traditional sense; it's more like *control* or *element* binding. This technique has been used in previous chapters.

WARNING

Be careful when binding to an entire UIElement!

When binding certain target properties to an entire UIElement, you might inadvertently be attempting to place the same element in multiple places of the visual tree. For example, the following XAML results in an InvalidOperationException explaining, "Specified element is already the logical child of another element."

```
<Label x:Name="one" Content="{Binding ElementName=two}"/>
<Label x:Name="two" Content="text"/>
```

However, you get no exception if you change the first Label to a TextBlock (and, therefore, the Content property to Text):

```
<TextBlock x:Name="one" Text="{Binding ElementName=two}"/>
<Label x:Name="two" Content="text"/>
```

Whereas Label.Content is of type Object, TextBlock.Text is a string. Therefore, the Label undergoes type conversion when assigned to a string and its ToString method is called. In this case, the TextBlock is rendered with a "System.Windows.Controls.Label: text" string, which is still not very useful. To copy the text from one Label or TextBlock to another, you should really be binding to the specific property (Label or Content).

Binding to a Collection

Binding a `Label` to `photos.Count` is nice, but it would be even better to bind the `ListBox` (the `Window`'s main piece of user interface) to the `photos` collection. This is the part of the Photo Gallery application that screams the loudest for data binding. The application, as presented in previous chapters, maintained the relationship between the collection of photos stored in the `ListBox` and the physical photos manually. When a new directory is selected, it clears the `ListBox` and creates a new `ListBoxItem` for each photo. If the user decides to delete or rename a photo, the change raises an event on the source collection (because it's internally using `FileSystemWatcher`), and an event handler manually refreshes the `ListBox` contents.

Fortunately, the procedure for replacing such logic with data binding is exactly the same as what we've already seen.

The Raw Binding

It would make sense to create a `Binding` with `ListBox.Items` as the target property, but, alas, `Items` is not a dependency property. But `ListBox` (and all other `ItemsControls`) have an `ItemsSource` dependency property that exists specifically for this data-binding scenario. `ItemsSource` is of type `IEnumerable`, so you can use the entire `photos` object as the source and set up the `Binding` as follows:

```
<ListBox x:Name="pictureBox"
  ItemsSource="{Binding Source={StaticResource photos}}" …>
  …
</ListBox>
```

For the target property to stay updated with changes to the source collection (that is, the adding and removing of elements), the source collection must implement an interface called `INotifyCollectionChanged`. Indeed, `ObservableCollection` implements both `INotifyPropertyChanged` and `INotifyCollectionChanged`, so the earlier change to make `Photos` derive from `ObservableCollection<Photo>` is necessary for making this binding work correctly.

The result of this data binding is shown in Figure 9.3.

Improving the Display

Clearly, the default display of the `photos` collection—a `ToString` rendering—is not acceptable. One way to improve this is to leverage the `DisplayMemberPath` property present on all `ItemsControls`, introduced in Chapter 4, "Introducing WPF's Controls." This property works hand in hand with `ItemsSource`. If you set it to an appropriate property path, the corresponding property value gets rendered for each item.

The collection in Photo Gallery consists of application-specific `Photo` objects, which have properties like `Name`, `DateTime`, and `Size`. Therefore, the following XAML produces the results in Figure 9.4, which is a slightly better rendering than Figure 9.3:

```
<ListBox x:Name="pictureBox" DisplayMemberPath="Name"
  ItemsSource="{Binding Source={StaticResource photos}}" …>
  …
</ListBox>
```

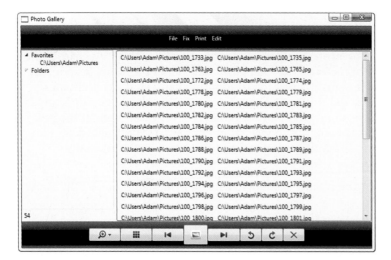

FIGURE 9.3   Binding the `ListBox` to the entire `photos` object shows the data in raw form.

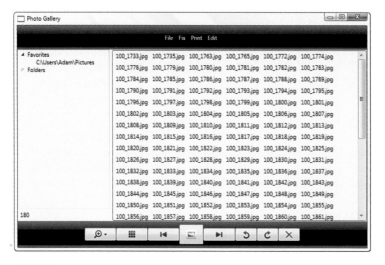

FIGURE 9.4   `DisplayMemberPath` is a simple mechanism for customizing the display of items in a data-bound collection.

However, because we're defining the `Photo` class ourselves, we could have just changed `Photo`'s implementation of `ToString` to return `Name` instead of the full path to get the same results.

For getting the actual images to display in the `ListBox`, you could add an `Image` property to the `Photo` class and use that as the `DisplayMemberPath`. But there are more flexible ways to control the presentation of bound data—ones that don't require changes to the source object. (This is important because you might not be the one defining the source object. Also, don't forget that one of the tenets of WPF is to separate look from logic!)

One way (not specific to data binding) is to use a data template, and another way is to use a value converter. The upcoming "Controlling Rendering" section looks at both of these options.

> ## WARNING
>
> ### ItemsControl's `Items` and `ItemsSource` properties can't be modified simultaneously!
>
> You must decide whether you want to populate an `ItemsControl` manually via `Items` or with data binding via `ItemsSource`, and you must not mix these techniques. `ItemsSource` can only be set when the `Items` collection is empty, and `Items` can only be modified when `ItemsSource` is null (otherwise, you'll get an `InvalidOperationException`). Therefore, if you want to add or remove items to/from a data-bound `ListBox`, you must do this to the underlying collection (`ItemsSource`) rather than at the UI level (`Items`). Note that regardless of which method is used to *set* items in an `ItemsControl`, you can always *retrieve* items via the `Items` collection.

Managing the Selected Item

As explained in Chapter 4, `Selectors` such as `ListBox` have a notion of a selected item or items. When binding a `Selector` to a collection (anything that implements `IEnumerable`), WPF keeps track of the selected item(s) so that other targets binding to the same source can make use of this information without the need for custom logic. This support can be used for creating master/detail user interfaces (as done in the final example in this chapter), or for synchronizing multiple `Selectors`, which we'll look at now.

To opt in to this support, set the `IsSynchronizedWithCurrentItem` property (inherited by all `Selectors`) to `true`. The following XAML sets this property on three `ListBoxes` that each displays a single property per item from the same photos collection:

```
<ListBox IsSynchronizedWithCurrentItem="True" DisplayMemberPath="Name"
  ItemsSource="{Binding Source={StaticResource photos}}"></ListBox>
<ListBox IsSynchronizedWithCurrentItem="True" DisplayMemberPath="DateTime"
  ItemsSource="{Binding Source={StaticResource photos}}"></ListBox>
<ListBox IsSynchronizedWithCurrentItem="True" DisplayMemberPath="Size"
  ItemsSource="{Binding Source={StaticResource photos}}"></ListBox>
```

Because each is marked with `IsSynchronizedWithCurrentItem="True"` *and each is pointing to the same source collection*, changing the selected item in any of them changes the selected item in the other two to match. (Although note that the scrolling of the `ListBoxes` is not synchronized automatically!) Figure 9.5 gives an idea of what this looks like. If any one of the `ListBoxes` omitted `IsSynchronizedWithCurrentItem` or set it to `false`, changing its own selected item would not impact the other two `ListBoxes`, nor would changing the selected item in the other two `ListBoxes` impact its own selection.

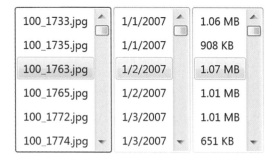

FIGURE 9.5   Three synchronized `ListBoxes`, thanks to data binding.

WARNING

`IsSynchronizedWithCurrentItem` does not support multiple selections!

When a `Selector` has multiple selected items (as with `ListBox`'s `SelectionMode` Multiple or Extended), only the first selected item is seen by other synchronized elements, even if they also support multiple selections!

Sharing the Source with `DataContext`

You've now applied data binding to several target properties, and all but one of them used the same source object (the `photos` collection). It's quite common for many elements in the same UI to bind to the same source object (different source *properties*, but the same source object). For this reason, WPF supports specifying an implicit data source rather than explicitly marking every `Binding` with a `Source`, `RelativeSource`, or `ElementName`. This implicit data source is also known as a *data context*.

To designate a source object such as the `photos` collection as a data context, simply find a common parent element and set its `DataContext` property to the source object. (All `FrameworkElements` and `FrameworkContentElements` have this `DataContext` property of type `Object`.) When encountering a `Binding` without an explicit source object, WPF traverses up the logical tree until it finds a nonnull `DataContext`.

Therefore, you can use `DataContext` as follows to make the `Label` and `ListBox` use it as the source object:

```
<StackPanel x:Name="parent" DataContext="{StaticResource photos}">
  <Label x:Name="numItemsLabel"
    Content="{Binding Path=Count}"
    DockPanel.Dock="Bottom" />

  …

  <ListBox x:Name="pictureBox" DisplayMemberPath="Name"
    ItemsSource="{Binding}" …>

    …
```

```
    </ListBox>
    …
</StackPanel>
```

Because `DataContext` is a simple property, it's also really easy to set from procedural code, eliminating the need to store the source object as a resource:

```
parent.DataContext = photos;
```

TIP

Encountering a property set to just `{Binding}` in XAML might look confusing, but it simply means that the source object is specified somewhere up the tree as a data context, and that the entire object is being bound rather than a single property on it.

FAQ

 When should I specify a source object using a data context versus specifying it explicitly in a `Binding`?

It's mostly just a matter of personal preference. If a source object is only being used by one target property, using a data context might be a bit of overkill and less readable. But if you are sharing a source object, using a data context to specify the object in only one place makes development less error-prone if you change the source.

One case where the use of a data context is really helpful is when plugging in resources defined elsewhere. Resources can assume that a parent data context exists (without knowing what it is), and can then be used in completely different contexts. (Although using `RelativeSource` to specify an explicit yet relative source also can provide this kind of flexibility.)

Controlling Rendering

Data binding is pretty simple when the source and target properties are compatible data types and the default rendering of the source is all you need to display. But often a bit of customization is required. The need for this in the previous section is obvious, as we want to display `Images` in Photo Gallery's `ListBox`, not raw strings!

These types of customizations would be easy *without* data binding because you're writing all the code to retrieve the data on your own (as done in the original version of Photo Gallery). But WPF provides two mechanisms for customizing how the source value is received and displayed, so you don't need to give up the benefits of data binding to get the desired results in more customized scenarios. These mechanisms are data templates and value converters.

Using Data Templates

A data template is a piece of UI that you'd like to apply to an arbitrary .NET object when it is rendered. Many WPF controls have properties (of type `DataTemplate`) for attaching a data template appropriately. For example, `ContentControl` has a `ContentTemplate` property for controlling the rendering of its `Content` object, `ItemsControl` has an

`ItemTemplate` that applies to each of its items, `HeaderedContentControl` and `HeaderedItemsControl` both define a `HeaderTemplate` property for controlling the look of their `Header` object, and so on.

By setting one of these properties to an instance of a `DataTemplate`, you can swap in a completely new visual tree. `DataTemplate`, like the `ItemsPanelTemplate` introduced in Chapter 4, derives from `FrameworkTemplate`. Therefore, it has a `VisualTree` content property that can be set to an arbitrary tree of `FrameworkElements`. This is easy to set in XAML but cumbersome to set in procedural code.

Let's try using a `DataTemplate` with Photo Gallery's `ListBox`, which, as of Figure 9.4, is showing raw strings rather than `Images`. The following snippet adds a simple `DataTemplate` by setting `ListBox`'s `ItemTemplate` property inline:

```
<ListBox x:Name="pictureBox"
  ItemsSource="{Binding Source={StaticResource photos}}" …>
<ListBox.ItemTemplate>
  <DataTemplate>
    <Image Source="placeholder.jpg" Height="35"/>
  </DataTemplate>
</ListBox.ItemTemplate>

  …
</ListBox>
```

Figure 9.6 shows that this is a good start. Although a generic `placeholder.jpg` image is shown for each item, at least the items are now `Images`!

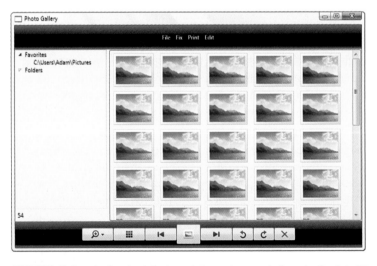

FIGURE 9.6   A simple data template makes each item in the `ListBox` appear as a place-holder `Image`.

With an `Image` data template in place, how do you set its `Source` property to the current `Photo` item's `FullPath` property? With data binding, of course! When you apply a data template, it is implicitly given an appropriate data context (that is, a source object). When applied as an `ItemTemplate`, the data context is implicitly the current item in `ItemsSource`. So, you can simply update the data template as follows to get the result shown in Figure 9.7:

```
<ListBox x:Name="pictureBox"
  ItemsSource="{Binding Source={StaticResource photos}}" …>
<ListBox.ItemTemplate>
  <DataTemplate>
    <Image Source="{Binding Path=FullPath}" Height="35"/>
  </DataTemplate>
</ListBox.ItemTemplate>

  …

</ListBox>
```

FIGURE 9.7   The updated data template gives the desired results—the right photo displayed for each item in the `ListBox`.

Of course, a `DataTemplate` doesn't have to be declared inline. They are most commonly used as a resource, so they can be shared by multiple elements. You can even get a `DataTemplate` to be automatically applied to a specific type wherever it might appear by setting its `DataType` property to the desired type.

A special subclass of `DataTemplate` exists for working with hierarchical data, such as XML or a file system. This class is called `HierarchicalDataTemplate`. It not only

> **TIP**
>
> Although data templates can be used on non-data-bound objects (such as a `ListBox` with a manually constructed set of items), you'll almost always want to use data binding *inside* the template to customize the appearance of the visual tree based on the underlying object(s).

enables you to change the presentation of such data, but enables you to directly bind a hierarchy of objects to an element that intrinsically understands hierarchies, such as a TreeView or Menu control. The "XmlDataProvider" section later in this chapter shows an example of using HierarchicalDataTemplate with XML data.

Using Value Converters

Whereas data templates can customize the way certain target values are rendered, value converters can morph the source value into a completely different target value. They enable you to plug in custom logic without giving up the benefits of data binding.

Value converters are often used to reconcile a source and target that are different data types. For example, you could change the background or foreground color of an element based on the value of some non-Brush data source, a la conditional formatting in Microsoft Excel. Or, you could use it to simply enhance the information being displayed without the need for separate elements, such as adding an "item(s)" suffix to a raw count. The following two sections explore examples of each of these.

Bridging Incompatible Data Types

Imagine that you want to change the Label's Background based on the number of items in the photos collection (the value of its Count property). The following Binding makes no sense because it tries to assign Background to a number rather than a Brush:

```
<Label Background="{Binding Path=Count, Source={StaticResource photos}}" …/>
```

To fix this, you can plug in a value converter using Binding's Converter property:

```
<Label Background="{Binding Path=Count, Converter={StaticResource myConverter},
  Source={StaticResource photos}}" …/>
```

This assumes that you've written a custom class that can convert an integer into a Brush and defined it as a resource:

```
<Window.Resources>
  <local:CountToBackgroundConverter x:Key="myConverter"/>
</Window.Resources>
```

To create this class called CountToBackgroundConverter, you must implement a simple interface called IValueConverter (in the System.Windows.Data namespace). This interface has two simple methods—Convert, which is passed the source instance that must be converted to the target instance, and ConvertBack, which does the opposite.

Therefore, CountToBackgroundConverter could be implemented in C# as follows:

```
public class CountToBackgroundConverter : IValueConverter
{
  public object Convert(object value, Type targetType, object parameter,
    CultureInfo culture)
  {
```

```
    if (targetType != typeof(Brush))
      throw new InvalidOperationException("The target must be a Brush!");

    // Let Parse throw an exception if the input is bad
    int num = int.Parse(value.ToString());

    return (num == 0 ? Brushes.Yellow : Brushes.Transparent);
  }
  public object ConvertBack(object value, Type targetType, object parameter,
    CultureInfo culture)
  {
    throw new NotSupportedException();
  }
}
```

The Convert method is called every time the source value changes. It's given the integral value and returns Brushes.Yellow if the value is zero, or Brushes.Transparent otherwise. (The idea is to highlight the Label's background when an empty folder is displayed.) The ConvertBack method is not needed, so CountToBackground-Converter simply throws an exception if it's ever called. The "Advanced Topics" section discusses situations in which ConvertBack is used. Figure 9.8 displays CountToBackgroundConverter in action.

FIGURE 9.8   The value converter makes the Label's Background yellow when there are no items in the photos collection, seen in the bottom-left corner of Photo Gallery's main Window.

TIP

To avoid confusion, it's a good idea to capture the semantics of a value converter in its name. I could have named CountToBackgroundConverter something like IntegerToBrushConverter because it technically can be used anywhere where the source data type is an integer and the target data type is a Brush. But it might only make sense when the source integer represents a count of items and when the Brush represents a Background. (For example, it's unlikely you'd ever want to set an element's Foreground to Transparent!) I might also want to define additional Integer-to-Brush converters with alternate semantics!

The methods of IValueConverter are passed a parameter and a culture. By default, parameter is set to null and culture is set to the value of the target element's Language property. This Language property (defined on FrameworkElement and

FrameworkContentElement, whose value is often inherited from the root element if set at all) uses "en-US" (American English) as its default value. However, the consumer of Bindings can control these two values via Binding.ConverterParameter and Binding.ConverterCulture. For example, rather than hard-coding Brushes.Yellow inside CountToBackgroundConverter.Convert, you could set it to the user-supplied parameter:

```
return (num == 0 ? parameter : Brushes.Transparent);
```

This assumes that parameter is always set as follows:

```
<Label Background="{Binding Path=Count, Converter={StaticResource myConverter},
  ConverterParameter=Yellow, Source={StaticResource photos}}" Content="…" />
```

Note that the value for ConvertParameter (like all markup extension parameters) undergoes type conversion, so a simple string like Yellow can be specified and the value converter will indeed receive the correct Brush object. Similarly, ConverterCulture can be set to an IETF language tag (like "ko-KR") and the converter will receive the appropriate CultureInfo object.

TIP

WPF ships with a handful of value converters to handle a few very common data-binding scenarios. One of these is BooleanToVisibilityConverter, which converts between the three-state Visibility enumeration (which can be Visible, Hidden, or Collapsed) and a Boolean or nullable Boolean. In the one direction, true is mapped to Visible, whereas false and null are mapped to Collapsed. In the other direction, Visible is mapped to true, whereas Hidden and Collapsed are mapped to false.

This is useful for toggling the visibility of elements based on the state of an otherwise unrelated element. For example, the following snippet of XAML implements a "Show Status Bar" CheckBox without requiring any procedural code:

```
<Window.Resources>
  <BooleanToVisibilityConverter x:Key="booltoVis"/>
</Window.Resources>
…
<CheckBox x:Name="checkBox">Show Status Bar</CheckBox>
…
<StatusBar Visibility="{Binding ElementName=checkBox, Path=IsChecked,
  Converter={StaticResource booltoVis}}">…</StatusBar>
```

In this case, the StatusBar is visible when (and only when) the CheckBox's IsChecked property is true.

> **WARNING**
>
> **Data-binding errors don't appear as unhandled exceptions!**
>
> Instead of throwing exceptions on data-binding errors, WPF dumps explanatory text via debug traces that can only be seen with an attached debugger (or other trace listeners). Therefore, when data binding doesn't work as expected, try running it under a debugger and be sure to check for traces. In Visual Studio, these can be found in the Output window.
>
> The previous example of a nonsensical binding (hooking up Background directly to photos.Count) produces the following debug trace:
>
> ```
> System.Windows.Data Error: 5 : Value produced by BindingExpression is not valid
> for target property.; Value='39' BindingExpression:Path=Count; DataItem='Photos'
> (HashCode=58961324); target element is 'Label' (Name='numItemsLabel'); target
> property is 'Background' (type 'Brush')
> ```
>
> Even exceptions thrown by the source object (or value converter) get swallowed and displayed as debug traces by default!
>
> Because the tracing is implemented with System.Diagnostics.TraceSource objects (introduced in the .NET Framework 2.0), there are several standard options for capturing these same traces outside the debugger. Mike Hillberg, a WPF architect, shares details at http://blogs.msdn.com/mikehillberg/archive/2006/09/14/WpfTraceSources.aspx. You can capture traces WPF emits in a number of areas (that aren't even enabled by default under a debugger), such as information about event routing, dependency property registration, resource retrieval, and much more.

Customizing Data Display

Sometimes, value converters are useful in cases where the source and target data types are already compatible. Earlier when we set the Content of numItemsLabel to the Count property of the photos collection (shown in Figure 9.1), it displayed just fine but requires some additional text for the user to not be confused by what that number means. Although this could be accomplished with an additional Label with static content like "item(s)," we can do better. (I don't know about you, but when I see a user interface report something like "1 item(s)," it just looks lazy to me.)

A value converter enables us to customize the text based on the value, so we can display "1 item" (singular) versus "2 items" (plural). And we can do this without the use of an additional element! The following RawCountToDescriptionConverter does just that:

```
public class RawCountToDescriptionConverter : IValueConverter
{
  public object Convert(object value, Type targetType, object parameter,
    CultureInfo culture)
  {
    // Let Parse throw an exception if the input is bad
    int num = int.Parse(value.ToString());
    return num + (num == 1 ? " item" : " items");
```

6

```
  }
  public object ConvertBack(object value, Type targetType, object parameter,
    CultureInfo culture)
  {
    throw new NotSupportedException();
  }
}
```

Note that this uses hard-coded English strings, whereas a production-quality converter would make use of the passed-in `culture` parameter. That's one downside of dynamically building the string; a static " item(s)" `Label` is more natural to localize.

TIP

Value converters are the key to plugging in any kind of custom logic into the data-binding process. Whether you want to apply some sort of transformation to the source value before displaying it or you want to change how the target gets updated based on the value of the source, you can easily accomplish this with a class that implements `IValueConverter`.

TIP

You can make a value converter temporarily cancel a data binding by returning the sentinel value `Binding.DoNothing`. This is different from returning `null`, as `null` might be a perfectly valid value for the target property.

`Binding.DoNothing` effectively means, "I don't want to bind right now; pretend the `Binding` doesn't exist." In this case, the value of the target property doesn't change from its current value unless there's some other entity that happens to be influencing its value (an animation, a trigger, and so on). This only affects the current call to `Convert` or `ConvertBack`, so unless the `Binding` is cleared (via a call to `ClearBinding`, for example), the value converter will continue to be called every time the source value changes.

FAQ

 How do I use a value converter to convert each item when binding to a collection?

You can apply a data template to the `ItemsControl`'s `ItemTemplate` property and then apply the value converter to the `Binding` done *inside the data template*. If you were to apply the value converter to the `ItemsControl`'s `Binding` instead, an update to the source collection would prompt the `Convert` method to be called once *for the entire collection* (not on a per-item basis). You could implement such a converter that accepts a collection and returns a morphed collection, but that would not be a very efficient approach.

Customizing the View of a Collection

In the previous "Binding to a Collection" section, we saw that with the flip of a switch (setting IsSynchronizedWithCurrentItem to true), multiple Selectors pointing to the same source collection can see the same selected item. This behavior seems almost magical, at least when you're watching it in person. (It's hard to capture the synchronized motion in a static screenshot!) The source collection has no notion of a current item, so where is this information coming from and where is the state being maintained?

It turns out that whenever you bind to a collection (anything that implements IEnumerable), a default *view* is implicitly inserted between the source and target objects. This view (which is an object implementing the ICollectionView interface) stores the notion of a current item, but it also has support for sorting, grouping, filtering, and item navigation. This section digs into these four topics as well as working with multiple views for the same source object.

> **TIP**
>
> Views are automatically associated with each source collection, *not* with the targets consuming the source. The result is that changes to the view (such as sorting or filtering it) are automatically seen by all targets.

Sorting

ICollectionView has a SortDescriptions property that provides a way to control how the view's items are sorted. The basic idea is that you choose a property on the collection items to sort by (such as Name, DateTime, or Size on the Photo object) and you choose whether you want that property to be sorted ascending or descending. This choice is captured by a SortDescription object, which you can construct with a property name and a ListSortDirection. For example:

```
SortDescription sort = new SortDescription("Name", ListSortDirection.Ascending);
```

The SortDescriptions property, however, is a *collection* of SortDescription objects. It was designed this way so you can sort by multiple properties simultaneously. The first SortDescription in the collection represents the most significant property and the last SortDescription represents the least significant property. For example, if you add the following two SortDescriptions to the collection, the items get sorted descending by DateTime, but if there are any ties, the Name (in ascending order) is used as the tiebreaker:

```
view.SortDescriptions.Add(new SortDescription("DateTime",
  ListSortDirection.Descending));
view.SortDescriptions.Add(new SortDescription("Name",
  ListSortDirection.Ascending));
```

The SortDescriptions collection has a Clear method for returning the view to the default sort. A view's default sort is simply the order in which items are placed in the source collection, which might not be sorted at all!

Listing 9.1 demonstrates how Photo Gallery could implement logic to sort its photos by Name, DateTime, or Size when the user clicks a corresponding Button. As in Windows Explorer, a repeated click toggles the sort between ascending and descending.

LISTING 9.1   Sorting by Three Different Properties

```
// Click event handlers for three different Buttons:
void sortByName_Click(object sender, RoutedEventArgs e)
{
  SortHelper("Name");
}
void sortByDateTime_Click(object sender, RoutedEventArgs e)
{
  SortHelper("DateTime");
}
void sortBySize_Click(object sender, RoutedEventArgs e)
{
  SortHelper("Size");
}


void SortHelper(string propertyName)
{
  // Get the default view
  ICollectionView view = CollectionViewSource.GetDefaultView(
    this.FindResource("photos"));

  // Check if the view is already sorted ascending by the current property
  if (view.SortDescriptions.Count > 0
      && view.SortDescriptions[0].PropertyName == propertyName
      && view.SortDescriptions[0].Direction == ListSortDirection.Ascending)
  {
    // Already sorted ascending, so "toggle" by sorting descending
    view.SortDescriptions.Clear();
    view.SortDescriptions.Add(new SortDescription(
      propertyName, ListSortDirection.Descending));
  }
  else
  {
    // Sort ascending
    view.SortDescriptions.Clear();
    view.SortDescriptions.Add(new SortDescription(
      propertyName, ListSortDirection.Ascending));
  }
}
```

> ## DIGGING DEEPER
>
> ### Custom Sorting
>
> If you want more control over the sorting process than what
> `ICollectionView.SortDescriptions` gives you (which frankly seems unlikely), you can
> usually take advantage of custom sorting support. If the underlying collection implements
> `IList` (as most collections do), the `ICollectionView` returned by `CollectionViewSource.`
> `GetDefaultView` is actually an instance of the `ListCollectionView` class. If you can cast
> the `ICollectionView` to a `ListCollectionView`, you can assign a custom object imple-
> menting `IComparer` to its `CustomSort` property. When this is done, your implementation of
> `IComparer.Compare` will be called to determine the sort order. Inside your `Compare` method,
> you can use any method you want for sorting the items.

Notice that this code has no explicit relationship with the `ListBox` displaying the photos.
The view being operated on is associated with the source `photos` collection and is
retrieved by a simple call to the static `CollectionViewSource.GetDefaultView` method.
Indeed, if additional `ItemsControls` bound to the same `photos` collection, they would
pick up the same view by default and would all sort together.

Grouping

`ICollectionView` has a `GroupDescriptions` property that works much like
`SortDescriptions`. You can add any number of `PropertyGroupDescription` objects to it
to arrange the source collection's items into groups and potential subgroups.

For example, the following code groups items in the `photos` collection by the value of
their `DateTime` property:

```
// Get the default view
ICollectionView view = CollectionViewSource.GetDefaultView(
  this.FindResource("photos"));
// Do the grouping
view.GroupDescriptions.Clear();
view.GroupDescriptions.Add(new PropertyGroupDescription("DateTime"));
```

Unlike sorting, however, the effects of grouping are not noticeable unless you modify the
`ItemsControl` displaying the data. To get grouping to behave properly, you must set the
`ItemsControl`'s `GroupStyle` property to an instance of a `GroupStyle` object. This object
has a `HeaderTemplate` property that should be set to a data template defining the look of
the grouping header.

Photo Gallery's `ListBox` could be given the following `GroupStyle` to support the preceding grouping code:

```
<ListBox x:Name="pictureBox"
  ItemsSource="{Binding Source={StaticResource photos}}" …>
<ListBox.GroupStyle>
  <GroupStyle>
```

6

```
    <GroupStyle.HeaderTemplate>
      <DataTemplate>
        <Border BorderBrush="Black" BorderThickness="1">
          <TextBlock Text="{Binding Path=Name}" FontWeight="Bold"/>
        </Border>
      </DataTemplate>
    </GroupStyle.HeaderTemplate>
  </GroupStyle>
</ListBox.GroupStyle>
  …
</ListBox>
```

Notice the use of data binding inside the data template. In this case, the data template is given a data context of a special CollectionViewGroup object that's instantiated behind the scenes. The details of this class aren't important, other than the fact that it has a Name property representing the value defining each group. Therefore, the data template uses data binding to display this Name in the grouping header. Figure 9.9 shows the result of running the preceding code with the updated XAML.

After doing this, we see that perhaps grouping by Photo.DateTime is not a great idea. Because DateTime includes both a date and a time, each Photo tends to have a unique value, leaving us with many groups of one!

To fix this, we can leverage an overloaded constructor of the PropertyGroupDescription class that enables us to tweak the property value before using it as the basis for grouping. To do this, the constructor allows us to pass in a value converter! Therefore, we can write a DateTimeToDateConverter class that converts the raw DateTime into a string more suitable for grouping:

```
public class DateTimeToDateConverter : IValueConverter
{
  public object Convert(object value, Type targetType, object parameter,
    CultureInfo culture)
  {
    return ((DateTime)value).ToString("MM/dd/yyyy");
  }
  public object ConvertBack(object value, Type targetType, object parameter,
    CultureInfo culture)
  {
    throw new NotSupportedException();
  }
}
```

In this case, the returned string simply strips out the time component of the input DateTime. But you could imagine supporting much fancier groupings with this mechanism, such as calculating date ranges and returning strings like "Last Week," "Last Month," and so on. (Again, you should use the passed-in culture to tweak the formatting of the returned string.)

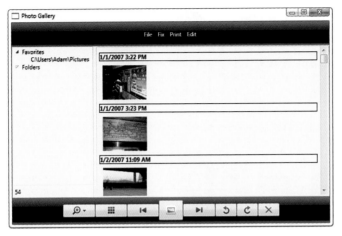

FIGURE 9.9   A first attempt at grouping items in the ListBox.

> **TIP**
>
> If you want to group items of an ItemsControl yet you don't care about creating a fancy GroupStyle, you can use a built-in GroupStyle that ships with WPF. It's exposed as a static GroupStyle.Default property. Therefore, you can reference it in XAML as follows:
>
> ```
> <ListBox x:Name="pictureBox"
>   ItemsSource="{Binding Source={StaticResource photos}}" …>
> <ListBox.GroupStyle>
>   <x:Static Member="GroupStyle.Default">
> </ListBox.GroupStyle>
>   …
> </ListBox>
> ```

With this value converter defined, we can use it for grouping as follows:

```
// Get the default view
ICollectionView view = CollectionViewSource.GetDefaultView(
  this.FindResource("photos"));
// Do the grouping
view.GroupDescriptions.Clear();
view.GroupDescriptions.Add(
  new PropertyGroupDescription("DateTime", new DateTimeToDateConverter()));
```

The result of this change is shown in Figure 9.10.

To sort groups, you can use the same mechanism described in the preceding section. Sorting is always applied before grouping. The result is that the primary SortDescription applies to the groups and any remaining SortDescriptions apply to items within each group. Just make sure that the property (or custom logic) used to do the sorting matches the property (or custom logic) used to do the grouping, otherwise the resulting arrangement of items is not intuitive.

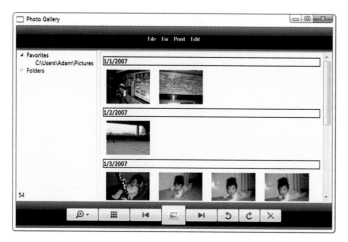

FIGURE 9.10   Improved grouping based on the date component of `Photo.DateTime`.

> **TIP**
>
> Perhaps you want to implement custom grouping based on the values of several properties. You can accomplish this by constructing `PropertyGroupDescription` with a null property name. When you do this, the `value` parameter passed to your value converter is the entire source item (a `Photo` object, in the Photo Gallery example) rather than a single property value.

Filtering

As with sorting and grouping, `ICollectionView` has a property that enables *filtering*— selective removal of items based on an arbitrary condition. This property is called `Filter`, and is a `Predicate<Object>` type (in other words, a delegate that accepts a single `Object` parameter and returns a Boolean).

When `Filter` is `null` (which it is by default), all items in the source collection are shown in the view. But when it's set to a delegate, the delegate is instantly called back for every item in the source collection. The delegate's job is to determine whether each item should be shown (by returning `true`) or should be hidden (by returning `false`).

By using an anonymous delegate in C#, specifying a filter can be done pretty compactly. For example, the following code filters out all `Photo` items whose `DateTime` is older than 7 days ago:

```
ICollectionView view = CollectionViewSource.GetDefaultView(this.FindResource
  ("photos"));
view.Filter = delegate(object o) {
  return ((o as Photo).DateTime - DateTime.Now).Days <= 7;
};
```

To remove the filter, simply set `view.Filter` back to `null`.

Navigating

In this context, *navigating* a view refers to managing the current item; not the kind of navigation discussed in Chapter 7. `ICollectionView` not only has a `CurrentItem` property (and a corresponding `CurrentPosition` property that exposes the current item's zero-based index), but it also has a handful of methods for programmatically changing the `CurrentItem`. The data-binding version of Photo Gallery uses these methods to implement handlers for the Next Photo/Previous Photo `Button`s as follows:

```
void previous_Click(object sender, RoutedEventArgs e)
{
  // Get the default view
  ICollectionView view = CollectionViewSource.GetDefaultView(
    this.FindResource("photos"));
  // Move backward
  view.MoveCurrentToPrevious();
  // Wrap around to the end
  if (view.IsCurrentBeforeFirst) view.MoveCurrentToLast();
}
void next_Click(object sender, RoutedEventArgs e)
{
  // Get the default view
  ICollectionView view = CollectionViewSource.GetDefaultView(
    this.FindResource("photos"));
  // Move forward
  view.MoveCurrentToNext();
  // Wrap around to the beginning
  if (view.IsCurrentAfterLast) view.MoveCurrentToFirst();
}
```

Although a bit wordy, these navigation methods are straightforward to use. These handlers not only update the selected item in the `ListBox` without explicitly referencing it, but any additional elements that wish to display information about the current item can be automatically updated as well as long as they bind to the same source. Note that until an item is selected on the source collection, `CurrentItem` is `null` and `CurrentPosition` is -1.

> **WARNING**
>
> **Default view navigation isn't exposed automatically!**
>
> Unlike sorting, grouping, and filtering, the effects of navigation on the default view can only be seen on `Selectors` that have `IsSynchronizedWithCurrentItem` set to true. Without this setting, the `Selector`'s `SelectedItem` and the default view's `CurrentItem` are detached; they can be updated independently without affecting one another. The WPF team wanted synchronization of the selected item to be an explicit choice to expose developers to the concept of a view and avoid potentially confusing behavior. But frankly, I find the inconsistency with the other "automatic" aspects of the default view to be confusing.

> **TIP**
>
> Property paths used in `Bindings` support referencing a collection's current item with special forward-slash syntax. For example, the following `Binding` binds to the current item, assuming the data source is a collection:
>
> ```
> "{Binding Path=/}"
> ```
>
> The following binds to the `DateTime` property on the current item:
>
> ```
> "{Binding Path=/DateTime}"
> ```
>
> The following binds to the current item of a collection exposed by a property called `Photos` on a different data source that isn't a collection itself:
>
> ```
> "{Binding Path=Photos/}"
> ```
>
> And finally, the following binds to the `DateTime` property on the current item from the preceding example:
>
> ```
> "{Binding Path=Photos/DateTime}"
> ```
>
> This functionality is incredibly useful for implementing master/detail user interfaces without any procedural code.

Working with Additional Views

The previous examples of sorting, grouping, filtering, and navigating always operated on the default view associated with the source collection. But it's conceivable that you want elements to have *different* views of the same source collection. It turns out that the `CollectionViewSource` class has more uses than just returning the default view; it can also construct a brand-new view over any source. This view can then be selectively applied to any target, overriding the default view.

To create a new view over Photo Gallery's `photos` collection, you could do the following:

```
CollectionViewSource viewSource = new CollectionViewSource();
viewSource.Source = photos;
// viewSource.View now points to a nondefault ICollectionView implementation
```

A design goal of `CollectionViewSource` is to make it easy to create custom views declaratively, so you can alternatively use the following XAML:

```
<Window.Resources>
  <local:Photos x:Key="photos"/>
  <CollectionViewSource x:Key="viewSource" Source="{StaticResource photos}"/>
</Window.Resources>
```

To apply the custom view to a target property, simply bind to the `CollectionViewSource` rather than the underlying source object:

```
<ListBox x:Name="pictureBox"
  ItemsSource="{Binding Source={StaticResource photos viewSource}}" …>
  …
</ListBox>
```

Note that although the original source is now wrapped by a `CollectionViewSource`, WPF special-cases the `CollectionViewSource` class so that you don't have to change any `Binding Paths`. Binding to the `Count` property, for example, still refers to the property of the underlying `Photos` object rather than the `CollectionViewSource` object.

Such a `ListBox` is now exempt from any sorting/grouping/filtering/navigating being done on the default view. If you want to perform any of these actions on the custom view, you can follow all the same techniques outlined previously using the `ICollectionView` returned by the `CollectionViewSource.View` instance property rather than the `CollectionViewSource.GetDefaultView` static method.

To enable a custom view to be configured with sorting and grouping entirely within XAML, `CollectionViewSource` has its own `SortDescriptions` and `GroupDescriptions` properties that work just like the corresponding properties on `ICollectionView`. It also has its own `Filter` member, but it's defined as an event rather than a delegate property so it can also be set inside XAML. (Of course, it must be set to an event handler written in procedural code.) Sorting, grouping, and filtering can, therefore, all be expressed in XAML as follows:

```
<CollectionViewSource x:Key="viewSource" Filter="viewSource_Filter"          ─── Filtering
    Source="{StaticResource photos}">
<CollectionViewSource.SortDescriptions>
  <componentModel:SortDescription PropertyName="DateTime" Direction="Descending"/>
</CollectionViewSource.SortDescriptions>
<CollectionViewSource.GroupDescriptions>                                         Sorting
  <PropertyGroupDescription PropertyName="DateTime"/>
</CollectionViewSource.GroupDescriptions>                                     ─── Grouping
</CollectionViewSource>
```

The `SortDescription` class happens to live in a .NET namespace not included in the standard XML namespace, so the following directive is needed:

```
xmlns:componentModel="clr-namespace:System.ComponentModel;assembly=WindowsBase"
```

The `viewSource_Filter` method referenced by the XAML could be implemented as follows, which is a translation of the previous filtering delegate that excludes all photos older than 7 days from today's date:

```
void viewSource_Filter(object sender, FilterEventArgs e)
{
  e.Accepted = ((e.Item as Photo).DateTime - DateTime.Now).Days <= 7;
}
```

6

Rather than getting the source item passed in directly, the event handler receives it as
e.Item. Rather than *returning* a Boolean, it must set the Boolean e.Accepted property to
communicate whether the item is in or out.

TIP

Even if you don't require multiple views over the same source collection, you can opt to
create and apply a custom view with the explicit CollectionViewSource simply so you can
sort and group items without any procedural code!

FAQ

 **If my application contains a collection, and nobody ever data binds directly to
it (but rather to a CollectionViewSource), does the default view still exist?**

No. For performance reasons, the default view is created on demand. This is unlike a tree
falling in a forest, which I'm told still makes a sound even if nobody is around to hear it.

WARNING

Navigation works differently in a custom view!

Changing the current item on a custom view automatically impacts any Selectors binding to
that view by default; the Selector's IsSynchronizedWithCurrentItem property must be
explicitly set to false in order to opt out of the synchronized navigation. This is the exact
opposite behavior of the default view!

Although the default value for IsSynchronizedWithCurrentItem is false, WPF automatically sets it to true when a Selector's ItemsSource is set to a custom view unless it has
been given an explicit value (or the Selector's SelectionMode isn't Single). The idea is
that using a custom view is an explicit acknowledgment of the view's existence, so you
should get the expected view navigation behavior by default. (This monkey business is yet
another reason I wish that IsSynchronizedWithCurrentItem defaulted to true for all
views.)

Data Providers

Because the source object can be any arbitrary .NET object, you can perform just about
any data binding imaginable with enough code. You can imagine binding to a database,
the Windows Registry, an Excel spreadsheet, and so on. All you need is an appropriate
.NET object that exposes the right set of properties and notifications and handles all the
messy implementation details! (That said, the work involved in creating such code might
outweigh the benefits of data binding if you're writing everything yourself!)

To cut down on the need for custom code, WPF ships with two classes that provide a generic "data binding–friendly" way to expose common items: XmlDataProvider and ObjectDataProvider.

FAQ

 How do I use data binding to bind to a relational database?

Unfortunately, WPF does not include a data provider for databases. (In beta versions, WPF did have an experimental ADO.NET data provider, but it was removed for version 3.0.) However, nothing is stopping you from using an ADO.NET DataSet (for example) as a data source. If you fill a DataSet and set it as an element's DataContext, you can bind to it fairly seamlessly. The Windows SDK has a sample of using WPF data binding with ADO.NET.

XmlDataProvider

The XmlDataProvider class provides an easy way to data bind to a chunk of XML, whether it's an in-memory fragment or a complete file. Listing 9.2 shows an example of using XmlDataProvider to bind to an embedded data island.

LISTING 9.2   Binding to an Embedded XML Data Island

```xml
<Window xmlns="http://schemas.microsoft.com/winfx/2006/xaml/presentation"
        xmlns:x="http://schemas.microsoft.com/winfx/2006/xaml"
        Title="XML Data Binding">
  <Window.Resources>
    <XmlDataProvider x:Key="dataProvider" XPath="GameStats">
      <x:XData>
        <GameStats xmlns="">
          <!-- One stat per game type -->
          <GameStat Type="Beginner">
            <HighScore>1203</HighScore>
          </GameStat>
          <GameStat Type="Intermediate">
            <HighScore>1089</HighScore>
          </GameStat>
          <GameStat Type="Advanced">
            <HighScore>541</HighScore>
          </GameStat>
        </GameStats>
      </x:XData>
    </XmlDataProvider>
  </Window.Resources>
  <Grid>
```

XML data island

LISTING 9.2   Continued

```
<ListBox ItemsSource="{Binding Source={StaticResource dataProvider},    Binding to
    XPath=GameStat/HighScore}" />                                        the XML
  </Grid>
</Window>
```

The XML data island is set as XmlDataProvider's content property and contained within the XData element, which is a requirement to distinguish it from the surrounding XAML. (You'll get a compiler error if you omit the XData tags.) The XmlDataProvider's XPath property is set to an XPath query that tells it where the relevant data resides inside the XML tree. XPath, short for XML Path Language, is a W3C Recommendation published at http://www.w3.org/TR/xpath.

> **TIP**
>
> When embedding an XML data island inside XAML, you should mark its root node with an empty xmlns attribute, as done in Listing 9.2. Otherwise, the elements get polluted with the default namespace (http://schemas.microsoft.com/winfx/2006/xaml/presentation in this example), preventing XPath queries from working as expected.

The consumption of the XmlDataProvider looks like the consumption of any source object, except that Binding's XPath property is used rather than Path to extract the relevant pieces of the source. This listing uses XPath to display the content of each HighScore node as an item in the ListBox, as shown in Figure 9.11.

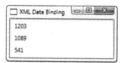

FIGURE 9.11   The result of the XML data binding performed in Listing 9.2.

If the XML resides in a separate file (which is usually the case), you can simply set XmlDataProvider's Source property to the appropriate Uri rather than setting its content property. Just like other Uris, this could refer to a local file, a file from the Internet, an embedded resource, and so on. For Listing 9.2, you could replace the XmlDataProvider with the following:

```
<XmlDataProvider x:Key="dataProvider" XPath="GameStats" Source="GameStats.xml"/>
```

XPath is a powerful query language—much more powerful than the property paths used in previous bindings. For example, Listing 9.2 could set XPath to "GameStat/@Type" to fill the ListBox with the values of each GameStat's Type attribute (Beginner, Intermediate, and Advanced). It could even use the expression "comment()" to show the contents of the first XML comment!

> **DIGGING DEEPER**
>
> **Interactions Between `XPath` and `Path`**
>
> You can actually use XPath and Path simultaneously on the same `Binding`! The XML data provided by `XmlDataProvider` is in the form of objects defined in `System.Xml.dll` (in the `System.Xml` namespace), such as `XmlNode`. This is important to know if you're interacting with the data programmatically, but it also means that you can give `Binding` a `Path` that refers to the current XmlNode or XmlNodeList instance retrieved. For example, the following `Label` uses XmlNode's OuterXml property to display `<HighScore>1203</HighScore>` rather than simply 1203 when used with the previously defined data provider:
>
> ```
> <Label Content="{Binding Source={StaticResource dataProvider},
>                   XPath=GameStat/HighScore, Path=OuterXml}"/>
> ```
>
> In addition to this support, `ItemsControl`'s `DisplayMemberPath` property supports both Path and XPath syntax.

If you want to bind the entire set of XML data to an element that understands hierarchies (TreeView or Menu) without custom code, you must use one or more `HierarchicalDataTemplates`. Listing 9.3 is an update to Listing 9.2 that adds three data templates (two `HierarchicalDataTemplates` and one plain `DataTemplate`) and changes the `ListBox` to a `TreeView` with an updated XPath that includes all the XML content.

LISTING 9.3   Binding to a Hierarchy Using `HierarchicalDataTemplate`

```
<Window xmlns="http://schemas.microsoft.com/winfx/2006/xaml/presentation"
        xmlns:x="http://schemas.microsoft.com/winfx/2006/xaml"
        Title="XML Data Binding">
  <Window.Resources>
    <HierarchicalDataTemplate DataType="GameStats"
      ItemsSource="{Binding XPath=*}">
      <TextBlock FontStyle="Italic" Text="All Game Stats"/>
    </HierarchicalDataTemplate>
    <HierarchicalDataTemplate DataType="GameStat" ItemsSource="{Binding XPath=*}">
      <TextBlock FontWeight="Bold" FontSize="20" Text="{Binding XPath=@Type}"/>
    </HierarchicalDataTemplate>
    <DataTemplate DataType="HighScore">
      <TextBlock Foreground="Blue" Text="{Binding XPath=.}"/>
    </DataTemplate>
    <XmlDataProvider x:Key="dataProvider" XPath="GameStats">
      <x:XData>
        <GameStats xmlns="">
          <!-- One stat per game type -->
          <GameStat Type="Beginner">
            <HighScore>1203</HighScore>
```

LISTING 9.3   Continued

```
          </GameStat>
          <GameStat Type="Intermediate">
            <HighScore>1089</HighScore>
          </GameStat>
          <GameStat Type="Advanced">
            <HighScore>541</HighScore>
          </GameStat>
        </GameStats>
      </x:XData>
    </XmlDataProvider>
  </Window.Resources>
  <Grid>
    <TreeView ItemsSource="{Binding Source={StaticResource dataProvider},
      XPath=.}" />
  </Grid>
</Window>
```

The idea is to use a HierarchicalDataTemplate for every data type in the hierarchy but then use a simple DataTemplate for any leaf nodes. Each data template gives you the option to customize the rendering of the data type, but HierarchicalDataTemplate also enables you to specify its children in the hierarchy by setting its ItemsSource property. Both HierarchicalDataTemplates in Listing 9.3 bind ItemsSource to a XPath expression of * to include all children in the XML data source.

The DataType value on each data template makes each one automatically affect any instances of the specified type within its scope (the Window in this example). When used with XmlDataProvider, the value of DataType corresponds to an XML element name. Note that the three data templates are not given explicit keys despite being in a ResourceDictionary. This works because internally the value of DataType is used for the template's key.

Figure 9.12 shows the rendered XAML from Listing 9.3. It also shows what happens if you replace the single occurrence of TreeView with Menu, leaving the rest of the listing alone.

TreeView in Listing 9.3   Changing TreeView to Menu

FIGURE 9.12   The use of HierarchicalDataTemplates can automatically fill TreeView and Menu with a hierarchy of data-bound objects.

> **TIP**
>
> Often, XML data defines its own namespace for its elements. For example, the Really Simple Syndication (RSS) feed from my blog defines three:
>
> ```
> <rss version="2.0" xmlns:dc="http://purl.org/dc/elements/1.1/"
>                     xmlns:slash="http://purl.org/rss/1.0/modules/slash/"
>                     xmlns:wfw="http://wellformedweb.org/CommentAPI/">
>
>   ...
> </rss>
> ```
>
> To reference elements in these namespaces (like wfw:commentRss) in an XPath, you can set an XmlNamespaceManager property on the XmlDataProvider or on individual Bindings. For example:
>
> ```
> <XmlDataProvider Source="http://blogs.msdn.com/adam_nathan/rss.xml"
>   XmlNamespaceManager="{StaticResource namespaceMapping}"
>   XPath="rss/channel" x:Key="dataProvider"/>
> ```
>
> The typical way to get an instance of an XmlNamespaceManager is to use the derived XmlNamespaceMappingCollection class, which assigns a prefix to each namespace. For example:
>
> ```
> <XmlNamespaceMappingCollection x:Key="namespaceMapping">
>   <XmlNamespaceMapping Uri="http://purl.org/dc/elements/1.1/" Prefix="dc"/>
>   <XmlNamespaceMapping Uri="http://purl.org/rss/1.0/modules/slash/"
>     Prefix="slash"/>
>   <XmlNamespaceMapping Uri="http://wellformedweb.org/CommentAPI/" Prefix="wfw"/>
> </XmlNamespaceMappingCollection>
> ```
>
> Although it's natural to choose prefixes that match the ones in the XML, you can choose any prefixes you want. The prefixes you choose can be used in XPath expressions, such as:
>
> ```
> "{Binding XPath=wfw:commentRss}"
> ```
>
> Whenever an XPath value has no prefix, the empty namespace is assumed to be the namespace URI. Therefore, even if your XML source has a default namespace, you must assign an XmlNamespaceManager for the queries to work.

6

ObjectDataProvider

Whereas XmlDataProvider exposes XML as a data source, ObjectDataProvider exposes a .NET object as a data source. "But that doesn't make any sense," you're probably thinking to yourself! "I can already use any arbitrary .NET object as a data source. What good does ObjectDataProvider do?" It opens up a few additional capabilities that you don't get by binding to the raw object. For example, it enables you to:

▶ Declaratively instantiate the source object with a parameterized constructor

▶ Bind to a *method* on the source object

▶ Have more options for asynchronous data binding

> ## DIGGING DEEPER
>
> **Asynchronous Data Binding**
>
> Whenever binding to data isn't a quick operation, it should be done asynchronously to avoid freezing your user interface. WPF exposes two independent knobs for making binding happen asynchronously: Binding has an IsAsync property and both XmlDataProvider and ObjectDataProvider have an IsAsynchronous property. (Don't you just love the consistency?)
>
> When IsAsynchronous is true, the data provider creates the source object on a background thread. IsAsynchronous is false by default for ObjectDataProvider but true by default for XmlDataProvider (because the latter is often used with remote XML files such as RSS feeds that are slow to retrieve). On the other hand, when IsAsync (which is always false by default) is true, the source *property* is invoked on a background thread.
>
> Therefore, it's best to set IsAsynchronous to true when the source object is slow to construct, and it's best to set IsAsync to true when the source property accessor is slow (which is rare).

Using a Parameterized Constructor in XAML

Most data sources that you'd use probably have a default constructor, such as the photos collection used earlier in the chapter. The following XAML "wraps" this collection in an ObjectDataProvider:

```
<Window.Resources>
  <local:Photos x:Key="photos"/>
  <ObjectDataProvider x:Key="dataProvider"
    ObjectInstance="{StaticResource photos}"/>
</Window.Resources>
```

In this case, whether you bind to photos or dataProvider, you get the exact same results. Even the Binding Path to use is identical because Binding automatically "unwraps" objects inside data providers such as ObjectDataProvider.

ObjectDataProvider also can be given the desired type of its object to wrap (rather than an instance) and construct it on your behalf:

```
<Window.Resources>
  <!-- The collection object is instantiated internally by ObjectDataProvider: -->
  <ObjectDataProvider x:Key="dataProvider" ObjectType="{x:Type local:Photos}"/>
</Window.Resources>
```

When using ObjectDataProvider in this fashion, you can get it to instantiate an object via its parameterized constructor by setting its ConstructorParameters property to a collection of objects. For example, if the Photos constructor required a capacity to be passed in, you could use ObjectDataProvider as follows:

```
<ObjectDataProvider x:Key="dataProvider" ObjectType="{x:Type local:Photos}">
<ObjectDataProvider.ConstructorParameters>
  <sys:Int32>23</sys:Int32>
</ObjectDataProvider.ConstructorParameters>
</ObjectDataProvider>
```

This is useful for data sources whose definition you don't control because directly declaring an object in XAML only works with a default constructor. (If you did control the definition of the data source, presumably you'd just add an appropriate default constructor to it.) Of course, if declaring the source in XAML isn't important to you, you could always construct it programmatically and easily set it as a data context for any XAML-defined elements.

Binding to a Method

One scenario that ObjectDataProvider enables that you otherwise can't easily achieve declaratively or programmatically is binding to a method. As with support for parameterized constructors, this is mostly useful for existing classes that aren't data binding–friendly and can't be changed. For your own types, you might as well expose potential data sources as properties. But imagine that the photos collection exposed a method called GetFolderName that returned a string representing the folder containing all the current items. You could expose this method as a data source as follows:

```
<ObjectDataProvider x:Key="dataProvider" ObjectType="{x:Type local:Photos}"
  MethodName="GetFolderName"/>
```

If parameters need to be passed to the method, you can use ObjectDataProvider's MethodParameters property (which works just like its ConstructorParameters property).

To bind to this method, simply bind to the entire ObjectDataProvider:

```
<TextBlock Text="{Binding Source={StaticResource dataProvider}}"/>
```

Specifying a Path in this case would apply to the instance returned by the method.

DIGGING DEEPER

Suppressing the Automatic Unwrapping of Data Providers

If you want to bind directly to properties of ObjectDataProvider rather than the wrapped data source, you can set Binding's BindsDirectlyToSource property to true to suppress the automatic unwrapping. This works for any DataSourceProvider-derived source (as well as CollectionViewSource), so it includes ObjectDataProvider, XmlDataProvider, and any custom derived classes you might write.

Advanced Topics

The final section of this chapter outlines some of the more esoteric but incredibly useful features of data binding. This includes customizing the flow of data between the source and target, plugging in custom validation logic, and combining disjoint sources into a single bindable entity.

Customizing the Data Flow

In all the data-binding examples you've seen so far, data updates flow from the source to the target. But, in some cases, the target property can be directly changed by users, and it would be useful to support flowing such changes back to the source.

Indeed, Binding supports this (and more) via its Mode property, which can be set to one of the following values of the BindingMode enumeration:

- ▶ **OneWay**—The target is updated whenever the source changes.

- ▶ **TwoWay**—A change to either the target or source updates the other.

- ▶ **OneWayToSource**—The opposite of OneWay. The source is updated whenever the target changes.

- ▶ **OneTime**—This works just like OneWay, except changes to the source are not reflected at the target. The target retains a snapshot of the source at the time the Binding is initiated.

TwoWay binding is appropriate for data-bound forms, where you might have TextBoxes that get filled with data that the user is allowed to change. In fact, whereas most dependency properties default to OneWay binding, dependency properties such as TextBox.Text default to TwoWay binding.

WARNING

Watch out for different default BindingModes!

The fact that different dependency properties have different default BindingModes can easily trip you up. For example, unlike with Label.Content, binding TextBox.Text to a collection's Count property fails unless you explicitly set BindingMode to OneWay (or OneTime) because the Count property is read-only. TwoWay and OneWayToSource require a writable source property.

These different modes are the reason that value converters have both a Convert and a ConvertBack method. Both are called when performing TwoWay binding, and only ConvertBack is called when doing OneWayToSource binding.

FAQ

 Why would I ever use a `Binding` with a `Mode` of `OneWayToSource`? In such a case, it sounds like the target should really be the source and the source should really be the target.

One reason could be that you're using multiple `Bindings`, some with data flowing from the source to the target and others with data flowing from the target to the source. For example, you might want to share a source among many data-bound targets, but want one of these target elements to update that source via data binding.

`OneWayToSource` can also be used as a sneaky way to get around the restriction that a `Binding`'s target property must be a dependency property. If you want to bind a source dependency property to a target property that is *not* a dependency property, `OneWayToSource` enables you to accomplish this by marking your "real source" as the target and your "real target" as the source!

When using `TwoWay` or `OneWayToSource` binding, you might want different behaviors for when and how the source gets updated. For example, if a user types in a `TwoWay` data-bound `TextBox`, do you want the source to be updated with each keystroke, or only when the user is done typing? Binding enables you to control such behavior with its `UpdateSourceTrigger` property.

`UpdateSourceTrigger` can be set to a member of the `UpdateSourceTrigger` enumeration, which has the following values:

▶ **`PropertyChanged`**—The source is updated whenever the target property value changes.

▶ **`LostFocus`**—When the target property value changes, the source is only updated after the target element loses focus.

▶ **`Explicit`**—The source is only updated when you make an explicit call to `BindingExpression.UpdateSource`. You can get an instance of `BindingExpression` by calling the static `BindingOperations.GetBindingExpression` method or calling `GetBindingExpression` on any `FrameworkElement` or `FrameworkContentElement`.

Just as different properties have different default `Mode` settings, they also have different default `UpdateSourceTrigger` settings. `TextBox.Text` defaults to `LostFocus`.

DIGGING DEEPER

Dependency Properties and Default Settings

The default settings for dependency properties are stored in a special set of metadata, as shown in Chapter 3. To programmatically check the setting for any dependency property, you can call its `GetMetadata` method (for example, `TextBox.TextProperty.GetMetadata()`) and then check the value of properties such as `BindsTwoWayByDefault` or `DefaultUpdateSourceTrigger`.

> **TIP**
>
> Although the source and/or target data gets updated automatically when using data binding, you might want to take additional actions when a data update occurs. Perhaps you want to write some data to a log, or show a visual effect indicating the data change.
>
> Oddly enough, all `FrameworkElements` and `FrameworkContentElements` have `SourceUpdated` and `TargetUpdated` events that you can handle. But they only get raised for `Bindings` that have their `NotifyOnSourceUpdated` and/or `NotifyOnTargetUpdated` Boolean properties set to `true`.

Adding Validation Rules to Binding

When you accept user input, it's a good idea to reject invalid data and give feedback to the user in a timely fashion. The early days of form filling on the Web were filled with horror stories of inappropriate validation, such as only detecting errors after everything was submitted and then requiring the user to type everything in again from scratch! Fortunately, data binding has a built-in validation mechanism that makes it relatively easy to create a rich and interactive experience. There are so many different ways to accomplish this and so many different knobs to configure, however, that it's more confusing than it should be.

Imagine that you want the user to type the name of an existing `.jpg` file into a data-bound `TextBox`. There are two obvious error conditions here: The user could enter a nonexistent filename or a non-`.jpg` filename. If the `TextBox` weren't data bound, you could insert custom validation logic that checks for these two conditions to the code that updates the data source. But when data binding propagates updates automatically, you need a way to inject validation logic into the process. You could write a value converter that performs the logic and throws an exception for bad data, but besides the fact that value converters aren't meant for that purpose, it still doesn't solve the part about displaying the error to the user.

You can handle this situation in a few different ways. One way is to write your own validation rule, and another is to take advantage of exceptions that might already be thrown from attempts to update the source incorrectly.

> **TIP**
>
> The techniques described in this section only apply to propagating changes from the target to the source. Therefore, these features only work with a `BindingMode` of `OneWayToSource` or `TwoWay`.

Writing Your Own Validation Rule

`Binding` has a `ValidationRules` property that can be set to one or more `ValidationRule`-derived objects. Each rule can check for specific conditions and mark the data as invalid. We could write the following `JpgValidationRule` class that enforces our requirements by deriving from `ValidationRule` and overriding its abstract `Validate` method:

```
public class JpgValidationRule : ValidationRule
{
  public override ValidationResult Validate(object value, CultureInfo cultureInfo)
```

```
  {
    string filename = value.ToString();

    // Reject nonexistent files:
    if (!File.Exists(filename))
      return new ValidationResult(false, "Value is not a valid file.");

    // Reject files that don't end in .jpg:
    if (!filename.EndsWith(".jpg", StringComparison.InvariantCultureIgnoreCase))
      return new ValidationResult(false, "Value is not a .jpg file.");

    // The input passes the test!
    return new ValidationResult(true, null);
  }
}
```

Invalid data is reported by returning a `false` `ValidationResult`, and valid data is reported by returning a `true` `ValidationResult`. (The check for the ".jpg" suffix is more restrictive than it has to be, but it still gets the point across.)

With this class in place, it can be applied to a `Binding` as follows:

```
<TextBox>
<TextBox.Text>
  <Binding …>
  <Binding.ValidationRules>
    <local:JpgValidationRule/>
  </Binding.ValidationRules>
  </Binding>
</TextBox.Text>
</TextBox>
```

The validation check is invoked during any attempt to update the underlying data (which, in this case, is when the `TextBox` loses focus because of the `LostFocus` default for `UpdateSourceTrigger`). This happens before a value converter is called (if present), and it only takes one rule to veto the update and mark the data as invalid.

So, what happens when data is marked as invalid? By default, the element with the target property is given a new control template so it renders with a thin red border. But you can assign a custom control template to be used in such conditions by setting the `Validation.ErrorTemplate` attached property on the target element. (Control templates are covered in the next chapter.) If you use validation, you'll want to assign a custom template because the default one is not very satisfactory.

In addition, when data is marked as invalid, the target element's `Validation.HasError` attached property becomes `true` and its `Validation.Error` attached event is raised (but only if `Binding`'s `NotifyOnValidationError` property is set to `true`). Therefore, you could implement rich error notification logic with an appropriate trigger or event handler.

6

You can get detailed information about the validation failures, such as the strings returned by the `JpgValidationRule` class, by checking the target element's `Validation.Errors` attached property. These properties are automatically cleared when a subsequent successful bind occurs.

Sending Exceptions Through the Validation System

Writing a custom validation rule might duplicate error-checking logic that is already performed by the data source (or a value converter). If either of these already throws an exception for the same conditions you want to treat as invalid, you can use a built-in `ExceptionValidationRule` object. (This is the only `ValidationRule` that WPF ships.) For example:

```
<TextBox>
<TextBox.Text>
  <Binding …>
  <Binding.ValidationRules>
    <ExceptionValidationRule/>
  </Binding.ValidationRules>
  </Binding>
</TextBox.Text>
</TextBox>
```

`ExceptionValidationRule` simply marks the data as invalid if any exception is thrown when attempting to update the source property. Therefore, this mechanism enables us to react properly to the exception rather than having it swallowed and emitted as a debug trace.

DIGGING DEEPER

There's More Than One Way to Handle Exceptions

Another way to handle exceptions in source updates is to attach a delegate to `Binding`'s `UpdateSourceExceptionFilter` property. The delegate gets called whenever an exception occurs from attempting to update the source property, and that `Exception` object is passed to the delegate. Therefore, you can implement a custom error notification scheme without using any of the `ValidationRule` features. `UpdateSourceExceptionFilter` might be simpler to use programmatically, but only the `ExceptionValidationRule` approach can be used declaratively.

Interestingly, there is still a connection between the `UpdateSourceExceptionFilter` delegate and the other validation scheme. If you return a `ValidationError` from your delegate, it will treat your delegate like a custom validation rule, and add the `ValidationError` to the target element's `Validation.Errors` collection, set `Validation.HasError` to true, and potentially raise the `Validation.Error` event.

To summarize, if the data source or a value converter in use already has logic to throw an exception on bad data, you can do one of the following:

▶ Use `UpdateSourceExceptionFilter` to plug in custom notification logic

▶ Use `ExceptionValidationRule`, defining an `ErrorTemplate` and/or plugging in additional notification logic by monitoring `Validation.HasError` or `Validation.Error` (when `NotifyOnValidationError` is true)

If the data source or value converter doesn't have such logic, you can use the latter approach but with a custom validation rule rather than `ExceptionValidationRule`.

Working with Disjoint Sources

WPF provides a few interesting ways to combine multiple sources of data. The key to these approaches is the following classes:

▶ `CompositeCollection`

▶ `MultiBinding`

▶ `PriorityBinding`

CompositeCollection

The `CompositeCollection` class provides an easy way to expose separate collections and/or arbitrary items as a single collection. This can be useful when you want to bind to a collection of items that come from more than one source. The following XAML defines a `CompositeCollection` with all the contents of the photos collection plus two more items:

```
<CompositeCollection>
  <CollectionContainer Collection="{Binding Source={StaticResource photos}}"/>
  <local:Photo …/>
  <local:Photo …/>
</CompositeCollection>
```

The photos collection is wrapped in a `CollectionContainer` object so that its items are considered part of the `CompositeCollection` rather than the collection itself. If the photos collection were added directly to the `CompositeCollection` instead, the `CompositeCollection` would only contain three items!

MultiBinding

`MultiBinding` enables you to aggregate multiple `Binding`s together and spit out a single target value. It requires that you use a value converter because otherwise WPF would have no idea how to combine the multiple input values. The following XAML shows how `MultiBinding` could be used to calculate a `ProgressBar`'s value by adding together the progress values of three independent data-bound sources, assuming the presence of a value converter and three source objects as resources:

```
<ProgressBar …>
<ProgressBar.Value>
  <MultiBinding Converter="{StaticResource converter}">
    <Binding Source="{StaticResource worker1}"/>
    <Binding Source="{StaticResource worker2}"/>
    <Binding Source="{StaticResource worker3}"/>
  </MultiBinding>
</ProgressBar.Value>
  </ProgressBar>
```

Value converters used in a MultiBinding are a little different than ones used in a plain
old Binding, however. They must implement the IMultiValueConverter interface, whose
methods accept/return an *array* of values rather than just one. Therefore, here is an appropriate definition of the value converter used in the previous XAML snippet:

```
public class ProgressConverter : IMultiValueConverter
{
  public object Convert(object[] values, Type targetType, object parameter,
    CultureInfo culture)
  {
    int totalProgress = 0;

    // Require that each input value is an instance of a Worker
    foreach (Worker worker in values)
      totalProgress += worker.Progress;

    return totalProgress;
  }
  public object[] ConvertBack(object value, Type[] targetTypes, object parameter,
    CultureInfo culture)
  {
    throw new NotSupportedException();
  }
}
```

PriorityBinding

PriorityBinding looks a lot like MultiBinding, in that it encapsulates multiple Binding
objects. But rather than aggregating Bindings together, the idea of PriorityBinding is to
let multiple Bindings *compete* for setting the target value!

If you are data binding to a slow data source, you might want to allow faster sources to
provide a "rough" version of the data while you wait. This technique can be seen in lots
of software. For example, if you open a large document in Microsoft Word, you might
first see something like "77,257 characters (an approximate value)" display in the
lower-left corner for a few seconds, then something like "Page: 1 of 3," which is still not
the correct page count, then finally the expected "Page: 1 of 46." For the Photo Gallery

application, this technique could be used to quickly bind to a collection of thumbnail images, then replace that with a collection of full-fidelity images after that slower bind completes.

The following XAML demonstrates a typical declaration of `PriorityBinding`:

```
<PriorityBinding>
  <Binding Source="HighPri" Path="SlowSpeed" IsAsync="True"/>
  <Binding Source="MediumPri" Path="MediumSpeed" IsAsync="True"/>
  <Binding Source="LowPri" Path="FastSpeed"/>
</PriorityBinding>
```

The `Binding`s are processed from beginning to end, so the first `Binding` listed has the highest priority (and, therefore, should be the slowest one to complete) and the last `Binding` listed has the lowest priority (and should be the quickest one). As different values get returned, higher-priority values overwite the lower-priority ones.

> **TIP**
>
> When using `PriorityBinding`, all but the last `Binding`s should set `IsAsync` to `true` so they are processed in the background. Without this setting, the highest-priority `Binding` would execute synchronously (probably freezing the UI) and after it returned, there would be no reason to consult the lower-priority `Binding`s!

Putting It All Together: The Pure-XAML RSS Reader

The canonical example of the power of WPF data binding is a fully functioning RSS reader written without any procedural code. Listing 9.4 has my version of such an implementation. The result is shown in Figure 9.13.

LISTING 9.4   The Entire Implementation of an RSS Reader

```
<Window xmlns="http://schemas.microsoft.com/winfx/2006/xaml/presentation"
        xmlns:x="http://schemas.microsoft.com/winfx/2006/xaml" Title="RSS Reader">
<Window.Resources>
  <XmlDataProvider x:Key="Blog"
    Source="http://blogs.msdn.com/adam_nathan/rss.aspx"/>
</Window.Resources>
  <DockPanel
    DataContext="{Binding Source={StaticResource Blog}, XPath=/rss/channel/item}">
    <TextBox DockPanel.Dock="Top" Text="{Binding Source={StaticResource Blog},
      BindsDirectlyToSource=true, Path=Source,
      UpdateSourceTrigger=PropertyChanged}"/>
    <Label DockPanel.Dock="Top" Content="{Binding XPath=/rss/channel/title}"
```

LISTING 9.4   Continued

```
       FontSize="14" FontWeight="Bold"/>
    <Label DockPanel.Dock="Top"
      Content="{Binding XPath=/rss/channel/description}"/>
    <ListBox DockPanel.Dock="Left" DisplayMemberPath="title"
      ItemsSource="{Binding}" IsSynchronizedWithCurrentItem="True" Width="300"/>
    <Frame Source="{Binding XPath=link}"/>
  </DockPanel>
</Window>
```

FIGURE 9.13   The all-XAML RSS reader implemented in Listing 9.4.

As expected, XmlDataProvider is used to retrieve the RSS feed.

Here are some of the interesting points about this application:

▶ The default TwoWay binding of TextBox.Text is leveraged to initially fill the TextBox
  with the XmlDataProvider's Source, and also enable the user to change the Source
  at runtime.

▶ To enable the XmlDataProvider's Source to be bound, the TextBox's Binding has
  BindsDirectlyToSource set to true. Otherwise, its Path would incorrectly refer to
  the RSS feed.

▶ The TextBox's Binding uses an UpdateSourceTrigger of PropertyChanged so an
  attempt to refresh the data is made with each keystroke. The best solution would
  probably be to use an UpdateSourceTrigger of Explicit instead and provide a Go
  button that manually refreshes the source. But that would require a line of procedural code, which goes against the point of this example!

- ▶ The value of `ListBox`'s `DisplayMemberPath` is an XPath expression to extract the `title` element for each item in the XML source.

- ▶ The `ListBox` and `Frame` provide a master/detail view simply by sharing the same data source.

- ▶ Rather than using `Frame`, the raw content of each RSS item could have been displayed in something like a `TextBlock`. But that would give us raw HTML that would be difficult to read. And there's no easy way to render HTML properly other than using a `Frame` with a persisted file (which the feed's `link` element conveniently provides us).

- ▶ As different RSS items (or whole RSS feeds) are selected, `Frame`'s navigation buttons keep track of our actions automatically.

Conclusion

Data binding is a very powerful feature, although its use is also completely optional. After all, it's not hard to write code that the ties two objects together. But writing such code can be tedious, error-prone, and a maintenance hassle, especially when managing multiple data sources that might need to be synchronized as items are added, removed, and changed. Such code also tends to make your business logic tightly coupled with your user interface, which makes your software more brittle.

`XmlDataProvider` could be considered a "killer app" for data binding, as it makes retrieving, parsing, navigating, and displaying remote XML data incredibly easy. The ability to get asynchronous behavior on any `Binding` or data provider simply by setting a Boolean property also makes data binding a compelling alternative to performing such work manually.

But there's more to data binding than cutting down on the amount of code you need to write. Much of the appeal of WPF's data binding comes from the fact that the majority of it can be done declaratively. This has some important implications. Design tools like Expression Blend can (and do) surface data-binding functionality, so nonprogrammers can add sophisticated functionality to any user interface. It also enables loose XAML pages, which can't use procedural code, to take advantage of functionality that makes them feel less like documents and more like miniature applications.

CHAPTER 10

Styles, Templates, Skins, and Themes

Arguably the most celebrated feature in WPF is the ability to give any user interface element a radically different look without having to give up all of the built-in functionality that it provides. HTML lacks this power, which is the reason most websites use images to represent buttons rather than "real buttons." Of course, it's pretty easy to simulate a button's behavior with an image in HTML, but what if you want to give a completely different look to a SELECT element (HTML's version of ComboBox)? It's a lot of work if you want to do more than change simple properties (such as its foreground and background colors).

This chapter explains the four main components of WPF's restyling support:

▶ **Styles**—A simple mechanism for separating property values from user interface elements (similar to the relationship between Cascading Style Sheets [CSS] and HTML). They're also the foundation for applying the other mechanisms in this chapter.

▶ **Templates**—Powerful objects that most people are really referring to when they talk about "restyling" in WPF.

▶ **Skins**—Application-specific collections of styles and/or templates, typically with the ability to be replaced dynamically.

▶ **Themes**—Visual characteristics of the host operating system, with potential customizations by the end user.

As you'll see, an important enabler of WPF's restyling support is the semantics of resources, covered in Chapter 8, "Resources."

FAQ

 Why does WPF allow people to completely customize the look of standard controls? The inconsistencies from one application to another are going to confuse users!

This "celebrated" feature of WPF also makes many people nervous. Is this power and flexibility going to usher in a new age of beautiful software, or is it going to be abused in ways that annoy and frustrate users (such as the BLINK element in HTML)?

The answer is certainly "both." I, too, was skeptical about WPF back in 2003 when most demos consisted of bouncing buttons and spinning rainbow-filled list boxes. But, it's good to know that you *could* create a completely insane UI, even if you shouldn't. WPF's philosophy is to make an application's experience limited only by the skill of its designers rather than limited by the underlying platform. It's hard to disagree with that stance.

If you can't hire graphic designers, fortunately the default visual appearance of a WPF application looks consistent with the expectations of Windows users. If you *can* hire designers, WPF makes it easy for them to have an impact across the entire application (not just on icons or a splash screen).

As for inconsistencies between applications, the same could be said about web applications, which tend to infuse their own branding into the entire user experience much more than traditional Windows applications. Despite the lack of consistency (or even *because of* lack of consistency), websites with good user experiences can do very well. Also, people try to create non-standard-looking Windows applications *anyway*. And with lack of platform support, they have to jump through many hoops to get the desired effect, often producing buggy behavior or weird side effects.

Styles

A *style*, represented by the System.Windows.Style class, is a pretty simple entity. Its main function is to group together property values that could otherwise be set individually. The intent is to then share this group of values among multiple elements.

Take, for example, the three customized Buttons in Figure 10.1. This look is achieved by setting seven properties. Without a Style, you would need to duplicate these identical assignments on all three Buttons, as shown in Listing 10.1.

FIGURE 10.1   Three Buttons whose look has been customized.

LISTING 10.1   Copy/Paste Galore!

```xml
<StackPanel Orientation="Horizontal">
  <Button FontSize="22" Background="Purple" Foreground="White"
    Height="50" Width="50" RenderTransformOrigin=".5,.5">
  <Button.RenderTransform>
    <RotateTransform Angle="10"/>
  </Button.RenderTransform>
    1
  </Button>
  <Button FontSize="22" Background="Purple" Foreground="White"
    Height="50" Width="50" RenderTransformOrigin=".5,.5">
  <Button.RenderTransform>
    <RotateTransform Angle="10"/>
  </Button.RenderTransform>
    2
  </Button>
  <Button FontSize="22" Background="Purple" Foreground="White"
    Height="50" Width="50" RenderTransformOrigin=".5,.5">
  <Button.RenderTransform>
    <RotateTransform Angle="10"/>
  </Button.RenderTransform>
    3
  </Button>
</StackPanel>
```

But with a Style, you can add a level of indirection—setting them in one place and pointing each Button to this new element, as shown in Listing 10.2. Style uses a collection of Setters to set the target properties. Creating a Setter is just a matter of specifying the name of a dependency property (qualified with its class name) and its desired value.

This is nice for several reasons, such as having only one spot to change if you later have second thoughts about rotating the Buttons or if you want to change their Background. Defining a Style as a resource also gives you all the flexibility that the resource mechanism provides. For example, you could define one version of buttonStyle at the application level, but override it with a different Style (still with a key of buttonStyle) in an individual Window's Resources collection.

Note that despite its name, there's nothing inherently visual about a Style. But it's typically used for setting properties that affect visuals. Indeed, Style only enables the setting of dependency properties, which tend to be visual in nature.

10

LISTING 10.2   Consolidating Property Assignments Inside a `Style`

```
<StackPanel Orientation="Horizontal">
<StackPanel.Resources>
  <Style x:Key="buttonStyle">
    <Setter Property="Button.FontSize" Value="22"/>
    <Setter Property="Button.Background" Value="Purple"/>
    <Setter Property="Button.Foreground" Value="White"/>
    <Setter Property="Button.Height" Value="50"/>
    <Setter Property="Button.Width" Value="50"/>
    <Setter Property="Button.RenderTransformOrigin" Value=".5,.5"/>        Style
    <Setter Property="Button.RenderTransform">                             definition
    <Setter.Value>
      <RotateTransform Angle="10"/>
    </Setter.Value>
    </Setter>
  </Style>
</StackPanel.Resources>
  <Button Style="{StaticResource buttonStyle}">1</Button>
  <Button Style="{StaticResource buttonStyle}">2</Button>                  Applying
  <Button Style="{StaticResource buttonStyle}">3</Button>                  the Style
</StackPanel>
```

> **TIP**
>
> Styles can even inherit from one another! The following `Style` adds bold text to
> buttonStyle defined in Listing 10.2 by using the `BasedOn` property:
>
> ```
> <Style x:Key="buttonStyleWithBold" BasedOn="{StaticResource buttonStyle}">
>   <!-- The seven properties set by buttonStyle are inherited -->
>   <Setter Property="Button.FontWeight" Value="Bold"/>
> </Style>
> ```

Sharing Styles

Although you could set an element's `Style` property directly in its XAML definition
(using property element syntax), the whole point of using a `Style` is to share it among
multiple elements, as done in Listing 10.2. `Style` supports a few different mechanisms
that enable you to control exactly how that sharing occurs.

Sharing Among Heterogeneous Elements

Although the `Style` in Listing 10.2 is shared among three `Button`s, with some tweaks it
can also be shared among heterogeneous elements. Listing 10.3 accomplishes this by
changing each `Button.XXX` referenced inside the `Style` to `Control.XXX`, and then applying
the new style to many elements. The result is shown in Figure 10.2.

FIGURE 10.2   Heterogeneous elements given the same Style.

LISTING 10.3   Sharing a Single Style with Heterogeneous Elements

```xml
<StackPanel Orientation="Horizontal">
<StackPanel.Resources>
  <Style x:Key="controlStyle">
    <Setter Property="Control.FontSize" Value="22"/>
    <Setter Property="Control.Background" Value="Purple"/>
    <Setter Property="Control.Foreground" Value="White"/>
    <Setter Property="Control.Height" Value="50"/>
    <Setter Property="Control.Width" Value="50"/>
    <Setter Property="Control.RenderTransformOrigin" Value=".5,.5"/>
    <Setter Property="Control.RenderTransform">
    <Setter.Value>
      <RotateTransform Angle="10"/>
    </Setter.Value>
    </Setter>
  </Style>
</StackPanel.Resources>
  <Button Style="{StaticResource controlStyle}">1</Button>
  <ComboBox Style="{StaticResource controlStyle}">
  <ComboBox.Items>2</ComboBox.Items>
  </ComboBox>
  <Expander Style="{StaticResource controlStyle}" Content="3"/>
  <TabControl Style="{StaticResource controlStyle}">
  <TabControl.Items>4</TabControl.Items>
  </TabControl>
  <ToolBar Style="{StaticResource controlStyle}">
  <ToolBar.Items>5</ToolBar.Items>
  </ToolBar>
  <InkCanvas Style="{StaticResource controlStyle}"/>
  <TextBox Style="{StaticResource controlStyle}" Text="7"/>
</StackPanel>
```

10

You don't need to worry if a Style is applied to an element that doesn't have all the listed dependency properties; the properties that exist are set and the ones that don't are ignored. For example, InkCanvas doesn't have Foreground or FontSize properties. Yet when the Style is applied to it in Listing 10.3, all the relevent properties (Background, Height, Width, and so on) are correctly applied. Similarly, adding the following Setter to the Style in Listing 10.3 affects the TextBox but leaves all the other elements looking as they do in Figure 10.2:

```
<Setter Property="TextBox.TextAlignment" Value="Right"/>
```

DIGGING DEEPER

Strange (but True) Setter Behavior

An astute reader might wonder how *any* of the Setters in Listing 10.3 are able to affect the InkCanvas, given that they are all properties of Control and InkCanvas doesn't even derive from Control! This happens because of one of the more "magical" aspects of dependency properties (which reinforces how different they are from normal .NET properties).

Although InkCanvas registers several of its own dependency properties (with DependencyProperty.Register), it also has several—such as Background—whose "owner-ship" is shared with other types (so it calls DependencyProperty.AddOwner instead). When multiple types own the same dependency property, it doesn't matter which type name you use in Setter.Property as long as it's one of the owners. Unfortunately, the ownership of dependency properties is an implementation detail that (at least at the time of writing) is not documented.

The implications of this can produce even more baffling results. For example, the Setters in Listing 10.3 didn't even need to change from Listing 10.2. If they reference Button.*XXX* rather than Control.*XXX*, the result is identical. Also, if you add a TextBlock to Listing 10.3, you'd see that setting Button.Foreground successfully changes TextBlock's Foreground property, but setting Button.Background *does not* change TextBlock's Background property! That's because TextBlock and all Controls share an implementation of their Foreground dependency property, but don't share a Background implementation. (Control shares its Background with types such as Panel and InkCanvas, whereas TextBlock shares its completely independent implementation with TextElement, FlowDocument, and other types.)

My advice is to avoid all this nonsense and create distinct Styles for distinct types.

TIP

Any individual element can override aspects of its Style by directly setting a property to a local value. For example, the Button in Listing 10.3 could do the following to retain the rotation, size, and so on from controlStyle yet have a red Background rather than a purple one:

```
<Button Style="{StaticResource controlStyle}" Background="Red">1</Button>
```

This works because of the order of precedence for dependency property values presented in Chapter 3, "Important New Concepts in WPF." The local value trumps anything set from a Style.

> **TIP**
>
> To enable sharing of complex property values even *within* a Style, Style has its own Resources property. You can leverage this collection to make your Style self-contained, rather than creating a potentially brittle dependency to resources defined elsewhere.

Restricting the Use of Styles

If you want to enforce that a Style can only be applied to a particular type, you can set its TargetType property accordingly. For example, the following Style can only be applied to a Button (or a subclass of Button):

```xml
<Style x:Key="buttonStyle" TargetType="{x:Type Button}">
  <Setter Property="Button.FontSize" Value="22"/>
  <Setter Property="Button.Background" Value="Purple"/>
  <Setter Property="Button.Foreground" Value="White"/>
  <Setter Property="Button.Height" Value="50"/>
  <Setter Property="Button.Width" Value="50"/>
  <Setter Property="Button.RenderTransformOrigin" Value=".5,.5"/>
  <Setter Property="Button.RenderTransform">
  <Setter.Value>
    <RotateTransform Angle="10"/>
  </Setter.Value>
  </Setter>
</Style>
```

Any attempt to apply this Style to a non-Button generates a compile-time error. Therefore, TargetType="{x:Type Control}" could be applied to the Style in Listing 10.3 and it would still work with all the elements except InkCanvas.

In addition, when you apply a TargetType to a Style, you no longer need to prefix the property names inside Setters with the type name. So, the previous XAML snippet could be rewritten as follows and have the exact same meaning:

```xml
<Style x:Key="buttonStyle" TargetType="{x:Type Button}">
  <Setter Property="FontSize" Value="22"/>
  <Setter Property="Background" Value="Purple"/>
  <Setter Property="Foreground" Value="White"/>
  <Setter Property="Height" Value="50"/>
  <Setter Property="Width" Value="50"/>
  <Setter Property="RenderTransformOrigin" Value=".5,.5"/>
  <Setter Property="RenderTransform">
  <Setter.Value>
    <RotateTransform Angle="10"/>
  </Setter.Value>
  </Setter>
</Style>
```

10

Creating Implicit Styles

Applying a TargetType to a Style gives you another feature as well. If you omit its Key, the Style gets implicitly applied to all elements of that target type within the same scope. This is typically called a *typed style* as opposed to a *named style*, which is the only kind of Style we've seen so far.

The scope of a typed Style is determined by the location of the Style resource. For example, it could implicitly apply to all relevant elements in a Window if it's a member of Window.Resources. Or, it could apply to an entire application by defining it as an application-level resource as follows:

```
<Application …>
<Application.Resources>
  <Style TargetType="{x:Type Button}">                              No x:Key!
    <Setter Property="FontSize" Value="22"/>
    <Setter Property="Background" Value="Purple"/>
    <Setter Property="Foreground" Value="White"/>
    <Setter Property="Height" Value="50"/>
    <Setter Property="Width" Value="50"/>
    <Setter Property="RenderTransformOrigin" Value=".5,.5"/>
    <Setter Property="RenderTransform">
    <Setter.Value>
      <RotateTransform Angle="10"/>
    </Setter.Value>
    </Setter>
  </Style>
</Application.Resources>
</Application>
```

In such an application, all Buttons get this style by default. But each Button can still override its appearance by explicitly setting a different Style or explicitly setting individual properties. Any Button can restore its default Style by setting its Style property to null.

WARNING

TargetType must match exactly for a typed style to be applied!

With a named style, it's okay for the target element to be a subclass of the TargetType. But a typed style typically only gets applied to elements whose type matches exactly! This is done to prevent surprises. For example, you might have created a Style for all ToggleButtons in your application but don't want it applied to any CheckBoxes (which is a subclass of ToggleButton). This behavior is controlled by each element (by its selection of a default style key covered in the "Themes" section at the end of this chapter). Therefore, it's possible to write a custom element that inherits the typed style from its base class.

DIGGING DEEPER

The Magic Behind a Keyless Resource

You might be curious how `Style` is able to get away with being a member of a `ResourceDictionary` without having a key. It actually *does* have a key—it's just set implicitly. And the implicit key is simply the value of `TargetType` (which is a `Type` rather than a string). To explicitly access a keyless `Style` whose `TargetType` is `Button`, you could refer to it as follows:

```
<Button Style="{StaticResource {x:Type Button}}" …/>
```

Only one keyless `Style` can be defined in the same `ResourceDictionary` for each distinct `TargetType`; otherwise, you'll get an error from attempting to have duplicate keys in the same collection.

TIP

`Styles` can be applied in multiple places. For example, all `FrameworkElements` and `FrameworkContentElements` have a `FocusVisualStyle` property in addition to their `Style` property. A `Style` assigned to `FocusVisualStyle` is only active when the element has keyboard focus, and is very handy for overriding the look of the standard dotted rectangle that indicates keyboard focus (which can look weird when the control has been drastically altered).

Some controls have their own additional places to plug in a `Style`. For example, `ItemsControl` has an `ItemContainerStyle` property that applies to each item's container (such as `ListBoxItem` or `ComboBoxItem`). Other controls, like `ToolBar`, expose `ResourceKey` properties that represent the keys for several `Styles` used internally, such as `ButtonStyleKey` and `TextBoxStyleKey`. Although these *XXX*StyleKey properties are read-only, you can leverage these keys to define your own `Styles` that override the default ones. For example:

```
<Application …>
<Application.Resources>
  <Style x:Key="{x:Static ToolBar.ButtonStyleKey}" TargetType="{x:Type Button}">
    …
  </Style>
</Application.Resources>
</Application>
```

One reason `ToolBar` uses `ResourceKey` properties instead of `Style` properties is that dependency properties do not support dynamic resource references as their default value. `ItemsControl` can get away with giving `ItemContainerStyle` a default value of `null` because the default style for its item container is always the same. `ToolBar`, however, requires different default styles depending on the theme.

10

Triggers

Triggers, first introduced in Chapter 3, have a collection of Setters just like Style (and/or collections of TriggerActions). But whereas a Style applies its values unconditionally, a trigger performs its work based on one or more conditions.

Recall that there are three types of triggers:

- **Property triggers**—Invoked when the value of a dependency property changes
- **Data triggers**—Invoked when the value of a plain .NET property changes
- **Event triggers**—Invoked when a routed event is raised

FrameworkElement, Style, DataTemplate, and ControlTemplate (covered in the next section) all have a Triggers collection, but whereas Style and the template classes accept all three types, FrameworkElement only accepts event triggers. (This is simply because the team didn't have enough time to implement the support for version 3.0.) Fortunately, Style happens to be the logical place to put triggers even if you had a choice because of the ease in sharing them and their direct tie to the visual aspects of elements.

So, let's look at a few examples of property triggers and data triggers inside styles. We'll save event triggers for Chapter 13, "Animation."

Property Triggers

A property trigger (represented by the Trigger class) executes a collection of Setters when a specified property has a specified value. And when the property no longer has this value, the property trigger "undoes" the Setters.

For example, the following update to buttonStyle makes the rotation only happen when the mouse pointer is hovering over the Button (and sets the Foreground to Black rather than White):

```
<Style x:Key="buttonStyle" TargetType="{x:Type Button}">
<Style.Triggers>
  <Trigger Property="IsMouseOver" Value="True">
    <Setter Property="RenderTransform">
    <Setter.Value>
      <RotateTransform Angle="10"/>
    </Setter.Value>
    </Setter>
    <Setter Property="Foreground" Value="Black"/>
  </Trigger>
</Style.Triggers>
  <Setter Property="FontSize" Value="22"/>
  <Setter Property="Background" Value="Purple"/>
  <Setter Property="Foreground" Value="White"/>
  <Setter Property="Height" Value="50"/>
```

```
  <Setter Property="Width" Value="50"/>
  <Setter Property="RenderTransformOrigin" Value=".5,.5"/>
</Style>
```

The result of applying this Style to a Button is shown in Figure 10.3. The trigger sets the Foreground to Black so the content is more readable against the light blue background that Buttons get by default on Windows Vista while the mouse is hovering. This "hover background" is not baked into Button, but rather comes from a trigger on Button's

IsMouseOver=false IsMouseOver=true

FIGURE 10.3   A simple property trigger can change Button's visuals while hovering.

theme style (discussed in the "Themes" section at the end of the chapter). It can be overridden by explicitly setting the Background property inside the trigger we just created.

A more complicated example of a property trigger is one that works with data-binding validation rules. In the preceding chapter, we created a JpgValidationRule class that was attached to a data-bound TextBox and ensured that the user only typed in a valid .jpg filename. To declaratively and visually show the results of a failed validation, we can create a property trigger based on the Validation.HasError attached property as follows:

```
<Style x:Key="textBoxStyle" TargetType="{x:Type TextBox}">
<Style.Triggers>
  <Trigger Property="Validation.HasError" Value="True">
    <Setter Property="Background" Value="Red"/>
    <Setter Property="ToolTip"
      Value="{Binding RelativeSource={RelativeSource Self},
      Path=(Validation.Errors)[0].ErrorContent}"/>
  </Trigger>
</Style.Triggers>
</Style>
```

In this property trigger, data binding is used to provide an appropriate message inside the ToolTip. Notice the handy use of RelativeSource to grab the Validation.Errors attached property from whatever element this Style ends up being applied to.

Applying this Style to a TextBox such as the following produces the result in Figure 10.4 when a validation error is raised:

```
<TextBox Style="{StaticResource textBoxStyle}">
<TextBox.Text>
  <Binding …>
  <Binding.ValidationRules>
    <local:JpgValidationRule/>
```

```
  </Binding.ValidationRules>
  </Binding>
</TextBox.Text>
</TextBox>
```

c:\xxx.jpg|		c:\xxx.jpg

> Value is not a valid file.

No validation errors   Validation error

FIGURE 10.4   Declaratively reacting to a validation rule error.

Data Triggers

Data triggers are just like property triggers, except that they can be triggered by *any* .NET property rather than just dependency properties. (The Setters inside a data trigger are still restricted to setting dependency properties, however.)

To use a data trigger, add a DataTrigger object to the Triggers collection and specify the property/value pair. To support plain .NET properties, you specify the relevant property with a Binding rather than a simple property name.

The following TextBox has a Style that triggers the setting of IsEnabled based on the value of its Text property, which is not a dependency property. When Text is the string "disabled," IsEnabled is set to false (which is admittedly an unusual application of a data trigger):

```
<StackPanel Width="200">
<StackPanel.Resources>
  <Style TargetType="{x:Type TextBox}">
  <Style.Triggers>
    <DataTrigger
      Binding="{Binding RelativeSource={RelativeSource Self}, Path=Text}"
      Value="disabled">
      <Setter Property="IsEnabled" Value="False"/>
    </DataTrigger>
  </Style.Triggers>
    <Setter Property="Background"
      Value="{Binding RelativeSource={RelativeSource Self}, Path=Text}"/>
  </Style>
</StackPanel.Resources>
  <TextBox Margin="3"/>
</StackPanel>
```

The same Binding to the Text property happens to be used outside of the trigger, which sets the TextBox's Background to whatever the Text value is (thanks to the string-to-Brush type converter). If Text isn't set to a valid color name, Background reverts to its default color because of the way errors in data binding are handled. (The addition of data binding to a normal Setter such as this can make it seem like it's part of a trigger when it's really not.) This TextBox is shown in Figure 10.5 with a few different Text values.

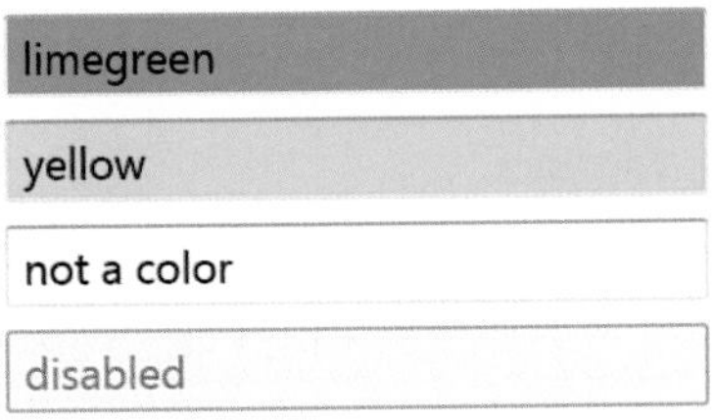

FIGURE 10.5   The TextBox Style's data trigger disables it when its text is "disabled."

Expressing More Complex Logic with Triggers

The logic expressed with the previous triggers has been of the form "when *property=value*, set the following properties." But more powerful options exist:

▶ Multiple triggers can be applied to the same element (to get a logical OR).

▶ Multiple properties can be evaluated for the same trigger (to get a logical AND).

Logical OR

Because Style.Triggers can contain multiple triggers, you can create more than one with the exact same Setters to express a logical OR relationship:

```
<Style.Triggers>
  <Trigger Property="IsMouseOver" Value="True">
    <Setter Property="RenderTransform">
    <Setter.Value>
      <RotateTransform Angle="10"/>
    </Setter.Value>
    </Setter>
    <Setter Property="Foreground" Value="Black"/>
  </Trigger>
  <Trigger Property="IsFocused" Value="True">
    <Setter Property="RenderTransform">
    <Setter.Value>
      <RotateTransform Angle="10"/>
    </Setter.Value>
    </Setter>
    <Setter Property="Foreground" Value="Black"/>
  </Trigger>
</Style.Triggers>
```

This means, "if IsMouseOver is true *or* if IsFocused is true, apply the rotation and black foreground."

DIGGING DEEPER

Conflicting Triggers

If multiple triggers that have conflicting Setters are active simultaneously, the last one wins. The same is true of conflicting Setters inside a single trigger.

Logical AND

To express a logical AND relationship, you can use a variation of Trigger called MultiTrigger, or a variation of DataTrigger called MultiDataTrigger. MultiTrigger and MultiDataTrigger have a collection of Conditions that contain the information you would normally put directly inside a Trigger or DataTrigger. Therefore, you can use MultiTrigger as follows:

```
<Style.Triggers>
  <MultiTrigger>
  <MultiTrigger.Conditions>
    <Condition Property="IsMouseOver" Value="True"/>
    <Condition Property="IsFocused" Value="True"/>
  </MultiTrigger.Conditions>
    <Setter Property="RenderTransform">
    <Setter.Value>
      <RotateTransform Angle="10"/>
    </Setter.Value>
    </Setter>
    <Setter Property="Foreground" Value="Black"/>
  </MultiTrigger>
</Style.Triggers>
```

This means, "if IsMouseOver is true *and* if IsFocused is true, apply the rotation and black foreground." MultiDataTrigger works the same way as MultiTrigger, but with support for plain .NET properties.

TIP

If you want to add even more complex event-driven behavior to a Style, you can make use of an EventSetter (which shares a common base class with Setter) to attach an event handler to any element that makes use of the Style. EventSetters can be added to a Style just like Setters:

```
<Style x:Key="buttonStyle" TargetType="{x:Type Button}">
  <Setter Property="FontSize" Value="22"/>
  <EventSetter Event="MouseEnter" Handler="Button_MouseEnter"/>
</Style>
```

Although this requires procedural code to handle the event, it is, nevertheless, a handy way to share a common handler among many elements without resorting to copying and pasting.

Templates

Controls expose many properties to customize their look: Button has configurable Background and Foreground Brushes (which can even be fancy gradients), TabControl's tabs can be relocated by setting its TabStripPlacement property, and so on. But you can only do so much with such properties.

A template, on the other hand, allows you to completely replace an element's visual tree with anything you can dream up, while keeping all of its functionality intact. And templates (like many things in WPF) aren't just some add-on mechanism for third parties; the default visuals for every Control in WPF are defined in templates (and customized for each Windows theme). The source code for every control is completely separated from its default visual tree representations (or "visual source code").

Templates (and the desire to separate visuals from logic) are also the reason that WPF's controls don't expose more simple properties to tweak their look. For example, it would be nice to change the color of the Expander's arrow back in Figure 10.2, as the gray color doesn't show up nicely against the purple background. This relatively simple change can only be accomplished by defining a new template for Expander, however. Expander has no ArrowBrush or ArrowColor property because an Expander with a custom template might not even have an arrow!

There are a few different kinds of templates. What has been described so far is the focus of this section: *control templates*. Control templates are represented by the ControlTemplate class that derives from the abstract FrameworkTemplate class. The other FrameworkTemplate-derived classes were covered in previous chapters: DataTemplate (described in the preceding chapter) and ItemsPanelTemplate (described in Chapter 4, "Introducing WPF's Controls"). Data templates customize the look of any .NET object, which is especially important for non-UIElements, whose default template is simply a TextBlock containing a string returned by its ToString method. ItemsPanelTemplates can be assigned to an ItemsControl's ItemsPanel as an easy way to alter its layout.

Slick custom visuals undoubtedly involve using 2D (or 3D!) graphics, animation, or other rich media covered in the next part of the book. This chapter sticks to some simple 2D drawings.

Introducing Control Templates

The important piece of the ControlTemplate class is its VisualTree content property, which contains the tree of elements that define the desired look. After you define a ControlTemplate (undoubtedly in XAML), you can attach it to any Control or Page by setting its Template property. Listing 10.4 defines a simple yet slick control template as a resource, and then applies it to a single Button. The result of this is shown in Figure 10.6.

FIGURE 10.6   A fancy round Button, created with a custom ControlTemplate.

LISTING 10.4   A Simple `ControlTemplate` Applied to a `Button`

```xml
<Grid>
<Grid.Resources>
  <ControlTemplate x:Key="buttonTemplate">
    <Grid>
      <Ellipse Width="100" Height="100">
      <Ellipse.Fill>
        <LinearGradientBrush StartPoint="0,0" EndPoint="0,1">
          <GradientStop Offset="0" Color="Blue"/>
          <GradientStop Offset="1" Color="Red"/>
        </LinearGradientBrush>
      </Ellipse.Fill>
      </Ellipse>
      <Ellipse Width="80" Height="80">
      <Ellipse.Fill>
        <LinearGradientBrush StartPoint="0,0" EndPoint="0,1">
          <GradientStop Offset="0" Color="White"/>
          <GradientStop Offset="1" Color="Transparent"/>
        </LinearGradientBrush>
      </Ellipse.Fill>
      </Ellipse>
    </Grid>
  </ControlTemplate>
</Grid.Resources>
  <Button Template="{StaticResource buttonTemplate}">OK</Button>
</Grid>
```

To get this look, the template's visual tree uses two circles (created with `Ellipse` elements) placed inside a single-cell `Grid`. Despite the custom look, the resultant `Button` still has a `Click` event, an `IsDefault` property, and all the other functionality you'd expect. After all, it still is an instance of the `Button` class!

> **TIP**
>
> In Listing 10.4, the `Button` is considered the *templated parent* of the elements in the control template's visual tree. `FrameworkElement` and `FrameworkContentElement` both have a `TemplatedParent` property that represents this relationship.

Getting Interactivity with Triggers

As with `Styles`, `Templates` can contain all types of triggers in a `Triggers` collection. Listing 10.5 adds triggers to the preceding `ControlTemplate` to visually respond to a mouse hover and click. A trigger on `Button.IsMouseOver` makes the `Button` orange, and a trigger on `Button.IsPressed` shrinks the button with a `ScaleTransform` to give it a "pushed in" look. The result is shown in Figure 10.7.

IsMouseOver=true   IsPressed=true
                    (and IsMouseOver=true)

FIGURE 10.7   The hover and pushed-in effects for the `ControlTemplate` in Listing 10.5.

LISTING 10.5   A `ControlTemplate` Enhanced with Triggers

```xml
<Grid>
<Grid.Resources>
  <ControlTemplate x:Key="buttonTemplate">
    <Grid>
      <Ellipse x:Name="outerCircle" Width="100" Height="100">
      <Ellipse.Fill>
        <LinearGradientBrush StartPoint="0,0" EndPoint="0,1">
          <GradientStop Offset="0" Color="Blue"/>
          <GradientStop Offset="1" Color="Red"/>
        </LinearGradientBrush>
      </Ellipse.Fill>
      </Ellipse>
      <Ellipse Width="80" Height="80">
      <Ellipse.Fill>
        <LinearGradientBrush StartPoint="0,0" EndPoint="0,1">
          <GradientStop Offset="0" Color="White"/>
          <GradientStop Offset="1" Color="Transparent"/>
        </LinearGradientBrush>
      </Ellipse.Fill>
      </Ellipse>
    </Grid>
  <ControlTemplate.Triggers>
    <Trigger Property="Button.IsMouseOver" Value="True">
      <Setter TargetName="outerCircle" Property="Fill" Value="Orange"/>
    </Trigger>
    <Trigger Property="Button.IsPressed" Value="True">
      <Setter Property="RenderTransform">
      <Setter.Value>
        <ScaleTransform ScaleX=".9" ScaleY=".9"/>
      </Setter.Value>
      </Setter>
```

LISTING 10.5   Continued

```
        <Setter Property="RenderTransformOrigin" Value=".5,.5"/>
      </Trigger>
    </ControlTemplate.Triggers>
  </ControlTemplate>
</Grid.Resources>
  <Button Template="{StaticResource buttonTemplate}">OK</Button>
</Grid>
```

Notice that the larger circle in the template's visual tree is given a name of outerCircle. This is done so it can be referenced by a trigger. The first trigger uses Setter's TargetName property (which only makes sense inside a template) to make its setting of Fill to Orange apply to only the outerCircle element. Omitting the TargetName would cause an error in this case because the trigger would apply to the entire Button, which doesn't have a Fill property. The capability to target subelements of a template with triggers is essential for sophisticated templates.

> **TIP**
>
> Analogous to Setter's TargetName property, Trigger (and EventTrigger and Condition) has a SourceName property that enables you to react to a change on a specific subelement of a template rather than the entire thing. For example, you could have triggers for IsMouseOver on individual subelements to get a richly customized hover effect.

The second trigger doesn't need to target a subelement, however. The ScaleTransform (applied as a RenderTransform) applies to the entire Button, as does the setting of RenderTransformOrigin to center the scaling. It's hard to convey in Figure 10.7, but a slight centered shrinkage (10% in this case) is a very effective visual effect for a Button press.

DIGGING DEEPER

Named Elements in Templates

Naming an element with x:Name inside a template does not make it become a field to access programmatically, unlike its behavior outside of a template. This is because a template can be applied to multiple elements in the same scope. The main purpose of naming elements in a template is for referencing them from triggers (typically defined in XAML). But if you want programmatic access to a named element inside a template, you can use the template's FindName method after the template has been applied to a target.

Restricting the Target Type

As with Style, ControlTemplate has a TargetType property that can restrict where the template can be applied. It also enables you to remove the class name qualifications on any property references inside a template (such as the values of `Trigger.Property` and `Setter.Property`). Therefore, the template from Listing 10.5 could be rewritten as

```xml
<ControlTemplate x:Key="buttonTemplate" TargetType="{x:Type Button}">
  <Grid>

    …
  </Grid>
<ControlTemplate.Triggers>
  <Trigger Property="IsMouseOver" Value="True">
    <Setter TargetName="outerCircle" Property="Fill" Value="Orange"/>
  </Trigger>
  <Trigger Property="IsPressed" Value="True">
    <Setter Property="RenderTransform">
    <Setter.Value>
      <ScaleTransform ScaleX=".9" ScaleY=".9"/>
    </Setter.Value>
    </Setter>
    <Setter Property="RenderTransformOrigin" Value=".5,.5"/>
  </Trigger>
</ControlTemplate.Triggers>
</ControlTemplate>
```

Note that in this example, the `Setters` already had unqualified `Property` values in previous listings. That's because the properties are either qualified by the use of `TargetName`, or they are common to all `Controls`. (Without an explicit `TargetType`, the target type is implicitly `Control`.)

Unlike a `Style`, the use of `TargetType` does not enable you to remove the template's `x:Key` (when used in a dictionary). There is no such thing as a default control template; you have to set the template inside a typed `Style` to get such behavior.

Respecting the Templated Parent's Properties

There's a bit of a problem with the templates we've created so far. Any `Buttons` they're applied to look exactly the same, no matter what the values of its properties are. For example, in the last two listings the `Button` has "OK" as content, but it never gets displayed. If you're creating a control template that's meant to be broadly reusable, you need to do some work to respect various properties of the target `Control`.

Respecting `ContentControl`'s `Content` Property

The key to inserting property values from the target element inside a control template is data binding. Fortunately, a class called `TemplateBindingExtension` makes this easy.

`TemplateBindingExtension` is a markup extension that is similar to `Binding`, but simpler, more lightweight, and customized for templates. It's often referred to as simply `TemplateBinding` because of the tendency to omit the `Extension` suffix when used in XAML.

10

The "data source" for TemplateBinding is always the target element, and the "path" is any of its dependency properties, selected by setting TemplateBinding's Property property. Therefore, we could add a TextBlock to the control template in Listing 10.5 that contains the target Button's Content as follows:

```
<TextBlock Text="{TemplateBinding Property=Button.Content}"/>
```

Or, because TemplateBinding has a constructor that accepts a dependency property, we could simply write:

```
<TextBlock Text="{TemplateBinding Button.Content}"/>
```

And if TargetType is used to restrict the template's use for Buttons (or other ContentControls), we could simplify this even further as:

```
<TextBlock Text="{TemplateBinding Content}"/>
```

Of course, a Button can contain nontext Content, so using a TextBlock to display it creates an artificial limitation. To ensure that all types of Content get displayed properly in the template, we can use a generic ContentControl instead of a TextBlock. Listing 10.6 does just that. The ContentControl is given a Margin and wrapped in a Viewbox so it's displayed at a reasonable size relative to the rest of the Button.

LISTING 10.6   An Updated ControlTemplate That Displays the Target Button's Content

```
<ControlTemplate x:Key="buttonTemplate" TargetType="{x:Type Button}">
  <Grid>
    <Ellipse x:Name="outerCircle" Width="100" Height="100">
    <Ellipse.Fill>
      <LinearGradientBrush StartPoint="0,0" EndPoint="0,1">
        <GradientStop Offset="0" Color="Blue"/>
        <GradientStop Offset="1" Color="Red"/>
      </LinearGradientBrush>
    </Ellipse.Fill>
    </Ellipse>
    <Ellipse Width="80" Height="80">
    <Ellipse.Fill>
      <LinearGradientBrush StartPoint="0,0" EndPoint="0,1">
        <GradientStop Offset="0" Color="White"/>
        <GradientStop Offset="1" Color="Transparent"/>
      </LinearGradientBrush>
    </Ellipse.Fill>
    </Ellipse>
    <Viewbox>
      <ContentControl Margin="20" Content="{TemplateBinding Content}"/>
    </Viewbox>
  </Grid>
```

LISTING 10.6   Continued

```
<ControlTemplate.Triggers>
  <Trigger Property="IsMouseOver" Value="True">
    <Setter TargetName="outerCircle" Property="Fill" Value="Orange"/>
  </Trigger>
  <Trigger Property="IsPressed" Value="True">
    <Setter Property="RenderTransform">
    <Setter.Value>
      <ScaleTransform ScaleX=".9" ScaleY=".9"/>
    </Setter.Value>
    </Setter>
    <Setter Property="RenderTransformOrigin" Value=".5,.5"/>
  </Trigger>
</ControlTemplate.Triggers>
</ControlTemplate>
```

Figure 10.8 shows what two Buttons look like with this new control template applied. One Button has simple "OK" text content, whereas the other has an Image. In both cases, the content is reflected in the new visuals as expected.

FIGURE 10.8   Two different Buttons with the control template defined in Listing 10.6.

> **WARNING**
>
> **TemplateBinding only works inside a template's visual tree, and doesn't work with properties on Freezables!**
>
> TemplateBinding doesn't work outside of a template or outside of its VisualTree property, so you can't even use TemplateBinding inside a template's trigger. Furthermore, in the current version of WPF, TemplateBinding doesn't work when applied to a Freezable (for mostly artificial reasons). For example, attempting to bind the Color property of any explicit Brush fails.
>
> However, TemplateBinding is just a less-powerful but convenient shortcut for using a regular Binding. You can get the same effect by using a regular Binding with a RelativeSource equal to {RelativeSource TemplatedParent} and a Path equal to whatever dependency property whose value you want to retrieve. Such a Binding works in the cases mentioned where TemplateBinding does not.

> **TIP**
>
> Rather than using a `ContentControl` inside a control template, you should use the lighter-weight `ContentPresenter` element. `ContentPresenter` displays content just like `ContentControl`, but was designed specifically for use in control templates. `ContentPresenter` is a primitive building block, whereas `ContentControl` is a full-blown control with its own control template (that contains a `ContentPresenter`)!
>
> In Listing 10.6, you can replace
>
> ```
> <ContentControl Margin="20" Content="{TemplateBinding Content}"/>
> ```
>
> with
>
> ```
> <ContentPresenter Margin="20" Content="{TemplateBinding Content}"/>
> ```
>
> `ContentPresenter` even has a built-in shortcut; if you omit setting its `Content` to `{TemplateBinding Content}`, it implicitly assumes that's what you want. So, you can replace the preceding line of code with simply
>
> ```
> <ContentPresenter Margin="20"/>
> ```
>
> This only works when the control template is given an explicit `TargetType` of `ContentControl` or a `ContentControl`-derived class (like `Button`).
>
> The remaining templates in this chapter use `ContentPresenter` instead of `ContentControl`, as that's what real-world templates use.

Respecting Other Properties

No matter what type of control you're creating a control template for, there are undoubtedly other properties on the target control that should be honored if you want the template to be reusable: `Height` and `Width`, perhaps `Background`, `Padding`, and so on. Some properties (such as `Foreground`, `FontSize`, `FontWeight`, and so on) might automatically inherit their desired values thanks to property value inheritance in the visual tree, but other properties need explicit attention.

Listing 10.7 is an update to Listing 10.6 that respects the `Background`, `Padding`, and `Content` properties of the target `Button`. It also implicitly respects the size of the target element by *removing* the explicit `Height` and `Width` settings and letting the layout system do its job. This listing uses a `ContentPresenter` rather than a `ContentControl`, although either one produces the same result.

LISTING 10.7   Updates to the `ControlTemplate` That Make It More Reusable

```
<ControlTemplate x:Key="buttonTemplate" TargetType="{x:Type Button}">
  <Grid>
    <Ellipse x:Name="outerCircle">
    <Ellipse.Fill>
      <LinearGradientBrush StartPoint="0,0" EndPoint="0,1">
        <GradientStop Offset="0"
```

LISTING 10.7   Continued

```
              Color="{Binding RelativeSource={RelativeSource TemplatedParent},
                Path=Background.Color}"/>
          <GradientStop Offset="1" Color="Red"/>
        </LinearGradientBrush>
      </Ellipse.Fill>
    </Ellipse>
    <Ellipse RenderTransformOrigin=".5,.5">
    <Ellipse.RenderTransform>
      <ScaleTransform ScaleX=".8" ScaleY=".8"/>
    </Ellipse.RenderTransform>
    <Ellipse.Fill>
      <LinearGradientBrush StartPoint="0,0" EndPoint="0,1">
        <GradientStop Offset="0" Color="White"/>
        <GradientStop Offset="1" Color="Transparent"/>
      </LinearGradientBrush>
    </Ellipse.Fill>
    </Ellipse>
    <Viewbox>
      <ContentPresenter Margin="{TemplateBinding Padding}"/>
    </Viewbox>
  </Grid>
<ControlTemplate.Triggers>
  <Trigger Property="IsMouseOver" Value="True">
    <Setter TargetName="outerCircle" Property="Fill" Value="Orange"/>
  </Trigger>
  <Trigger Property="IsPressed" Value="True">
    <Setter Property="RenderTransform">
    <Setter.Value>
      <ScaleTransform ScaleX=".9" ScaleY=".9"/>
    </Setter.Value>
    </Setter>
    <Setter Property="RenderTransformOrigin" Value=".5,.5"/>
  </Trigger>
</ControlTemplate.Triggers>
</ControlTemplate>
```

The target Button's Padding is now used as the ContentPresenter's Margin. It's common to use the element's Padding in a template as the Margin of an inner element. After all, that's basically the definition of Padding!

In addition to this, a few nonintuitive changes have been made to the template's visual tree to accommodate an externally specified size and Background. We could have simply used {TemplateBinding Background} as the Fill for outerCircle, giving each Button the flexibility to specify a solid color, a gradient, and so on. But perhaps the "red glow" at the bottom is a characteristic that we'd like to keep consistent wherever the template is used. In other words, we only want to replace the blue part of the gradient with the externally specified Background. However, GradientStop.Color can't be directly set to {TemplateBinding Background} because Color is of type Color, whereas Background is of type Brush (and because GradientStop derives from Freezable)! Therefore, the listing uses a normal Binding instead, which supports referencing the Color subproperty. (Note that this Binding only works when Background is set to a SolidColorBrush because other Brushes don't have a Color property.)

Both Ellipses (or the parent Grid) could have been given an explicit Height and Width matching the target Button by binding to its ActualHeight and ActualWidth properties. Instead, these values are omitted altogether because the root element is implicitly given the templated parent's size anyway! This means that an individual target Button has the power to make itself look like an ellipse by specifying different values for Width and Height. If we wanted to preserve the perfect circular look, we could have wrapped the entire visual tree in a Viewbox.

The final trick used by Listing 10.7 is the ScaleTransform on the inner circle to make it 80% of the size of the outer circle. In previous listings, this transform is unnecessary because both the outer and inner circles have a hard-coded size. But with a dynamic size, ScaleTransform enables us to effectively perform a little math on the size. (If we wanted a fixed-size difference between the circles, a simple Margin would do the trick.)

Figure 10.9 shows the rendered result for the following Buttons that make use of this new control template:

```
<StackPanel Orientation="Horizontal">
  <Button Template="{StaticResource buttonTemplate}"
    Height="100" Width="100" FontSize="80" Background="Black"
    Padding="20" Margin="5">1</Button>
  <Button Template="{StaticResource buttonTemplate}"
    Height="150" Width="250" FontSize="80" Background="Yellow"
    Padding="20" Margin="5">2</Button>
  <Button Template="{StaticResource buttonTemplate}"
    Height="200" Width="200" FontSize="80" Background="White"
    Padding="20" Margin="5">3</Button>
</StackPanel>
```

Each Button has values for Background, Padding, and Content that are explicitly used by the control template. Their values for Height and Width are implicitly respected by the template, and their FontSize setting is implicitly picked up by the template's ContentPresenter. The size of the font isn't directly reflected in the rendered output because the template wraps the ContentPresenter inside a Viewbox to keep it within the bounds of the outer circle. The Margin specified on each Button is not used by the template, but it still affects the StackPanel layout as usual, giving a little bit of space between each Button.

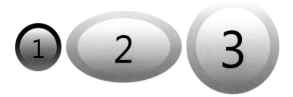

FIGURE 10.9   Buttons that tweak the look of their custom template from Listing 10.7.

DIGGING DEEPER

`TemplateBinding` and **Value Converters**

Just like `Binding`, `TemplateBinding` also supports a value converter. `TemplateBinding` has `Converter`and `ConverterParameter` properties, but oddly enough no `ConverterCulture` property. If you require the use of `ConverterCulture`, you can simply use a `Binding` instead.

Hijacking Existing Properties for New Purposes

Sometimes, you might want to parameterize some aspect of a control template, despite there being no corresponding property on the target control. For example, the template in Listing 10.7 has a hard-coded orange `Brush` representing the hover state. What can we do to allow individual `Buttons` to customize this `Brush`? There's no corresponding property already on `Button` to be set!

One option is to define a custom control using the techniques described in Chapter 16, "User Controls and Custom Controls." It wouldn't be too much work to write a new class that derives from `Button` and adds a single `HoverBrush` property. But that's a bit heavyweight for such a simple task. Another option is to define several control templates that each uses a different hover `Brush`. But that would only be reasonable if the set of desired `Brushes` is small and known.

Instead, what most people resort to is a devious little hack known as *hijacking* a dependency property. This involves looking at the target control for any dependency properties of the desired type, and seeing if you can leverage them in an unintended way. For example, all `Controls` have three properties of type `Brush`: `Background`, `Foreground`, and `BorderBrush`. Because `Background` and `Foreground` already play important roles in Listing 10.7, neither one would look very good as a hover `Brush`. (There would also be no way to set the hover `Brush` independently of the other two.) But `BorderBrush` is a different story. It's completely unused by the template in Listing 10.7, so why not use that?

There really is no reason not to use it, other than the fact that it makes the usage of the template confusing and less readable. Nevertheless, here's how you could update the `IsMouseOver` trigger from Listing 10.7 to hijack `BorderBrush`:

```
<Trigger Property="IsMouseOver" Value="True">
  <Setter TargetName="outerCircle" Property="Fill"
    Value="{Binding RelativeSource={RelativeSource TemplatedParent},
      Path=BorderBrush}"/>
</Trigger>
```

A Binding must be used in this case rather than a TemplateBinding because the Trigger is outside of the visual tree.

If this hack leaves a bad taste in your mouth, then by all means use an alternative approach. This hack is definitely not recommended by the WPF team! But it's a useful trick to know about, just in case you're looking for a quick fix.

Respecting Visual States

When creating a control template for Buttons, visually reacting to hover and pressed states with corresponding triggers is a nice touch, but purely optional. Imagine using the template from Listing 10.7 on a CheckBox or ToggleButton, however. (This can be done simply by changing the TargetType.) Because the template doesn't show different visuals for the Checked versus Unchecked versus Indeterminate states, it's a pretty lousy template for these controls!

In fact, the template in Listing 10.7 is still incomplete, even for a Button! The fact that it doesn't show any different visuals when IsEnabled is false or IsDefaulted is true makes it a pretty lousy template!

Therefore, you should consider all the visual states a control should expose when designing a control template for it. This might take the form of triggers on the appropriate properties or events, or it could just be a matter of binding them appropriately.

For example, a control template for ProgressBar must show the current value to be useful. Listing 10.8 contains a control template (defined as an application-level resource) for ProgressBar that makes it look like a pie chart. The most important aspect of the template—filling up the pie according to the current Value—is accomplished by binding to the templated parent and using value converters to do the necessary trigonometry. In addition to this, triggers on IsEnabled and IsIndeterminate alter the visuals for these states. The results are shown in Figures 10.10 and 10.11 for ProgressBars such as the following:

```
<ProgressBar Foreground="{StaticResource foregroundBrush}" Width="100"
  Height="100" Value="10" Template="{StaticResource progressPie}"/>
```

The foregroundBrush resource is defined as a simple green gradient:

```
<LinearGradientBrush x:Key="foregroundBrush" StartPoint="0,0" EndPoint="1,1">
  <GradientStop Offset="0" Color="LightGreen"/>
  <GradientStop Offset="1" Color="DarkGreen"/>
</LinearGradientBrush>
```

FIGURE 10.10   Customized `ProgressBar` visuals for various stages of progress.

IsEnabled=false   IsIndeterminate=true

FIGURE 10.11   Customized `ProgressBar` visuals for disabled and indeterminate states.

LISTING 10.8   The "Pie Chart" Control Template for `ProgressBar`

```
<Application x:Class="WindowsApplication1.App"
  xmlns="http://schemas.microsoft.com/winfx/2006/xaml/presentation"
  xmlns:x="http://schemas.microsoft.com/winfx/2006/xaml"
  xmlns:local="clr-namespace:WindowsApplication1"
  StartupUri="Window1.xaml">
  <Application.Resources>

    <ControlTemplate x:Key="progressPie" TargetType="{x:Type ProgressBar}">

    <!-- Resources -->
    <ControlTemplate.Resources>
      <local:ValueMinMaxToPointConverter x:Key="converter1"/>
      <local:ValueMinMaxToIsLargeArcConverter x:Key="converter2"/>
    </ControlTemplate.Resources>

    <!-- Visual Tree -->
    <Viewbox>
      <Grid Width="20" Height="20">
        <Ellipse x:Name="background" Stroke="{TemplateBinding BorderBrush}"
          StrokeThickness="{TemplateBinding BorderThickness}"
          Width="20" Height="20" Fill="{TemplateBinding Background}"/>
        <Path x:Name="pie" Fill="{TemplateBinding Foreground}">
        <Path.Data>
          <PathGeometry>
            <PathFigure StartPoint="10,10" IsClosed="True">
              <LineSegment Point="10,0"/>
              <ArcSegment Size="10,10" SweepDirection="Clockwise">
              <ArcSegment.Point>
                <MultiBinding Converter="{StaticResource converter1}">
```

LISTING 10.8   Continued

```xml
                        <Binding RelativeSource="{RelativeSource TemplatedParent}"
                          Path="Value"/>
                        <Binding RelativeSource="{RelativeSource TemplatedParent}"
                          Path="Minimum"/>
                        <Binding RelativeSource="{RelativeSource TemplatedParent}"
                          Path="Maximum"/>
                      </MultiBinding>
                    </ArcSegment.Point>
                    <ArcSegment.IsLargeArc>
                      <MultiBinding Converter="{StaticResource converter2}">
                        <Binding RelativeSource="{RelativeSource TemplatedParent}"
                          Path="Value"/>
                        <Binding RelativeSource="{RelativeSource TemplatedParent}"
                          Path="Minimum"/>
                        <Binding RelativeSource="{RelativeSource TemplatedParent}"
                          Path="Maximum"/>
                      </MultiBinding>
                    </ArcSegment.IsLargeArc>
                    </ArcSegment>
                </PathFigure>
              </PathGeometry>
            </Path.Data>
            </Path>
        </Grid>
      </Viewbox>

      <!-- Triggers -->
      <ControlTemplate.Triggers>
        <Trigger Property="IsIndeterminate" Value="True">
          <Setter TargetName="pie" Property="Visibility" Value="Hidden"/>
          <Setter TargetName="background" Property="Fill">
          <Setter.Value>
            <LinearGradientBrush StartPoint="0,0" EndPoint="1,1">
              <GradientStop Offset="0" Color="Yellow"/>
              <GradientStop Offset="1" Color="Brown"/>
            </LinearGradientBrush>
          </Setter.Value>
          </Setter>
        </Trigger>
        <Trigger Property="IsEnabled" Value="False">
          <Setter TargetName="pie" Property="Fill">
          <Setter.Value>
```

LISTING 10.8   Continued

```
          <LinearGradientBrush StartPoint="0,0" EndPoint="1,1">
            <GradientStop Offset="0" Color="Gray"/>
            <GradientStop Offset="1" Color="White"/>
          </LinearGradientBrush>
        </Setter.Value>
      </Setter>
    </Trigger>
  </ControlTemplate.Triggers>
  </ControlTemplate>

  </Application.Resources>
</Application>
```

The root of the visual tree is a Viewbox, so the 20x20 single-cell Grid can scale appropriately. The background circle (which has a radius of 10 prior to scaling) is given the templated parent's Background, BorderBrush, and BorderThickness. The "pie" is a Path (an element covered in the next chapter) that is given the templated

> **TIP**
>
> Notice that Listing 10.8 defines value converters in ControlTemplate's Resources collection. Like Style, all FrameworkTemplates have their own Resources collection. It can be used to keep templates self-contained.

parent's Foreground and relies on two MultiBindings with value converters defined in Listing 10.9 to get the right shape. MultiBinding is used rather than a simple TemplateBinding or Binding so the pie gets updated when any of ProgressBar's three relevant properties change: Value, Minimum, and Maximum. The two triggers create the results in Figure 10.11 by filling an element with a hard-coded Brush (and in the case of IsIndeterminate, hiding the pie). A more appropriate effect for IsIndeterminate is probably an animation that spins the pie around, but at least there's *some* visual distinction as is. Note that not all of ProgressBar's properties are honored by this template. For example, Orientation is unused, but there's not a great way to honor it considering the visual representation.

LISTING 10.9   The Value Converters Used in Listing 10.8

```
public class ValueMinMaxToIsLargeArcConverter : IMultiValueConverter
{
  public object Convert(object[] values, Type targetType, object parameter,
    CultureInfo culture)
  {
    double value = (double)values[0];
    double minimum = (double)values[1];
    double maximum = (double)values[2];
```

LISTING 10.9   Continued

```csharp
    // Only return true if the value is 50% of the range or greater
    return ((value * 2) >= (maximum - minimum));
  }

  public object[] ConvertBack(object value, Type[] targetTypes, object parameter,
    CultureInfo culture)
  {
    throw new NotSupportedException();
  }
}

public class ValueMinMaxToPointConverter : IMultiValueConverter
{
  public object Convert(object[] values, Type targetType, object parameter,
    CultureInfo culture)
  {
    double value = (double)values[0];
    double minimum = (double)values[1];
    double maximum = (double)values[2];

    // Convert the value to one between 0 and 360
    double current = (value / (maximum - minimum)) * 360;

    // Adjust the finished state so the ArcSegment gets drawn as a whole circle
    if (current == 360)
      current = 359.999;

    // Shift by 90 degrees so 0 starts at the top of the circle
    current = current - 90;

    // Convert the angle to radians
    current = current * 0.017453292519943295;

    // Calculate the circle's point
    double x = 10 + 10 * Math.Cos(current);
    double y = 10 + 10 * Math.Sin(current);
    return new Point(x, y);
  }

  public object[] ConvertBack(object value, Type[] targetTypes, object parameter,
    CultureInfo culture)
  {
    throw new NotSupportedException();
  }
}
```

The first value converter is pretty simple. ArcSegment's IsLargeArc property (from Listing 10.8) must be true when the pie is more than half full and false otherwise. Therefore, ValueMinMaxToIsLargeArcConverter does this simple calculation based on the three values from the target ProgressBar and returns the appropriate Boolean value.

The second value converter is much more complicated. Its job is to return the proper Point along the circle's circumference according to the current values. To do this, it first converts the ProgressBar's Value to an angle (in degrees), makes some adjustments, and then converts it to radians. With this angle, a little trigonometry is used to get the point, based on the fixed radius of 10 and the center point of (10,10).

DIGGING DEEPER

Magical PART_XXX Names in Templates

You'll often hear claims of WPF's controls being "lookless" and having an implementation that's completely independent from their visuals. (I even made that claim earlier in this chapter!) It turns out that this isn't *entirely* true! Some WPF controls have built-in logic to control their visual behavior, but only when the template performs the correct "secret handshake" to enable this logic.

On the one hand, this is an implementation detail that you don't need to know about. On the other hand, by learning about this mechanism, you can sometimes create control templates with much less effort by taking advantage of this built-in logic!

The "secret handshake" performed by several controls is to look for elements in the control template's visual tree with specific names (always of the form "PART_XXX") and sometimes with specific types. If such elements are found, extra behavior is applied to them. The specific names and behaviors depend on the control. For example:

▶ If a ProgressBar control template has elements named PART_Indicator and PART_Track, the control ensures that the Width (or Height, based on ProgressBar's Orientation) of PART_Indicator remains the correct percentage of the Width (or Height) of PART_Track, based on ProgressBar's Value, Minimum, and Maximum properties. For the pie chart template, this behavior is clearly undesirable. But for a template that more closely matches the standard ProgressBar look, taking advantage of this support greatly simplifies it (and removes the need for procedural code to do the math).

▶ If a ComboBox control template has a Popup named PART_Popup, ComboBox's DropDownClosed event gets automatically raised when the Popup is closed. If it has a TextBox named PART_EditableTextBox, it integrates automatically with ComboBox's ability to update the selection as the user types.

▶ Controls such as TextBox and PasswordBox have most of their functionality tied to an element in the control template called PART_ContentHost. If you don't have an element with this name in your control template, you'll have to reimplement the entire editable surface!

10

Mixing Templates with `Styles`

Although all the control templates thus far are applied directly to elements for simplicity, it's more common to set a `Control`'s `Template` property inside a `Style` and then apply that style to the desired elements. For example:

```
<Style TargetType="{x:Type Button}">
  <Setter Property="Template">
  <Setter.Value>
    <ControlTemplate TargetType="{x:Type Button}">
      …
    </ControlTemplate>
  </Setter.Value>
  </Setter>
  …
</Style>
```

Besides the convenience of combining a template with arbitrary property settings, there are important advantages to doing this:

▶ It gives you the effect of default templates. For example, when a typed `Style` gets applied to elements by default, and that `Style` contains a custom control template, the control template gets applied without any explicit markings on those elements!

▶ It enables you to provide default yet overridable property values that control the look of the template. In other words, it enables you to respect the templated parent's properties but still provide your own default values.

The final point is very relevant for the templates we've examined so far. For the `ProgressBar` pie chart template, I wanted the pie to be filled with a green gradient by default. If such a `Brush` is hard-coded inside the template, consumers would have no way to customize the fill. On the other hand, by binding to the templated parent's `Foreground` (which is what Listing 10.8 does), the onus is on every `ProgressBar` to set its `Foreground` appropriately. `ProgressBar`'s default `Foreground` is a solid green color, not the desired gradient!

By placing the green gradient in a `Style`'s `Setter`, however, you get the desired default look while still allowing individual `ProgressBar`s to override the fill by explicitly setting their `Foreground` property locally. And the `{TemplateBinding Foreground}` expression inside the template doesn't need to change. The `Style` could look as follows:

```
<Style x:Key="pieStyle" TargetType="{x:Type ProgressBar}">
  <Setter Property="Foreground">
  <Setter.Value>
    <LinearGradientBrush StartPoint="0,0" EndPoint="1,1">
      <GradientStop Offset="0" Color="LightGreen"/>
      <GradientStop Offset="1" Color="DarkGreen"/>
    </LinearGradientBrush>
```

```xaml
      </Setter.Value>
    </Setter>
    <Setter Property="Template">
    <Setter.Value>
      <ControlTemplate TargetType="{x:Type ProgressBar}">
        …
          <Path x:Name="pie" Fill="{TemplateBinding Foreground}">
        …
      </ControlTemplate>
    </Setter.Value>
    </Setter>
</Style>
```

Consumers of the Style could do the following:

```xaml
<!-- Use the default gradient fill -->
<ProgressBar Style="{StaticResource pieStyle}"
  Width="100" Height="100" Value="10"/>
<!-- Use a solid red fill instead -->
<ProgressBar Style="{StaticResource pieStyle}" Foreground="Red"
  Width="100" Height="100" Value="10"/>
```

Of course, the same approach can be used for other properties, such as Width and Height.

DIGGING DEEPER

Interactions Between Styles and Their Templates

When a Style contains a control template, it's possible to see the same property set from several different places: from triggers in the Style, from triggers in the Style's template, and from a Setter in the Style! The order of precedence is the order just listed in the preceding sentence. So, Style triggers override template triggers, and all triggers override Style Setters.

FAQ

 How do I make small tweaks to an existing control template, rather than creating a brand-new one from scratch?

There is no mechanism for tweaking existing templates (like Style's BasedOn). Instead, you can easily retrieve a XAML representation for any existing Style or template, modify it, and then apply it as a brand-new Style or template. In fact, even if you want to create a completely different look, the best way to become familiar with how to design robust control templates is to look at the built-in WPF control templates used by their theme styles.

Continues

10

FAQ

Continued

To obtain the "visual source code" in XAML for any control template, simply use code like the following (after the control has undergone layout, so the template gets applied):

```
string xaml = XamlWriter.Save(someControl.Template);
```

Or, you can retrieve the entire `Style` for any element by programmatically grabbing the correct resource. The following code grabs the theme style of an element by using a dependency property called `DefaultStyleKey` (described in the "Themes" section) to identify the `Style` resource:

```
// Get the default style key
object defaultStyleKey = someElement.GetValue(
  FrameworkElement.DefaultStyleKeyProperty);
// Retrieve the resource with that key
Style style = (Style)Application.Current.FindResource(defaultStyleKey);
// Serialize its XAML representation into a string
string xaml = System.Windows.Markup.XamlWriter.Save(style);
```

Alternatively, you can just consult the Windows SDK, which contains XAML files with all the theme styles used by WPF's controls.

For other types of `Styles`, you could call `FindResource` with the appropriate key, such as `typeof(Button)` for a typed `Button` style (if it exists).

Skins

Skinning refers to the act of changing an application's appearance (or *skin*) on the fly, typically by third parties. WPF doesn't have a distinct concept called a *skin*, nor does it have a formal notion of *skinning*, but it doesn't need one. You can easily write an application or component that supports dynamic skinning by using WPF's dynamic resource mechanism (described in Chapter 8) combined with `Styles` and/or templates.

To support skinning in your application, one of the first things you need to do is decide on a data format. Whereas it might make sense to invent a format for Win32 or Windows Forms applications, XAML is a no-brainer data format for skins in WPF applications. But what should such XAML files look like?

Often, the initial instinct is to load an entire `Window` or `Page` dynamically from a loose XAML file and hook it up to the appropriate logic (using the technique shown at the end of Chapter 2, "XAML Demystified"). Loading your entire UI on the fly gives complete flexibility, but, in most cases, it's probably *too much* flexibility. Authors of such XAML files would need a lot of discipline to include all the right elements with all the right names and all the right event handlers, and so on. (Either that or the code to connect the UI to the application logic needs to be extremely forgiving.)

For environments that aren't highly controlled, the best approach is to make `ResourceDictionary` the root of a skin representation. `ResourceDictionary` makes a great extensibility point in general because of the ease in which it can be swapped in and out or merged with others. When defining a skin, it makes sense for the `ResourceDictionary` to contain `Styles` and/or templates.

To demonstrate skinning, the following `Window` is a hypothetical progress dialog, shown in Figure 10.12:

```xml
<Window x:Class="WindowsApplication1.Window1"
  xmlns="http://schemas.microsoft.com/winfx/2006/xaml/presentation"
  xmlns:x="http://schemas.microsoft.com/winfx/2006/xaml"
  Title="Please Wait" Height="200" Width="300" ResizeMode="NoResize">
  <Grid>
    <StackPanel Style="{DynamicResource DialogStyle}">
      <Label Style="{DynamicResource HeadingStyle}">Loading...</Label>
      <ProgressBar Value="35" MinHeight="20" Margin="20"/>
      <Button Style="{DynamicResource CancelButtonStyle}" Width="70"
        Click="Cancel_Click">Cancel</Button>
    </StackPanel>
  </Grid>
</Window>
```

Notice that most of the `Window`'s elements are given explicit `Styles`. This is not a requirement for skinning, but it's often a nice touch for giving skin authors more control over the visual experience. For example, suppose you want to give a specific look to a Cancel `Button` that's different from the look you want for all other `Buttons`. Marking all Cancel `Buttons` with an explicit `CancelButtonStyle` allows you to do just that. Referencing the explicit `Styles` as *dynamic* resources is critical to enable them to be updated at arbitrary times.

To compile successfully (and give the look shown in Figure 10.12), the preceding `Window` is paired with the following `App.xaml` file that provides a default definition of each `Style` resource:

FIGURE 10.12   A dialog box, shown with its default skin.

> **TIP**
>
> When giving an element a `Style` that you expect to be reskinned dynamically, don't forget to reference it as a dynamic resource!

```xml
<Application xmlns="http://schemas.microsoft.com/winfx/2006/xaml/presentation"
    xmlns:x="http://schemas.microsoft.com/winfx/2006/xaml"
    StartupUri="Window1.xaml">
  <Application.Resources>
```

10

```
    <Style x:Key="DialogStyle" TargetType="{x:Type StackPanel}">
      <Setter Property="Margin" Value="20"/>
    </Style>
    <Style x:Key="HeadingStyle" TargetType="{x:Type Label}">
      <Setter Property="FontSize" Value="16"/>
      <Setter Property="FontWeight" Value="Bold"/>
    </Style>
    <Style x:Key="CancelButtonStyle" TargetType="{x:Type Button}"/>
  </Application.Resources>
</Application>
```

Notice that `CancelButtonStyle` is empty, so applying it to a `Button` has no effect. This is perfectly valid because the expectation is that a skin might replace this `Style` with something more meaningful.

With this in place, a skin file could simply look like the following:

```
<ResourceDictionary
  xmlns="http://schemas.microsoft.com/winfx/2006/xaml/presentation"
  xmlns:x="http://schemas.microsoft.com/winfx/2006/xaml">
  <Style x:Key="DialogStyle" TargetType="{x:Type StackPanel}">
    …
  </Style>
  <Style x:Key="HeadingStyle" TargetType="{x:Type Label}">
    …
  </Style>
  <Style x:Key="CancelButtonStyle" TargetType="{x:Type Button}">
    …
  </Style>
  Any additional styles…
</ResourceDictionary>
```

Then all the host application needs to do is dynamically load the skin XAML file and assign it as the new `Application.Resources` dictionary. The following code does this for a `.xaml` file sitting in the current directory:

```
ResourceDictionary resources = null;
using (FileStream fs = new FileStream("CustomSkin.xaml", FileMode.Open,
  FileAccess.Read))
{
  // Get the root element, which must be a ResourceDictionary
  resources = (ResourceDictionary)XamlReader.Load(fs);
}
Application.Current.Resources = resources;
```

You could alternatively use code like the following to retrieve a skin file from the Internet at an arbitrary URL:

```
ResourceDictionary resources = null;
System.Net.WebClient client = new System.Net.WebClient();
using (Stream s = client.OpenRead("http://adamnathan.net/wpf/CustomSkin.xaml"))
{
  // Get the root element, which must be a ResourceDictionary
  resources = (ResourceDictionary)XamlReader.Load(s);
}
Application.Current.Resources = resources;
```

Because assigning a dictionary to `Application.Current.Resources` code wipes out the
current dictionary, you should also store the default `ResourceDictionary` if you want to
restore it later!

FAQ

 **What happens if a skin doesn't define a named `Style` expected by
the application?**

If you take the approach of completely replacing the current `Application.Resources` dictionary with a new `ResourceDictionary`, and if the new dictionary is missing `Styles`, then the
affected controls will silently revert to their default appearance. This is true of any dynamic
resource that gets removed while the application is running. The dynamic resource mechanism does emit a debug trace, however, similar to how data binding reports errors. For
example, applying a skin missing a `Style` called `CancelButtonStyle` causes the following
message to be emitted inside a debugger:

```
System.Windows.ResourceDictionary Warning: 9 : Resource not found;
ResourceKey='CancelButtonStyle'
```

The progress dialog sample (whose full source code is included with the rest of the book's
code) switches the skin when you click the Cancel `Button` for demonstration purposes,
but for a real application this action would likely be taken when a user initiates it from
some skin-choosing user interface.

In this book's source code, you'll find two alternative skins for the progress dialog in
Figure 10.12. The dialog is shown with these two skins in Figure 10.13.

"Electric" skin   "Light and Fluffy" skin

FIGURE 10.13   Two alternate skins for the dialog.

Notice that the "electric" skin restyles the `ProgressBar` (using the pie chart template from the previous section) even though the application didn't give it an explicit `Style`. It does this by making it a typed `Style` that applies to all `ProgressBars`. Fortunately, any additions of, removals of, or changes to typed styles in a `ResourceDictionary` get automatically reflected the same way that explicit dynamic resources do. The skin's `CancelButtonStyle` uses a `TranslateTransform` to reposition it next to the `ProgressBar` rather than below it. It also does something quite unique for the `Label`'s `Style`; it uses a template to send the `Label`'s content through a "jive translator" web service. (This, of course, only works if the `Label` contains text.)

DIGGING DEEPER

Skins That Require Procedural Code

The "electric" skin's `ProgressBar` template requires procedural code (as seen in the previous section), so it can't be implemented in a loose XAML file. In such cases, you can compile the `ResourceDictionary` into an assembly and still expose it as a skin. The key is to use `Application.LoadComponent` to retrieve the compiled resource. The resource can be compiled into the same assembly or a different assembly, as explained in Chapter 8.

The progress dialog sample compiles both skins into the same assembly, so it uses code like the following to load them:

```
ResourceDictionary resources = (ResourceDictionary)Application.LoadComponent(
  new Uri("CustomSkin.xaml", UriKind.RelativeOrAbsolute));
Application.Current.Resources = resources;
```

The "light and fluffy" skin has its own set of fairly radical changes. The complete source for this skin is shown in Listing 10.10.

LISTING 10.10   The "Light and Fluffy" Skin

```xml
<ResourceDictionary
  xmlns="http://schemas.microsoft.com/winfx/2006/xaml/presentation"
  xmlns:x="http://schemas.microsoft.com/winfx/2006/xaml">
  <!-- Make the background a simple gradient -->
  <Style x:Key="DialogStyle" TargetType="{x:Type StackPanel}">
    <Setter Property="Margin" Value="0"/>
    <Setter Property="Background">
    <Setter.Value>
      <LinearGradientBrush StartPoint="0,0" EndPoint="1,1">
        <GradientStop Offset="0" Color="LightBlue"/>
        <GradientStop Offset="1" Color="White"/>
      </LinearGradientBrush>
    </Setter.Value>
    </Setter>
  </Style>
```

LISTING 10.10   Continued

```xml
<!-- Rotate and move the main text -->
<Style x:Key="HeadingStyle" TargetType="{x:Type Label}">
  <Setter Property="Foreground" Value="White"/>
  <Setter Property="FontSize" Value="30"/>
  <Setter Property="FontFamily" Value="Segoe Print"/>
  <Setter Property="RenderTransform">
  <Setter.Value>
    <TransformGroup>
      <RotateTransform Angle="-35"/>
      <TranslateTransform X="-19" Y="55"/>
    </TransformGroup>
  </Setter.Value>
  </Setter>
  <Setter Property="BitmapEffect">
  <Setter.Value>
    <DropShadowBitmapEffect ShadowDepth="2" Softness=".2"/>
  </Setter.Value>
  </Setter>
</Style>

<!-- Remove the Cancel button -->
<Style x:Key="CancelButtonStyle" TargetType="{x:Type Button}">
  <Setter Property="Visibility" Value="Collapsed"/>
</Style>

<!-- Wrap the ProgressBar in an Expander -->
<Style TargetType="{x:Type ProgressBar}">
  <Setter Property="Height" Value="100"/>
  <Setter Property="Template">
  <Setter.Value>
    <ControlTemplate TargetType="{x:Type ProgressBar}">
      <Expander Header="More Details" ExpandDirection="Left">
        <ProgressBar Style="{x:Null}"
          Height="30" Value="{TemplateBinding Value}"
          Minimum="{TemplateBinding Minimum}"
          Maximum="{TemplateBinding Maximum}"
          IsEnabled="{TemplateBinding IsEnabled}"
          IsIndeterminate="{TemplateBinding IsIndeterminate}"/>
      </Expander>
    </ControlTemplate>
  </Setter.Value>
  </Setter>
</Style>
</ResourceDictionary>
```

10

The customized `DialogStyle` and `HeadingStyle` are pretty straightforward (although the latter uses a slick bitmap effect introduced in the next chapter). But this skin, to keep a minimalistic user interface, uses `CancelButtonStyle` to *completely hide* the Cancel `Button`! In this case, doing so is appropriate (assuming that closing the `Window` behaves the same way). In other cases, users might not appreciate a skin that hides pieces of the user interface!

The typed `Style` for `ProgressBar` also performs an interesting trick for the purpose of simplifying the user interface. It defines a custom template to wrap the `ProgressBar` inside an `Expander` (that's collapsed by default)! The wrapped `ProgressBar` has several `TemplateBindings` to keep its display in sync with the templated parent. Notice that this inner `ProgressBar` is given a null `Style`. This is necessary to avoid a nasty recursion problem. Without the explicit `Style`, the inner `ProgressBar` gets the default typed `Style` that it's a part of, making it an `Expander` inside an `Expander` inside an `Expander`, and so on.

FAQ

 How can I prevent a user-contributed skin from acting maliciously?

There is no built-in mechanism to do this. You could try to write your own logic to examine a user-supplied `ResourceDictionary` and remove things that you consider to be malicious, but this is basically a futile task. For example, if you want to prevent a skin from hiding elements, you could pretty easily remove `Setters` that operate on `Visibility`. But what about a skin that makes text the same color as the background? Or a skin that gives controls an empty-looking template? There's more than one way to skin a cat! (Pun intended.)

And making your UI unusable is the least of your concerns. Imagine a skin that finds a way to send private information displayed by the application back to a web server. There's an inherent risk whenever arbitrary code (or XAML!) is executed inside a full-trust application.

If you're concerned about this, you're probably better off defining your own skin data format that is much more limited in expressiveness. But if you provide an easy way for a user to remove a "malicious skin," then perhaps you don't need to worry about this in the first place.

Themes

Whereas *skins* are application specific, *themes* generally refer to visual characteristics of the operating system that are reflected in user interface elements of all programs. For example, changing your Windows theme to "Windows Classic" gives buttons and scroll-bars a flat and rectangular look. On Windows XP, switching the default theme's color scheme between Blue, Olive Green, and Silver affects the color and sheen of standard controls. To maintain consistency with the user's chosen Windows theme, the built-in WPF controls have a separate control template for each theme, as you saw with `Button` in Chapter 4.

Consistency with the OS theme is important for the default control templates. But when somebody creates custom control templates, they are typically doing so to *avoid* consistency with the rest of the operating system! Nevertheless, it can still be a nice touch to incorporate elements of the user's OS theme to prevent the customized controls from sticking out like a sore thumb.

This section examines how easy it is to create Styles and templates (and, therefore, skins) that adapt to the current theme. There are basically two ways to do this. The first is simple but not as powerful, and the second is a bit more work but completely flexible.

Using System Colors, Fonts, and Parameters

The fields exposed by the SystemColors, SystemFonts, and SystemParameters classes automaticallyget updated when the Windows theme changes. Therefore, incorporating these into your Styles and templates is an easy way to blend them in with the user's theme.

The following updated ProgressBar pie chart Style makes use of the SystemColors class to control the colors in its default fill (using the technique explained in Chapter 8):

```
<Style TargetType="{x:Type ProgressBar}">
<Style.Resources>
  <LinearGradientBrush x:Key="foregroundBrush" StartPoint="0,0" EndPoint="1,1">
    <GradientStop Offset="0"
      Color="{DynamicResource {x:Static SystemColors.InactiveCaptionColorKey}}"/>
    <GradientStop Offset="0.5"
      Color="{DynamicResource {x:Static SystemColors.InactiveCaptionColorKey}}"/>
    <GradientStop Offset="1"
      Color="{DynamicResource {x:Static SystemColors.ActiveCaptionColorKey}}"/>
  </LinearGradientBrush>
</Style.Resources>
<Setter Property="Foreground" Value="{StaticResource foregroundBrush}"/>
<Setter Property="Background"
  Value="{DynamicResource {x:Static SystemColors.ControlBrushKey}}"/>
...
</Style>
```

Figure 10.14 shows how the appearance of this Style subtly changes when switching Windows themes.

Windows Vista (Aero)   Windows Classic

FIGURE 10.14   The same control with the same Style, viewed under two different themes.

10

Per-Theme Styles and Templates

Many of the built-in WPF controls differ from theme to theme in richer ways than just colors, fonts, and simple measurements. For example, they're generally shinier in the Windows Vista theme and dull in Windows Classic. This is accomplished by having a separate control template for each theme.

The ability to define your own styles and templates that differ in interesting ways based on the current theme can be quite useful. For example, it could be argued that the Windows Classic version of ProgressBar in Figure 10.14 is *too* pretty! Someone who uses the Windows Classic theme probably isn't going to appreciate fancy gradients and other effects!

If you want to create your own per-theme styles and templates, you could programmatically load and swap them whenever the theme changes (using the techniques discussed in the "Skins" section). WPF doesn't expose a theme-changing event, however, so this would involve intercepting the Win32 WM_THEMECHANGE message (the same way WM_DWMCOMPOSITIONCHANGED was intercepted in Chapter 7, "Structuring and Deploying an Application"). Fortunately, WPF does expose a theming mechanism built on top of the low-level Win32 APIs, enabling you to provide per-theme resources with almost no procedural code.

The first step is to organize your theme-specific resources into distinct resource dictionary XAML files (one per theme) that get compiled into your assembly. You can then designate each resource dictionary as a *theme dictionary* by placing it in a themes subfolder (which must be in the root of your project!) and naming it *ThemeName*.*ThemeColor*.xaml (case insensitive). A theme dictionary can be loaded and applied automatically by WPF when your application launches and whenever the theme changes. Styles inside a theme dictionary are called *theme styles*.

The following are themes that Microsoft has created, and the corresponding valid theme dictionary URIs:

- The Windows Vista theme: themes\Aero.NormalColor.xaml
- The default Windows XP theme: themes\Luna.NormalColor.xaml
- The olive green Windows XP theme: themes\Luna.Homestead.xaml
- The silver Windows XP theme: themes\Luna.Metallic.xaml
- The Windows XP Media Center Edition 2005 and Windows XP Tablet PC Edition 2005 theme: themes\Royale.NormalColor.xaml
- The Windows Classic theme: themes\Classic.xaml
- The Zune Windows XP theme: themes\Zune.NormalColor.xaml

Note that Windows Classic is a bit special, as it doesn't have the *ThemeColor* part of the URI.

Furthermore, you can specify a fallback
resource dictionary that gets used if you
don't have a dictionary corresponding
to the current theme and color. This fallback dictionary, often called the *generic
dictionary*, must be named
themes\Generic.xaml.

With one or more theme dictionaries and/or a generic dictionary in place, you must now
opt in to the automatic theming mechanism with an assembly level `ThemeInfoAttribute`.
This attribute's constructor takes two parameters of type `ResourceDictionaryLocation`.
The first one specifies where WPF should find the theme dictionaries, and the second one
specifies where WPF should find the generic dictionary. Each one can independently be
set to the following values:

- **None** (default)—Don't look for a resource dictionary.

- **SourceAssembly**—Look for them inside the current assembly.

- **ExternalAssembly**—Look for them inside a different assembly, which must be
  named *AssemblyName.ThemeName*.dll (where *AssemblyName* matches the current
  assembly's name). WPF uses this scheme for its built-in theme dictionaries, found
  inside `PresentationFramework.Aero.dll`, `PresentationFramework.Luna.dll`, and so
  on. This is a nice way to avoid having extra copies of resources loaded in memory at
  all times.

Therefore, a typical usage of `ThemeInfoAttribute` looks like the following:

```
// Look for the theme dictionaries and the generic dictionary inside this assembly
[assembly:ThemeInfo(ResourceDictionaryLocation.SourceAssembly,
                    ResourceDictionaryLocation.SourceAssembly)]
```

There's one final catch to the theming support. It's designed to provide the *default styles*
for elements. As `ThemeInfoAttribute` indicates, theme styles must exist in the same
assembly defining the target element or a specific companion assembly. Unlike
application-level (or lower) resource dictionaries, you can't define a typed style for exter-
nally-defined elements such as `Button` or `ProgressBar` in a theme dictionary or generic
dictionary in your own application and have it override the default style—unless you use
an additional mechanism involving `ThemeDictionaryExtension`.

`ThemeDictionaryExtension` is a markup extension that enables you to override the theme
styles for any elements. It can reference any assembly containing a set of theme dictionaries, even the current application. You can apply `ThemeDictionaryExtension` as the `Source`
for a `ResourceDictionary` to affect everything under its scope. For example:

```
<Application …>
<Application.Resources>
  <ResourceDictionary>
  <ResourceDictionary.MergedDictionaries>
```

```
    <ResourceDictionary …/>
    <ResourceDictionary Source="{ThemeDictionary MyApplication}"/>
  </ResourceDictionary.MergedDictionaries>
  </ResourceDictionary>
</Application.Resources>
</Application>
```

Imagine that you want to make the pie chart style for ProgressBar vary based on the Windows theme. If the MyApplication assembly contains per-theme styles with a TargetType of {x:Type ProgressBar}, all ProgressBars in this application get the customized per-theme style by default thanks to the use of ThemeDictionaryExtension.

Another approach for attaching per-theme styles to existing elements is to define a custom subclass. Creating custom controls is the subject of Chapter 16, but creating a custom control (or other element) solely for the purpose of giving it a theme style is pretty simple. For the per-theme pie chart style example, you could create a custom control called ProgressPie as follows:

```
public class ProgressPie : ProgressBar
{
  static ProgressPie()
  {
    DefaultStyleKeyProperty.OverrideMetadata(
      typeof(ProgressPie),
      new FrameworkPropertyMetadata(typeof(ProgressPie)));
  }
}
```

Because ProgressPie derives from ProgressBar, it automatically has all the necessary functionality. But having a unique type gives us the ability to support a new theme style distinct from ProgressBar's theme style. The only magic incantation is the single line of code in ProgressPie's static constructor that sets the DefaultStyleKey dependency property. DefaultStyleKey is a protected dependency property on FrameworkElement and FrameworkContentElement that determines the key to use for its default style. (The terms *default style* and *theme style* are often used interchangeably.)

WPF's built-in elements set this property to their own type, so their corresponding theme dictionaries use typed styles. If the preceding code didn't set a DefaultStyleKey, ProgressPie would inherit the value from ProgressBar, which is typeof(ProgressBar). Therefore, ProgressPie makes typeof(ProgressPie) its DefaultStyleKey.

This book's source code contains a Visual Studio project that contains the preceding definition of ProgressPie, the preceding usage of ThemeInfoAttribute, and a handful of theme dictionaries that get compiled into the application. Each theme dictionary is a standalone XAML file with the following structure:

```
<ResourceDictionary
  xmlns="http://schemas.microsoft.com/winfx/2006/xaml/presentation"
  xmlns:x="http://schemas.microsoft.com/winfx/2006/xaml"
  xmlns:local="clr-namespace:ThemedProgressPie">
  <Style TargetType="{x:Type local:ProgressPie}">
    ...
  </Style>
</ResourceDictionary>
```

Figure 10.15 displays a theme-styled ProgressPie under two different themes. Although you can dig into how each Style was created, the point is that theme styles give you the flexibility to completely change an element's visuals when the theme changes. Unlike the visuals in Figure 10.14, I think Figure 10.15 succeeds in making the Windows Vista ProgressPie extra sexy and the

Windows Vista (Aero)   Windows Classic

FIGURE 10.15   The same control with its theme style, viewed under two different themes.

Windows Classic ProgressPie extra boring. All kidding aside, making theme styles *too* different from each other will probably confuse your users more than help them.

DIGGING DEEPER

Understanding Windows Vistas Themes and Color Schemes

Windows Vista has a long list of color schemes, found on the advanced Appearance Settings dialog. Whether a user chooses Windows Aero or Windows Vista Basic, WPF uses your Aero.NormalColor theme dictionary. (This is still true when a user's window color is no longer "normal" because of color customizations made via Control Panel.) And whether a user chooses Windows Standard, Windows Classic, or one of the eyeball-melting High Contrast schemes, WPF uses your Classic theme dictionary. If you want to distinguish between these color schemes that map to the same theme, your best bet is to incorporate SystemColors into your styles and templates.

Conclusion

The combination of Styles, templates, skins, and themes is very powerful and often confusing to someone learning about WPF. Adding to the confusion is the fact that Styles can (and often do) contain templates, elements in templates all have Styles (whether marked explicitly or inherited implicitly), and theme styles are managed separately from normal Styles (so an element like Button's Style property is null by default even though it clearly has a theme style applied).

These mechanisms are so powerful, in fact, that often you can restyle an existing control as an alternative to writing your own custom control. This is great news, as restyling an existing control is significantly easier than writing a custom control, and perhaps can be done entirely by a graphic designer rather than a programmer. If you do find that you need to write a custom control (the topic of Chapter 16), the lessons learned here about creating robust templates and adapting to themes are still very applicable.

PART IV

Going Beyond Today's Applications with Rich Media

CHAPTER 11

2D Graphics

Applications and components can have many reasons for drawing rectangles, ellipses, lines, or other shapes and paths. Most custom control templates tend to require some drawing to get their custom look, as was done in the previous chapter with Button and ProgressBar templates. But applications might simply want to provide an experience with custom rendering, regardless of whether it's done in the context of controls. This could be in the form of a product logo or simple curves to separate areas of a Window. On the Web, these types of experiences are typically created by embedding images, but with the drawing capabilities of WPF, you can do all of this with vector drawings that scale perfectly to any size.

The ability to create and use vector-based 2D graphics is not unique to WPF; even GDI enabled the drawing of paths and shapes. The main difference with drawing in WPF versus GDI or any previous Windows technology is that WPF is a completely *retained-mode* graphics system rather than an *immediate-mode* graphics system.

In an immediate-mode system (GDI, GDI+, DirectX, and so on), you can draw "directly" onto the screen, but you must maintain the state of all visuals. In other words, it's your responsibility to draw the correct pixels when a region of the screen is invalidated. This invalidation can be caused by user actions, such as resizing the window, or by application-specific actions that require updated visuals.

In a retained mode system, you can describe higher-level concepts such as "place a 10x10 blue square at (0,0)," and the system remembers and maintains the state for you. So, what you're really saying is, "place a 10x10 blue square at (0,0) *and keep it there*." You don't need to worry about invalidation and repainting, so this can save a significant amount of work. It's also the key to WPF's seamless support for overlapping objects, transparency, video, resolution independence, effective UI remoting, and so on.

As with many things in WPF, there are multiple ways to create and use two-dimensional graphics. The heart of this chapter focuses on three important data types: Drawings, Visuals, and Shapes. Their relationship to each other is complex. For the most part, Drawings are simple descriptions of paths and shapes with associated fill and outline Brushes. Visuals are one way to draw Drawings onto the screen, but Visuals also unlock a lower-level and lighter-weight approach for drawing that enable you to ditch Drawing objects altogether. Finally, Shapes are prebuilt Visuals that are the easiest (but most heavyweight) approach for drawing custom artwork onto the screen. As we examine Drawings, Visuals, and Shapes, we'll look at a simple piece of clip art and see what it means to create and use it in all three contexts.

The end of the chapter covers Brushes and special effects known as *bitmap effects*. Brushes are a vital part of all the topics in this chapter, and have been used throughout the book for mundane tasks such as setting a control's Foreground and Background. WPF has many different feature-rich Brushes, which is why they deserve a dedicated section. Finally, the bitmap effects such as drop shadows or blurring are not commonly used features (nor should they be in the current version of WPF because of performance issues), but they can add really slick touches to your user interface that would be difficult to create without them.

Drawings

The abstract Drawing class represents a two-dimensional drawing. Drawing—specifically its GeometryDrawing subclass—was designed to be WPF's version of clip art. It's sufficient for representing any 2D illustration, and, as with all classes deriving from Animatable, it even supports animation, data binding, resource references, and more!

WPF includes five concrete subclasses of Drawing:

▶ **GeometryDrawing**, the one most relevant for this chapter, combines a Geometry with a Brush that fills it and a Pen that outlines it.

▶ **ImageDrawing** combines an ImageSource with a Rect that defines its bounds.

▶ **VideoDrawing** combines a MediaPlayer (discussed in Chapter 14, "Audio, Video, Speech, and Documents") with a bounding Rect.

▶ **GlyphRunDrawing** combines a GlyphRun, a low-level text class, with a Brush for its foreground.

▶ **DrawingGroup** contains a collection of Drawings and has a handful of properties for altering them in bulk (Opacity, Transform, and so on). DrawingGroup is itself a Drawing so it can be plugged in wherever a Drawing can be used. (This is just like the relationship between TransformGroup and Transform.)

Here's an example of a `GeometryDrawing` containing a `Geometry` describing an ellipse (`EllipseGeometry`), an orange `Brush`, and a black `Pen`:

```
<GeometryDrawing Brush="Orange">                                    ───── Brush
<GeometryDrawing.Pen>
  <Pen Brush="Black" Thickness="10"/>                               ───── Pen
</GeometryDrawing.Pen>
<GeometryDrawing.Geometry>
  <EllipseGeometry RadiusX="100" RadiusY="50"/>                     ───── Geometry
</GeometryDrawing.Geometry>
</GeometryDrawing>
```

Drawings are not `UIElements`; they don't have any rendering behavior on their own. Therefore, if you try to place the preceding `GeometryDrawing` inside a `Window` or other `ContentControl`, you'll get a simple `TextBlock` containing the string "System.Windows.Media.GeometryDrawing" (the fallback `ToString` rendering).

To get `Drawings` rendered appropriately, you can place them inside one of three different host objects:

▶ **DrawingImage**—Derives from `ImageSource`, so it can be used inside an `Image` rather than the typical `BitmapImage`

▶ **DrawingBrush**—Derives from `Brush`, so it can be applied in many places, such as the Foreground, Background, or BorderBrush on a `Control`

▶ **DrawingVisual**—Derives from `Visual`, and is covered in the "Visuals" section

Therefore, you can use `DrawingImage` with the preceding `GeometryDrawing` as follows to get it drawn on the screen:

```
<Image>
<Image.Source>
  <DrawingImage>
  <DrawingImage.Drawing>
    <GeometryDrawing Brush="Orange">
    <GeometryDrawing.Pen>
      <Pen Brush="Black" Thickness="10"/>
    </GeometryDrawing.Pen>
    <GeometryDrawing.Geometry>
      <EllipseGeometry RadiusX="100" RadiusY="50"/>
    </GeometryDrawing.Geometry>
    </GeometryDrawing>
  </DrawingImage.Drawing>
  </DrawingImage>
</Image.Source>
</Image>
```

Figure 11.1 shows the rendered result of this `Image` that ultimately contains the `GeometryDrawing`.

FIGURE 11.1   A simple `EllipseGeometry` inside a `GeometryDrawing`, inside a `DrawingImage`, inside an `Image`.

DIGGING DEEPER

`DrawingImage` Versus `ImageDrawing`

It can be hard to keep the difference between `DrawingImage` and the previously mentioned `ImageDrawing` straight. They are both interesting, however, because they enable mixing and matching of vector-based content with bitmap-based content.

`DrawingImage` is an `ImageSource`, enabling a typically vector-based `Drawing` to be its content rather than something bitmap-based. Conversely, `ImageDrawing` is a `Drawing`, enabling a typically bitmap-based `ImageSource` to be its content rather than something vector based.

WARNING

`DrawingImage` can't be used everywhere `ImageSource` is expected!

Because `DrawingImage` derives from `ImageSource`, you might try to use it wherever you might have used a `BitmapImage` (or other `BitmapSource`-derived objects). This works for `Image.Source`, but does *not* work for `Window.Icon`. This property enforces that it can only be set to a bitmap. To work around this limitation, you could dynamically render the vector-based content onto a bitmap using a `RenderTargetBitmap`.

Previous chapters have used `Brushes` enough times that you should be fairly comfortable with the concept. `Brushes` have a lot more functionality than discussed so far, however, and are not specific to `Drawings`. Therefore, the "Brushes" section near the end of this chapter examines these features. For now, we'll look at the two other components of a `GeometryDrawing`: the `Geometry` and the `Pen`.

Geometries

A `Geometry` is the simplest possible abstract representation of a shape or path. It exposes methods that enable you to ask it geometric questions, like "What is your area?" or "Do you intersect this point?" `Geometry` has a number of subclasses, which can be grouped into basic geometries and aggregate geometries.

> ## DIGGING DEEPER
>
> ### Uses for Geometries
>
> Although geometries are often used inside of Drawings, they show up in other places in WPF's APIs. For example, System.Windows.Ink.Stroke exposes ink strokes as geometries (via its GetGeometry method), and DrawingGroup and Visual-derived classes expose a Clip property that enables you to clip the visuals according to an arbitrary Geometry instance.

Basic Geometries

The four basic geometries are as follows:

▶ **RectangleGeometry**—Has a Rect property for defining its dimensions and even RadiusX and RadiusY properties for defining rounded corners

▶ **EllipseGeometry**—Has RadiusX and RadiusY properties, plus a Center property

▶ **LineGeometry**—Has StartPoint and EndPoint properties to define a line segment

▶ **PathGeometry**—Contains a collection of PathFigure objects in its Figures content property; a general-purpose Geometry

The first three geometries are really just special cases of PathGeometry provided for convenience. You can express any rectangle, ellipse, or line segment in terms of a PathGeometry. So, let's dig a little more into the components of this powerful PathGeometry class.

PathFigures and PathSegments

Each PathFigure in a PathGeometry contains one or more connected PathSegments in its Segments content property. A PathSegment is simply a straight or curvy line segment, represented by one of seven derived classes:

▶ **LineSegment**—A class for representing a line segment (of course!)

▶ **PolyLineSegment**—A shortcut for representing a connected sequence of LineSegments

▶ **ArcSegment**—A class for representing a segment that curves along the circumference of an imaginary ellipse

▶ **BezierSegment**—A class for representing a cubic Bézier curve

▶ **PolyBezierSegment**—A shortcut for representing a connected sequence of BezierSegments

▶ **QuadraticBezierSegment**—A class for representing a quadratic Bézier curve

▶ **PolyQuadraticBezierSegment**—A shortcut for representing a connected sequence of QuadraticBezierSegments

---

DIGGING DEEPER

Bézier Curves

Bézier curves (named after engineer Pierre Bézier) are commonly used in computer graphics for representing smooth curves. Bézier curves are even used by fonts to mathematically describe curves in their glyphs!

The basic idea is that in addition to two endpoints, a Bézier curve has one or more *control points* that give the line segment its curve. These control points are not visible (and not necessarily on the curve itself) but rather are used as input to a formula that dictates where each point on the curve exists. Intuitively, each control point acts like a center of gravity, so the line segment appears to be "pulled" toward these points.

Despite the scarier-sounding name, QuadraticBezierSegment is actually simpler than a BezierSegment and computationally cheaper. A quadratic Bézier curve only has one control point, whereas a cubic Bézier curve has two. Therefore, a quadratic Bézier curve can only form a U-like shape (or a straight line), but a cubic Bézier curve can also take the form of an S-like shape.

The following GeometryDrawing contains a PathGeometry with two simple LineSegments that create the "L" shape in Figure 11.2:

```
<GeometryDrawing>
<GeometryDrawing.Pen>
  <Pen Brush="Black" Thickness="10"/>
</GeometryDrawing.Pen>
<GeometryDrawing.Geometry>
  <PathGeometry>
    <PathFigure>
      <LineSegment Point="0,100"/>
      <LineSegment Point="100,100"/>
    </PathFigure>
  </PathGeometry>
</GeometryDrawing.Geometry>
</GeometryDrawing>
```

Of course, to produce the visuals in Figure 11.2, the GeometryDrawing must be hosted in something like a DrawingImage, as done previously.

FIGURE 11.2   A GeometryDrawing that ultimately contains a pair of LineSegments.

Notice that the definition for each LineSegment only includes a single Point. That's because it implicitly connects the previous point to the current one. The first LineSegment connects the default starting point of (0,0) to (0,100), then the second LineSegment connects (0,100) to (100,100). (The other six PathSegments act the same way as well.) If you want to provide a custom starting point, you can simply set PathFigure's StartPoint property to a Point other than (0,0).

You might expect that applying a Brush to this GeometryDrawing is meaningless, but Figure 11.3 shows that it actually fills it as a polygon, pretending that a line segment exists to connect the last point back to the starting point. Figure 11.3 was created by adding the following Brush to the preceding XAML:

FIGURE 11.3   The GeometryDrawing from Figure 11.2 filled with an orange Brush.

```xaml
<GeometryDrawing Brush="Orange">
  ...
</GeometryDrawing>
```

To turn the imaginary line segment into a real one, you could add a third LineSegment to the PathFigure explicitly, or you could simply set PathFigure's IsClosed property to true. The result of doing either is shown in Figure 11.4.

FIGURE 11.4   The GeometryDrawing from Figure 11.3, but with IsClosed="True".

Because all PathSegments within a PathFigure must be connected, you can place multiple PathFigures in a PathGeometry if you want disjoint shapes or paths in the same Geometry. You could also overlap PathFigures to create results that would be complicated to replicate in a single PathFigure. For example, the following XAML overlaps the triangle from Figure 11.4 with a triangle that is given a different StartPoint but is otherwise identical:

```xaml
<GeometryDrawing Brush="Orange">
<GeometryDrawing.Pen>
  <Pen Brush="Black" Thickness="10"/>
</GeometryDrawing.Pen>
<GeometryDrawing.Geometry>
  <PathGeometry>
    <!-- Triangle #1 -->
    <PathFigure IsClosed="True">
      <LineSegment Point="0,100"/>
      <LineSegment Point="100,100"/>
    </PathFigure>
    <!-- Triangle #2 -->
    <PathFigure StartPoint="70,0" IsClosed="True">
      <LineSegment Point="0,100"/>
      <LineSegment Point="100,100"/>
    </PathFigure>
  </PathGeometry>
```

```
</GeometryDrawing.Geometry>
</GeometryDrawing>
```

This dual-`PathFigure` `GeometryDrawing` is displayed in Figure 11.5. If you don't want the sharp point at each corner, you can set each `LineSegment`'s `IsSmoothJoin` property (inherited by all `PathSegments`) to true. Figure 11.6 shows the result of doing this.

FIGURE 11.5   Overlapping triangles created by using two `PathFigures`.

FIGURE 11.6   Overlapping triangles with `IsSmoothJoin="True"` on all `LineSegments`.

The behavior of the orange fill might not be what you expected to see. `PathGeometry` enables you to control this fill behavior with its `FillRule` property.

FillRule

Whenever you have a `Geometry` with intersecting points, whether via multiple overlapping `PathFigures` or overlapping `PathSegments` in a single `PathFigure`, there can be multiple interpretations of which area is *inside* a shape (and can, therefore, be filled) and which area is *outside* a shape.

With `PathGeometry`'s `FillRule` property (which can be set to a `FillRule` enumeration), you have two choices on how filling is done:

▶ **EvenOdd** (default)—Fills a region only if you would cross an odd number of segments to travel from that region to the area outside the entire shape.

▶ **NonZero**—Is a more complicated algorithm that takes into consideration the direction of the segments you would have to cross to get outside the entire shape. For many shapes, it is likely to fill all enclosed areas.

The difference between `EvenOdd` and `NonZero` is illustrated in Figure 11.7 with the same overlapping triangles from Figure 11.6.

EvenOdd   NonZero

FIGURE 11.7   Overlapping triangles with different values for `PathGeometry.FillRule`.

Aggregate Geometries

WPF's two classes for aggregating geometries—`GeometryGroup` and `CombinedGeometry`—sound similar but behave quite differently. But like `TransformGroup`'s relationship to `Transform` and `DrawingGroup`'s relationship to `Drawing`, both aggregate geometry classes derive from `Geometry`, so they can be used anywhere that a simpler `Geometry` can be used.

DIGGING DEEPER

StreamGeometry

For complex geometries that don't need to be modified after they are created, you should consider using StreamGeometry rather than PathGeometry as a performance optimization. StreamGeometry works like PathGeometry, except that it can only be filled via procedural code. Its odd name refers to an implementation detail: To use less memory (and less of the CPU), its PathFigures and PathSegments are stored as a compact byte stream rather than a graph of .NET objects.

The following code constructs a StreamGeometry with overlapping triangles that is identical to the PathGeometry used to create Figure 11.6:

```
StreamGeometry g = new StreamGeometry();
using (StreamGeometryContext context = g.Open())
{
  // Triangle #1
  context.BeginFigure(new Point(0, 0), true /*isFilled*/, true /*isClosed*/);
  context.LineTo(new Point(0, 100), true /*isStroked*/, true /*isSmoothJoin*/);
  context.LineTo(new Point(100, 100), true /*isStroked*/, true /*isSmoothJoin*/);

  // Triangle #2
  context.BeginFigure(new Point(70, 0), true /*isFilled*/, true /*isClosed*/);
  context.LineTo(new Point(0, 100), true /*isStroked*/, true /*isSmoothJoin*/);
  context.LineTo(new Point(100, 100), true /*isStroked*/, true /*isSmoothJoin*/);
}
// Apply this Geometry to an existing GeometryDrawing:
geometryDrawing.Geometry = g;
```

Rather than creating LineSegments, ArcSegments, BezierSegments, and so on, you call methods such as LineTo, ArcTo, and BezierTo.

GeometryGroup

GeometryGroup composes one or more Geometry instances together. For example, the previously shown XAML for creating the overlapping triangles in Figure 11.5 could be rewritten to use two geometries (each with a single PathFigure) rather than one:

```
<GeometryDrawing Brush="Orange">
<GeometryDrawing.Pen>
  <Pen Brush="Black" Thickness="10"/>
</GeometryDrawing.Pen>
<GeometryDrawing.Geometry>
  <GeometryGroup>
    <!-- Triangle #1 -->
    <PathGeometry>
      <PathFigure IsClosed="True">
```

```
        <LineSegment Point="0,100"/>
        <LineSegment Point="100,100"/>
      </PathFigure>
    </PathGeometry>
    <!-- Triangle #2 -->
    <PathGeometry>
      <PathFigure StartPoint="70,0" IsClosed="True">
        <LineSegment Point="0,100"/>
        <LineSegment Point="100,100"/>
      </PathFigure>
    </PathGeometry>
  </GeometryGroup>
</GeometryDrawing.Geometry>
</GeometryDrawing>
```

GeometryGroup, like PathGeometry, has a FillRule property set to EvenOdd by default. It takes precedence over any FillRule settings of its children.

This, of course, begs the question, "Why would I create a GeometryGroup when I can just as easily create a single PathGeometry with multiple PathFigures?" One minor advantage is that GeometryGroup enables you to aggregate other geometries such as RectangleGeometry and EllipseGeometry, which can be easier to use. But the major advantage of using GroupGeometry is that you can set various Geometry properties independently on each child.

For example, the following GeometryGroup composes two identical triangles, but sets the Transform on one of them to rotate it 25°:

```
<GeometryDrawing Brush="Orange">
<GeometryDrawing.Pen>
  <Pen Brush="Black" Thickness="10"/>
</GeometryDrawing.Pen>
<GeometryDrawing.Geometry>
  <GeometryGroup>
    <!-- Triangle #1 -->
    <PathGeometry>
      <PathFigure IsClosed="True">
        <LineSegment Point="0,100" IsSmoothJoin="True"/>
        <LineSegment Point="100,100" IsSmoothJoin="True"/>
      </PathFigure>
    </PathGeometry>
    <!-- Triangle #2 -->
    <PathGeometry>
    <PathGeometry.Transform>
      <RotateTransform Angle="25"/>
    </PathGeometry.Transform>
      <PathFigure IsClosed="True">
```

```
      <LineSegment Point="0,100" IsSmoothJoin="True"/>
      <LineSegment Point="100,100" IsSmoothJoin="True"/>
    </PathFigure>
  </PathGeometry>
 </GeometryGroup>
</GeometryDrawing.Geometry>
</GeometryDrawing>
```

The result of this is shown in Figure 11.8. Creating such a Geometry with a single PathGeometry and a single PathFigure would be difficult. Creating it with a single PathGeometry containing two PathFigures would be easier, but would still require manually doing the math to perform the rotation. With GeometryGroup, however, creating it is very straightforward.

FIGURE 11.8   A GeometryGroup with two identical triangles, except that one is rotated.

> **TIP**
>
> Because Brush and Pen are specified at the Drawing level rather than at the Geometry level, GeometryGroup doesn't enable you to combine shapes with different fills or outlines. To achieve this, you can use a DrawingGroup to combine multiple drawings (which might or might not have multiple geometries).

> **TIP**
>
> Unlike UIElements, which can only have a single parent, instances of Geometry, PathFigure, and related classes can be shared. Sharing these objects when possible can result in a major performance improvement, especially for complex geometries.
>
> For the GeometryGroup used for Figure 11.8, there's no need to duplicate the identical PathFigure instances. Instead, with the PathFigure defined as a resource with the key figure, you could rewrite the GeometryGroup as follows:
>
> ```
> <GeometryGroup>
>   <!-- Triangle #1 -->
>   <PathGeometry>
>     <StaticResource ResourceKey="figure"/>
>   </PathGeometry>
>   <!-- Triangle #2 -->
>   <PathGeometry>
>   <PathGeometry.Transform>
>     <RotateTransform Angle="25"/>
>   </PathGeometry.Transform>
>     <StaticResource ResourceKey="figure"/>
>   </PathGeometry>
> ```

CombinedGeometry

CombinedGeometry, unlike GeometryGroup, is not a general-purpose aggregator. Instead, it merges two (and only two) geometries using one of the approaches designated by the GeometryCombineMode enumeration:

- ▶ **Union** (default)—Gives the combined geometry the entire area of both geometries

- ▶ **Intersect**—Only gives the combined geometry the area shared by both geometries

- ▶ **Xor**—Only gives the combined geometry the area that is *not* shared by both geometries

- ▶ **Exclude**—Only gives the combined geometry the area that is unique to the first geometry

CombinedGeometry defines Geometry1 and Geometry2 properties to hold the two inputs and a GeometryCombineMode property accepting one of the preceding values. Figure 11.9 demonstrates the result of using each GeometryCombineMode value with the overlapping triangles from Figure 11.8 as follows:

```
<GeometryDrawing Brush="Orange">
<GeometryDrawing.Pen>
  <Pen Brush="Black" Thickness="10"/>
</GeometryDrawing.Pen>
<GeometryDrawing.Geometry>
  <CombinedGeometry GeometryCombineMode="XXX">
  <CombinedGeometry.Geometry1>
    <!-- Triangle #1 -->
    <PathGeometry>

      …
    </PathGeometry>
  </CombinedGeometry.Geometry1>
  <CombinedGeometry.Geometry2>
    <!-- Triangle #2 -->
    <PathGeometry>

      …
    </PathGeometry>
  </CombinedGeometry.Geometry2>
  </CombinedGeometry>
</GeometryDrawing.Geometry>
</GeometryDrawing>
```

Representing Geometries as Strings

Representing each segment in a Geometry with a separate element is fine for simple shapes and paths, but for complicated artwork it can get very verbose. Although most people use a design tool to emit XAML-based geometries rather than crafting them by hand, it makes sense to keep the resultant file size as small as reasonably possible.

Union   Intersect   Xor   Exclude

FIGURE 11.9   CombinedGeometry with each of the GeometryCombineMode settings, with a surrounding square to provide a frame of reference.

Therefore, WPF has a GeometryConverter type converter that supports a flexible syntax for representing just about any PathGeometry as a string. For programmatic scenarios, Geometry even exposes a static Parse method that accepts the same syntax and returns a Geometry instance.

For example, the PathGeometry representing the simple triangle displayed back in Figure 11.4:

```
<GeometryDrawing>
<GeometryDrawing.Pen>
  <Pen Brush="Black" Thickness="10"/>
</GeometryDrawing.Pen>
<GeometryDrawing.Geometry>
  <PathGeometry>
    <PathFigure IsClosed="True">
      <LineSegment Point="0,100"/>
      <LineSegment Point="100,100"/>
    </PathFigure>
  </PathGeometry>
</GeometryDrawing.Geometry>
</GeometryDrawing>
```

can be represented with the following compact syntax:

```
<GeometryDrawing Geometry="M 0,0 L 0,100 L 100,100 Z">
<GeometryDrawing.Pen>
  <Pen Brush="Black" Thickness="10"/>
</GeometryDrawing.Pen>
</GeometryDrawing>
```

Representing the overlapping triangles from Figure 11.5 requires a slightly longer string:

```
<GeometryDrawing Geometry="M 0,0 L 0,100 L 100,100 Z M 70,0 L 0,100 L 100,100 Z">
<GeometryDrawing.Pen>
  <Pen Brush="Black" Thickness="10"/>
</GeometryDrawing.Pen>
</GeometryDrawing>
```

These strings contain a series of commands that control properties of the `PathGeometry` and its `PathFigures`, plus commands that fill one or more `PathFigures` with `PathSegments`. The syntax is pretty simple but very powerful. Table 11.1 describes all of the available commands.

TABLE 11.1   Geometry String Commands

Command	Meaning
`PathGeometry` and `PathFigure` Properties	
F *n*	Set `FillRule`, where 0 means `EvenOdd` and 1 means `NonZero`. If you use this, it must be at the beginning of the string.
M *x,y*	Start a new `PathFigure` and set `StartPoint` to (*x,y*). This must be specified before using any other commands (excluding F). The M stands for *move*.
Z	End the `PathFigure` and set `IsClosed` to `true`. You can begin another disjoint `PathFigure` after this with an M command, or use a different command to start a new `PathFigure` originating from the current point. If you don't want the `PathFigure` to be closed, you can emit the Z command entirely.
`PathSegments`	
L *x,y*	Create a `LineSegment` to (*x,y*).
A *rx,ry d f1 f2 x,y*	Create an `ArcSegment` to (*x,y*) based on an ellipse with radii *rx* and *yx*, rotated *d* degrees. The *f1* and *f2* flags can be set to 0 (`false`) or 1 (`true`) to control two of `ArcSegment`'s properties: `IsLargeArc` and `Clockwise`, respectively.
C *x1,y1 x2,y2 x,y*	Create a `BezierSegment` to (*x,y*) using control points (*x1,y1*) and (*x2,y2*). The C stands for *cubic Bézier curve*.
Q *x1,y1 x,y*	Create a `QuadraticBezierSegment` to (*x,y*) using control point (*x1,y1*).
Additional Shortcuts	
H *x*	Create a `LineSegment` to (*x,y*), where *y* is taken from the current point. The H stands for *horizontal line*.
V *y*	Create a `LineSegment` to (*x,y*), where *x* is taken from the current point. The V stands for *vertical line*.
S *x2,y2 x,y*	Create a `BezierSegment` to (*x,y*) using control points (*x1,y1*) and (*x2,y2*), where *x1* and *y1* are automatically calculated to guarantee smoothness. (This point is either the second control point of the previous segment or the current point if the previous segment is not a `BezierSegment`.) The S stands for *smooth cubic Bézier curve*.
Lowercase commands	Any command can be specified in lowercase to make its relevant parameters be interpreted as *relative* to the current point rather than absolute coordinates. This doesn't change the meaning of the F, M, and Z commands, but they can also be specified in lowercase.

DIGGING DEEPER

Spaces and Commas in Geometry Strings

The spaces between commands and parameters are optional, and all commas are optional. But you must have at least one space or comma between parameters. Therefore, the string `M 0,0 L 0,100 L 100,100 Z` is equivalent to the much more confusing `M0 0L0 100L100 100Z`.

Pens

Looking at the three components of a GeometryDrawing, geometries and Brushes are large topics but Pens are relatively simple. A Pen is basically a Brush with a Thickness. Indeed, the two Pen properties used in previous examples are Brush (of type Brush) and Thickness (of type double). But Pen defines a few more properties for controlling its appearance:

▶ **StartLineCap** and **EndLineCap**—Customize any open segment endpoints with a value from the PenLineCap enumeration: Flat (the default), Square, Round, or Triangle. For any endpoints that join two segments, you can customize their appearance with LineJoin instead.

▶ **LineJoin**—Affects corners with a value from the PenLineJoin enumeration: Miter (the default), Round, or Bevel. A separate **MiterLimit** property can be used to limit how far a Miter join extends, which can otherwise be very large for small angles. Its default value is 10.

▶ **DashStyle**—Can make the Pen's stroke a nonsolid line. It can be set to an instance of a DashStyle object. The endpoints of each dash can be customized with Pen's **DashCap** property, which works just like StartLineCap and EndLineCap except that its default value is Square instead of Flat.

FAQ

❓ What's the difference between PenLineCap's Flat and Square values?

A Flat line cap ends exactly on the endpoint, whereas a Square line cap extends beyond the endpoint. Similar to the Round line cap, you can imagine a square with the same dimensions as the Pen's Thickness centered on the endpoint. Therefore, the line ends up extending *half* the length of the Pen's Thickness.

Figure 11.10 shows each of the PenLineCap values applied to a LineSegment's StartLineCap and EndLineCap. Figure 11.11 demonstrates each of the LineJoin values on the corners of a triangle. Using a LineJoin of Round is like setting IsSmoothJoin to

Flat
Square
Round
Triangle

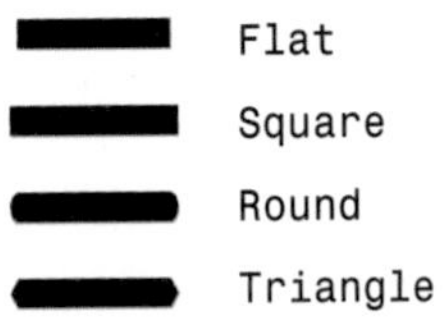

FIGURE 11.10   Each type of PenLineCap on both ends of a LineSegment.

true on all PathSegments. The latter approach enables you to customize each corner indi-vidually, whereas setting Pen's LineJoin applies to the entire Geometry.

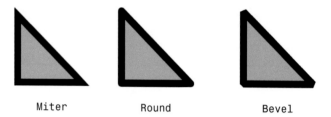

Miter   Round   Bevel

FIGURE 11.11   Each type of LineJoin applied to the familiar triangle.

The DashStyle class defines a Dashes property, which is a simple DoubleCollection that can contain a pattern of numbers that represents the widths of dashes and the spaces between them. The odd values represent the widths (relative to the Pen's Thickness) of dashes and the even values represent the relative widths of spaces. Whatever pattern you choose is then repeated indefinitely. DashStyle also has a double Offset property that controls where the pattern begins.

The confusing thing about DashStyle is that because DashCap is set to Square by default, each dash is naturally wider when given the same numeric value as a space. Furthermore, giving a dash a width of 0 is common because it simply becomes the DashCap itself. However, a DashStyles class defines a few common patterns in static DashStyle proper-ties. For example, you can use a DashDotDot pattern as follows:

```
<Pen Brush="Black" Thickness="10" DashStyle="{x:Static DashStyles.DashDotDot}"/>
```

Figure 11.12 shows each of the built-in DashStyles, along with the numeric Dashes values they use internally.

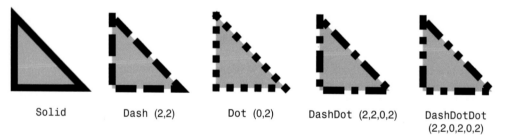

Solid   Dash (2,2)   Dot (0,2)   DashDot (2,2,0,2)   DashDotDot
                                                                  (2,2,0,2,0,2)

FIGURE 11.12   Each of the built-in DashStyles properties applied to a Pen, with the default Square DashCap and Miter LineJoin.

Clip Art Example

Now that you know everything there is to know about GeometryDrawings, you can create a simple piece of clip art. Listing 11.1 contains an Image-hosted DrawingGroup with three GeometryDrawings to render the ghost shown in Figure 11.13.

FIGURE 11.13   A ghost created with a DrawingGroup containing three GeometryDrawings.

LISTING 11.1   The Drawing-Based Implementation of a Ghost, Hosted in an Image

```
<Image>
<Image.Source>
  <DrawingImage>
  <DrawingImage.Drawing>
    <DrawingGroup>

        <!-- The body -->
        <GeometryDrawing Brush="Blue" Geometry="M 240,250
          C 200,375 200,250 175,200
          C 100,400 100,250 100,200
          C 0,350   0,250   30,130
          C 75,0    100,0   150,0
          C 200,0   250,0   250,150 Z"/>

        <!-- The eyes -->
        <GeometryDrawing Brush="Black">
        <GeometryDrawing.Pen>
          <Pen Brush="White" Thickness="10"/>
        </GeometryDrawing.Pen>
        <GeometryDrawing.Geometry>
          <GeometryGroup>
            <!-- Left eye -->
            <EllipseGeometry RadiusX="15" RadiusY="15" Center="95,95"/>
            <!-- Right eye -->
            <EllipseGeometry RadiusX="15" RadiusY="15" Center="170,105"/>
          </GeometryGroup>
        </GeometryDrawing.Geometry>
        </GeometryDrawing>

        <!-- The mouth -->
        <GeometryDrawing>
        <GeometryDrawing.Pen>
```

LISTING 11.1   Continued

```
      <Pen Brush="Black" StartLineCap="Round" EndLineCap="Round"
        Thickness="10"/>
    </GeometryDrawing.Pen>
    <GeometryDrawing.Geometry>
      <LineGeometry StartPoint="75,160" EndPoint="175,150"/>
    </GeometryDrawing.Geometry>
    </GeometryDrawing>

  </DrawingGroup>
 </DrawingImage.Drawing>
 </DrawingImage>
</Image.Source>
</Image>
```

Visuals

Visual, the abstract base class of UIElement (which is the base class of FrameworkElement), contains the low-level infrastructure required to draw anything onto the screen. The previous section uses Image elements as a way to render all Drawings onto the screen. Image ultimately derives from Visual, but its two intermediate base classes—FrameworkElement and UIElement—contain a number of features that often aren't required for drawings: Styles, data binding, resources, participation in layout, support for keyboard/mouse/stylus input and focus, support for routed events, and so on.

Now imagine an application or component that might want to perform a lot of custom rendering: perhaps a side-scrolling game in the style of Super Mario Bros. or a mapping program like Google Maps or Virtual Earth. If implemented with WPF, such programs could have hundreds or thousands of Drawings on the screen at any point in time. If they were all hosted in a single Image, you would not be able to support fine-grained interactivity with individual Drawings. But if each one were hosted in a separate Image, there would be an unacceptable amount of overhead for unnecessary features.

Fortunately, a different Visual subclass provides a lightweight mechanism for rendering Drawings onto the screen: DrawingVisual. DrawingVisual has a few handy properties for controlling rendering aspects, such as Opacity and Clip (which DrawingGroup also happens to have). But it also has support for a minimal amount of interaction with input devices. This comes in a form of hit testing called *visual hit testing*.

Because DrawingVisual operates at a much lower level than typical WPF features, its use is not very obvious. This section explains how to fill a DrawingVisual with content, how to get that content rendered to the screen, and how to perform visual hit testing.

Filling a `DrawingVisual` with Content

`DrawingVisual` does not have a simple `Drawing` property to which you can attach a `Drawing`. (It actually *does* have a `Drawing` property, but it's read-only.) Instead, you must call its `RenderOpen` method, which returns an instance of a `DrawingContext`. You can draw into this object and then close it with its `Close` method.

For example, the following code places the entire ghost `Drawing` from Listing 11.1 inside a `DrawingVisual`, assuming it's defined as a resource with a ghostDrawing key:

```
DrawingGroup ghostDrawing = FindResource("ghostDrawing") as DrawingGroup;
DrawingVisual ghostVisual = new DrawingVisual();
using (DrawingContext dc = ghostVisual.RenderOpen())
{
  dc.DrawDrawing(ghostDrawing);
}
```

This code makes use of the fact that `DrawingContext` implements `IDisposable`, mapping its `Close` method to `Dispose` (which is implicitly called in a `finally` block when exiting the using scope).

Listing 11.1 used a `DrawingGroup` to combine the three `GeometryDrawings` defining the ghost simply so it could be set as the single `Drawing` inside a `DrawingImage`. With `DrawingVisual`, however, consolidating the `GeometryDrawings` in a `DrawingGroup` is not necessary. The following code adds each of the three `GeometryDrawings` to the `DrawingContext` individually, assuming they are defined as resources with their own keys:

```
GeometryDrawing bodyDrawing = FindResource("bodyDrawing") as GeometryDrawing;
GeometryDrawing eyesDrawing = FindResource("eyesDrawing") as GeometryDrawing;
GeometryDrawing mouthDrawing = FindResource("mouthDrawing") as GeometryDrawing;
DrawingVisual ghostVisual  = new DrawingVisual();
using (DrawingContext dc = ghostVisual.RenderOpen())
{
  dc.DrawDrawing(bodyDrawing);
  dc.DrawDrawing(eyesDrawing);
  dc.DrawDrawing(mouthDrawing);
}
```

Later drawings are placed on top of earlier drawings, so this code preserves the proper z-ordering.

Just as you could get rid of the extra `DrawingGroup` layer and get the same result, you can also get rid of the `Drawing` objects altogether! Drawings are essentially just wrappers on top of the drawing commands that you can perform directly on `DrawingContext`. `DrawingContext` contains several methods for drawing geometries, images, and even video or text. (In other words, these methods cover the functionality provided by the entire list of Drawing types shown earlier in the chapter: `GeometryDrawing`, `ImageDrawing`, `VideoDrawing`, and `GlyphRunDrawing`.) It also supports pushing and popping a variety of effects. Table 11.2 lists all the `DrawingContext` methodst.

TABLE 11.2   DrawingContext Methods

Drawing a Simple GeometryDrawing Without a Geometry or Drawing Instance:
DrawRectangle, DrawRoundedRectangle, DrawEllipse, DrawLine
Drawing Arbitrary Drawings Without a Drawing Instance:
DrawGeometry, DrawImage, DrawVideo, DrawGlyphRun, DrawText
Drawing Arbitrary Drawings with a Drawing Instance:
DrawDrawing
Applying Effects to Drawing Commands:
PushClip, PushEffect, PushGuidelineSet, PushOpacity, PushOpacityMask, PushTransform, Pop
Finishing the Sequence of Drawing Commands:
Close

The PushXXX and Pop methods enable you to not only apply the same effect such as translucency or rotation to a series of commands, but also to nest them.

Listing 11.2 contains a new implementation of the ghost clip art from Listing 11.1 entirely in procedural code. In the Window's constructor, the DrawingVisual is created and filled in without the aid of any Drawing instances. Note that the Window in this listing is still completely blank because we actually haven't taken any steps to render the DrawingVisual! That task is saved for the next section.

LISTING 11.2   WindowHostingVisual.cs—The DrawingContext-based Implementation of the Ghost from Listing 11.1

```csharp
using System;
using System.Windows;
using System.Windows.Media;

public class WindowHostingVisual : Window
{
  public WindowHostingVisual()
  {
    Title = "Hosting DrawingVisuals";
    Width = 300;
    Height = 350;

    DrawingVisual ghostVisual = new DrawingVisual();
    using (DrawingContext dc = ghostVisual.RenderOpen())
    {
      // The body
      dc.DrawGeometry(Brushes.Blue, null, Geometry.Parse(
        @"M 240,250
          C 200,375 200,250 175,200
          C 100,400 100,250 100,200
```

LISTING 11.2   Continued

```
      C 0,350    0,250    30,130
      C 75,0     100,0    150,0
      C 200,0    250,0    250,150 Z"));
    // Left eye
    dc.DrawEllipse(Brushes.Black, new Pen(Brushes.White, 10),
      new Point(95, 95), 15, 15);
    // Right eye
    dc.DrawEllipse(Brushes.Black, new Pen(Brushes.White, 10),
      new Point(170, 105), 15, 15);
    // The mouth
    Pen p = new Pen(Brushes.Black, 10);
    p.StartLineCap = PenLineCap.Round;
    p.EndLineCap = PenLineCap.Round;
    dc.DrawLine(p, new Point(75, 160), new Point(175, 150));
  }
 }
}
```

This listing calls DrawGeometry to draw the ghost's body, which is the simplest method for drawing a complex shape. Notice that Geometry.Parse is used so the path can be described as the same string used in Listing 11.1 rather than an explicit PathFigure containing a bunch of BezierSegment instances. The drawing of the eyes and mouth doesn't even require using Geometry instances; DrawEllipse and DrawLine are used. A few extra lines of code are needed to initialize the Pen for the mouth because Pen's constructor doesn't let you specify advanced features such as the line caps.

Unlike the XAML-based Drawing in Listing 11.1, Listing 11.2 is not a particularly great way to share clip art. But it's a valuable technique for drawing-heavy applications. Going back to the mapping program example, DrawingContext's DrawGeometry method could be used to draw paths representing roads, lakes, and boundaries, and DrawText could be used to add labels on top of this content. Or, if the maps use satellite images, DrawImage can be used to position such images without the overhead of an Image element for each one. (DrawImage accepts an ImageSource rather than an Image.)

Therefore, the DrawingContext class is WPF's closest analog to the Win32 device context or the Windows Forms Graphics object. Note that the use of DrawingContext doesn't change the fact that you're operating within a retained-mode system. The specified drawing doesn't happen immediately; the commands are persisted by WPF until they are needed.

> **TIP**
>
> Using DrawingContext is the most lightweight way to perform drawing because it can avoid the overhead of allocating a Drawing object on the managed heap for every line, shape, and so on. Therefore, it's the best choice for rendering tens of thousands of items.

Displaying a `Visual` on the Screen

Displaying a `Visual` on the screen that happens to also be a `UIElement` is easy; if you add it as the `Content` of a `ContentControl` like `Window`, or a child in a `Panel`, or an item in an `ItemsControl`, and so on, it gets rendered appropriately based on its `OnRender` implementation. But if you've got a non-`UIElement` `Visual`, such as our ghostly `DrawingVisual`, all you would see rendered if you take one of these actions is the unsatisfactory `ToString` rendering.

To get such a `Visual` properly rendered, you need to manually add it to some `UIElement`'s visual tree. "Now wait just a minute," you might be saying, "I thought the whole point of using `DrawingVisual` was to avoid the extra overhead of `UIElement`!" Yes, but you still need at least one `UIElement`, even if that's simply the top-level `Window`. In the mapping program example, you could host thousands of `Visual`s in a single `Canvas` or `Window` rather than having thousands of `UIElement`s in that same host.

The tricky part about adding `Visual`s to an element is that you have to derive your own custom class from an existing `UIElement` and then override two protected virtual members: `VisualChildrenCount` and `GetVisualChild`. Listing 11.3 does this for the `Window` previously defined in Listing 11.2. This is all the code needed to display the `DrawingVisual`, as shown in Figure 11.14. Notice that the background is black, unlike when hosting a `DrawingImage` inside an `Image` element.

FIGURE 11.14   The ghost `DrawingVisual` is rendered inside the `Window` after `VisualChildrenCount` and `GetVisualChild` are overridden

LISTING 11.3   WindowHostingVisual.cs—Update for Rendering the Ghost `DrawingVisual`

```
using System;
using System.Windows;
using System.Windows.Media;

public class WindowHostingVisual : Window
{
  DrawingVisual ghostVisual = null;

  public WindowHostingVisual()
  {
    Title = "Hosting DrawingVisuals";
    Width = 300;
    Height = 350;
```

LISTING 11.3   Continued

```
    ghostVisual = new DrawingVisual();
    using (DrawingContext dc = ghostVisual.RenderOpen())
    {
      The same drawing commands from Listing 11.2…
    }

    // Bookkeeping:
    AddVisualChild(ghostVisual);
    AddLogicalChild(ghostVisual);
  }

  // The two necessary overrides, implemented for the single Visual:
  protected override int VisualChildrenCount
  {
      get { return 1; }
  }
  protected override Visual GetVisualChild(int index)
  {
    if (index != 0)
      throw new ArgumentOutOfRangeException("index");

    return ghostVisual;
  }
}
```

VisualChildrenCount must return the number of Visuals contained by the Window. This
simple example only has the one DrawingVisual, so this property always returns 1.
GetVisualChild must return the actual Visual associated with a zero-based index.
Therefore, this method is implemented to return the DrawingVisual when the input is 0
and throw an exception otherwise. If you want to support multiple Visuals, you could
maintain a collection of them and update these two members to use that collection. If
you want to interact with the layout system, you must override two additional
members—MeasureOverride and ArrangeOverride—covered in Chapter 17, "Layout with
Custom Panels."

Be aware that the VisualChildrenCount/GetVisualChild implementation in Listing 11.3
causes the Window's Content property to never be rendered, even if it's set. If that's not
acceptable, an easy solution is to move this Visual-hosting code to a different UIElement
and then place that element in the Window as desired. For the mapping program example,
this could mean hosting your custom Visuals in a Canvas-derived class, and then placing
that in a Window's Grid (or other Panel) so you can overlay Buttons and other controls.

Besides overriding the two members of Visual, Listing 11.3 also passes the DrawingVisual
to two protected methods defined on Window's base classes: AddVisualChild (defined on
Visual) and AddLogicalChild (defined on FrameworkElement). Calling both of these isn't

strictly necessary for rendering the DrawingVisual, but it should be done to "register" the existence of this visual with the appropriate logical and visual trees. That way, features like event routing, hit testing, and property inheritance work as expected. If you are maintaining a collection of Visual children and ever remove one of these children, you should call RemoveVisualChild and RemoveLogicalChild.

WARNING

Calling a Visual.AddVisualChild is not enough for adding a visual child!

The name of the AddVisualChild method makes it sound like calling it is all you need to do to add a Visual child to your element. But that is not the case. You must still implement VisualChildrenCount and GetVisualChild to return the appropriate information.

DIGGING DEEPER

Other Uses for Visuals

Although non-UIElement Visuals must be hosted in a UIElement to be rendered on the screen, you can do other things with these lightweight Visuals without requiring a UIElement host. For example, any Visual can be sent to a printer with PrintDialog's PrintVisual method, and you can host any Visual in a Win32 application (as described in Chapter 15, "Interoperability with Win32, Windows Forms, and ActiveX").

DIGGING DEEPER

Another Option for Performing Custom Rendering

If your application or component only uses a single DrawingVisual, which means that you don't require its drawings to be independently interactive, you might as well host it in a UIElement instead. The extra overhead of UIElement compared to DrawingVisual is not significant when dealing with a single instance. And working with a custom UIElement is easier than working with a DrawingVisual; simply override its OnRender method, draw into its DrawingContext parameter, and host it anywhere, such as Content in a ContentControl. That said, hosting a Drawing inside an Image is even easier still, doesn't require any procedural code, and has insignificant overhead over a UIElement if you're only dealing with one.

Visual Hit Testing

The term *hit testing* refers to determining whether a point (or set of points) intersects with a given object. This is typically done in the context of a mouse-related event, where the point in question is the location of the mouse pointer.

In WPF, there are two kinds of hit testing: *visual hit testing*, which is supported by all Visuals, and *input hit testing*, which is only supported by UIElements. This section describes only visual hit testing; input hit testing is covered in the "Shapes" section.

Visual hit testing is crucial for enabling a `Visual` to respond to user actions such as mouse clicks or hovering because it doesn't have any of the input events that `UIElements` have (`MouseLeftButtonDown`, `MouseEnter`, `MouseLeave`, `MouseMove`, and so on). By handling such events on the host `UIElement` and then using visual hit testing to determine if relevant child `Visual`s were "hit," you can make any `Visual` respond appropriately to any or all of these events.

Simple Hit Testing

Visual hit testing can be performed with the static `VisualTreeHelper.HitTest` method. The simplest overload of this method accepts a root `Visual` whose visual tree should be searched and the coordinate being tested (which must be expressed relative to the passed-in root). It returns a `HitTestResult`, which contains the topmost `Visual` hit by that point.

Therefore, the following method could be added to the `Window` in Listing 11.3 to process clicks on the ghost `DrawingVisual` and respond by rotating it by 1° each time (just for demonstration purposes):

```
protected override void OnMouseLeftButtonDown(MouseButtonEventArgs e)
{
  base.OnMouseLeftButtonDown(e);

  // Retrieve the mouse pointer location relative to the Window
  Point location = e.GetPosition(this);

  // Perform visual hit testing for the entire Window
  HitTestResult result = VisualTreeHelper.HitTest(this, location);

  // If we hit the ghostVisual, rotate it
  if (result.VisualHit == ghostVisual)
  {
    if (ghostVisual.Transform == null)
      ghostVisual.Transform = new RotateTransform();

    (ghostVisual.Transform as RotateTransform).Angle++;
  }
}
```

Because `Image` is ultimately a `Visual`, you could have implemented the same scheme with the `Image` hosting the `DrawingImage` version of the ghost back in Listing 11.1. (Or, you could have simply attached an event handler to `Image`'s `MouseLeftButtonDown` event.) There's an important difference between doing this with an `Image` versus doing the visual hit testing with a `DrawingVisual`, however. The preceding code only considers the `DrawingVisual` to be hit for coordinates physically within the ghost's body, whereas an `Image` is considered to be hit for any coordinates within the `Image`'s rectangular bounds.

Hit Testing with Multiple Visuals

Having nonrectangular hit testing is nice, but perhaps you want to hit test for individual portions of the ghost, such as the eyes versus the mouth versus the body. To accomplish this, you need to split the single DrawingVisual into three DrawingVisuals. Listing 11.4 does just that, and performs the 1° rotation on any DrawingVisual each time it is clicked. Figure 11.15 shows the result of this ability to manipulate visuals independently, with a ghost that is starting to look like a Picasso painting!

FIGURE 11.15   The ghost represented by three independent DrawingVisuals, after a few clicks on the body and several clicks on the eyes.

LISTING 11.4   WindowHostingVisual.cs—Splitting the Ghost into Three DrawingVisuals for Independent Hit Testing

```
using System;
using System.Windows;
using System.Windows.Input;
using System.Windows.Media;
using System.Collections.Generic;

public class WindowHostingVisual : Window
{
  List<Visual> visuals = new List<Visual>();

  public WindowHostingVisual()
  {
    Title = "Hosting DrawingVisuals";
    Width = 300;
    Height = 350;

    DrawingVisual bodyVisual = new DrawingVisual();
    DrawingVisual eyesVisual = new DrawingVisual();
    DrawingVisual mouthVisual = new DrawingVisual();

    using (DrawingContext dc = bodyVisual.RenderOpen())
    {
      // The body
      dc.DrawGeometry(Brushes.Blue, null, Geometry.Parse(
        @"M 240,250
          C 200,375 200,250 175,200
          C 100,400 100,250 100,200
          C 0,350   0,250   30,130
          C 75,0    100,0   150,0
```

LISTING 11.4   Continued

```
      C 200,0   250,0   250,150 Z"));
  }
  using (DrawingContext dc = eyesVisual.RenderOpen())
  {
    // Left eye
    dc.DrawEllipse(Brushes.Black, new Pen(Brushes.White, 10),
      new Point(95, 95), 15, 15);
    // Right eye
    dc.DrawEllipse(Brushes.Black, new Pen(Brushes.White, 10),
      new Point(170, 105), 15, 15);
  }
  using (DrawingContext dc = mouthVisual.RenderOpen())
  {
    // The mouth
    Pen p = new Pen(Brushes.Black, 10);
    p.StartLineCap = PenLineCap.Round;
    p.EndLineCap = PenLineCap.Round;
    dc.DrawLine(p, new Point(75, 160), new Point(175, 150));
  }

  visuals.Add(bodyVisual);
  visuals.Add(eyesVisual);
  visuals.Add(mouthVisual);

  // Bookkeeping:
  foreach (Visual v in visuals)
  {
    AddVisualChild(v);
    AddLogicalChild(v);
  }
}

// The two necessary overrides, implemented for the single Visual:
protected override int VisualChildrenCount
{
  get { return visuals.Count; }
}
protected override Visual GetVisualChild(int index)
{
  if (index < 0 || index >= visuals.Count)
    throw new ArgumentOutOfRangeException("index");

  return visuals[index];
}
```

LISTING 11.4   Continued

```
protected override void OnMouseLeftButtonDown(MouseButtonEventArgs e)
{
  base.OnMouseLeftButtonDown(e);

  // Retrieve the mouse pointer location relative to the Window
  Point location = e.GetPosition(this);

  // Perform visual hit testing
  HitTestResult result = VisualTreeHelper.HitTest(this, location);

  // If we hit any DrawingVisual, rotate it
  if (result.VisualHit.GetType() == typeof(DrawingVisual))
  {
    DrawingVisual dv = result.VisualHit as DrawingVisual;
    if (dv.Transform == null)
      dv.Transform = new RotateTransform();

    (dv.Transform as RotateTransform).Angle++;
  }
}
}
```

Because this Window now has three Visual children instead of one, it uses a List<Visual> collection to store them for the sake of the VisualChildrenCount and GetVisualChild implementation. Drawing into three DrawingVisuals instead of one is a simple change; the DrawingContext commands are simply split into three using blocks, one per DrawingVisual. In the processing of the HitTestResult, the code applies the rotation logic to any Visual as long as it's a DrawingVisual.

DIGGING DEEPER

DrawingVisuals as Children of a DrawingVisual

DrawingVisual derives from ContainerVisual, which can contain any number of Visuals in its Children collection. (ContainerVisual really should have been called VisualGroup, for consistency with WPF classes such as TransformGroup, DrawingGroup, and GeometryGroup.) Therefore, another way to implement Listing 11.4 would be to add eyesVisual and mouthVisual as children of bodyVisual *instead of* adding them to the Window's visuals collection. This also means that the listing could go back to the approach of managing a single Visual rather than a collection! Rendering and hit testing automatically work for children of a DrawingVisual because ContainerVisual overrides and implements VisualChildrenCount and GetVisualChild similarly to how Listing 11.4 implements them. You just need to hook up your Window to the root DrawingVisual, and let the DrawingVisual handle the rest!

Hit Testing with Overlapping Visuals

Visual hit testing can inform you about *all* Visuals that intersect a location, not just the topmost Visual. For the three-Visuals ghost example, you can set up hit testing such that clicking on the eyes tells you that the eyes were hit *and* the body underneath the eyes was hit. It doesn't matter if a Visual is completely obscured; it can still be hit.

To take advantage of this functionality, you must use a more powerful form of the HitTest method that accepts a HitTestResultCallback delegate. Before this version of HitTest returns, the delegate is invoked once for each relevant Visual, starting from the topmost and ending at the bottommost.

The following code is an update to the OnMouseLeftButtonDown method from Listing 11.4 that supports hit testing on overlapping Visuals:

```
protected override void OnMouseLeftButtonDown(MouseButtonEventArgs e)
{
  base.OnMouseLeftButtonDown(e);

  // Retrieve the mouse pointer location relative to the Window
  Point location = e.GetPosition(this);

  // Perform visual hit testing
  VisualTreeHelper.HitTest(this, null,
    new HitTestResultCallback(HitTestCallback),
    new PointHitTestParameters(location));
}


public HitTestResultBehavior HitTestCallback(HitTestResult result)
{
  // If we hit any DrawingVisual, rotate it
  if (result.VisualHit.GetType() == typeof(DrawingVisual))
  {
    DrawingVisual dv = result.VisualHit as DrawingVisual;
    if (dv.Transform == null)
      dv.Transform = new RotateTransform();

    (dv.Transform as RotateTransform).Angle++;
  }
  // Keep looking for hits
  return HitTestResultBehavior.Continue;
}
```

There are a few differences here. The most noticeable one is that the logic to process HitTestResult is moved to the callback method because this overload of HitTest doesn't return anything. The callback method must return one of two HitTestResultBehavior values: Continue or Stop. Therefore, you can stop the probing for further Visuals at any time. If the callback *always* returns Stop, only the topmost Visual is processed, just like with the simpler hit testing approach. The second parameter of this `HitTest` overload, where `null` is passed, can be set to a `HitTestFilterCallback` delegate to skip the processing of certain parts of a visual tree without stopping the processing altogether. You can implement very sophisticated hit-testing schemes with this approach.

Notice that this overload of `HitTest` isn't given the relevant `Point` directly but rather is passed a `PointHitTestParameters` object wrapping the `Point`. That's because the method accepts an abstract `HitTestParameters` instance, and WPF has two subclasses: `PointHitTestParameters` and `GeometryHitTestParameters`. The latter can be used to hit test against an arbitrary region. This is useful for supporting more complicated input actions, such as dragging a selection rectangle or drawing a "lasso" to select multiple objects.

FAQ

 Why does the more powerful form of visual hit testing involve an awkward callback mechanism instead of simply returning an array of `HitTestResults`?

The callback scheme was chosen for performance reasons. This way, WPF doesn't have to allocate any extra memory, which is important when dealing with high numbers of `Visual`s or frequent hit testing. In addition, the callback scheme allows for scenario-specific optimizations by giving callback methods the power to halt processing by returning `HitTestResultBehavior.Stop`.

TIP

If you want visual hit testing to report a hit anywhere within a `Visual`'s bounding box rather than its precise geometry, you can override `Visual`'s `HitTestCore` method, which is called whenever the bounding box is hit. (This method enables you to customize hit testing in other ways as well.)

A simpler way to accomplish this is to simply draw a transparent rectangle matching the size of the bounding box inside the `Visual`. That's because visual hit testing doesn't care about the transparency of objects; they get hit just the same (as if they are panes of glass).

WARNING

Don't modify the visual tree in your hit-testing callback methods!

Hit-testing callback methods are called while the visual tree is in the process of being walked, so altering the tree can cause incorrect behavior. If you must modify the visual tree based on certain `Visual`s being hit, you should store the information you need during the callbacks so that you can act on it after `HitTest` returns. This is pretty easy to do because `HitTest` doesn't return until after all callbacks have been called.

Shapes

A Shape, like a GeometryDrawing, is a basic 2D drawing that combines a Geometry with a Pen and Brush. Unlike GeometryDrawing, however, Shape derives from FrameworkElement, so it can be directly placed in a user interface without custom code or a complex hierarchy of objects. For example, Chapter 2, "XAML Demystified," showed how easy it is to embed a square in a Button by using Rectangle (which derives from Shape):

```
<Button MinWidth="75">
  <Rectangle Height="20" Width="20" Fill="Black"/>
</Button>
```

WPF provides six classes that derive from the abstract System.Windows.Shapes.Shape class:

- ▶ Rectangle
- ▶ Ellipse
- ▶ Line
- ▶ Polyline
- ▶ Polygon
- ▶ Path

Most of these should look pretty familiar, as they mirror the Geometry classes discussed earlier in the chapter. The following sections examine each one individually because they work slightly differently than their Geometry counterparts (and Polyline and Polygon are Shape-specific abstractions over a PathGeometry). Shape itself defines many properties for controlling the appearance of its concrete subclasses. The two most important ones are Fill and Stroke, both of type Brush.

FAQ

 Why is Shape.Stroke a Brush rather than a Pen?

Shape's Fill and Stroke properties have the same role as GeometryDrawing's Brush and Pen properties: Fill is for the inner area, and Stroke is for the outline. Internally, a Pen is indeed used to create the outline of the Shape. But rather than exposing the Pen directly, Shape defines Stroke as a Brush and exposes eight additional properties to tweak the settings of the internal Pen wrapping the Stroke Brush: StrokeStartLineCap, StrokeEndLineCap, StrokeThickness, and so on.

This unfortunate inconsistency was created because setting the Pen-related properties directly on the Shape is simpler than using a separate Pen object, especially for the common case in which all you're setting is the Brush and the Thickness.

> **WARNING**
>
> **Overuse of Shapes can lead to performance problems!**
>
> It's so tempting to use Shapes as the building blocks for any 2D drawings. They are much more discoverable and easier to work with than Drawings, and they work with the content model that WPF developers take for granted. Design tools and XAML exporters also tend to represent artwork as Shapes by default, so Shapes can sneak into your applications without you even realizing it. For example, when you select the XAML Export menu item in Microsoft Expression Design, the resultant .xaml file contains Shapes in a Canvas unless you explicitly change the Document Format option to Resource Dictionary. At this point, you can choose between a DrawingImage and a DrawingBrush.
>
> When you have Shape-based artwork, *every single Shape* supports Styles, data binding, resources, layout, keyboard/mouse/stylus input and focus, routed events, and so on. It's nice that you can take advantage of all this without extra work, but as discussed in the "Visuals" section, this is typically unnecessary overhead. Keep this in mind if you find yourself using more than a small number of Shapes.

Rectangle

RectangleGeometry, discussed earlier, has a Rect property for defining its dimensions. Rectangle, on the other hand, delegates to WPF's layout system for controlling its size and position. This could involve using its Width and Height properties (among others) inherited from FrameworkElement, or controlling its location with Canvas.Left and Canvas.Top, for example.

Just like RectangleGeometry, however, Rectangle defines its own RadiusX and RadiusY properties of type double that enable you to give it rounded corners. Figure 11.16 shows the following Rectangles in a StackPanel with various values of RadiusX and RadiusY:

```
<StackPanel>
  <Rectangle Width="200" Height="100"
    Fill="Orange" Stroke="Black" StrokeThickness="10" Margin="4"/>
  <Rectangle Width="200" Height="100" RadiusX="10" RadiusY="30"
    Fill="Orange" Stroke="Black" StrokeThickness="10" Margin="4"/>
  <Rectangle Width="200" Height="100" RadiusX="30" RadiusY="10"
    Fill="Orange" Stroke="Black" StrokeThickness="10" Margin="4"/>
  <Rectangle Width="200" Height="100" RadiusX="100" RadiusY="50"
    Fill="Orange" Stroke="Black" StrokeThickness="10" Margin="4"/>
</StackPanel>
```

RadiusX can be at most half the Width of the Rectangle, and RadiusY can be at most half the Height. Setting them any higher makes no difference.

WARNING

You must explicitly set Stroke or Fill for a Shape to be seen!

This might sound obvious for someone used to working with GeometryDrawings, but it's a common pitfall for people who think of Shapes like they think of Buttons and ListBoxes. Although each Shape internally contains the appropriate Geometry, its Stroke and Fill are both set to null by default.

Ellipse

After discovering the flexibility of Rectangle and realizing that it can be made to look like an ellipse (or circle), you'd think that a separate Ellipse class would be redundant. And you'd be right! All Ellipse does is make it easier to get an elliptical shape. It defines no settable properties above and beyond what Shape and its base classes provide. Unlike EllipseGeometry, which exposes RadiusX, RadiusY, and Center properties, Ellipse simply fills its rectangular region with the largest possible elliptical shape.

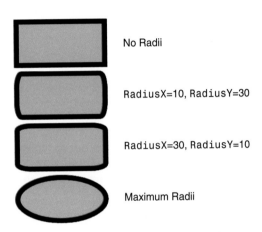

No Radii

RadiusX=10, RadiusY=30

RadiusX=30, RadiusY=10

Maximum Radii

FIGURE 11.16   Four Rectangles with different values for RadiusX and RadiusY.

The following Ellipse could replace the last Rectangle in the previous XAML snippet and Figure 11.16 would look identical:

```
<Ellipse Width="200" Height="100"
  Fill="Orange" Stroke="Black" StrokeThickness="10" Margin="4"/>
```

The only change is replacing the element name and removing the references to RadiusX and RadiusY.

DIGGING DEEPER

How Shapes Work

Shapes internally override UIElement's OnRender method and use DrawingContext methods to draw the appropriate geometry. For example, Ellipse has an OnRender implementation effectively like the following:

```
protected override void OnRender(DrawingContext drawingContext)
{
  Pen pen = …;   // Fabricate a Pen based on all the StrokeXXX properties
  Rect rect = …; // Layout determines the size of this rectangle
  drawingContext.DrawGeometry(this.Fill, pen, new EllipseGeometry(rect));
}
```

Continues

DIGGING DEEPER

Continued

Furthermore, Rectangle has an OnRender implementation effectively like the following:

```
protected override void OnRender(DrawingContext drawingContext)
{
    Pen pen = …;    // Fabricate a Pen based on all the StrokeXXX properties
    Rect rect = …; // Layout determines the size of this rectangle
    drawingContext.DrawRoundedRectangle(this.Fill, pen, rect, this.RadiusX,
        this.RadiusY);
}
```

The bulk of the code inside a Shape is the plumbing needed to interact with the layout system. This plumbing is covered in Chapter 17.

Line

Line defines four double properties to represent a line segment connecting points $(x1,y1)$ and $(x2,y2)$. These properties are called X1, Y1, X2, and Y2. These are defined as four properties rather than two Point properties (as in LineGeometry) for ease of use in data-binding scenarios.

The values of Line's properties are not absolute coordinates. They are relative to the space given to the Line element by the layout system. For example, the following StackPanel contains three Lines, rendered in Figure 11.17:

```
<StackPanel>
    <Line X1="0" Y1="0"    X2="100" Y2="100" Stroke="Black" StrokeThickness="10"
        Margin="4"/>
    <Line X1="0" Y1="0"    X2="100" Y2="0"    Stroke="Black" StrokeThickness="10"
        Margin="4"/>
    <Line X1="0" Y1="100" X2="100" Y2="0"    Stroke="Black" StrokeThickness="10"
        Margin="4"/>
</StackPanel>
```

Notice that each Line is given the space needed by its bounding box, so the horizontal line only gets 10 units (for the thickness of its Stroke) plus the specified Margin. Line inherits Shape's Fill property, but it is meaningless because there is never any area to fill.

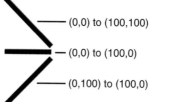

FIGURE 11.17   Three Lines in a StackPanel, demonstrating that their coordinates are relative.

Polyline

Polyline represents a sequence of lines, expressed in its Points property (a collection of Point objects). The following four Polylines are rendered in Figure 11.18:

```
<StackPanel>
<Polyline Points="0,0 100,100" Stroke="Black" StrokeThickness="10" Margin="4"/>
<Polyline Points="0,0 100,100 200,0" Stroke="Black" StrokeThickness="10"
  Margin="4"/>
<Polyline Points="0,0 100,100 200,0 300,100" Stroke="Black" StrokeThickness="10"
  Margin="4"/>
<Polyline Points="0,0 100,100 200,0 300,100 100,100" Stroke="Black"
  StrokeThickness="10" Margin="4"/>
</StackPanel>
```

A type converter enables Points to be specified as a simple list of alternating *x* and *y* values. The commas can help readability, but are optional. You can place a comma between every value or use no commas at all.

Figure 11.19 demonstrates that setting Polyline's Fill fills it like an open PathGeometry, pretending that a line segment exists that connects the first Point with the last Point. This happens because, internally, Polyline is using a PathGeometry! Figure 11.19 was created simply by taking the Polylines from Figure 11.18 and marking them with Fill="Orange".

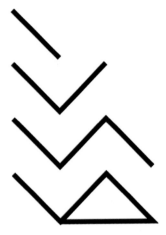

FIGURE 11.18   Four Polylines, ranging from two to five points.

Polygon

Just as Rectangle makes Ellipse redundant, Polyline makes Polygon redundant. The only difference between Polyline and Polygon is that Polygon automatically adds a line segment connecting the first and last Points. (In other words, it sets IsClosed to true in its internal PathGeometry's PathFigure.)

If you take the Polylines from Figure 11.19 and simply change each element name to Polygon, you get the result in Figure 11.20. Notice that the initial line segment in the first and last Polygons is noticeably longer than in Figure 11.19. This is because of the Miter corners joining the initial line segment with the

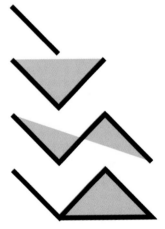

FIGURE 11.19   The same Polylines from Figure 11.18 but with an explicit Fill.

final line segment (which happens to share the same coordinates). Because the angle between the two line segments is 0°, the corner would be infinitely long if not for the StrokeMiterLimit property limiting it to 10 units by default.

Both Polygon and Polyline expose the underlying PathGeometry's FillRule with their own FillRule property.

Path

As you probably expected, just like all basic geometries can be represented as a PathGeometry, all the other Shapes can be alternatively represented with the general purpose Path. Path only adds a single Data property to Shape, which can be set to an instance of any Geometry. Therefore, Path turns out to be the easiest (and most fully featured)

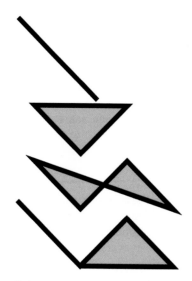

FIGURE 11.20   Polygons are just like Polylines, except that they always form a closed shape.

way to embed an arbitrary Geometry directly into a user interface. There's no need for an explicit Drawing object or low-level DrawingContext techniques; you simply set the Data, Fill, and Stroke-related properties.

The following Path produces the same result as the overlapping triangles from Figure 11.5:

```
<Path Fill="Orange" Stroke="Black" StrokeThickness="10">
<Path.Data>
  <PathGeometry>
    <!-- Triangle #1 -->
    <PathFigure IsClosed="True">
      <LineSegment Point="0,100"/>
      <LineSegment Point="100,100"/>
    </PathFigure>
    <!-- Triangle #2 -->
    <PathFigure StartPoint="70,0" IsClosed="True">
      <LineSegment Point="0,100"/>
      <LineSegment Point="100,100"/>
    </PathFigure>
  </PathGeometry>
</Path.Data>
</Path>
```

Or, you can take advantage of Geometry's type converter and express the whole thing as follows:

```
<Path Fill="Orange" Stroke="Black" StrokeThickness="10"
  Data="M 0,0 L 0,100 L 100,100 Z M 70,0 L 0,100 L 100,100 Z"/>
```

Clip Art Based on Shapes

It's now time to revisit the ghost clip art that was represented as a DrawingImage in Listing 11.1 and as a sequence of DrawingContext commands in Listings 11.2 through 11.4. Listing 11.5 places the pieces of the ghost, which are now independent Shapes, on a Canvas. The result looks identical to hosting the DrawingImage in an Image, as shown in Figure 11.13.

LISTING 11.5   The Ghost Represented as Four Independent Shapes

```
<Canvas xmlns="http://schemas.microsoft.com/winfx/2006/xaml/presentation">
  <Path Fill="Blue" Data="M 240,250
    C 200,375 200,250 175,200
    C 100,400 100,250 100,200
    C 0,350   0,250   30,130
    C 75,0    100,0   150,0
    C 200,0   250,0   250,150 Z"/>
    <Ellipse Fill="Black" Stroke="White" StrokeThickness="10"
      Width="40" Height="40" Canvas.Left="75" Canvas.Top="75"/>
    <Ellipse Fill="Black" Stroke="White" StrokeThickness="10"
      Width="40" Height="40" Canvas.Left="150" Canvas.Top="85"/>
    <Line X1="75" Y1="160" X2="175" Y2="150" StrokeStartLineCap="Round"
      StrokeEndLineCap="Round" Stroke="Black" StrokeThickness="10"/>
</Canvas>
```

The numeric data used for the Path (body) and the Line (mouth) is identical to the data used in the original DrawingImage. The property values for both Ellipses, however, needed a bit of translation to map from the original EllipseGeometry objects to the Ellipse objects. The original eyes had a radius of 15 and a Pen thickness of 10. Because the Pen outline is centered on any Geometry's edge, it only extended the total radius to 20. That's why the Ellipses in Listing 11.5 are given a Height and Width of 40 (the radius multiplied by 2). In this case, the entire Shape, including its outline, fits inside the bounds. As for the values chosen for Canvas.Left and Canvas.Top, they are the original EllipseGeometry Center values minus the total radius of 20.

Unlike previous implementations of the ghost, this one supports *input hit testing* independently on each of its four pieces (each eye is even treated separately!) because they all derive from UIElement. Input hit testing differs from visual hit testing in that it more closely represents what a user can physically hit with her mouse, keyboard, or stylus. It only supports hitting the topmost element at any coordinate, and only allows elements to be hit if IsEnabled and IsVisible (properties introduced by UIElement) are both true. (It also only supports hit testing against a single point rather than a Geometry, but that's just an artificial limitation rather than a philosophical difference.)

To perform input hit testing, you simply call InputHitTest on an instance of a UIElement whose visual tree you want to be tested. You can pass it a Point, and it returns an IInputElement instance (an interface implemented by UIElement and ContentElement). But input hit testing is rarely performed directly because all UIElements already have a host of events exposing whether they've been pressed, clicked, and so on: GotKeyboardFocus, KeyDown, KeyUp, GotMouseCapture, MouseEnter, MouseLeave, MouseMove, MouseWheel, GotStylusCapture, StylusEnter, StylusLeave, StylusInAirMove, and so on. And if the policy enforced by input hit testing is too restrictive for your needs, you can always perform visual hit testing with any Shape.

DIGGING DEEPER

Input Hit Testing's Dirty Little Secret

Input hit testing is really just a special case of visual hit testing. In fact, the implementation of InputHitTest simply calls VisualTreeHelper.HitTest with its own internal callbacks for filtering and results processing! Its filter callback prunes disabled and invisible UIElements from the visual tree traversal, and its results callback stops the search after it finds the first match.

Brushes

It's not obvious when programming with WPF via XAML, but WPF elements almost never interact directly with colors. Instead, most uses of color are wrapped inside objects known as Brushes. This is an extremely powerful indirection because WPF contains six different kinds of Brushes that can do just about everything imaginable. There are three *color brushes* and three *tile brushes*. Although this section mostly demonstrates Brushes on a Drawing or Window, keep in mind that Brushes can be used as the background, foreground, or outline of just about anything you can put on the screen.

Color Brushes

WPF's three color brushes are SolidColorBrush, LinearGradientBrush, and RadialGradientBrush. You might think you already know everything there is to know about these Brushes from their limited use in the book so far, but all of these Brushes are more flexible than most people realize.

SolidColorBrush

The SolidColorBrush, used implicitly throughout this book, fills the target area with a single color. It has a simple Color property of type System.Windows.Media.Color. Because of the type converter that converts strings like "Blue" or "#FFFFFF" into SolidColorBrushes, they are indistinguishable from their underlying Color in XAML.

The Color structure has more functionality than you might expect. It natively supports two color spaces:

▶ **sRGB**—The standard RGB color space designed for CRT monitors and familiar to most programmers and web designers. The values for red, green, and blue are each represented as a byte, so there are only 256 possible values.

▶ **scRGB**—An enhanced RGB color space that represents red, green, and blue as floating-point values. This enables a much wider gamut (a subset of colors that can be accurately represented). Red, green, and blue values of 0.0 represent black, whereas three values of 1.0 represent white. However, scRGB allows for values outside of this range, so information isn't lost if you apply transformations to Colors that temporarily push any channel outside of its normal range.

Color exposes sets of properties (one per channel) for both color spaces: A, R, G, and B of type Byte for the more familiar sRGB, and ScA, ScR, ScG, and ScB of type Single for the more flexible scRGB. (A and ScA represent the alpha channel, for varying the opacity.) Whenever any of these properties are set, Color updates both of its internal representations. Therefore, you can mix and match these properties with the same Color instance and everything stays in sync. You can also leverage this behavior to easily convert sRGB values to scRGB values, and vice versa.

Color defines operators that enable you to add, subtract, and multiply two instances, and compare them for equality. However, because scRGB uses floating-point values (which should never be tested for strict equality), Color defines a static AreClose method that accepts two colors and returns true if all of their channels are within a very small epsilon of each other.

Color's type converter supports several different string representations:

▶ A name, like Red, Khaki, or DodgerBlue, matching one of the static properties on the Colors class.

▶ The sRGB representation #argb, where a, r, g, b are hexadecimal values for the A, R, G, and B properties. For example, opaque Red is #FFFF0000 or more simply #FF0000 (because A is assumed to be the maximum 255, by default).

▶ The scRGB representation sc#a r g b, where a, r, g, b are *decimal* values for the ScA, ScR, ScG, and ScB properties. In this representation, opaque Red is sc#1.0 1.0 0.0 0.0 or more simply sc#1.0 0.0 0.0. Commas are also allowed between each value.

LinearGradientBrush

LinearGradientBrush, which has been used a few times already in the book, fills an area with a gradient defined by colors at specific points along an imaginary line segment, with linear interpolation between those points.

LinearGradientBrush contains a collection of GradientStop objects in its GradientStops content property, each of which contains a Color and an Offset. The offset is a double value relative to the bounding box of the area being filled, where 0 is the beginning and 1 is the end. Therefore, the following LinearGradientBrush can be applied to any version of the ghost clip art to create the result in Figure 11.21:

```
<LinearGradientBrush>
  <GradientStop Offset="0" Color="Blue"/>
  <GradientStop Offset="1" Color="Red"/>
</LinearGradientBrush>
```

By default, the gradient starts at the top-left corner of the area's bounding box and ends at the bottom-right corner. You can customize these points, however, with LinearGradientBrush's StartPoint and EndPoint properties. The values of these points are relative to the bounding box, just like the Offset in each GradientStop. Therefore, the default values for StartPoint and EndPoint are (0,0) and (1,1), respectively.

FIGURE 11.21   A simple blue-to-red LinearGradientBrush applied to the ghost.

DIGGING DEEPER

Custom Color Space Profiles

Advanced developers or designers can specify Colors based on a custom ICC profile. (ICC is the International Color Consortium that has defined the cross-platform profile format.) In procedural code, you can construct such a Color by calling the static Color.FromValues method that accepts an array of Singles and a Uri pointing to the profile file. In XAML, you can take advantage of Color's type converter that accepts a string of the form ContextColor *Uri Values*.

For example, the following SolidColorBrush gives a Button a red Background by using the sRGB profile file that you should have in your Windows system32 directory under spool\drivers\color:

```
<Button>
<Button.Background>
  <SolidColorBrush Color="ContextColor
file://C:/WINDOWS/system32/spool/drivers/color/sRGB%20Color%20Space%20Profile.icm
    1.0,1.0,0.0,0.0"/>
</Button.Background>
</Button>
```

If you want to use absolute units instead of relative ones, set MappingMode to Absolute (rather than the default RelativeToBoundingBox). Note that this only applies to StartPoint and EndPoint; the Offset values in each GradientStop are always relative!

Figure 11.22 shows a few different settings of `StartPoint` and `EndPoint` on the `LinearGradientBrush` used in Figure 11.22 (with the default relative `MappingMode`). Notice that the relative values are not limited to a range of 0 to 1. You can specify smaller or larger numbers to make the gradient logically extend *past* the bounding box. (This applies to `GradientStop Offset` values as well.)

The default interpolation of colors is done using the sRGB color space, but you can set `ColorInterpolationMode` to `ScRgbLinearInterpolation` to use the scRGB color space instead. The result is a much smoother gradient, as shown in Figure 11.23.

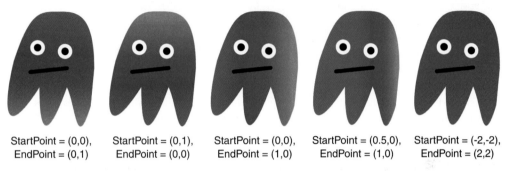

| StartPoint = (0,0),
EndPoint = (0,1) | StartPoint = (0,1),
EndPoint = (0,0) | StartPoint = (0,0),
EndPoint = (1,0) | StartPoint = (0.5,0),
EndPoint = (1,0) | StartPoint = (-2,-2),
EndPoint = (2,2) |

FIGURE 11.22   Various settings of `StartPoint` and `EndPoint`.

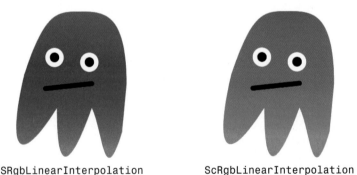

SRgbLinearInterpolation   ScRgbLinearInterpolation

FIGURE 11.23   The `ColorInterpolationMode` affects the appearance of the gradient.

The final property for controlling `LinearGradientBrush` is `SpreadMethod`, which determines how any leftover area not covered by the gradient should be filled. This only makes sense when the `LinearGradientBrush` is explicitly set to *not* cover the entire bounding box. The default value (from the `GradientSpreadMethod` enumeration) is `Pad`, meaning that the remaining space should be filled with the color at the endpoint. You could alternatively set it to `Repeat` or `Reflect`. Both of these values repeat the gradient in a never-ending pattern, but `Reflect` reverses every other gradient to maintain a smooth transition. Figure 11.24 demonstrates each of these `SpreadMethod` values on the following `LinearGradientBrush` that forces the gradient to cover only the middle 10% of the bounding box:

```
<LinearGradientBrush StartPoint=".45,.45" EndPoint=".55,.55" SpreadMethod="XXX">
  <GradientStop Offset="0" Color="Blue"/>
  <GradientStop Offset="1" Color="Red"/>
</LinearGradientBrush>
```

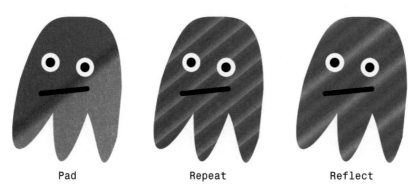

| Pad | Repeat | Reflect |

FIGURE 11.24   Different values of SpreadMethod can create vastly different effects.

And don't forget, because Pens use a Brush rather than a simple Color to fill their area, Drawings, Shapes, Controls, and many other elements in WPF can be outlined with complicated fills. Figure 11.25 shows a version of the ghost that uses the following Pen on the GeometryDrawing defining its body:

```
<Pen Thickness="20">
<Pen.Brush>
  <LinearGradientBrush>
    <GradientStop Offset="0" Color="Red"/>
    <GradientStop Offset="0.2" Color="Orange"/>
    <GradientStop Offset="0.4" Color="Yellow"/>
    <GradientStop Offset="0.6" Color="Green"/>
    <GradientStop Offset="0.8" Color="Blue"/>
    <GradientStop Offset="1" Color="Purple"/>
  </LinearGradientBrush>
</Pen.Brush>
</Pen>
```

Notice that the Pen's LinearGradientBrush uses six GradientStops spaced equally along the gradient path, rather than just two.

FIGURE 11.25   Outlining the ghost with a Pen using a LinearGradientBrush.

> **TIP**
>
> To get crisp lines inside a gradient brush, you can simply add two GradientStops at the same Offset with different Colors. The following LinearGradientBrush does this at Offsets 0.2 *and* 0.6 to get two distinct lines defining the DarkBlue region:
>
> ```
> <LinearGradientBrush EndPoint="0,1">
>   <GradientStop Offset="0" Color="Aqua"/>
>   <GradientStop Offset="0.2" Color="Blue"/>
>   <GradientStop Offset="0.2" Color="DarkBlue"/>
>   <GradientStop Offset="0.6" Color="DarkBlue"/>
>   <GradientStop Offset="0.6" Color="Blue"/>
>   <GradientStop Offset="1" Color="Aqua"/>
> </LinearGradientBrush>
> ```
>
> When applied to the ghost's body, the result is shown in Figure 11.26.
>
>
>
> FIGURE 11.26
> Two crisp lines inside the gradient, enabled by duplicate Offsets.

RadialGradientBrush

RadialGradientBrush works like LinearGradientBrush, except it has a single starting point with each GradientStop emanating from it in the shape of an ellipse. RadialGradientBrush and LinearGradientBrush share a common GradientBrush base class, which defines the GradientStops, SpreadMethod, ColorInterpolationMode, and MappingMode properties that we already examined on LinearGradientBrush.

Figure 11.27 shows the following simple RadialGradientBrush applied to the ghost:

```
<RadialGradientBrush>
  <GradientStop Offset="0" Color="Blue"/>
  <GradientStop Offset="1" Color="Red"/>
</RadialGradientBrush>
```

By default, the imaginary ellipse controlling the gradient is centered in the bounding box, with a width and height matching the width and height of the bounding box. This can clearly be seen on the ghost by setting SpreadMethod to Repeat, as shown in Figure 11.28.

To customize the size and position of the imaginary ellipse, RadialGradientBrush defines Center, RadiusX, and RadiusY properties. These

FIGURE 11.27   A simple blue-to-red RadialGradientBrush applied to the ghost.

have default values of (0.5,0.5), 0.5, and
0.5, respectively, because they're
expressed as coordinates relative to the
bounding box. Because the default size
of the ellipse often doesn't cover the
corner of the area being filled (as in
Figure 11.28), increasing the radii is a
simple way to cover the area without
relying on `SpreadMethod`.

`RadialGradientBrush` also has a
`GradientOrigin` property that specifies
where the gradient should originate
independently of the defining ellipse. To

FIGURE 11.28   Setting `SpreadMethod` to
`Repeat` clearly reveals the bounds of the
ellipse.

avoid getting strange results, it should be set to a point within the defining ellipse. Its
default value is (0.5,0.5), the center of the default ellipse, but Figure 11.29 shows what
happens when set to a different value, such as (0,0):

```
<RadialGradientBrush GradientOrigin="0,0" SpreadMethod="Repeat">
  <GradientStop Offset="0" Color="Blue"/>
  <GradientStop Offset="1" Color="Red"/>
</RadialGradientBrush>
```

If you set `MappingMode` to `Absolute`, the
values for all four of these
`RadialGradientBrush`-specific properties
(`Center`, `RadiusX`, `RadiusY`, and
`GradientOrigin`) are treated as absolute
coordinates instead of relative to the
bounding box.

Because all `Colors` have an alpha
channel, you can incorporate transparency and translucency into any
gradient by changing the alpha channel
on any `GradientStop`'s `Color`. The
following `RadialGradientBrush` uses
two blue colors with different alpha values:

FIGURE 11.29   Shifting the gradient's origin
within the ellipse with the `GradientOrigin`
property.

```
<RadialGradientBrush RadiusX="0.7" RadiusY="0.7">
  <GradientStop Offset="0" Color="#990000FF"/>
  <GradientStop Offset="1" Color="#000000FF"/>
</RadialGradientBrush>
```

Figure 11.30 shows the result of applying this `RadialGradientBrush` (quite appropriately!)
to the ghost drawing, on top of a photographic background so the transparency is
apparent.

FIGURE 11.30   A ghost with translucency, accomplished by using colors with nonopaque alpha channels.

WARNING

When it comes to gradients, not all transparent colors are equal!

Notice that the second GradientStop for Figure 11.30 uses a "transparent blue" color rather than simply specifying Transparent as the color. That's because Transparent is defined as white with a 0 alpha channel (#00FFFFFF). Although both colors are completely invisible, the interpolation to each color does not behave the same way. If Transparent were used for the second GradientStop for Figure 11.30, you would not only see the alpha value gradually change from 0x99 to 0, but you would also see the red and green values gradually change from 0 to 0xFF, giving the brush more of a gray look.

Tile Brushes

In addition to color brushes, WPF defines three *tile brushes*, which all derive from an abstract TileBrush base class. A tile brush fills the target area with a repeating pattern. Depending on which tile brush you choose to use, the source of the pattern can be any Drawing, Image, or Visual.

All three brushes act identically except for the type that they operate on. Therefore, the following section examines the main functionality of all tile brushes using DrawingBrush as an example. Then we'll briefly look at the other two tile brushes: ImageBrush and VisualBrush.

DrawingBrush

Hosting a Drawing in a DrawingBrush is just like hosting one in a DrawingImage. The following XAML uses the ghost DrawingGroup from Listing 11.1 and sets it as a DrawingImage's Drawing to be used as a the Background of a Window:

```
<Window xmlns="http://schemas.microsoft.com/winfx/2006/xaml/presentation"
        Title="DrawingBrush as the Background">
```

```
<Window.Background>
  <DrawingBrush>
    <DrawingBrush.Drawing>
      <DrawingGroup>
        The three GeometryDrawings from Listing 11.1…
      </DrawingGroup>
    </DrawingBrush.Drawing>
  </DrawingBrush>
</Window.Background>
</Window>
```

Figure 11.31 shows the result of doing this. Unlike `DrawingImage`, `DrawingBrush`'s default background is black instead of white.

By default, the `Drawing` is stretched to fill the area (or its bounding box if the area is nonrectangular), but this behavior can be adjusted with the `Stretch` property, which can be set to one of the `Stretch` enumeration values covered in Chapter 6, "Layout with Panels," with `Viewbox`. Figure 11.32 shows the effect of each of these values.

FIGURE 11.31   The default appearance of a DrawingBrush background containing the ghost Drawing.

When `Stretch` is set to a value other than `Fill`, the `Drawing` is centered both horizontally and vertically. But this behavior can also be customized by setting `AlignmentX` to `Left`, `Center`, or `Right` and `AlignmentY` to `Top`, `Center`, or `Bottom`.

The most interesting part of `DrawingBrush`, and the reason it's called a tile brush, is its `TileMode` property. If you set it to `Tile` rather than its default value of `None`, the `Drawing` can repeat itself indefinitely in both directions. For this to work, however, you must specify a `Rect` for the first "tile" to occupy. This is done with `DrawingBrush`'s `Viewport` property. Figure 11.33 demonstrates the effect of setting `Viewport` to a few different `Rect` values (shown with the *x,y,width,height* syntax supported by `Rect`'s type converter). The incredible thing about the third `Window` in Figure 11.33 is that you can zoom in (using `Magnifier` on Windows Vista or later) and see each ghost `Drawing` in full fidelity!

Just like with some of the gradient brush properties, the units of `Viewport` are relative to the bounding box by default. This enables you to effectively specify how many tiles you want horizontally and how many you want vertically. But you can also switch `Viewport` to use absolute coordinates by changing the value of `ViewportUnits` (a property of the familiar `BrushMappingMode` type).

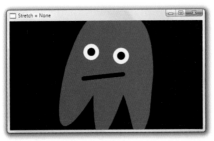

None

Fill (default)

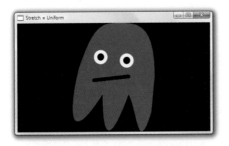

Uniform

UniformToFill

FIGURE 11.32   Applying different Stretch values to a DrawingBrush.

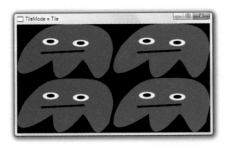

Viewport = 0, 0, 0.5, 0.5

Viewport = 0, 0, 0.1, 0.2

Viewport = 0, 0, 0.02, 0.02

FIGURE 11.33   Different Viewport values with TileMode=Tile and Stretch=Fill.

The `TileMode` enumeration used by the `TileMode` property has more values than just `Tile` and `None`, however. It supports three more values that flip tiles in different ways:

▶ **FlipX** flips the tiles in every other column horizontally.

▶ **FlipY** flips the tiles in every other row vertically.

▶ **FlipXY** does both of the above.

Figure 11.34 demonstrates these three settings. Although these settings might not be very interesting for the ghost `Drawing`, you could use them with certain types of `Drawings` to help create the illusion of a continuous fill.

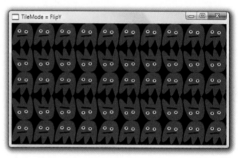

FlipX   FlipY

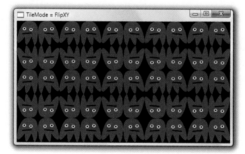

FlipXY

FIGURE 11.34   The three "Flip" settings for `TileMode`.

The final piece of customization is the `Viewbox` property, which enables you to specify a subset of the `Drawing` to use as the source of each tile (or the entire brush, if `TileMode` is set to `None`). `Viewbox` is a rectangle specified in bounding-box-relative units by default, just like `Viewport`. And a separate `ViewboxUnits` property can be set to make `Viewbox` use absolute coordinates, independently of the `ViewportUnits` setting.

Figure 11.35 sets the `DrawingBrush`'s `Viewbox` property to the top-left quadrant of the ghost `Drawing` by giving it the `Rect` value `0, 0, 0.5, 0.5`, and then mixes that setting with two different `TileModes`.

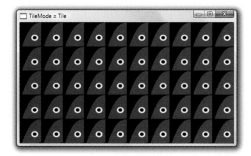
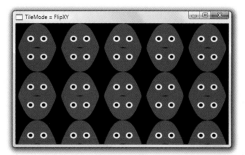

Tile   FlipXY

FIGURE 11.35   Setting Viewbox to retrieve only the top-left quadrant of the drawing, used with two different TileModes.

As a final note on DrawingBrush, remember that its Drawing does not have to be a GeometryDrawing. It could be a VideoDrawing, for example!

ImageBrush

ImageBrush is identical to DrawingBrush, except it has an ImageSource property of type ImageSource rather than a Drawing property of type Drawing. It is meant to hold bitmap content rather than vector content. (That said, with the existence of DrawingImage and ImageDrawing discussed earlier in the chapter, you can make DrawingBrush contain bitmap content and ImageBrush contain vector content!)

The following XAML uses an ImageBrush as the Background of a Window. The bitmap content comes from the Winter Leaves.jpg file that ships with Windows Vista:

```
<Window xmlns="http://schemas.microsoft.com/winfx/2006/xaml/presentation"
        Title="ImageBrush with TileMode = FlipXY">
<Window.Background>
  <ImageBrush TileMode="FlipXY" Viewport="0,0,0.1,0.2">
  <ImageBrush.ImageSource>
    <BitmapImage UriSource="C:\Users\Public\Pictures\Sample Pictures\Winter
      Leaves.jpg"/>
  </ImageBrush.ImageSource>
  </ImageBrush>
</Window.Background>
</Window>
```

The resulting Window is shown in Figure 11.36.

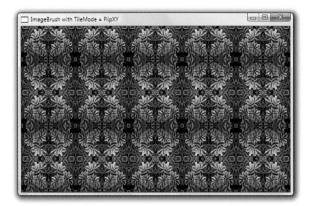

FIGURE 11.36   The `ImageBrush` Background, using `TileMode=FlipXY` to create an interesting pattern.

VisualBrush

`VisualBrush` is also identical to `DrawingBrush`, except it has a `Visual` property of type `Visual` instead of a `Drawing` property of type `Drawing`. The power to paint with *any* `Visual` however, even `FrameworkElements` like `Buttons` and `TextBoxes`, makes `VisualBrush` very unique and powerful.

The following XAML paints a `Window`'s `Background` with a `VisualBrush` containing a simple `Button`. The rendered result is shown in Figure 11.37.

```
<Window xmlns="http://schemas.microsoft.com/winfx/2006/xaml/presentation"
        Title="ImageBrush with TileMode = FlipXY">
<Window.Background>
  <VisualBrush TileMode="FlipXY" Viewport="0,0,0.5,0.5">
  <VisualBrush.Visual>
    <Button>OK</Button>
  </VisualBrush.Visual>
  </VisualBrush>
</Window.Background>
</Window>
```

Note that the `Button` inside this `VisualBrush` can never be clicked. `VisualBrush` simply paints the appearance of `Visuals`; there is no interactivity within the area that is painted.

Rather than embedding elements directly in a `VisualBrush`, it's more common to set its `Visual` to an instance of a `UIElement` already on the screen and available for user interaction. This

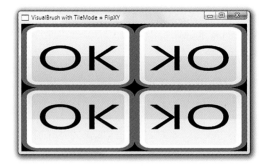

FIGURE 11.37   The `VisualBrush` Background based on a `Button`.

could be done with procedural code or a simple `Binding`, as demonstrated in the following `Window`:

```xml
<Window xmlns="http://schemas.microsoft.com/winfx/2006/xaml/presentation"
  xmlns:x="http://schemas.microsoft.com/winfx/2006/xaml"
  Title="VisualBrush with TileMode = FlipXY">
  <DockPanel>
    <StackPanel Margin="10" x:Name="stackPanel">
      <Button>Button</Button>
      <CheckBox>CheckBox</CheckBox>
    </StackPanel>
    <Rectangle>
    <Rectangle.Fill>
      <VisualBrush TileMode="FlipXY" Viewport="0,0,0.5,0.5"
        Visual="{Binding ElementName=stackPanel}"/>
    </Rectangle.Fill>
    </Rectangle>
  </DockPanel>
</Window>
```

This `Window` produces the result in Figure 11.38. The entire `StackPanel` docked on the left is used as the `VisualBrush`'s `Visual`. The `VisualBrush` is applied as the `Fill` of a `Rectangle` that occupies the remainder of the `Window`. The "real" instances of the `Button` and `CheckBox` on the left support interactivity, but the visual copies do not. The visual copies do, however, reflect any changes to the `Button` and `CheckBox` visuals as they happen.

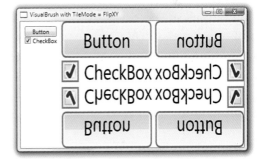

FIGURE 11.38   Copying the appearance of live `Visuals` inside a `VisualBrush`.

These examples probably haven't done a good job at convincing you that there can actually be a reasonable use for such an unusual `Brush`! But there are some good ones. Applications can leverage `VisualBrush` to provide "live previews" of inner content (perhaps documents) in a smaller, browseable form. Internet Explorer does this with its Quick Tabs view (in versions 7 or later). In addition, Windows Vista leverages the technology underlying `VisualBrush` to create its live preview of each window when you hover over a taskbar item, or switch between windows using Alt+Tab or Windows+Tab.

Another popular use of `VisualBrush` is the creation of a live reflection effect. The following `Window` creates a simple reflection below a `TextBox`, using essentially the same technique employed in the previous XAML snippet:

```xml
<Window xmlns="http://schemas.microsoft.com/winfx/2006/xaml/presentation"
  xmlns:x="http://schemas.microsoft.com/winfx/2006/xaml"
```

```
    Title="TextBox with Reflection" Width="500" Height="200" Background="DarkGreen">
  <StackPanel Margin="40">
    <TextBox x:Name="textBox" FontSize="30"/>
    <Rectangle Height="{Binding ElementName=textBox, Path=ActualHeight}"
      Width="{Binding ElementName=textBox, Path=ActualWidth}">
    <Rectangle.Fill>
      <VisualBrush Visual="{Binding ElementName=textBox}"/>
    </Rectangle.Fill>
    <Rectangle.LayoutTransform>
      <ScaleTransform ScaleY="-0.75"/>
    </Rectangle.LayoutTransform>
    </Rectangle>
  </StackPanel>
</Window>
```

The Rectangle containing the
VisualBrush reflection is flipped upside
down by using a ScaleTransform. But
rather than setting ScaleY to -1, the
value of -0.75 is used to give the reflection a little bit of perspective. The result
is shown in Figure 11.39.

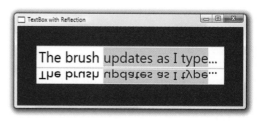

This effect isn't quite satisfactory,
however, because the reflection is too
crisp and clear. We can improve this
with an opacity mask, covered in the next section.

FIGURE 11.39   A simple live reflection
effect.

Brushes as Opacity Masks

All Visual subclasses (and DrawingGroup) have an Opacity property that affects the entire
object evenly, but they also have an OpacityMask that can be used to apply custom
opacity effects. OpacityMask can be set to any Brush, and that Brush's alpha channel is
used to determine which parts of the object should be opaque, which parts should be
transparent, and which parts should be somewhere in-between.

The alpha channel used by OpacityMask can come from the colors in a color brush, from
drawings in a DrawingBrush, from images in an ImageBrush (for example, PNG transparency), and so on. The following Window uses a LinearGradientBrush as an OpacityMask
to create the obnoxious-looking Button in Figure 11.40:

```
<Window xmlns="http://schemas.microsoft.com/winfx/2006/xaml/presentation"
  Title="LinearGradientBrush OpacityMask">
<Window.Background>
  <LinearGradientBrush>
    <GradientStop Offset="0" Color="Orange"/>
    <GradientStop Offset="1" Color="Brown"/>
```

```
    </LinearGradientBrush>
</Window.Background>
  <Button Margin="40" FontSize="80">OK
  <Button.OpacityMask>
    <LinearGradientBrush EndPoint="0.1,0.1" SpreadMethod="Reflect">
      <GradientStop Offset="0" Color="Blue"/>
      <GradientStop Offset="1" Color="Transparent"/>
    </LinearGradientBrush>
  </Button.OpacityMask>
  </Button>
</Window>
```

The LinearGradientBrush used for the OpacityMask defines a repetitive gradient between blue and transparent, but the blue color is immaterial. All that matters is that it's a completely opaque color.

Figure 11.41 shows what this same Button would look like if the OpacityMask were instead set to a DrawingBrush containing the familiar ghost Drawing. On the left, the ghost's body is filled with a completely opaque color. The result is no different than what you could accomplish with clip-

FIGURE 11.40   A Button with a striped OpacityMask, courtesy of a LinearGradientBrush.

ping the Button to the ghost body's Geometry. On the right, the ghost's body is filled with a translucent color (but its eyes and mouth are still opaque). This gives a result that you could not achieve with clipping alone.

FIGURE 11.41   Using the ghost as DrawingBrush OpacityMask, with two different body fill colors.

With the features for creating a gadget-style application (setting `AllowsTransparency` to true and so on) described in Chapter 7, "Structuring and Deploying an Application," you can even apply an `OpacityMask` to the top-level `Window`!

As promised, here's how you could use `OpacityMask` to improve the live reflection effect from Figure 11.39:

```xml
<Window xmlns="http://schemas.microsoft.com/winfx/2006/xaml/presentation"
  xmlns:x="http://schemas.microsoft.com/winfx/2006/xaml"
  Title="TextBox with Reflection" Width="500" Height="200" Background="DarkGreen">
  <StackPanel Margin="40">
    <TextBox x:Name="textBox" FontSize="30"/>
    <Rectangle Height="{Binding ElementName=textBox, Path=ActualHeight}"
      Width="{Binding ElementName=textBox, Path=ActualWidth}">
    <Rectangle.Fill>
      <VisualBrush Visual="{Binding ElementName=textBox}"/>
    </Rectangle.Fill>
    <Rectangle.LayoutTransform>
      <ScaleTransform ScaleY="-0.75"/>
    </Rectangle.LayoutTransform>
    <Rectangle.OpacityMask>
      <LinearGradientBrush EndPoint="0,1">
        <GradientStop Offset="0" Color="Transparent"/>
        <GradientStop Offset="1" Color="#77000000"/>
      </LinearGradientBrush>
    </Rectangle.OpacityMask>
    </Rectangle>
  </StackPanel>
</Window>
```

The result of this change, which is undoubtedly the most tasteful use of `OpacityMask` in this chapter, is shown in Figure 11.42.

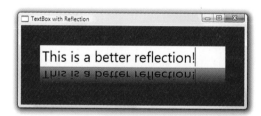

FIGURE 11.42   The live reflection effect, enhanced with an `OpacityMask`.

Bitmap Effects

WPF has five special visual effects built in to the `System.Windows.Media.Effects` namespace that can be applied to any `UIElement`, `DrawingGroup`, and a few other types (such as `Viewport3DVisual`, covered in the next chapter). These effects are called *bitmap effects* because the effect is applied to the rendered rasterized output as a postprocessing step.

FIGURE 11.43   The five bitmap effects in the `System.Windows.Media.Effects` namespace applied to a `Button`.

Figure 11.43 shows each of the five built-in bitmap effects applied to a simple `Button`: `BevelBitmapEffect`, `BlurBitmapEffect`, `DropShadowBitmapEffect`, `EmbossBitmapEffect`, and `OuterGlowBitmapEffect`.

To apply a bitmap effect to a relevant object, simply set its `BitmapEffect` property to an instance of one of the `BitmapEffect`-derived classes. For example, the first `Button` in Figure 11.43 was created as follows:

```
<Button Width="100">
  OK
<Button.BitmapEffect>
  <BevelBitmapEffect/>
</Button.BitmapEffect>
</Button>
```

The bevel effect is not very satisfactory on a `Button` because it subtly affects the edges of the inner `TextBlock` as well. Blurring by itself might seem like an odd effect, but it could be part of an animation that brings elements into or out of focus. Or, it could be used as a visually interesting way to temporarily disable pieces of UI. Blurring would also be a great addition to the reflection effect in Figure 11.42, but unfortunately applying a bitmap effect to the lower `Rectangle` prevents its `VisualBrush` from refreshing automatically! (This is simply a bug that should be fixed in a future version of WPF.) The bump mapping done by the emboss effect generally doesn't make much sense for typical controls like `Button` (at least with their default control templates), but it provides interesting results on `Images`.

Figure 11.44 shows three of the effects applied to an `Image` (which is nonrectangular because it uses PNG transparency). In this case, the bevel effect doesn't work very well, but the drop shadow looks slick. The emboss effect makes an already frightening photo downright terrifying.

FIGURE 11.44   `BevelBitmapEffect`, `DropShadowBitmapEffect`, and `EmbossBitmapEffect` applied to an `Image`.

Much like `TransformGroup`, `DrawingGroup`, and `GeometryGroup` provide the ability to compose multiple Transforms, Drawings, and geometries, WPF defines a `BitmapEffectGroup` class that groups together multiple bitmap effects. It derives from `BitmapEffect` so you can plug in a collection of effects wherever you set the `BitmapEffect` property. For example, the following `Button` uses three effects simultaneously, which is pictured in Figure 11.45:

```
<Button Width="100">
  Three Effects
<Button.BitmapEffect>
  <BitmapEffectGroup>
    <OuterGlowBitmapEffect/>
    <DropShadowBitmapEffect/>
    <BevelBitmapEffect/>
  </BitmapEffectGroup>
</Button.BitmapEffect>
</Button>
```

You can even apply the same effect multiple times to magnify its impact. The following `Button` has six `DropShadowBitmapEffect`s, causing the huge shadow shown in Figure 11.46:

```
<Button Width="100">
  6 DropShadows
<Button.BitmapEffect>
  <BitmapEffectGroup>
    <DropShadowBitmapEffect/>
```

> ## DIGGING DEEPER
>
> ### Custom Bitmap Effects
>
> WPF enables you to write your own bitmap effects, but only via a set of low-level unmanaged APIs defined in `mileffects.h` (and `mileffects.idl`). The Windows SDK contains reference documentation and a sample for building a custom effect with these APIs.

Three Effects

FIGURE 11.45   Three effects— `BevelBitmapEffect`, `DropShadowBitmap-Effect`, and `OuterGlowBitmapEffect`— applied simultaneously to a `Button`.

```
    <DropShadowBitmapEffect/>
    <DropShadowBitmapEffect/>
    <DropShadowBitmapEffect/>
    <DropShadowBitmapEffect/>
    <DropShadowBitmapEffect/>
  </BitmapEffectGroup>
</Button.BitmapEffect>
</Button>
```

FIGURE 11.46   Six DropShadowBitmap-Effects is about five too many!

WARNING

Use bitmap effects sparingly!

At least for version 3.0 of WPF, the use of bitmap effects can significantly degrade performance. That's because they are always rendered in software, and they actually render directly on the UI thread rather than the render thread! Their performance impact is proportional to the size of the item it is applied to. Therefore, it's best to use them only on small and static content.

The last four figures have all used the bitmap effects with their default settings. However, each class provides a handful of properties to customize their appearance. Table 11.3 summarizes these properties and their values.

TABLE 11.3   Properties on the Bitmap Effects

Effect	Properties	Default Values
BevelBitmapEffect	BevelWidth: A nonnegative double	5
	EdgeProfile: BulgedUp, CurvedIn, CurvedOut, or Linear	Linear
	LightAngle: A double representing an angle (in degrees)	135
	Relief: A double between 0 (flat) and 1 (tall)	0.3
	Smoothness: A double between 0 (crisp) and 1 (blurry)	0.2
BlurBitmapEffect	Radius: A nonnegative double	5
	KernelType: Box or Gaussian	Gaussian
DropShadowBitmapEffect	Color: Any Color (even one with a nonopaque alpha)	Black
	Direction: A double representing an angle (in degrees)	315
	Noise: A double between 0 (smooth) and 1 (grainy)	0
	Opacity: A double between 0 (transparent) and 1 (opaque)	1

TABLE 11.3   Continued

Effect	Properties	Default Values
	ShadowDepth: A nonnegative double	5
	Softness: A double between 0 (crisp) and 1 (blurry)	0.5
EmbossBitmapEffect	LightAngle: A double representing an angle (in degrees)	45
	Relief: A double between 0 and 1	0.44
OuterGlowBitmapEffect	GlowColor: Any Color (even one with a nonopaque alpha)	Gold
	GlowSize: A nonnegative double	5
	Noise: A double between 0 (smooth) and 1 (grainy)	0
	Opacity: A double between 0 (transparent) and 1 (opaque)	1

Figure 11.47 shows some of the effects that can be accomplished with a few of these properties set to nondefault values, based on the following XAML:

```
<StackPanel>
  <Button Width="100">
    BulgedUp Bevel
  <Button.BitmapEffect>
    <BevelBitmapEffect EdgeProfile="BulgedUp"/>
  </Button.BitmapEffect>
  </Button>
  <Button Width="100" Margin="20">
    Big, Noisy Glow
  <Button.BitmapEffect>
    <OuterGlowBitmapEffect GlowSize="20" Noise="1" GlowColor="Red"/>
  </Button.BitmapEffect>
  </Button>
  <TextBlock FontSize="20" HorizontalAlignment="Center"
    FontFamily="Segoe Print" Foreground="White">
    Small Glow
  <TextBlock.BitmapEffect>
    <OuterGlowBitmapEffect GlowColor="Black" GlowSize="1"/>
  </TextBlock.BitmapEffect>
  </TextBlock>
</StackPanel>
```

FIGURE 11.47   Setting a few properties can drastically alter the appearance of bitmap effects.

Conclusion

Although it might have initially seemed like a stretch to include a chapter about 2D graphics in a section about "rich media," you hopefully now understand just how rich WPF's 2D support is. Unlike the 2D drawing support in previous Windows technologies, WPF gives you the power of DirectX (including hardware acceleration and antialiasing) mixed with the ease-of-use of a retained-mode graphics system.

This chapter focused on vector graphics, but it also highlighted where bitmap-based images fit seamlessly into the same picture. You've also seen the first few hints of video support, which is covered further in Chapter 14.

As with many features in WPF, a big part of the power of 2D graphics comes from the tight integration with the rest of WPF. The same drawing primitives used to create lines, shapes, and ghosts are the same ones used to create `Buttons`, `Menus`, and `ListBoxes`. In the next chapter, we'll see how to expand on this support to take WPF into the third dimension.

The 3D APIs in Windows Presentation Foundation were designed to be as approachable and easy to use as other parts of the .NET Framework. Because 3D is a truly integrated part of the WPF platform, many concepts are shared and reused from 2D graphics and elsewhere. This significantly reduces the learning curve for 2D developers approaching 3D for the first time because the 3D APIs often follow familiar patterns and conventions. This makes WPF an excellent tool for learning about 3D graphics.

This chapter focuses primarily on the aspects of the APIs which are unique to 3D, but it is important to remember that much of the power of the 3D features comes from deep integration with the rest of the platform. This integration spans everything from UI remoting, to printing, to running in partial-trust web applications.

Like 2D, the 3D features are available from both procedural code and XAML. To display a 3D scene in WPF, you build a graph of objects similar to how you build 2D artwork out of Shapes or Drawings. Once you have described your scene, the system takes care of invalidation and repainting on your behalf. All the features of the property engine, such as data binding and animation, work identically with 3D objects.

3D content is not constrained to a box. Scenes contained within a Viewport3D are composed seamlessly with other UI elements in your application and can be included in templates and ItemsControls. Likewise, 2D media such as video, Drawings, and Visuals can be displayed on the surfaces of 3D models. Services such as hit testing automatically continue into the 3D portions of the Visual tree.

This chapter has three purposes. First, it is an introduction to 3D graphics for developers who have no prior experience with 3D. Second, it is a reference for the 3D APIs in WPF. Third, it is a road map for experienced 3D developers familiar with other platforms like DirectX or who need to write tools that interoperate with WPF.

Getting Started with 3D Graphics

The purpose of 3D graphics is to produce 2D images from 3D models suitable for display-ing on an output device such as your computer screen. Creating images from 3D models is a different paradigm than most 2D developers are used to. When working in two dimensions, you usually draw the exact shape that you want using absolute coordinates. If you want a rectangle at (50,75) that is 100 units wide by 30 units tall, you typically create a `Rectangle` element (or a `GeometryDrawing` with a `RectangleGeometry` that has the corresponding bounds). Consider the house drawn in Listing 12.1 using the 2D `Drawing` classes. The output is shown in Figure 12.1.

LISTING 12.1   Drawing a House with 2D Drawings

```
<Page Background="Black"
  xmlns="http://schemas.microsoft.com/winfx/2006/xaml/presentation"
  xmlns:x="http://schemas.microsoft.com/winfx/2006/xaml">
  <Image>
  <Image.Source>
    <DrawingImage>
    <DrawingImage.Drawing>
      <DrawingGroup x:Name="House">
        <GeometryDrawing x:Name="Front" Brush="Red"
          Geometry="M0,260 L0,600 L110,670 L110,500 L190,550 L190,710 L300,775
            L300,430 L150,175"/>
        <GeometryDrawing x:Name="Side" Brush="Green"
          Geometry="M300,430 L300,775 L600,600 L600,260"/>
        <GeometryDrawing x:Name="Roof" Brush="Blue"
          Geometry="M150,175 L300,430 L600,260 L450,0"/>
      </DrawingGroup>
    </DrawingImage.Drawing>
    </DrawingImage>
  </Image.Source>
  </Image>
</Page>
```

Although the house might have been drawn to look somewhat three-dimensional, the data from which the image was produced is two-dimensional. From the system's point of view, you've drawn some flat 2D polygons. Although you can rotate the polygons within a 2D plane, you cannot turn the house to see the back or generate images of the inside of the house. No information exists for the parts of the house you cannot see. If you want to be able to create images of the house from multiple vantage points (without creating independent 2D drawings for each view), you have to give the system more information.

Listing 12.2 gives a preview of how the same image would be produced using Model3Ds instead of 2D Drawings. Although Listing 12.2 is longer than its 2D counterpart, you've gained a great deal of flexibility in what you can do with your house. Using your 3D model, you can now generate 2D images from any vantage point just by tweaking a few properties, as shown in Figure 12.2.

FIGURE 12.1   A simple house drawn using 2D Drawings.

LISTING 12.2   A House Drawn Using Model3Ds

```
<Page Background="Black"
  xmlns="http://schemas.microsoft.com/winfx/2006/xaml/presentation"
  xmlns:x="http://schemas.microsoft.com/winfx/2006/xaml">
  <Viewport3D>
  <Viewport3D.Camera>
    <OrthographicCamera Position="5,5,5" LookDirection="-1,-1,-1" Width="5"/>
  </Viewport3D.Camera>
  <Viewport3D.Children>
    <ModelVisual3D x:Name="Light">
    <ModelVisual3D.Content>
      <AmbientLight/>
    </ModelVisual3D.Content>
    </ModelVisual3D>
    <ModelVisual3D>
    <ModelVisual3D.Content>
      <Model3DGroup x:Name="House">

        <GeometryModel3D x:Name="Roof">
        <GeometryModel3D.Material>
          <DiffuseMaterial Brush="Blue"/>
        </GeometryModel3D.Material>
        <GeometryModel3D.Geometry>
          <MeshGeometry3D Positions="-1,1,1 0,2,1 0,2,-1 -1,1,-1 0,2,1 1,1,1
                          1,1,-1 0,2,-1"
                     TriangleIndices="0 1 2 0 2 3 4 5 6 4 6 7"/>
```

LISTING 12.2   Continued

```
</GeometryModel3D.Geometry>
</GeometryModel3D>

<GeometryModel3D x:Name="Sides">
<GeometryModel3D.Material>
  <DiffuseMaterial Brush="Green"/>
</GeometryModel3D.Material>
<GeometryModel3D.Geometry>
  <MeshGeometry3D Positions="-1,1,1 -1,1,-1 -1,-1,-1 -1,-1,1 1,1,-1
                             1,1,1 1,-1,1 1,-1,-1"
                  TriangleIndices="0 1 2 0 2 3 4 5 6 4 6 7"/>
</GeometryModel3D.Geometry>
</GeometryModel3D>

<GeometryModel3D x:Name="Ends">
<GeometryModel3D.Material>
  <DiffuseMaterial Brush="Red"/>
</GeometryModel3D.Material>
<GeometryModel3D.Geometry>
  <MeshGeometry3D
    Positions="-0.25,0,1 -1,1,1 -1,-1,1 -0.25,-1,1 -0.25,0,1
      -1,-1,1 0.25,0,1 1,-1,1 1,1,1 0.25,0,1 0.25,-1,1 1,-1,1
      1,1,1 0,2,1 -1,1,1 -1,1,1 -0.25,0,1 0.25,0,1 1,1,1 1,1,-1
      1,-1,-1 -1,-1,-1 -1,1,-1 1,1,-1 -1,1,-1 0,2,-1"
    TriangleIndices="0 1 2 3 4 5 6 7 8 9 10 11 12 13 14 15 16 17 15
      17 18 19 20 21 19 21 22 23 24 25"/>
</GeometryModel3D.Geometry>
</GeometryModel3D>

    </Model3DGroup>
  </ModelVisual3D.Content>
  </ModelVisual3D>
 </Viewport3D.Children>
 </Viewport3D>
</Page>
```

FIGURE 12.2   Several views of the house.

Listing 12.2 gives you a peek at most of the objects that are discussed in the remainder of the chapter. While many of the classes in the listing are new, they are straightforward extensions of the 2D types covered in Chapter 11. Table 12.1 shows how some of the 3D types map to their nearest 2D equivalent.

TABLE 12.1   Mapping 2D Types to the Nearest 3D Equivalent

2D Type	3D Type	Description
Drawing	Model3D	Drawings represent pieces of 2D content, such as clip art, which may be rendered by a Visual.
		Model3Ds represent pieces of 3D models, which may be rendered by a Visual3D.
Geometry	Geometry3D	A Geometry represents a 2D shape. Geometries can answer questions about bounds and intersections. By itself, a Geometry cannot be rendered. A GeometryDrawing combines a Geometry with a Brush to give it an appearance.
		A Geometry3D represents a 3D surface. To render a Geometry3D it is combined with a Material using a GeometryModel3D.
Visual	Visual3D	Visual is the base class for elements that render 2D content. This includes DrawingVisual and all FrameworkElements such as Controls and Shapes.
		Visual3D is the base class for elements that render 3D content. ModelVisual3D is a concrete Visual3D that renders 3D content represented as Model3Ds.
Transform	Transform3D	Subclasses of the 2D Transform class are used to position, rotate, and size 2D Drawings and Visuals.
		There were no Transform3Ds in Listing 12.2, but when you encounter the 3D transform objects later in this chapter you will see that they perform the same function for Model3Ds and Visual3Ds.

While most of the 3D objects are straightforward extensions of the 2D API, there are two concepts that are unique to 3D in WPF and which also appear in Listing 12.2.

▶ **Cameras**—To generate images of 3D models, you place a virtual Camera within the scene. Like a real camera, the position, orientation, and other properties of the Camera determine your view of the scene.

▶ **Materials & Lights**—In 2D, you use Brushes to specify the appearance of a filled Geometry. In 3D you also use Brushes, but there is an extra lighting step that influences the appearance of 3D surfaces.

As you will see in the upcoming sections, the Camera, Materials, and Lights all play important roles in enabling you to quickly render views of dynamic 3D scenes.

Cameras and Coordinate Systems

In the real world, what you see depends on where you stand, the direction you look, how you tilt your head, and so on. In WPF, you place a virtual Camera into your 3D scene to control what will appear in the Viewport3D. This is done by positioning and orienting the Camera in the world coordinate system (sometimes called *world space* for short). Figure 12.3 shows the 2D and 3D coordinate systems used by WPF.

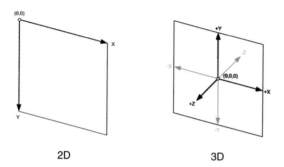

2D	3D

FIGURE 12.3   The 2D and 3D coordinate systems.

Besides the extra z-axis, a couple of additional differences exist between the 2D and 3D coordinate systems.

In 3D, the y-axis typically points up instead of down. Also, negative coordinates, which are rarely used in 2D, are quite common in 3D. Because of this, you usually consider the origin to be at the center of space as opposed to the top-left corner as you do in 2D. Of course, these are merely conventions and you are free to use transformations to map into whatever system is most convenient for you.

The two common Camera classes you will use, OrthographicCamera and PerspectiveCamera, expose a set of properties to position and orient your Camera in world space. The upcoming sections discuss these properties and how you can use them to control what part of the 3D scene is visible.

The Position Property

The Position property controls where the Camera is positioned in space. By moving the Camera, you can create different views of your scene. The Position property is of type Point3D. Point3Ds contain x, y, and z coordinates and define a location in a coordinate system. When rendering the model of the house, Listing 12.2 used the position (5,5,5):

```
<Viewport3D.Camera>
  <OrthographicCamera Position="5,5,5" LookDirection="-1,-1,-1" Width="5"/>
</Viewport3D.Camera>
```

DIGGING DEEPER

WPF Uses a Right-Handed Coordinate System

The *handedness* of a coordinate system refers to the relationship of the z-axis to the x- and y-axes. If the positive x- and y-axes are arranged as shown in Figure 12.4, there are two directions the z-axis could point. In a left-handed coordinate system, the positive z-axis points away from the viewer, as shown on the left. In a right-handed system, the positive z-axis points toward the viewer, as shown on the right.

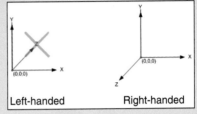

WPF standardized on a right-handed coordinate system. The right-handed coordinate system derives its name from the *right-hand rule*: If your index finger points in the direction of the positive x-axis and your middle finger points in the direction of the positive y-axis, your thumb indicates the direction of the positive z-axis, as shown in Figure 12.5.

FIGURE 12.4   Left-handed versus right-handed coordinate systems.

This is an easy, if not somewhat awkward, way to remember the relationship between the axes. Later in this chapter, you'll discover a different version of the right-hand rule to remember the winding order of triangles in a MeshGeometry3D.

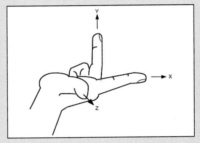

FIGURE 12.5   The right-hand rule.

This means that the Camera is positioned five units to the right on the x-axis, five units up on the y-axis, and five units forward on the z-axis. Looking at Figure 12.6, you can see that this locates the Camera above the house looking at what we will call the southeast side. (There is no standard connection between the axes and the cardinal directions, but you can assign one for your application for convenience.)

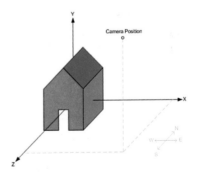

FIGURE 12.6   Camera positioned to view southeast side.

If you want to see the southwest side of the house, you would position the Camera at (-5,5,5). The new position is shown in Figure 12.7.

```
<Viewport3D.Camera>
  <OrthographicCamera Position="-5,5,5" LookDirection="-1,-1,-1" Width="5"/>
</Viewport3D.Camera>
```

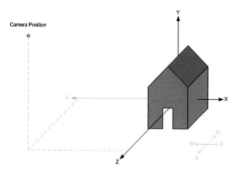

FIGURE 12.7   Camera positioned to view southwest side.

However, setting the Camera to this new position alone would not give you the desired view without adjusting the LookDirection. To use a physical analogy, this is like looking at your friend through the viewfinder of a camera and then taking 10 giant steps to the left. Unless you turn to face your friend again, you will now be taking a picture of the wall. You use the LookDirection property to control which direction the Camera is looking.

LookDirection

The LookDirection property specifies which direction the Camera is facing. LookDirection is of type Vector3D. Like Point3Ds, Vector3Ds also contain x, y, and z coordinates, but rather than specify a location in space, a Vector3D specifies a direction and a magnitude. The magnitude of a Vector3D is called its Length and is given by

$$\sqrt{x^2 + y^2 + z^2}$$

The Camera in Listing 12.2 uses a LookDirection of <-1,-1,-1>:

```
<Viewport3D.Camera>
  <OrthographicCamera Position="5,5,5" LookDirection="-1,-1,-1" Width="5"/>
</Viewport3D.Camera>
```

WARNING

Remember, `Cameras` have a blind spot!

Surfaces closer than the `Camera`'s `NearPlaneDistance` will be clipped. You need to be careful when setting the `Camera`'s `Position` that any objects you want to see are at least `NearPlaneDistance` units ahead of the `Camera` in the `LookDirection`. Figure 12.8 shows you what would happen if you move the `Camera` too close to the model of the house.

The purpose of a `Camera`'s `NearPlaneDistance` is to work around the limited floating point precision of the GPU's Z-Buffer. When the precision of the Z-Buffer is exhausted, a phenomenon known as *Z-fighting* occurs, in which the GPU is unable to determine which surfaces are nearer to the `Camera`. Figure 12.9 shows an example of the type of rendering artifacts Z-fighting causes. The pattern of the artifacts usually changes with the viewing angle.

Z-fighting is typically caused by attempting to render objects too close to the `Camera`'s `Position`. The `NearPlaneDistance` property of the `Camera` works around Z-fighting by clipping objects closer than a certain distance from the `Camera`. `NearPlaneDistance` defaults to 0.125, which is a good setting.

There are other, less common ways that Z-fighting may occur. One is attempting to render objects that are *really* far away from the `Camera`. There is a corresponding `FarPlaneDistance`, which can be used to work around this if it should occur, but, as it is rare, this property defaults to positive infinity.

FIGURE 12.8   House clipped by the Camera's Near Plane.

FIGURE 12.9   Z-Fighting Artifacts.

Finally, Z-fighting can occur when you render two surfaces that are nearly, but not quite on top of each other. The only way to fix this case is to move the surfaces sufficiently far apart, such that one is clearly closer to the `Camera` than the other. If two surfaces are exactly on top of each other, however, the rendering order is deterministic and Z-fighting will not occur. In this case, the surface rendered second will always appear on top.

The x, y, and z coordinates of this vector tell the camera to look downward toward the northwest as shown in Figure 12.10.

It was mentioned previously that if you moved the Position of the Camera to (-5,5,5), the house would no longer be visible. Figure 12.11 shows you why. Moving the Camera does not change the LookDirection, so the Camera is no longer facing the house in its new location.

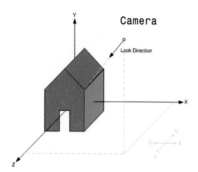

FIGURE 12.10　Camera looking downward toward the northwest.

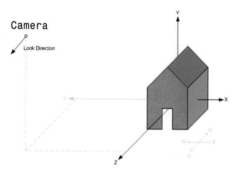

FIGURE 12.11　Moving the Camera does not change the LookDirection.

An easy way to figure out the required LookDirection for the Camera is to find a point in world space that you want to see and subtract it from the Camera's Position. In this case, the model of the house is roughly around the origin (0,0,0). Subtracting (-5,5,5) from (0,0,0) gives us a vector in the direction of <5,-5,-5>, as shown in Figure 12.12.

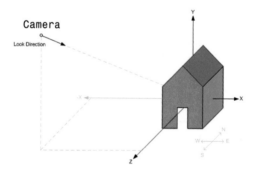

FIGURE 12.12　The new LookDirection.

Using this new LookDirection generates the image in Figure 12.13:

```xml
<Viewport3D.Camera>
  <OrthographicCamera Position="-5,5,5" LookDirection="5,-5,-5" Width="5"/>
</Viewport3D.Camera>
```

If you are moving the Camera a lot, it might make sense to write a small utility method to assign the new LookDirection for the Camera based on its Position and the point you want to look at:

```csharp
private void LookAt(ProjectionCamera camera, Point3D lookAtPoint)
{
  camera.LookDirection = lookAtPoint - camera.Position;
}
```

FIGURE 12.13   Viewing the other side of the house.

> **TIP**
>
> WPF APIs that take a Vector3D to indicate direction are only interested in the direction of the Vector3D, not the Length. A LookDirection of <1,-1,-1> produces an identical image to the one shown in Figure 12.13. If the Length of the Vector3D needs to be normalized for internal calculations, WPF does this for you automatically.
>
> In general, you only need to be concerned that Vector3Ds define a direction (that is, they are not the zero vector <0,0,0>), unless you are using them to calculate Point3Ds. When adding a Vector3D to a Point3D to find a new Point3D, the Length determines how far away the new Point3D will be. You should be aware that the Length of Vector3Ds influences the direction during linear interpolation. Specifically, Vector3DAnimation does not normalize the Vector3Ds first.

UpDirection

The LookDirection tells us which direction the Camera is facing, but this does not completely specify the Camera's orientation. You can still twist the Camera while keeping the LookDirection fixed on the same point in space, as shown in Figure 12.14. This is what you do with a physical camera to go from landscape to portrait orientation. You can use the UpDirection property to disambiguate this final component of the Camera's orientation.

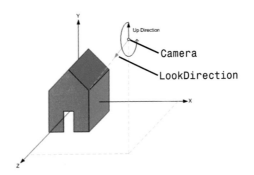

FIGURE 12.14   The UpDirection property.

The UpDirection property defaults to <0,1,0>. By specifying a different direction such as <1,0,0>, you can turn the Camera on its side. Figure 12.15 shows the image produced with this UpDirection.

```
<Viewport3D.Camera>
  <OrthographicCamera Position="5,5,5" LookDirection="-1,-1,-1"
    UpDirection="1,0,0" Width="5"/>
</Viewport3D.Camera>
```

FIGURE 12.15   Specifying the positive x-axis as the UpDirection.

In this section, you manipulated the Camera in the scene using the Position, UpDirection, and LookDirection properties. Although this is often the most convenient way to set up a static Camera in a scene, most scenarios that involve moving or rotating the Camera are more easily accomplished using the Camera.Transform property.

> **TIP**
>
> The Camera.Transform property is especially helpful if you want the Camera to follow an object moving through the scene as the same Transform3D can be applied to both the Camera and the object you want to follow.

The key advantage of the Camera.Transform property is that it enables the Camera to be positioned and animated like other 3D objects in the scene. Keep this in mind when Transform3Ds are discussed later in this chapter.

WARNING

Don't forget to transform the UpDirection!

If you are rotating the Camera around an object and the view abruptly flips over as you pass a certain spot, chances are that you forgot to adjust the UpDirection. The trouble happens if you move the LookDirection past the UpDirection, as shown in Figure 12.16.

As the Camera approaches the house, the LookDirection is adjusted so that you are looking downward. As the Camera goes over the roof, you would expect to be looking at the far side of the house upside down. However, because UpDirection is still pointing at the positive y-axis, the Camera instead spins in place right as you cross the center of the roof. Worse, when you are directly above the roof, the LookDirection and UpDirection are on the same line and the result is undefined. The correct way to rotate the Camera like this is to rotate the UpDirection along with the LookDirection, as illustrated in Figure 12.17.

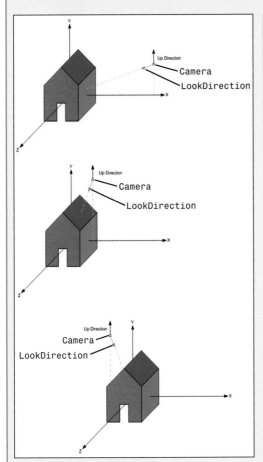

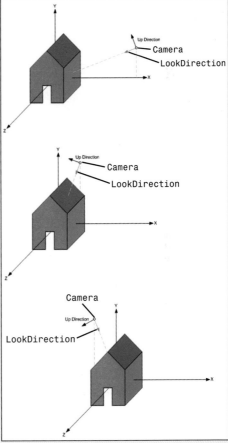

FIGURE 12.16   Camera passing over the house incorrectly.

FIGURE 12.17   UpDirection adjusted to preserve view as Camera passes house.

Orthographic Versus Perspective

WPF has two types of Cameras that most applications choose from. The PerspectiveCamera creates a realistic image in which objects farther from the Camera appear smaller than those closer to the Camera. This models the way humans see things in the real world. The other type of Camera, OrthographicCamera, is more useful for editing tools and some visualizations because objects appear the same size regardless of their distance from the Camera, allowing for precise measurement and analysis. Technical or manufacturing drawings frequently use OrthographicCameras. Figure 12.18 shows the same model rendered with an OrthographicCamera and a PerspectiveCamera.

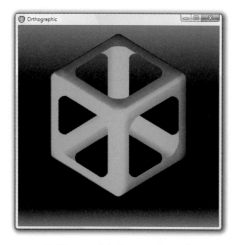

OrthographicCamera example   PerspectiveCamera example

FIGURE 12.18   OrthographicCamera and PerspectiveCamera examples

All Cameras work by projecting the 3D models in the scene onto an image plane that is then displayed to the user. With an OrthographicCamera, each point on the image plane shows you what is straight behind it, as shown in Figure 12.19. This enables you to view a section of space shaped like a rectangular right prism. The width of the viewable space is controlled by the OrthographicCamera.Width property. The height is computed automatically from the Viewport3D's bounding rectangle to preserve an aspect ratio of 1:1.

```
<Viewport3D.Camera>
  <OrthographicCamera Position="5,5,5" LookDirection="-1,-1,-1" Width="5"/>
</Viewport3D.Camera>
```

With a PerspectiveCamera, the width of the viewable area is not constant. As the distance from the Camera increases, more of the 3D world space is visible. This enables you to view a square frustum-shaped region of the scene, as shown in Figure 12.20. Because the viewable area expands as you get farther from the Camera, objects farther away appear smaller in a perspective projection. You control the rate of expansion with the FieldOfView property. In WPF, FieldOfView controls the horizontal angle at which the field of view expands.

```
<Viewport3D.Camera>
  <PerspectiveCamera Position="5,5,5" LookDirection="-1,-1,-1" FieldOfView="45"/>
</Viewport3D.Camera>
```

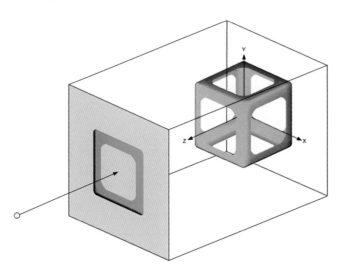

FIGURE 12.19   Orthographic projection.

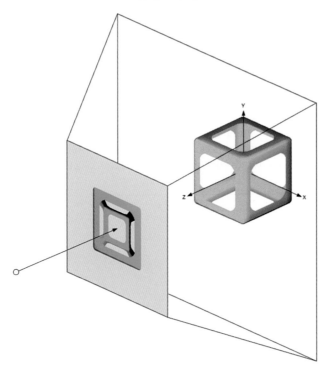

FIGURE 12.20   Perspective projection.

The `FieldOfView` property is comparable to the zoom lens on a physical camera. The `Width` property is the analogous concept for an `OrthographicCamera`. Small values for `Width` and `FieldOfView` "zoom in" on a small part of a 3D object. Larger values of `Width` and `FieldOfView` show more of the scene.

DIGGING DEEPER

MatrixCamera

WPF supports a third type of `Camera`, the `MatrixCamera`, which enables you to specify the view and projection transforms as `Matrix3Ds`. The mathematics behind projective transforms is a fascinating topic, but beyond the scope of this chapter.

`MatrixCamera` is provided to aid with porting code from other platforms like Direct3D. An advanced user can use `MatrixCamera` to create `Cameras` not directly supported by the other WPF `Camera` types, such as a frustum `Camera`.

The layout of the matrices used with a `MatrixCamera` is identical to what Direct3D uses. This makes it easy to port methods to construct view and projection matrices from utility libraries like D3DX. These matrices are well documented in the DirectX SDK.

Transform3Ds

As with `Transforms` in 2D, `Transform3Ds` allow you to position, rotate, and size 3D objects in space. `Transform3Ds` can be applied to `Model3Ds`, `ModelVisual3Ds`, and the `Camera`. This is done by setting their respective `Transform` properties. When you set the `Transform` property on a 3D object, you are mapping your object's coordinate space into a new coordinate space. This is no different than what happens when you position an element in 2D using the `Canvas.Left` and `Canvas.Top` properties.

Figure 12.21 displays the 2D drawing of a ghost from Chapter 11, "2D Graphics." All of the drawing instructions that make up the ghost are relative to the ghost's local coordinate system. Using a 2D `TranslateTransform`, you can change the ghost's frame of reference so that the point (0,0) in the ghost's coordinate system is no longer the same as point (0,0) in the container's coordinate system. This is shown on the right side of Figure 12.21.

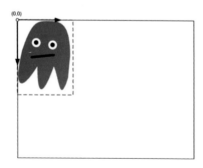

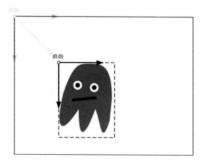

The ghost's coordinate system is the same as the container's.

The ghost's coordinate system is offset relative to the container's.

FIGURE 12.21   The ghost's coordinate system versus the container's coordinate system.

The TranslateTransform causes the ghost and any child Visuals it might contain to move on the screen, but as far as the ghost is concerned, it's business as usual. None of the ghost's drawing instructions are modified, just its frame of reference. This is actually how a Canvas moves elements around—by constructing a TranslateTransform for its contained Visuals behind the scenes.

The same principles apply to 3D transforms. In 3D, there is a top-level world coordinate system. To position, size, and orient 3D objects within the world coordinate system, you use the five subclasses of Transform3D:

▶ **TranslateTransform3D**—Offsets a 3D object relative to its container.

▶ **ScaleTransform3D**—Scales a 3D object relative to its container.

▶ **RotateTransform3D**—Rotates a 3D object relative to its container.

▶ **MatrixTransform3D**—Transforms a 3D object by a Matrix3D.

▶ **Transform3DGroup**—Contains a collection of Transform3Ds. The Transform3DGroup is itself a Transform3D and is used to apply multiple transforms to a 3D object.

This section applies these transforms to the simple model of a house shown at the beginning of this chapter. Listing 12.3 presents the same XAML as before except with two emphasized changes. First, we've added a transform (currently the identity transform which does nothing). Second, we've increased our Camera's Width so that we'll be able to see the effect of applying various transforms.

LISTING 12.3 Updates to the House Drawn Using Model3Ds

```
<Page Background="Black"
  xmlns="http://schemas.microsoft.com/winfx/2006/xaml/presentation"
  xmlns:x="http://schemas.microsoft.com/winfx/2006/xaml">
  <Viewport3D>
  <Viewport3D.Camera>
    <OrthographicCamera Position="5,5,5" LookDirection="-1,-1,-1" Width="10"/>
  </Viewport3D.Camera>
  <Viewport3D.Children>
    <ModelVisual3D x:Name="Light">
    <ModelVisual3D.Content>
      <AmbientLight/>
    </ModelVisual3D.Content>
    </ModelVisual3D>
    <ModelVisual3D>
    <ModelVisual3D.Transform>
      <x:Static Member="Transform3D.Identity"/>
    </ModelVisual3D.Transform>
    <ModelVisual3D.Content>
      <Model3DGroup x:Name="House">
```

LISTING 12.3   Continued

```
        <GeometryModel3D x:Name="Roof">
        <GeometryModel3D.Material>
          <DiffuseMaterial Brush="Blue"/>
        </GeometryModel3D.Material>
        <GeometryModel3D.Geometry>
          <MeshGeometry3D Positions="-1,1,1 0,2,1 0,2,-1 -1,1,-1 0,2,1 1,1,1
                          1,1,-1 0,2,-1"
                          TriangleIndices="0 1 2 0 2 3 4 5 6 4 6 7"/>
        </GeometryModel3D.Geometry>
        </GeometryModel3D>

        <GeometryModel3D x:Name="Sides">
        <GeometryModel3D.Material>
          <DiffuseMaterial Brush="Green"/>
        </GeometryModel3D.Material>
        <GeometryModel3D.Geometry>
          <MeshGeometry3D Positions="-1,1,1 -1,1,-1 -1,-1,-1 -1,-1,1 1,1,-1
                          1,1,1 1,-1,1 1,-1,-1"
                          TriangleIndices="0 1 2 0 2 3 4 5 6 4 6 7"/>
        </GeometryModel3D.Geometry>
        </GeometryModel3D>

        <GeometryModel3D x:Name="Ends">
        <GeometryModel3D.Material>
          <DiffuseMaterial Brush="Red"/>
        </GeometryModel3D.Material>
        <GeometryModel3D.Geometry>
          <MeshGeometry3D
            Positions="-0.25,0,1 -1,1,1 -1,-1,1 -0.25,-1,1 -0.25,0,1
              -1,-1,1 0.25,0,1 1,-1,1 1,1,1 0.25,0,1 0.25,-1,1 1,-1,1
              1,1,1 0,2,1 -1,1,1 -1,1,1 -0.25,0,1 0.25,0,1 1,1,1 1,1,-1
              1,-1,-1 -1,-1,-1 -1,1,-1 1,1,-1 -1,1,-1 0,2,-1"
            TriangleIndices="0 1 2 3 4 5 6 7 8 9 10 11 12 13 14 15 16 17 15
              17 18 19 20 21 19 21 22 23 24 25"/>
        </GeometryModel3D.Geometry>
        </GeometryModel3D>

      </Model3DGroup>
    </ModelVisual3D.Content>
    </ModelVisual3D>
  </Viewport3D.Children>
  </Viewport3D>
</Page>
```

TranslateTransform3Ds

TranslateTransform3D moves your object by an offset relative to its container. The offset is specified by the OffsetX, OffsetY, and OffsetZ properties. For example, setting the OffsetZ property to 3 slides the house forward on the z-axis by three units, as shown in Figure 12.22:

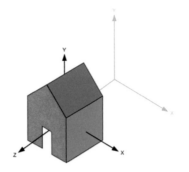

FIGURE 12.22   Translating the house forward three units on the z-axis.

```
<ModelVisual3D.Transform>
  <TranslateTransform3D OffsetZ="3"/>
</ModelVisual3D.Transform>
```

Note that you can make positioning 3D objects easier by constructing your models such that the origin is at a convenient location. For example, the house model has the origin roughly at the center. To move the house so that the center is at the point (3,2,1), you can translate it as follows:

```
<ModelVisual3D.Transform>
  <TranslateTransform3D OffsetX="3" OffsetY="2" OffsetZ="1"/>
</ModelVisual3D.Transform>
```

ScaleTransform3Ds

ScaleTransform3Ds are used to change the size of 3D objects. The scale factor is expressed in each dimension by the ScaleX, ScaleY, and ScaleZ properties. Because you can specify different scale factors for each dimension, it is possible to stretch an object using a ScaleTransform3D. For example, the following transform makes the house twice as wide along the x-axis, as shown in Figure 12.23:

FIGURE 12.23   Scaling the house along the x-axis.

```
<ModelVisual3D.Transform>
  <ScaleTransform3D ScaleX="2"/>
</ModelVisual3D.Transform>
```

To change the size of a 3D object while maintaining its proportions, set the ScaleX, ScaleY, and ScaleZ properties to the same value. This is called a *uniform scale*. A uniform scale factor of 2 doubles the size of an object. A uniform scale factor of 0.5 halves the size of an object.

> **WARNING**
>
> **Scale by 1, not 0, when you want to keep the original size!**
>
> To keep an object at its original size, you want a 1:1 scale—not a 1:0 scale. Setting ScaleX, ScaleY, or ScaleZ to 0 flattens the object in one or more directions. Flattening in one dimension can sometimes be useful, for example to flatten a sphere into a disk. But flattening in two dimensions collapses the 3D object into an invisible line, and flattening three dimensions reduces the object into an invisible point!

When you apply a scale, you are expanding and contracting space. This causes all points to move except for the center of the scale. By default, this center is the origin. In Figure 12.23, the house remained in place because the center of the house is the origin. If you move the house so that the center is at (0,0,3) and then scale it to half of the size, the center of the house would move to (1.5,0,0) as space contracted toward the origin. This is shown in the following XAML, and the results are shown in Figure 12.24:

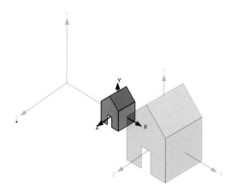

FIGURE 12.24   The house moves as space contracts toward the origin.

```xml
<ModelVisual3D.Transform>
  <Transform3DGroup>
    <TranslateTransform3D OffsetX="3"/>
    <ScaleTransform3D ScaleX="0.5" ScaleY="0.5" ScaleZ="0.5"/>
  </Transform3DGroup>
</ModelVisual3D.Transform>
```

One way to prevent the house from moving during the scale is to specify a different point in space to be the center of the scale. You do this by setting the CenterX, CenterY, and CenterZ properties. The following XAML illustrates how to do this by choosing the scale center to be the new center of the house. This causes the house to shrink "in place" as shown in Figure 12.25.

```xml
<ModelVisual3D.Transform>
  <Transform3DGroup>
    <TranslateTransform3D
      OffsetX="3"/>
```

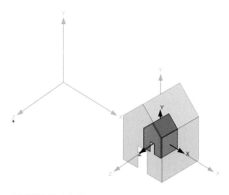

FIGURE 12.25   The scale is centered at the center of the house.

```
        <ScaleTransform3D ScaleX="0.5" ScaleY="0.5" ScaleZ="0.5" CenterX="3"/>
      </Transform3DGroup>
</ModelVisual3D.Transform>
```

Another way to keep the house from moving is to reorder the translate and scale transforms:

```
<ModelVisual3D.Transform>
   <Transform3DGroup>
      <ScaleTransform3D ScaleX="0.5" ScaleY="0.5" ScaleZ="0.5"/>
      <TranslateTransform3D OffsetX="3"/>
   </Transform3DGroup>
</ModelVisual3D.Transform>
```

If you perform the translation after the scale, the scale does not affect the offset of the translation. This is because the house is first shrunk while it is still at the origin. After the house is the desired size, it is then moved three units on the x-axis.

Looking at Figure 12.24, you might have noticed that as the scale factor approaches zero, the house moves toward the center of the scale. You might wonder what happens if the scale factor goes past zero to negative numbers. This causes the object to be reflected. Figure 12.26 shows how a negative ScaleZ causes the house model to be mirrored in the XY plane.

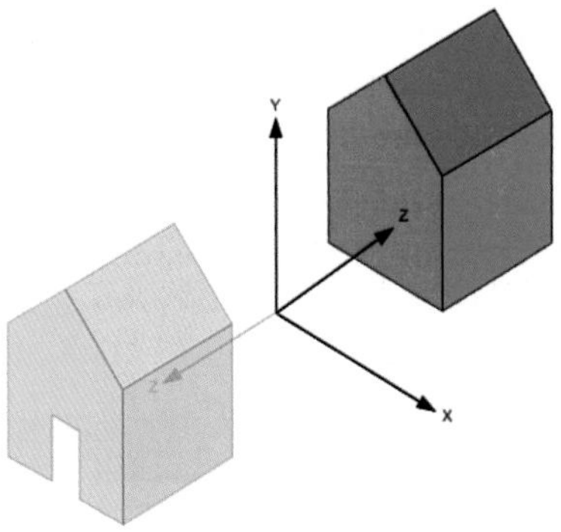

FIGURE 12.26   Reflecting along the z-axis.

```
<ModelVisual3D.Transform>
   <Transform3DGroup>
      <TranslateTransform3D OffsetZ="3"/>
      <ScaleTransform3D ScaleZ="-1"/>
   <Transform3DGroup>
</ModelVisual3D.Transform>
```

Notice that the reflection changes the direction of the z-axis. If you were to apply a translation after the scale, the OffsetZ property would now move the object in the opposite direction.

DIGGING DEEPER

Scaling About a Nonprinciple Axis

Under the covers, the CenterX, CenterY, and CenterZ properties work by first translating the object so that the specified point is at the origin. The scale is then performed and the object is translated back so the center point is at its original position.

You can use a similar technique to scale an object along a direction other than the x-, y-, or z-axes. First, use a RotationTransform3D to rotate the object so that the desired scale direction rests on one of the x-, y-, or z-axes. After performing the scale, apply the opposite rotation to restore the newly scaled object back to its original orientation.

RotateTransform3Ds

RotateTransform3Ds are used to rotate 3D objects in space. The rotation is described by a Rotation3D object. Rotation3D is an abstract class with two concrete implementations:

▶ **AxisAngleRotation3D**—Rotates the object around the specified Axis by the number of degrees given by the Angle property. This is usually the most convenient and human-readable way to describe 3D rotations.

▶ **QuaternionRotation3D**—Specifies the rotation as a Quaternion. Quaternions are a clever encoding of an Axis/Angle rotation that has some nice properties that make them popular with many 3D systems and tools.

FAQ

 Why doesn't WPF standardize on one way to specify rotations?

Early releases of WPF only had support for Quaternions, but Quaternions turned out to be difficult for 2D developers approaching 3D for the first time. A common mistake was to create a rotation from 0 to 360°, which resulted in no movement during a Rotation3DAnimation because it started and ended in the same orientation. Rotating an object more than 179.9999...° required either cumulative animations or multiple key frames.

Later releases added Axis/Angle rotations to make the trivial spinning in place animation easier for developers new to 3D. A simple spin could then be created by animating the Angle property with a DoubleAnimation. However, support for Quaternions was kept as an aid for people writing exporters for modeling packages that often represent rotations as Quaternions.

To support "layout-to-layout" animations where you might have defined one rotational configuration using Axis/Angle and another using Quaternions, WPF defines AxisAngleRotation3D and QuaternionRotation3D that derive from the common Rotation3D base class. You can animate between any two Rotation3Ds using a Rotation3DAnimation, which always takes the shortest path between the two orientations.

Continued

One form of rotation not directly supported by WPF is Euler angles. An Euler angle rotation takes the form of three angles that represent rotations about three axes. Which three axes, the order in which the rotations are applied, and the direction of the rotation are not standardized.

There is no `EulerAngleRotation3D` in version 3.0 of WPF, but you can construct an equivalent `Transform3D` by using a `Transform3DGroup` containing three `RotateTransform3D`s as in the following XAML. Note that you might need to tweak the axes to match the ordering you want.

```
<Transform3DGroup>
  <RotateTransform3D>
  <RotateTransform3D.Rotation>
    <AxisAngleRotation3D x:Name="RotateX" Axis="1,0,0" Angle="0"/>
  </RotateTransform3D.Rotation>
  </RotateTransform3D>
  <RotateTransform3D>
  <RotateTransform3D.Rotation>
    <AxisAngleRotation3D x:Name="RotateY" Axis="0,1,0" Angle="0"/>
  </RotateTransform3D.Rotation>
  </RotateTransform3D>
  <RotateTransform3D>
  <RotateTransform3D.Rotation>
    <AxisAngleRotation3D x:Name="RotateZ" Axis="0,0,1" Angle="0"/>
  </RotateTransform3D.Rotation>
  </RotateTransform3D>
</Transform3DGroup>
```

Figure 12.27 shows the result of rotating the house model 45° around the y-axis. In a right-handed coordinate system, a positive `Angle` of rotation rotates the coordinate space counterclockwise.

```
<ModelVisual3D.Transform>
  <RotateTransform3D>
  <RotateTransform3D.Rotation>
    <AxisAngleRotation3D Axis="0,1,0"
      Angle="45"/>
  </RotateTransform3D.Rotation>
  </RotateTransform3D>
</ModelVisual3D.Transform>
```

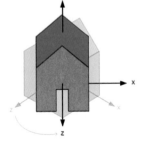

FIGURE 12.27   Rotation of 45° about positive y-axis.

Note that after the rotation, the x- and z-axes are pointing in new directions. If you had applied a translation prior to the rotation, you would have encountered behavior similar

to what was observed with the
`ScaleTransform3D`. Rotations rotate space
around a point. By default, that point is
at the origin. If your model is not
centered at the point of rotation, you
will find it has moved, as shown in
Figure 12.28.

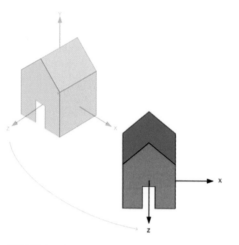

```
<ModelVisual3D.Transform>
  <Transform3DGroup>
    <TranslateTransform3D OffsetZ="3"/>
    <RotateTransform3D>
    <RotateTransform3D.Rotation>
      <AxisAngleRotation3D Axis="0,1,0"
        Angle="45"/>
    </RotateTransform3D.Rotation>
    </RotateTransform3D>
  </Transform3DGroup>
</ModelVisual3D.Transform>
```

FIGURE 12.28   Side effect of the rotation.

Again, if you want the house to spin "in place," one option is to change the center of
rotation using the `CenterX`, `CenterY`, and `CenterZ` properties:

```
<ModelVisual3D.Transform>
  <Transform3DGroup>
    <TranslateTransform3D OffsetZ="3"/>
    <RotateTransform3D CenterZ="3">
    <RotateTransform3D.Rotation>
      <AxisAngleRotation3D Axis="0,1,0" Angle="45"/>
    </RotateTransform3D.Rotation>
    </RotateTransform3D>
  </Transform3DGroup>
</ModelVisual3D.Transform>
```

Another way to work around this is to reorder the translate and rotate transforms. If you
perform the translation after the rotation, the rotation does not affect the offset of the
translation:

```
<ModelVisual3D.Transform>
  <Transform3DGroup>
    <RotateTransform3D>
    <RotateTransform3D.Rotation>
      <AxisAngleRotation3D Axis="0,1,0" Angle="45"/>
    </RotateTransform3D.Rotation>
    </RotateTransform3D>
    <TranslateTransform3D OffsetZ="3"/>
  </Transform3DGroup>
</ModelVisual3D.Transform>
```

Combining `Transform3Ds`

Unlike in 2D where the common case is to apply just a translation, the common case in 3D is to apply three transforms: scale, rotate, and translate (generally in that order). To apply multiple transforms, use a `Transform3DGroup`. The following XAML shows the typical usage of a `Transform3DGroup`:

```
<Transform3DGroup>
  <ScaleTransform3D x:Name="Size" ScaleX="1" ScaleY="1" ScaleZ="1"/>
  <RotateTransform3D>
  <RotateTransform3D.Rotation>
    <AxisAngleRotation3D x:Name="Orientation" Axis="0,1,0" Angle="0"/>
  </RotateTransform3D.Rotation>
  </RotateTransform3D>
  <TranslateTransform3D x:Name="Position" OffsetX="0" OffsetY="0" OffsetZ="0"/>
</Transform3DGroup>
```

DIGGING DEEPER

`MatrixTransform3D`

There is a fifth type of `Transform3D` supported by WPF: the `MatrixTransform3D`. The `MatrixTransform3D` enables you to specify a projective 3D transform as a `Matrix3D`. Here *projective* refers to the fact that a `Matrix3D` is a full 4x4 matrix. This does not necessarily mean that you must specify a `Camera` style projection matrix, although you can. `MatrixTransform3Ds` are useful for defining transforms not directly supported by the other `Transform3D` objects, or for porting code which calculates transforms as matrices.

It is worth noting that any of the `Transform3D` objects can be converted to a `Matrix3D` via the `Value` property. This includes `Transform3DGroups`, so it is possible to collapse a graph of `Transform3Ds` into a single `MatrixTrasform3D`.

Model3Ds

`Model3Ds` are the building blocks out of which you build a 3D model for your scene. Multiple `Model3Ds` are often grouped together to make a single 3D model. The `Model3D` classes are analogous to the 2D `Drawing` classes. However, unlike in 2D where `Drawings` are one of many ways to add 2D content to a WPF application, `Model3Ds` are the *only* way to declare 3D content in the current version of WPF.

WPF includes three subclasses of `Model3D`:

► **`Light`**—Has several subclasses that emit light into the scene. It is often overlooked that `Lights` are, in fact, `Model3Ds`, which is very convenient for scenarios such as attaching the headlights to a car with a `Model3DGroup`.

► **`GeometryModel3D`**—Renders a surface (described as a `Geometry3D`) with a given `Material`. `GeometryModel3D` is analogous to the 2D `GeometryDrawing`.

▶ **Model3DGroup**—Contains a collection of Model3Ds. The Model3DGroup is itself a Model3D and is often used to group multiple GeometryModel3Ds and Lights into a single 3D model.

You have already seen all of these classes in use in Listings 12.2 and 12.3, which rendered the simple house.

TIP

Entering XAML by hand is very educational and might be useful for creating simple models or "stand-in" art such as cubes, but it's not a good long-term strategy for creating 3D models.

Just as most bitmaps are created in a paint program, most 3D models are created using modeling software. Those that are not modeled in an application are usually generated procedurally.

When you need shapes more complex than planes and cubes, you will want to find a 3D modeling program with a XAML exporter. At the time of this writing, third-party exporters for the most popular 3D modeling packages are beginning to appear, including some free packages. There are also 3D modeling programs like Zam3D, which are explicitly targeted at WPF and speak XAML natively. There are pointers to tools and exporters in the appendix, "Helpful Tools."

Lights

Lighting is one of the concepts unique to 3D in WPF. In 2D, the colors that appear from the screen usually come directly from the Brush or Pen used. In 3D, there is an extra lighting step, which dynamically calculates the shading of the 3D objects depending on their proximity to light sources in the scene. Dynamic lighting makes it far easier to create and animate realistic looking scenes.

There are three components to lighting: Light objects, which emit light into the scene, Materials, which reflect the light back to the Camera, and the geometry of the model, which determines the angles involved. This section introduces the various Light types supported by WPF:

▶ **DirectionalLight**—Casts parallel rays into the scene from an origin at infinity. DirectionalLights approximate a far-away light source such as the sun.

▶ **PointLight**—Radiates light uniformly in all directions from a point in the scene. The intensity of the light attenuates as distance from the point increases. PointLights approximate unfocused light sources such as light bulbs.

▶ **SpotLight**—Emits a cone of light from a point in the scene. Like a PointLight, the intensity of the light attenuates as distance from the point increases. SpotLights approximate focused light sources such as the beam of a flashlight.

► **AmbientLight**—Lights every surface uniformly. Bright AmbientLights create flat-looking images because of lack of shading, but a low intensity AmbientLight approximates the effect of light that has been scattered by reflecting between diffuse surfaces in the scene.

You might have noticed that each of the previous descriptions contains the word "approximate." It's important to understand the goal of lighting in real-time graphics systems such as WPF is not to produce an accurate physical simulation of the way light behaves in the real world. To achieve real-time frame rates, graphics systems use clever tricks and rough estimations. Two common approximations are that surfaces do not block light (that is, they do not cast shadows) and lighting is only computed at the vertices of a mesh and then interpolated across the face. WPF uses both of these.

There is an element of artistry in creating a scene that appears to be realistically lit. To accomplish the desired effect, you might need to do unrealistic things such as adding extra light sources, baking lighting effects into your Materials, and so on. Don't feel bad about doing these things. Although the lighting and material APIs use real-world metaphors, they are just tools.

DirectionalLights

A DirectionalLight approximates a light source so far away that the rays have become parallel, such as light from the sun striking the Earth. Figure 12.29 illustrates the effect of the following DirectionalLight shining down on a sphere:

```
<DirectionalLight Direction="1,-1,-0.5" Color="White"/>
```

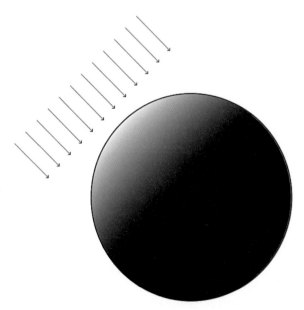

FIGURE 12.29   DirectionalLight shining on a sphere.

The direction of the light entering the scene is controlled by the `Direction` property. Of course, the `Transform` property inherited from `Model3D` also influences the direction of the light. The color of the `Light` is controlled by the `Color` property.

TIP

You can control the intensity of lights using the `Color` property. For example, #FFFFFF is a full-intensity white light. #808080 is a half-intensity white light. The alpha component of the light color has no effect.

Lights work additively. Two identical (same `Position`, same `Direction`, and so on) half-intensity lights yield the same effect as one full-intensity light.

Images created with a single `DirectionalLight` often look somewhat unnatural, and for good reason. In the real world, even when light enters a scene from a single direction (such as sunlight), it generally bounces around between objects in the scene causing some illumination. One way to approximate this is to add a low-intensity `AmbientLight`, covered later in this section.

PointLights

A `PointLight` approximates a light source that radiates light uniformly in all directions from a point in space, such as a naked light bulb. Unlike a `DirectionalLight`, the intensity of the light from a `PointLight` diminishes as distance from its position increases. Figure 12.30 illustrates the effect of the following `PointLight` illuminating a nearby sphere:

```
<PointLight Color="White" Position="2,2,2"
  ConstantAttenuation="0"
  LinearAttenuation="0"
  QuadraticAttenuation="0.125"/>
```

The location of a `PointLight` is specified by its `Position` property. The rate at which the light intensity attenuates as distance increases is controlled by a combination of the `ConstantAttenuation`, `LinearAttenuation`, and `QuadraticAttenuation` properties.

The formula for attenuation is

$$Attenuation = \frac{1}{\max(1,\ C + Ld + Qd^2)}$$

where C, L, and Q are `ConstantAttenuation`, `LinearAttenuation`, and `QuadraticAttenuation`, respectively. d is the distance between the `Light`'s position and the point being lit. You can derive some useful information from this formula. For example, C=1, L=0, Q=0 gives you a `PointLight` with constant intensity regardless of distance. However, these properties are usually set by trial and error.

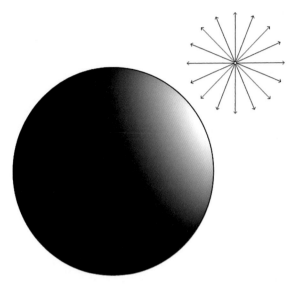

FIGURE 12.30   `PointLight` shining on a sphere.

`PointLights` also have a `Range` property, which specifies an abrupt cutoff radius outside of which the `PointLight` has no effect. `Range` is unrelated to the attenuation properties in that it does not affect the intensity of the light inside of the cutoff. The default value of `Range` is positive infinity.

SpotLights

`SpotLights` are `PointLights` that have been focused in to a beam. In the real world, light is focused using lenses and reflectors. In real-time computer graphics, this is approximated by limiting the emissions from a `PointLight` to a cone. Figure 12.31 shows how a `SpotLight` is just a `PointLight` whose rays have been constrained to an angular spread.

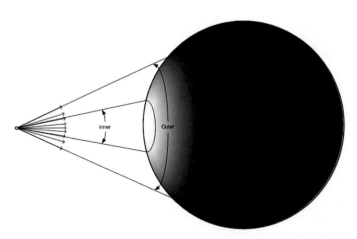

FIGURE 12.31   `SpotLight` shining on a sphere.

The `Direction` property specifies the direction in which the cone is pointing. The shape of the cone is controlled by the `OuterConeAngle` and `InnerConeAngle` properties. For example:

```
<SpotLight Color="White" Position="2,2,2"
  Direction="-1,-1,-1"
  InnerConeAngle="45"
  OuterConeAngle="90" />
```

FAQ

 Why doesn't my `SpotLight` or `PointLight` light my model?

The beginning of this section mentioned that real-time lighting uses clever tricks and rough estimations to achieve real-time frame rates. One of the approximations used by WPF is to only compute the intensity of lights at the vertices.

This approximation can sometimes causes surprising results with `PointLights` and `SpotLights`, as shown in Figure 12.32. The red circle shows where the light intersects the quadrilateral. This could be either the cone of a `SpotLight` or the lit sphere of a `PointLight` with limited `Range`. The surface remains unlit because the light did not extend to the vertices at the corners.

To work around this, the surface can be subdivided into a grid of quadrilaterals, as shown in Figure 12.33. Adding vertices increases the number of sample points at which lighting is computed and you will begin to see the effect of the `SpotLight`.

As you continue to subdivide the mesh, the detail increases. However, to create a perfect circle of light, you need to subdivide until you have about one vertex per pixel.

If you have a reasonably sized falloff area similar to the one shown in Figure 12.31, a small number of subdivisions usually does the trick. If you need a hard boundary between your lit and unlit areas, it might be better to bake the lighting into your `Material`. This can work especially well if the lighting in your scene is static.

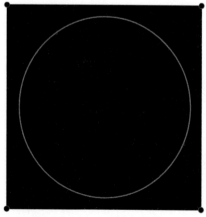

FIGURE 12.32   Light inside a quadrilateral.

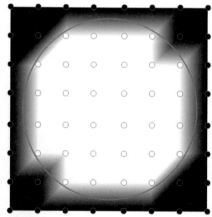

FIGURE 12.33   Light inside a subdivided grid.

The area inside the `InnerConeAngle` receives light that is the color and intensity specified by the `Color` property. The intensity of the light diminishes between the `InnerConeAngle` and `OuterConeAngle`. By adjusting the difference between the `InnerConeAngle` and `OuterConeAngle`, you can vary the size of the falloff area. By setting the `InnerConeAngle` to be equal or greater than the `OuterConeAngle`, you can create a `SpotLight` with no falloff area.

AmbientLights

`AmbientLights` are typically used to approximate the effect of light that has been scattered by reflecting off of multiple diffuse surfaces in the scene. Rays from an `AmbientLight` strike all surfaces from all directions, as shown in Figure 12.34.

FIGURE 12.34   `AmbientLight` shining on a sphere.

`AmbientLights` have only one interesting property, `Color`, which controls the intensity and the color of the light emitted. The `Transform` property inherited from `Model3D` has no effect on `AmbientLights`.

Adding a full intensity `AmbientLight` like the following to the scene usually produces a flat-looking image such as the one shown in Figure 12.35:

```
<AmbientLight Color="White"/>
```

However, a low-intensity `AmbientLight` added to the scene brightens the unlit areas in the scene to produce a softer image that resembles a scene which receives some natural lighting. Figure 12.36 shows a lit scene with and without the following `AmbientLight`:

```
<Model3DGroup>
  <DirectionalLight Direction="1,-1,-1" Color="White"/>
  <AmbientLight Color="#FF333333"/>
</Model3DGroup>
```

FIGURE 12.35   Full-intensity `AmbientLight`.

DirectionalLight only   With a low-intensity AmbientLight

FIGURE 12.36   Lit scene with and without `AmbientLight`.

12

A good rule of thumb to prevent the scene from appearing flat is to only use one `AmbientLight` per scene and keep the intensity at less than one-third white (#555555 or lower).

To control how much the `AmbientLight` affects specific objects in your scene, use the `DiffuseMaterial.AmbientColor` property. For example, setting the `AmbientColor` to black prevents models rendered with that `DiffuseMaterial` from being affected by any `AmbientLights` in the scene.

GeometryModel3Ds

The shape of visible objects in a 3D scene is defined by their geometry. In WPF, you specify 3D geometry using `Geometry3D` objects. However, a `Geometry3D` by itself defines a 3D surface with no appearance. In order to see the 3D surface you need to combine it with a `Material`. A `GeometryModel3D` is a `Model3D` that combines both using the `Geometry` and `Material` properties.

The following is an example of a `GeometryModel3D`, which renders a square (described as a `MeshGeometry3D`) using a blue `DiffuseMaterial`:

```
<GeometryModel3D>
<GeometryModel3D.Material>
  <DiffuseMaterial Brush="Blue"/>
</GeometryModel3D.Material>
<GeometryModel3D.Geometry>
  <MeshGeometry3D Positions="-1,1,0 -1,-1,0 1,-1,0 1,1,0"
                  TriangleIndices="0 1 2, 0 2 3"/>
</GeometryModel3D.Geometry>
</GeometryModel3D>
```

This section first covers the various `Material` types and then examines `MeshGeometry3D`.

Materials

As discussed earlier, properties of `Light` objects determine the orientation and color of light rays in the scene. The properties of `Materials` select which of those rays are reflected back to the viewer to create the image we see. In the real world, materials absorb some wavelengths of light and reflect others. An apple appears red to us because the skin of the fruit reflects red light and absorbs other wavelengths. In WPF, the type and properties of the `Material` objects determine which colors are reflected back to the `Camera` to create the image. This section discusses the various `Material` types supported by WPF:

▶ **DiffuseMaterial**—Scatters light striking the surface in all directions, producing a flat, matte appearance such as newsprint.

▶ **SpecularMaterial**—Reflects light at the same angle as the incident ray. `SpecularMaterials` are used to create glossy highlights present on smooth surfaces like plastic or metal.

▶ **EmissiveMaterial**—Approximates a surface that is emitting light. EmissiveMaterials always appear to be lit regardless of the light objects in the scene; however, they will not cast light onto other objects. Often, EmissiveMaterials are combined with a Light to achieve this effect. EmissiveMaterials are also often used to create objects that are always shown at full intensity and for which no shading is desired, such as in many UI type experiences.

▶ **MaterialGroup**—Applies multiple Materials to a model. Each Material is rendered in order, with the last Material in the group appearing on top.

DiffuseMaterials

DiffuseMaterial is the most commonly used type of Material. When light strikes a DiffuseMaterial, it is scattered in all directions, producing a matte appearance. Figure 12.37 shows a teapot rendered with a red DiffuseMaterial.

The scattering is uniform and does not depend on the viewing angle of the Camera. However, the angle between the light and the surface does affect the intensity of the reflected light, as shown in Figure 12.38. When the ray strikes the surface directly, it is reflected at maximum intensity. The reflection diminishes as the angle between the light and surface decreases. This is what causes the parts of the teapot facing the light to be illuminated while the parts facing away from the light source remain unlit.

The color reflected by the Material is controlled by the Material's Brush property. The image of the red teapot in Figure 12.37 was created by shining a white light on a DiffuseMaterial, which only reflects red light:

FIGURE 12.37   DiffuseMaterial on a teapot model.

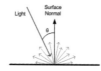

More light is reflected   Less light is reflected

FIGURE 12.38   Intensity of reflected light.

```
<DiffuseMaterial Brush="Red"/>
```

Which colors are reflected by the Material can vary over the object's surface by using one of the nonsolid color Brushes. For example, the left side of Figure 12.39 shows the same teapot with zebra stripes applied by an ImageBrush:

```
<DiffuseMaterial>
<DiffuseMaterial.Brush>
```

```
<ImageBrush ImageSource="C:\ZebraStripes.png" ViewportUnits="Absolute"/>
</DiffuseMaterial.Brush>
</DiffuseMaterial>
```

Which part of the Brush appears on which part of the 3D surface is controlled by the texture coordinates (sometimes called UV coordinates) of the geometry. Texture coordinates are discussed in more detail in the TextureCoordinates section under Geometry3Ds.

ImageBrush

ImageBrush tinted orange

FIGURE 12.39   ImageBrush and the ImageBrush tinted orange.

WARNING

If you're not using a SolidColorBrush, you need TextureCoordinates!

If you attempt to use a GradientBrush, ImageBrush, DrawingBrush, or VisualBrush without specifying texture coordinates, your model will not render. Without texture coordinates, there is no mapping between points on the surface to the colors in the Brush. This is not a problem for SolidColorBrushes because all points on the surface map to the same color.

Missing or bad texture coordinates are usually easy to diagnose. If switching your Material to use a SolidColorBrush causes the model to appear, the odds are good that your geometry is missing texture coordinates.

TIP

By allowing you to use Brushes rather than static images as your texture source, texture mapping is made far more expressive in WPF. Not only can the 3D models themselves be data bound and animated, so can the content of their Brushes, which might be animated 2D Drawings, video, or even 2D Controls like a DocumentViewer!

The right side of Figure 12.39 shows the same ImageBrush tinted orange, to look like tiger stripes. There are three ways this effect could be achieved:

▶ Modify the image used by the ImageBrush.

▶ Change the Color of the Lights in the scene to orange. White regions of a DiffuseMaterial reflect any color of light. If only orange light exists in the scene, orange light is reflected.

▶ Change the Color property on the Material to orange. Effectively, this is equivalent to changing the Light Color to orange except that it only affects this specific Material instead of all of the Materials in the scene.

Typically, you will want to use the Color property on the Lights to vary the light intensity in the scene. You might also want to tint the Lights to match the ambient light of the environment, for example green Lights for a scene in the forest, blue for underwater, and so on.

The Color property on Materials is useful when you want to filter the light that is reflected by specific objects. You might use this to tweak the lighting in your scene by darkening specific objects. Another use for this property is to get extra mileage out of your ImageSource by tinting it, as in Figure 12.39 to create tiger stripes from our zebra texture:

```
<DiffuseMaterial Color="Orange">
<DiffuseMaterial.Brush>
  <ImageBrush ImageSource="C:\ZebraStripes.png" ViewportUnits="Absolute"/>
</DiffuseMaterial.Brush>
</DiffuseMaterial>
```

This technique can be especially helpful if you want the user to be able to pick a custom color for a 3D model, such as selecting the paint job of a car.

DIGGING DEEPER

Calculating the Final Reflected Color

The final color that is reflected to the user is given by the formula

$$\left(\sum_{i=0}^{n} Lc_i Mc_i\right) Mb$$

where Lc is the Color property of each Light, Mc is the Color property of the Material, and Mb is the color sampled from the Material's Brush. The alpha components of the Material's Color property and the color sampled from the Brush are multiplied together. The alpha component of the Light is ignored.

FAQ

 Why can you only sometimes see through translucent DiffuseMaterials?

There are a number of ways to create a translucent DiffuseMaterial, including using an ImageSource with alpha, using the Brush.Opacity property, or using Alpha in the DiffuseMaterial.Color. If you create a translucent DiffuseMaterial you might be surprised to find that objects behind it are sometimes not rendered.

This behavior is the result of how overlapping surfaces are handled by WPF. Rather than sort all of the triangles in the scene and render them back to front, WPF uses a depth buffer to ensure that the surface nearest the Camera is rendered last (that is, on top). Depth buffers are much faster than sorting the scene (and potentially subdividing interpenetrating geometry), but they have the side effect that once a surface near the Camera is rendered surfaces further away are skipped. This is bad news if your nearer surface was intended to be translucent.

In order to ensure that translucent DiffuseMaterials render as intended, you will need to take care when constructing your scene. Just like in 2D, objects in the 3D scene are rendered in the order they appear in the Children property. By placing the translucent objects at the end of the Children collection, you can ensure that the objects behind the translucent objects are rendered first.

Another possibility is to create a translucent-like effect using EmissiveMaterials. EmissiveMaterials are blended additively and therefore do not use the depth buffer. EmissiveMaterials are discussed in the next section.

FAQ

 Where is WPF's AmbientMaterial class?

People porting code or importing file formats that are based on the fixed function lighting from Direct3D or other 3D platforms might wonder why there is no AmbientMaterial class in WPF. Traditional fixed function lighting allows the user to specify four material colors: ambient, diffuse, emissive, and specular, which are used to calculate the lighting contributions at the vertices.

Ambient and diffuse are similar, but are specified separately so that users can limit the contributions of the omnipresent AmbientLight to portions of the scene. For example, you might have an outdoor scene that you want to brighten with an AmbientLight, but you do not want AmbientLight inside of the entrance to a cave in a hillside. You would set the ambient color of the Material inside the cave to black to prevent AmbientLights from having an effect.

WPF exposes an AmbientColor property on DiffuseMaterial for this purpose. The normal Color property controls how the DiffuseMaterials reflect light from all Light types in the scene except AmbientLight. The AmbientColor limits the color of the light reflected from AmbientLights only.

Therefore the diffuse, specular, and emissive materials colors in the traditional pipeline map to the Color properties of the DiffuseMaterial, SpecularMaterial, and EmissiveMaterial, respectively. The ambient color maps to the AmbientColor property on DiffuseMaterial.

EmissiveMaterials

EmissiveMaterials always emit light visible to the Camera. They do not, however, emit light to other surfaces in the scene the way a Light does. The left side of Figure 12.40 shows the effect of the following EmissiveMaterial on the teapot model:

```
<EmissiveMaterial Brush="Green"/>
```

EmissiveMaterial   EmissiveMaterial over Black DiffuseMaterial

FIGURE 12.40   EmissiveMaterial on a teapot model.

EmissiveMaterials are additively blended into the image. Additive blending adds light to the image, but does not occlude light from objects behind the material. This is why the checkered background is visible through the teapot on the left side of Figure 12.40. The bright green regions come from overlapping geometry that you wouldn't normally see. (This is the rim of the lid, plus the handle and spout extend a small amount into the body of the teapot.)

To prevent you from being able to see through your model, the EmissiveMaterial can be combined with a DiffuseMaterial using a MaterialGroup:

```
<MaterialGroup>
  <DiffuseMaterial Brush="Black"/>
  <SpecularMaterial Brush="Green"/>
</MaterialGroup>
```

The result of this change is shown on the right side of Figure 12.40.

In this case, the EmissiveMaterial is still additively blended with the image. However, by rendering a black teapot underneath, the end result is black plus the emissive color, resulting in just the emissive color. Also, note that you can no longer see the overlapping geometry inside the teapot. This is because the near side of the black teapot prevents us from seeing through to the overlapping lid, handle, and spout.

SpecularMaterials

SpecularMaterials reflect light back to the viewer when the Camera is close to the angle of reflection between the light and the surface. SpecularMaterial is also additively blended and by itself looks glasslike, as demonstrated by the following one shown on the left side of Figure 12.41:

```
<SpecularMaterial Brush="White" SpecularPower="10"/>
```

Often, a SpecularMaterial is combined with a DiffuseMaterial to add a bright highlight characteristic of hard, shiny surfaces, as follows (shown on the right side of Figure 12.41):

```
<MaterialGroup>
  <DiffuseMaterial Brush="Red"/>
  <SpecularMaterial Brush="White" SpecularPower="40"/>
</MaterialGroup>
```

Compare this with the image of the red DiffuseMaterial alone in Figure 12.37.

The "hardness" of the highlight is controlled by the SpecularPower property. The larger the value for this property, the more focused the specular highlight is.

SpecularMaterial by itself

SpecularMaterial over a red DiffuseMaterial

FIGURE 12.41   SpecularMaterial on a teapot model.

> **TIP**
>
> To make plastic-looking surfaces, combine a bright DiffuseMaterial with a white SpecularMaterial. To create metal-looking surfaces, use a dark DiffuseMaterial with a bright SpecularMaterial of the same hue.

Unlike a `DiffuseMaterial` which scatters light uniformly, a `SpecularMaterial` reflects light in the opposite direction of the incident ray. As shown in Figure 12.42, the reflected light bounces off a `SpecularMaterial` like a mirror and is only visible when the `Camera` is close to the reflected ray.

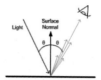

FIGURE 12.42   Light bounces off a `SpecularMaterial`.

Note that because `AmbientLights` are directionless, they have no effect on `SpecularMaterials`.

Like the `DiffuseMaterial`, the final color reflected to the viewer is a combination of the `Color` properties of the `Lights` in the scene, the `Brush` of the `SpecularMaterial`, and the `Material`'s `Color` property. See the "DiffuseMaterials" section for more details on how the final color is computed.

> **TIP**
>
> Unlike traditional fixed-function lighting, which only allowed you to specify a color for the specular highlight, WPF allows you to use any Brush. Using alpha in the image, you can create a Material where specularity varies over the surface. This technique is called gloss mapping and can be used to add shininess only to the metallic parts of a texture for a car, fingerprints on glass, and so on.

Combining Materials

As you've seen in previous examples, `MaterialGroup` enables you to apply multiple materials to a surface. Materials in a `MaterialGroup` are rendered on top of each other in the order specified. Common uses include applying an `EmissiveMaterial` or `SpecularMaterial` over a `DiffuseMaterial`, as was done to create the `Materials` for the teapot in this section.

Geometry3Ds

Similar to the 2D `Geometry` class, `Geometry3Ds` are used to define the shape of 3D objects. By themselves, `Geometry3Ds` have no appearance. `Geometry3Ds` are combined with `Materials` using a `GeometryModel3D` to create a `Model3D` that can be rendered. In the current version of WPF, there is only one concrete `Geometry3D` class: the `MeshGeometry3D`.

A `MeshGeometry3D` represents a set of 3D surfaces specified as a list of triangles. `MeshGeometry3D` is composed of the following properties:

- ▶ **Positions**—Defines the vertices of the triangles contained in the mesh.

- ▶ **TriangleIndices**—Describes the connections between the vertices to form triangles. If `TriangleIndices` is not specified, it is implied that the positions should be connected in the order they appear: 0 1 2, then 3 4 5, and so on.

- ▶ **Normals**—Allows you to optionally tweak the lighting of the mesh.

- ▶ **TextureCoordinates**—Provides a 3D-to-2D mapping for each position used by the Materials.

Each of the Positions, Normals, and TextureCoordinates properties is a collection with one entry for each vertex in the mesh. For example, the position for the 0th vertex comes from the 0th entry in the Positions collection, the normal for the 0th vertex comes from the 0th entry in the Normals collection, and so on.

Positions

The triangles in the mesh are defined by specifying the 3D coordinates of their vertices. The coordinates are stored in the Positions collection of the MeshGeometry3D. By default, each group of three Point3Ds in the Positions collection is drawn as a triangle. The following snippet produces the triangle illustrated in Figure 12.43:

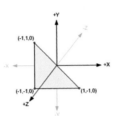

FIGURE 12.43   A triangle described by a MeshGeometry3D.

```
<MeshGeometry3D Positions="-1,1,0 -1,-1,0 1,-1,0"/>
```

You can create a square by adding a second triangle, shown in Figure 12.44:

```
<MeshGeometry3D Positions="-1,1,0 -1,-1,0 1,-1,0 -1,1,0 1,-1,0 1,1,0"/>
```

Front Versus Back

One of the things about 3D geometry that often surprises 2D developers is that the triangles in a MeshGeometry3D have separate front and back sides. Each side can be rendered using a different material. You also might choose to not render a side by leaving the Material property null. Which side of a triangle is the front is determined by the winding of the vertices. Figure 12.45 illustrates the winding of the triangles in the square as viewed from the front and back.

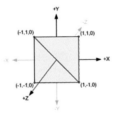

FIGURE 12.44   A square described by a MeshGeometry3D.

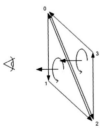 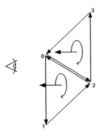

Square from the front   Square from the back

FIGURE 12.45   Viewing the square from two different perspectives.

The winding is determined by the order in which the points are connected in the triangle. For example, connecting point 0 to point 1 creates a directed edge starting at 0 and ending at 1. The direction of the edges wind in a counterclockwise direction when viewed from the front, shown on the left of Figure 12.45.

DIGGING DEEPER

Winding Order and Handedness

The section about Cameras introduced a right-hand rule to remember which direction the z-axis points in a right-handed coordinate system. There is a second right-hand rule that tells you which side of a triangle is the front. The direction your fingers curl when looking at your thumb indicate the winding direction. As illustrated in Figure 12.46, this is counterclockwise for a right-handed system.

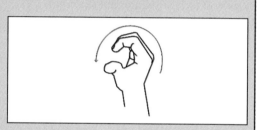

FIGURE 12.46   The other right-hand rule.

The right-hand rule is also useful for remembering the positive direction of rotation in a right-handed coordinate system.

TIP

If you suspect you have an issue with the winding in your mesh, you can always set both the Material and BackMaterial properties so that the triangle will be visible regardless of which side you view it from.

If it is acceptable to have the same material on both the front and back, you can ignore the issue of winding. However, it is sometimes very useful to be able to specify different Materials for the front and the back. It is also faster to avoid rendering the BackMaterial if it will not be visible in the scene.

TriangleIndices

A mesh is built into the desired shape by adding triangles. Even curved surfaces are approximated by lots of little triangles. As the number of triangles in your mesh increases, so does the number of shared edges.

TriangleIndices enables you to share positions between triangles. When the TriangleIndices collection is empty, it is implied that the points should be connected in the order they appear in the Positions collection. When TriangleIndices exist, the points are connected in groups of three as specified by the TriangleIndices. For example, you can create a square using only four unique points, as illustrated in Figure 12.47:

```
<MeshGeometry3D Positions="-1,1,0 -1,-1,0 1,-1,0 1,1,0"
                TriangleIndices="0 1 2, 0 2 3"/>
```

Sharing the position between triangles has a slightly different semantic meaning than declaring the same point multiple times. When the position is shared, the triangles are considered to be part of a single continuous surface. When the positions are separate, the triangles are separate abutting surfaces that can have different normals or texture coordinates.

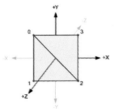

FIGURE 12.47   Indices of the vertices.

> **TIP**
>
> Regardless of whether you use `TriangleIndices`, you do not need to worry about cracks appearing between triangles within a single `MeshGeometry3D`. WPF has strict rendering rules that guarantee triangles sharing points are rendered as adjacent without a seam.
>
> However, you *do* need to be aware that transforms are not always exact. If you are using different transforms on two `MeshGeometry3D`s to make them adjacent, it is possible that floating-point error in the transformations might create small gaps between the meshes.
>
> Sometimes, this error can be worked around by fudging the transform to create a small amount of overlap. Other times, you will need to construct the `MeshGeometry3D`s with points that are adjacent rather than transforming them to be so.

Normals

A *normal* is a vector that is perpendicular to a surface at a point. You specify normals at the vertices to tell the system whether triangles represent flat surfaces or are approximating curved surfaces. Figure 12.48 shows the difference between flat and smooth shading on a tube approximated as 12 quadrilaterals.

Flat shaded tube   Smooth shaded tube

FIGURE 12.48   Two tubes approximated as 12 quadrilaterals.

> **TIP**
>
> If you do not specify normals, the system generates them for you by averaging the face normals of each triangle that shares each vertex. If vertices are not shared between triangles, the result is the face normals, which gives the flat shaded appearance shown on the left side of Figure 12.48. If the vertices are shaded between adjacent triangles using `TriangleIndices`, the averaging results in the smooth shaded appearance shown on the right side of Figure 12.47.

When the normals for each vertex in a triangle are parallel, as illustrated in the cross section of the tube on the left side of Figure 12.49, the rendered surface appears flat. If the normals point in different directions, the shading is smoothly interpolated across the face of the triangle. To create a smooth surface like that illustrated on the right side of Figure 12.49, the normals of the adjacent triangles should be the same to prevent a crease from appearing.

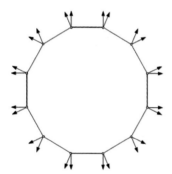
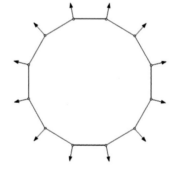

Cross section of the flat tube   Cross section of the smooth tube

FIGURE 12.49   Cross sections of the tubes from Figure 12.48.

Let's consider the simple square mesh you have been building. If you want the square to appear flat, specify all of the normals perpendicular to the surface, as illustrated on the left side of Figure 12.50:

```
<MeshGeometry3D Positions="-1,1,0 -1,-1,0 1,-1,0 1,1,0"
                TriangleIndices="0 1 2, 0 2 3"
                Normals="0,0,1 0,0,1 0,0,1 0,0,1"/>
```

If you want the square to be lit as if it were an approximation of a slightly curved surface, specify the normals to match the curvature of the surface, as illustrated on the right side of Figure 12.50:

```
<MeshGeometry3D Positions="-1,1,0 -1,-1,0 1,-1,0 1,1,0"
                TriangleIndices="0 1 2, 0 2 3"
                Normals="-0.25,0.25,1 -0.25,-0.25,1 0.25,-0.25,1 0.25,0.25,1"/>
```

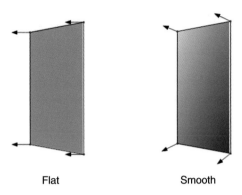

Flat   Smooth

FIGURE 12.50   The result of using two different Normals values.

TextureCoordinates

When you set the Fill property on a 2D Shape, it is assumed that you want the Brush to map to the 2D bounds of the Shape. In 3D, you need to provide this mapping yourself. Each entry in the TextureCoordinates collection is a 2D point in Brush space. These points map triangles in 3D space to triangles in Brush space. The triangles in Brush space provide the colors for the materials when the surface is rendered. Figure 12.51 illustrates how you would map the vertices in your square to stretch an image across it:

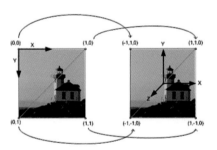

FIGURE 12.51   Mapping between 2D Brush space and 3D surface.

```
<MeshGeometry3D Positions="-1,1,0 -1,-1,0 1,-1,0 1,1,0"
                TriangleIndices="0 1 2, 0 2 3"
                TextureCoordinates="0,0 0,1 1,1 1,0"/>
```

Keep in mind that in the 2D coordinate system used by WPF, the origin is at the top-left corner and the positive y-axis extends downward. By convention, the source image is usually considered to extend from 0 to 1 in both the X and Y directions.

Model3DGroup

Model3DGroup derives from Model3D. Model3DGroups are used to group together a collection of Model3Ds into a single model. Grouping multiple GeometryModel3Ds together with a Model3DGroup is the way you build a model that uses multiple materials. Listing 12.4 shows how six GeometryModel3Ds can be combined to form a model of a cube.

WARNING

By default, WPF texture coordinates are interpreted differently than what you might expect!

You should be aware of a couple of quirks with the way WPF handles texture coordinates. The default behavior of WPF texture coordinates closely matches the default behavior of 2D geometry, which is very convenient for 2D/3D integration scenarios. However, when you are attempting to use a mesh containing texture coordinates generated for a different system there are a couple of Brush settings you will want to change.

The first is that, by default, Brush space is mapped to the bounds of the texture coordinates. This means that the following will not show the top-left quarter of the Brush as you might expect:

```
<MeshGeometry3D Positions="-1,1,0 -1,-1,0 1,-1,0 1,1,0"
                TriangleIndices="0 1 2, 0 2 3"
                TextureCoordinates="0,0 0,0.5 0.5,0.5 0.5,0"/>
```

Instead, the bounds (0,0) – (0.5,0.5) become the relative bounds of the source and the entire Brush is displayed. To prevent this, set the ViewportUnits of the Brush to absolute.

```
<ImageBrush ViewportUnits="Absolute"/>
```

You will almost always want to do this when applying Brushes to 3D meshes. The default behavior is useful in 2D to map Brush space to the bounds of the 2D geometry being filled. In 3D, it is rarely used.

The second issue to be aware of is that some systems specify their y-axis as pointing upward in 2D instead of downward as WPF uses. If you are using texture coordinates generated for such a system, your Brushes will be applied upside down. You can correct for this with a simple Brush transform:

```
<ImageBrush ViewportUnits="Absolute" Transform="1,0,0,-1,0,1"/>
```

Finally, if your mesh has texture coordinates that extend outside of the 0-to-1 range, it is likely that the intent was to tile. TileMode needs to be turned on explicitly in WPF:

```
<ImageBrush ViewportUnits="Absolute" Transform="1,0,0,-1,0,1" TileMode="Tile"/>
```

ImageBrush is shown as an example, but these tips apply to all Brushes that use TextureCoordinates.

TIP

Some 3D systems have an object called a "mesh," which contains not only geometry information, but materials as well. Sometimes, even multiple materials are permitted in a "mesh." In WPF, this corresponds to a Model3DGroup containing multiple GeometryModel3Ds, one for each Material.

LISTING 12.4   A Cube

```
<Model3DGroup x:Name="Cube">

  <GeometryModel3D x:Name="Front">
  <GeometryModel3D.Material>
    <DiffuseMaterial Brush="Orange"/>
  </GeometryModel3D.Material>
  <GeometryModel3D.Geometry>
    <MeshGeometry3D Positions="1,1,1 -1,1,1 -1,-1,1 1,-1,1"
                    TextureCoordinates="1,1 0,1 0,0 1,0"
                    TriangleIndices="0 1 2 0 2 3"/>
  </GeometryModel3D.Geometry>
  </GeometryModel3D>

  <GeometryModel3D x:Name="Right">
  <GeometryModel3D.Material>
    <DiffuseMaterial Brush="Yellow"/>
  </GeometryModel3D.Material>
  <GeometryModel3D.Geometry>
    <MeshGeometry3D Positions="1,1,-1 -1,1,-1 -1,1,1 1,1,1"
                    TextureCoordinates="0,0 1,0 1,1 0,1"
                    TriangleIndices="0 1 2 0 2 3"/>
  </GeometryModel3D.Geometry>
  </GeometryModel3D>

  <GeometryModel3D x:Name="Back">
  <GeometryModel3D.Material>
    <DiffuseMaterial Brush="Red"/>
  </GeometryModel3D.Material>
  <GeometryModel3D.Geometry>
    <MeshGeometry3D Positions="-1,-1,-1 -1,1,-1 1,1,-1 1,-1,-1"
                    TextureCoordinates="1,0 1,1 0,1 0,0"
                    TriangleIndices="0 1 2 0 2 3"/>
  </GeometryModel3D.Geometry>
  </GeometryModel3D>

  <GeometryModel3D x:Name="Left">
  <GeometryModel3D.Material>
    <DiffuseMaterial Brush="Blue"/>
  </GeometryModel3D.Material>
  <GeometryModel3D.Geometry>
    <MeshGeometry3D Positions="-1,1,1 -1,1,-1 -1,-1,-1 -1,-1,1"
                    TextureCoordinates="1,1 0,1 0,0 1,0"
                    TriangleIndices="0 1 2 0 2 3"/>
  </GeometryModel3D.Geometry>
```

LISTING 12.4   Continued

```
  </GeometryModel3D>

  <GeometryModel3D x:Name="Top">
  <GeometryModel3D.Material>
    <DiffuseMaterial Brush="Green"/>
  </GeometryModel3D.Material>
  <GeometryModel3D.Geometry>
    <MeshGeometry3D Positions="1,-1,1 1,-1,-1 1,1,-1 1,1,1"
                    TextureCoordinates="1,1 0,1 0,0 1,0"
                    TriangleIndices="0 1 2 0 2 3"/>
  </GeometryModel3D.Geometry>
  </GeometryModel3D>

  <GeometryModel3D x:Name="Bottom">
  <GeometryModel3D.Material>
    <DiffuseMaterial Brush="Purple"/>
  </GeometryModel3D.Material>
  <GeometryModel3D.Geometry>
    <MeshGeometry3D Positions="-1,-1,1 -1,-1,-1 1,-1,-1 1,-1,1"
                    TextureCoordinates="0,1 0,0 1,0 1,1"
                    TriangleIndices="0 1 2 0 2 3"/>
  </GeometryModel3D.Geometry>
  </GeometryModel3D>

</Model3DGroup>
```

Visual3Ds

All elements that draw 2D content to the screen inherit their ability to render from the Visual base class. Similarly, Visual3Ds are nodes in the visual tree that can display 3D content. The visual services such as hit testing, bounding, and so on, extend to Visual3Ds as well and are accessible via the VisualTreeHelper class.

There is only one concrete Visual3D class in the current version of WPF: the ModelVisual3D.

ModelVisual3Ds

The ModelVisual3D is similar to the 2D DrawingVisual. To set the content of a ModelVisual3D, you use the Content property:

```
<Viewport3D>
<Viewport3D.Camera>
  <OrthographicCamera Position="5,5,5" LookDirection="-1,-1,-1" Width="5"/>
</Viewport3D.Camera>
```

```
<Viewport3D.Children>
  <ModelVisual3D Content="{StaticResource CubeModel}"/>
</Viewport3D.Children>
</Viewport3D>
```

ModelVisual3D also has a Children property. Therefore, you use ModelVisual3Ds to compose multiple models into a scene inside of your Viewport3D:

```
<Viewport3D>
<Viewport3D.Camera>
  <OrthographicCamera Position="5,5,5" LookDirection="-1,-1,-1" Width="5"/>
</Viewport3D.Camera>
<Viewport3D.Children>
  <ModelVisual3D Transform="{DynamicResource SquadronTransform}">
    <ModelVisual3D Content="{StaticResource AirplaneModel}"
      Transform="{DynamicResource PlaneTransform1}"/>
    <ModelVisual3D Content="{StaticResource AirplaneModel}"
      Transform="{DynamicResource PlaneTransform2}"/>
  </ModelVisual3D>
</Viewport3D.Children>
</Viewport3D>
```

Children (and not Content!) is designated as ModelVisual3D's content property, so the preceding XAML added the two children directly to the parent element. Keep in mind that Model3Ds can be reused between ModelVisual3Ds.

FAQ

 When should I use Model3DGroup versus ModelVisual3D?

Although you could put your entire scene together using a Model3DGroup displayed under a single ModelVisual3D, you will be missing out on some important performance optimizations if you do this. ModelVisual3Ds are optimized to be scene nodes. They cache bounds and other information that lightweight Model3DGroups do not.

Going to the other extreme, you could use ModelVisual3Ds for each and every GeometryModel3D in your scene. This is inadvisable because it unnecessarily increases the working set of your application. Model3DGroups are lightweight constructs intended for grouping multiple GeometryModel3Ds into a single model.

In general, you should use Model3DGroups to combine the various pieces of a single model (for example, the tires, windshield, and body of a car). ModelVisual3Ds should be used for displaying instances of 3D models (for example, use a ModelVisual3D for each car you add to the scene).

> **TIP**
>
> Whereas rendering primitives like Drawing and Model3D are sealed for extension, Visuals are not. ModelVisual3D is the right class to extend from if you want to create a reusable 3D element that renders and potentially has some custom behaviors.

3D Hit Testing

Like their 2D counterparts, Visual3Ds participate in visual hit testing. Typically hit testing is used to answer questions about which visual is under the mouse pointer. The easiest way to do this is to handle an appropriate mouse event on a 2D Visual that contains your 3D scene, such as the Viewport3D element:

```
<Viewport3D MouseDown="MouseDownHandler">
```

When your event handler is called, issue a visual hit test at that point.

```
private void MouseDownHandler(object sender, MouseButtonEventArgs e)
{
  base.OnMouseLeftButtonDown(e);

  Viewport3D viewport = (Viewport3D)sender;
  Point location = e.GetPosition(viewport);

  HitTestResult result = VisualTreeHelper.HitTest(viewport, location);

  if (result != null && result.VisualHit is Visual3D)
  {
    MessageBox.Show("Hit Visual3D!");
  }
}
```

Of course, the overload of VisualTreeHelper.HitTest shown in Chapter 11, which uses callback delegates to report multiple results also works with Visual3Ds. Like in 2D, the results are returned in front to back order. If you would like to start a hit test from within the 3D scene, you can use the overload of VisualTreeHelper.HitTest that takes a Visual3D and a HitTestParameters3D.

> **DIGGING DEEPER**
>
> **Getting Detailed Hit Test Information**
>
> The HitTestResult type is the base class for a number of types such as PointHitTestResult and GeometryHitTestResult. The type of HitTestResult returned to you depends on the type of hit test you initiated and what the hit test ended up intersecting in the scene. If you issue a point hit test that ends up hitting a 3D mesh, you may cast the HitTestResult to a RayMeshGeometry3DHitTestResult. RayMeshGeometry3DHitTest-Result has a wealth of information about the details of the intersection.

12

The `Viewport3D` Element

`Viewport3D` is the 2D `FrameworkElement` that provides the bridge between the 2D and 3D trees. The parent of a `Viewport3D` is always a 2D element such as a `Window` or `Grid`. The children of the `Viewport3D` are `Visual3D`s. The 3D scene described by the `Visual3D` children is rendered inside of the rectangular layout bounds of the `Viewport3D`. The `Camera` property on the `Viewport3D` controls the view of the 3D scene you will see inside of the `Viewport3D`.

TIP

Many container-like elements are normally sized during the layout system's measure pass (described in Chapter 17, "Layout with Custom Panels") to fit their contents. For example, a `Button` is typically sized to accommodate the text or whatever content is inside of it. `Viewport3D`s work the other way around. `Viewport3D`s adjust the view of the 3D scene to fit whatever its layout bounds turn out to be.

For this reason, you need to set the `Width` and `Height` properties of `Viewport3D` elements unless it is already being stretched to fit an area by layout. If you forget to do this, the `Viewport3D` defaults to a size of 0 by 0 and the 3D scene does not appear.

One of the neat things about a `Viewport3D` being a fully featured `FrameworkElement` that participates in layout is that you can easily integrate 3D elements into your application almost anywhere. In fact, it is possible for designers to use features like `Styles` and `ControlTemplates` to replace the default appearance of controls with interactive 3D content. Figure 12.52 shows the result of applying such a style to the Photo Gallery example introduced in Chapter 7. Note that the text and background that appears in the cube faces is data-bound to the templated `Button`. You can update the text and background and the cubes update in real time! When you click on the `Button`, the cube spins.

LISTING 12.5   The Cube `Button` Style

```xml
<!-- This style replaces the appearance of all Buttons with 3D cubes.
     Because the Viewport3D has no "natural size", you need to set
     the Width and Height properties on your Buttons if they are not
     stretched to fit their container. -->
<Style TargetType="{x:Type Button}">
  <Setter Property="Template">
  <Setter.Value>
    <ControlTemplate>
    <ControlTemplate.Triggers>
      <!-- When the button is pressed, spin the cube -->
      <Trigger Property="Button.IsPressed" Value="true">
      <Trigger.EnterActions>
        <BeginStoryboard>
          <Storyboard TargetName="RotateY" TargetProperty="Angle">
```

LISTING 12.5   Continued

```xml
            <DoubleAnimation Duration="0:0:1" From="0" To="360"
                             DecelerationRatio="1.0"/>
        </Storyboard>
      </BeginStoryboard>
    </Trigger.EnterActions>
    </Trigger>
 </ControlTemplate.Triggers>
  <Viewport3D>
  <Viewport3D.Camera>
    <PerspectiveCamera Position="2.9,2.65,2.9" LookDirection="-1,-1,-1"/>
  </Viewport3D.Camera>
  <Viewport3D.Children>
    <ModelVisual3D x:Name="Light">
    <ModelVisual3D.Content>
      <DirectionalLight Direction="-0.3,-0.4,-0.5"/>
    </ModelVisual3D.Content>
    </ModelVisual3D>
    <ModelVisual3D x:Name="Cube">
    <ModelVisual3D.Transform>
      <RotateTransform3D>
      <RotateTransform3D.Rotation>
        <AxisAngleRotation3D x:Name="RotateY" Axis="0,1,0" Angle="0"/>
      </RotateTransform3D.Rotation>
      </RotateTransform3D>
    </ModelVisual3D.Transform>
    <ModelVisual3D.Content>
      <GeometryModel3D>
      <GeometryModel3D.Material>
        <DiffuseMaterial>
        <DiffuseMaterial.Brush>
          <!-- Use a VisualBrush to display the Button's original
               Background and Content on the faces of the cube. -->
          <VisualBrush ViewportUnits="Absolute" Transform="1,0,0,-1,0,1">
          <VisualBrush.Visual>
            <Border Background="{Binding Path=Background,
              RelativeSource={RelativeSource TemplatedParent}}">
              <Label Content="{Binding Path=Content,
                RelativeSource={RelativeSource TemplatedParent}}"/>
            </Border>
          </VisualBrush.Visual>
          </VisualBrush>
        </DiffuseMaterial.Brush>
        </DiffuseMaterial>
      </GeometryModel3D.Material>
```

LISTING 12.5   Continued

```
        <GeometryModel3D.Geometry>
          <MeshGeometry3D
            Positions="1,1,-1 1,-1,-1 -1,-1,-1 -1,1,-1 1,1,1 -1,1,1 -1,-1,1
              1,-1,1 1,1,-1 1,1,1 1,-1,1 1,-1,-1 1,-1,-1 1,-1,1 -1,-1,1 -1,-1,-1
              -1,-1,-1 -1,-1,1 -1,1,1 -1,1,-1 1,1,1 1,1,-1 -1,1,-1 -1,1,1"
            TriangleIndices="0 1 2 0 2 3 4 5 6 4 6 7 8 9 10 8 10 11 12
              13 14 12 14 15 16 17 18 16 18 19 20 21 22 20 22 23"
            TextureCoordinates="0,1 0,0 1,0 1,1 1,1 0,1 0,-0 1,0 1,1
              0,1 0,-0 1,0 1,0 1,1 0,1 0,-0 0,0 1,-0 1,1 0,1 1,-0
              1,1 0,1 0,0"/>
        </GeometryModel3D.Geometry>
        </GeometryModel3D>
      </ModelVisual3D.Content>
      </ModelVisual3D>
    </Viewport3D.Children>
    </Viewport3D>
  </ControlTemplate>
  </Setter.Value>
  </Setter>
</Style>
```

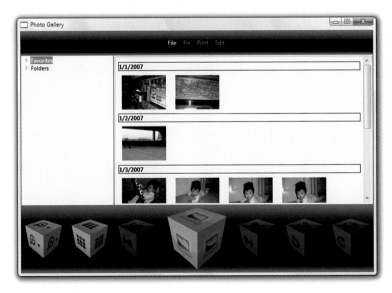

FIGURE 12.52   The cube Button Style applied to Photo Gallery.

DIGGING DEEPER

The `Viewport3DVisual`

Under the covers, the `Viewport3D` element uses a `Viewport3DVisual` to bridge the 2D visual tree with the 3D visual tree. The `Viewport3DVisual` is primarily an implementation detail, but if you choose to program at the `Visual` level instead of at the `FrameworkElement` level, the `Viewport3DVisual` is the 2D `Visual` you will need to connect the `Visual3D` tree. The properties of the `Viewport3DVisual` are identical to the `Viewport3D` with the addition of the `Viewport` property. `Viewport` is used to set the bounds in which the 3D scene will be displayed, because there is no concept of layout at the `Visual` layer.

Conclusion

Hopefully you now understand how the 3D APIs in WPF are a straightforward extension of the 2D APIs you are already familiar with. As shown in Table 12.1 at the beginning of this chapter, most of the 3D types are direct corollaries of the classes discussed in previous chapters. This makes WPF an ideal platform for applications that need to mix 3D graphics with 2D UI.

Although the 3D features of WPF might seem basic at a glance, there is hidden power derived from being a tightly integrated component of the platform. WPF 3D transforms can be data-bound. You can display video, `Drawings`, or even 2D `Controls` on the surfaces of a 3D object. Entire 3D scenes can be used as `DataTemplates` and `ControlTemplates`. And all this works when printing, remoting, or running as a partial-trust web application.

This chapter focused on the 3D-specific APIs, but this is only part of the story. Many of the best 3D features are general features of the platform. As you learn about animation and media in the upcoming chapters, keep in mind that these features can also be applied to 3D objects.

CHAPTER 13

Animation

WPF's animation functionality makes it very straightforward to add dynamic effects to your applications or components. It's also one of the most obvious features in WPF to abuse! But rather than worrying about a future of applications filled with bouncing Buttons and spinning Menus, think instead of all the ways in which animation can be put to good use. Certainly you've come across an Adobe Flash-enabled website with a slick animation that left a good impression, or watched a baseball game or newscast on TV in which scrolling text or animated transitions enhanced the viewing experience. Sure, animation might not be appropriate for every piece of software, but there are many that can benefit from its judicious use.

When exposed via design tools like Microsoft Expression Blend, WPF's animation support provides capabilities much like Adobe Flash. But because it's a core part of the WPF platform with APIs that are fairly simple, you can easily create a wide range of animations without the help of such a tool. Indeed, this chapter demonstrates several different animation techniques with nothing more than short snippets of C# or XAML.

This chapter begins by examining WPF's animation classes and their use from procedural code. After that, we'll see how to use the same classes from XAML, which involves a few additional concepts. After covering both approaches, the chapter concludes by examining a more powerful form of animation that uses keyframes.

Animations in Procedural Code

When most people think about animation, they think of a cartoon-like mechanism, where movement is simulated by displaying images in rapid succession. In WPF, animation has a more specific definition: varying the value of a property over time. This could be related to motion, such as making an element grow by increasing its Width, or it could be something like varying the value of a color.

Such animation can be accomplished without the special support discussed in this chapter, and even without much work—thanks to WPF's retained-mode graphics model. This section begins by examining the options for performing this work manually. It then introduces WPF's many classes that can do almost all of the animation work for you.

Performing Animation "By Hand"

The classic way to implement such an animation scheme is to set up a timer and a callback function that is periodically called back based on the frequency of the timer. Inside the callback function, you can manually update the target property (doing a little math to determine the current value based on the elapsed time) until it reaches the final value. At that point, you could stop the timer and/or remove the event handler.

Of course, nothing is stopping you from following this classic approach in WPF. WPF even has its own DispatcherTimer class that can be used for implementing such a scheme. You get to choose DispatcherTimer's frequency by setting its Interval property, and can attach an event handler to its Tick event.

Although this approach may be familiar to Windows programmers, performing animation with a timer is not recommended. The timers are not in sync with the monitor's vertical refresh rate nor are they in sync with the WPF rendering engine.

Instead of implementing custom timer-based animation, you could perform custom frame-based animation by attaching an event handler to the static Rendering event on System.Windows.Media.CompositionTarget. Rather than being raised at a customizable interval, this event is raised post-layout and pre-render *once per frame*. (This is like using enterFrame when developing Adobe Flash animations.)

Using the frame-based Rendering event is not only preferred over a timer-based approach, but it's even preferred over the animation classes that are the focus of this chapter when dealing with hundreds of objects that require high-fidelity animations. For example, collision detection or other physics-based animations should be done using this approach. Animations that morph a panel's elements from one layout to another are also usually implemented using this approach. The Rendering event generally gives the best performance and the most customizations (because you can write arbitrary code in the event handler), although there are tradeoffs. In normal conditions WPF only renders frames when part of the UI is invalidated. But as long as any event handler is attached to Rendering, WPF renders frames continuously. Therefore, Rendering is best for short-lived animations.

DIGGING DEEPER

The Difference Between `DispatcherTimer` and Other .NET Timers

The key difference between `DispatcherTimer` and other timers like
`System.Threading.Timer` or `System.Timers.Timer` is that handlers for `DispatcherTimer`
are invoked on the UI thread. This is important for WPF applications because UI elements
can be manipulated inside the handler without worrying about threading. If you use one of
the other timers, you need to partition your update logic into a different function and use the
Dispatcher to invoke it on the UI thread. For example:

```
void Callback(object sender, EventArgs e)
{
  this.Dispatcher.Invoke(DispatcherPriority.Normal,
    new TimerDispatcherDelegate(DoTheRealWork));
}
```

instead of simply:

```
void Callback(object sender, EventArgs e)
{
  // Update the property directly in the callback
}
```

By default, `DispatcherTimer` callbacks are handled with a `DispatcherPriority` of
Background, but you can construct a `DispatcherTimer` with an explicit
`DispatcherPriority` if you want the callbacks to be handled differently.

Introducing the Animation Classes

Although using the `CompositionTarget.Rendering` event is a reasonable way to implement animations, the designers of WPF wanted animation to be a simpler and more
declarative process. So, WPF has many classes in the `System.Windows.Media.Animation`
namespace that enable you to describe and apply an animation without doing the
manual work to perform it. These classes are extremely useful when you know how you
want your animation to behave for large amounts of time in advance.

There are two important aspects to these animation classes:

> ▸ **They can only vary the value of a *dependency* property.** So, the definition
> of WPF animation is slightly more constrained than previously stated, unless you
> use one of the manual approaches with `DispatcherTimer` or the `Rendering` event.

> ▸ **They enable animations that are "time resolution independent."** Similar
> in spirit to the resolution independence of WPF's graphics, animations using the
> WPF animation classes do not speed up as hardware gets faster; they simply get
> smoother! WPF can vary the frame rate based on a variety of conditions, and you as
> the animation developer don't need to care.

System.Windows.Media.Animation contains many similar-looking animation classes because distinct data types are animated with a distinct animation class. For example, if you want to vary the value of an element's `double` dependency property over time, you could use an instance of `DoubleAnimation`. Instead, if you want to vary the value of an element's `Thickness` dependency property over time, you could use an instance of `ThicknessAnimation`. WPF contains built-in animation classes for 22 different data types, listed in Table 13.1.

TABLE 13.1   Data Types with Built-In Animation Classes

Core .NET Data Types	WPF Data Types
Boolean	Thickness
Byte	Color
Char	Size
Decimal	Rect
Int16	Point
Int32	Point3D
Int64	Vector
Single	Vector3D
Double	Rotation3D
String	Matrix
Object	Quaternion

Using an Animation

To understand how the animation classes work, let's look at the `double` data type. Animating a `double` is not only easy to understand, but it's a very common scenario because of the number of useful `double` dependency properties on many elements.

Imagine we want a `Button`'s `Width` property to grow from `50` to `100`. For demonstration purposes, we can place the `Button` inside a simple `Window` with a `Canvas`:

```
<Window x:Class="Window1" Title="Animation" Width="300" Height="300"
  xmlns="http://schemas.microsoft.com/winfx/2006/xaml/presentation"
  xmlns:x="http://schemas.microsoft.com/winfx/2006/xaml">
  <Canvas>
    <Button x:Name="b">OK</Button>
  </Canvas>
</Window>
```

DIGGING DEEPER

Animation Classes and the Lack of Generics

The `System.Windows.Media.Animation` namespace has the following classes:

- 22 *XXX*AnimationBase classes
- 17 *XXX*Animation classes
- 22 *XXX*AnimationUsingKeyFrames classes
- 22 *XXX*KeyFrameCollection classes
- 22 *XXX*KeyFrame classes
- 22 Discrete*XXX*KeyFrame classes
- 17 Linear*XXX*KeyFrame classes
- 17 Spline*XXX*KeyFrame classes
- 3 *XXX*AnimationUsingPath classes

(*XXX* represents a data type from Table 13.1.)

The classes within each of these nine buckets are almost identical to each other, so nine basic concepts have been exploded into a whopping 164 classes! When people familiar with .NET come across this design, the first reaction is often, "Why didn't the WPF team use generics?" In other words, why isn't there a single Animation<T> class that enables double to be animated with an Animation<double>, Thickness to be animated with an Animation<Thickness>, and so on?

One obvious (but not very satisfactory) reason is the lack of complete support for generics in XAML. But even if generics were completely supported, there are aspects of these classes that make them a bad fit for generics. For example, the presence of an Animation<T> class implies that you could construct it with any data type, such as Animation<Window>. But there is no support for such an animation, nor is there a constraint that can be placed on the generic class that would sufficiently express what it supports.

In the code-behind file, we can use `DoubleAnimation` to very simply express what I said in English ("animate Width from 50 to 100"):

```
using System.Windows;
using System.Windows.Controls;
using System.Windows.Media.Animation;

public partial class Window1 : Window
{
  public Window1()
  {
    InitializeComponent();
```

```
    // Define the animation
    DoubleAnimation a = new DoubleAnimation();
    a.From = 50;
    a.To = 100;

    // Start animating
    b.BeginAnimation(Button.WidthProperty, a);
  }
}
```

The instance of `DoubleAnimation` contains the initial and end values for a `double` property—*any* `double` property. The `Button`'s `BeginAnimation` method is then called to associate the animation with its `Width` dependency property *and* to initiate the animation at the point in time. If you were to compile and run this code, you would see the width of the `Button` smoothly grow from `50` to `100` over the course of one second.

Animation classes have a number of properties in addition to `From` and `To` that can customize their behavior in interesting ways. We'll be examining these properties throughout this section. They also have a handful of simple events, such as a `Completed` event that gets raised as soon the target property reaches its final value.

Linear Interpolation

It's important to note that `DoubleAnimation` takes care of smoothly changing the `double` value over time via *linear interpolation*. (Otherwise, the animation would appear to be no different than a simple property set!) In other words, for this one-second animation, the value of `Width` is `55` when 0.1 seconds have elapsed (5% progress in both the value and time elapsed), `75` when 0.5 seconds have elapsed (50% progress in both the value and time elapsed), and so on. Internally, there is a function being called at regular intervals performing the calculations that you would have to do if performing an animation the "raw" way. This is why most of the data types in Table 13.1 are numeric. (The nonnumeric data types like `Boolean` and `String` require further explanation later in this chapter.)

Figuring out how to apply an animation to get the desired results can take a little practice. Here are some examples:

▶ If you want to make an element fade in, it doesn't make sense to animate its `Visibility` property because there's no middle ground between `Hidden` and `Visible`. Instead, you should animate its `Opacity` property of type `double` from `0` to `1`.

▶ If you want an element inside a `Grid` to slide across the screen, you *could* animate its `Grid.Column` attached property with an `Int32Animation`, but the transition from column to column would be choppy. Instead, you could give the element a `TranslateTransform` as a `RenderTransform`, and then animate its `X` property (of type `double`) with a `DoubleAnimation`.

▶ Animating the `Width` of a `Grid`'s column (which is useful for the "Creating a Visual Studio-Like Collapsible, Dockable, Resizable Pane" example at the end of Chapter 6) is not straightforward because `ColumnDefinition.Width` is defined as a `GridLength` structure, which has no corresponding animation class built in. Instead, you could animate `ColumnDefinition`'s `MinWidth` and/or `MaxWidth` properties, both of type `double`, or you could set `ColumnDefinition`'s `Width` to `Auto` and then insert an element in that column whose `Width` you animate.

Reusing Animations

The preceding code attached the animation to the `Button` with a `BeginAnimation` call. You can call `BeginAnimation` multiple times to apply the exact same animation to multiple elements or even multiple properties of the same element. For example, adding the following line of code to the preceding code-behind animates the `Height` of the `Window` in sync with the `Button`'s `Width`:

```
this.BeginAnimation
  (Window.HeightProperty, a);
```

The result of this addition is shown in Figure 13.1. (Before you sneer at the thought of a `Window` that grows, keep in mind that there could actually be legitimate uses for such a mechanism. For example, you might want to enlarge a dialog when the user expands an inner `Expander`, and a simple animation is more visually pleasing than an abrupt jump to the new size.)

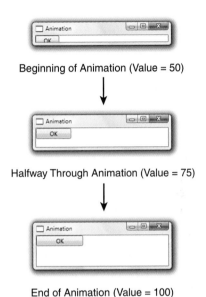

Beginning of Animation (Value = 50)

Halfway Through Animation (Value = 75)

End of Animation (Value = 100)

FIGURE 13.1   The same `DoubleAnimation` makes both the `Button`'s `Width` and the `Window`'s `Height` grow from 50 to 100.

Controlling Duration

The simple `DoubleAnimation` used thus far has the default duration of one second, but you can change the duration of an animation by setting its `Duration` property:

```
DoubleAnimation a = new DoubleAnimation();
a.From = 50;
a.To = 100;
a.Duration = new Duration(TimeSpan.Parse("0:0:5"));
```

This makes the animation from Figure 13.1 take five seconds rather than one. The typical way to construct a `Duration` instance is with a standard `TimeSpan` object, which is a part of the .NET Framework that predates WPF. By using the static `TimeSpan.Parse` method, you can specify the length of time with a string of the format *days.hours:minutes: seconds.fraction.*

> **WARNING**
>
> **Be careful when specifying the length of a `Duration` or `TimeSpan` as a string!**
>
> `TimeSpan.Parse`, which is also used by a type converter for `Duration` for the benefit of XAML, accepts shortcuts in its syntax so you don't need to specify every piece of `days.hours:minutes:seconds.fraction`. However, the behavior is not what you might expect. The string `"2"` means two *days*, not two seconds! The string `"2.5"` means two *days* and five *hours*! And the string `"0:2"` means two *minutes*. Given that most animations are no more than a few seconds long, the typical syntax used is *hours:minutes:seconds* or *hours:minutes:seconds.fraction*. So, two seconds can be expressed as `"0:0:2"` and half a second can be expressed as `"0:0:0.5"` or `"0:0:.5"`.

> **DIGGING DEEPER**
>
> **The Difference Between a `Duration` and a `TimeSpan`**
>
> The reason WPF defines a `Duration` type rather than just using `TimeSpan` is that `Duration` has two special values that can't be expressed by a `TimeSpan`: `Duration.Automatic` and `Duration.Forever`. Both of these values are designed for more complex classes like `Storyboard` described later in this chapter.
>
> `Automatic` is the default value for every animation class's `Duration` property, however, which is equivalent to a one-second `TimeSpan`. `Forever` is nonsensical for a simple animation like `DoubleAnimation`, because such a `Duration` would make it stay at its initial value indefinitely. WPF has no way to interpolate values between now and the end of time!

Flexibility with `From` and `To`

Right before the animation used in Figure 13.1 changes the `Button`'s `Width` and the `Window`'s `Height` from `50` to `100`, these properties must jump from their natural values to `50`. This isn't noticeable for animations that begin as soon as the `Window` is shown. But if we were to call `BeginAnimation` in response to an event, the "jump" effect would be jarring.

We could fix this by setting `To` to the current `Width`/`Height` instead of `50`, but this would require splitting the animation into two distinct objects—one that animates from the `Button`'s `ActualWidth` to `100`, and another that animates from the `Window`'s `ActualHeight` to `100`. Fortunately, there's an alternative. Specifying the `From` field of the animation can be optional. If you omit it, the animation begins with the current value of the target property, whatever that might be. For example, you might try to update the previous animation as follows:

```
DoubleAnimation a = new DoubleAnimation();
// Comment out: a.From = 50;
a.To = 100;
a.Duration = new Duration(TimeSpan.Parse("0:0:5"));
```

You might expect this to animate the Button's Width from its default value (just wide enough to fit the "OK" content with a little padding) to 100 over the course of five seconds. Instead, this produces an AnimationException that explains the following (in its inner exception):

```
'System.Windows.Media.Animation.DoubleAnimation' cannot use default origin value
of 'NaN'.
```

Because Width is unset, it has a value of NaN. And the animation can't interpolate any values between NaN and 100! Furthermore, applying the animation to ActualWidth (which is set to the true width rather than NaN) rather than Width isn't an option because it's read-only and it's not a dependency property. Instead, you must explicitly set the Width of the target Button somewhere for the preceding animation to work. For example:

```
<!-- Now the animation can grow the Button without a From value: -->
<Button x:Name="b" Width="20">OK</Button>
```

The Window from Figure 13.1 works with the From-less animation as is because its Height is already set to 300. But note that the same animation now grows the Button's Width from 20 to 100 yet *shrinks* the Window's Height from 300 to 100! Similarly, if you set the Button's Width to a value larger than 100, the animation would shrink its Width to 100.

> **TIP**
>
> Omitting an explicit From setting is important for getting smooth animations, especially when an animation is initiated in response to a repeatable user action. For example, if the animation to grow a Button's Width from 50 to 100 is started whenever the Button is clicked, rapid clicks would make the Width jump back to 50 each time. By omitting From, however, subsequent clicks make the animation continue from its current animated value, keeping the visual smoothness of the effect. Similarly, if you have an element grow on MouseEnter then shrink on MouseLeave, omitting From on both animations prevents the size of the element from jumping if the mouse pointer leaves the element before it's done growing, or if it reenters before it's done shrinking.

In fact, specifying the To field can also be optional! If the following animation is applied to the preceding Button, its Width changes from 50 to 20 (its explicitly marked Width) over five seconds:

```
DoubleAnimation a = new DoubleAnimation();
a.From = 50;
// Comment out: a.To = 100;
a.Duration = new Duration(TimeSpan.Parse("0:0:5"));
```

Each animation class also has a By field that can be set instead of the To field. The following animation means "animate the value *by* 100 (to 150)" instead of "animate the value *to* 100":

```
DoubleAnimation a = new DoubleAnimation();
a.From = 50;
a.By = 100; // Equivalent to a.To = 50 + 100;
```

Using By without From is a flexible way to express "animate the value from its current value to 100 units larger":

```
DoubleAnimation a = new DoubleAnimation();
a.By = 100; // Equivalent to a.To = currentValue + 100;
```

Negative values are supported for shrinking the current value:

```
DoubleAnimation a = new DoubleAnimation();
a.By = -100; // Equivalent to a.To = currentValue - 100;
```

Simple Animation Tweaks

You've seen the core properties of animation classes: From, To, Duration, and By. But there are a lot more properties that can alter an animation's behavior in more interesting ways.

As with the By property, some of these properties might look like silly tricks that could easily be accomplished manually with a little bit of code. That is true, but the main point of all these properties is to enable a lot of these easy-to-code tweaks purely from XAML.

BeginTime

If you don't want an animation to begin immediately when you call BeginAnimation, you can insert a delay by setting BeginTime to an instance of a TimeSpan:

```
DoubleAnimation a = new DoubleAnimation();
// Delay the animation by 5 seconds:
a.BeginTime = TimeSpan.Parse("0:0:5");
a.From = 50;
a.To = 100;
a.Duration = new Duration(TimeSpan.Parse("0:0:5"));
```

Besides being potentially useful in isolation, setting BeginTime can be useful for specifying a sequence of animations that start one after the other.

You can even set BeginTime to a negative value:

```
DoubleAnimation a = new DoubleAnimation();
// Start the animation half-way through:
a.BeginTime = TimeSpan.Parse("-0:0:2.5");
a.From = 50;
a.To = 100;
a.Duration = new Duration(TimeSpan.Parse("0:0:5"));
```

This starts the animation immediately, but at 2.5 seconds into the timeline (as if the animation really started 2.5 seconds previously). Therefore, the preceding animation is equivalent to one with `From` set to 75, `To` set to 100, and `Duration` set to 2.5 seconds.

Note that `BeginTime` is of type `Nullable<TimeSpan>` rather than `Duration` because the extra expressiveness of `Duration` is not needed. (It would be nonsensical to set a `BeginTime` of `Forever`!)

> **TIP**
>
> The code in this section uses `TimeSpan.Parse` because it supports the same syntax used by `TimeSpan`'s type converter (and therefore the same syntax used in XAML). Procedural code can benefit by using other `TimeSpan` methods, however, such as its static `FromSeconds` or `FromMilliseconds` methods.

SpeedRatio

The `SpeedRatio` property is a multiplier applied to `Duration`. It's set to 1 by default, but you can set it to any `double` value greater than 0:

```
DoubleAnimation a = new DoubleAnimation();
a.BeginTime = TimeSpan.Parse("0:0:5");
// Make the animation twice as long:
a.SpeedRatio = 2;
a.From = 50;
a.To = 100;
a.Duration = new Duration(TimeSpan.Parse("0:0:5"));
```

A value less than 1 slows down the animation, and a value greater than 1 speeds it up. `SpeedRatio` does not affect `BeginTime`; the preceding animation still has a 5-second delay, but the transition from 50 to 100 takes only 2.5 seconds rather than 5.

AutoReverse

If `AutoReverse` is set to `true`, the animation "plays backward" as soon as it completes. The reversal takes the same amount of time as the forward progress. For example, the following animation makes the value go from 50 to 100 in the first 5 seconds, then from 100 back to 50 over the course of 5 more seconds:

```
DoubleAnimation a = new DoubleAnimation();
a.AutoReverse = true;
a.From = 50;
a.To = 100;
a.Duration = new Duration(TimeSpan.Parse("0:0:5"));
```

`SpeedRatio` affects the speed of *both* the forward animation and backward animation. Therefore, giving the preceding animation a `SpeedRatio` of 2 would make the entire animation run for 5 seconds and giving it a `SpeedRatio` of 0.5 would make it run for 20 seconds. Note that any delay specified via `BeginTime` does *not* delay the reversal; it always happens immediately after the normal part of the animation completes.

RepeatBehavior

By setting RepeatBehavior, you can accomplish one of three different behaviors:

- ▶ Making the animation repeat itself a certain number of times, regardless of its duration
- ▶ Making the animation repeat itself until a certain amount of time has elapsed
- ▶ Cutting off the animation early

To repeat the animation a certain number of times, you can set RepeatBehavior to an instance of a RepeatBehavior class constructed with a double value:

```
DoubleAnimation a = new DoubleAnimation();
// Perform the animation twice in a row:
a.RepeatBehavior = new RepeatBehavior(2);

a.AutoReverse = true;
a.From = 50;
a.To = 100;
a.Duration = new Duration(TimeSpan.Parse("0:0:5"));
```

If AutoReverse is true, the reversal is repeated as well. So, the preceding animation goes from 50 to 100 to 50 to 100 to 50 over the course of 20 seconds. If BeginTime is set to introduce a delay, that delay is *not* repeated. Because RepeatBehavior can be initialized with a double, you can even repeat by a fractional amount.

To repeat the animation until a certain amount of time has elapsed, you can construct RepeatBehavior with a TimeSpan instead of a double. The following animation is equivalent to the preceding one:

```
DoubleAnimation a = new DoubleAnimation();
// Perform the animation twice in a row:
a.RepeatBehavior = new RepeatBehavior(TimeSpan.Parse("0:0:20"));
a.AutoReverse = true;
a.From = 50;
a.To = 100;
a.Duration = new Duration(TimeSpan.Parse("0:0:5"));
```

Twenty seconds is needed to make the animation complete two full cycles because of the setting of AutoReverse to true. Note that the TimeSpan-based RepeatBehavior is not scaled by SpeedRatio; if you set SpeedRatio to two in the preceding animation, it performs the full cycle four times rather than two.

To use RepeatBehavior as a way to cut off an animation early, simply construct it with a TimeSpan value shorter than the natural duration. The following animation makes the value go from 50 to 75 over 2.5 seconds:

```
DoubleAnimation a = new DoubleAnimation();
// Stop the animation halfway through:
a.RepeatBehavior = new RepeatBehavior(TimeSpan.Parse("0:0:2.5"));
a.From = 50;
a.To = 100;
a.Duration = new Duration(TimeSpan.Parse("0:0:5"));
```

TIP

You can make an animation repeat indefinitely by setting `RepeatBehavior` to the static `RepeatBehavior.Forever` field:

```
a.RepeatBehavior = RepeatBehavior.Forever;
```

DIGGING DEEPER

The Total Timeline Length of an Animation

With all the different adjustments that can be made to an animation with properties such as `BeginTime`, `SpeedRatio`, `AutoReverse`, and `RepeatBehavior`, it can be hard to keep track of how long it will take an animation to finish after it is initiated. Its `Duration` value certainly isn't adequate for describing the true length of time! Instead, the following formula describes an animation's true duration:

$$\text{Total Timeline Length} = \text{BeginTime} + \left(\frac{\text{Duration} * (\text{AutoReverse ? 2 : 1})}{\text{SpeedRatio}} * \text{RepeatBehavior} \right)$$

This applies if `RepeatBehavior` is specified as a double value (or left as its default value of one). If `RepeatBehavior` is specified as a `TimeSpan`, the total timeline length is simply the value of `RepeatBehavior` plus the value of `BeginTime`.

AccelerationRatio and DecelerationRatio

By default, animations update the target value in a linear fashion. When the animation is 25% done, the value is 25% of the way toward the final value, and so on. By changing the values of `AccelerationRatio` and `DecelerationRatio`, however, you can make the interpolation nonlinear. This is a popular technique for causing elements to "spring" to the final value, making the animation more lifelike.

Both properties can be set to a `double` value from 0 to 1 (with 0 being their default value). The `AccelerationRatio` value represents the percentage of time that the target value should accelerate from being stationary. Similarly, the `DecelerationRatio` value represents the percentage of time that the target value should decelerate to being stationary. Therefore, the sum of both properties must be less than or equal to one (100%).

Figure 13.2 illustrates what various values of `AccelerationRatio` and `DecelerationRatio` mean in practice.

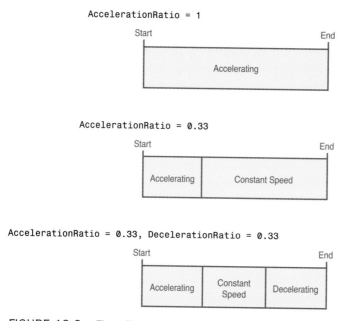

FIGURE 13.2   The effects of `AccelerationRatio` and `DecelerationRatio` as the value changes from start to end.

IsAdditive and IsCumulative

You can set `IsAdditive` to true to implicitly add the target property's current value (post-animation) to the animation's `From` and `To` properties. This doesn't affect repeating an animation with `RepeatBehavior`, but rather applies to manually repeating an animation at some later point in time. In essence, this makes an animation operate on a dependency property's post-animation value rather than continuing to operate on its pre-animation value.

`IsCumulative` is similar to `IsAdditive`, except that it works with `RepeatBehavior` (and *only* works with `RepeatBehavior`). For example, if you use `RepeatBehavior` to repeat an animation from 50 to 100 three times, the default behavior is to see the value go from 50 to 100, jump back to 50 then go to 100, then jump back to 50 one last time before ending at 100. With `IsCumulative` set to true, the animation instead smoothly changes the value from 50 to 200 over the same amount of time. If you take that same animation and set `AutoReverse` to true, you'll see the value go from 50 to 100 to 50, then jump to 100 and go from 100 to 150 to 100, then jump to 150 and go from 150 to 200 to 150.

FillBehavior

By default, when an animation completes, the target property remains at the final animated value unless some other mechanism later changes the value. This is typically the desired behavior, but if you want the property to jump back to its pre-animated value after the animation completes, you can set FillBehavior to Stop (rather than its default value of HoldEnd).

Animations in XAML

Given that animation classes consist of a bunch of useful properties, it's easy to imagine defining one in XAML. For example:

```
<DoubleAnimation From="50" To="100" Duration="0:0:5" AutoReverse="True"/>
```

But where do you place such an object? One option is to define it as a resource, so that you can retrieve it from procedural code and call BeginAnimation at the right time. You could even adjust properties on the animation to get different effects as conditions in your application change.

But, unsurprisingly, WPF supports initiating animations purely in XAML. The key to this support lies in triggers and their ability to contain more than just Setters but also *actions*.

All three types of triggers can contain actions, but this chapter focuses on event triggers because actions are the *only* things they can contain.

EventTriggers Containing Storyboards

As mentioned in Chapter 3, "Important New Concepts in WPF," an event trigger (represented by the EventTrigger class) is activated when a routed event is raised. The event is specified by the trigger's RoutedEvent property, and it can contain one or more actions (objects deriving from the abstract TriggerAction class) in its Actions collection. Animation classes such as DoubleAnimation are not actions themselves, so you can't add them directly to an EventTrigger's Actions collection. Instead, animations are placed inside an object known as a Storyboard, which is wrapped in an action called BeginStoryboard.

Therefore, placing the preceding DoubleAnimation inside an event trigger that is activated when a Button is clicked can look as follows:

```
<Button>
  OK
<Button.Triggers>
  <EventTrigger RoutedEvent="Button.Click">
  <EventTrigger.Actions>
    <BeginStoryboard>
      <Storyboard TargetProperty="Width">
        <DoubleAnimation From="50" To="100"
          Duration="0:0:5" AutoReverse="True"/>
      </Storyboard>
    </BeginStoryboard>
```

```
    </EventTrigger.Actions>
    </EventTrigger>
  </Button.Triggers>
</Button>
```

These two extra objects fill the two roles that BeginAnimation plays in procedural code: Storyboard specifies the dependency property that the animation operates on with TargetProperty, and

> **TIP**
>
> An animation can't be initiated in XAML unless it is placed inside a Storyboard.

BeginStoryboard specifies when the animation begins by attaching the Storyboard to the trigger.

The BeginStoryboard object might feel superfluous, but WPF ships with other TriggerAction-derived classes. One action is for playing sounds (covered in the next chapter), and several other actions work in concert with BeginStoryboard for declaratively pausing a storyboard, seeking it, stopping it, and so on. (These are called PauseStoryboard, SeekStoryboard, and so on.)

Specifying the Target Property

In the preceding XAML, Storyboard's TargetProperty property is set to the name of a property (Width) directly on the target object. But TargetProperty's type is PropertyPath, which supports more complicated expressions (as seen in Chapters 4 and 9), such as a property with a chain of subproperties.

The following Button has a LinearGradientBrush with three GradientStops as a Background. It uses a ColorAnimation to make the middle Color repeatedly animate from black to white and back. (The idea of animating a Color might sound strange, but internally it has floating-point values representing the ScA, ScR, ScB, and ScG components, so ColorAnimation can interpolate those values much like DoubleAnimation does for its single value.) To animate the middle Color of the LinearGradientBrush, the Storyboard must have a complex TargetProperty expression:

```
<Button Padding="30">
  OK
<Button.Background>
  <LinearGradientBrush>
    <GradientStop Color="Blue" Offset="0"/>
    <GradientStop Color="Black" Offset="0.5"/>
    <GradientStop Color="Blue" Offset="1"/>
  </LinearGradientBrush>
</Button.Background>
<Button.Triggers>
  <EventTrigger RoutedEvent="Button.Loaded">
  <EventTrigger.Actions>
    <BeginStoryboard>
```

```
    <Storyboard TargetProperty="Background.GradientStops[1].Color">
      <ColorAnimation From="Black" To="White" Duration="0:0:2"
        AutoReverse="True" RepeatBehavior="Forever"/>
    </Storyboard>
   </BeginStoryboard>
  </EventTrigger.Actions>
  </EventTrigger>
</Button.Triggers>
</Button>
```

The syntax for `TargetProperty` mimics what you would have to type to access the property in C#, although without casting. This `Storyboard` assumes that the `Button`'s `Background` is set to some object with a `GradientStops` property that can be indexed, assumes that it has at least two items, and assumes that the second item has a `Color` property of type `Color`. If any of these assumptions were wrong, the animation would fail. Of course, in this case these are all correct assumptions, so the `Button` successfully animates, as shown in Figure 13.3.

FIGURE 13.3   Animating the middle `Color` in a `LinearGradientBrush`.

Similarly, you could attach a `DoubleAnimation` to a `TargetProperty` of `Background.GradientStops[1].Offset` and give the Brush an animated "gleam" by making the highlight move from 0 to 1. If you want to animate *both* `Color` and `Offset` in response to the same `Loaded` event, you can add two `BeginStoryboard` actions to the trigger as follows:

```
<EventTrigger RoutedEvent="Button.Loaded">
<EventTrigger.Actions>
  <BeginStoryboard>
    <Storyboard TargetProperty="Background.GradientStops[1].Color">
      <ColorAnimation From="Black" To="White" Duration="0:0:2"
        AutoReverse="True" RepeatBehavior="Forever"/>
    </Storyboard>
  </BeginStoryboard>
  <BeginStoryboard>
    <Storyboard TargetProperty="Background.GradientStops[1].Offset">
      <DoubleAnimation From="0" To="1" Duration="0:0:2"
        AutoReverse="True" RepeatBehavior="Forever"/>
    </Storyboard>
```

13

```
    </BeginStoryboard>
  </EventTrigger.Actions>
</EventTrigger>
```

Fortunately, WPF provides a mechanism for animating different properties within the same Storyboard. First of all, a Storyboard can contain multiple animations. Storyboard's content property is Children, a collection of Timeline objects (a base class of all animation classes). Second, the TargetProperty property is not only a normal dependency property, but also an attached property that can be applied to Storyboard's children! Therefore, the previous XAML could be rewritten as follows:

```
<EventTrigger RoutedEvent="Button.Loaded">
<EventTrigger.Actions>
  <BeginStoryboard>
    <Storyboard>
      <ColorAnimation From="Black" To="White" Duration="0:0:2"
        Storyboard.TargetProperty="Background.GradientStops[1].Color"
        AutoReverse="True" RepeatBehavior="Forever"/>
      <DoubleAnimation From="0" To="1" Duration="0:0:2"
        Storyboard.TargetProperty="Background.GradientStops[1].Offset"
        AutoReverse="True" RepeatBehavior="Forever"/>
    </Storyboard>
  </BeginStoryboard>
</EventTrigger.Actions>
</EventTrigger>
```

This single Storyboard contains two animations, with each one targeting a different property on the target object. Both animations start simultaneously, but if you want a storyboard to contain animations that begin at different times, you can simply give each animation a different BeginTime value.

Specifying the Target Object

In the Storyboards shown so far, the target object containing the target property has been implicit. By default, it's the object containing the triggers or, in the case of a Style, the templated parent. But you can specify a different target object using Storyboard's TargetName property. And just like TargetProperty, TargetName can be applied directly to a Storyboard or to individual children as an attached property.

Here's a fun example using TargetName that "morphs" one picture to another by animating the opacity of the second picture that sits on top of the first:

```
<Grid xmlns="http://schemas.microsoft.com/winfx/2006/xaml/presentation">
<Grid.Triggers>
  <EventTrigger RoutedEvent="Grid.Loaded">
    <BeginStoryboard>
```

```
        <Storyboard TargetName="jim2" TargetProperty="Opacity">
          <DoubleAnimation From="1" To="0" Duration="0:0:4"
            AutoReverse="True" RepeatBehavior="Forever"/>
        </Storyboard>
      </BeginStoryboard>
    </EventTrigger>
  </Grid.Triggers>
    <Image Name="jim1" Source="jim1.gif"/>
    <Image Name="jim2" Source="jim2.gif"/>
</Grid>
```

Jim, the subject of these photos, shaved his impressive beard and got a long-overdue haircut, but took before and after photos that are eerily similar. The result of this animation is shown in Figure 13.4.

Opacity = 1   Opacity = 0.5   Opacity = 0

FIGURE 13.4   Animating an Image's Opacity to morph between two similar photos.

In this example, the use of TargetName is a little contrived because the event trigger could have been placed directly on jim2 rather than the parent Grid. But in larger examples (like perhaps a slide show of Images), it can be desirable to accumulate animations in a single location with a single event trigger, perhaps even with a single Storyboard by using TargetName as an attached property on each animation.

EventTriggers Inside a Style
Although each XAML snippet in this section adds an event trigger directly to elements, it's more common to see event triggers used inside of a Style. Listing 13.1 applies a Style with built-in animations to eight Buttons in a StackPanel. The animations make each Button grow to twice their size on MouseEnter and shrink back to normal size on MouseLeave, resulting in a simplified version of a "fisheye" effect. The result is shown in Figure 13.5.

FIGURE 13.5   Each Button is restyled with grow and shrink animations.

LISTING 13.1   Styling Buttons with Built-In Animations

```xml
<Window xmlns="http://schemas.microsoft.com/winfx/2006/xaml/presentation"
  xmlns:x="http://schemas.microsoft.com/winfx/2006/xaml"
  Title="Animation">
<Window.Resources>
  <Style TargetType="{x:Type Button}">
    <Setter Property="VerticalAlignment" Value="Bottom"/>
    <Setter Property="LayoutTransform">
    <Setter.Value>
      <ScaleTransform/>
    </Setter.Value>
    </Setter>
  <Style.Triggers>
    <EventTrigger RoutedEvent="Button.MouseEnter">
    <EventTrigger.Actions>
      <BeginStoryboard>
        <Storyboard>
          <DoubleAnimation Storyboard.TargetProperty="LayoutTransform.ScaleX"
            To="2" Duration="0:0:0.25"/>
          <DoubleAnimation Storyboard.TargetProperty="LayoutTransform.ScaleY"
            To="2" Duration="0:0:0.25"/>
        </Storyboard>
      </BeginStoryboard>
    </EventTrigger.Actions>
    </EventTrigger>
    <EventTrigger RoutedEvent="Button.MouseLeave">
    <EventTrigger.Actions>
      <BeginStoryboard>
        <Storyboard>
          <DoubleAnimation Storyboard.TargetProperty="LayoutTransform.ScaleX"
            To="1" Duration="0:0:0.25"/>
          <DoubleAnimation Storyboard.TargetProperty="LayoutTransform.ScaleY"
            To="1" Duration="0:0:0.25"/>
        </Storyboard>
      </BeginStoryboard>
    </EventTrigger.Actions>
    </EventTrigger>
  </Style.Triggers>
  </Style>
</Window.Resources>
  <StackPanel Orientation="Horizontal">
    <Button>1</Button>
    <Button>2</Button>
    <Button>3</Button>
    <Button>4</Button>
```

LISTING 13.1   Continued

```
    <Button>5</Button>
    <Button>6</Button>
    <Button>7</Button>
    <Button>8</Button>
  </StackPanel>
</Window>
```

This listing leverages `TargetProperty` as an attached property to animate both `ScaleX` and `ScaleY` in the same `Storyboard`. Both animations assume that `LayoutTransform` is set to an instance of a `ScaleTransform`. If `LayoutTransform` were instead set to a `TransformGroup` with a `ScaleTransform` as its first child, these animations could use the expressions `LayoutTransform.Children[0].ScaleX` and `LayoutTransform.Children[0].ScaleY` to access the desired properties.

> **TIP**
>
> The best way to animate the size and location of an element is to attach a `ScaleTransform` and/or `TranslateTransform` and animate its properties. Animating `ScaleTransform`'s `ScaleX` and `ScaleY` is generally more useful than animating `Width` and `Height` because it enables you to change the element size by a percentage rather than a fixed number of units. And animating `TranslateTransform` is better than animating something like `Canvas.Left` and `Canvas.Top` because it works regardless of the `Panel` containing the element.

To animate each `Button` via a `ScaleTransform` without requiring each `Button` to explicitly have one, Listing 13.1 sets `LayoutTransform` to an instance of `ScaleTransform` inside the `Style`. (Of course, this scheme breaks down if an individual `Button` has its `LayoutTransform` explicitly set.) `From` is omitted on all animations to keep the effect smooth. `Duration` is set with a simple string thanks to a type converter that accepts `TimeSpan.Parse` format (or `"Automatic"` or `"Forever"`).

> **TIP**
>
> Like `Duration`, `RepeatBehavior` has a type converter that makes it easy to use in XAML. A `TimeSpan`-formatted string can be used to set a fixed time, `"Forever"` can be used to indicate `RepeatBehavior.Forever`, and a number followed by `"x"` (for example, `"2x"` or `"3x"`) is treated as a multiplier.

DIGGING DEEPER

Starting Animations from Property Triggers

You can replace the `Style.Triggers` collection from Listing 13.1 with the following equivalent one that uses a single property trigger on `IsMouseOver`:

```
<Style.Triggers>
  <Trigger Property="IsMouseOver" Value="True">
  <Trigger.EnterActions>
    <BeginStoryboard>
      <Storyboard>
        <DoubleAnimation Storyboard.TargetProperty="LayoutTransform.ScaleX"
          To="2" Duration="0:0:0.25"/>
        <DoubleAnimation Storyboard.TargetProperty="LayoutTransform.ScaleY"
          To="2" Duration="0:0:0.25"/>
      </Storyboard>
    </BeginStoryboard>
  </Trigger.EnterActions>
  <Trigger.ExitActions>
    <BeginStoryboard>
      <Storyboard>
        <DoubleAnimation Storyboard.TargetProperty="LayoutTransform.ScaleX"
          To="1" Duration="0:0:0.25"/>
        <DoubleAnimation Storyboard.TargetProperty="LayoutTransform.ScaleY"
          To="1" Duration="0:0:0.25"/>
      </Storyboard>
    </BeginStoryboard>
  </Trigger.ExitActions>
  </Trigger>
</Style.Triggers>
```

Instead of a simple `Actions` collection, a property trigger has two collections: `EnterActions` and `ExitActions`. Actions inside `EnterActions` are activated when the trigger itself is activated (which is when any `Setters` would be applied). Actions inside `ExitActions` are activated when the trigger is deactivated (which is when any `Setters` would be undone). In this example, because the effect can be accomplished with either event triggers or a property trigger, the choice is simply one of personal preference.

Using Storyboard as a Timeline

A `Storyboard` is more than just a simple container that associates one or more animations with one or more target objects and their properties. `Storyboard` derives from `Timeline`, a base class shared with all the animation classes (`DoubleAnimation`, `ColorAnimation`, and so on). This means that `Storyboard` has many of the same properties and events discussed earlier in the chapter: `Duration`, `BeginTime`, `SpeedRatio`, `AutoReverse`, `RepeatBehavior`, `AccelerationRatio`, `DecelerationRatio`, `FillBehavior`, and so on.

Listing 13.2 contains a `Storyboard` that fades one `TextBlock` in and out at a time, for an effect somewhat like watching a movie trailer. The `Storyboard` itself is marked with a `RepeatBehavior` to make the entire sequence of animation repeat indefinitely. Figure 13.6 shows how this listing is rendered at three different spots of the sequence.

FIGURE 13.6   Snapshots of the movie-trailer-like title sequence.

LISTING 13.2   A Storyboard Containing Several Animations

```xml
<Grid xmlns="http://schemas.microsoft.com/winfx/2006/xaml/presentation"
  Background="Black" TextBlock.Foreground="White" TextBlock.FontSize="30">
<Grid.Triggers>
  <EventTrigger RoutedEvent="Grid.Loaded">
    <BeginStoryboard>
      <Storyboard TargetProperty="Opacity" RepeatBehavior="Forever">
        <DoubleAnimation Storyboard.TargetName="title1" BeginTime="0:0:2"
          From="0" To="1" Duration="0:0:2" AutoReverse="True"/>
        <DoubleAnimation Storyboard.TargetName="title2" BeginTime="0:0:6"
          From="0" To="1" Duration="0:0:2" AutoReverse="True"/>
        <DoubleAnimation Storyboard.TargetName="title3" BeginTime="0:0:10"
          From="0" To="1" Duration="0:0:2" AutoReverse="True"/>
        <DoubleAnimation Storyboard.TargetName="title4" BeginTime="0:0:14"
          From="0" To="1" Duration="0:0:2" AutoReverse="True"/>
        <DoubleAnimation Storyboard.TargetName="title5" BeginTime="0:0:18"
          From="0" To="1" Duration="0:0:2" AutoReverse="True"/>
      </Storyboard>
    </BeginStoryboard>
  </EventTrigger>
</Grid.Triggers>
  <TextBlock HorizontalAlignment="Center" VerticalAlignment="Center" Opacity="0"
    Name="title1">In a world</TextBlock>
  <TextBlock HorizontalAlignment="Center" VerticalAlignment="Center" Opacity="0"
    Name="title2">where user interfaces need to be created</TextBlock>
  <TextBlock HorizontalAlignment="Center" VerticalAlignment="Center" Opacity="0"
    Name="title3">one book</TextBlock>
  <TextBlock HorizontalAlignment="Center" VerticalAlignment="Center" Opacity="0"
    Name="title4">will explain it all...</TextBlock>
  <TextBlock HorizontalAlignment="Center" VerticalAlignment="Center" Opacity="0"
    Name="title5">WPF Unleashed</TextBlock>
</Grid>
```

Setting the Timeline-inherited properties on Storyboard affects the entire set of child animations, although in a slightly different way than setting the same property individually on all children. For example, if Listing 13.2 set RepeatBehavior="Forever" on every child animation rather than the Storyboard itself, it would wreak havoc. The first title would fade in and out as expected, but then at 6 seconds, *both* title1 and title2 would fade in and out together. At 10 seconds, title1, title2, and title3 would fade in and out simultaneously. And so on.

Similarly, setting SpeedRatio="2" on each DoubleAnimation would make each fade take 1 second rather than 2, but the final animation would still start 18 seconds after the animation starts. On the other hand, setting SpeedRatio="2" on the Storyboard would speed up the entire animation by a factor of two, including the BeginTimes. Therefore, the final animation would start 9 seconds after the animation starts. Setting AccelerationRatio="1" on the Storyboard would make each animation (and the time between them) faster than the previous one. Setting Duration to a time shorter than the natural duration can cut off the entire sequence of animations early.

Keyframe Animations

The normal animation classes only support linear interpolation from one value to another (or limited forms of nonlinear interpolation thanks to AccelerationRatio and DecelerationRatio). If you want to represent a more complicated animation, you can specify *keyframes*, which provide specific values at specific times. The use of keyframes requires a keyframe-enabled animation class. For example, DoubleAnimation has a companion class called DoubleAnimationUsingKeyFrames, as do all the other XXXAnimation classes.

The keyframe animation classes have the same properties and events as their counterparts, except for the From, To, and By properties. Instead, they have a KeyFrames collection that can hold keyframe instances specific to the type being animated. WPF has three types of keyframes, which this section examines.

Linear Keyframes

Listing 13.3 uses DoubleAnimationUsingKeyFrames to help move an Image of a house fly in a zigzag pattern, as illustrated in Figure 13.7. Because the Image is inside a Canvas, the motion is accomplished by animating the Canvas.Left and Canvas.Top attached properties rather than using a more versatile TranslateTransform.

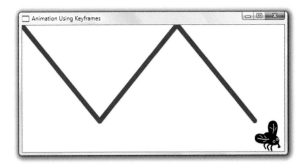

FIGURE 13.7   Zigzag motion is easy to create with a keyframe animation.

13

LISTING 13.3   The Zigzag Animation for Figure 13.7

```xml
<Window xmlns="http://schemas.microsoft.com/winfx/2006/xaml/presentation"
  Title="Animation Using Keyframes" Height="300" Width="580">
  <Canvas>
    <Image Source="fly.png">
    <Image.Triggers>
      <EventTrigger RoutedEvent="Image.Loaded">
      <EventTrigger.Actions>
        <BeginStoryboard>
          <Storyboard>
            <DoubleAnimation Storyboard.TargetProperty="(Canvas.Left)"
              From="0" To="500" Duration="0:0:3"/>
            <DoubleAnimationUsingKeyFrames Storyboard.TargetProperty="(Canvas.Top)"
              Duration="0:0:3">
              <LinearDoubleKeyFrame Value="0" KeyTime="0:0:0"/>
              <LinearDoubleKeyFrame Value="200" KeyTime="0:0:1"/>
              <LinearDoubleKeyFrame Value="0" KeyTime="0:0:2"/>
              <LinearDoubleKeyFrame Value="200" KeyTime="0:0:3"/>
            </DoubleAnimationUsingKeyFrames>
          </Storyboard>
        </BeginStoryboard>
      </EventTrigger.Actions>
      </EventTrigger>
    </Image.Triggers>
    </Image>
  </Canvas>
</Window>
```

The fly's motion consists of two animations that begin in parallel when the image loads. One is a simple DoubleAnimation that increases its horizontal position linearly from 0 to 500. The other is the keyframe-enabled animation, which oscillates the vertical position from 0 to 200 then back to 0 then back to 200.

DIGGING DEEPER

Animation and Data Binding

To simplify the discussions in this section, Listing 13.3 uses hard-coded values when animating Canvas.Left and Canvas.Top. Alternatively, you could use data binding to set the various To values to match the dimensions of the Window or Canvas. For example:

```
<DoubleAnimation Storyboard.TargetProperty="(Canvas.Left)" From="0"
  To="{Binding RelativeSource={RelativeSource FindAncestor,
  AncestorType={x:Type Canvas}}, Path=ActualWidth}"
  Duration="0:0:3"/>
```

Unfortunately, such an animation can't be performed in a trigger on Image.Loaded because the event is raised before the Window or Canvas is assigned its ActualHeight. (The value is still NaN, causing an AnimationException to be thrown.) You can perform such binding in animations associated with later events, however.

WARNING

Attached properties must be wrapped in parentheses when specified as a TargetProperty!

Notice that in Listing 13.3, both Canvas.Left and Canvas.Top are referenced inside parentheses when used as the value for Storyboard's TargetProperty property. This is a requirement for any attached properties used in a property path. Without the parentheses, the animation would look for a property on Image called Canvas (expecting it to return an object with Left and Top properties) and throw an exception because it doesn't exist.

Each keyframe instance (LinearDoubleKeyFrame) in Listing 13.3 gives a specific value and a time for that value to be applied. Setting KeyTime is optional, however. If you omit one, WPF assumes the keyframe occurs halfway between the surrounding keyframes. If you omit the KeyTime on all keyframes, they are spaced evenly across the duration of the animation. (This can also be specified explicitly by setting KeyTime to KeyTimeType.Uniform, or just "Uniform" in XAML.)

Although the keyframes in Listing 13.3 specify the exact vertical position of the fly at 0, 1, 2, and 3 seconds, WPF still needs to calculate intermediate values between these "key times." Because each keyframe is represented with an instance of *Linear*DoubleKeyFrame, the intermediate values are derived from simple linear interpolation. For example, at 0.5, 1.5, and 2.5 seconds, the calculated value is 100.

> **TIP**
>
> KeyTimes can be specified as percentages rather than TimeSpan values. This is handy for expressing the timing of keyframes independently from the duration of the animation. For example, the DoubleAnimationUsingKeyFrames from Listing 13.3 can be replaced with the following to obtain the same result:
>
> ```
> <DoubleAnimationUsingKeyFrames Storyboard.TargetProperty="(Canvas.Top)"
>   Duration="0:0:3">
>   <LinearDoubleKeyFrame Value="0" KeyTime="0%"/>
>   <LinearDoubleKeyFrame Value="200" KeyTime="33.3%"/>
>   <LinearDoubleKeyFrame Value="0" KeyTime="66.6%"/>
>   <LinearDoubleKeyFrame Value="200" KeyTime="100%"/>
> </DoubleAnimationUsingKeyFrames>
> ```
>
> KeyTime can also be set to Paced, which arranges the keyframes in such a way that gives the target property a constant rate of change. In other words, a pair of keyframes that changes the value from 0 to 200 is spaced twice as far apart as a pair of keyframes that changes the value from 0 to 100.

But DoubleAnimationUsingKeyFrames's KeyFrames property is a collection of (abstract) DoubleKeyFrame objects, so it can be filled with other types of keyframe objects. In addition to LinearDoubleKeyFrame, DoubleKeyFrame has two other subclasses: SplineDoubleKeyFrame and DiscreteDoubleKeyFrame.

Spline Keyframes

Every Linear*XXX*KeyFrame class has a corresponding Spline*XXX*KeyFrame class. It can be used just like its linear counterpart, so updating DoubleAnimationUsingKeyFrames from Listing 13.3 as follows produces the exact same result:

```
<DoubleAnimationUsingKeyFrames Storyboard.TargetProperty="(Canvas.Top)"
  Duration="0:0:3">
  <SplineDoubleKeyFrame Value="0" KeyTime="0:0:0"/>
  <SplineDoubleKeyFrame Value="200" KeyTime="0:0:1"/>
  <SplineDoubleKeyFrame Value="0" KeyTime="0:0:2"/>
  <SplineDoubleKeyFrame Value="200" KeyTime="0:0:3"/>
</DoubleAnimationUsingKeyFrames>
```

The spline keyframe classes have an additional KeySpline property that differentiates themselves from the linear classes. KeySpline can be set to an instance of a KeySpline object, which describes the desired motion as a cubic Bézier curve. KeySpline has two properties of type Point that represent the curve's control points. (The start point of the curve is always 0 and the end point is always 1.) A type converter enables you to specify a KeySpline in XAML as a simple list of two points. For example, the following update changes the fly's motion from the simple zigzag in Figure 13.7 to the more complicated motion in Figure 13.8:

```
<DoubleAnimationUsingKeyFrames Storyboard.TargetProperty="(Canvas.Top)"
  Duration="0:0:3">
  <SplineDoubleKeyFrame KeySpline="0,1 1,0" Value="0" KeyTime="0:0:0"/>
  <SplineDoubleKeyFrame KeySpline="0,1 1,0" Value="200" KeyTime="0:0:1"/>
  <SplineDoubleKeyFrame KeySpline="0,1 1,0" Value="0" KeyTime="0:0:2"/>
  <SplineDoubleKeyFrame KeySpline="0,1 1,0" Value="200" KeyTime="0:0:3"/>
</DoubleAnimationUsingKeyFrames>
```

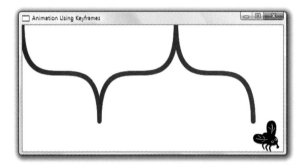

FIGURE 13.8   With KeySpline specified, the interpolation between keyframes is now based on cubic Bézier curves.

Finding the right value for KeySpline that gives the desired effect can be tricky, and almost certainly requires the use of a design tool like Expression Blend. But several free tools can be found online that help you visualize Bézier curves based on the specified control points.

Discrete Keyframes

A discrete keyframe simply indicates that no interpolation should be done from the previous keyframe. Updating DoubleAnimationUsingKeyFrames from Listing 13.3 as follows produces the motion illustrated in Figure 13.9:

```
<DoubleAnimationUsingKeyFrames Storyboard.TargetProperty="(Canvas.Top)"
  Duration="0:0:3">
  <DiscreteDoubleKeyFrame Value="0" KeyTime="0:0:0"/>
  <DiscreteDoubleKeyFrame Value="200" KeyTime="0:0:1"/>
  <DiscreteDoubleKeyFrame Value="0" KeyTime="0:0:2"/>
  <DiscreteDoubleKeyFrame Value="200" KeyTime="0:0:3"/>
</DoubleAnimationUsingKeyFrames>
```

Of course, all three types of keyframes can be mixed into the same animation. The following mixture makes the fly follow the path shown in Figure 13.10:

```
<DoubleAnimationUsingKeyFrames Storyboard.TargetProperty="(Canvas.Top)"
  Duration="0:0:3">
  <DiscreteDoubleKeyFrame Value="0" KeyTime="0:0:0"/>
```

```
  <LinearDoubleKeyFrame Value="200" KeyTime="0:0:1"/>
  <DiscreteDoubleKeyFrame Value="0" KeyTime="0:0:2"/>
  <SplineDoubleKeyFrame KeySpline="0,1,1,0" Value="200" KeyTime="0:0:3"/>
</DoubleAnimationUsingKeyFrames>
```

Because the first keyframe's time is at the very beginning, its type is actually irrelevant. That's because each frame only indicates how interpolation is done *before* that frame.

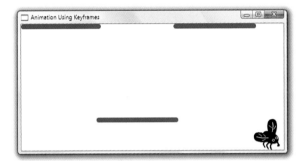

FIGURE 13.9   Discrete keyframes makes the fly's vertical position jump from one key value to the next with no interpolation.

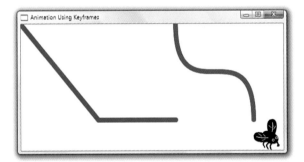

FIGURE 13.10   Mixing all three types of keyframes into a single animation.

As with Spline*XXX*KeyFrame, every Linear*XXX*KeyFrame class has a corresponding Discrete*XXX*KeyFrame. But WPF has five additional discrete keyframe classes that have no linear or spline counterpart. These classes enable you to animate Boolean, Char, Matrix, Object, and String. WPF only supports discrete keyframe animations with these data types because interpolation would not be meaningful (or even possible, as with the case of Boolean).

For example, here's an animation that could be applied to a TextBlock to animate its Text from a lowercase string to an uppercase string (with each keyframe using the default KeyTime of Uniform):

```
<StringAnimationUsingKeyFrames Storyboard.TargetProperty="Text" Duration="0:0:.5">
  <DiscreteStringKeyFrame Value="play"/>
  <DiscreteStringKeyFrame Value="Play"/>
  <DiscreteStringKeyFrame Value="PLay"/>
  <DiscreteStringKeyFrame Value="PLAy"/>
  <DiscreteStringKeyFrame Value="PLAY"/>
</StringAnimationUsingKeyFrames>
```

TIP

If you want to simply set a property value inside an event trigger rather than animate it in the traditional sense, you might be able to use a keyframe animation to simulate a `Setter`. For example, the following animation makes the `Button` disappear instantly when clicked by setting the `Opacity` to 0 with a keyframe at the beginning of an otherwise empty animation:

```
<Button>
  Click Me Once
<Button.Triggers>
  <EventTrigger RoutedEvent="Button.Click">
  <EventTrigger.Actions>
    <BeginStoryboard>
      <Storyboard>
        <DoubleAnimationUsingKeyFrames Storyboard.TargetProperty="Opacity">
          <DiscreteDoubleKeyFrame Value="0" KeyTime="0"/>
        </DoubleAnimationUsingKeyFrames>
      </Storyboard>
    </BeginStoryboard>
  </EventTrigger.Actions>
  </EventTrigger>
</Button.Triggers>
</Button>
```

DIGGING DEEPER

Path-Based Animations

WPF has yet another built-in alternative for animating `Double`, `Point`, and `Matrix` types. The `DoubleAnimationUsingPath`, `PointAnimationUsingPath`, and `MatrixAnimationUsingPath` classes enable you to specify a `PathGeometry` that dictates how the target value changes (with linear interpolation used between its points). Although they can technically be used with any properties of the right type, these classes are designed for animating the position of an object, using the `PathGeometry` as the "road" on which the object travels. (In the case of `DoubleAnimationUsingPath`, you would use a pair of these animations. One can apply the current X value from the `PathGeometry` to the target X value, whereas the other does the same for the Y value.)

Conclusion

With animation, you can do something as simple as a subtle rollover effect (which is becoming commonplace for even standard user interfaces) or as complex as an animated cartoon. Storyboards, which are a necessary part of performing animations purely in XAML, help to orchestrate complex series of animations.

The same could be said for other areas of WPF, but going overboard with animation can harm the usability and accessibility of your application or component. Another factor to consider is the performance implication of animation. Too much animation could make an otherwise-useful application become unusable on a less-powerful computer.

Fortunately, WPF enables you to provide rich animations (or other functionality) on powerful computers while scaling back the experience on less-powerful systems. The key to this is the RenderCapability class in the System.Windows.Media namespace. It defines a static Tier property and a static TierChanged event. When you're running on a tier 0 computer, everything is rendered in software. On a tier 1 computer, hardware rendering is sometimes used. And on a tier 2 computer (the top tier), everything that *can be* rendered in hardware is rendered in hardware. Therefore, you should be reluctant to use multiple simultaneous animations (or complicated gradients or 3D) on a tier 0 system. Besides removing animations, another way to adjust to running in the bottom tier is to reduce the natural frame rate (which tends to be 60 fps) with Storyboard's DesiredFrameRate attached property. This can decrease CPU utilization on such systems.

TIP

If you find yourself doing a lot of animation (or complicated static graphics, whether 2D or 3D), use RenderCapability.Tier to adjust your behavior. Note that although Tier is a 32-bit integer, the main value is stored in the high word. Therefore, you need to shift the value by 16 bits to see the true tier:

```
int tier = RenderCapability.Tier >> 16
```

This was done to enable subtiers in the future, but the result is pretty confusing for anyone using the API!

CHAPTER 14

Audio, Video, Speech, and Documents

This chapter is a grab bag of topics that aren't closely related, other than the fact that they each represent a specific domain of rich media that most applications don't even attempt to include. (Audio, video, and speech are also similar in that it's hard to demonstrate them in a physical book with static pictures!) In all four of these areas, Windows Presentation Foundation lowers the bar of difficulty significantly compared to previous technologies. So, although you might not have considered incorporating these feature areas in the past, you might change your mind after reading this chapter!

Audio

The audio support in WPF is simple to use. But unlike most of WPF, it's not revolutionary or next-generation, nor does it exploit the latest advances in hardware (at least in version 3.0). Instead, it's a thin layer over existing functionality in Win32 and Windows Media Player that covers the most common audio needs. You won't be able to build a professional audio application solely using WPF, but you can easily enhance an application with music and sound effects!

As with many tasks in WPF, you can accomplish playing audio in multiple ways, each with its own pros and cons. The choices for audio are represented by several different classes:

▸ SoundPlayer

▸ MediaPlayer

▶ SoundPlayerAction

▶ MediaElement and MediaTimeline

SoundPlayer

The easiest way to play audio files in a WPF application is to use the same mechanism used by non-WPF applications: the System.Media.SoundPlayer class. SoundPlayer, a part of the .NET Framework since version 2.0, is a simple wrapper for the Win32 PlaySound API. This means that it has a bunch of limitations, such as

▶ It only supports .wav audio files.

▶ It has no support for playing multiple sounds simultaneously. (Any new sound being played interrupts a currently playing sound.)

▶ It has no support for varying the volume of sounds.

It is, however, the most lightweight approach for playing a sound, so it's very appropriate to use for simple sound effects. The following code shows how to use SoundPlayer to play a sound:

```
SoundPlayer player = new SoundPlayer("tada.wav");
player.Play();
```

The string passed to SoundPlayer's constructor can be any filename or a URL. Calling Play plays the sound asynchronously, but you can also call PlaySync to play it on the current thread, or PlayLooping to make the sound repeat asynchronously until you call Stop (or until any other sound is played from any instance of SoundPlayer, or even direct calls to the underlying Win32 API).

For performance reasons, the audio file isn't loaded until the first time the sound is played. But this behavior could cause an unwanted pause, especially if you're retrieving a large audio file over the network. Therefore, SoundPlayer also defines Load and LoadAsynch methods for performing the loading at any point in time prior to the first playing.

If you want to play a familiar system sound without worrying about its filename and path on the target computer, the System.Media namespace also contains a SystemSounds class with static Asterisk, Beep, Exclamation, Hand, and Question properties. Each property is of type SystemSound, which has its own Play method (for asynchronous nonlooping playing only). That said, I would use these sparingly (if at all) to avoid annoying users with sounds that they only expect to come from Windows itself!

SoundPlayerAction

If you want to use SoundPlayer to add simple sound effects to user interface events such as hovering over or clicking a Button, you could easily define the appropriate event handlers that use SoundPlayer in their implementation. However, WPF defines a

SoundPlayerAction class (which derives from TriggerAction) that enables you to use SoundPlayer without writing any procedural code.

The following XAML snippet adds EventTriggers directly to a Button that play an audio file when the Button is clicked or the mouse pointer enters its bounds:

```
<Button>
<Button.Triggers>
  <EventTrigger RoutedEvent="Button.Click">
  <EventTrigger.Actions>
    <SoundPlayerAction Source="click.wav"/>
  </EventTrigger.Actions>
  </EventTrigger>
  <EventTrigger RoutedEvent="Button.MouseEnter">
  <EventTrigger.Actions>
    <SoundPlayerAction Source="hover.wav"/>
  </EventTrigger.Actions>
  </EventTrigger>
</Button.Triggers>
</Button>
```

SoundPlayerAction simply wraps SoundPlayer in a trigger-friendly way, so it has all the same limitations. Actually, it has even *more* limitations because you can't customize how it interacts with SoundPlayer. SoundPlayerAction internally constructs a SoundPlayer instance with its Source value and calls Play whenever the action is invoked. You can't play the sound synchronously (but why would you want to?), make it loop, or preload the audio file.

MediaPlayer

If the limitations of SoundPlayer and SoundPlayerAction are not acceptable, you can use the WPF-specific MediaPlayer class in the System.Windows.Media namespace. It is built on top of Windows Media Player, so it supports all of its audio formats (.wav, .wma, .mp3, and so on). Multiple sounds can be played simultaneously (although via different instances of MediaPlayer), and the volume can be controlled by setting its Volume property to a double between 0 and 1 (with 0.5 as the default value).

But MediaPlayer has even more features for giving you a lot of control over the audio:

► You can pause the audio with its Pause method (if CanPause is true).

► You can mute the audio by setting its IsMuted property to true.

► You shift the balance toward the left or right speaker by setting its Balance property to a value between -1 and 1. -1 means that all the audio is sent to the left speaker, 0 (the default) means that all the audio is sent to both speakers, and 1 means that all the audio is sent to the right speaker.

▸ For audio formats that support it, you can speed up or slow down the audio (without affecting its pitch) by setting its SpeedRatio property to any nonnegative double value. 1.0 is the default value, so a value less than 1.0 slows it down, whereas a value greater than 1.0 speeds it up.

▸ You can get the length of the audio clip with its NaturalDuration property (which is unaffected by SpeedRatio) and get the current position with the Position property.

▸ If the audio format supports seeking, you can even *set* the current position with the Position property.

Here is the simplest way to use MediaPlayer to play an audio file:

```
MediaPlayer player = new MediaPlayer();
player.Open(new Uri("music.wma", UriKind.Relative));
player.Play();
```

A single instance can play multiple audio files, but only one at a time. After you open a file with Open, methods such as Play, Pause, and Stop apply to that file. You can also call Close to release the file (which also stops the audio if it's currently playing). The file is always

> **TIP**
>
> For more details and quirks related to MediaPlayer, be sure to read the upcoming "Video" section, even if you have no intention of using WPF's video support.

played asynchronously, so you would not want to call Close immediately after the preceding code because you wouldn't hear anything get played!

MediaElement and MediaTimeline

MediaPlayer gives you a lot more flexibility than SoundPlayer, but it is designed for procedural code only. (Its main functionality is exposed through methods, its properties are not dependency properties, and its events are not routed events.) Somewhat like how SoundPlayerAction wraps SoundPlayer for declarative use, WPF provides a MediaElement class that wraps MediaPlayer for declarative use.

MediaElement is a full-blown FrameworkElement in the System.Windows.Controls namespace, so it's meant to be embedded in your user interface, it participates in layout, and so on. (This sounds odd until you realize that MediaElement is also used for video, discussed in the next section.) MediaElement exposes most of the properties and events of MediaPlayer as dependency properties and routed events.

You can set MediaElement's Source property to the URI of an audio file, but it would play as soon as the element is loaded. Instead, to declaratively play sounds at arbitrary times, you should set Source on the fly using animation with a MediaTimeline.

Just like the earlier example that uses SoundPlayerAction, the following XAML shows how to use MediaElement and MediaTimeline to play an audio file when a Button is clicked or the mouse pointer enters its bounds:

```
<MediaElement x:Name="audio"/>
...
<Button>
<Button.Triggers>
  <EventTrigger RoutedEvent="Button.Click">
  <EventTrigger.Actions>
    <BeginStoryboard>
      <Storyboard>
        <MediaTimeline Source="click.wma" Storyboard.TargetName="audio"/>
      </Storyboard>
    </BeginStoryboard>
  </EventTrigger.Actions>
  </EventTrigger>
  <EventTrigger RoutedEvent="Button.MouseEnter">
  <EventTrigger.Actions>
    <BeginStoryboard>
      <Storyboard>
        <MediaTimeline Source="hover.wma" Storyboard.TargetName="audio"/>
      </Storyboard>
    </BeginStoryboard>
  </EventTrigger.Actions>
  </EventTrigger>
</Button.Triggers>
</Button>
```

In addition to the BeginStoryboard action, you can use the same Storyboard with the PauseStoryboard, ResumeStoryboard, SeekStoryboard, and StopStoryboard actions to pause/resume/seek/stop the audio.

TIP

To create continuously looping background audio, you can set MediaTimeline's RepeatBehavior to Forever, and use it in a trigger on MediaElement's Loaded event. For example:

```
<MediaElement x:Name="audio">
<MediaElement.Triggers>
  <EventTrigger RoutedEvent="MediaElement.Loaded">
  <EventTrigger.Actions>
    <BeginStoryboard>
      <Storyboard>
        <MediaTimeline Source="music.mp3" Storyboard.TargetName="audio"
          RepeatBehavior="Forever"/>
      </Storyboard>
    </BeginStoryboard>
```

Continues

> **TIP**
>
> **Continued**
>
> ```
>     </EventTrigger.Actions>
>     </EventTrigger>
>   </MediaElement.Triggers>
> </MediaElement>
> ```
>
> Unfortunately, a slight pause might be heard every time the audio reaches the end, before it is played again from the beginning. One (weird) workaround for this is to create a video with the desired audio then replace the Source with the video file (and keep the MediaElement hidden from view). That's because WPF has tighter integration with video and supports seamless looping in this case.

Video

WPF's video support is built on the same MediaPlayer class described in the previous section, and its companion classes such as MediaElement and MediaTimeline. Therefore, all file formats supported by Windows Media Player can be easily used in WPF applications as well (.wmv, .avi, .mpg, and so on). Also, much of the discussion in this section also applies to playing audio with MediaPlayer and/or MediaElement.

> **WARNING**
>
> **WPF's audio and video support requires Windows Media Player 10 or higher!**
>
> Without at least version 10 installed, the use of MediaPlayer (and related classes) throws an exception.

> **WARNING**
>
> **Prior to Windows Vista, Windows Media Player is 32-bit only!**
>
> The 64-bit versions of Windows (prior to Windows Vista) contain only a 32-bit version of Windows Media Player. Because WPF's video (and richer audio) support is built on Windows Media Player, you can't use it from a 64-bit application running on these platforms. Instead, you must ensure that your application runs as 32-bit. In this case, your application can automatically use the 32-bit version of the .NET Framework (which is installed alongside the 64-bit version).

Controlling the Visual Aspects of MediaElement

Like Viewbox and Image, MediaElement has Stretch and StretchDirection properties that control how the video fills the space given to it. Figure 14.1 shows the three different Stretch values operating on a MediaElement placed directly inside a Window:

```
<Window xmlns="http://schemas.microsoft.com/winfx/2006/xaml/presentation">
  <MediaElement Source="C:\Users\Public\Videos\Sample Videos\butterfly.wmv"
    Stretch="XXX"/>
</Window>
```

Uniform (default)   Fill   UniformToFill

FIGURE 14.1   MediaElement in a Window with three different Stretch settings.

Of course, the neat thing about MediaElement is that it enables video to be manipulated in richer ways, like most other FrameworkElements. The following XAML, rendered in Figure 14.2, places two instances of a video on top of each other, both half-transparent, both clipped with a circle, and one rotated 180°:

```
<Canvas>
  <MediaElement Source="C:\Users\Public\Videos\Sample Videos\butterfly.wmv"
    Opacity="0.5">
  <MediaElement.Clip>
    <EllipseGeometry Center="220,220" RadiusX="220" RadiusY="220"/>
  </MediaElement.Clip>
  <MediaElement.LayoutTransform>
    <RotateTransform Angle="180"/>
  </MediaElement.LayoutTransform>
  </MediaElement>

  <MediaElement Source="C:\Users\Public\Videos\Sample Videos\butterfly.wmv"
    Opacity="0.5">
  <MediaElement.Clip>
    <EllipseGeometry Center="220,220" RadiusX="220" RadiusY="220"/>
  </MediaElement.Clip>
  </MediaElement>
</Canvas>
```

Furthermore, by placing MediaElement inside a VisualBrush, you can easily use video just about anywhere—as a background for a ListBox, a material on a 3D surface, and so on. Just be sure to measure the performance implications before going overboard with VisualBrush and video!

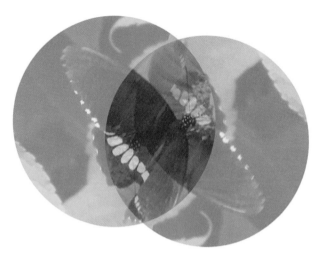

FIGURE 14.2   Clipped, rotated, and half-transparent video inside two MediaElements.

FAQ

 How do I take snapshots of individual video frames?

You can set the Position of video to a specific point to "freeze frame" it. But if you want to persist that frame as a separate Image, you render a MediaElement into a RenderTargetBitmap (just like any other Visual). For example:

```
MediaElement mediaElement = …;
Size desiredSize = …;
Size dpi = …;
RenderTargetBitmap bitmap = new RenderTargetBitmap(desiredSize.Width,
  desiredSize.Height, dpi.Width, dpi.Height, PixelFormats.Pbgra32);
bitmap.Render(mediaElement);
Image image = new Image();
image.Source = BitmapFrame.Create(bitmap);
```

If you are working with MediaPlayer rather than MediaElement, you could create a DrawingVisual to pass to RenderTargetBitmap's Render method as follows:

```
DrawingVisual visual = new DrawingVisual();
MediaPlayer mediaPlayer = …;
Size desiredSize = …;
using (DrawingContext dc = visual.RenderOpen())
{
  dc.DrawVideo(mediaPlayer, new Rect(0, 0, desiredSize.Width,
    desiredSize.Height));
}
```

The key to this code is DrawingContext's DrawVideo method, which accepts an instance of MediaPlayer and a Rect. In fact, MediaElement uses DrawVideo inside its OnRender method to do its own video rendering!

Controlling the Underlying Media

The previous two XAML snippets use the simple approach of setting MediaElement's Source directly. This causes the media to play immediately when the element is loaded. It's more likely that you'll want to play/pause/stop the video at specific times. As in the "Audio" section, the following XAML accomplishes this with a trigger that uses MediaTimeline. It also contains triggers that use PauseStoryboard and ResumeStoryboard to provide the functionality for a simple media player:

```
<Grid>
<Grid.Triggers>
  <EventTrigger RoutedEvent="Button.Click" SourceName="playButton">
  <EventTrigger.Actions>
    <BeginStoryboard Name="beginStoryboard">
      <Storyboard>
        <MediaTimeline Source="C:\Users\Public\Videos\Sample Videos\butterfly.wmv"
          Storyboard.TargetName="video"/>
      </Storyboard>
    </BeginStoryboard>
  </EventTrigger.Actions>
  </EventTrigger>
  <EventTrigger RoutedEvent="Button.Click" SourceName="pauseButton">
  <EventTrigger.Actions>
    <PauseStoryboard BeginStoryboardName="beginStoryboard"/>
  </EventTrigger.Actions>
  </EventTrigger>
  <EventTrigger RoutedEvent="Button.Click" SourceName="resumeButton">
  <EventTrigger.Actions>
    <ResumeStoryboard BeginStoryboardName="beginStoryboard"/>
  </EventTrigger.Actions>
  </EventTrigger>
</Grid.Triggers>

  <MediaElement x:Name="video"/>
  <StackPanel Orientation="Horizontal" VerticalAlignment="Bottom">
    <Button x:Name="playButton" Background="#55FFFFFF" Height="40">Play</Button>
    <Button x:Name="pauseButton" Background="#55FFFFFF" Height="40">Pause</Button>
    <Button x:Name="resumeButton" Background="#55FFFFFF" Height="40">Resume
    </Button>
  </StackPanel>
</Grid>
```

The user interface includes three translucent Buttons for controlling the video playing underneath them, as shown in Figure 14.3.

14

Although the default behavior for media specified as the Source of a MediaElement is to begin playing when the element is loaded, you can change this behavior with MediaElement's LoadedBehavior and UnloadedBehavior properties, both of type MediaState. MediaState is an enumeration with the values Play (the default for LoadedBehavior), Pause, Stop, Close (the default for UnloadedBehavior), and Manual.

FIGURE 14.3   A simple video player, with Buttons that use storyboards to control the video.

If you want to control the media from procedural code, MediaElement exposes the methods of the MediaPlayer it wraps (Play, Stop, and so on) but you can only call these when LoadedBehavior and UnloadedBehavior are set to Manual. In addition, you can only set the Position and SpeedRatio properties when the element is in this manual mode.

Note that manual mode is only applicable when you don't have any MediaTimelines in triggers attached to the MediaElement. When MediaElement is an animation target, its behavior is *always* driven by an animation clock (exposed as its Clock property of type MediaClock) and can't be altered manually unless you interact with the clock.

TIP

When combining a MediaTimeline with other animations inside the same Storyboard, you might want to customize the way in which these animations are synchronized. Playing media often has an initial delay from loading and buffering, causing it to fall behind other animations. And if you give your Storyboard a fixed duration, it might cut off the end of the media because of such delays.

To change this behavior, you can set Storyboard's SlipBehavior property to Slip rather than its default value of Grow. This causes all animations to wait until the media is ready before doing anything.

TIP

To include streaming audio or video in your application, simply set the Source to a streaming URL. Any encoding supported by Windows Media Player works, such as ASF-encoded .wmv files. If you want to include a live video feed from a local webcam (which doesn't have a URL you can point to), Chapter 15, "Interoperability with Win32, Windows Forms, and ActiveX," shows a way to accomplish this.

> # WARNING
>
> ## Media files can't be embedded resources!
>
> The URIs given as Source values to MediaPlayer, MediaElement, and MediaTimeline are not as general-purpose as the URIs used elsewhere in WPF. They must be paths understood by Windows Media Player, such as absolute or relative file system paths, or a URL. This means that there's no built-in support for referencing a media file embedded as a resource. Ironically, the only mechanism discussed in this chapter that supports specifying media as an arbitrary stream is the otherwise very-limited SoundPlayer! (It has a constructor that accepts a Stream rather than a string path.)
>
> This also means you can't refer to files at the site of origin using the pack://siteOfOrigin syntax. Instead, you can simply hard-code the appropriate path or URL, or programmatically retrieve the site of origin using ApplicationDeployment.CurrentDeployment. ActivationUri (in the System.Deployment.Application namespace defined in System.Deployment.dll) and then prepend it to a filename to form a fully qualified URI.

> # TIP
>
> To diagnose any errors when using MediaPlayer or MediaElement, you should attach an event handler to the MediaFailed event defined by both classes. This could look like the following:
>
> ```
> <MediaElement Source="nonExistentFile.wmv" MediaFailed="OnMediaFailed"/>
> ```
>
> where the OnMediaFailed code-behind function is defined as
>
> ```
> void OnMediaFailed(object o, ExceptionRoutedEventArgs e)
> {
>   MessageBox.Show(e.ErrorException.ToString());
> }
> ```
>
> If the Source file doesn't exist, you'll now see the following exception rather than silent failure:
>
> ```
> System.IO.FileNotFoundException: Cannot find the media file. --->
> System.Runtime.InteropServices.COMException (0xC00D1197):
> Exception from HRESULT: 0xC00D1197
> ```
>
> Most people are surprised when they learn that you need to opt in to this behavior rather than seeing such exceptions by default. But because of the asynchronous nature of media processing, a directly thrown exception might not be catchable anywhere outside of a global handler.

> **FAQ**
>
> **How can I get metadata associated with audio or video, such as Artist or Genre?**
>
> WPF does not expose a way to retrieve this metadata. Instead, you must use unmanaged Windows Media Player APIs to access this information.

Speech

The .NET Framework 3.0 includes a new set of speech APIs in the `System.Speech` namespace. These APIs make it easy to incorporate both speech recognition and speech synthesis. They are built on top of Microsoft SAPI APIs and use W3C standard formats for synthesis and recognition grammars, so they integrate very well with existing engines.

The `System.Speech` APIs are not tied to WPF; you won't find any dependency properties, routed events, the built-in ability to animate voice, and so on. Therefore, you can easily use them in any .NET application, whether WPF-based, Windows Forms-based, or even console-based.

Speech Synthesis

Speech synthesis, also known as *text-to-speech*, is the process of turning text into audio. This requires a "voice" to speak the text. Windows Vista has a great voice installed by default, called Microsoft Anna. Microsoft's SAPI SDK (a free download at http://www.microsoft.com/speech/download/sdk51) includes Microsoft Anna and other voices, such as the more robotic-sounding Microsoft Sam, and can be installed on just about all versions of Windows.

Bringing Text to Life

To get started, add a reference to `System.Speech.dll` to your project. The relevant APIs are in the `System.Speech.Synthesis` namespace. Getting text to be spoken is as simple as follows:

```
SpeechSynthesizer synthesizer = new SpeechSynthesizer();
synthesizer.Speak("I love WPF!");
```

This speaks the text synchronously using the voice, rate, and volume settings chosen in the Text to Speech area of Control Panel. To speak text asynchronously, you can call `SpeakAsync` instead of `Speak`:

```
synthesizer.SpeakAsync("I love WPF!");
```

You can change the rate and volume of the spoken text by setting `SpeechSynthesizer`'s `Rate` and `Volume` properties. They are both integers, but `Rate` has a range of -10 to 10, whereas `Volume` has a range of 0 to 100. You can also cancel pending asynchronous speech by calling `SpeakAsyncCancelAll`.

If you have multiple voices installed, you can change the voice at any time by calling
SelectVoice:

```
synthesizer.SelectVoice("Microsoft Sam");
```

You can enumerate them with GetInstalledVoices, or even attempt to select a voice with
a desired gender and age (which, for some reason, feels a little creepy):

```
synthesizer.SelectVoiceByHints(VoiceGender.Female, VoiceAge.Adult);
```

You can even send its output to a .wav file rather than your speakers. For example:

```
synthesizer.SetOutputToWaveFile("c:\Users\Adam\Documents\speech.wav");
```

This affects any subsequent calls to Speak or SpeakAsync. You can point the synthesizer
back to the speakers by calling SetOutputToDefaultAudioDevice.

SSML and PromptBuilder

You can do a lot by passing simple strings to SpeechSynthesizer and using its various
members to change voices, rate, volume, and so on. But SpeechSynthesizer also supports
input in the form of a standard XML-based language known as Speech Synthesis Markup
Language (SSML). This enables you to encapsulate complex speech in a single chunk, and
have more control over the synthesizer's behavior. You can pass SSML content to
SpeechSynthesizer directly via its SpeakSsml and SpeakSsmlAsync methods, but
SpeechSynthesizer also has overloads of Speak and SpeakAsync that accept an instance of
PromptBuilder.

PromptBuilder is a handy class that
makes it easy to programmatically build
complex speech input. With
PromptBuilder, you can express most of
what you could accomplish with an
SSML file, but it's generally simpler to
learn than SSML.

> **TIP**
>
> Speech Synthesis Markup Language (SSML)
> is a W3C Recommendation published at
> http://www.w3.org/TR/speech-synthesis.

The following code builds a simple dialog with PromptBuilder and then speaks it by
passing it to SpeakAsync:

```
SpeechSynthesizer synthesizer = new SpeechSynthesizer();
PromptBuilder promptBuilder = new PromptBuilder();

promptBuilder.AppendTextWithHint("WPF", SayAs.SpellOut);
promptBuilder.AppendText("sounds better than WPF.");

// Pause for 2 seconds
promptBuilder.AppendBreak(new TimeSpan(0, 0, 2));

promptBuilder.AppendText("The time is");
```

14

```
promptBuilder.AppendTextWithHint(DateTime.Now.ToString("hh:mm"), SayAs.Time);

// Pause for 2 seconds
promptBuilder.AppendBreak(new TimeSpan(0, 0, 2));

promptBuilder.AppendText("Hey Sam, can you spell queue?");

promptBuilder.StartVoice("Microsoft Sam");
promptBuilder.AppendTextWithHint("queue", SayAs.SpellOut);
promptBuilder.EndVoice();

promptBuilder.AppendText("Do it faster!");

promptBuilder.StartVoice("Microsoft Sam");
promptBuilder.StartStyle(new PromptStyle(PromptRate.ExtraFast));
promptBuilder.AppendTextWithHint("queue", SayAs.SpellOut);
promptBuilder.EndStyle();
promptBuilder.EndVoice();

// Speak all the content in the PromptBuilder
synthesizer.SpeakAsync(promptBuilder);
```

After you instantiate a `PromptBuilder`, you keep appending different types of content. The preceding code makes use of `AppendTextWithHint` to spell out some words (which produces a better pronunciation of WPF) and to pronounce a string representing time (such as "08:25") more naturally. You can also surround chunks of content with Start*XXX*/End*XXX* methods that change the voice or style of the surrounding text, or denote where paragraphs and sentences begin and end. These chunks can be nested, just like the XML elements you would create if you were writing raw SSML.

TIP

SpeechSynthesizer even supports playing .wav audio files! You can do this in two easy ways. One is using `PromptBuilder`'s AppendAudio method:

```
promptBuilder.AppendAudio("sound.wav");
```

(You could also include the equivalent directive in an SSML file and pass it to `SpeakSsml`/`SpeakSsmlAsync`.)

Another way is to use an overload of Speak or SpeakAsync that accepts a Prompt instance such as FilePrompt. With FilePrompt, you can speak content of a file, whether it's a plain text file, an SSML file, or a .wav file:

```
synthesizer.SpeakAsync(new FilePrompt("text.txt", SynthesisMediaType.Text);
synthesizer.SpeakAsync(new FilePrompt("content.ssml", SynthesisMediaType.Ssml);
synthesizer.SpeakAsync(new FilePrompt("sound.wav", SynthesisMediaType.WaveAudio);
```

DIGGING DEEPER

Converting a `PromptBuilder` to SSML

You can get the SSML representation of a `PromptBuilder` by calling its ToXml method (as long as the result is well formed at the time you call it, for example, there are no StartXXX calls without matching EndXXX calls). Here's the result when calling it on the `PromptBuilder` from the preceding code (at 8:25 PM):

```xml
<speak version="1.0" xmlns="http://www.w3.org/2001/10/synthesis"
  xml:lang="en-US">
  <say-as interpret-as="characters">WPF</say-as>
  sounds better than WPF
  <break time="2000ms"/>
  The time is
  <say-as interpret-as="time">08:25</say-as>
  <break time="2000ms"/>
  Hey Bob, can you spell queue?
  <voice name="Microsoft Sam">
    <say-as interpret-as="characters">queue</say-as>
  </voice>
  Do it faster!
  <voice name="Microsoft Sam">
    <prosody rate="x-fast">
      <say-as interpret-as="characters">queue</say-as>
    </prosody>
  </voice>
</speak>
```

This can be a handy way to persist content that you want spoken at a later time.

Speech Recognition

Speech recognition is the exact opposite of speech synthesis. Recognition is all about extracting speech sounds from an audio input and turning it into text.

TIP

For speech recognition to work, you need to have a speech recognition engine installed and running. Windows Vista comes with one, and Office XP or later comes with one as well. You can also install a free one from http://www.microsoft.com/speech/download/sdk51. You can start the Windows Vista engine by selecting Windows Speech Recognition from the Start menu under Accessories, Ease of Access.

14

Converting Spoken Words into Text

To use speech recognition, you must add a reference to System.Speech.dll to your project (just like with speech synthesis). This time, the relevant APIs are in the System.Speech.Recognition namespace. The simplest form of recognition is demonstrated by the following code, which instantiates a SpeechRecognizer and attaches an event handler to its SpeechRecognized event:

```
SpeechRecognizer recognizer = new SpeechRecognizer();
recognizer.SpeechRecognized +=
  new EventHandler<SpeechRecognizedEventArgs>(recognizer_SpeechRecognized);
```

SpeechRecognized gets called whenever spoken words or phrases are converted to text, so a simple implementation could be written as follows:

```
void recognizer_SpeechRecognized(object sender, SpeechRecognizedEventArgs e)
{
  textBox.Text += e.Result.Text;
}
```

When instantiating SpeechRecognizer, you'll see a dialog similar to Figure 14.4 if you haven't previously configured speech recognition via Control Panel. Therefore, this is probably not something you want to do in the normal flow of your application!

FIGURE 14.4   Using speech recognition for the first time summons a wizard that helps you configure your microphone and train the computer for the sound of your voice.

The preceding code is adequate for dictating text into a TextBox, but it's unnecessary on Windows Vista because you already get that functionality for free! For example, if you enable Windows Vista speech recognition and give any WPF TextBox focus, the words you speak into the microphone auto-matically appear, as shown in Figure 14.5. This works because the Windows Vista speech recognition system inte-grates with the UI Automation interfaces exposed by WPF elements. You can even invoke actions such as clicking on Buttons by speaking their automation names! (This is not specific to WPF, but also true of Windows Forms or any other UI frameworks with built-in inte-gration with Windows accessibility.)

FIGURE 14.5   Dictating content into a WPF TextBox using the Windows Speech Recognition program.

The typical usage of speech recognition is to add custom spoken commands to your program that are more sophisticated than the default functionality exposed through accessibility. Such commands typically consist of a few words or phrases that an applica-tion knows in advance. To handle this efficiently, you'll want to give SpeechRecognizer more information about your expectations. That's where SRGS comes in.

Specifying a Grammar with SRGS

If you want to programmatically act on certain words or phrases, writing a SpeechRecognized event handler is tricky if you don't constrain the input. You need to ignore irrelevant phrases and possibly pick out relevant words from larger phrases that can't be easily predicted. For example, if one of the words you want to act on is "go," do you accept words like "goat," assuming that the recognizer simply misunderstood the user?

To avoid this kind of grunt-work and guesswork, SpeechRecognizer supports specifying a grammar based on the Speech Recognition Grammar Specification (SRGS). With a grammar that captures your possible valid inputs,

> **TIP**
>
> Speech Recognition Grammar Specification (SRGS) is a W3C Recommendation published at http://www.w3.org/TR/speech-grammar.

the recognizer can automatically ignore meaningless results and improve the accuracy of its recognition.

To attach a grammar to a SpeechRecognizer, you can call its LoadGrammar method. SRGS-based grammars can be described in XML, so the following code loads a custom grammar from an SRGS XML file in the current directory:

```
SpeechRecognizer recognizer = new SpeechRecognizer();
SrgsDocument doc = new SrgsDocument("grammar.xml");
recognizer.LoadGrammar(new Grammar(doc));
```

SrgsDocument (and other SRGS-related types) are defined in the System.Speech.Recognition.SrgsGrammar namespace.

An SrgsDocument can also be built in-memory using a handful of APIs. The following code builds a grammar that only allows two commands: *stop* and *go*:

14

```
SpeechRecognizer recognizer = new SpeechRecognizer();
SrgsDocument doc = new SrgsDocument();
SrgsRule command = new SrgsRule("command", new SrgsOneOf("stop", "go"));
doc.Rules.Add(command);
doc.Root = command;
recognizer.LoadGrammar(new Grammar(doc));
```

You can express much more intricate grammars, however. The following example could be used by a card game, enabling a user to give commands like *three of hearts* or *ace of spaces* to play those cards:

```
SpeechRecognizer recognizer = new SpeechRecognizer();
SrgsDocument doc = new SrgsDocument();
SrgsRule command = new SrgsRule("command");
SrgsRule rank = new SrgsRule("rank");
SrgsItem of = new SrgsItem("of");
SrgsRule suit = new SrgsRule("suit");
SrgsItem card = new SrgsItem(new SrgsRuleRef(rank), of, new SrgsRuleRef(suit));
command.Add(card);
rank.Add(new SrgsOneOf("two", "three", "four", "five", "six", "seven",
  "eight", "nine", "ten", "jack", "queen", "king", "ace"));
of.SetRepeat(0, 1);
suit.Add(new SrgsOneOf("clubs", "diamonds", "spades", "hearts"));
doc.Rules.Add(command, rank, suit);
doc.Root = command;
recognizer.LoadGrammar(new Grammar(doc));
```

This grammar defines the notion of a card as *"rank of suit"* where *rank* has 13 possible values, *suit* has 4 possible values, and "of" can be omitted (hence the SetRepeat call that allows it to be said zero or one time).

Specifying a Grammar with GrammarBuilder

Specifying grammars with the APIs in System.Speech.Recognition.SrgsGrammar or with an SRGS XML file (whose syntax is not covered here) can be complicated. Therefore, the System.Speech.Recognition namespace also contains a GrammarBuilder class that exposes the most commonly used aspects of recognition grammars via much simpler APIs. Grammar (the type passed to SpeechRecognizer.LoadGrammar) has an overloaded constructor that accepts an instance of GrammarBuilder, so it can easily be plugged in wherever you can use an SrgsDocument.

For example, here's the first grammar from the previous section reimplemented using GrammarBuilder:

```
SpeechRecognizer recognizer = new SpeechRecognizer();
GrammarBuilder builder = new GrammarBuilder(new Choices("stop", "go"));
recognizer.LoadGrammar(new Grammar(builder));
```

And here's the reimplemented card game grammar:

```
SpeechRecognizer recognizer = new SpeechRecognizer();
GrammarBuilder builder = new GrammarBuilder();
builder.Append(new Choices("two", "three", "four", "five", "six", "seven",
  "eight", "nine", "ten", "jack", "queen", "king", "ace"));
builder.Append("of", 0, 1);
builder.Append(new Choices("clubs", "diamonds", "spades", "hearts"));
recognizer.LoadGrammar(new Grammar(builder));
```

GrammarBuilder doesn't expose all the power and flexibility of SrgsDocument, but it's often all that you need. In the card game example, the user can speak "two clubs" or perhaps something that sounds like "two uh cubs" and your SpeechRecognized event handler should receive the canonical "two of clubs" string. You can get even fancier in your grammars and tag pieces with semantic labels, so the event handler can pick out concepts like the rank and suit without having to parse even the canonical string.

Documents

Previous chapters have used elements such as TextBlock and Label for displaying read-only text and TextBox for displaying editable text. But when it comes to text, WPF includes much more functionality than what is provided by these simple elements!

FAQ

? How does WPF's flow document support relate to XPS (XML Paper Specification)?

Unlike the dynamic-layout documents described in this section, XPS documents have a fixed layout and always look the same, whether on screen or on paper. The .NET Framework includes APIs for creating and viewing XPS documents (in the System.Windows.Xps and System.Windows.Documents namespaces), or you can use tools like Microsoft Word to create and view them. In WPF applications, XPS documents are typically represented as instances of FixedDocument and viewed in a DocumentViewer control.

You can think of XPS documents much like Adobe PDF documents; they both have standalone viewers (available on multiple platforms) and are often viewed in a web browser (with the right plug-in installed). One area where XPS is unique is that it's also a native Windows Vista spool file format. This ensures that XPS documents can be printed without loss of quality or fidelity, and without any extra work done by the application initiating the printing. In general, XPS is a very compelling technology for creating digital reading experiences, thanks to its tight integration with WPF.

The specifications for XPS and the Open Packaging Conventions used by XPS (whose APIs are in the System.IO.Packaging namespace) can be found at http://www.microsoft.com/xps.

WPF contains a rich set of classes for creating, viewing, modifying, packaging, and storing high-quality documents. These classes, combined with core platform enhancements to the readability of digital text (such as subpixel ClearType and advanced OpenType font features), can create a very powerful and compelling experience.

The focus of this section is what WPF calls *flow documents*. A flow document (represented by the FlowDocument element) contains text and other content that can adjust to make optimal use of the space given to the document. For example, on a wide-screen monitor, this could mean automatically adding extra columns.

Creating Flow Documents

FlowDocument (and FixedDocument) is a FrameworkContentElement, the content-centric parallel to FrameworkElement. FrameworkContentElements, like FrameworkElements, support data binding, animation, and other WPF mechanisms, but they do not participate in WPF's layout mechanism. FrameworkContentElements are ultimately housed in a FrameworkElement when displayed on the screen.

Another type of FrameworkContentElement is TextElement, an abstract class that represents content that can be placed inside a FlowDocument. This section examines the various TextElements (from the System.Windows.Documents namespace) and demonstrates how to compose them to create rich and flexible documents.

A Simple FlowDocument

The following XAML shows what a straightforward FlowDocument looks like, which is simply a collection of Paragraphs (a type of TextElement) representing a draft of Chapter 1 from this book:

```
<FlowDocument>
  <Paragraph FontSize="22" FontWeight="Bold">Chapter 1</Paragraph>
  <Paragraph FontSize="35" FontWeight="Bold">Why WPF?</Paragraph>
  <Paragraph>
    In movies and on TV, the …
  </Paragraph>
  <Paragraph>…</Paragraph>
  <Paragraph>…</Paragraph>

  …
</FlowDocument>
```

Figure 14.6 shows the rendered result of this XAML. You can use a FlowDocument such as this as the root of a XAML file, and it gets automatically displayed in an appropriate viewer.

Two main types of TextElements exist—Blocks and Inlines. (Both of these are abstract classes derived from TextElement.) A Block is a rectangular region that can't be separated (except when it spans multiple pages), whereas an Inline is a region that flows more freely with text, potentially occupying a nonrectangular space (flowing from the end of one line to the beginning of the next). FlowDocument only supports Blocks, such as

Paragraph, as its children. (Its content property is called `Blocks`, which is a `BlocksCollection`.) We'll look at the role of `Inlines` after examining `Blocks` more closely.

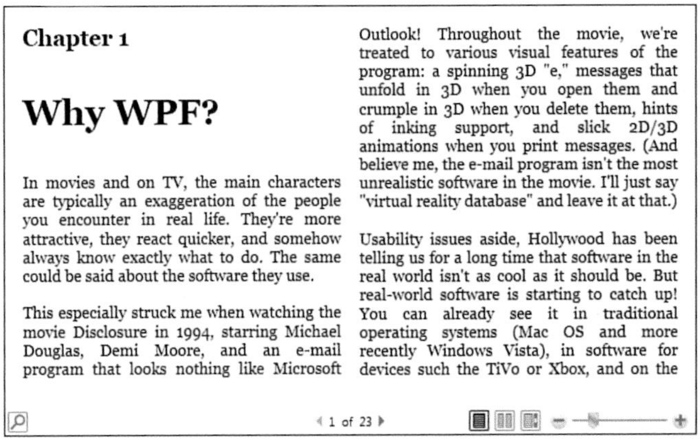

FIGURE 14.6   A simple `FlowDocument`.

Blocks

WPF has five different types of `Blocks`:

▶ `Paragraph`—Contains a collection of `Inlines`, which typically have the "meat" of the document. In XAML, you often see `Paragraph`'s content set to simple text, but internally an `Inline` called `Run` is created with that content and added to the `Paragraph`'s `Inlines` collection.

▶ `Section`—Groups one or more `Blocks` together without imposing any additional structure. This is handy if you want to set the same property values for multiple `Blocks`, such as a `Background` and `Foreground`.

▶ `List`—Presents a collection of `ListItems` as a bulleted, numbered, or plain list. Each `ListItem` can contain a collection of `Blocks`, so creating a typical text-based `List` involves placing a `Paragraph` inside each `ListItem`. `List`'s `MarkerStyle` property (of type `TextMarkerStyle`) provides plenty of formatting options for bullets—`Box`, `Circle`, `Disc` (the default bullet), and `Square`—or for numbers—`Decimal`, `LowerLatin`, `UpperLatin`, `LowerRoman`, and `UpperRoman`. A plain list can be achieved by setting `MarkerStyle` to `None`.

▶ `Table`—Organizes content into rows and columns, sort of like `Grid` but closer to an HTML `TABLE`. `Table`, unlike `Grid`, can only contain `Blocks` (and elements defining the `Table`'s structure).

▶ `BlockUIContainer`—Hosts a single `UIElement`. Therefore, `BlockUIContainer` is the key to embedding a wide range of WPF content into a `FlowDocument`, whether it's an `Image`, a `MediaElement`-hosted video, a `Button`, 3D content in a `Viewport3D`, and so on.

Listing 14.1 demonstrates the use of all five types of Blocks inside a FlowDocument. The resulting document is displayed in Figure 14.7.

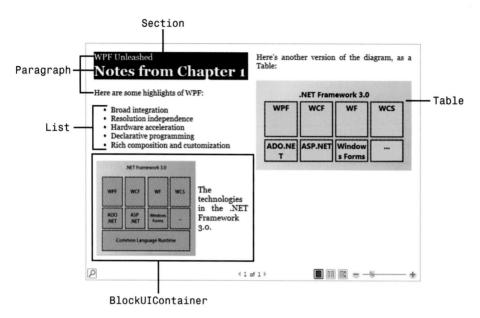

FIGURE 14.7   A FlowDocument that uses all five types of Blocks.

LISTING 14.1   The FlowDocument in Figure 14.7

```
<FlowDocument xmlns="http://schemas.microsoft.com/winfx/2006/xaml/presentation"
              xmlns:x="http://schemas.microsoft.com/winfx/2006/xaml">
  <Section LineHeight="2" Foreground="White" Background="Black">
    <Paragraph FontSize="18">WPF Unleashed</Paragraph>
    <Paragraph FontSize="30" FontWeight="Bold">Notes from Chapter 1</Paragraph>
  </Section>
  <Paragraph>Here are some highlights of WPF:</Paragraph>
  <List>
    <ListItem>
      <Paragraph>Broad integration</Paragraph>
    </ListItem>
    <ListItem>
      <Paragraph>Resolution independence</Paragraph>
    </ListItem>
    <ListItem>
      <Paragraph>Hardware acceleration</Paragraph>
    </ListItem>
    <ListItem>
      <Paragraph>Declarative programming</Paragraph>
```

LISTING 14.1   Continued

```xml
      </ListItem>
      <ListItem>
        <Paragraph>Rich composition and customization</Paragraph>
      </ListItem>
    </List>
    <BlockUIContainer>
      <Viewbox>
        <StackPanel Orientation="Horizontal">
          <Image Source="diagram.jpg" Margin="5"/>
          <TextBlock VerticalAlignment="Center" Width="100" TextWrapping="Wrap">
            The technologies in the .NET Framework 3.0.
          </TextBlock>
        </StackPanel>
      </Viewbox>
    </BlockUIContainer>
    <Paragraph>
      Here's another version of the diagram, as a Table:
    </Paragraph>
    <Table CellSpacing="5" Padding="15" FontFamily="Segoe UI">
    <Table.Background>
      <LinearGradientBrush>
        <GradientStop Color="Yellow" Offset="0"/>
        <GradientStop Color="Orange" Offset="1"/>
      </LinearGradientBrush>
    </Table.Background>

    <!-- Define four columns: -->
    <Table.Columns>
      <TableColumn/>
      <TableColumn/>
      <TableColumn/>
      <TableColumn/>
    </Table.Columns>

    <!-- Create three rows: -->
      <TableRowGroup>
        <TableRow>
          <TableCell ColumnSpan="4" TextAlignment="Center">
            <Paragraph FontWeight="Bold">.NET Framework 3.0</Paragraph>
          </TableCell>
        </TableRow>

        <TableRow>
          <TableCell BorderBrush="Black" BorderThickness="2" Background="LightGray"
```

LISTING 14.1   Continued

```
                TextAlignment="Center" LineHeight="70">
                <Paragraph FontWeight="Bold">WPF</Paragraph>
            </TableCell>
            <TableCell BorderBrush="Black" BorderThickness="2" Background="LightGray"
                TextAlignment="Center">
                <Paragraph FontWeight="Bold">WCF</Paragraph>
            </TableCell>
            <TableCell BorderBrush="Black" BorderThickness="2" Background="LightGray"
                TextAlignment="Center">
                <Paragraph FontWeight="Bold">WF</Paragraph>
            </TableCell>
            <TableCell BorderBrush="Black" BorderThickness="2" Background="LightGray"
                TextAlignment="Center">
                <Paragraph FontWeight="Bold">WCS</Paragraph>
            </TableCell>
        </TableRow>

        <TableRow>
            <TableCell BorderBrush="Black" BorderThickness="2" Background="LightGray"
                TextAlignment="Center">
                <Paragraph FontWeight="Bold">ADO.NET</Paragraph>
            </TableCell>
            <TableCell BorderBrush="Black" BorderThickness="2" Background="LightGray"
                TextAlignment="Center">
                <Paragraph FontWeight="Bold">ASP.NET</Paragraph>
            </TableCell>
            <TableCell BorderBrush="Black" BorderThickness="2" Background="LightGray"
                TextAlignment="Center">
                <Paragraph FontWeight="Bold">Windows Forms</Paragraph>
            </TableCell>
            <TableCell BorderBrush="Black" BorderThickness="2" Background="LightGray"
                TextAlignment="Center">
                <Paragraph FontWeight="Bold">...</Paragraph>
            </TableCell>
        </TableRow>
    </TableRowGroup>
  </Table>
</FlowDocument>
```

Paragraphs are used throughout the document, but Section is used at the beginning to give two Paragraphs different Foreground, Background, and LineHeight. List is then used with its default settings for a straightforward bulleted list. BlockUIContainer is used to not only contain an Image, but a corresponding caption in the form of a TextBlock. They are arranged in a `StackPanel` and then placed inside a `Viewbox` so both items scale nicely as the width of the document changes.

Finally, for demonstration purposes, the content of the `Image` is mimicked with a `Table`. Notice that the APIs exposed by `Table` (and, therefore, the structure of elements inside `Table` in XAML) differ considerably from `Grid`. Columns are defined by placing `TableColumn` elements inside `Table`'s `Columns` collection (similar to `Grid`'s `ColumnDefinitions` collection), but the rows are defined directly with the content they contain. `Table` contains a `TableRowGroup` with a bunch of `TableRows` placed in the order that they appear, from top to bottom. Each `TableCell` inside a `TableRow` fills the next available column sequentially, unless `ColumnSpan` is set to give different behavior. `TableCell` is the only element that can contain the `Blocks` that form the content of the `Table`, which, in this case, are all `Paragraphs`.

`Table` can even contain multiple `TableRowGroups`! The content of each one gets placed directly below the previous one.

Figure 14.7 shows that the `Table` ends up looking pretty similar to the `Image` embedded in the document. Of course, the two have very different behaviors. The text in the `Table` is selectable and scales perfectly as you zoom in to the document. But whereas the `Image` is never split between pages, the `Table` can be. The inner text content can also wrap when space is tight. This splitting and wrapping is shown in Figure 14.8.

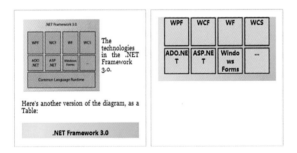

FIGURE 14.8   A different view of the `FlowDocument` from Figure 14.7, with the `Table` split between pages two and three.

Inlines

`Inlines` are elements that can be placed inside a `Paragraph` to make its content more interesting than plain text. As mentioned in the previous section, `Paragraphs` don't really contain a simple string, but rather a collection of `Inlines`. And when a `Paragraph` defined in XAML appears to contain plain text, it really contains a single `Inline` known as `Run`. `Run` has a simple `Text` string property and a constructor that accepts a string.

Therefore, the following `Paragraph` defined in XAML:

```
<Paragraph>Here are some highlights of WPF:</Paragraph>
```

is equivalent to the following C# code:

```
Paragraph p = new Paragraph(new Run("Here are some highlights of WPF:"));
```

What other Inlines exist that can enhance a paragraph? They fall into three categories: spans, anchored blocks, and everything else.

Spans

The most common spans are Bold, Italic, Underline, and the familiar Hyperlink from Chapter 7, "Structuring and Deploying an Application." They all fittingly derive from Span, which can also be used directly in a Paragraph for applying additional effects to text. Although Paragraphs already support making their text bold, italic, and so on by setting properties such as FontWeight and FontStyle, these spans make it possible to apply these effects to smaller regions within the Paragraph.

The following Paragraph, which is rendered in Figure 14.9, demonstrates all of these spans:

```
<Paragraph>
  <Bold>bold</Bold>
  <Italic>italic</Italic>
  <Underline>underline</Underline>
  <Hyperlink>hyperlink</Hyperlink>
  <Span BaselineAlignment="Superscript">superscript</Span>
  <Span BaselineAlignment="Subscript">subscript</Span>
  <Span>
  <Span.TextDecorations>
    <TextDecoration Location="Strikethrough" />
  </Span.TextDecorations>
    strikethrough
  </Span>
</Paragraph>
```

The BaselineAlignment and TextDecorations properties used on Span are common to all Inlines, so they can easily be combined with Bold, Italic, or other effects. In addition, like Paragraph, the content of any span is actually a collection of Inlines rather than a simple string. In the previous XAML, this means that there's an implicit Run inside every child of Paragraph. This also means that you can easily embed spans within spans, such as in the following Paragraph, rendered in Figure 14.10:

```
<Paragraph>
a<Bold>b<Italic>c<Underline>d<Hyperlink>e</Hyperlink>f</Underline>g</Italic>h
</Bold>i
</Paragraph>
```

> **TIP**
>
> Even the familiar `TextBlock` element stores its contents as a collection of `Inlines`! Therefore, you could replace the `Paragraph` tags in the previous XAML snippets with `TextBlock` tags and they would still work. `Label`, on the other hand, does not directly support such content.

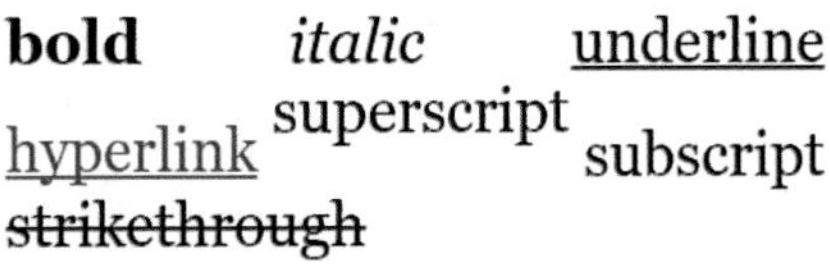

bold   *italic*   <u>underline</u>

<u>hyperlink</u> ^{superscript}   _{subscript}

~~strikethrough~~

FIGURE 14.9   Applying different spans to text in a paragraph.

ab<u>*cdef*</u>ghi

FIGURE 14.10   Nesting a `Hyperlink` inside `Underline` inside `Italic` inside `Bold`.

Anchored Blocks

WPF contains two `Inlines` that are a bit unusual because they are designed to contain `Blocks`! They are `Figure` and `Floater`, and both derive from an abstract `AnchoredBlock` class.

`Figure` is like a mini-`FlowDocument` that can be embedded in the outer `FlowDocument`. The inner content is isolated from the outer content, which flows around the `Figure`. For example, the `FlowDocument` representing Chapter 1 might want to have its paragraphs flow around images (just like the figures in this book). This could be done as follows:

```
<FlowDocument>
  <Paragraph FontSize="22" FontWeight="Bold">Chapter 1</Paragraph>
  <Paragraph FontSize="35" FontWeight="Bold">Why WPF?</Paragraph>
  <Paragraph>
    <Figure Width="130">
      <BlockUIContainer>
        <Image Source="wpf.png"/>
      </BlockUIContainer>
    </Figure>
    In movies and on TV, the …
  </Paragraph>
  <Paragraph>…</Paragraph>
  <Paragraph>…</Paragraph>
  …
</FlowDocument>
```

Because a `Figure` contains `Blocks`, you can place a `Table`, `Paragraphs`, and so on inside it. But using `BlockUIContainer` to hold an `Image` is all we need in this case. The result is shown in Figure 14.11.

Chapter 1

Why WPF?

In movies and on TV, the main characters are typically an exaggeration of the people you encounter in real life. They're more attractive, they react quicker, and somehow always know exactly what to do. The same could be said about the software they use.

This especially struck me when watching the movie Disclosure in 1994, starring Michael Douglas, Demi Moore, and an e-mail program that looks nothing like Microsoft Outlook! Throughout the movie, we're treated to various visual features of the program: a spinning 3D "e," messages that unfold in 3D when you open them and crumple in 3D when you delete them, hints of inking support, and slick 2D/3D animations when you print messages. (And believe me, the e-mail program isn't the most unrealistic software in the movie. I'll just say "virtual reality database" and leave it at that.)

Usability issues aside, Hollywood has been telling us for a long time that software in the real world isn't as cool as it should be. But real-world software is starting to catch up!

‹ 1 of 23 ›

FIGURE 14.11   A Figure containing an Image inside the third Paragraph of the FlowDocument.

You can adjust the placement of a Figure with its HorizontalAnchor and VerticalAnchor properties (of type FigureHorizontalAnchor and FigureVerticalAnchor, respectively). The default value for HorizontalAnchor is ColumnRight, and the default value for VerticalAnchor is ParagraphTop. Both properties provide many options for placement based on the current column or Paragraph, or even relative to the bounds of the entire page. Figure 14.12 demonstrates some alternative placements for the Figure in Figure 14.11 by explicitly setting HorizontalAnchor and/or VerticalAnchor.

Floater is a simplified form of Figure. It can contain arbitrary Blocks, but it does not support positioning relative to the page bounds or even spanning columns. Rather than having HorizontalAnchor and VerticalAnchor properties, it has a simple HorizontalAlignment property (of type HorizontalAlignment) that can be set to Left, Center, Right, or Stretch. If you don't require the full functionality of Figure, you might as well use the lighter-weight Floater instead.

Other Inlines

The two remaining Inlines don't have anything in common other than the fact that they don't derive from Span or AnchoredBlock. One of them is LineBreak, which functions as a newline. Simply place an empty LineBreak element between any two characters in a paragraph, and the second character will start on the following line.

TIP

To place a *page* break rather than a *line* break in a FlowDocument, set the BreakPageBefore property to true on the first Paragraph you want after the break. BreakPageBefore is defined on Block, so this also applies to Section, List, BlockUIContainer, and Table.

Chapter 1

Why WPF?

In movies and on TV, the main characters are typically an exaggeration of the people you encounter in real life. They're more attractive, they react quicker, and somehow always know exactly what to do. The same could be said about the software they use.

This especially struck me when watching the movie Disclosure in 1994, starring Michael Douglas, Demi Moore, and an e-mail program that looks nothing like Microsoft Outlook! Throughout the movie, we're treated to various visual features of the program: a spinning 3D "e," messages that unfold in 3D when you open them and crumple in 3D when you delete them, hints of inking support, and slick 2D/3D animations when you print messages. (And believe me, the e-mail program isn't the most unrealistic software in the movie. I'll just say "virtual reality database" and leave it at that.)

Usability issues aside, Hollywood has been telling us for a long time that software in the real world isn't as cool as it should be. But real-world software is starting to catch up!

1 of 23

`HorizontalAnchor="ColumnLeft"`

Chapter 1

Why WPF?

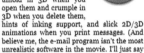

In movies and on TV, the main characters are typically an exaggeration of the people you encounter in real life. They're more attractive, they react quicker, and somehow always know exactly what to do. The same could be said about the software they use.

This especially struck me when watching the movie Disclosure in 1994, starring Michael Douglas, Demi Moore, and an e-mail program that looks nothing like Microsoft Outlook! Throughout the movie, we're treated to various visual features of the program: a spinning 3D "e," messages that unfold in 3D when you open them and crumple in 3D when you delete them, hints of inking support, and slick 2D/3D animations when you print messages. (And believe me, the e-mail program isn't the most unrealistic software in the movie. I'll just say "virtual reality database" and leave it at that.)

Usability issues aside, Hollywood has been telling us for a long time that software in the real world isn't as cool as it should be. But real-world software is

1 of 23

`HorizontalAnchor="PageCenter"`

Chapter 1

Why WPF?

In movies and on TV, the main characters are typically an exaggeration of the people you encounter in real life. They're more attractive, they react quicker, and somehow always know exactly what to do. The same could be said about the software they use.

This especially struck me when watching the movie Disclosure in 1994, starring Michael Douglas, Demi Moore, and an e-mail program that looks nothing like Microsoft Outlook! Throughout the movie, we're treated to various visual features of the program: a spinning 3D "e," messages that unfold in 3D when you open them and crumple in 3D when you delete them, hints of inking support, and slick 2D/3D animations when you print messages. (And believe me, the e-mail program isn't the most unrealistic software in the movie. I'll just say "virtual reality database" and leave it at that.)

Usability issues aside, Hollywood has been telling us for a long time that software in the real world isn't as cool as it should be. But real-world software is starting to catch up! You can already see it in traditional

1 of 23

`HorizontalAnchor="PageRight"` and `VerticalAnchor="PageTop"`

FIGURE 14.12   Controlling the placement of a `Figure` with `HorizontalAnchor` and `VerticalAnchor`.

The last `Inline` is `InlineUIContainer`, which is just like `BlockUIContainer` except with the ability to be inserted into a `Paragraph` and flow with the rest of the text. As with `BlockUIContainer`, it can contain a `MediaElement`-hosted video, a `Button`, 3D content in a `Viewport3D`, and so on, but it's often handy simply to include a little inline `Image`. The following `Paragraph`, rendered in Figure 14.13, demonstrates this with an inline RSS icon next to a `Hyperlink` to an RSS feed:

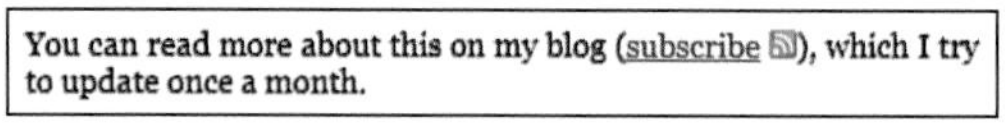

> You can read more about this on my blog (underline subscribe ▨), which I try to update once a month.

FIGURE 14.13   A `Paragraph` with an inline `Image`, thanks to `InlineUIContainer`.

```
<Paragraph>
  You can read more about this on my blog (
  <Hyperlink NavigateUri="http://blogs.msdn.com/adam_nathan/rss.xml">
    subscribe
  </Hyperlink>
  <InlineUIContainer>
    <Image Width="14" Source="rss.gif"/>
  </InlineUIContainer>
  ), which I try to update once a month.
</Paragraph>
```

Displaying Flow Documents

As mentioned in Chapter 4, "Introducing WPF's Controls," a `FlowDocument` can be viewed (and edited) inside a `RichTextBox`. Although you can prevent user edits by setting `RichTextBox`'s `IsReadOnly` property to `true`, `RichTextBox` is not meant to be the typical control that applications use for document reading!

Instead, WPF provides *three* additional controls for displaying flow documents. They can be hard to keep straight at first, but the differences are straightforward:

▶ `FlowDocumentScrollViewer` displays the document as one continuous file with a scrollbar, similar to the "Web Layout" mode in Microsoft Word (and similar to a read-only `RichTextBox` inside a `ScrollViewer`).

▶ `FlowDocumentPageViewer` displays the document as discrete pages, similar to the "Full Screen Reading" mode in Microsoft Word.

▶ `FlowDocumentReader` combines `FlowDocumentScrollViewer` and `FlowDocumentPageViewer` into a single control, and exposes additional functionality such as built-in text search. (This is the control you get by default if you use `FlowDocument` as the root element in your XAML file.)

Figure 14.14 shows the differences between them by displaying the `FlowDocument` containing Chapter 1. `FlowDocumentReader` is a rich control (somewhat like the common viewers for XPS or PDF files), but if you don't require switching between scrolling and pagination, you might as well use one of the more lightweight viewers. Both `FlowDocumentPageViewer` and `FlowDocumentReader` (in pagination mode) automatically add/remove columns as you zoom out/in to maximize the use of available space.

> ### Chapter 1
>
> # Why WPF?
>
> In movies and on TV, the main characters are typically an exaggeration of the people you encounter in real life. They're more attractive, they react quicker, and somehow always know exactly what to do. The same could be said about the software they use.
>
> This especially struck me when watching the movie Disclosure in 1994, starring Michael Douglas, Demi Moore, and an e-mail program that looks nothing like Microsoft Outlook! Throughout the movie, we're treated to various visual features of the program: a spinning 3D "e," messages that unfold in 3D when you open them and crumple in 3D when you delete them, hints of inking support, and slick 2D/3D animations when you print messages. (And believe me, the e-mail program isn't the most unrealistic software in the movie. I'll just say "virtual reality database" and leave it at that.)
>
> Usability issues aside, Hollywood has been telling us for a long time that software in the real world isn't as cool as it should be. But real-world software is starting to catch up! You

FlowDocumentScrollViewer

> ### Chapter 1
>
> # Why WPF?
>
> In movies and on TV, the main characters are typically an exaggeration of the people you encounter in real life. They're more attractive, they react quicker, and somehow always know exactly what to do. The same could be said about the software they use.
>
> This especially struck me when watching the movie Disclosure in 1994, starring Michael Douglas, Demi Moore, and an e-mail program that looks nothing like Microsoft
>
> Outlook! Throughout the movie, we're treated to various visual features of the program: a spinning 3D "e," messages that unfold in 3D when you open them and crumple in 3D when you delete them, hints of inking support, and slick 2D/3D animations when you print messages. (And believe me, the e-mail program isn't the most unrealistic software in the movie. I'll just say "virtual reality database" and leave it at that.)
>
> Usability issues aside, Hollywood has been telling us for a long time that software in the real world isn't as cool as it should be. But real-world software is starting to catch up! You can already see it in traditional operating systems (Mac OS and more recently Windows Vista), in software for devices such the TiVo or Xbox, and on the
>
> ◂ 1 of 23 ▸

FlowDocumentPageViewer

> ### Chapter 1
>
> # Why WPF?
>
> In movies and on TV, the main characters are typically an exaggeration of the people you encounter in real life. They're more attractive, they react quicker, and somehow always know exactly what to do. The same could be said about the software they use.
>
> This especially struck me when watching the movie Disclosure in 1994, starring Michael Douglas, Demi Moore, and an e-mail program that looks nothing like Microsoft
>
> Outlook! Throughout the movie, we're treated to various visual features of the program: a spinning 3D "e," messages that unfold in 3D when you open them and crumple in 3D when you delete them, hints of inking support, and slick 2D/3D animations when you print messages. (And believe me, the e-mail program isn't the most unrealistic software in the movie. I'll just say "virtual reality database" and leave it at that.)
>
> Usability issues aside, Hollywood has been telling us for a long time that software in the real world isn't as cool as it should be. But real-world software is starting to catch up! You can already see it in traditional operating systems (Mac OS and more recently Windows Vista), in software for devices such the TiVo or Xbox, and on the
>
>  Type text to find... ◂ ▸ ▾   ◂ 1 of 23 ▸

FlowDocumentReader

FIGURE 14.14   Chapter 1 displayed in each of the FlowDocument containers.

Notice that `FlowDocumentScrollViewer` doesn't show the zoom functionality that appears in the other two, but you can enable this by setting its `IsToolBarVisible` property to true.

Adding Annotations

The three viewers for `FlowDocument` (plus `DocumentViewer`, the viewer for `FixedDocument`) support *annotations*, which enable users to highlight content or attach notes in the form of text or ink. The strange thing about this support is that you have to define your own user interface for enabling it; there are no default controls to reveal.

Although crafting your own custom UI for annotations is tedious, it's not very difficult. That's because an `AnnotationService` class in the `System.Windows.Annotations` namespace exposes a command for each of the important annotation-controlling features. For example:

▶ `CreateTextStickyNoteCommand` attaches a new text-based `StickyNoteControl` as an annotation on the selected text.

▶ `CreateInkStickyNoteCommand` attaches a new ink-based `StickyNoteControl` as an annotation on the selected text.

▶ `DeleteStickyNotesCommand` deletes the currently selected `StickyNoteControl`(s).

▶ `CreateHighlightCommand` highlights the selected text in the color passed as the command's parameter.

▶ `ClearHighlightsCommand` removes any highlighting from the currently selected text.

Listing 14.2 defines a `Window` that adds a few simple `Button`s on top of a `FlowDocumentReader`. Each of these `Button`s is assigned to one of the previously described commands.

LISTING 14.2   Window1.xaml—The UI for an Annotation-Enabled `FlowDocumentReader`

```
<Window
  xmlns="http://schemas.microsoft.com/winfx/2006/xaml/presentation"
  xmlns:x="http://schemas.microsoft.com/winfx/2006/xaml"
  xmlns:a=
    "clr-namespace:System.Windows.Annotations;assembly=PresentationFramework"
  Title="FlowDocumentReader + Annotations"
  x:Class="Window1" Initialized="OnInitialized" Closed="OnClosed">
  <StackPanel>
    <StackPanel Orientation="Horizontal">
      <Label>Control Annotations:</Label>
      <Button Command="a:AnnotationService.CreateTextStickyNoteCommand"
              CommandTarget="{Binding ElementName=reader}">
```

LISTING 14.2   Continued

```
        Create Text Note
      </Button>
      <Button Command="a:AnnotationService.CreateInkStickyNoteCommand"
              CommandTarget="{Binding ElementName=reader}">
        Create Ink Note
      </Button>
      <Button Command="a:AnnotationService.DeleteStickyNotesCommand"
              CommandTarget="{Binding ElementName=reader}">
        Remove Note
      </Button>
      <Button Command="a:AnnotationService.CreateHighlightCommand"
              CommandParameter="{x:Static Brushes.Yellow}"
              CommandTarget="{Binding ElementName=reader}">
        Create Yellow Highlight
      </Button>
      <Button Command="a:AnnotationService.ClearHighlightsCommand"
              CommandTarget="{Binding ElementName=reader}">
        Remove Highlight
      </Button>
    </StackPanel>

    <FlowDocumentReader x:Name="reader">
      <FlowDocument>
        …
      </FlowDocument>
    </FlowDocumentReader>
  </StackPanel>
</Window>
```

The System.Windows.Annotations namespace is given an XML namespace prefix of a, used to refer to each of the commands on AnnotationService. Although AnnotationService is part of PresentationFramework, this namespace happens to not be included in WPF's standard XML namespace. For the commands to work, each of these Buttons uses the FlowDocumentReader element as the command target. The Buttons become enabled and disabled automatically, based on the context in which each command is valid.

The only thing missing is the definition of the OnInitialized and OnClosed methods referenced in the XAML file. Listing 14.3 contains the code-behind file for Listing 14.2.

LISTING 14.3   `Window1.xaml.cs`—The Logic for an Annotation-Enabled `FlowDocumentReader`

```csharp
using System;
using System.IO;
using System.Windows;
using System.Windows.Annotations;
using System.Windows.Annotations.Storage;

public partial class Window1 : Window
{
  FileStream stream;

  public Window1()
  {
    InitializeComponent();
  }

  protected void OnInitialized(object sender, EventArgs e)
  {
    // Enable and load annotations
    AnnotationService service = AnnotationService.GetService(reader);
    if (service == null)
    {
      stream = new FileStream("storage.xml", FileMode.OpenOrCreate);
      service = new AnnotationService(reader);
      AnnotationStore store = new XmlStreamStore(stream);
      store.AutoFlush = true;
      service.Enable(store);
    }
  }

  protected void OnClosed(object sender, EventArgs e)
  {
    // Disable and save annotations
    AnnotationService service = AnnotationService.GetService(reader);
    if (service != null && service.IsEnabled)
    {
      service.Disable();
      stream.Close();
    }
  }
}
```

The main purpose of the `OnInitialized` and `OnClosed` methods is to enable and disable the `AnnotationService` associated with the `FlowDocumentReader`. However, when enabling the service you must also specify a `Stream` that persists the annotations. This listing uses a standalone XML file in the current directory. When the application is closed, any annotations are saved and reappear the next time the application is run (as long as the `storage.xml` file remains untouched).

Figure 14.15 shows an instance of this annotation-enabled `Window` in action.

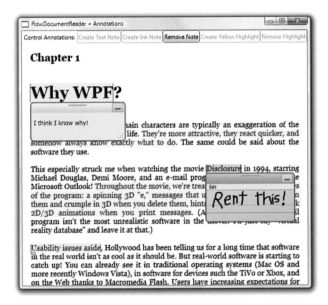

FIGURE 14.15   Annotations on a `FlowDocument`, enabled by the custom `Buttons` at the top of the `Window`.

Conclusion

WPF's support for audio, video, speech, and documents rounds out its rich media offerings. The audio support is limited, but is enough to accomplish the most common tasks. The video support is only a subset of what's provided by the underlying Windows Media Player APIs, but the seamless integration with the rest of WPF (so you can transform or animate video just like any other content) makes it extremely compelling.

WPF's speech synthesis and recognition support is state of the art, but at the same time it's mainly just a wrapper on top of the unmanaged Microsoft SAPI APIs. Contrary to the other three areas, however, WPF's rich support for documents is brand-new functionality that you can't find anywhere else in Microsoft's technology offerings. Many people see documents support as WPF's "killer app." It is the technology behind the Times Reader application from the *New York Times*, and will undoubtedly be used in other applications that push the boundaries of user experiences.

PART V

Advanced Topics

Interoperability with Win32, Windows Forms, and ActiveX

Windows Presentation Foundation, especially in its first release, lacks some features that previous technologies already have. When creating a WPF-based user interface, you might want to exploit such features. For example, WPF currently doesn't include some of the standard controls that Windows Forms already has: DateTimePicker, MonthCalendar, NumericUpDown, MaskedTextBox, NotifyIcon, DataGridView, and more. Windows Forms also has support for multiple document interface (MDI) window management, wrappers over additional Win32 dialogs and APIs, and various handy APIs like Screen.AllScreens (which returns an array of screens with information about their bounds). Win32 has controls like an IP Address text box (SysIPAddress32) that have no equivalent in either Windows Forms or WPF. Windows Vista introduces Win32-based "glass" effects, task dialogs, and a new wizard framework that don't have first-class exposure to WPF. And tons of ActiveX controls exist for the purpose of embedding rich functionality into your own software.

Perhaps you've already put a lot of effort into developing your own pre-WPF user interfaces or controls. If so, you might want to leverage some of your own work that's already in place. Maybe you have developed an application in a non-WPF technology with an extremely complicated main surface (like a CAD program) and just want to "WPFize" the outer edges of the applications with rich menus, toolbars, and so on. Maybe you've created a web application with tons of HTML content that you want to enhance but not replace.

In earlier chapters, you've already seen WPF's "HTML interoperability." Given that HTML can be hosted inside a WPF Frame and WPF content can be hosted inside HTML (as a XAML Browser Application or a loose XAML page), you can leverage existing HTML content alongside new WPF content. Fortunately, WPF's support for interoperability goes much deeper than that. It's fairly easy for WPF applications and controls to leverage all kinds of non-WPF content or APIs, such as all the examples in the previous two paragraphs. Some of these scenarios are possible thanks to the features described in this chapter, some are possible thanks to the .NET Framework's interoperability between managed and unmanaged code, and (in the case of calling miscellaneous Windows Forms APIs from WPF) some are possible simply because the other technology defines managed APIs that just happen to live in non-WPF assemblies.

Figure 15.1 summarizes the different UI technologies and the paths you can take to mix and match them. Win32 is a general bucket that includes any technology that runs on Windows: DirectX, MFC, WTL, OpenGL, and so on. Notice that there's a direct path between each set of technologies except for WPF and ActiveX. In that case, you must use another technology as an intermediate layer.

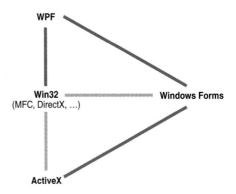

FIGURE 15.1   The relationship between various Windows UI technologies.

All of the blue lines connecting the technologies are discussed in this chapter. The line between Win32 and Windows Forms is enabled by standard .NET Framework interoperability technologies for mixing managed and unmanaged code (and the fact that Windows Forms is based on Win32), and the line between Win32 and ActiveX is somewhat artificial because there are no real barriers separating Win32 and ActiveX.

This chapter focuses on embedding controls of one type inside applications of another type. It first examines both directions of WPF/Win32 interoperability, and then both directions of WPF/Windows Forms interoperability. The chapter ends by examining the options with WPF/ActiveX interoperability. Although the focus is on embedding controls, we'll look at another important scenario at the end of each section that isn't as straightforward as you might imagine: launching heterogeneous dialogs.

> **WARNING**
>
> **You cannot overlap WPF content with non-WPF content!**
>
> As with hosting HTML content in Frame, any non-WPF content that's hosted in a WPF application has extra limitations that don't apply to native WPF content. For example, you can't apply Transforms to non-WPF content. Furthermore, you cannot overlap content from one technology over content from another. You can arbitrarily nest (for example) Win32 inside WPF inside Windows Forms inside WPF, and so on, but every pixel must have one and only one technology responsible for its rendering.

Embedding Win32 Controls in WPF Applications

In Win32, all controls are considered to be "windows," and Win32 APIs interact with them via window handles known as HWNDs. All Windows-based UI technologies (DirectX, MFC, and so on) ultimately use HWNDs to some degree, so the ability to work with HWNDs gives the ability to work with all of these technologies.

Although WPF's subsystems (layout, animation, and so on) don't know how to interact directly with HWNDs, WPF defines a FrameworkElement that can host an arbitrary HWND. This FrameworkElement is System.Windows.Interop.HwndHost, and makes HWND-based controls look and act almost exactly like WPF controls.

To demonstrate the use of HwndHost in a WPF application, let's look at embedding a custom Win32 control to add webcam functionality to WPF. As the previous chapter mentioned, WPF's video support doesn't include anything for interacting with local video capture devices such as a simple webcam. Microsoft's DirectShow technology has support for this, so Win32 interoperability enables us to leverage that same webcam support in a WPF application.

> **FAQ**
>
> **? Because WPF is built on top of DirectX, isn't there a more direct way to have WPF interoperate with DirectX surfaces?**
>
> In version 3.0 of WPF, there is no direct "DirectX interoperability" feature. Although there are managed APIs for DirectX, you should not try to call them within WPF applications. But because all DirectX content (like WPF content) must ultimately be hosted in an HWND, you can use HWND interoperability as the means for mixing these two technologies.

A Win32 Webcam Control

Listing 15.1 contains the unmanaged C++ definition for a custom Win32 Webcam control that wraps a few DirectShow COM objects.

LISTING 15.1   Webcam.h—Definition of Some Webcam Win32 APIs

```
#if !defined(WEBCAM_H)
#define WEBCAM_H

#include <wtypes.h>

class Webcam
{
public:
  static HRESULT Initialize(int width, int height);
  static HRESULT AttachToWindow(HWND hwnd);
  static HRESULT Start();
  static HRESULT Pause();
  static HRESULT Stop();
  static HRESULT Repaint();
  static HRESULT Terminate();
  static int GetWidth();
  static int GetHeight();
};
#endif // !defined(WEBCAM_H)
```

The Webcam class is designed to work with a computer's default video capture device, so it contains a set of simple static methods for controlling this device. It is initialized with a width and height (which can be later retrieved via GetWidth and GetHeight methods). Then, after telling Webcam (via AttachToWindow) what HWND to render itself on, the behavior can be controlled with simple Start/Pause/Stop methods.

Listing 15.2 contains the implementation of the Webcam class. The complete implementations of Webcam::Initialize and Webcam::Terminate are omitted for brevity, but the entire implementation can be found with this book's source code.

LISTING 15.2   Webcam.cpp—Implementation of the Webcam APIs

```
LRESULT WINAPI WndProc(HWND hwnd, UINT msg, WPARAM wParam, LPARAM lParam)
{
  switch (msg)
  {
    case WM_ERASEBKGND:
      DefWindowProc(hwnd, msg, wParam, lParam);
      Webcam::Repaint();
      break;
    default:
      return DefWindowProc(hwnd, msg, wParam, lParam);
  }
  return 0;
}
```

LISTING 15.2   Continued

```cpp
HRESULT Webcam::Initialize(int width, int height)
{
  _width = width;
  _height = height;

  // Create and register the Window Class
  WNDCLASS wc;
  wc.style          = CS_VREDRAW | CS_HREDRAW;
  wc.lpfnWndProc    = WndProc;
  wc.cbClsExtra     = 0;
  wc.cbWndExtra     = 0;
  wc.hInstance      = GetModuleHandle(NULL);
  wc.hIcon          = LoadIcon(NULL, IDI_APPLICATION);
  wc.hCursor        = LoadCursor(NULL, IDC_ARROW);
  wc.hbrBackground  = (HBRUSH)(COLOR_SCROLLBAR+1);
  wc.lpszMenuName   = 0;
  wc.lpszClassName  = L"WebcamClass";
  RegisterClass(&wc);

  HRESULT hr = CoCreateInstance(CLSID_FilterGraph, NULL, CLSCTX_INPROC_SERVER,
    IID_IGraphBuilder, (void **)&_graphBuilder);

  ...Create and interact with several COM objects...
  return hr;
}

HRESULT Webcam::AttachToWindow(HWND hwnd)
{
  if (!_initialized || !_windowlessControl)
    return E_FAIL;

  _hwnd = hwnd;

  // Position and size the video
  RECT rcDest;
  rcDest.left = 0;
  rcDest.right = _width;
  rcDest.top = 0;
  rcDest.bottom = _height;
  _windowlessControl->SetVideoClippingWindow(hwnd);
  return _windowlessControl->SetVideoPosition(NULL, &rcDest);
}
```

15

LISTING 15.2   Continued

```
HRESULT Webcam::Start()
{
  if (!_initialized || !_graphBuilder || !_mediaControl)
    return E_FAIL;

  _graphBuilder->Render(_pin);
  return _mediaControl->Run();
}

HRESULT Webcam::Pause()
{
  if (!_initialized || !_mediaControl)
    return E_FAIL;

  return _mediaControl->Pause();
}

HRESULT Webcam::Stop()
{
  if (!_initialized || !_mediaControl)
    return E_FAIL;

  return _mediaControl->Stop();
}

HRESULT Webcam::Repaint()
{
  if (!_initialized || !_windowlessControl)
    return E_FAIL;

  return _windowlessControl->RepaintVideo(_hwnd, GetDC(_hwnd));
}

HRESULT Webcam::Terminate()
{
  HRESULT hr = Webcam::Stop();

  …Release several COM objects…
  return hr;
}

int Webcam::GetWidth()
{
```

LISTING 15.2   Continued

```
  return _width;
}

int Webcam::GetHeight()
{
  return _height;
}
```

The implementation begins with a simple Win32 window procedure, which makes sure to repaint the video whenever a WM_ERASEBKGND message is received. Inside Initialize, a Win32 window class called WebcamClass is defined and registered, and a bunch of DirectShow-specific COM objects are created and initialized. (The Terminate method releases all of these COM objects.) AttachToWindow not only tells DirectShow which window to render on, but it sets the size of the video to match the dimensions passed to Initialize. The other methods are simple wrappers for the underlying DirectShow methods.

Using the Webcam Control in WPF

The first step in using the Webcam control in a WPF application is to create a project that is able to "see" this unmanaged control from the WPF-specific managed code that must be written. Many options exist for integrating managed code into an unmanaged codebase. But if you're comfortable with C++, using C++/CLI to seamlessly mix managed and unmanaged code is usually the best approach. This is especially true for the Webcam class because it doesn't expose any functionality outside of the DLL in which it is compiled.

FAQ

 What Is C++/CLI?

C++/CLI is a version of the C++ language that supports managed code. Ignoring the now-deprecated "Managed C++" features in earlier versions of Visual C++, C++/CLI is *the way* for C++ developers to consume and produce .NET components. (CLI stands for Common Language Infrastructure, which is the name of the Ecma-standardized pieces of the .NET Framework's common language runtime.) In fact, C++/CLI is undergoing Ecma standardization at the time of writing (like the CLI and C#). Just to put some context around these standards: Visual C++ is Microsoft's implementation of C++/CLI, Visual C# is Microsoft's implementation of C#, and the common language runtime (CLR) is Microsoft's implementation of the CLI. Using the managed code features in Visual C++ is often as simple as adding the /clr compilation switch to relevant source files or projects, and learning some new bits of syntax specific to managed data types.

DIGGING DEEPER

Mixing Managed and Unmanaged Code

C++/CLI is a language-specific mechanism for mixing managed and unmanaged code (and managed and unmanaged data) at the source code level. But the .NET Framework provides two language-neutral technologies for integrating managed and unmanaged code (meaning that they work in any .NET-based language):

▶ Platform Invoke (or PInvoke), which enables calling any static entry points in any managed language as long as the unmanaged signature is redeclared in managed code. This is similar to the `Declare` functionality in Visual Basic 6.

▶ COM Interoperability, which enables using COM components in any managed language in a manner similar to using normal managed components, and vice versa.

Some of the general advantages to using C++/CLI over PInvoke and COM Interoperability are as follows:

▶ The unmanaged and managed code can easily be compiled into the same DLL.

▶ Consuming DLLs with static entry points can be done directly rather than having to redefine the unmanaged signatures.

▶ If unmanaged APIs are changed, you get compile-time errors for callers that need to be updated. With PInvoke, you need to remember to update the managed signature to match the unmanaged one; otherwise, you can get subtle runtime errors.

▶ COM objects can be accessed directly, so various limitations of the COM Interoperability layer are avoided. On the flip side, directly accessing COM objects from managed code can be error-prone, but Visual C++ ships a few templates (like `com_handle`) that make this easier.

Listing 15.3 defines a WPF `Window`—all in C++/CLI—and uses the `HwndHost` type to integrate the Win32 `Webcam` control. Because it is using and defining managed data types, it must be compiled with the `/clr` compiler option.

WARNING

Visual C++ currently does not support compiled XAML!

This is why Listing 15.3 defines the `Window` entirely in procedural code. Other options would be to load and parse XAML at runtime (as shown in Chapter 2, "XAML Demystified"), or to define the `Window` in a different language that supports compiled XAML.

LISTING 15.3   Window1.h—A WPF `Window` Using an `HwndHost`-Derived Class

```
#include "stdafx.h"
#include "Webcam.h"

#using <mscorlib.dll>
#using <PresentationFramework.dll>
```

LISTING 15.3   Continued

```cpp
#using <WindowsBase.dll>
#using <PresentationCore.dll>

using namespace System;
using namespace System::Windows;
using namespace System::Windows::Controls;
using namespace System::Windows::Interop;
using namespace System::Runtime::InteropServices;

ref class MyHwndHost : HwndHost
{
protected:
  virtual HandleRef BuildWindowCore(HandleRef hwndParent) override
  {
    HWND hwnd = CreateWindow(L"WebcamClass", // Registered class
      NULL,                                   // Title
      WS_CHILD,                               // Style
      CW_USEDEFAULT, 0,                       // Position
      Webcam::GetWidth(),                     // Width
      Webcam::GetHeight(),                    // Height
      (HWND)hwndParent.Handle.ToInt32(),      // Parent
      NULL,                                   // Menu
      GetModuleHandle(NULL),                  // hInstance
      NULL);                                  // Optional parameter

    if (hwnd == NULL)
      throw gcnew ApplicationException("CreateWindow failed!");

    Webcam::AttachToWindow(hwnd);

    return HandleRef(this, IntPtr(hwnd));
  }

  virtual void DestroyWindowCore(HandleRef hwnd) override
  {
    // Just a formality:
    ::DestroyWindow((HWND)hwnd.Handle.ToInt32());
  }
};

ref class Window1 : Window
{
```

15

LISTING 15.3   Continued

```cpp
public:
  Window1()
  {
    DockPanel^ panel = gcnew DockPanel();
    MyHwndHost^ host = gcnew MyHwndHost();
    Label^ label = gcnew Label();
    label->FontSize = 20;
    label->Content = "The Win32 control is docked to the left.";
    panel->Children->Add(host);
    panel->Children->Add(label);
    this->Content = panel;

    if (FAILED(Webcam::Initialize(640, 480)))
    {
      ::MessageBox(NULL, L"Failed to communicate with a video capture device.",
        L"Error", 0);
    }
    Webcam::Start();
  }

  ~Window1()
  {
    Webcam::Terminate();
  }
};
```

The first thing to notice about Listing 15.3 is that it defines a subclass of HwndHost called MyHwndHost. This is necessary because HwndHost is actually an abstract class! It contains two methods that need to be overridden:

▶ BuildWindowCore, in which you must return the HWND to be hosted. This is typically where initialization is done as well. The parent HWND is given to you as a parameter to this method. If you do not return a child HWND whose parent matches the passed-in parameter, WPF throws an InvalidOperationException.

▶ DestroyWindowCore, which gives you the opportunity to do any cleanup/termination when the HWND is no longer needed.

For both methods, HWNDs are represented as HandleRef types. HandleRef is a lightweight wrapper (in the System.Runtime.InteropServices namespace) that ties the lifetime of the HWND to a managed object. You'll typically pass this as the managed object when constructing a HandleRef.

Listing 15.3 calls the Win32 CreateWindow API inside BuildWindowCore to create an instance of the WebcamClass window that was registered in Listing 15.2, passing the input

HWND as the parent. The HWND returned by CreateWindow is not only returned by BuildWindowCore (inside a HandleRef), but it is also passed to the Webcam::AttachToWindow method so the video is rendered appropriately. Inside DestroyWindowCore, the Win32 DestroyWindow API is called to signify the end of the HWND's lifespan.

> **TIP**
>
> A typical implementation of an HwndHost subclass calls CreateWindow inside BuildWindowCore and DestroyWindow inside DestroyWindowCore. Note, however, that calling DestroyWindow isn't really necessary. That's because a child HWND is automatically destroyed by Win32 when the parent HWND is destroyed. So in Listing 15.3, the implementation of DestroyWindowCore could be left empty.

Inside the Window's constructor, the MyHwndHost is instantiated and added to a DockPanel just like any other FrameworkElement. The Webcam is then initialized and the video stream is started.

> **TIP**
>
> For some applications, initialization of the Win32 content might need to wait until all the WPF content has been rendered. In such cases, you can perform this initialization from Window's ContentRendered event.

Listing 15.4 contains the final piece needed for the WPF webcam application, which is the main method that creates the Window and runs the Application. It is also compiled with the /clr option. The running application is shown in Figure 15.2.

LISTING 15.4   HostingWin32.cpp—The Application's Entry Point

```cpp
#include "Window1.h"

using namespace System;
using namespace System::Windows;
using namespace System::Windows::Media;

[STAThreadAttribute]
int main(array<System::String ^> ^args)
{
  Application^ application = gcnew Application();
  Window^ window = gcnew Window1();
  window->Title = "Hosting Win32 DirectShow Content in WPF";
  window->Background = Brushes::Orange;
  application->Run(window);
  return 0;
}
```

15

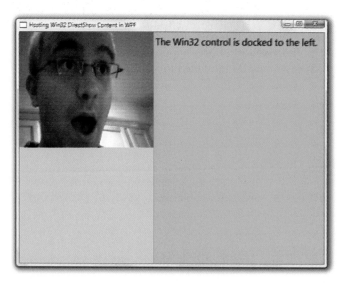

FIGURE 15.2   A live webcam feed is embedded in the WPF window.

TIP

With Visual C++'s /clr compiler option, you can compile entire projects or individual source files as managed code. It's tempting to simply compile entire projects as managed code, but it's usually best if you decide on a file-by-file basis what should be compiled as managed and what should be compiled as unmanaged. Otherwise, you could create extra work for yourself without any real gain.

The /clr option works well, but it often increases build time and can sometimes require code changes. For example, .C files must be compiled as C++ under /clr, but .C files often require some syntax changes to be compiled as such. Also, managed code can't run under the Windows loader lock, so compiling DllMain (or any code called by it) as managed results in a (fortunately quite descriptive) runtime error.

Visual Studio makes source-file-by-source-file /clr settings a bit more work than applying it at a project level. When turning /clr on and off for an entire project, other settings that need to be changed (/RTC1, /Gm, /EHsc) get changed back and forth automatically. When doing this at a file level, however, you need to manually change the other compiler switches. Fortunately, the compiler gives clear error messages telling you what needs to be done.

Notice the gray area underneath the video stream in Figure 15.2. The reason this appears is quite simple. The MyHwndHost element is docked to the left side of the DockPanel in Listing 15.3, but the Webcam control is initialized with a fixed size of 640x480.

If the implementation of Webcam::AttachToWindow in Listing 15.2 were changed to discover the size of the HWND, the video could stretch to fill that area. This change is shown in the following code, with the result shown in Figure 15.3:

```
HRESULT Webcam::AttachToWindow(HWND hwnd)
{
  if (!_initialized || !_windowlessControl)
    return E_FAIL;

  _hwnd = hwnd;

  // Position and size the video
  RECT rcDest;
  GetClientRect(hwnd,&rcDest);
  _windowlessControl->SetVideoClippingWindow(hwnd);
  return _windowlessControl->SetVideoPosition(NULL, &rcDest);
}
```

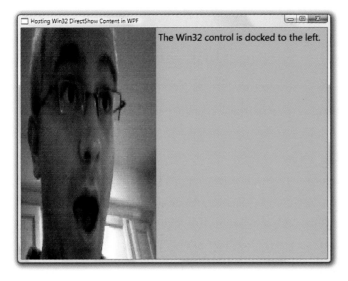

FIGURE 15.3   The Webcam control, altered to fill the entire rectangle given to it.

Although the best solution for a webcam application is probably to give the HwndHost-derived element a fixed (or at least unstretched) size, it's important to understand that WPF layout applies only to the HwndHost. Within its bounds, you need to play by Win32 rules to get the layout you desire.

Supporting Keyboard Navigation

In addition to the two abstract methods that must be implemented, HwndHost has a few virtual methods that can optionally be overridden if you want to handle seamless keyboard navigation between WPF elements and hosted Win32 content. This doesn't apply to the hosted Webcam control as is, as it never needs to gain keyboard focus. But for controls that accept input, there are some common features that you'd undoubtedly want to support:

▶ Tabbing into the hosted Win32 content

▶ Tabbing out of the hosted Win32 content

▶ Supporting access keys

Figure 15.4 illustrates contents of a hypothetical WPF Window with two WPF controls surrounding a Win32 control (hosted in HwndHost) with four child Win32 controls. We'll use this illustration when discussing each of these three features. The numbers represent the expected order of navigation. For the three WPF controls (1, 6, and the HwndHost containing 2-5), the ordering could come implicitly from the way in which they were added to their parent or it could come from an explicit TabIndex being set for each control. For the four Win32 controls (2-5), the order is defined by application-specific logic.

FIGURE 15.4   A scenario in which keyboard navigation is important with hosted Win32 content.

Tabbing Into the Hosted Win32 Content

"Tabbing into" the Win32 content means two things:

▶ When the *previous* WPF element has focus, pressing Tab moves focus to the *first* item in the Win32 control. In Figure 15.4, this means focus moves from 1 to 2.

▶ When the *next* WPF element has focus, pressing Shift+Tab moves focus back to the *last* item in the Win32 control. In Figure 15.4, this means focus moves from 6 to 5.

Both of these actions can be supported fairly easily by overriding HwndHost's TabInto method, which is called when HwndHost receives focus via Tab or Shift+Tab. In C++/CLI, a typical implementation would look like the following:

```
virtual bool TabInto(TraversalRequest^ request) override
{
  if (request->FocusNavigationDirection == FocusNavigationDirection::Next)
    SetFocus(hwndForFirstWin32Control);
  else
    SetFocus(hwndForLastWin32Control);
  return true;
}
```

TabInto's parameter reveals whether the user has just pressed Tab (giving FocusNavigationDirection.Next) or Shift+Tab (giving FocusNavigationDirection. Previous). Therefore, this code uses this information to decide whether to give focus to its first child or last child. It does this using the Win32 SetFocus API. After setting focus to the correct element, it returns true to indicate that it successfully handled the request.

Tabbing Out of the Hosted Win32 Content

Supporting tabbing into a Win32 control is not enough, of course. If you don't also support tabbing *out of* the control, keyboard navigation can get "stuck" inside of the Win32 control. For Figure 15.4, tabbing out of the control means being able to navigate from 5 to 6 with Tab, or from 2 to 1 with Shift+Tab.

Supporting this direction is a little more complicated than the other direction. That's because after focus enters Win32 content, WPF no longer has the same kind of control over what's going on. The application still receives Windows messages that are ultimately passed along to HwndHost, but WPF's keyboard navigation functionality can't "see" what's going on with focus.

Therefore, there is no TabOutOf method to override. Instead, there is a TranslateAccelerator method, which gets called whenever the application receives WM_KEYDOWN or WM_SYSKEYDOWN message from Windows (much like the Win32 API with the same name). Listing 15.5 shows a typical C++/CLI implementation of TranslateAccelerator for the purpose of supporting tabbing out of Win32 content (and tabbing within it).

LISTING 15.5   A Typical C++/CLI Implementation for TranslateAccelerator

```cpp
virtual bool TranslateAccelerator(MSG% msg, ModifierKeys modifiers) override
{
  if (msg.message == WM_KEYDOWN && msg.wParam == IntPtr(VK_TAB))
  {
    // Handle Shift+Tab
    if (GetKeyState(VK_SHIFT))
    {
      if (GetFocus() == hwndOfFirstControl)
      {
        // We're at the beginning, so send focus to the previous WPF element
        return this->KeyboardInputSite->OnNoMoreTabStops(
          gcnew TraversalRequest(FocusNavigationDirection::Previous));
      }
      else
        return (SetFocus(hwndOfPreviousControl) != NULL);
    }
    // Handle Shift without Tab
    else
    {
```

LISTING 15.5   Continued

```
    if (GetFocus() == hwndOfLastControl)
    {
      // We're at the end, so send focus to the next WPF element
      return this->KeyboardInputSite->OnNoMoreTabStops(
        gcnew TraversalRequest(FocusNavigationDirection::Next));
    }
    else
      return (SetFocus(hwndOfNextControl) != NULL);
  }
 }
}
```

TranslateAccelerator is passed a reference to a "raw" Windows message (represented as a managed System.Windows.Interop.MSG structure) and a ModifierKeys enumeration that reveals if the user is pressing Shift, Alt, Control, and/or the Windows key. (This information can also be retrieved using the Win32 GetKeyState API.)

In this listing, the code only takes action if the message is WM_KEYDOWN and if Tab is being pressed (which includes Shift+Tab). After determining whether the user pressed Tab or Shift+Tab using GetKeyState, the code must determine if it is time to tab *out of* the control or *within* the control. Tabbing out should occur if focus is already on the first child control and the user pressed Shift+Tab, or if focus is already on the last child control and the user pressed Tab. So in these cases, the implementation calls OnNoMoreTabStops on HwndHost's KeyboardInputSite property. This is the way to tell WPF that focus should return under its control. OnNoMoreTabStops needs to be passed a FocusNavigationDirection value so it knows which WPF element should get focus (1 or 6 in Figure 15.4). The implementation of TranslateAccelerator must return true if it handles the keyboard event. Otherwise, the event bubbles or tunnels to other elements. One point that Listing 15.5 glosses over is that setting the values of hwndOfPreviousControl and hwndOfNextControl appropriately involves a small amount of application-specific code to determine what the previous/next Win32 control is based on the HWND that currently has focus.

With such an implementation of TranslateAccelerator and TabInto (from the previous section), a user of the application represented by Figure 15.4 would now be able to navigate all the way from 1 to 6 and back from 6 to 1 using Tab and Shift+Tab, respectively.

Supporting Access Keys

The final piece of keyboard navigation to support is jumping to a control via an access key (sometimes called a *mnemonic*). For example, the text boxes in Figure 15.4 would likely have corresponding labels with an access key (indicated by an underlined letter). When hosted in a WPF application, we still want focus to jump to the corresponding controls when the user presses Alt and the access key.

> **WARNING**
>
> **C++/CLI compilation is likely to run into a conflict with `TranslateAccelerator`!**
>
> The standard Windows header file `winuser.h` defines `TranslateAccelerator` as an alias for the Win32 `TranslateAcceleratorW` function (if compiling with `UNICODE` defined) or the Win32 `TranslateAcceleratorA` function (if compiling with `UNICODE` undefined). Therefore, this is likely to conflict with the WPF-based `TranslateAccelerator` method in a Win32-based C++ project. To prevent compilation errors, you can undefine this symbol immediately before your `TranslateAccelerator` method. For example:
>
> `#undef TranslateAccelerator`

To support this, you can override `HwndHost`'s `OnMnemonic` method. Like `TranslateAccelerator`, it is given a raw Windows message and a `ModifierKeys` enumeration. So you could implement it as follows, if you want to support two access keys—a and b:

```
virtual bool OnMnemonic(MSG% msg, ModifierKeys modifiers) override
{
  // Ensure that we got the expected message
  if (msg.message == WM_SYSCHAR && (modifiers | ModifierKeys.Alt))
  {
    // Convert the IntPtr to a char
    char key = (char)msg.wParam.ToPointer();

    // Only handle the 'a' and 'b' characters
    if (key == 'a')
      return (SetFocus(someHwnd) != NULL);
    else if (key == 'b')
      return (SetFocus(someOtherHwnd) != NULL);
  }
  return false;
}
```

> **TIP**
>
> Because C++/CLI was introduced with Visual C++ 2005, you might find yourself needing to upgrade an older codebase to a later compiler to take advantage of it. This can sometimes be tricky because of increased ISO standard compliance in the compiler and various changes to Windows libraries and headers. However, the following website can help with most issues that come up:
>
> http://msdn.microsoft.com/visualc/previous/migrating
>
> Although it might not be an automatic process, there are many benefits to upgrading to the latest Visual C++ compiler, even for your unmanaged code!

15

FAQ

 How do I launch a Win32 modal dialog from a WPF application?

You can still use your favorite Win32 technique for showing the dialog (such as calling the Win32 `DialogBox` function). With C++/CLI, this can be a direct call. Or with a language like C#, you can use PInvoke to call the relevant function(s). The only trick is to get the `HWND` of a WPF `Window` to pass as the dialog's parent.

Fortunately, you can get the `HWND` for any WPF `Window` by using the `WindowInteropHelper` class from the `System.Windows.Interop` namespace.

This looks like the following in C++/CLI:

```
WindowInteropHelper^ helper = gcnew WindowInteropHelper(wpfParentWindow);
HWND hwnd = (HWND)helper->Handle.ToPointer();
DialogBox(hinst, MAKEINTRESOURCE(MYDIALOG), hwnd, (DLGPROC)MyDialogProc);
```

Embedding WPF Controls in Win32 Applications

Lots of compelling WPF features can be integrated into a Win32 application: 3D, rich documents support, animation, easy restyling, and so on. Even if you don't require this extra "flashiness," you can still take advantage of important features, such as flexible layout and resolution independence.

WPF's HWND interoperability is bidirectional, so WPF controls can be embedded in Win32 applications much like how Win32 controls are embedded in WPF applications. In this section, we'll take a built-in WPF control—`DocumentViewer`, the viewer for XPS documents—and embed it in a simple Win32 window using a class called `HwndSource`.

Introducing HwndSource

`HwndSource` does the opposite of `HwndHost`—it exposes any WPF `Visual` as an `HWND`. Listing 15.6 demonstrates the use of `HwndSource` with the relevant C++ source file from a Win32 project included with this book's source code. It is compiled with `/clr`, so it is managed code that uses both managed and unmanaged data types.

LISTING 15.6   HostingWPF.cpp—Embedding a WPF Control in a Win32 Dialog

```
#include "stdafx.h"
#include "HostingWPF.h"
#include "commctrl.h"

#using <PresentationFramework.dll>
#using <PresentationCore.dll>
#using <WindowsBase.dll>
```

LISTING 15.6   Continued

```cpp
LRESULT CALLBACK DialogFunction(HWND hDlg, UINT message, WPARAM wParam,
  LPARAM lParam)
{
  switch (message)
  {
    case WM_INITDIALOG:
    {
      // Describe the HwndSource
      System::Windows::Interop::HwndSourceParameters p;
      p.WindowStyle = WS_VISIBLE | WS_CHILD;
      p.PositionX = 10;
      p.PositionY = 10;
      p.Width = 500;
      p.Height = 350;
      p.ParentWindow = System::IntPtr(hDlg);

      System::Windows::Interop::HwndSource^ source =
        gcnew System::Windows::Interop::HwndSource(p);

      // Attach a new DocumentViewer to the HwndSource
      source->RootVisual = gcnew System::Windows::Controls::DocumentViewer();

      return TRUE;
    }

    case WM_CLOSE:
      EndDialog(hDlg, LOWORD(wParam));
      return TRUE;
  }
  return FALSE;
}

[System::STAThread]
int APIENTRY _tWinMain(HINSTANCE hInstance, HINSTANCE hPrevInstance,
  LPTSTR lpCmdLine, int nCmdShow)
{
  DialogBox(hInstance, (LPCTSTR)IDD_MYDIALOG, NULL, (DLGPROC)DialogFunction);
  return 0;
}
```

15

In this project, a simple dialog is defined via a Win32 resource script (not shown here). The application's entry point (_tWinMain) simply shows this dialog via the Win32 DialogBox function, specifying DialogFunction as the window procedure that receives the Win32 messages.

Inside DialogFunction, only two messages are processed—WM_INITDIALOG, which creates and embeds the WPF control on initialization, and WM_CLOSE, which terminates the dialog appropriately. Inside the processing of WM_INITDIALOG, an HwndSourceParameters structure is created, and some of its fields are initialized to give the HwndSource an initial size, position, and style. Most important, it is given a parent HWND (which, in this case, is the dialog itself). For Win32 programmers, this type of initialization should look very familiar. It's mostly the same kind of information that you would pass to the Win32 CreateWindow function.

After HwndSourceParameters is populated, the code only needs to do two simple steps to put the WPF content in place. It instantiates an HwndSource object with the HwndSourceParameters data, and then it sets HwndSource's RootVisual property (of type System.Windows.Media.Visual) to an appropriate instance. Here, a DocumentViewer is instantiated. The result is shown in Figure 15.5.

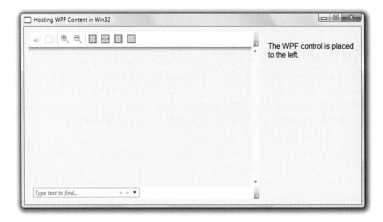

FIGURE 15.5   The WPF DocumentViewer control hosted in a simple Win32 dialog.

Although this example uses a built-in WPF control, you can follow the same approach with your own arbitrarily complex WPF content. Just take the top-level element (like a Grid or a Page) and use HwndSource to expose it to the rest of Win32 as one big HWND.

WARNING

WPF must run on an STA thread!

As with Windows Forms and earlier technologies, the main thread in an application using WPF must live in a single-threaded apartment. In Listing 15.6, the STAThreadAttribute must be applied to the entry point because the entire file is compiled as managed code, and managed code defaults to MTA.

However, the most reliable way to force the main thread to be STA in Visual C++ is to use the linker option /CLRTHREADATTRIBUTE:STA. This works regardless of whether the application's entry point is managed or unmanaged. STAThreadAttribute, on the other hand, can only be used when the entry point is managed.

> **WARNING**
>
> **Be sure to set the Visual C++ debugger mode to Mixed!**
>
> For large Win32 applications, it can often make sense to integrate WPF (and managed code in general) into DLLs loaded by the executable but to leave the executable as entirely unmanaged. This can cause a few development-time gotchas, however.
>
> The debugger in Visual C++ defaults to an Auto mode, which means that it performs unmanaged-only or managed-only debugging based on the type of executable. But when an unmanaged EXE loads a DLL with managed code, you aren't able to properly debug that managed code with unmanaged-only debugging. The solution is simply to set the project's debugger mode to Mixed instead.

> **TIP**
>
> If you don't specify a parent HWND when creating an HwndSource, the result is a top-level Win32 window, with HwndSourceParameters.Name used as the window title. So creating a parent-less HwndSource and setting its RootVisual property to arbitrary WPF content gives pretty much the same result as creating a WPF Window and setting its Content property to that same content. In fact, Window is really just a rich wrapper over HwndSource. By using HwndSource directly to create a top-level window, you have more control over the various style bits used when creating the HWND, but you lack all sorts of handy members defined by Window and related classes (such as the automatic message loop handled by Application.Run).

Getting the Right Layout

Because you're in the world of Win32 when doing this type of integration, there's no special layout support for the top-level WPF control. In Listing 15.6, the DocumentViewer is given an initial placement of (10,10) and a size of (500,350). But that placement and size is never going to change without some explicit code to change them. For example, Listing 15.7 makes the DocumentViewer occupy the entire space of the window, even as the window is resized. The result is shown in Figure 15.6.

FIGURE 15.6   The WPF DocumentViewer control hosted and resized in a simple Win32 dialog.

LISTING 15.7   `HostingWPF.cpp`—Updating the Size of the WPF Control

```cpp
#include "stdafx.h"
#include "HostingWPF.h"
#include "commctrl.h"

#using <PresentationFramework.dll>
#using <PresentationCore.dll>
#using <WindowsBase.dll>

ref class Globals
{
public:
  static System::Windows::Interop::HwndSource^ source;
};

LRESULT CALLBACK DialogFunction(HWND hDlg, UINT message, WPARAM wParam,
  LPARAM lParam)
{
  switch (message)
  {
    case WM_INITDIALOG:
    {
      System::Windows::Interop::HwndSourceParameters p;
      p.WindowStyle = WS_VISIBLE | WS_CHILD;
      // Initial size and position don't matter due to WM_SIZE handling:
      p.PositionX = 0; p.PositionY = 0;
      p.Width = 100; p.Height = 100;
      p.ParentWindow = System::IntPtr(hDlg);

      Globals::source = gcnew System::Windows::Interop::HwndSource(p);
      Globals::source->RootVisual =
        gcnew System::Windows::Controls::DocumentViewer();
      return TRUE;
    }

    case WM_SIZE:
      RECT r;
      GetClientRect(hDlg, &r);
      SetWindowPos((HWND)Globals::source->Handle.ToPointer(), NULL,
        r.left, r.top, r.right - r.left, r.bottom - r.top, 0);
      return TRUE;
```

LISTING 15.7   Continued

```
    case WM_CLOSE:
      EndDialog(hDlg, LOWORD(wParam));
      return TRUE;
  }
  return FALSE;
}

[System::STAThreadAttribute]
int APIENTRY _tWinMain(HINSTANCE hInstance, HINSTANCE hPrevInstance,
  LPTSTR lpCmdLine, int nCmdShow)
{
  DialogBox(hInstance, (LPCTSTR)IDD_MYDIALOG, NULL, (DLGPROC)DialogFunction);
  return 0;
}
```

The most important code is the handling of the WM_SIZE message. It uses the Win32 GetClientRect API to get the current window size, and then it applies it to the HwndSource using the Win32 SetWindowPos API. There are two interesting points about this new implementation:

▶ The HwndSource variable is now "global," so it can be shared by multiple places in the code. But C++/CLI does not allow a managed variable to be truly global, so the listing uses a common technique of making it a static variable of a managed class.

▶ To operate on the HwndSource with Win32 APIs such as SetWindowPos, you need its HWND. This is exposed via a Handle property of type IntPtr. In C++/CLI, you can call its ToPointer method (which returns a void*) and then cast the result to an HWND.

15

TIP

You don't need to share an HwndSource globally as long as you have its corresponding HWND! HwndSource defines a static FromHwnd method, which returns an HwndSource instance corresponding to any HWND (assuming the HWND belongs to an HwndSource in the first place). This is very handy when retrofitting Win32 codebases with WPF content because HWNDs are often passed around as parameters. With this technique, you can avoid the need to define a managed Globals class, as was done in Listing 15.7.

TIP

You can use HwndSource with a pure WPF application to respond to obscure Windows messages! In pure WPF applications, you don't need to define a window procedure and respond to Windows messages. But that's not because Windows messages don't exist; the top-level window still has an HWND and still plays by Win32 rules. As mentioned in a previous tip, WPF's Window object actually uses HwndSource to host any content inside the top-level HWND. And internally, WPF has a window procedure that exposes relevant messages in its own way. For example, WPF handles WM_SIZE messages and raises a SizeChanged event.

There are, however, Windows messages that WPF does not expose. But you can use HwndSource with any WPF Window to get exposure to all messages. The key is to use the System.Windows.Interop.WindowInteropHelper class, which exposes the HWND for any WPF Window. After you have this handle, you can get the corresponding HwndSource object (using HwndSource.FromHwnd) and attach a window procedure using HwndSource's AddHook method.

Chapter 7 performed these actions to discover WM_DWMCOMPOSITIONCHANGED messages. The following Window intercepts WM_TCARD, an obscure message that can be sent by HtmlHelp when certain directives are selected inside an application's help file:

```
public partial class AdvancedWindow : Window
{
  …

  void AdvancedWindow_Loaded(object sender, RoutedEventArgs e)
  {
    // Get the HWND for the current Window
    IntPtr hwnd = new WindowInteropHelper(this).Handle;
    // Get the HwndSource corresponding to the HWND
    HwndSource source = HwndSource.FromHwnd(hwnd);
    // Add a window procedure to the HwndSource
    source.AddHook(new HwndSourceHook(WndProc));
  }

  private static IntPtr WndProc(
    IntPtr hwnd, int msg, IntPtr wParam, IntPtr lParam, ref bool handled)
  {
    // Handle any Win32 message
    if (msg == WM_TCARD)
    {
      …
      handled = true;
    }
    return IntPtr.Zero;
  }

  // Define any Win32 message constants
  private const int WM_TCARD = 0x0052;
}
```

FAQ

How do I launch a WPF modal dialog from a Win32 application?

To launch a WPF `Window`, whether from Win32 code or WPF code, you can instantiate it and call its `ShowDialog` method. The trick, as with the reverse direction, is assigning the proper parent to the WPF `Window`. Correctly setting the parent of a modal dialog is important to get the desired behavior: ensuring it remains on top of the parent window at all times, that both windows minimize together, and so on.

The problem is that `Window`'s `Owner` property is of type `Window`, and it has no other property or method that enables its parent to be set to an arbitrary `HWND`. Furthermore, you can't fabricate a `Window` object from an arbitrary `HWND`.

The solution to this dilemma is to use the `WindowInteropHelper` class in the `System.Windows.Interop` namespace. This class not only exposes the `HWND` for any WPF `Window`, but enables you to set its owner to an arbitrary `HWND`! This looks like the following in C++/CLI:

```cpp
Nullable<bool> LaunchWpfDialogFromWin32Window(Window^ dialog, HWND parent)
{
  WindowInteropHelper^ helper = gcnew WindowInteropHelper(dialog);
  helper->Owner = parent;
  return dialog->ShowDialog();
}
```

15

Embedding Windows Forms Controls in WPF Applications

You've seen that WPF can host Win32 controls by wrapping any `HWND` inside an `HwndHost`. And Windows Forms controls can easily be exposed as Win32 controls. (Unlike WPF controls, they are all `HWND`-based, so `System.Windows.Forms.Control` directly defines a `Handle` property exposing the `HWND`.) Therefore, you could imagine using the same techniques previously discussed to host Windows Forms controls inside WPF.

However, there is the opportunity for much richer integration between Windows Forms and WPF, without delving into the underlying `HWND`-based plumbing. Sure, they have different rendering engines and different controls. But they both have rich .NET-based object models with similar properties and events, and both have services (such as layout and data binding) that go above and beyond their Win32 common denominator.

Indeed, WPF takes advantage of this opportunity and also has built-in functionality for direct interoperability with Windows Forms. This support is still built on top of the Win32 `HWND` interoperability described in the last two sections, but with many features to make the integration much simpler. The hard work is done for you, so you can communicate more directly between the technologies, usually without the need to write any unmanaged code.

As with Win32 interoperability, WPF defines a pair of classes to cover both directions of communication. The analog to HwndHost is called WindowsFormsHost, and appears in the System.Windows.Forms.Integration namespace (in the WindowsFormsIntegration.dll assembly).

Embedding a `PropertyGrid` with Procedural Code

This chapter's introduction mentioned that Windows Forms has several interesting built-in controls that WPF lacks in its first version. One control—the powerful PropertyGrid—helps to highlight the deep integration between Windows Forms and WPF, so let's use that inside a WPF Window. (Of course, you can also create custom Windows Forms controls and embed them in WPF Windows as well.)

The first step is to add a reference to System.Windows.Forms.dll and WindowsFormsIntegration.dll to your WPF-based project. After you've done this, your Window's Loaded event is an appropriate place to create and attach a hosted Windows Forms control. For example, let's take a simple Window containing a Grid called grid:

```
<Window x:Class="HostingWindowsFormsControl.Window1"
  xmlns="http://schemas.microsoft.com/winfx/2006/xaml/presentation"
  xmlns:x="http://schemas.microsoft.com/winfx/2006/xaml"
  Title="Hosting a Windows Forms Property Grid in WPF"
  Loaded="Window_Loaded">
    <Grid Name="grid"/>
</Window>
```

The following handler of the Loaded event adds the PropertyGrid to the Grid, using WindowsFormsHost as the intermediate element:

```
private void Window_Loaded(object sender, RoutedEventArgs e)
{
  // Create the host and the PropertyGrid control
  System.Windows.Forms.Integration.WindowsFormsHost host =
    new System.Windows.Forms.Integration.WindowsFormsHost();
  System.Windows.Forms.PropertyGrid propertyGrid =
    new System.Windows.Forms.PropertyGrid();

  // Add the PropertyGrid to the host, and the host to the WPF Grid
  host.Child = propertyGrid;
  grid.Children.Add(host);

  // Set a PropertyGrid-specific property
  propertyGrid.SelectedObject = this;
}
```

The integration-specific code is as simple as instantiating WindowsFormsHost and setting its Child property to the desired object. WindowsFormsHost's Child property can be set to any object that derives from System.Windows.Forms.Control.

The last line, which sets PropertyGrid's SelectedObject property to the instance of the current WPF Window, enables a pretty amazing scenario. PropertyGrid displays the properties of any .NET object, and, in some cases, enables the editing of the object's values. It does this via .NET reflection. Because WPF objects are .NET objects, PropertyGrid provides a fairly rich way to edit the current Window's properties on the fly without writing any extra code. Figure 15.7 shows the previously defined Window in action. When running this application, you can see values change as you resize the Window, you can type in new property values to resize the Window, you can change its background color or border style, and so on.

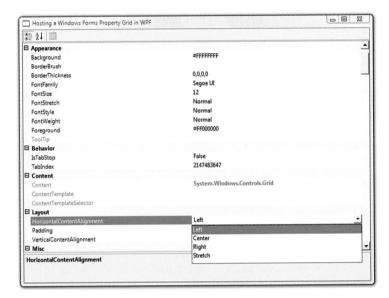

FIGURE 15.7   The hosted Windows Forms PropertyGrid enables you to change properties of the WPF Window on the fly.

Notice that the enumeration values for properties such as HorizontalContentAlignment are automatically populated in a drop-down list, thanks to the standard treatment of .NET enums. But Figure 15.7 highlights some additional similarities between Windows Forms and WPF, other than being .NET-based. Notice that Window's properties are grouped into categories such as "Behavior," "Content," and "Layout." This comes from CategoryAttribute markings that are used both by Windows Forms and WPF. The type converters used by WPF are also compatible with Windows Forms, so you can type in "red" as a color, for example, and it gets automatically converted to the hexadecimal ARGB representation (#FFFF0000). Another neat thing about the PropertyGrid used in this manner is that you can see attached properties that could be applied to the object, with the syntax you would expect.

> **TIP**
>
> The WindowsFormsHost class actually derives from HwndHost, so it supports the same HWND interoperability features described earlier, just in case you want to dig into lower-level mechanics, such as overriding its WndProc method.

Embedding a `PropertyGrid` with XAML

There's no reason that you have to instantiate a `WindowsFormsHost` instance in procedural code; you could alternatively define it right inside your XAML file. Furthermore, there's nothing to stop you from using Windows Forms controls inside of XAML, other than limitations of the expressiveness of XAML. (The controls must have a default constructor, useful instance properties to set, and so on.)

Not all Windows Forms controls work well within XAML, but `PropertyGrid` works reasonably well. For example, the previous XAML can be replaced with the following XAML:

```
<Window x:Class="HostingWindowsFormsControl.Window1"
  xmlns="http://schemas.microsoft.com/winfx/2006/xaml/presentation"
  xmlns:x="http://schemas.microsoft.com/winfx/2006/xaml"
  xmlns:swf="clr-namespace:System.Windows.Forms;assembly=System.Windows.Forms"
  Title="Hosting a Windows Forms Property Grid in WPF"
  Loaded="Window_Loaded">
  <Grid>
    <WindowsFormsHost>
      <swf:PropertyGrid x:Name="propertyGrid"/>
    </WindowsFormsHost>
  </Grid>
</Window>
```

The `System.Windows.Forms.Integration` .NET namespace is already included as part of WPF's standard XML namespace, so `WindowsFormsHost` can be used without any additional work. And with the `System.Windows.Forms` .NET namespace given the prefix of swf, the `PropertyGrid` object can be instantiated directly in the XAML file. Notice that the `PropertyGrid` can be added as a child element to `WindowsFormsHost` because its `Child` property is marked as a content property. `PropertyGrid`'s properties can generally be set in XAML rather than C#. We still need some procedural code, however, to set the `SelectedObject` property:

```
private void Window_Loaded(object sender, RoutedEventArgs e)
{
  propertyGrid.SelectedObject = this;
}
```

TIP

By default, Windows Forms controls hosted in WPF applications might look old-fashioned. That's because they use the "classic" Win32 Common Controls library unless you explicitly enable the Windows XP-era visual styles. You can do this by embedding a special manifest file in your application, but it's easiest to just call the `System.Windows.Forms.Application.EnableVisualStyles` method before any of the Windows Forms controls are instantiated. The Visual Studio template for Windows Forms projects automatically inserts this method call, but the template for WPF projects does not.

FAQ

 How do I launch a Windows Forms modal dialog from a WPF application?

The answer seems like it should be simple: Instantiate your Form-derived class and call its ShowDialog method. But for it to behave like a correct modal dialog, you should call the overload of ShowDialog that accepts an owner. This owner, however, must be in the form of an IWin32Window, a type that's incompatible with a WPF Window.

As explained in the previous section, you can get the HWND for a WPF Window by using the WindowInteropHelper class from the System.Windows.Interop namespace, but how do you get an IWin32Window? You actually have to define a custom class that implements it. Fortunately, this is pretty easy because IWin32Window only defines a single Handle property. The following code defines an OwnerWindow class that can be used in this situation:

```
class OwnerWindow : IWin32Window
{
  private IntPtr handle;

  public IntPtr Handle
  {
    get { return handle; }
    set { handle = value; }
  }
}
```

With this class in place, you can write code like the following that launches a modal Windows Forms dialog using a WPF Window as its parent:

```
DialogResult LaunchWindowsFormsDialogFromWpfWindow(Form dialog, Window parent)
{
  WindowInteropHelper helper = new WindowInteropHelper(parent);
  OwnerWindow owner = new OwnerWindow();
  owner.Handle = helper.Handle;
  return dialog.ShowDialog(owner);
}
```

Embedding WPF Controls in Windows Forms Applications

WPF controls can be embedded inside a Windows Forms application thanks to a companion class of WindowsFormsHost called ElementHost. ElementHost is like HwndSource, but is customized for hosting WPF elements inside a Windows Forms Form rather than inside an arbitrary HWND. ElementHost is a Windows Forms control (deriving from System.Windows.Forms.Control) and internally knows how to display WPF content.

To demonstrate the use of ElementHost, we'll create a simple Windows Forms application that hosts a WPF Expander control. After creating a standard Windows Forms project in

Visual Studio, the first step is to add `ElementHost` to the Toolbox using the Tools, Choose Toolbox Items menu item. This presents the dialog shown in Figure 15.8.

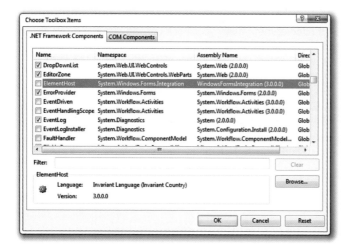

FIGURE 15.8   Adding `ElementHost` to the Toolbox in a Windows Forms project.

With `ElementHost` in the Toolbox, you can drag it onto a Windows Form just like any other Windows Forms control. Doing this automatically adds references to the necessary WPF assemblies (`PresentationFramework.dll`, `PresentationCore.dll`, and so on). Listing 15.8 shows the main source file to a Windows Forms project, whose `Form` contains an `ElementHost` called `elementHost` docked to the left and a `Label` on the right.

LISTING 15.8   `Form1.cs`—Embeds a WPF Expander in a Windows Forms Form

```
using System.Windows.Forms;
using System.Windows.Controls;

namespace WindowsFormsHostingWPF
{
  public partial class Form1 : Form
  {
    public Form1()
    {
      InitializeComponent();

      // Create a WPF Expander
      Expander expander = new Expander();
      expander.Header = "WPF Expander";
      expander.Content = "Content";
```

LISTING 15.8   Continued

```
    // Add it to the ElementHost
    elementHost.Child = expander;
  }
 }
}
```

This code uses the `System.Windows.Controls` namespace for `Expander`, which it simply instantiates and initializes inside the `Form`'s constructor. `ElementHost`, like `WindowsFormsHost`, has a simple `Child` property that can be set to any `UIElement`. This property must be set in source code rather than in the Windows Forms designer, so here it is set to the `Expander` instance. The result is shown in Figure 15.9. Notice that, by default, the `Expander` occupies all the space given to the `ElementHost`.

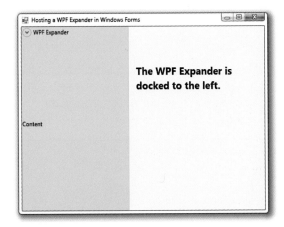

FIGURE 15.9   A Windows Forms application containing a WPF `Expander` control.

Taking this example one step further, we can use a combination of `ElementHost` *and* `WindowsFormsHost` to have a Windows Forms control embedded in a WPF control embedded in a Windows Forms application! All we need to do is set the `Content` of the WPF `Expander` to a `WindowsFormsHost`, which can contain an arbitrary Windows Forms control. Listing 15.9 does just that, placing a Windows Forms `MonthCalendar` inside a WPF `Expander`, all on the same Windows Forms `Form`. Figure 15.10 shows the result.

LISTING 15.9   `Form1.cs`—Uses Both Directions of Windows Forms and WPF Integration

```
using System.Windows.Forms;
using System.Windows.Controls;
using System.Windows.Forms.Integration;

namespace WindowsFormsHostingWPF
{
```

LISTING 15.9   Continued

```
public partial class Form1 : Form
{
  public Form1()
  {
    InitializeComponent();

    // Create a WPF Expander
    Expander expander = new Expander();
    expander.Header = "WPF Expander";

    // Create a MonthCalendar and wrap it in a WindowsFormsHost
    WindowsFormsHost host = new WindowsFormsHost();
    host.Child = new MonthCalendar();

    // Place the WindowsFormsHost in the Expander
    expander.Content = host;

    // Add the Expander to the ElementHost
    elementHost.Child = expander;
  }
}
```

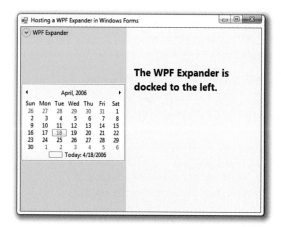

FIGURE 15.10   The Windows Forms MonthCalendar is inside the WPF Expander, which is on a Windows Forms Form.

DIGGING DEEPER

Converting Between Two Representations

One of the headaches of working with a hybrid Windows Forms/WPF application is dealing with the separate managed data types defined for the same concepts. For example, WPF has its own `Color`, `Cursor`, `Size`, `Rect`, and `Point` types that are different from the Windows Forms `Color`, `Cursor`, `Size`, `Rectangle`, and `Point` types. In most cases, however, converting between the two types is fairly simple. For example:

▶ Both `Color` types have a `FromArgb` static method, so you can create one `Color` from the other by passing this method the A, R, G, and B values from the source `Color`.

▶ To get a Windows Forms font size from a WPF font size, multiply the value by 0.75. To get a WPF font size from a Windows Forms font size, divide the value by 0.75.

In other cases, doing the conversion requires more work. In the case of converting from a `System.Drawing.Bitmap` to a `System.Windows.Media.Imaging.BitmapSource`, you need to work with a representation that both technologies understand—a Win32 `HBITMAP`.

The Windows Forms `Bitmap` object is based on an `HBITMAP`, so it has a simple `GetHbitmap` function that returns the handle (as an `IntPtr`). On the WPF side, `BitmapSource` has nothing to do with `HBITMAP`s, but fortunately the `System.Windows.Interop.Imaging` class defines three static helper methods for creating `BitmapSource`s from three different origins—a memory section, an `HICON`, and an `HBITMAP`. That last method, called `CreateBitmapSourceFromHBitmap`, can be given the handle and dimensions from the Windows Forms `Bitmap`, and it returns the desired WPF object.

15

FAQ

 How do I launch a WPF modal dialog from a Windows Forms application?

The technique for doing this is almost identical to launching a WPF modal dialog from Win32. You can instantiate your `Window`-derived class and call its `ShowDialog` method. But you also need to set the `Window`'s `Owner` property for it to behave correctly. `Owner` must be set to a `Window`, whereas in a Windows Forms application the owner is undoubtedly a `System.Windows.Forms.Form`.

Once again, you can use the `WindowInteropHelper` class to set its owner to an arbitrary `HWND`. Therefore, you can set it to the value returned by `Form`'s `Handle` property. The following code does just that:

```
bool? LaunchWpfDialogFromWindowsForm(Window dialog, Form parent)
{
  WindowInteropHelper helper = new WindowInteropHelper(dialog);
  helper.Owner = parent.Handle;
  return dialog.ShowDialog();
}
```

Embedding ActiveX Controls in WPF Applications

There must be thousands of ActiveX controls in existence, and they can be easily embedded in WPF applications. But that's not because of any hard work done by the WPF team. Ever since version 1.0, Windows Forms has had a bunch of plumbing built-in for interoperability with ActiveX controls. Rather than duplicating all of that plumbing natively inside WPF, the team decided to simply depend on Windows Forms for this scenario. WPF gets the functionality "for free" just by working well with Windows Forms.

Using Windows Forms as an intermediate layer between ActiveX and WPF might sound suboptimal, but the development experience is just about as pleasant as can be expected. To demonstrate how to embed an ActiveX control in a WPF application, we'll use the Microsoft Terminal Services Control that ships with Windows. This control contains basically all the functionality of Remote Desktop, but controllable via a few simple APIs.

The first step for using an ActiveX control is to get a managed and Windows Forms-compatible definition of the relevant types. This can be done in two different ways:

▶ Run the ActiveX Importer (AXIMP.EXE) on the ActiveX DLL. This utility is included in the .NET Framework component of the Windows SDK.

▶ In any Windows Forms project in Visual Studio, add the component to the Toolbox using the COM Components tab from the dialog shown by the Tools, Choose Toolbox Items menu item. Then drag the control from the Toolbox onto any Form. This process causes Visual Studio to invoke the ActiveX Importer behind the scenes.

No matter which approach you use, two DLLs get generated. You should add references to these in your WPF-based project (along with System.Windows.Forms.dll and WindowsFormsIntegration.dll). One is an Interop Assembly that contains "raw" managed definitions of the unmanaged interfaces, classes, enums, and structures defined in the type library contained inside the ActiveX DLL. The other is an assembly that contains a Windows Forms control corresponding to each ActiveX class. The first DLL is named with the library name from the original type library, and the second DLL is named the same but with an Ax prefix.

For the Microsoft Terminal Services Control, the original ActiveX DLL is called mstscax.dll and is found in Windows' system32 directory. (In the Choose Toolbox Items dialog, it shows up as "Microsoft Terminal Services Control.") Running the ActiveX Importer generates MSTSCLib.dll and AxMSTSCLib.dll.

With the four relevant two assemblies added to a project (MSTSCLib.dll, AxMSTSCLib.dll, System.Windows.Forms.dll, and WindowsFormsIntegration.dll), Listings 15.10 and 15.11 contain the XAML and C# code to host the control and get the resulting application shown in Figure 15.11.

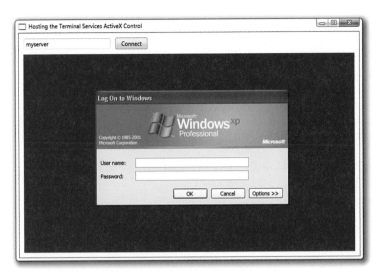

FIGURE 15.11   Hosting the Terminal Services ActiveX Control in a WPF Window.

LISTING 15.10   Window1.xaml—XAML for the Terminal Services WPF Application

```
<Window x:Class="HostingActiveX.Window1"
  xmlns="http://schemas.microsoft.com/winfx/2006/xaml/presentation"
  xmlns:x="http://schemas.microsoft.com/winfx/2006/xaml"
  Title="Hosting the Terminal Services ActiveX Control">
  <DockPanel Name="panel" Margin="10">
    <StackPanel Margin="0,0,0,10" DockPanel.Dock="Top" Orientation="Horizontal">
      <TextBox x:Name="serverBox" Width="180" Margin="0,0,10,0"/>
      <Button x:Name="connectButton" Click="connectButton_Click">Connect</Button>
    </StackPanel>
  </DockPanel>
</Window>
```

LISTING 15.11   Window1.xaml.cs—C# Code for Hosting the Terminal Services ActiveX
Control

```
using System;
using System.Windows;
using System.Windows.Forms.Integration;

namespace HostingActiveX
{
  public partial class Window1 : Window
  {
    AxMSTSCLib.AxMsTscAxNotSafeForScripting termServ;
```

LISTING 15.11   Continued

```
  public Window1()
  {
    InitializeComponent();

    // Create the host and the ActiveX control
    WindowsFormsHost host = new WindowsFormsHost();
    termServ = new AxMSTSCLib.AxMsTscAxNotSafeForScripting();

    // Add the ActiveX control to the host, and the host to the WPF panel
    host.Child = termServ;
    panel.Children.Add(host);
  }

  void connectButton_Click(object sender, RoutedEventArgs e)
  {
    termServ.Server = serverBox.Text;
    termServ.Connect();
  }
}
}
```

There's nothing special about the XAML in Listing 15.10; it simply contains a DockPanel with a TextBox and Button for choosing a server and connecting to it. In Listing 15.11, a WindowsFormsHost is added to the DockPanel, and the Windows Forms representation of the ActiveX control is added to the WindowsFormsHost. This control is called AxMsTscAxNotSafeForScripting. (In versions of Windows prior to Windows Vista, it has the somewhat simpler name of AxMsTscAx.) The interaction with the AxMsTscAxNotSafeForScripting control is quite simple. Its Server property can be set to a simple string, and you can connect to the server by calling Connect.

Of course, the instantiation of the WindowsFormsHost *and* the AxMsTscAxNotSafeForScripting control can be done directly in XAML, replacing the highlighted code in Listing 15.11. This is shown in Listing 15.12. You could go a step further and use data binding to replace the first line in connectButton_Click, but you would still need the event handler for calling the Connect method.

LISTING 15.12   Window1.xaml—Updated XAML for the Terminal Services WPF Application

```
<Window x:Class="HostingActiveX.Window1"
  xmlns="http://schemas.microsoft.com/winfx/2006/xaml/presentation"
  xmlns:x="http://schemas.microsoft.com/winfx/2006/xaml"
  xmlns:ax="clr-namespace:AxMSTSCLib;assembly=AxMSTSCLib"
  Title="Hosting the Terminal Services ActiveX Control">
  <DockPanel Name="panel" Margin="10">
```

LISTING 15.12   Continued

```
  <StackPanel Margin="0,0,0,10" DockPanel.Dock="Top" Orientation="Horizontal">
    <TextBox x:Name="serverBox" Margin="0,0,10,0"/>
    <Button x:Name="connectButton" Click="connectButton_Click">Connect</Button>
  </StackPanel>
  <WindowsFormsHost>
    <ax:AxMsTscAxNotSafeForScripting x:Name="termServ"/>
  </WindowsFormsHost>
 </DockPanel>
</Window>
```

TIP

It's possible to host ActiveX controls in a partial-trust XAML Browser Application or loose XAML page, but you can't use Windows Forms interoperability to do so (because this feature requires a higher level of trust). Instead, use a Frame that hosts a web page containing the ActiveX control. For example:

```
<Frame Source="pack://siteoforigin:,,,/webpage.html"/>
```

Where webpage.html contains:

```
<html>
  <body>
    <object Width="100%" Height="100%" ClassId="clsid:…"/>
  </body>
</html>
```

As far as security goes, you will see the same behavior as if you navigated to webpage.html directly in Internet Explorer. You might get security prompts, determined by the user's settings and the current zone. But you can avoid prompts in some cases with a signed, safe-for-scripting ActiveX control.

FAQ

What about the reverse direction of exposing WPF controls as ActiveX controls?

There is no built-in support for this above and beyond HWND interoperability, so your best bet is to use your favorite means of creating a non-WPF ActiveX control (using Active Template Library [ATL], for example) and injecting WPF content inside of it.

Conclusion

Most developers understand that it's possible to build really powerful applications with WPF. But with the HWND and Windows Forms interoperability features discussed in this chapter, there's essentially no limit to the power. That's because you can tap into decades of effort that has been poured into controls and functionality that are already developed, tested, and deployed. For organizations with huge investments in existing code, this is a critical feature.

The main scenarios discussed in this chapter boiled down to four classes. Their names are a bit confusing and inconsistent, so here's a summary that you can flip back to if you ever forget which class is which:

TABLE 15.1   The Four Main Interoperability Classes

Class Name	Usage
HwndHost	Hosting an HWND in WPF
WindowsFormsHost	Hosting Windows Forms in WPF
HwndSource	Hosting WPF in an HWND
ElementHost	Hosting WPF in Windows Forms

The benefits of interoperability are broader than the features discussed in this chapter, however. You could completely overhaul an application's user interface with WPF, but hook it up to back-end logic that was already in place with the old user interface—even if that logic was unmanaged code. This could be done with a number of techniques, such as using C++/CLI, PInvoke, or COM Interoperability.

And despite the ease and power of the features described in this chapter, there are still clear benefits for having an all-WPF user interface rather than a hybrid one. For example, in a pure WPF user interface, all the elements can be scaled, styled, and restyled in a similar fashion. They can be seamlessly overlaid on top of each other. In addition, you don't have to worry about mixing resolution-independent elements with resolution-dependent elements. A pure WPF user interface also opens the door to being able to run in a partial-trust environment (depending on how you separate your back-end logic).

Even complex applications with years of user-interface investment can easily benefit from WPF if they are well factored. For example, I once came across an MFC-based program that showed street maps across the United States. The application used various MFC (therefore GDI-based) primitives to draw each line and shape in the current scene. But by swapping in a WPF surface and performing the same drawing actions using the drawing APIs discussed in Chapter 11, "2D Graphics," the map could be replaced with a WPF version with relatively little code changes. After making the leap to WPF, the application could now easily support features that would have been difficult otherwise: crisp zooming, tilting the map in 3D, and so on.

Therefore, if you have developed a pre-WPF application, there are many ways to improve the look or functionality of it by using interoperability to incrementally add WPF features. If you've developed pre-WPF *controls*, there's another nice use of interoperability that doesn't necessarily involve updating end-user functionality: Simply wrap such controls in a WPF object model so consumers can treat it like a first-class WPF control without having to learn about WPF's interoperability features. Creating custom controls (whether pure WPF or not) is the topic of the next chapter.

CHAPTER 16

User Controls and Custom Controls

Chapter 4, "Introducing WPF's Controls," claimed that no modern presentation framework would be complete without a standard set of controls that enable you to quickly assemble traditional user interfaces. I think it's safe to say that no modern presentation framework would be complete without the ability to create your own reusable controls either. You might want to create a control because your own applications have custom needs, or because there's money to be made by selling unique controls to other software developers! This chapter is about two WPF mechanisms for writing your own controls: *user controls* (the easier of the two) and *custom controls* (the more-complicated but more-flexible variety).

The role that user controls and custom controls play in WPF is quite different than in other technologies. In other technologies, custom controls are often created simply to get a nonstandard look. But WPF has many options for achieving nonstandard-looking controls without creating brand-new controls. You can completely restyle built-in controls with WPF's style and template mechanisms demonstrated in Chapter 10, "Styles, Templates, Skins, and Themes." Or you can sometimes simply embed complex content inside built-in controls to get the look you want. In other technologies, a Button containing an Image or a TreeView containing ComboBoxes might necessitate a custom control, but not in WPF! (That's not to say that there are fewer opportunities for selling reusable components. It just means you've got more implementation options.)

Therefore, the decision to create a user control or custom control should be based on the APIs you want to expose rather than the look you want to achieve. If no existing control has a *programmatic* interface that naturally represents your concept, go ahead and create a user control or custom control. The biggest mistake people make with user controls and custom controls is creating one from scratch when an existing one can suffice!

FAQ

 I've concluded that I need to write my own control. But should I write a user control or a custom control?

The intention is that you should create a user control if its reuse will be limited and you don't care about exposing rich styling and theming support, whereas you should create a custom control if you want it to be a robust first-class control (like WPF's built-in controls). A user control tends to contain a logical tree defining its look, and tends to have logic that directly interacts with these child elements. A custom control, on the other hand, tends to get its look from a visual tree defined in a separate control template, and generally has logic that works even if a consumer changes its visual tree completely (using the techniques from Chapter 10).

This distinction is mostly imposed by the default development experience provided by Visual Studio, however. Visual Studio pushes you in a certain direction based on the type of control you add to your project. When you add a user control, you get a XAML file with a corresponding code-behind file, so you can easily build your user control much like you would build a Window or Page. But when you add a custom control to your project, you get a normal .cs (or .vb) code file plus a theme style with a simple control template injected into your project's generic dictionary (themes\generic.xaml).

Therefore, to answer this question with less hand-waving, let's look at the precise differences between user controls and custom controls. A custom control can derive from Control or any of its subclasses. The definition of a user control, on the other hand, is a class that derives from UserControl, which itself derives from ContentControl, which derives from Control. So, user controls are technically a type of custom control, but this chapter uses the term *custom control* to mean any Control-derived class that isn't a user control.

If the control you want to create would benefit by taking advantage of functionality already present in a non-ContentControl (such as RangeBase or Selector) or a ContentControl-derived class (such as HeaderedContentControl or Button), it's logical to derive your class from it. Or, if your control doesn't need any of the extra functionality that classes like ContentControl add on top of Control, deriving directly from Control makes sense. Both of these choices mean that you're writing a custom control rather than a user control.

But if neither of these conditions are true, the choice between deriving directly from ContentControl (which means you're writing a custom control) versus deriving from UserControl (which means you're writing a user control) is fairly insignificant if you ignore the development experience. That's because UserControl differs very little from its ContentControl base class; it has a different default control template, it has a default content alignment of Stretch in both directions (rather than Left and Top), it sets IsTabStop and Focusable to false by default, and it changes the source of any events raised from inner content to be the UserControl itself. And that's all. WPF does no special-casing of UserControl at runtime. Therefore, in this case, it makes sense to choose based on your intention to create a "lookless" control (which would be a custom control) versus a "look-filled" control (which would be a user control).

Creating a User Control

There's no better way to understand the process of creating a user control than actually creating one. So in this section, we'll create a user control called `FileInputBox`.

`FileInputBox` combines a `TextBox` with a Browse `Button`. The intention is that a user could type a raw filename in the `TextBox`, or click the `Button` to get a standard `OpenFileDialog`. If she chooses a file in this dialog box, its fully qualified name is automatically pasted into the `TextBox`. This control works exactly like `<INPUT TYPE="FILE"/>` in HTML.

Creating the User Interface

Listing 16.1 contains the user control's XAML file that defines the user interface, and Figure 16.1 shows the rendered result.

FIGURE 16.1   The `FileInputBox` user control combines a simple `TextBox` with a simple `Button`.

LISTING 16.1   `FileInputBox.xaml`—The User Interface for `FileInputBox`

```
<UserControl x:Class="Chapter16.FileInputBox"
    xmlns="http://schemas.microsoft.com/winfx/2006/xaml/presentation"
    xmlns:x="http://schemas.microsoft.com/winfx/2006/xaml">
  <DockPanel>
    <Button x:Name="theButton" DockPanel.Dock="Right" Click="theButton_Click">
      Browse...</Button>
    <TextBox x:Name="theTextBox"
      MinWidth="{Binding ActualWidth, ElementName=theButton}" Margin="0,0,2,0"/>
  </DockPanel>
</UserControl>
```

The `Button` is docked on the right and has an event handler for the `Click` event (covered in the next section). The `TextBox` fills the remaining space, except for a 2-unit margin on the right to give some space between itself and the `Button`. The XAML definition is very simple, but it handles every layout situation flawlessly. The setting of `MinWidth` on `TextBox` isn't necessary, but it's a slick way to ensure that the `TextBox` doesn't look too small in certain layout conditions. And by making its minimum width match the width of the `Button` (which is always just big enough to fit its content thanks to the right-docking), a hard-coded size is avoided.

Figure 16.2 shows what happens when an application uses an instance of `FileInputBox` and sets various properties inherited from `ContentControl` and `Control` as follows:

FIGURE 16.2   `FileInputBox` automatically respects visual properties from its base classes.

```
<local:FileInputBox BorderBrush="Orange" BorderThickness="4" Background="Blue"
  HorizontalContentAlignment="Right"/>
```

The fact that setting these properties works correctly seems like a no-brainer, but it's actually not as automatic as you might think. The appearance of FileInputBox depends on its control template, which it inherits from UserControl. Fortunately, UserControl's default control template respects properties such as the ones used in Figure 16.2:

```
<ControlTemplate TargetType="{x:Type UserControl}">
  <Border Background="{TemplateBinding Background}"
    BorderBrush="{TemplateBinding BorderBrush}"
    BorderThickness="{TemplateBinding BorderThickness}"
    Padding="{TemplateBinding Padding}">
    <ContentPresenter
      HorizontalAlignment="{TemplateBinding HorizontalContentAlignment}"
      VerticalAlignment="{TemplateBinding VerticalContentAlignment}"/>
  </Border>
</ControlTemplate>
```

If FileInputBox derived directly from ContentControl (UserControl's base class) instead, these properties would *not* be respected unless it was given a custom template. As is, FileInputBox can be restyled by its consumers, and individual elements (the TextBox, Button, and/or DockPanel) can even be restyled if the consumer creates typed styles for them!

> **TIP**
>
> If you want to prevent an application's typed styles from impacting elements inside your control, your best bet is to give them an explicit Style (which can be null to get the default look).

From a visual perspective, consuming a FileInputBox as follows

```
<Window xmlns="http://schemas.microsoft.com/winfx/2006/xaml/presentation"
  xmlns:x="http://schemas.microsoft.com/winfx/2006/xaml"
  xmlns:local="clr-namespace:Chapter16">
  <StackPanel Margin="20">
    <local:FileInputBox/>
  </StackPanel>
</Window>
```

is just a shortcut for plopping the logical tree of elements from FileInputBox.xaml into your user interface:

```
<Window xmlns="http://schemas.microsoft.com/winfx/2006/xaml/presentation"
  xmlns:x="http://schemas.microsoft.com/winfx/2006/xaml"
  xmlns:local="clr-namespace:Chapter16">
  <StackPanel Margin="20">
    <UserControl>
      <DockPanel>
        <Button DockPanel.Dock="Right">Browse...</Button>
        <TextBox MinWidth="{Binding ActualWidth, ElementName=theButton}"
```

```
                Margin="0,0,2,0"/>
        </DockPanel>
    </UserControl>
  </StackPanel>
</Window>
```

This alone can be handy, but is also achievable by giving an arbitrary existing control an explicit control template containing the DockPanel, Button, and TextBox (ignoring the subtle differences from the elements being in a visual tree rather than the logical tree). However, user controls typically add value by encapsulating custom behavior.

Creating the Behavior

Listing 16.2 contains the entire code-behind file for Listing 16.1. This gives FileInputBox the appropriate behavior when the Button is clicked, exposes the text from the TextBox as a read/write property, and exposes a simple FileNameChanged event corresponding to the TextChanged event exposed by the TextBox. The event handler for TextChanged marks the event as handled (to stop its bubbling) and raises the FileNameChanged event instead.

LISTING 16.2   FileInputBox.xaml.cs—The Logic for FileInputBox

```csharp
using System;
using System.Windows;
using System.Windows.Controls;
using Microsoft.Win32;

namespace Chapter16
{
  public partial class FileInputBox : UserControl
  {
    public FileInputBox()
    {
      InitializeComponent();
      theTextBox.TextChanged += new TextChangedEventHandler(OnTextChanged);
    }

    private void theButton_Click(object sender, RoutedEventArgs e)
    {
      OpenFileDialog d = new OpenFileDialog();
      if (d.ShowDialog() == true) // Result could be true, false, or null
        this.FileName = d.FileName;
    }

    public string FileName
    {
      get { return theTextBox.Text; }
```

16

LISTING 16.2   Continued

```
    set { theTextBox.Text = value; }
  }

  void OnTextChanged(object sender, TextChangedEventArgs e)
  {
    e.Handled = true;
    if (FileNameChanged != null)
      FileNameChanged(this, EventArgs.Empty);
  }

  public event EventHandler<EventArgs> FileNameChanged;
  }
}
```

That's all there is to it! If you don't care about broadly sharing your user control or maximizing the integration with WPF's subsystems, you can often expose plain .NET methods, properties, and events and have a control that's "good enough." Figure 16.3 shows the control in action.

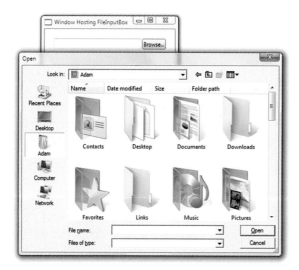

FIGURE 16.3   FileInputBox spawns a standard OpenFileDialog when its Button is clicked.

Consuming a user control is very straightforward. If you want to use it from a Window or Page in the same assembly, simply reference the appropriate namespace, which, in this case, is Chapter16:

```
<Window xmlns="http://schemas.microsoft.com/winfx/2006/xaml/presentation"
  xmlns:x="http://schemas.microsoft.com/winfx/2006/xaml"
```

```
  xmlns:local="clr-namespace:Chapter16">
  <StackPanel Margin="20">
    <local:FileInputBox/>
  </StackPanel>
</Window>
```

If you want to use it from a separate assembly, the `clr-namespace` directive simply needs to include the assembly information along with the namespace:

```
xmlns:local="clr-namespace:Chapter16;assembly=Chapter16Controls"
```

DIGGING DEEPER

Protecting User Controls from Accidental Usage

The following is a valid way to initialize `FileInputBox`, giving its `TextBox` an initial FileName value of `c:\Lindsay.htm`:

```
<local:FileInputBox FileName="c:\Lindsay.htm"/>
```

But because `FileInputBox` ultimately derives from `ContentControl`, here are two other ways a consumer might attempt to use `FileInputBox`:

```
<local:FileInputBox Content="c:\Lindsay.htm"/>
```

or

```
<local:FileInputBox>c:\Lindsay.htm</local:FileInputBox>
```

Can you guess what happens in these cases? The default value of `Content` (the `DockPanel` containing the `Button` and `TextBox`) gets completely replaced with this string! This is clearly not what the consumer intended; otherwise, they should have just used a `TextBlock` element!

Fortunately, you can take some actions to prevent such mistakes. For `FileInputBox`, you can designate `FileName` to be the content property instead of `Content`, as follows:

```
[ContentProperty("FileName")]
public partial class FileInputBox : UserControl
{
  …
}
```

This simple change makes:

```
<local:FileInputBox>c:\Lindsay.htm</local:FileInputBox>
```

equivalent to:

```
<local:FileInputBox FileName="c:\Lindsay.htm"/>
```

Continues

16

DIGGING DEEPER

Continued

But how can we change the explicit setting of `Content` from being disastrous? One way is to add the following method to `FileInputBox`:

```
protected override void OnContentChanged(object oldContent, object newContent)
{
  if (oldContent != null)
    throw new InvalidOperationException("You can't change Content!");
}
```

Another solution is to place your control's user interface inside a control template (rather than `Content`) and bind `TextBox.Text` to the `Content` property. But if you do that, you might as well write a custom control rather than a user control!

Adding Dependency Properties

One possible enhancement to `FileInputBox` is to change `FileName` from a plain .NET property to a dependency property. That way, consumers of the control can use it as a data-binding target, more easily use the value in a custom control template, and so on.

To turn `FileName` into a dependency property, you can add a `DependencyProperty` field to the class, initialize it appropriately, and change the implementation of the `FileName` property to use the dependency property mechanism:

```
public static readonly DependencyProperty FileNameProperty =
  DependencyProperty.Register("FileName", typeof(string), typeof(FileInputBox));

public string FileName
{
  get { return (string)GetValue(FileNameProperty); }
  set { SetValue(FileNameProperty, value); }
}
```

Giving the field a name of *PropertyName*`Property` is the convention followed by WPF's built-in objects, and should be followed by your own controls to avoid confusion.

The preceding implementation of `FileName` as a dependency property is flawed, however. It's no longer associated with the `Text` property of the control's inner `TextBox`! To update `FileName` when `Text` changes, you could add a line of code inside `OnTextChanged`:

```
void OnTextChanged(object sender, TextChangedEventArgs e)
{
  this.FileName = theTextBox.Text;
  e.Handled = true;
  if (FileNameChanged != null)
    FileNameChanged(this, EventArgs.Empty);
}
```

And to update `Text` when `FileName` changes, it's tempting to add a line of code to the `FileName` property's set accessor as follows:

```
set { theTextBox.Text = value; SetValue(FileNameProperty, value); }
```

But this isn't a good idea because, as explained in Chapter 3, the set accessor never gets called unless someone sets the .NET property in procedural code. When setting the property in XAML, data binding to it, and so on, WPF calls `SetValue` directly.

To respond properly to any value change in the `FileName` dependency property, you could register for a notification provided by the dependency property system. But the easiest way to keep `Text` and `FileName` in sync is to use data binding. Listing 16.3 contains the entire C# implementation of `FileInputBox`, updated with `FileName` as a dependency property. This assumes that the XAML for `FileInputBox` has been updated to take advantage of data binding as follows:

```
<UserControl x:Class="Chapter16.FileInputBox"
    xmlns="http://schemas.microsoft.com/winfx/2006/xaml/presentation"
    xmlns:x="http://schemas.microsoft.com/winfx/2006/xaml"
    x:Name="root">
  <DockPanel>
    <Button x:Name="theButton" DockPanel.Dock="Right" Click="theButton_Click">
      Browse...</Button>
    <TextBox x:Name="theTextBox"
      MinWidth="{Binding ActualWidth, ElementName=theButton}"
      Text="{Binding FileName, ElementName=root}" Margin="0,0,2,0"/>
  </DockPanel>
</UserControl>
```

LISTING 16.3   `FileInputBox.xaml.cs`—An Alternate Version of Listing 16.2, in Which `FileName` is a Dependency Property

```
using System;
using System.Windows;
using System.Windows.Controls;
using Microsoft.Win32;

namespace Chapter16
{
  public partial class FileInputBox : UserControl
  {
    public FileInputBox()
    {
      InitializeComponent();
      theTextBox.TextChanged += new TextChangedEventHandler(OnTextChanged);
    }
```

LISTING 16.3   Continued

```
  private void theButton_Click(object sender, RoutedEventArgs e)
  {
    OpenFileDialog d = new OpenFileDialog();
    if (d.ShowDialog() == true) // Result could be true, false, or null
      this.FileName = d.FileName;
  }

  public string FileName
  {
    get { return (string)GetValue(FileNameProperty); }
    set { SetValue(FileNameProperty, value); }
  }


  private void OnTextChanged(object sender, TextChangedEventArgs e)
  {
    e.Handled = true;
    if (FileNameChanged != null)
      FileNameChanged(this, EventArgs.Empty);
  }

  public static readonly DependencyProperty FileNameProperty =
  DependencyProperty.Register("FileName", typeof(string), typeof(FileInputBox));
  public event EventHandler<EventArgs> FileNameChanged;
  }
}
```

With the data binding in place on TextBox.Text (which is two-way by default), the standard dependency property implementation works with no extra code, despite the fact that the value for FileName is stored separately from the TextBox.

> **WARNING**
>
> **Avoid implementing logic in a dependency property's property wrapper other than calling GetValue and SetValue!**
>
> If you deviate from the standard implementation, you'll introduce semantics that only apply when the property is directly set from procedural code. To react to calls to SetValue, regardless of the source, register for a dependency property changed notification and place your logic in the callback method instead. Or find another mechanism to respond to property value changes with the help of data binding, as done in Listing 16.3.

> **TIP**
>
> `FrameworkPropertyMetadata`, an instance of which can be passed to `DependencyProperty.Register`, contains several properties for customizing the behavior of the dependency property. Besides attaching a property changed handler, you can set a default value, control whether the property gets inherited by child elements, set the default data flow for data binding, control whether a value change should refresh the control's layout or rendering, and so on.

Adding Routed Events

If you go to the effort of giving your user control appropriate dependency properties, you should probably make the same effort to transform appropriate events into routed events. Consumers can write triggers based on a routed event you expose, but they can't directly do that for normal .NET events. For `FileInputBox`, it makes sense for its `FileNameChanged` event to be a bubbling routed event, especially because the `TextChanged` event it's wrapping is itself a bubbling routed event!

As discussed in Chapter 3, defining a routed event is much like defining a dependency property: You define a `RoutedEvent` field (with an `Event` suffix by convention), register it, and optionally provide a .NET event that wraps the `AddHandler` and `RemoveHandler` APIs. Listing 16.4 shows what it looks like to update the `FileNameChanged` event from the previous two listings to be a bubbling routed event. In addition to the routed event implementation, the private `OnTextChanged` method is updated to raise the routed event with the `RaiseEvent` method inherited from `UIElement`.

LISTING 16.4   `FileInputBox.xaml.cs`—An Update to Listing 16.3, Making FileNameChanged a Routed Event

```
using System;
using System.Windows;
using System.Windows.Controls;
using Microsoft.Win32;

namespace Chapter16
{
  public partial class FileInputBox : UserControl
  {
    public FileInputBox()
    {
      InitializeComponent();
      theTextBox.TextChanged += new TextChangedEventHandler(OnTextChanged);
    }

    private void theButton_Click(object sender, RoutedEventArgs e)
    {
```

LISTING 16.4   Continued

```
    OpenFileDialog d = new OpenFileDialog();
    if (d.ShowDialog() == true) // Result could be true, false, or null
      this.FileName = d.FileName;
  }

  public string FileName
  {
    get { return (string)GetValue(FileNameProperty); }
    set { SetValue(FileNameProperty, value); }
  }


  private void OnTextChanged(object sender, TextChangedEventArgs e)
  {
    e.Handled = true;
    RoutedEventArgs args = new RoutedEventArgs(FileNameChangedEvent);
    RaiseEvent(args);
  }

  public event RoutedEventHandler FileNameChanged
  {
    add { AddHandler(FileNameChangedEvent, value); }
    remove { RemoveHandler(FileNameChangedEvent, value); }
  }

  public static readonly DependencyProperty FileNameProperty =
  DependencyProperty.Register("FileName", typeof(string), typeof(FileInputBox));
  public static readonly RoutedEvent FileNameChangedEvent =
    EventManager.RegisterRoutedEvent("FileNameChanged",
    RoutingStrategy.Bubble, typeof(RoutedEventHandler), typeof(FileInputBox));
  }
}
```

Creating a Custom Control

Just as the previous section used FileInputBox to illustrate creating a user control, this section uses a PlayingCard control to illustrate the process of creating a custom control. Whereas the tendency for designing a user control is to start with the user interface then later add behavior, it usually makes more sense to start with the behavior when designing a custom control. That's because a good custom control has a pluggable UI.

Creating the Behavior

The `PlayingCard` control should have a notion of a *face*, which can be set to one of 52 possible values. It should be clickable. It could also have a notion of being *selected*, for which each click toggles its state between selected and unselected.

Before going off and implementing the control, it helps to think about the similarities between your control and any of the built-in WPF controls. That way, you can choose a base class more specific than just `Control`, leveraging as much built-in support as possible.

For `PlayingCard`, the notion of a *face* is sort of like the `Foreground` property that all controls have. But `Foreground` is a `Brush`, and I want to enable setting the control's face to a simple string like "H2" for two of hearts or "SQ" for queen of spades. We could hijack some control's existing property of type string (like `TextBlock.Text`), as described in Chapter 10, but such a hack would be a poor experience for consumers of the control. Therefore, it feels logical to implement our own `Face` property.

The notion of being clickable is what defines a `Button`, so it seems obvious that `Button` should be the base class we choose. But what about the notion of being *selected*? `ToggleButton` already has that in the form of an `IsChecked` property, as well as the notion of being clickable! So `ToggleButton` sounds like an ideal base class.

A First Attempt

Listing 16.5 contains an implementation of a `ToggleButton`-derived `PlayingCard` control.

LISTING 16.5   `PlayingCard.cs`—Logic for the `PlayingCard` Custom Control

```
using System.Windows.Media;
using System.Windows.Controls.Primitives;

namespace Chapter16
{
  public class PlayingCard : ToggleButton
  {
    public string Face
    {
      get { return face; }
      set { face = value; Foreground = (Brush)TryFindResource(face); }
    }
    private string face;
  }
}
```

With the `Click`, `Checked`, and `Unchecked` events and `IsChecked` property inherited from `ToggleButton`, all `PlayingCard` needs to do is implement a `Face` property. Listing 16.5 uses the input string as the key to a resource used for the control's `Foreground`. By using `TryFindResource`, any invalid strings result in the `Foreground` being set to `null`, which is reasonable behavior. But this also implies that we need to store valid resources somewhere with the keys "HA," "H2," "H3," and so on. That's not a problem; we could store them in PlayingCard's Resources collection and the TryFindResource call will find them.

To create the visuals for PlayingCard, I designed 52 drawings in Adobe Illustrator—one for each possible face—then exported them to XAML using an exporter mentioned in the appendix, "Helpful Tools." Each of the 52 resources is a DrawingBrush with a number of GeometryDrawing objects. These are the resources that I want to add to PlayingCard's Resources collection. It would be ridiculous to attempt to convert such a large chunk of XAML to C# code, so one approach I could take is to split the definition of PlayingCard between a XAML file and a C# file, making the code in Listing 16.5 the code-behind file. Listings 16.6 and 16.7 show what this would look like.

LISTING 16.6   PlayingCard.xaml.cs—The Code from Listing 16.5, Now as a Code-Behind File

```
using System.Windows.Media;
using System.Windows.Controls.Primitives;

namespace Chapter16
{
  public partial class PlayingCard : ToggleButton
  {
    public PlayingCard()
    {
      InitializeComponent();
    }

    public string Face
    {
      get { return face; }
      set { face = value; Foreground = (Brush)TryFindResource(face); }
    }
    private string face;
  }
}
```

LISTING 16.7   PlayingCard.xaml—Resources for the PlayingCard Custom Control

```
<ToggleButton x:Class="Chapter16.PlayingCard"
  xmlns="http://schemas.microsoft.com/winfx/2006/xaml/presentation"
  xmlns:x="http://schemas.microsoft.com/winfx/2006/xaml"
  xmlns:local="clr-namespace:Chapter16">
<ToggleButton.Resources>
  <DrawingBrush x:Key="HA" Stretch="Uniform">
  <DrawingBrush.Drawing>
    …
```

LISTING 16.7   Continued

```xml
</DrawingBrush.Drawing>
</DrawingBrush>
<DrawingBrush x:Key="H2" Stretch="Uniform">
<DrawingBrush.Drawing>

  ...
</DrawingBrush.Drawing>
</DrawingBrush>

...
<Style TargetType="{x:Type local:PlayingCard}">

  ...
  <Setter Property="Template">
  <Setter.Value>
    <ControlTemplate TargetType="{x:Type local:PlayingCard}">

      ...
      <Rectangle Fill="{TemplateBinding Foreground}"/>

      ...
    </ControlTemplate>
  </Setter.Value>
  </Setter>
</Style>
</ToggleButton.Resources>
</ToggleButton>
```

The changes to the C# code are straightforward additions needed to support the compilation of PlayingCard across both files. Listing 16.7 fills the Resources collection with all 52 DrawingBrushes, plus a typed Style with a template that improves the visual appearance (so PlayingCard looks even less like a Button) and triggers that start animations based on the Checked, Unchecked, MouseEnter, and MouseLeave events. The key to the template is that the control's Foreground, which is assigned to one of the DrawingBrush resources whenever Face is assigned a value, fills a Rectangle. Showing the entire contents of Listing 16.7 would occupy *over 100 pages* (I kid you not!) because of the size and number of DrawingBrushes. But this book's source code includes it in its entirety.

Figure 16.4 shows instances of PlayingCard in action, using the following Window that assigns a unique Face to each instance and rotates them in a "fan" formation:

```xml
<Window xmlns="http://schemas.microsoft.com/winfx/2006/xaml/presentation"
  xmlns:x="http://schemas.microsoft.com/winfx/2006/xaml"
  xmlns:local="clr-namespace:Chapter16"
  Title="Window Hosting PlayingCards">
<Window.Background>

  ...
</Window.Background>
  <Viewbox>
    <Canvas Width="220" Height="400">
```

16

```
    <local:PlayingCard Face="C3" Width="100" Height="140" Canvas.Left="0"
      Canvas.Top="100">
      <local:PlayingCard.RenderTransform>
        <RotateTransform CenterX="50" CenterY="140" Angle="300"/>
      </local:PlayingCard.RenderTransform>
    </local:PlayingCard>
    <local:PlayingCard Face="CQ" Width="100" Height="140" Canvas.Left="10"
      Canvas.Top="100">
      <local:PlayingCard.RenderTransform>
        <RotateTransform CenterX="50" CenterY="140" Angle="310"/>
      </local:PlayingCard.RenderTransform>
    </local:PlayingCard>
    ...
    </Canvas>
  </Viewbox>
</Window>
```

PlayingCard "springs out" at you when you hover over it.   PlayingCard jumps up or down when you click to select or unselect it.

FIGURE 16.4   A hand of PlayingCard instances, which individually react to hover and selection.

This approach for implementing `PlayingCard` works, and the output looks just fine on paper. But if you run the application shown in Figure 16.4, you'll probably notice that the performance is sluggish. It also consumes a lot of memory. And both of these issues get worse for every additional `PlayingCard` you place in the `Window`! The problem is that the 52 `DrawingBrush` resources are stored inside the control, so every instance has its own copy of all of them! (100 book pages of resources x 13 instances = a lot of memory!)

This approach also suffers from unexpected behavior for consumers of the control. For example, if the preceding `Window` attempts to set an individual `PlayingCard`'s `Resources` property in XAML, an exception is thrown explaining that the `ResourceDictionary` can't be reinitialized.

There was a warning sign that might have indicated to a savvy reader that we were heading down the wrong path (other than the title of this section being "A First Attempt"): The logic in Listings 16.5 and 16.6 does not purely focus on the behavior of the `PlayingCard` control. Instead, it dictates a visual implementation detail by requiring resources with specific keys and by assigning them to `Foreground`.

A quick fix is to take the contents of `PlayingCard.Resources` and slap them into any consumer's `Application.Resources` instead. This avoids the performance and memory problems, but it breaks the encapsulation of the control. If the application pictured in Figure 16.4 accidentally omitted these resources, it would look like Figure 16.5.

The bottom line is that when creating this version of `PlayingCard`, we were still thinking in terms of the user control model, in which the control "owns" its UI. We need to break free of that thinking, and reorganize the code.

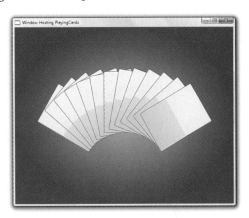

FIGURE 16.5   A hand of `PlayingCard` instances looks no different than `ToggleButtons` when the necessary resources aren't present.

The Recommended Approach

Looking back at Listing 16.5, we should remove the resource retrieval and setting of `Foreground`, leaving that detail to the `Style` applied to `PlayingCard`:

```
public string Face
{
  get { return face; }
  set { face = value; Foreground = (Brush)TryFindResource(face); }
}
```

The reasonable place to put PlayingCard's Style is inside the assembly's generic dictionary (themes\generic.xaml, covered in Chapter 10). Therefore, to apply the custom Style to PlayingCard (and avoid it looking as it does in Figure 16.5), we should place the following line of code in PlayingCard's static constructor:

```
DefaultStyleKeyProperty.OverrideMetadata(typeof(PlayingCard),
  new FrameworkPropertyMetadata(typeof(PlayingCard)));
```

Also, to facilitate the use of Face with WPF subsystems, we should turn it into a dependency property. Listing 16.8 contains all three of these changes, giving us the final implementation of PlayingCard.

LISTING 16.8   PlayingCard.cs—The Final Logic for the PlayingCard Custom Control

```
using System.Windows;
using System.Windows.Media;
using System.Windows.Controls.Primitives;

namespace Chapter16
{
  public class PlayingCard : ToggleButton
  {
    static PlayingCard()
    {
      // Override style
      DefaultStyleKeyProperty.OverrideMetadata(typeof(PlayingCard),
        new FrameworkPropertyMetadata(typeof(PlayingCard)));
      // Register Face dependency property
      FaceProperty = DependencyProperty.Register("Face",
        typeof(string), typeof(PlayingCard));
    }

    public string Face
    {
      get { return (string)GetValue(FaceProperty); }
      set { SetValue(FaceProperty, value); }
    }
    public static DependencyProperty FaceProperty;
  }
}
```

It almost seems too simple, but that's all the logic you need. The code captures the essence of PlayingCard: The only way it's unique from ToggleButton is that it has a string Face property. The rest is just a difference in default visuals.

> **TIP**
>
> When you create a WPF Custom Control project in Visual Studio or use Add, New Item to add a WPF Custom Control to an existing project, Visual Studio automatically creates a code file with the correct `DefaultStyleKeyProperty.OverrideMetadata` call, a placeholder `Style` and template inside your generic dictionary (generating the file if it doesn't already exist), and does *not* give you a XAML file that shares the class definition. Therefore, if you use these mechanisms, you're unlikely to fall into implementation traps such as the first attempt at implementing `PlayingCard`.

Creating the User Interface

To give the final implementation of `PlayingCard` an appropriate user interface, we need to fill our assembly's generic dictionary with the appropriate `Style` and supporting resources. (We should also fill one or more theme dictionaries if we care about customizing the visuals for specific Windows themes, as explained in Chapter 10.) To get the same visual results achieved in Figure 16.4, we should move all the resources that we originally defined *inside* `PlayingCard` (in Listing 16.7) into the generic dictionary.

The following line of the control template from Listing 16.7 needs to be modified, however:

```
<Rectangle Fill="{TemplateBinding Foreground}"/>
```

Filling the main `Rectangle` with `Foreground`'s value isn't appropriate anymore because `PlayingCard` itself doesn't set its value, and it would be too much of a burden to require consumers of the control to set this `Brush`.

What we want to do instead is set `Fill` to the appropriate `DrawingBrush` resource in the generic dictionary based on the current value of `Face`. We should use `StaticResource` to do this because the `DynamicResource` mechanism won't find resources inside a generic or theme dictionary. Because `Face` is a dependency property, my first instinct was to change the value of `Fill` as follows:

```
<Rectangle>
<Rectangle.Fill>
  <StaticResource ResourceKey="{TemplateBinding Face}"/>
</Rectangle.Fill>
</Rectangle>
```

Unfortunately, this produces an exception at runtime with the horribly confusing message:

```
Cannot convert the value in attribute 'ResourceKey' to object of type ''.
```

If you replace TemplateBinding with the equivalent Binding:

```
<Rectangle>
<Rectangle.Fill>
  <StaticResource ResourceKey=
    "{Binding Face, RelativeSource={RelativeSource TemplatedParent}}"/>
</Rectangle.Fill>
</Rectangle>
```

you'll still get an exception but at least its message makes sense:

```
'Binding' cannot be set on the 'ResourceKey' property of type
'StaticResourceExtension'. A 'Binding' can only be set on a DependencyProperty
of a DependencyObject.
```

ResourceKey isn't a dependency property (and couldn't possibly be because StaticResourceExtension doesn't even derive from DependencyObject), so we can't use it as the target of data binding.

If we define the key to each DrawingBrush as a ComponentResourceKey (with the PlayingCard type as the TypeInTargetAssembly and the face name as the ResourceId) rather than a simple string, we could restore the C# code that programmatically sets Foreground by calling TryFindResource and leave the TemplateBinding to Foreground intact. (The use of ComponentResourceKey is important because otherwise FindResource and TryFindResource can't find resources inside a generic or theme dictionary.) There's another option, however, that enables us to keep the C# code as shown in Listing 16.8 and keep the resource keys as simple strings: Define 52 property triggers (one per valid Face value) that assign Fill to a resource specified at compile time. Although this is verbose, it's also simple. Listing 16.9 shows 13 of these 52 triggers.

LISTING 16.9   Generic.xaml—The Generic Dictionary Containing PlayingCard's Default Style and Control Template

```
<ResourceDictionary
    xmlns="http://schemas.microsoft.com/winfx/2006/xaml/presentation"
    xmlns:x="http://schemas.microsoft.com/winfx/2006/xaml"
    xmlns:local="clr-namespace:Chapter16">
  …
  <Style TargetType="{x:Type local:PlayingCard}">
    …
   <Setter Property="Template">
   <Setter.Value>
    <ControlTemplate TargetType="{x:Type local:PlayingCard}">
     …
     <Rectangle Name="faceRect"/>
     …
    <ControlTemplate.Triggers>
     <Trigger Property="Face" Value="HA">
```

LISTING 16.9   Continued

```xml
      <Setter TargetName="faceRect" Property="Fill" Value="{StaticResource HA}"/>
    </Trigger>
    <Trigger Property="Face" Value="H2">
     <Setter TargetName="faceRect" Property="Fill" Value="{StaticResource H2}"/>
    </Trigger>
    <Trigger Property="Face" Value="H3">
     <Setter TargetName="faceRect" Property="Fill" Value="{StaticResource H3}"/>
    </Trigger>
    <Trigger Property="Face" Value="H4">
     <Setter TargetName="faceRect" Property="Fill" Value="{StaticResource H4}"/>
    </Trigger>
    <Trigger Property="Face" Value="H5">
     <Setter TargetName="faceRect" Property="Fill" Value="{StaticResource H5}"/>
    </Trigger>
    <Trigger Property="Face" Value="H6">
     <Setter TargetName="faceRect" Property="Fill" Value="{StaticResource H6}"/>
    </Trigger>
    <Trigger Property="Face" Value="H7">
     <Setter TargetName="faceRect" Property="Fill" Value="{StaticResource H7}"/>
    </Trigger>
    <Trigger Property="Face" Value="H8">
     <Setter TargetName="faceRect" Property="Fill" Value="{StaticResource H8}"/>
    </Trigger>
    <Trigger Property="Face" Value="H9">
     <Setter TargetName="faceRect" Property="Fill" Value="{StaticResource H9}"/>
    </Trigger>
    <Trigger Property="Face" Value="H10">
     <Setter TargetName="faceRect" Property="Fill" Value="{StaticResource H10}"/>
    </Trigger>
    <Trigger Property="Face" Value="HJ">
     <Setter TargetName="faceRect" Property="Fill" Value="{StaticResource HJ}"/>
    </Trigger>
    <Trigger Property="Face" Value="HQ">
     <Setter TargetName="faceRect" Property="Fill" Value="{StaticResource HQ}"/>
    </Trigger>
    <Trigger Property="Face" Value="HK">
     <Setter TargetName="faceRect" Property="Fill" Value="{StaticResource HK}"/>
    </Trigger>

    ...
   </ControlTemplate.Triggers>
  </Setter.Value>
  </Setter>
 </Style>
</ResourceDictionary>
```

16

Of course, as long as we are manually mapping values of Face to resource keys, we might as well redefine Face as an integer from 0 to 51, to be friendlier to typical algorithms that operate on playing cards. We could then add properties such as Suit and Rank to make working with the information easier.

This approach fixes the performance problems of the first attempt because the generic resources are shared among all instances of PlayingCard. (And if you don't want to share a certain resource, you can mark it with x:Shared="False".) But more than that, the complete separation of UI and logic enables PlayingCard to be restyled with maximum flexibility. Unlike the first version of the code, it doesn't require a Brush for each face, so you could even plug in a control template that represents each card as a simple TextBlock. If you want to advertise the customizable resources from a control such as PlayingCard and encourage them to be overridden by others, you could define 52 static properties that return an appropriate ComponentResourceKey for each resource.

DIGGING DEEPER

Other Approaches for Designing PlayingCard

Rather than embedding the notion of being selected into PlayingCard itself, you could place PlayingCards into a ListBox and rely on its selection behavior. You could then change its SelectionMode to automatically switch between allowing single selections or multiple selections!

If you host the items in a ListBox, however, you won't get the nice "fan" layout in Figures 16.4 and 16.5 by default. But using the techniques described in the next chapter, you could write a custom "fan" panel and plug it into the ListBox as its ItemsPanel template.

You could also rewrite PlayingCard as a simple object rather than a custom control and use a data template to give it the appropriate visuals. You could even use simple strings as long as a data template is in place to treat them like card faces!

TIP

The "Creating the Behavior" section discussed reusing as much existing logic as possible by choosing an appropriate base class for your custom control. On the UI side of things, WPF also has many built-in elements that you should try to leverage in your control template. For the nontraditional UI inside PlayingCard, it makes sense to start from scratch. But for other controls, you might find a lot of unfamiliar reusable components to leverage in the System.Windows.Controls.Primitives namespace, such as BulletDecorator, ResizeGrip, ScrollBar, Thumb, Track, and so on.

Considerations for More Sophisticated Controls

The `PlayingCard` control has minimal interactivity that could be handled in the control template with some simple triggers. But controls with more interactivity need to use other techniques. For example, imagine that we want to change `FileInputBox` from the beginning of this chapter from a user control to a custom control. This implies that we'll move its user interface (repeated in the following XAML) into a control template:

```
<DockPanel>
  <Button x:Name="theButton" DockPanel.Dock="Right" Click="theButton_Click">
    Browse...</Button>
  <TextBox x:Name="theTextBox"
    MinWidth="{Binding ActualWidth, ElementName=theButton}"
    Text="{Binding FileName, ElementName=root}" Margin="0,0,2,0"/>
</DockPanel>
```

But how should we attach the clicking of the `Button` to `FileInputBox`'s `theButton_Click` event handler? We can't set the `Click` event the same way inside the control template. (Well, we could if we redefined `theButton_Click` in a code-behind file for the generic dictionary. But that would effectively reimplement all the control's logic, and it would mean that anyone overriding the default template with their own would have to do the same thing!)

We can handle this kind of interactivity using two reasonable approaches, both of which are employed by WPF's built-in controls in different situations:

▶ Using named template parts

▶ Using commands

Using Named Template Parts

Chapter 10 mentioned template parts, which are a loose contract between a control and its template. A control can retrieve an element in its template with a given name, and then do whatever it desires with that element.

After you decide on elements to designate as template part(s), you should choose a name for each one. The convention is a name of the form "PART_*XXX*." You should then document each part's existence by marking your class with `TemplatePartAttribute` (one for each part). This looks like the following for a version of `FileInputBox` that expects a "Browse" `Button` in its control template:

```
[TemplatePart(Name="PART_Browse", Type=typeof(Button))]
public class FileInputBox : Control
{
  …
}
```

16

WPF doesn't do anything with `TemplatePartAttribute`, but it serves as documentation that design tools can leverage.

To process your specially designated template parts, you should override the `OnApplyTemplate` method inherited from `FrameworkElement`. This method is called any time a template is applied, so it gives you the opportunity to handle dynamic template changes gracefully. To retrieve the instances of any elements inside your control template, you can call `GetTemplateChild`, also inherited from `FrameworkElement`. The following implementation retrieves the designated Browse `Button` and attaches the necessary logic to its `Click` event.

```
public override void OnApplyTemplate()
{
  base.OnApplyTemplate();

  // Retrieve the Button from the current template
  Button browseButton = base.GetTemplateChild("PART_Browse") as Button;

  // Hook up the event handler
  if (browseButton != null)
    browseButton.Click += new RoutedEventHandler(theButton_Click);
}
```

Note that this implementation gracefully handles templates that omit `PART_Browse`, causing the `Button` variable to be null. This is the recommended approach, making your control handle any control template with varying degrees of functionality. After all, it's quite reasonable to imagine someone wanting to restyle `FileInputBox` such that it doesn't have a Browse `Button`. If you want to go against recommendations and be stricter, you could always throw an exception in `OnApplyTemplate` if the template doesn't contain the parts that you require. But such a control likely won't work well inside graphic design tools such as Expression Blend.

Using Commands

A more flexible way to attach logic to pieces of a template is to define and use commands. With a command on `FileInputBox` representing the notion of browsing, a control template could associate a subelement with it as follows:

```
<Button Command="{x:Static local:FileInputBox.BrowseCommand}">Browse...</Button>
```

This not only avoids the need for magical names, but the element triggering this command no longer has to be a `Button`!

To implement this command, `FileInputBox` needs a static .NET property of type `RoutedCommand` or `RoutedUICommand` (with a static backing field that can be private):

```
private static RoutedUICommand browseCommand = new
  RoutedUICommand("Browse...", "BrowseCommand", typeof(FileInputBox));

public static RoutedUICommand BrowseCommand
{
  get { return browseCommand; }
}
```

The control should bind this command to the desired custom logic (theButton_Click in this case) in its static constructor:

```
static FileInputBox()
{
  // Specify the gesture that triggers the command:
  CommandManager.RegisterClassInputBinding(typeof(FileInputBox),
    new MouseGesture(MouseAction.LeftClick));

  // Attach the command to custom logic:
  CommandManager.RegisterClassCommandBinding(typeof(FileInputBox),
    new CommandBinding(browseCommand, theButton_Click));
}
```

DIGGING DEEPER

Supporting UI Automation

To make your custom control truly first-class, it should support UI Automation. The pattern for doing this is to create a companion class that derives from FrameworkElementAutomationPeer named *ControlName*AutomationPeer that describes your control to the automation system. You should then override OnCreateAutomationPeer (inherited from UIElement) in your custom control, making it return an instance of your companion class:

```
protected override AutomationPeer OnCreateAutomationPeer()
{
  return new FileInputBoxAutomationPeer(this);
}
```

Whenever an event occurs that should be communicated to the automation system, you can retrieve the companion class and raise an automation-specific event, as follows:

```
FileInputBoxAutomationPeer peer =
  UIElementAutomationPeer.FromElement(myControl) as FileInputBoxAutomationPeer;
if (peer != null)
  peer.RaiseAutomationEvent(AutomationEvents.StructureChanged);
```

16

TIP

A sophisticated control might wish to determine if it is running in *design mode* (for example, being displayed in the Visual Studio or Expression Blend designer). The static `System.ComponentModel.DesignerProperties` class exposes an `IsInDesignMode` attached property that gives you this information. Design tools simply change the default value when appropriate, so a custom control can call the static `GetIsInDesignMode` method with a reference to itself to obtain the value.

Conclusion

If you're reading this book in order, you should be familiar enough with WPF to find the process of creating a custom control fairly understandable. For WPF beginners, however, creating a custom control—even when guided by Visual Studio—involves too many unorthodox concepts. And if such a user doesn't care about restyling and theming but rather just wants to build simple applications and controls as they could with Windows Forms, all that extra complication doesn't even add much value! That's why WPF takes a bifurcated view of custom controls versus user controls.

Of course, even these two approaches are not your only options for plugging in reusable pieces into WPF applications. For example, you could create a custom lower-level element that derives directly from `FrameworkElement`. A common non-`Control` to derive from is `Panel`, for creating custom layout schemes. And that's the topic of the next (and final) chapter.

CHAPTER 17

Layout with Custom Panels

Chapter 6, "Layout with Panels," examined the variety of panels included with WPF. If none of the built-in panels do exactly what you want, you have the option of writing your own panel. Of course, with all the flexibility of the built-in panels, the layout properties on child elements (discussed in Chapter 5, "Sizing, Positioning, and Transforming Elements"), plus the ability to embed panels within other panels to create arbitrarily complex layout, it's unlikely you're going to need a custom panel. Actually, you never *need* a custom panel; with enough procedural code, you can achieve any layout with just a Canvas. It's just a matter of how easy and automatic you want to be able to repetitively apply certain types of layout.

For example, perhaps you want to create a version of WrapPanel that stacks or wraps in a different direction than the two built-in directions. Or perhaps you want to create a version of StackPanel that stacks bottom-up, although you could alternatively get this effect pretty easily with a DockPanel by giving each element a Dock value of Bottom. UI virtualization might be a good incentive for creating a custom panel, such as creating a VirtualizingWrapPanel much like the VirtualizingStackPanel that already exists. You could also create a custom panel that incorporates automatic drag and drop, similar to ToolBarTray.

To understand the steps involved in creating a custom panel, we'll create a simple panel inspired by the Ribbon in the 2007 Microsoft Office System. The good news is that there is no special mechanism for creating a custom panel; you use the exact same approach used by the built-in panels. But this also means we should take a closer look at how panels and their children communicate, which was glossed over in Chapters 5 and 6.

Communication Between Parents and Children

Chapters 5 and 6 explain that parent panels and their children work together to determine their final sizes and positions. To strike a reasonable balance between the needs of the parent and its children, layout is a recursive two-pass process. The first pass is called *measure*, and the second pass is called *arrange*.

The Measure Step

In the measure step, parents ask their children how big they want to be, given the amount of space available. Panels (and children, when appropriate) do this by overriding the MeasureOverride method from FrameworkElement. For example:

```
protected override Size MeasureOverride(Size availableSize)
{
  …
  // Ask each child how big it would like to be, given a certain amount space
  foreach (UIElement child in Children)
  {
    child.Measure(new Size(…));
    // The child's answer is now in child.DesiredSize
    …
  }
  …
  // Tell my parent how big I would like to be given the passed-in availableSpace
  return new Size(…);
}
```

All children can be accessed via the panel's Children collection (a UIElementCollection), and asking each child for its desired size is done by simply calling its Measure method (inherited from UIElement). Measure doesn't return a value, but after the call, the child's DesiredSize property contains its answer. As the parent, you can decide if you want to alter your behavior based on the desired sizes of any of your children.

WARNING

In MeasureOverride, panels must always call Measure on each child!

You might want to implement a panel that simply doesn't care how big its children want to be, and doesn't have any use for checking their DesiredSize values. Still, all panels *must* ask their children anyway (by calling Measure) because some elements don't work correctly if their Measure method never gets called. This is somewhat like asking your spouse "How was your day?" when you really don't care about the answer, just to avoid the repercussions. (Or so I'm told. Personally, I always care about the answer!)

The preceding snippet of C# code, like all MeasureOverride implementations, uses two important Size values discussed in the following sections.

The Size Passed to Each Child's Measure Method

This should represent the amount of space you're planning to give the child. It could be all the space given to you (captured in MeasureOverride's availableSize parameter), some fraction of your space, or some absolute value, depending on your desires.

In addition, you can use Double.PositiveInfinity for either or both of Size's dimensions to find out how large the child wants to be in an ideal situation. In other words, this line of code:

```
child.Measure(new Size(Double.PositiveInfinity, Double.PositiveInfinity));
```

means, "How big do you want to be given all the space in the world?"

The layout system automatically handles the child layout properties discussed in Chapter 5, such as Margin, so the size ultimately passed to the child's implementation of MeasureOverride is the size you passed to Measure minus any margins. This also means that the availableSize parameter passed to your own MeasureOverride implementation represents whatever *your* parent allocated for you minus your own margins.

The Size Returned by MeasureOverride

The Size you return represents how big you want to be (answering your parent's request just like your children have already answered it for you). You could return an absolute size, but that would ignore the requests from your children. More likely, you'd pick a value that enables you to "size to content," being big enough to fit all your children in their ideal sizes but no bigger.

If you only have one child, sizing to your content is as simple as returning that child's DesiredSize as your own desired size. For multiple children, you would need to combine the widths and heights of your children according to how you plan to arrange them.

17

WARNING

You can't simply return availableSize from MeasureOverride!

Whether because of its simplicity or because of your own greediness, it's tempting to use the passed-in availableSize parameter as the return value for MeasureOverride. This basically means, "Give me all the space you've got."

However, whereas a Size with Double.PositiveInfinity in both dimensions is a legal value for availableSize, it is not a valid value for DesiredSize! Even when given unlimited space, you must choose a concrete size. If you ever end up returning an infinite size, UIElement's Measure implementation throws an InvalidOperationException with a helpful message: "Layout measurement override of element 'XXX' should not return PositiveInfinity as its DesiredSize, even if Infinity is passed in as available size."

The Arrange Step

After measurement has been completed all the way through the element tree, it's time for the physical arranging of elements. In the arrange step, parents *tell* their children where they are getting placed and how much space they are given (which might be a different Size than the one given earlier). Panels (and children, when appropriate) do this by overriding the ArrangeOverride method from FrameworkElement. For example:

```
protected override Size ArrangeOverride(Size finalSize)
{
    …
    // Tell each child how much space it is getting
    foreach (UIElement child in Children)
    {
        child.Arrange(new Rect(…));
        // The child's size is now in child.ActualHeight & child.ActualWidth

        …
    }
    …
    // Set my own actual size (ActualHeight & ActualWidth)
    return new Size(…);
}
```

You tell each child its location and size by passing a Rect and a Size to its Arrange method (inherited from UIElement). For example, you can give each child its desired size simply by passing the value of its DesiredSize property to Arrange. You can be certain that this size is set appropriately because all measuring is done before any arranging begins.

Unlike with Measure, you cannot pass an infinite size to Arrange (and the finalSize passed to you will never be infinite). The child can choose to occupy a different amount of space than what you've specified (such as a subset of the space). Parents can determine what actions (if any) they want to take if this happens. The actual size chosen by each child can be obtained from its ActualHeight and ActualWidth properties after the call to Arrange.

As with your children, the size you return from ArrangeOverride becomes the value of your RenderSize and ActualHeight/ActualWidth properties. The size must not be infinite, but unlike with MeasureOverride it's valid to simply return the passed-in Size if you want to take up all the available space because finalSize can never be infinite.

As with the measure step, properties such as Margin are handled automatically, so the information getting passed to children (and the finalSize passed to you) has any margins subtracted. In addition, alignment is automatically handled by the arrange step. When a child is given the exact amount of space it needs (for example, passing its DesiredSize to its Arrange method), alignment appears to have no effect because there's no extra space for the element to align within. But when you give a child more space than it occupies, the results of its HorizontalAlignment and/or VerticalAlignment settings are seen.

> ## WARNING
>
> ### Don't do anything in `MeasureOverride` or `ArrangeOverride` that invalidates layout!
>
> You can do some exotic things in MeasureOverride or ArrangeOverride, such as applying additional transforms to children (either as LayoutTransforms or RenderTransforms). But be sure that you don't invoke any code that invalidates layout; otherwise, you could wind up in an infinite loop!
>
> Any method or property invalidates layout if it calls UIElement.InvalidateMeasure or UIElement.InvalidateArrange. These are public methods, however, so it can be hard to know what code calls them. Within WPF, dependency properties that use these methods document this fact with one or more metadata flags from the FrameworkPropertyMetadataOptions enumeration: AffectsMeasure, AffectsArrange, AffectsParentArrange, and/or AffectsParentMeasure.

Creating a 2007 Office-Like `RibbonPanel`

The Ribbon contains a lot of interesting functionality that is not easy to duplicate. As far as layout is concerned, however, the control is basically a set of toolbars arranged on tabs, but with flexible layout that enables the important features to be large and additional features to be small. Each tab contains a number of distinct groups, and it is these groups that we're going to encapsulate in a custom panel called RibbonPanel.

RibbonPanel, like most panels, could be easily created using a combination of more primitive ones. And its usefulness is constrained to a small number of scenarios (similar to ToolBarTray or TabPanel). But creating such a panel can still be useful when you want to repetitively arrange controls in a unique way. Encapsulating the custom logic in a panel can make the arrangement of a user interface less error-prone, and help to enforce consistency.

As with creating a custom control, you should spend a little time determining the appropriate base class for your custom panel. The choices for panels are easy, however. Most of the time, it makes sense to simply derive from Panel. If you plan on supporting UI virtualization, then you should derive from VirtualizingPanel, the abstract base class of VirtualizingStackPanel. Otherwise, it could be handy to derive from a different Panel subclass (such as Canvas or DockPanel) if you plan on supporting the same set of attached properties that these classes define.

RibbonPanel Behavior

RibbonPanel mimics a basic layout used by many groups of the Ribbon in various 2007 Office applications. Figure 17.1 shows what eight simple Buttons placed inside a RibbonPanel looks like.

FIGURE 17.1 The custom RibbonPanel containing eight Buttons.

The first element is placed on the left, given the entire height of the panel and as much width as it desires. Subsequent elements fill a gridlike arrangement in column major order. This grid always has three rows but an unbounded number of columns. The cells are all of equal size, so each cell's height is one-third the height of the panel, and each cell's width depends on the number of columns and the available space. Therefore, except for the specially treated first element, RibbonPanel is essentially like a column-major version of UniformGrid with an extra constraint on the number of rows.

In the following example, RibbonPanels are used within a TabControl to mimic Microsoft Word, as shown in Figure 17.2. Although it doesn't look exactly like Word's user interface, the layout is correct. The remaining step to get the correct appearance would be to style the elements, using the techniques from Chapter 10, "Styles, Templates, Skins, and Themes."

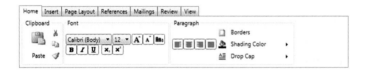

FIGURE 17.2 RibbonPanel can be used to create a Microsoft Word-like user interface.

RibbonPanel Implementation

Implementing RibbonPanel (or any custom panel) consists of only the following three easy steps:

1. Create a class that derives from Panel.

2. Override MeasureOverride and measure each child.

3. Override ArrangeOverride and arrange each child.

Listing 17.1 contains the entire implementation of RibbonPanel.

LISTING 17.1 RibbonPanel.cs—The Implementation of RibbonPanel

```
using System;
using System.Windows;
using System.Windows.Controls;

namespace CustomPanel
{
```

LISTING 17.1   Continued

```csharp
public class RibbonPanel : Panel
{
  protected override Size MeasureOverride(Size availableSize)
  {
    if (Children.Count < 1) return new Size(0, 0);

    // Ask the first child for its desired size, given unlimited space
    UIElement firstChild = Children[0];
    firstChild.Measure(new Size(Double.PositiveInfinity,
      Double.PositiveInfinity));

    // If there's only one child, the panel would like to be the exact same size
    if (Children.Count < 2) return firstChild.DesiredSize;

    // If not, calculate the desired width based on all children
    double numRows = Math.Ceiling((Children.Count - 1) / 3d);
    double maxWidthForEachRemainingChild = 0;

    for (int i = 1; i < Children.Count; i++)
    {
      // Ask each child for its desired size, given unlimited space
      UIElement child = Children[i];
      child.Measure(new Size(Double.PositiveInfinity, Double.PositiveInfinity));

      // Keep track of the maximum width
      maxWidthForEachRemainingChild = Math.Max(child.DesiredSize.Width,
        maxWidthForEachRemainingChild);
    }

    return new Size(
      // total width
      firstChild.DesiredSize.Width + maxWidthForEachRemainingChild * numRows,
      // height = desired height of the first child
      firstChild.DesiredSize.Height);
  }

  protected override Size ArrangeOverride(Size finalSize)
  {
    if (Children.Count < 1) return finalSize;

    // Give the first child its desired width but the height of the panel
    UIElement firstChild = Children[0];
    Point childOrigin = new Point(0, 0);
    Size firstChildSize = new Size(firstChild.DesiredSize.Width,
      finalSize.Height);
```

LISTING 17.1   Continued

```
    firstChild.Arrange(new Rect(childOrigin, firstChildSize));

    if (Children.Count < 2) return finalSize;

    // Determine the size for all the remaining children
    double numRows = Math.Ceiling((Children.Count - 1) / 3d);
    Size childSize = new Size(
      (finalSize.Width - firstChildSize.Width) / numRows,
      finalSize.Height / 3);
    childOrigin.X += firstChildSize.Width;

    for (int i = 1; i < Children.Count; i++)
    {
      UIElement child = Children[i];
      child.Arrange(new Rect(childOrigin, childSize));

      if (i % 3 == 0)
      {
        // Start a new column
        childOrigin.X += childSize.Width;
        childOrigin.Y = 0;
      }
      else
        childOrigin.Y += childSize.Height;
    }

    // Fill all the space given
    return finalSize;
    }
  }
}
```

The calculations in MeasureOverride and ArrangeOverride are a straightforward way to get the results shown in Figures 17.1 and 17.2. You can see that the panel doesn't need to care about any of the children's layout properties (Height, MinHeight, MaxHeight, Width, MinWidth, MaxWidth, Margin, Padding, Visibility, HorizontalAlignment, VerticalAlignment, LayoutTransform, and so on). In addition, tabbing between child elements is handled automatically. The tab order is defined by the order that children are added to the parent.

Listing 17.2 uses three instances of RibbonPanel in XAML to form the Microsoft Word-like user interface shown in Figure 17.2.

LISTING 17.2   UsingRibbonPanel.cs—The Word-Like UI in Figure 17.2

```
<Window xmlns="http://schemas.microsoft.com/winfx/2006/xaml/presentation"
        xmlns:x="http://schemas.microsoft.com/winfx/2006/xaml"
        xmlns:c="clr-namespace:CustomPanel"
        Title="CustomPanel"
>
  <DockPanel>
    <TabControl DockPanel.Dock="Top" Height="130">
      <TabItem Header="Write">
        <StackPanel Orientation="Horizontal">
          <GroupBox Header="Clipboard" Padding="2">
            <c:RibbonPanel>
              <Grid>
              <Grid.RowDefinitions>
                <RowDefinition/>
                <RowDefinition Height="Auto"/>
              </Grid.RowDefinitions>
                <Image Grid.Row="0" Stretch="none" Source="iconPaste.bmp"/>
                <Label Margin="10,0" Grid.Row="1">Paste</Label>
              </Grid>
              <Image Source="iconCut.bmp"/>
              <Image Source="iconCopy.bmp"/>
              <Image Source="iconFormatPainter.bmp"/>
            </c:RibbonPanel>
          </GroupBox>
          <GroupBox Header="Font">
            <c:RibbonPanel>
              <WrapPanel Width="220" VerticalAlignment="Center">
                ...
              </WrapPanel>
            </c:RibbonPanel>
          </GroupBox>
          <GroupBox Header="Paragraph">
            <c:RibbonPanel>
              <WrapPanel VerticalAlignment="Center">
                ...
              </WrapPanel>
              <MenuItem Header="Borders">
                ...
              </MenuItem>
              <MenuItem Header="Shading Color">
                ...
              </MenuItem>
              <MenuItem Header="Drop Cap">
                ...
```

17

LISTING 17.2   Continued

```
                </MenuItem>
            </c:RibbonPanel>
          </GroupBox>
        </StackPanel>
      </TabItem>
      ...
    </TabControl>
    ...
  </DockPanel>
</Window>
```

The XAML file in Listing 17.2 maps the CustomPanel .NET namespace to a c prefix, so RibbonPanel can be used with simple <c:RibbonPanel>...</c:RibbonPanel> syntax. Because RibbonPanel.cs is compiled into the same assembly, no Assembly value needs to be set with the clr-namespace directive.

The first RibbonPanel is filled with a Grid and three images to represent the expected usage of the panel. The middle RibbonPanel actually doesn't take advantage of its unique layout; it has a single WrapPanel child that fills the space and arranges its children in a custom manner. The last RibbonPanel is a mix of the previous two. It uses a WrapPanel as the first child, but adds three more children that get aligned as expected.

Conclusion

This chapter dug into the exact mechanism used by child elements and parent panels—how they compromise to give great results in a wide variety of situations. Implementing your own custom panels is really just an "advanced topic" because it's rare that you would need to do so. As you've seen, custom panels are pretty easy to write. Because of the measure/arrange protocol and all the work automatically handled by WPF, existing controls can be placed inside brand-new custom panels and they still behave very reasonably.

PART VI

Appendix

Helpful Tools

Because WPF introduces so many new concepts and new pieces of infrastructure, it's not practical to develop, design, build, debug, analyze, test, and deploy professional applications without a new wave of tools to help you. These tools fall into three major categories—professional development tools, free utilities, and professional design tools.

Professional Development Tools

Starting with version 2005, Visual Studio is the best development tool for WPF. And the support will undoubtedly get better with each new version. At the time of writing, two relevant versions are available:

▸ **Visual Studio 2005** is a good environment for building WPF applications after you've downloaded from http://msdn.com and installed the free Windows Software Development Kit (SDK) and the Visual Studio 2005 extensions for .NET Framework 3.0 development. These extensions not only add new project types specific to WPF, but also give you a visual designer, enabling you to drag, drop, and edit controls much like you can with Windows Forms. In addition, the extensions provide snippets support and IntelliSense for XAML, as shown in Figure A.1. These extensions are in prerelease form at the time of writing, so their name and functionality may change.

▸ **Visual Studio "Orcas,"** the successor to Visual Studio 2005 that is still in prerelease form at the time of writing, delivers a first-class WPF development environment with all the features from the .NET Framework 3.0 extensions built in.

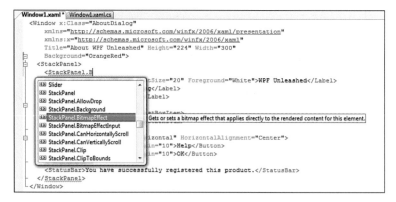

FIGURE A.1   IntelliSense almost makes typing XAML a pleasure!

Free Utilities

For developers who don't want to spend any money (other than on this book!) or who enjoy working with technologies at a lower level, several tools exist that can help you be productive inside or outside of an integrated development environment. Many of these tools are included in the Windows SDK available for download at http://msdn.com, but others can be found in various parts of the Internet:

▶ **Visual Studio Express** is a family of Visual Studio products intended for hobbyist developers. Express editions don't have all the features of Visual Studio Professional Edition, but are free and support WPF development reasonably well. (For 2005 editions, you must install the Windows SDK and the extensions for .NET Framework 3.0 development, described in the previous section.)

▶ **MSBuild** enables you to compile projects from a command prompt, using the same XML-based project format as Visual Studio. MSBuild is actually a core part of the .NET Framework redistributable, but you'll need the Windows SDK to use it for building WPF applications and components.

▶ **XamlPad** is a great tool for experimenting with XAML. It's basically a Notepad-style text editor, but with a pane that can render your WPF-specific XAML as you type it. XamlPad doesn't have IntelliSense, but the parser does give you decent error messages when you make mistakes. XamlPad is pictured in Figure A.2.

▶ **WpfPerf**, also known as Performance Profiling Tools for WPF, is a valuable set of tools bundled together for helping you understand performance issues in WPF applications. This includes

    ▶ Perforator, which enables you to tweak rendering settings, tint the areas of your user interface that aren't getting hardware accelerated, and more.

    ▶ Event Trace, which can produce an event log file with detailed low-level data emitted by the Windows kernel, the garbage collector, and WPF.

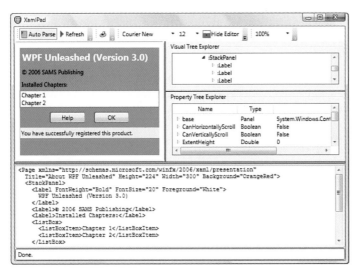

FIGURE A.2   XamlPad parses and displays user interfaces defined in XAML.

> ▶ Trace Viewer, which displays the data collected by Event Trace in a timeline view for easier analysis.

> ▶ Visual Profiler, which enables you to identify performance bottlenecks in terms of WPF elements rather than functions (as with a traditional profiler). It provides data and visualizations for determining the percentage of time an application spends doing rendering versus layout versus hit testing, and so on.

> ▶ Working Set Analyzer, which provides a user interface (with interactive pie charts) for the Virtual Address Dump (VaDump) command-line tool in the Windows SDK.

▶ **UISpy** inspects the UI elements in running WPF (and non-WPF) applications, using the UI Automation accessibility framework.

▶ **Snoop**, by Pete Blois (available at http://blois.us/Snoop), also enables inspection of running WPF applications, but with XamlPad-like features such as visual tree viewing and UI rendering/zooming. It also has extra features handy for troubleshooting, such as inspecting routed events and discovering binding errors.

▶ **LocBaml** is a *sample* in the Windows SDK (so you have to build the C# project to use it) that makes it easy to create localized versions of XAML-based UI. It can extract the strings used in your XAML (after it has been compiled into your assembly) and output a simple .csv file. You can then translate the strings into a different language and feed it back into LocBaml to generate the appropriate culture-specific resource DLL.

▶ **WICExplorer** enables the viewing of image metadata, pixel formats, CODEC information, and more. (WIC stands for Windows Imaging Component.)

A

▶ **IsXPS** is a simple command-line utility that can determine whether one or more files conform to the XML Paper Specification (XPS) and the Open Packaging Conventions (OPC) Specification.

▶ Familiar .NET development tools like **ILDASM** in the Windows SDK or **.NET Reflector** from http://www.aisto.com/roeder/dotnet/ are still just as handy for WPF. (The same is true for standard profiling tools like Visual Studio 2005 Performance Analyzer.)

Professional Design Tools

Several design tools either natively understand XAML or can import/export XAML. Although Visual Studio contains a developer-oriented visual designer for WPF, the following tools go much deeper into the full expressiveness enabled by XAML:

▶ **Microsoft Expression Blend**, not yet released at the time of writing, is the premier tool for creating rich user experiences in XAML. It was built from the ground up (in managed code) alongside and specifically for WPF. Blend shares the same project format as Visual Studio (and MSBuild), so developers and designers can work together on projects without any of the overhead typically associated with incorporating graphic designs into working software.

▶ **ZAM 3D** from Electric Rain is a complete 3D modeling application that natively supports XAML. This program nicely complements Blend for designers who are serious about making 3D an integral part of their user experience.

▶ **Microsoft Expression Design** is a tool for creating and editing 2D images, whether bitmap-based or vector-based. It supports exporting to XAML, so it can be helpful for WPF applications.

▶ **The 2007 Microsoft Office System** supports saving content as XPS documents. Independently of this, the **Microsoft XPS Document Writer** printer driver included in Windows Vista enables printing to an XPS document from any application.

▶ A number of other 2D/3D graphics and modeling tools can be helpful for WPF design because you can often find XAML exporters or converters for them. For example, Mike Swanson (a Microsoft employee) created a XAML exporter plug-in for **Adobe Illustrator**. He maintains a list of WPF-related converters and tools (and third-party WPF controls) at http://blogs.msdn.com/mswanson/articles/WPFToolsAndControls.aspx.

Index

How can we make this index more useful? Email us at indexes@samspublishing.com

How can we make this index more useful? Email us at indexes@samspublishing.com

THIS BOOK IS SAFARI ENABLED

INCLUDES FREE 45-DAY ACCESS TO THE ONLINE EDITION

The Safari® Enabled icon on the cover of your favorite technology book means the book is available through Safari Bookshelf. When you buy this book, you get free access to the online edition for 45 days.

Safari Bookshelf is an electronic reference library that lets you easily search thousands of technical books, find code samples, download chapters, and access technical information whenever and wherever you need it.

TO GAIN 45-DAY SAFARI ENABLED ACCESS TO THIS BOOK:

- Go to **http://www.samspublishing.com/safarienabled**
- Complete the brief registration form
- Enter the coupon code found in the front of this book on the "Copyright" page

If you have difficulty registering on Safari Bookshelf or accessing the online edition, please e-mail customer-service@safaribooksonline.com.

UNLEASHED

Unleashed takes you beyond the basics, providing an exhaustive, technically sophisticated reference for professionals who need to exploit a technology to its fullest potential. It's the best resource for practical advice from the experts, and the most in-depth coverage of the latest technologies.

ASP.NET 2.0 Unleashed
ISBN: 0672328232

OTHER UNLEASHED TITLES

Microsoft BizTalk Server 2006 Unleashed
ISBN: 0672329255

Microsoft SharePoint 2007 Development Unleashed
ISBN: 0672329034

Microsoft Exchange Server 2007 Unleashed
ISBN: 0672329204

Microsoft Small Business Server 2003 Unleashed
ISBN: 0672328054

Microsoft ISA Server 2006 Unleashed
ISBN: 0672329190

Microsoft Office Project Server 2007 Unleashed
ISBN: 0672329212

Microsoft Windows Server 2003 Unleashed (R2 Edition)
ISBN: 0672328984

Microsoft Windows Vista™ Unleashed
ISBN: 0672328941

Microsoft SQL Server 2005 Unleashed
ISBN: 0672328240

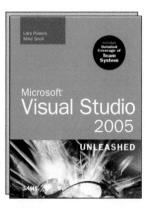

Microsoft Visual Studio 2005 Unleashed
ISBN: 0672328194

Microsoft Visual C# 2005 Unleashed
ISBN: 0672327767

SAMS

www.samspublishing.com